DEVELOPING COUNTRIES IN THE
WTO LEGAL SYSTEM

DEVELOPING COUNTRIES IN THE WTO LEGAL SYSTEM

EDITED BY CHANTAL THOMAS AND
JOEL P TRACHTMAN

Oxford University Press, Inc., publishes works that further Oxford University's objective of excellence in research, scholarship, and education.

Oxford   New York
Auckland   Cape Town   Dar es Salaam   Hong Kong   Karachi   Kuala Lumpur   Madrid   Melbourne
Mexico City   Nairobi   New Delhi   Shanghai   Taipei   Toronto

With offices in
Argentina   Austria   Brazil   Chile   Czech Republic   France   Greece   Guatemala   Hungary   Italy
Japan   Poland   Portugal   Singapore   South Korea   Switzerland   Thailand   Turkey   Ukraine
Vietnam

Copyright © 2009 by Oxford University Press, Inc.

Published by Oxford University Press, Inc.
198 Madison Avenue, New York, New York 10016

Oxford is a registered trademark of Oxford University Press
Oxford University Press is a registered trademark of Oxford University Press, Inc.

All rights reserved. No part of this publication may be reproduced, stored in a retrieval system, or transmitted, in any form or by any means, electronic, mechanical, photocopying, recording, or otherwise, without the prior permission of Oxford University Press, Inc.

Library of Congress Cataloging-in-Publication Data
Developing countries in the WTO legal system / edited by Chantal Thomas and Joel P. Trachtman.
  p. cm.
  Includes bibliographical references and index.
  ISBN 978-0-19-538361-4 ((hardback) : alk. paper)
1. World Trade Organization—Developing countries. 2. Foreign trade regulation—Developing countries.
3. Free trade—Developing countries. 4. Tariff—Law and legislation—Developing countries.
5. General Agreement on Tariffs and Trade (Organization) 6. Developing countries—Commercial policy.
7. International trade. I. Thomas, Chantal, 1971-
II. Trachtman, Joel P.
  K4610.D48 2009
  343'.087—dc22
                                                                    2008049653

1 2 3 4 5 6 7 8 9

Printed in the United States of America on acid-free paper

Note to Readers
This publication is designed to provide accurate and authoritative information in regard to the subject matter covered. It is based upon sources believed to be accurate and reliable and is intended to be current as of the time it was written. It is sold with the understanding that the publisher is not engaged in rendering legal, accounting, or other professional services. If legal advice or other expert assistance is required, the services of a competent professional person should be sought. Also, to confirm that the information has not been affected or changed by recent developments, traditional legal research techniques should be used, including checking primary sources where appropriate.

(Based on the Declaration of Principles jointly adopted by a Committee of the American Bar Association and a Committee of Publishers and Associations.)

You may order this or any other Oxford University Press publication by visiting the Oxford University Press website at www.oup.com

CONTENTS

List of Abbreviations   vii
Acknowledgments   xi

Chapter 1: Editors' Introduction   1
CHANTAL THOMAS AND JOEL P TRACHTMAN

I. THE WTO AND DEVELOPING COUNTRIES: SYSTEMIC PERSPECTIVES

Chapter 2: Developing Countries and the GATT/WTO System: Some Reflections on the Idea of Free Trade and Doha Round Trade Negotiations   21
BS CHIMNI

Chapter 3: Dysfunction, Diversion, and the Debate over Preferences: (How) Do Preferential Trade Policies Work?   45
JEFFREY L DUNOFF

Chapter 4: Trade and Development: Systemic Lessons from WTO Experience with Implementation, Trade Facilitation, and Aid for Trade   75
J MICHAEL FINGER

Chapter 5: Asymmetry in the Uruguay Round and in the Doha Round   105
SYLVIA OSTRY

Chapter 6: Developing Countries, the Doha Round, Preferences, and the Right to Regulate   111
JOEL P TRACHTMAN

II. INSTITUTIONAL CAPACITY AND DISPUTE SETTLEMENT

Chapter 7: Robert Hudec and the Theory of International Economic Law: The Law of Global Space   129
DAVID M TRUBEK AND M PATRICK COTTRELL

Chapter 8: Winners and Losers in the Panel Stage of the WTO Dispute Settlement System   151
BERNARD HOEKMAN, HENRIK HORN AND PETROS C MAVROIDIS

Chapter 9: Access to Justice in the WTO: A Case for a Small-Claims Procedure?   191
HÅKAN NORDSTRÖM AND GREGORY SHAFFER

Chapter 10: With a Little Help From Our Friends? Developing Country Complaints and Third-Party Participation 247
MARC L BUSCH AND ERIC REINHARDT

Chapter 11: MFN and the Third-Party Economic Interests of Developing Countries in GATT/WTO Dispute Settlement 265
CHAD P BOWN

Chapter 12: Economic Development and the World Trade Organization: Proposal for the Agreement on Development Facilitation and the Council for Trade and Development in the WTO 291
YONG-SHIK LEE

III. SUBSTANTIVE CHALLENGES

Chapter 13: Special and Differential Treatment in Agricultural Trade: Breaking the Impasse 323
TRACEY D EPPS AND MICHAEL J TREBILCOCK

Chapter 14: TRIPS 3.0: Policy Calibration and Innovation Displacement 363
DANIEL J GERVAIS

Chapter 15: Trade and Competition Policy in the Developing World: Is There a Role for the WTO? 395
DANIEL J GIFFORD AND ROBERT T KUDRLE

Chapter 16: The GATS and Developing Countries: Why Such Limited Traction? 437
BERNARD HOEKMAN

Chapter 17: Development by Moving People: Unearthing the Development Potential of a GATS Visa 457
SUNGJOON CHO

Chapter 18: Justice, the Bretton Woods Institutions, and the Problem of Inequality 475
FRANK J GARCIA

Index 511

LIST OF ABBREVIATIONS

A Pol Sci Rev	American Political Science Review
ADA	Anti-Dumping Agreement
AE Rev	American Economic Review
Am Bar Found Res J	American Bar Foundation Research Journal
Am Bus LJ	American Business Law Journal
Am J Pol Sci	American Journal of Political Science
Antitrust Bull	Antitrust Bulletin
Antitrust LJ	Antitrust Law Journal
Ari JICL	Arizona Journal of International and Comparative Law
Ari L Rev	Arizona Law Review
ASIL	American Society of International Law
ATC	Agreement on Textiles and Clothing
Atl Econ J	Atlantic Economic Journal
AUIL Rev	American University International Law Review
AUJIL & Pol	American University Journal of International Law and Policy
BCICL Rev	Boston College International and Comparative Law Review
BISD	GATT Basic Instruments and Selected Documents
Buffalo IPLJ	Buffalo Intellectual Property Law Journal
Can JEcon	Canadian Journal of Economics
Card JICL	Cardozo Journal of International and Comparative Law
Case West Res JIL	Case Western Reserve Journal of International Law
Cato J	Cato Journal
Chi-Kent JIP	Chicago-Kent Journal of Intellectual Property
Col JEL	Columbia Journal of European Law
Col JIL	Columbia Journal of International Law
Cont Econ Pol	Contemporary Economic Policy
CornILJ	Cornell International Law Journal
DePaul L Rev	DePaul Law Review
Dev Pol Rev	Development Policy Review
DSU	Understanding on Rules and Procedures Governing the Settlement of Disputes
Duke JCIL	Duke Journal of Comparative and International Law
EC	European Communities
Econ & Pol Weekly	Economic and Political Weekly

Econ & Pol	Economics and Politics
Econ Devl & Ch	Economic Development and Cultural Change
Econ J	Economic Journal
Econ Pol	Economic Policy
EJIL	European Journal of International Law
ELJ	European Law Journal
ELRev	European Law Review
EmILRev	Emory International Law Review
EU	European Union
Eur Econ Rev	European Economic Review
Flor St UJTL & Pol	Florida State University Journal of Transnational Law and Policy
Food Pol	Food Policy
Ford ILJ	Fordham International Law Journal
Ford L Rev	Fordham Law Review
Ford Urb LJ	Fordham Urban Law Journal
GATS	General Agreement on Trade in Services
GATT	General Agreement on Tariffs and Trade
GDP	Gross Domestic Product
Geo Wash IL Rev	George Washington International Law Review
GSoc	Global Society
GSP	Generalized System of Preferences
Harv ILJ	Harvard International Law Journal
Hastings ICL Rev	Hastings International and Comparative Law Review
Hous JIL	Houston Journal of International Law
Ind L Rev	Indiana Law Review
Int'l Econ L	International Economic Law
Int'l Leg Theo	International Legal Theory
Int'l Org	International Organizations
Int'l SQ	International Studies Quarterly
IPQ	Intellectual Property Quarterly
J Afr Econ	Journal of African Economies
J App Pract & Pro	Journal of Appellate Practice and Procedure
J Comp L & Econ	Journal of Competition Law and Economics
J ConR	Journal of Conflict Resolution
J Dev Stu	Journal of Development Studies
J Econ Pers	Journal of Economic Perspectives
J Int'l Econ	Journal of International Economics
J Int'l Pol Econ	Journal of International Political Economy
J Leg Stu	Journal of Legal Studies
Japan & W Econ	Japan and World Economy
JCMS	Journal of Common Market Studies
JDE	Journal of Development Economics

JE Pub Pol	Journal of European Public Policy
JEcon Growth	Journal of Economic Growth
JELit	Journal of Economic Literature
JIEL	Journal of International Economic Law
JIPL	Journal of Intellectual Property Law
JL & Econ	Journal of Law and Economics
JL Econ & Org	Journal of Law, Economics and Organizations
John Marshall Rev IPL	John Marshall Review of Intellectual Property Law
JWIP	Journal of World Intellectual Property
JWT	Journal of World Trade
JWTL	Journal of World Trade Law
Kansas L Rev	Kansas Law Review
L & Pol Int'l Bus	Law and Policy in International Business
L & Soc Rev	Law and Society Review
LDC	Least Developed Country
Lloyds Bank Rev	Lloyds Bank Review
MFA	Multi-Fiber Arrangement
MFN	Most Favored Nation
Mich JIL	Michigan Journal of International Law
Mich St LRev	Michigan State Law Review
Minn JGT	Minnesota Journal of Global Trade
Minn L Rev	Minnesota Law Review
NAMA	Non-Agricultural Market Access
NCJIL & Comm Reg	North Carolina Journal of International Law and Commercial Regulation
Nw JIL & Bus	Northwestern Journal of International Law and Business
NYUJIL & Pol	New York University Journal of International Law and Policy
O St JDR	Ohio State Journal on Dispute Resolution
OREP	Oxford Review of Economic Policy
Pac Econ Rev	Pacific Economic Review
Phil & Pub Affairs	Philosophy & Public Affairs
Pol Sci Q	Political Science Quarterly
Pol Theory	Political Theory
PTA	Preferential Trade Agreement
Pub Admin & Dev	Public Administration and Development
QJE	Quarterly Journal of Economics
Res Pol	Research Policy
Rev Econ Stats	The Review of Economics and Statistics
Rev Econ Stu	Review of Economic Studies
Rev Int'l Econ	Review of International Economics
RTA	Regional Trade Agreement

San Diego ILJ	San Diego International Law Journal
SCM Agreement	Agreement on Subsidies and Countervailing Measures
SG Agreement	Agreement on Safeguards
SPS Agreement	Agreement on Sanitary and Phytosanitary Measures
St Pol Q	State Politics and Policy Quarterly
Stan JIL	Stanford Journal of International Law
Sth Econ J	Southern Economic Journal
TBT Agreement	Agreement on Technical Barriers to Trade
Temp Int'l & Comp LJ	Temple International and Comparative Law Journal
Texas ILJ	Texas International Law Journal
TPRM	Trade Policy Review Mechanism
Transnat'l L & Cont Prob	Transnational Law and Contemporary Problems
TRIMS Agreement	Agreement on Trade Related Investment Measures
TRIPS Agreement	Agreement on Trade Related Intellectual Property Rights
U Cinn L Rev	University of Cincinnati Law Review
U San Fran L Rev	University of San Francisco Law Review
UC Davis Bus LJ	UC Davis Business Law Journal
UC Davis JIL & Pol	UC Davis Journal of International Law and Policy
UC Davis L Rev	UC Davis Law Review
UChig Leg For	University of Chicago Legal Forum
UDC L Rev	University of District of Columbia Law Review
UNSWLJ	University of New South Wales Law Journal
UPennJIEL	University of Pennsylvania Journal of International Economic Law
UPitt L Rev	University of Pittsburgh Law Review
URichL Rev	University of Richmond Law Review
US	United States
Va JIL	Virginia Journal of International Law
Vand JTL	Vanderbilt Journal of Transnational Law
W Comp	World Competition
W Econ	The World Economy
W Pol	World Politics
WB Econ Rev	World Bank Economic Rev
West Pol Q	Western Political Quarterly
WT Rev	World Trade Review
YaleLJ	Yale Law Journal

ACKNOWLEDGMENTS

The editors would like to thank the University of Minnesota Law School for its generous contributions to and support of this project. In particular, we thank Professors Guy Charles and Fred Morrison, who served as interim co-deans at the time that the conference for this book was convened, as well as Provost Thomas Sullivan. The editors also thank Marianne Hudec for her encouragement, and Jeremy Leong for his diligent research assistance.

1. EDITORS' INTRODUCTION

CHANTAL THOMAS AND JOEL P TRACHTMAN

A. Trade Liberalization and Poverty Reduction: the Role of Special and Differential Treatment 3
    I. Special and Differential Treatment: An Overview of the Pre-Uruguay Round Era 3
    II. Domestic Reform 5
    III. Market Access in Developed Countries 6
    IV. Special and Differential Treatment in the Uruguay Round 8
B. The WTO and the Right to Regulate for Development 10
    I. Balance-of-Payments Measures 12
    II. Other Protection 13
    III. Subsidies 13
    IV. TRIMS 14
    V. TRIPS 14
C. Moving Forward 15

The problem of poverty continues to plague many countries and the international system as a whole. The international trading system, governed primarily by a single multilateral organization—first the General Agreement on Tariffs and Trade (GATT) and then its successor, the World Trade Organization (WTO)—has served as a central forum for debate and decision making on the relationship between trade law and policy, on the one hand, and poverty reduction and development, on the other. Indeed, the Preamble to the Agreement Establishing the World Trade Organization avers the WTO's recognition that 'relations in the field of trade and economic endeavour should be conducted with a view to raising standards of living,' as well as a 'need for positive efforts designed to ensure that developing countries, and especially the least developed among them, secure a share in the growth in international trade commensurate with the needs of their economic development'.[1]

The question of how an international trading system premised on the foundational principles of nondiscrimination, as articulated in Article I and Article III, should address the special challenges facing developing economies precedes the 1995 establishment of the WTO by several decades and indeed has proved a defining question throughout the evolution of the post-World War II and postcolonial international arena. One of the most astute treatments of this question remains Robert Hudec's *Developing Countries in the GATT Legal System*.[2] The essays in the

---

1. Preamble, Agreement Establishing the World Trade Organization.
2. RE Hudec, *Developing Countries in the GATT Legal System* (Gower: Aldershot, 1987) 58.

present volume seek to respond to and expand Hudec's central insights and commemorate the twentieth anniversary of the book's publication.

Hudec's book can best be appreciated for two central achievements, one of substance and one of method—although they are intertwined—as the following discussion indicates. First, Hudec was perhaps among the first to apply a 'public choice' approach to the internal workings of international trade negotiations, shaped by a sensitivity to political economy and a realist's eye for internal organizational dynamics. From his experience working as a trade diplomat in Geneva, Hudec saw very well how national self-interest governed the strategies of trade negotiators, generating both the heavy reliance on reciprocity as a driver of progress in trade negotiations and pressures that often created diversions from the principles arising out of trade negotiations, primarily in the form of laxity instead of discipline in the application of the rules to certain political and economically sensitive sectors. Thus, *Developing Countries in the GATT Legal System* often recounts in fascinating detail the political and economic calculus adopted by trade negotiators as they both struggled toward and departed from progress in the trading regime.

Hudec's unique sensibility also caused him to endorse across-the-board liberalization, rather than special treatment, for developing countries. Given the pressures of internal political economy, a strong external impetus toward freer trade was necessary to ensure that negotiators would hew a liberalizing path that would ultimately benefit both their own economies and the global economy as a whole. Additionally, the reduction of global trade barriers would create countervailing domestic producer groups who could push for expanded foreign market access and therefore apply their disproportionate political influence to the greater good of trade liberalization. In this regard, Hudec warned against according preferential treatment to developing countries, fearing that the dangers of capture and self-interest would lead to the abuse of such arrangements to the detriment of both consumers and less advantaged and powerful producers within those countries.

Developing Countries in the GATT Legal System detailed the first few decades of dialogue and evolution in law and policy within the GATT on the question of trade and development. Since the 1987 publication of Hudec's original volume, much has changed within the international trading regime and in the contributions to this volume. Yet the WTO remains a critical forum for discussions of poverty focused on the role of international trade in helping people and countries to escape poverty, and an important role for trade scholars remains the assessment of the extent to which failure to modify the rules in favor of these constituencies may deny them the ability to escape poverty.

Trade, along with the WTO, is an engine for global growth. Although growth is expected to ameliorate poverty,[3] the WTO has not yet directly confronted questions regarding the global distribution of its benefits. However, various initiatives in connection with the Doha Development Agenda (DDA) may be

---

3. See the preamble language quoted above.

seen as opening up direct confrontation. The focus of the trading system's efforts on development has moved from special treatment for developing countries toward a commitment to nondiscriminatory liberalization in the agricultural and industrial products in which they may enjoy economic advantages. At the same time, the question of whether there is a continuing role for the principle of special and differential treatment (S&D treatment) retains significance in the ongoing WTO negotiations under the DDA.

Poor-country economies, like other economies, of course, include domestic producers interested in protection from competition, domestic producers interested in promoting exports, and domestic consumers interested in inexpensive goods. Standard political economy analysis suggests that domestic producers interested in protection would be able to overcome domestic consumers interested in inexpensive goods without the political intervention of domestic producers interested in promoting exports.

The WTO provides an occasion to motivate domestic producers interested in promoting exports to intervene by providing the possibility for commitments by other states to liberalize access for their exports. This promotes liberalization and the possibility of export-led growth. But the WTO also provides restrictions that are understood by some to limit the scope for industrial policy that can also induce growth. How can WTO rules be structured to limit the scope for protection by developing countries while maximizing the scope for industrial policy that may promote growth?

This volume provides a comprehensive, nuanced, and varied view of the position of developing countries in the WTO legal system. It comprises essays by a spectrum of contributors invited to comment on the issues at the heart of *Developing Countries in the GATT Legal System*. These scholars were invited to gather and discuss their work at the University of Minnesota in the spring of 2007 in celebration of the twentieth anniversary of Hudec's volume. One of our main goals as coconvenors of this conference was to create a forum for dialogue that would reflect the wide array of viewpoints, approaches, and substantive topics that have come to characterize debate over the WTO and its role in economic and social development. The contributors here are leading authors in trade law, law and economics, law and philosophy, and law and political economy.

In the remainder of this introduction, we offer a broad overview of current themes in the discourse on the WTO and developing countries and conclude by describing the contributing essays.

A. TRADE LIBERALIZATION AND POVERTY REDUCTION: THE ROLE OF SPECIAL AND DIFFERENTIAL TREATMENT

i. Special and Differential Treatment: An Overview of the Pre-Uruguay Round Era

Three issues relating to trade liberalization and development have been important since the early history of the GATT, particularly in the evolution of the concept of S&D treatment: (i) nonreciprocity for developing countries, (ii) 'permissive protection' for developing countries versus promotion of domestic liberalization and institutional reform, and (iii) increased market access for developing country products and services in developed country markets (as well as other developing country markets).

Although it features prominently in the DDA, it appears that S&D treatment, at least as applied so far, has had limited utility.[4] Special and differential treatment is a complex phenomenon—some aspects of S&D treatment are undoubtedly somewhat beneficial. It includes several specific rules and approaches that can be placed in three categories: nonreciprocity, preferential market access, and permissive protection.[5]

First, S&D treatment includes the concept, initially expressed in the mid-1960s, that poor countries will not be expected or requested to make reciprocal concessions in trade negotiations (nonreciprocity).[6] This concept has clearly been honored in the breach in connection with recent negotiations with larger developing countries, including Brazil, China, and India, with leading industrialized countries and even WTO officials calling on them to make concessions to promote the Doha Development Agenda. After its articulation in the 1960s, this vague principle was later incorporated in Part IV of GATT.[7] However, as several commentators have noted, those who are not required to reciprocate often find coincidentally that few concessions are accorded to them—even under conditions of most favored nation (MFN) status.[8] This is because the products of export

---

4. Paragraph 44 of the Doha Ministerial Declaration calls for a review of S&D treatment, with a view toward making the relevant provisions more precise, effective, and operational. For a proposal to revise S&D treatment in order to make it more favorable to poor countries, see WTO 'Communication from Cuba, Dominican Republic, Honduras, India, Indonesia, Kenya, Malaysia, Pakistan, Sri Lanka, Tanzania, Uganda, and Zimbabwe, Proposal for a Framework Agreement on Special and Differential Treatment' WT/GC/W/442 (2002). For the history of the concept of S&D treatment, see JH Jackson, *World Trade and the Law of the GATT: A Legal Analysis of the General Agreement on Tariffs and Trade* (Indianapolis: Bobbs-Merrill, 1969) 625–71. For an analysis of the S&D treatment principle, see P Lichtenbaum, 'Special Treatment' vs. 'Equal Participation': Striking a Balance in the Doha Negotiations' (2002) 17 AUIL Rev 1004. See also J Whalley, 'Special and Differential Treatment in a Millennium Round' (1999) CSGR Working Paper 30/99 <http://www.warwick.ac.uk/fac/soc/CSGR/wpapers/wp3099.PDF>; C Michalopoulos, 'The Role of Special and Differential Treatment for Developing Countries in GATT and the World Trade Organization' (2000) <http://www.worldbank.org/research/trade/archive.html>.

5. See WTO, 'Committee on Trade and Development, Implementation of Special and Differential Treatment Provisions in the WTO Agreements and Decisions' WT/COMTD/W/77 (2000).

6. WTO, BISD (13th Supp. 1965).

7. Hudec (n 2 above) 58.

8. See, eg, C Michalopoulous, 'Developing Country Strategies for the Millennium Round' (1999) 33(5) JWT 1, 25; Hudec (n 2 above) 46.

interest to developing countries often differ from those of interest to other countries and are not included in the give-and-take of negotiation over concessions.

Second, S&D treatment includes the aspiration to provide enhanced market access to developing country products. Partly because of the principle of non-reciprocity, this aspiration was often ignored. However, the area in which S&D treatment has had its greatest effect is in connection with the Generalized System of Preferences (GSP), which provides for reduced tariff treatment for certain developing country products.

Third, S&D treatment includes greater permission for protection, in particular under Articles XII and XVIII of GATT,[9] relating to balance of payments. While some economists, led by Dani Rodrik, believe that protection may foster domestic industries, there is a counterargument to the effect that protection may sustain geriatric or crony industries. Thus, the question about permission for protection is one of selectivity. Hudec believed that developing countries, like other countries, need the external constraints of WTO law in order to deny protection to undeserving industries.

ii. Domestic Reform

As Michael Finger has pointed out, '(p)erhaps the least development-friendly side of the Doha Declaration is its willingness to ladle out 'special and differential treatment' without a perception of where developing Members would be better off if *they themselves* observed the disciplines the negotiations aim to establish'.[10] For much of the past 20 years, a consensus—part of the 'Washington Consensus'—developed that poor countries would benefit from liberalization of their domestic markets. The debate about whether protection of domestic markets is good or bad for poor countries has recently been revived.[11] However, there still seem to be solid reasons for poor countries to liberalize at some point in their development path. The important issue here is *context*. In some cases, liberalization will be important to break the grip of oligopoly or cronyism, and provide investor inputs or consumer products more affordably or establish infrastructure for other productive activities. In other cases, there may be a legitimate basis for limiting the impact of imports—particularly if those imports are

---

9. See C Thomas, 'Balance-of-Payments Crises in the Developing World: Balancing Trade, Finance and Development in the New Economic Order' (2000) 15 AUIL Rev 1249, 1256.

10. JM Finger, 'A Diplomat's Economics: Development and Trade Perspectives on the Doha Agenda', working paper dated 10 May 2002 (emphasis in original).

11. See D Rodrik and F Rodríguez, 'Trade Policy and Economic Growth: A Skeptic's Guide to the Cross-National Evidence' in B Bernanke and KS Rogoff (eds), *Macroeconomics Annual 2000* (2001). Even more recently, see A Estevadeordal and AM Taylor, 'Is the Washington Consensus Dead? Growth, Openness, and the Great Liberalization, 1970s–2000s' (2008) NBER Working Paper No. W14264.

heavily subsidized, as in the case of some agriculture—to allow for the development of sustainable and competitive national industries, or to ease a process of economic reform or transition.

iii. Market Access in Developed Countries

There is a strong consensus that liberalization by the wealthy states in agriculture, textiles, and tropical products, even on an MFN basis, would assist growth in poor countries although there is wide variation in views regarding the magnitude of benefit.[12] For example, exports from developing countries are limited by continuing developed country tariffs (including quotas that were 'tariff-ied' in the Uruguay Round), domestic supports, and export subsidies. And indeed, market access in products of export interest to poor countries would be an important way to enhance livelihoods in those countries although it is not unambiguous. Easier exports to wealthy countries could mean higher prices at home. Reduction of wealthy country export subsidies on agriculture could hurt impoverished consumers in food-importing states. Import surges from wealthy countries with cheap agriculture developed as a product of superior technology and/or technologies of scale could remove or damage domestic food production—a sensitive political topic as most countries both attach special cultural significance to their rural agricultural communities and see self-reliance in the area of food production as of special importance.

Tariff peaks and tariff escalation in connection with goods of export interest to poor countries have restricted market access not only in agriculture, textiles, and tropical products, but also in other manufactured goods.[13] While developed country tariffs now average less than 5 percent, Hoekman points out that tariff peaks—higher tariffs—are 'often concentrated in products that are of interest to developing countries'.[14] Many of these apply to agricultural products, and they are often associated with tariff escalation, by which the tariffs on unprocessed products are disproportionately less than the tariffs on processed products, providing perverse incentives against manufacturing in poor countries. Tariff peaks may be a result of the principle of nonreciprocity or the result of 'simple political economy'[15] that is the result of some combination of a desire to protect the jobs of the relatively poor in rich countries and to respond to the other sociocultural values described earlier.

---

12. See *Make Trade Fair, Rigged Rules and Double Standards: Trade, Globalisation and the Fight Against Poverty* (2002) <www.maketradefair.com> [hereinafter the Oxfam Report].

13. Paragraph 16 of the Doha Declaration calls for the reduction of tariff peaks and tariff escalation.

14. B Hoekman, 'Strengthening the Global Trade Architecture for Development: The Post-Doha Agenda', working paper dated January 2002, 5.

15. J Bhagwati, 'The Poor's Best Hope' Economist (20 June 2002) 24.

While the GSP has provided modest benefits, it has not been applied to provide greater market access for many of the most important poor country products,[16] and the United States and European Communities (EC) have imposed substantial conditions on access to their Generalized System of Preferences (GSP) programs.[17] 'Graduation' policies including ceilings on eligible exports have also diminished the utility of GSP. Furthermore, as developed country tariffs have decreased to an average of less than 5 percent and with the formation of more free trade areas and customs unions, the preferences under the GSP have been greatly eroded and will be further eroded in future. The magnitude of the 'differential' has declined substantially. If benefits are unstable and are a wasting asset, they cannot form a sound basis for investment that would allow poor countries to actually achieve market access. The principle of nonreciprocity, as implemented through GSP, seems to have the effect of diminishing incentives for liberalization by beneficiary countries.[18] The dangers of relying on GSP programs and the lack of certainty that they will effectively create 'infant' industries that can become independently competitive was perhaps best demonstrated by the overhaul of tariff systems for textile industries, long an area in which developed countries maintained protectionist systems that benefited vulnerable domestic workforces, but within that supported benefits for particular developing country textile imports. With the removal of that system, certain powerfully expanding developing country economies, and most particularly China, threatened to eclipse the textile industries that had developed elsewhere. The textile example also demonstrates acutely the differences among developing countries and the dangers inherent in assuming that all countries have similar issues. The limitations on the GSP system and its perverse incentives to remain within primary-product industries had undoubtedly contributed to the fact that most of the benefits of such systems had gone to economies that already possessed the attributes necessary to succeed in export markets—namely the Newly Industrializing Countries (NICs).

In 2004, the WTO Appellate Body made an important decision regarding the scope of permissible conditionality—reciprocity—that may be applied in connection with GSP programs under WTO law. The *EC-Tariff Preferences* decision examined a complaint by India against the EC regarding the conditions under

---

16. Paragraph 42 of the Doha Ministerial Declaration provides a commitment to the *objective* of duty-free, quota-free market access for products originating from least developed countries. If realized, this commitment could be of some importance.

17. These conditions have been subject to challenge, and to some extent, revision. See discussion below.

18. C Ozden and E Reinhardt, 'The Perversity of Preferences: GSP and Developing Country Trade Policies, A1976–2000', working paper dated 24 May 2002 <http://userwww.service.emory.edu/~erein/research/gsp2.pdf>.

which the EC accords tariff preferences to developing countries.[19] The Appellate Body found that the requirement in the Enabling Clause for nondiscriminatory treatment does not require formally identical treatment but requires identical treatment of similarly situated beneficiaries. The distinction among beneficiaries must 'respond positively' to the needs of developing countries. Thus, reciprocity in the sense of developed countries extracting policy concessions in exchange for GSP treatment is sharply constrained. We may expect that the content and scope of this requirement will be tested in future litigation.

iv. Special and Differential Treatment in the Uruguay Round

As noted previously, prior to the Uruguay Round, S&D treatment included several specific rules and approaches that can be placed in three categories: nonreciprocity, preferential market access, and permissive protection.[20]

The principle of nonreciprocity was abandoned, or at least broadly modified, in the realization, as opposed to the rhetoric, of the Uruguay Round. This was partly due to a perception that S&D treatment had not provided significant benefits in the past.[21] It was also probably partly due to deep shifts in global political economy that had dissolved the political and theoretical basis for the major point of view arguing for nonreciprocity, a perspective that grew out of both radical dependency theory and reformist, UN-centered 'structuralist' reformers such as Raul Prebisch. While this point of view had reached a high point of sorts in the GATT context with the establishment of the GSP Waiver in 1974, over the ensuing two decades its effectiveness had waned for a variety of reasons.

First, the collective political force of developing countries acting as a bloc, as in the 'Group of 77,' had dissolved as a consequence of both internal stratifications and conflicts among developing countries and external alliances among individual or small groups of countries had dissolved that political reality. Examples abound but include the tension between the success of the Oil-Producing Exporting Countries' (OPEC) success in challenging developed-country economic control over oil prices and the deleterious effect of the OPEC price hikes on import prices for other, less well-off developing economies; the growth of a special trade system for former colonies in Africa, the Caribbean, and the Pacific (ACP) of European countries that became known as the Lome agreements; the creation of special arrangements between the United States and countries in the Latin American region of the Andes mountains, partially

---

19. WTO, *European Communities—Conditions for the Granting of Tariff Preferences to Developing Countries* (20 April 2004) WT/DS246/AB/R.

20. See WTO, 'Note by Secretariat, Implementation of Special and Differential Treatment Provisions in the WTO Agreements and Decisions' (2001) WT/COMTD/W/77/Rev.1.

21. See J Whalley, 'Special and Differential Treatment in the Millennium Round' (1999) 22 W Econ 1065.

intended to dissuade producers in those countries from turning to lucrative illegal drug markets; and so on. By the early 1980s, moreover, differences in fundamental underlying conditions had become all too clear. For example, whereas annual per capita income in Ghana roughly equaled that in South Korea three decades before *Developing Countries in the GATT Legal System*, by its year of publication, purchasing power in the latter country had increased to approximately ten times that of the former.[22] Thus, the underlying economic argument for developing countries to act as a bloc had, quite simply, weakened from many different directions.

The ability of developing countries to act collectively as a negotiating bloc in the GATT necessarily weakened further as many leading economies faced serious debt crises, requiring them to rely on developed-country governments and financial institutions, and as a consequence to internalize the prescriptions that became known as the 'Washington Consensus': liberalization, privatization, and fiscal austerity. Beyond the pressures exerted by the Bretton Woods Institutions and their developed-country leaders, however, many of these reforms were also welcomed domestically by populations who had failed to see the benefits of the infant-industry, structuralist/protectionist program.

Thus, by the beginning of the Uruguay Round, the climate in the global political economy and international institutional and legal landscape had changed such that the overall position of developing countries had transformed from one of demanding deep structural change toward a 'New International Economic Order',[23] sharply criticized by Hudec in his 1987 work, into one of reconciliation with the liberal values of the global North, toward what has been called 'deep integration.' Of course, to state the transformation in such terms ignores the complexity and compromise pervasive in both eras—from the limitations in the GSP that Hudec described to the difficulties with agricultural liberalization described in this volume.

Nevertheless, the birds-eye view revealed a marked shift in the Uruguay Round, from one of at least superficial recognition of the centrality of S&D treatment toward one of limiting the effects of S&D treatment in the categories of nonreciprocity, preferential market access, and permissive protection, as described at the beginning of this section.

One may argue that nonreciprocity was abandoned in the sense that developing countries were expected to reciprocate in terms of market access to goods and of the Agreement on Trade Related Aspects of Intellectual Property (TRIPS) and services. For example, in connection with the core GATT issue of tariffs,

---

22. H Werlin, 'Ghana and South Korea: Lessons from World Bank Case Studies' (1991) 11 Pub Admin & Dev 245, 246.

23. See, eg, Hudec (n 2 above) 22.

cuts were expected of developing countries at only a slightly lower level compared to those provided by developed countries.[24]

Preferential market access was reduced in the Uruguay Round by virtue of overall reductions in tariffs on industrial goods. The reduction in the value of preferences due to MFN tariff reductions became a significant impediment in the DDA negotiations. Furthermore, the Uruguay Round did nothing to reduce the erosion of preferential market access through conditionality imposed with respect to preference schemes (although the *EC-Tariff Preferences* decision has subsequently constrained conditionality). This conditionality might be understood as a type of broad reciprocity.

Third, permission for protection under the balance-of-payments exceptions was constrained and effectively reduced under the Uruguay Round Understanding on Balance-of-Payments Provisions.

In the Uruguay Round, a new type of S&D treatment emerged. This new type includes two facets: technical assistance in connection with implementation and transition periods. The Sanitary and Phytosanitary Agreement (SPS), Technical Barriers to Trade Agreement (TBT), and TRIPS Agreement all contain provisions for technical assistance. These provisions have varying degrees of binding force, but none of them may be characterized as clear and unconditional obligations. Important transition period provisions include those in the TRIPS Agreement, the Trade Related Investment Measures Agreement (TRIMS), the Subsidies and Countervailing Measures Agreement (SCM), the SPS Agreement, and the TBT Agreement. At the time of this writing, all of these transition periods contained in the Uruguay Round agreements had passed although some had been subsequently extended.

B. THE WTO AND THE RIGHT TO REGULATE FOR DEVELOPMENT

One of the critical questions about the GATT and the WTO has been the degree to which they have constrained the 'right to regulate,' in particular the degree to which they have constrained the ability of developing countries to implement development policy.[25] In 2004, Dani Rodrik wrote that

> '(a)lmost all successful cases of development in the last fifty years have been based on creative and often heterodox policy innovations . . . . nations combined their trade policy with unorthodox policies: high levels of tariff and non-tariff barriers, public ownership of large segments of banking and

---

24. JM Finger and LA Winters, 'Reciprocity in the WTO' in B Hoekman, A Mattoo and P English (eds) *Development, Trade and the WTO: a Handbook* (2002) 50, 58 and note 8.

25. See, eg, KP Gallagher (ed), *Putting Development First: The Importance of Policy Space in the WTO and International Financial Institutions* (2005).

industry, export subsidies, domestic content requirements, import-export linkages, patent and copyright infringements, directed credit, and restrictions on capital flows.... (T)rade liberalization was a gradual process....'[26]

Of course, the correlation of these heterodox policies with successful development would not necessarily indicate a causal relationship. Nor is there solid econometric evidence of correlation between heterodoxy and growth or of correlation between orthodoxy and growth. It is still worth assessing, as a descriptive if not a normative matter, which heterodox policies are constrained by WTO law.

The Uruguay Round agreements did much to reduce the scope of special exceptions from GATT disciplines available to developing countries. This meant that for the first time, developing countries would have effectively binding obligations in the GATT/WTO system. The enhancement of procedures for litigation under the Dispute Settlement Understanding (DSU) meant that these obligations would be judicially applicable, while the substantive changes in the obligations meant that these obligations would actually constrain developing country measures. They therefore reduced the policy flexibility of developing countries.

The Washington Consensus continued to erode after the conclusion of the Uruguay Round.[27] In fact, something of a backlash against the Washington Consensus took place. Part of this backlash included a return to arguments for infant-industry protection as a basis for export-led growth. While there seems to be wide agreement among economists that infant-industry protection in developing countries is not necessarily adverse to development, there are significant questions about the choice of industries for protection, the duration and magnitude of protection, and the effects of protection on reciprocal negotiations for liberalization. Importantly, even the backlash has not included a reversion to import substitution as a strategy for growth. An import substitution strategy would be aligned with maintenance of high import barriers, which would require a negotiating position of nonreciprocity if developed country import barriers are to be reduced.

The GATT 1947 obligations that developing countries incurred did not significantly restrict their development policy. As set forth, developing countries had few obligations to liberalize, could use balance-of-payments exceptions to protect domestic markets, and had few other obligations. This changed in the Uruguay Round, with increased tariff and other commitments, reduced access to balance-of-payments exceptions, greater additional obligations, and stronger

---

26. D Rodrik, 'How to Make the Trade Regime Work for Development' (2004) <http://ksghome.harvard.edu/~drodrik/How%20to%20Make%20Trade%20Work.pdf>.

27. See N Birdsall and A De La Torre, *Washington Contentious: Economic Policies for Social Equity in Latin America* (2001); JE Stiglitz, *Globalization and its Discontents* (2002).

dispute settlement. On the other hand, while many developing countries accepted broad tariff bindings in the Uruguay Round, for many of them the commitments were well above applied rates. Therefore, the developing countries could simply move up to bound rates in order to obtain an extra measure of protection.

In the paragraphs below, we focus generally on four types of measures: (a) balance-of-payments measures, (b) other protection, (c) subsidies, (d) TRIMS, and (e) TRIPS.

i. Balance-of-Payments Measures

During the pre-1994 GATT period, review of developing country balance-of-payments measures under Article XVIII lost the power to constrain action. Developing countries won wide discretion to determine their balance-of-payments problems and to impose quotas in response.

The Uruguay Round Understanding on the Balance-of-Payments Provisions of the General Agreement on Tariffs and Trade 1994 (the BOP Understanding) made several changes. First, it expressed a preference for price-based measures, such as surcharges, as compared to quotas. The BOP Understanding calls on members to avoid new quotas. Second, the BOP Understanding permits the imposition of balance-of-payments measures without advance approval but subjects them to requirements of subsequent consultations and periodic review. Of importance is that the BOP Understanding affirms that WTO dispute settlement 'may be invoked with respect to any matter arising from the application of restrictive import measures taken for balance-of-payment purposes.' The role of dispute settlement itself was disputed in a case brought against India in 1997. Given the inconclusive nature of most political consultations regarding balance-of-payment measures, binding dispute settlement brought the possibility of greater limitations on the freedom of action of developing countries.

The possibility of protection for balance of payments or infant-industry protection under Article XVIII of GATT has not been viewed as significant. The member states that by 2005 had engaged in consultations within the WTO Committee on Balance-of-Payments Restrictions are Bangladesh, Bulgaria, the Czech Republic, Hungary, India, Nigeria, Pakistan, Romania, the Slovak Republic, Sri Lanka, and Tunisia.

In the years after the conclusion of the Uruguay Round, there were some instances in which states asked whether the GATT-era practices relating to developing countries were really intended to end, countering clear legal text with diplomatic practice, and perhaps intent. This was the thrust of India's position in the *India—Quantitative Restrictions* case, in which India argued for continuity of the lax approach to developing country access to balance-of-payments exceptions that was followed under GATT. The Appellate Body in this case upheld the clear meaning of the Uruguay Round Understanding on Balance of Payments, subjecting member state claims of exceptions under Articles XII or XVIII to judicial scrutiny. Prior to the advent of the WTO, these claims were sometimes subjected to panel evaluation, but developing countries had become accustomed to undisciplined access to these exceptions.

In subsequent Doha Round negotiations, some developing countries have called for a decision to specify that only the BOP Committee would have authority to examine the justification of balance-of-payments measures.

ii. Other Protection

World Trade Organization law broadly constrains efforts at protection. However, it permits certain types of protection. These permitted types of protection include, most important, tariffs at or below bound rates (to the extent that bindings have been made). By selecting areas for higher tariff rates, states retain flexibility for industrial policy. Thus, the only constraint is that imposed by negotiated commitments. Other areas of permitted protection include contingent protection pursuant to antidumping; antisubsidies; safeguard laws; and protection through standards to the extent of compliance with Article III of GATT, the TBT Agreement, and the SPS Agreement. As tariffs have declined, nontariff measures seem to increase.

iii. Subsidies

The SCM Agreement extended the prohibition of export subsidies on manufactured goods to apply to developing countries and also introduced a prohibition on import substitution subsidies—subsidies contingent upon the use of domestic over imported goods. The prohibition on import substitution subsidies had been understood to be included in Article III of GATT.

The prohibition on export subsidies does not apply to least-developed member states designated as such by the United Nations, nor to those listed in Annex VII(b) of the SCM Agreement, until the GNP per capita of such members has reached $1,000 per annum.[28] Neither India nor China is eligible for this exception. For those developing countries that are not eligible for this exception, the SCM Agreement granted an eight-year transition period, which has now passed. Therefore, India and China are prohibited to use export subsidies on manufactured goods.

The prohibition on import substitution subsidies had no general exceptions but only contained transition periods of eight years for least developed countries and five years for developing countries. All developing countries are subject to the prohibition on import substitution subsidies.

---

28. The states listed are Bolivia, Cameroon, Congo, Côte d'Ivoire, Dominican Republic, Egypt, Ghana, Guatemala, Guyana, India, Indonesia, Kenya, Morocco, Nicaragua, Nigeria, Pakistan, Philippines, Senegal, Sri Lanka, and Zimbabwe. See the UN list of 50 least-developed countries at <http://www.un.org/special-rep/ohrlls/ldc/list.htm>.

The SCM Agreement also includes the concept of 'serious prejudice'. Serious prejudice occurs when a subsidy (a) displaces exports or imports, (b) results in significant price undercutting, or (c) results in an increase in the subsidizing country's market share. Where subsidies cause serious prejudice, they may be subject to dispute settlement procedures, with the result that they may be required to be withdrawn or their adverse effects removed.

iv. TRIMS

Within the Uruguay Round negotiations, the developed countries cut back significantly on their original demands with respect to investment liberalization and settled for the TRIMS Agreement that did little more than codify restrictions that had already been found,[29] or at least considered by some to exist, in Articles III and XI of GATT. Under these provisions, investment conditions that discriminate between imported and domestic goods or that restrict imports may be illegal. Thus, the TRIMS Agreement contains an 'illustrative list' of measures inconsistent with GATT. This illustrative list includes domestic content requirements, restrictions on importation of inputs, restrictions on importation of inputs by restricting access to foreign exchange by reference to inflows attributable to the enterprise, and restrictions on exportation of products. In *Indonesia-Autos*, the panel found that local content requirements imposed in connection with favorable treatment for investment violated the TRIMS Agreement.[30]

Notably, the TRIMS Agreement does not restrict the ability of states to impose export performance requirements as a condition for investment permission.[31] Some argue that export performance requirements are a useful second-best response to alleged anticompetitive practices by multinational corporations that might otherwise restrict production for export at their developing country facilities. For a broader discussion of responses to such anticompetitive practices, see the chapter by Daniel Gifford and Robert Kudrle in this volume.

v. TRIPS

The TRIPS Agreement raises a number of issues for developing countries. In this discussion, we focus on its restrictions on policy flexibility and on the ability to provide implicit benefits to local production through appropriation of

---

29. GATT, *Canada—Administration of the Foreign Investment Review Act* BISD 30S/140 (1984). The panel declined to find that export performance requirements violate GATT.

30. WTO, *Indonesia—Certain Measures Affecting the Automobile Industry* (23 July 1998) WT/DS 54, 55, 59, 64/R.

31. See D Rodrik, 'The Economics of Export-Performance Requirements' (1987) 102 QJE 633 (welfare effects of export performance requirements); P Low and A Subramanian, 'Beyond TRIMS: A Case for Multilateral Action on Investment Rules and Competition Policy?' in W Martin and LA Winters (eds), *The Uruguay Round and the Developing Countries* (1996) 380–88.

foreign-owned intellectual property. We do not focus on the absolute costs of the TRIPS Agreement in terms of implementation and payment of royalties, as discussed earlier.

The TRIPS Agreement established requirements for harmonization of intellectual property protection as well as minimum standards for enforcement of intellectual property rights. These provisions exceeded substantially the requirements set forth in the treaties administered by the World Intellectual Property Organization, including the Paris Convention and the Berne Convention, which contained no substantial requirements for harmonization or enforcement and no substantial dispute settlement mechanism.

We may understand the failure to protect foreign intellectual property rights as an implicit subsidy to domestic production, and therefore as a possible means to promote growth domestically. As the most valuable intellectual property rights are owned by persons or firms based in developed countries, the TRIPS Agreement denied developing countries the ability to provide these implicit subsidies at foreign expense. For a broader discussion of TRIPS, see the chapter by Daniel Gervais in this volume.

C. MOVING FORWARD

Given that most developing countries (Brazil, China, India, and a few others may be important exceptions) are unlikely to wield significant market power—to have effects on world prices—in most products, they would be unlikely to capture terms of trade benefits from protection. If they were able to select industries for protection accurately, developing countries might benefit from selective protection of infant industries until these industries become able to compete on world markets. Alice Amsden has argued that domestic 'reciprocal control mechanisms,' under which government support is conditioned upon the achievement of measurable goals, might allow governments to discipline domestic industries in exchange for subsidies.[32]

Like many others, Robert Hudec[33] was skeptical of the ability of developing country governments (and all other governments) to select industries to promote and to deny protection to industries that have little hope of attaining globally competitive efficiency. He felt that selective legal obligations—tariff schedules, restrictions on quotas and other balance-of-payments measures, and today, services commitments—would at least assist developing country governments in resisting calls for protection from these hopeless industries.

---

32. A Amsden, *The Rise of the Rest: Challenges to the West from Late Industrializing Countries* (2001).
33. Hudec (n 2 above).

One reading of Hudec's 1987 work might see it as supportive of the trade component of the Washington Consensus: the prescription for developing countries to liberalize.[34] However, this reading, while partially quite accurate, would miss important nuance. Hudec found that even assuming that some infant-industry protection or subsidization is good for developing countries, some legal commitments would also be good. The trick is in the discrimination: who discriminates and how?

Hudec assumed that the developing country governments themselves would discriminate between good and bad protection and would use their international legal obligations as a tool by which to bind themselves, or more accurately by which to plead to domestic lobbies that they are bound. Where commitments have been made, and now seem inconsistent with development goals of developing countries, what is to be done? Hudec was attracted to the GATT Article XVIII mechanism of multilateral review and chronicled its rise and fall as an effective mechanism for discriminating between valid and invalid protection.

In connection with the DDA, there are important initiatives toward intensifying special and differential treatment for developing countries—for increasing the preferences available to developing countries and reducing the commitments applicable to them. Hudec's work suggested that preferences, at least as heretofore structured, would do little to help developing countries in the real world. Hudec expected these preferences to be granted with strings attached or to develop strings over time; he did not expect the developed world to give something for nothing. While there may be greater political impetus today in developed countries to assist developing countries, it will be difficult to translate this impetus into useful preferences. Hudec also anticipated that these preferences would be granted in ways that resulted in trade diversion hurting other developing countries, rather than trade creation putting the adjustment burden on developed countries. At the 2005 Hong Kong ministerial meeting, ministers agreed to provide duty-free and quota-free access for products from least developed countries. This action accords with Hudec's prediction that preferential treatment would devolve into multiple tiers of preferential treatment. Finally, he understood that these preferences would be unstable, making them poor lures for investment, which is the critical factor in development.

Hoekman, Michalopoulos and Winters find that MFN liberalization of trade in goods and services that are of export interest to developing countries would be superior in global welfare terms to more selective preferences.[35] This is a critical point, and they argue that developing countries should not be placated by preferences but should demand MFN liberalization in areas where they hold actual or

---

34. While this prescription has been criticized and subject to important empirical challenge, the weight of evidence appears to support it.

35. B Hoekman, C Michalopolous, and LA Winters, 'Special and Differential Treatment in the WTO: Moving Forward' (2004) 27 W Econ 481.

potential advantage. This certainly includes trade in unskilled and semiskilled services under Mode 4 of the General Agreement on Trade in Services (GATS) and even more broadly suggests less reticence to put immigration on the table.

Hudec also suggested that reducing the commitments applicable to developing countries might not be helpful to their development. This is more than paternalism; it is based on a political economy perspective that understands that domestic import-competing producer interests are likely to be more influential than domestic consumer interests. Reciprocity is expected to co-opt domestic export producer interests to add their voice to that of the consumers in order to counter the force of the domestic import-competing producers.

This introduction has shown ambivalence regarding restrictions on the 'right to regulate' for industrial policy under WTO law. Some restrictions may be desirable, as Hudec suggested. Other restrictions may be undesirable. As Amsden and Hikino have argued,

> '(a)t close examination . . . the new rules of the World Trade Organization, a symbol of neoliberalism, are flexible and allow countries to continue to promote their industries under the banner of promoting science and technology. The success formula of late industrialization—allocating subsidies in exchange for monitorable, result-oriented performance standards—is still condoned'.[36]

Substantively, the contributions in this book and their responses to and extensions of the central questions in Hudec's 1987 work can be divided into four categories. The first category features a number of essays that respond directly to Hudec's original arguments. This set of papers by Chimni, Dunoff, Finger, and Ostry evaluate the situation of developing countries generally in the WTO. The second and third essay groups take on issues that influence or stem from current and ongoing negotiations and debates on trade and development. The second group of essays includes David Trubek and Patrick Cottrell's broad analysis of the consequences of Hudec's perspective for the international legal system in general and for development policy in particular. It also includes Yong-Shik Lee's call for reform of the organization of the WTO for development policy. This group also features essays with an empirical or law and economics approach; these essays look at institutional challenges for developing-country capacity to benefit from the WTO dispute settlement system, which has now emerged as an undeniably important force in the evolution of international trade law, even if its long-term implications are still far from measurable. Shaffer and Nordstrom, Mavroidis, Hoekman and Horn, Busch and Reinhardt, and Bown examine the situation of developing countries in WTO dispute settlement. Shaffer and Nordstrom examine the problem of developing country capacity to litigate and

---

36. AH Amsden and T Hikino, 'The Bark is Worse than the Bite: New WTO Law and Late Industrialization' (2000) Annals AAPSS 570.

recommend a small-claims-type procedure for the WTO. Mavroidis, Hoekman and Horn provide an empirical analysis of the level of developing country participation in WTO dispute settlement.[37] Busch and Reinhardt, and also Bown, examine the question of developing countries as third-party participants in WTO dispute settlement.

The third group of papers looks at a variety of substantive challenges that are relatively new, as topics of concentrated attention in the context of trade negotiations. Some of these papers examine the issue of market access for developing countries, addressing the central question of the benefits of special and differential treatment in market access for developing countries. Cho's paper focuses on market access within the GATS for unskilled and skilled labor. Hoekman's paper examines more broadly the possibility for increased market access in services under the GATS. Trebilcock and Epps focus on the essential field of agriculture and provide a detailed analysis of the problem of special and differential treatment in that context. Kudrle and Gifford examine the issue of competition law as it pertains to market access. Gervais examines special arrangements in the TRIPS Agreement, the intellectual property agreement within the WTO. Garcia examines the complementary competences and activities of the international financial institutions, focusing on issues of justice that are also applicable to trade institutions.

These chapters address the most pressing and interesting issues in connection with the situation of developing countries in the WTO legal system.

---

37. The Horn-Mavroidis dataset is publicly available from the World Bank. Their paper represents just one possible use of this very rich dataset, which they hope others will use.

PART ONE

THE WTO AND DEVELOPING COUNTRIES

SYSTEMIC PERSPECTIVES

2. DEVELOPING COUNTRIES AND THE GATT/WTO SYSTEM
Some Reflections on the Idea of Free Trade and Doha Round Trade Negotiations

BS CHIMNI[*]

A. Introduction 21
B. Free Trade and Developing Countries 24
    I. Historical and Economic Objections 24
    II. Ethical and Political Objections 28
    III. Nature and Character of GATT/WTO 30
C. Beyond GATT 33
    I. NAMA 33
    II. Services 35
    III. The Special and Differential Treatment Principle 39
D. Conclusion 43

A. INTRODUCTION

Robert Hudec's *Developing Countries in the GATT Legal System* remains, more than two decades after its publication, a most insightful text on the subject.[1] While critical of the trade policies of developing countries, the book considers these sympathetically. Hudec was no less disapproving of the hypocritical policies of the developed countries that preach free trade while practicing protectionism. But his book is, as he himself noted, essentially about what developing countries should do rather than about the trade policies of the developed countries. Through a combination of meticulous attention to detail and generalizations based on a profound understanding of the relevant economic, political, and legal factors, Hudec made out a persuasive case that developing countries should 'in their own economic interest' respond with a fuller commitment to

---

[*] Professor of Law, Jawaharlal Nehru University. I would like to thank Professor Joel Trachtman and participants at the conference for their comments. The usual caveat applies.

[1] R Hudec, *Developing Countries in the GATT Legal System* (Aldershot: Gower, 1987) For a recent appreciation of the work of Hudec, see DM Trubek and CM Patrick, 'Robert Hudec and the Theory of International Economic Law: The Law of Global Space' (2008) paper published by the Society of International Economic Law <http://ssrn.com/abstract=1144724>.

GATT/WTO law.[2] He argued that 'the current policy of non-reciprocity has . . . (had) a deleterious effect on trade policy of developing countries' as it had encouraged inefficient modes of protection.[3] Developing countries have simply become "non-paying participants" in unilateral preferential schemes that cannot be enforced.[4] Hudec firmly believed that 'the MFN obligation is the only foundation on which can be built a legal policy that will be effective in promoting and protecting market access for developing countries that lack economic power'.[5] The developing countries were therefore urged to invest their diplomatic capital not in seeking the expansion of the GSP and other preferential regimes but in ensuring the strict adherence of developed countries to the MFN obligation within GATT/WTO.[6] Bhagwati, a leading trade theorist of our time, agrees when he observes:

'...through much of the postwar period the developing countries were treated with kid gloves on trade liberalization because of the pervasive doctrine of infant-industry protection and the notion that the benefits of open trade did not apply to countries that were behind the curve of development.'[7]

The Bhagwati-Hudec thesis raises the broader question why, despite the convincing case made out on behalf of free trade since the days of Adam Smith and David Ricardo, it does not find adequate support among policy makers and civil society in the developing countries?[8] Why do developing countries continue to

---

2. Ibid 203.
3. Ibid 199.
4. C Ozden and E Reinhardt, 'Unilateral Preference Programs: The Evidence' in SJ Evenett and BM Hoekman (eds), *Economic Development & Multilateral Trade Cooperation* (London and Washington, DC: Palgrave Macmillan, CEPR and World Bank, 2006) 189–211, 209. Ozden and Reinhardt reviewing 'unilateral preference programs' conclude:
. . . .only a few countries are actual beneficiaries, and utilization levels are not high, even in eligible product categories, due largely to rules of origin restrictions. The most interesting finding is that superior export performance is one of the reasons for removal from GSP programs, and that these countries adopt less protectionist trade policies themselves after removal. The link between export performance and removal from GSP is an explicit part of the preference schemes. The evidence suggests that developing countries may find it in their interest to revisit the insistence on SDT and nonreciprocal preferential access to export markets.
5. Hudec (n 1 above) 199.
6. Ibid.
7. Cited in Hudec (n 1 above) 258.
8. A Keck and P Low, 'Special and Differential Treatment in the WTO: Why, When, and How?' in SJ Evenett and BM Hoekman (eds), *Economic Development & Multilateral Trade Cooperation* (London and Washington, DC: Palgrave Macmillan, CEPR and World Bank, 2006) 147–89, 155. The Bhagwati-Hudec thesis has the support of many commentators. Thus, for instance, Keck and Low write:
A particular problem arising from a generalized insistence on the political right to enjoy SDT is the tendency to assume that the best contribution the WTO can make to

pitch for S&D treatment despite the evidence that it has not delivered? A principal objective of this paper is to sketch the *general* or *popular* sources of free trade skepticism among ordinary citizens, civil society organizations, and policy makers in the developing countries. It is contended that the sentiment against free trade in developing countries is not simply a function of rent-seeking special interests. Free trade skepticism is rooted in a profound appreciation of the historical, ethical, legal, and political contexts in which the idea of free trade has been advanced and practiced. Section B therefore rehearses the reasons for free trade skepticism in developing countries.

Section C addresses in this backdrop the critical question raised by Trachtman in his contribution to this volume, that is, 'which obligations should not be imposed on/accepted by developing countries, which obligations should be imposed on/accepted by developing countries, and how and when should these later obligations be contingently relaxed'.[9] While raising the question, Trachtman rightly draws attention to the fact that Hudec's original book 'only addressed GATT, and did not address the WTO'.[10] Therefore, 'significantly, his analysis does not apply directly to TRIPS or TRIMS commitments, or perhaps to certain subsidies commitments'.[11] But in Trachtman's view it would 'seem to apply to GATS liberalization commitments'.[12] The GATT focus on international trade in goods, it is worth noting, also characterizes trade theory in general. On the other hand, the opposition to GATT/WTO law in developing countries is often to the TRIPS, TRIMS, and GATS texts.

In so far as trade in goods is concerned, the central question today is whether developing countries will be compelled to make 'more than reciprocal' concessions in the ongoing Non-Agricultural Market Access (NAMA) Negotiations of the Doha Round of Trade Negotiations? This would, in the light of the arguments made in Section B, be unfortunate from a welfare point of view. A distinct issue is whether the Hudec insights on goods apply to the area of trade in services. It is argued in Section C that since specific commitments undertaken

---

development is to ensure that developing countries assume minimum obligations under the system—the fewer the better. To the extent that developing countries limit their commitment to the system in this manner, they weaken their negotiating position and lessen the degree to which the trading partners are willing to pursue policies that support development. They limit their ability to fashion new rules in a development-friendly manner. They also weaken the scope for challenging elements in the system that are arguably unbalanced, independent of any consideration of SDT. Developing countries also forgo the opportunity to use a commitment to WTO obligations as a weapon against narrowly based domestic pressure to pursue policies that do not reflect the national interests.

9. J Trachtman, Chapter 6 of this collection of essays.
10. Ibid.
11. Ibid.
12. Ibid.

under GATS are difficult to withdraw or modify; enough is not known about the consequences of liberalizing trade in services; and 'services' include key social sectors like education and health: developing countries should err on the side of caution at least where key social sectors are concerned. Finally, the section looks at the question whether keeping the Hudec thesis in view, a fundamentally different S&D treatment principle can be adopted in the WTO? In this respect it is contended that from the perspective of developing countries, the recent formulations which recommend the phasing in of GATT/WTO obligations rather than carving out exceptions to them, may be helpful but difficult to institutionalize.

In sum, it is argued that the principle of free trade may not necessarily lead to just consequences in a world in which countries are at different stages of economic development and power is unequally distributed in internal and international relations. This paper does not contest the fact that there are good reasons for promoting free trade viz., benefits to consumers and increased efficiency/competitiveness of domestic industries. The difficult questions relate to the timing, extent, and distributive consequences of trade liberalization. It makes the 'local context' in which free trade obligations are undertaken of crucial import. It is these that must engage us. For this reason, the paper begins by identifying the basis of free trade skepticism in developing countries.

B. FREE TRADE AND DEVELOPING COUNTRIES

The popular sources of free trade skepticism in developing countries may be considered under three broad heads: (i) Historical and Economic, (ii) Ethical and Political, and (iii) Nature and Character of WTO.[13]

i. Historical and Economic Objections

First, it may be noted that the critique of the principle of free trade is a historically contingent critique. Free trade skeptics ask why developing countries should not pursue policies that the developed countries have *successfully* followed in the past rather than their narration in the *official* history of free trade? The unofficial history of free trade reveals that most developed countries used the instruments of tariffs and subsidies in the nineteenth and much of the twentieth century to strengthen their economies.[14] Thus, for example, the United States maintained average applied industrial tariffs 'of 40 to 50 percent from

---

13. It is worth stressing that the perception of different groups in developing countries is not necessarily the same. Thus, the views of the subaltern classes are different from that of the capitalist classes. See generally BS Chimni, 'The World Trade Organization, Democracy and Development: A View From the South' (2006) 40 JWT 5.

14. H Chang, *Why Developing Countries Need Tariffs: How WTO NAMA Negotiations Could Deny Developing Countries' Right to a Future* (Geneva: South Centre, 2005) xii–xiii.

1820 to 1931'.[15] Indeed, contrary to popular belief, the "notorious" Smoot-Hawley Tariff of 1930 'only marginally (if at all) increased the degree of protectionism in the United States economy".[16] Skeptics also point out that the success stories among developing countries over the last 50 years, including the Republic of Korea and more recently China, India, and Vietnam, have come through the use of tariff walls or other measures of protectionism. The case of Japan was no different.[17] In short, not only historical but also contemporary experience tells us that free trade may be good in principle, but free trade policies need to be implemented gradually as an economy gathers strength and particular sectors become competitive.[18] Bhagwati himself advises that 'the optimal speed at which one

---

15. The infant-industries argument 'was centrally relied on by the USA and Canada in maintaining a high tariff policy throughout most of the nineteenth century and the first quarter of the twentieth century... It is also, more controversially, claimed to have been a central strategic element in the rise of Japan as a major industrial power'. See MJ Trebilcock and R Howse, *The Regulation of International Trade* (3rd edn 1995) 8. It may also be noted that France had average tariffs of 20 to 30 percent from 1913 to 1931. Spain had a 41 percent tariff in 1913 and 1925, rising to 63 percent in 1931. Germany's tariff was 20–21 percent in 1925 and 1931 and 26 percent in 1950'. M Khor, *WTO's Doha Negotiations and Impasse: A Development Perspective* (Penang; Third World Network, 2006) 13.

16. Chang (n 14 above) 41.

'The average tariff rate for manufactured goods that resulted from this bill was 48 per cent, and it still falls within the range of the average rates that had prevailed in the United States since the Civil War, albeit in the upper region of this range. It is only in relation to the brief "liberal" interlude of 1913–1929 that the 1930 tariff bill can be interpreted as increasing protectionism, although even then it was not by very much (from 37 per cent in 1925 to 48 per cent in 1931)'

See Chang (n 14 above) xii–xiii. For a different view, see J Bhagwati, *In Defense of Globalization* (2004) 60–64; K Dam, 'Cordell Hull, the Reciprocal Trade Agreements Act, and the WTO' in E Petersmann (ed), *Reforming the World Trading System* (2005) 83–99, 85. Dam writes that 'the Smoot-Hawley tariff legislation' 'had led to such great general increase in US tariffs in that 1930 legislation that Hull felt that it had been the cause of the Great Depression'.

17. Chang (n 14 above) xii–xiii. Chang therefore aptly observes:

Success stories such as the Japanese and Korean auto industries, or Korean steel conform to the historical pattern established by almost all successful industrial countries from 18th Century Britain onwards. Without protection, Japan and the Republic of Korea would still be exporting silk and wigs made with human hair respectively. Anyone who drives a Japanese or a Korean car is living proof that infant-industry protection is still a very much valid argument in today's world. More recently, China's take-off in the 1990s took place behind average tariffs of over 30 per cent, while Viet Nam has used state trading, import monopolies, import quotas and high tariffs in generating annual growth rates of 8 per cent since the mid 1980s.

18. As Dani Rodrik observes: 'Policy "A" is to be recommended only if conditions "x" "y" and "z" obtain'. India and China have adopted this perspective. See D Rodrick, 'Goodbye Washington Consensus. Hello, Washington Confusion?' <http://209.85.175.104/

liberalizes is not necessarily the fastest'.[19] Thus, China's decision to lock in after a certain stage means that it can reap the benefits that increased competition brings in the wake of its membership of WTO. On the other hand, it is doubtful if the Chinese industry would have developed without state support.[20]

Second, the general historical lesson is reinforced by the colonial experience of developing countries that finds little mention in the official history of free trade. In the colonial era, contrary to the prescriptions of trade theory, the comparative advantage of colonies was coercively restructured. The story of Indian silks and calicoes that were imported into England is widely known: from being an exporter of the finest textiles, India turned into an exporter of raw cotton in the nineteenth century. The economic historian Carlo Coppola has therefore wryly noted that it was 'fortunate for England that no Indian Ricardo arose to convince the English people that, according to the law of comparative costs, it would be advantageous for them to turn into shepherds and import from India all the textiles that were needed. Instead, England passed a series of acts designed to prevent importation of Indian textiles and some "good results" were achieved.'[21] Metropolitan powers greatly benefited from unequal exchange in the colonial period.[22] This is at least true of the trade between Britain and large colonies like India.[23] In the absence of the possibility of developing countries today benefiting from such unequal exchange, what is required is more policy flexibility, be it in terms of giving infant-industry protection or receiving S&D treatment.

Third, the advocates of free trade do not always assess free trade policies in the light of other economic policies that developing countries are often compelled/ coerced to adopt. To be sure, there is the danger here of embracing what Bhagwati calls the *fallacy of aggregation*. He rightly points out that it is mistaken to believe that if you are for free trade you are also for capital account convertibility, direct foreign investment, etc. Bhagwati, however, assumes that developing countries are entirely free to reject or accept certain economic policies. But often these countries are unable, for reasons beyond their control (eg, primary commodity

---

search?q=cache:wylTNamLKZ8J:ksghome.harvard.edu/~drodrik/lessons%25200f%252 othe%25201990s%2520review%2520_jel_.pdf+Dani+Rodrik,+%22Goodbye+Washingt on+Consensus.+Hello,+Washington+Confusion%22&hl=en&ct=clnk&cd=1>.

19. J Bhagwati, *Free Trade Today* (2002) 90.

20. Rodrick (n 18 above).

21. CM Coppola, *European Culture and European Expansion* (1970) 152.

22. Therefore, even as Hudec advised against drawing the wrong lessons in the contemporary world, he noted that 'those that had been colonies had been taught by their parent countries that economic benefit was maximized by controlling trade and suppressing competition from alternative suppliers.' See Hudec (n 1 above) 29.

23. D Naoroji, *Poverty and Un-British Rule in India* (Delhi: Government of India, 1962); B Chandra, The *Rise and Growth of Economic Nationalism in India* (Delhi: People's Publishing House, 1966); and Sumit Sarkar, *Modern India* (Delhi: Macmillan India Ltd, 1983).

crisis, rise of oil prices), including conditionalities imposed by the international financial institutions, to have this policy space. Indeed, if the list of recommendations that eminent trade theorists like Bhagwati advance on global economic policy are accepted by the developed countries, the case against free trade would lose some of its force. These include (a) a liberal immigration policy, and for this purpose create an International Migration Organization; (b) an agreement not to compel a turn to capital account convertibility; and (c) the regulation of transnational corporations through a mandatory code on corporate social responsibility.[24] But these recommendations have found little favor with policy makers of developed countries.

Fourth, there is the problem of providing adjustment assistance to individuals/ communities negatively affected by policies of free trade. The lowering of trade barriers, it is universally recognized, can harm domestic industries with consequences for employees.[25] Therefore, the United States provides for trade adjustment assistance. Under the Trade Act of 2002, the scope of those protected is "far-reaching": 'it includes secondary workers and self-employed persons such as farmers and ranchers. It covers income support for two years as well as a 65 percent tax credit for health insurance while these workers are in re-training'.[26] While this may be far from being an ideal scheme and may also require to be extended to the service sector, it does offer some protection to workers negatively affected by trade liberalization. Developing countries, on the other hand, go in for trade liberalization without the provision of adjustment assistance since they do not have the resources to provide it.[27] The possibility of introducing adjustment assistance will recede further in the future. Many developing countries rely on customs revenues for 20 to 30 percent of government revenue. These would shrink when tariffs are lowered further under the ongoing Doha Round Trade

---

24. Bhagwati (n 16 above); Chimni (n 13 above) 390–91.

25. Indeed, free trade may even accentuate poverty at times Bhagwati (n 19 above) 90.

26. J Gathii, "Insulating Domestic Policy Through International Legal Minimalism: A Re-Characterization of the Foreign Affairs Trade Doctrine" (2004) 25 UPennJIEL 1, 46; US Department of Labor, *Employment & Training Administration* (2007) <http://www.doleta.gov/tradeact/2002act_index.cfm>. The scope of the coverage is sought to be enhanced by those anticipating the effects of further trade liberalization. F Bergsten, 'Rescuing the Doha Round' *Foreign Affairs (WTO Special Edition)*(December 2005) 1, 5.

27. R Chadha and others, 'Computational Analysis of the Impact on India of the Uruguay Round and the Doha Development Agenda Negotiations' in A Mattoo and RM Stern (eds), *India and the WTO* (2003) 13, 14. In sum, as Gathii notes, 'the theory of comparative advantage overstates the benefits of trade liberalization and thereby understates its distributional consequences, especially on those who bear the losses attendant with rising prosperity from freer trade'. JT Gathii, 'Re-characterizing the Social in the Constitutionalization of the WTO: A Preliminary Analysis' (2001) VII Widener Law Symposium Journal 137, 144.

Negotiations on NAMA.[28] It is said that the developing countries may suffer losses worth $63.4 billion under the formula presently proposed in NAMA negotiations, which is incidentally almost four times the possible benefits that may accrue from trade liberalization to developing countries.[29] In these circumstances, trade theorists have called upon international financial institutions 'to provide grant funds to make possible a welfare-enhancing, poverty-reducing transition to free trade'.[30] But the problem in this case may be, as Hoekman notes, the unwillingness to borrow from these institutions. He suggests, instead, 'dedicated grant-based funding' to strengthen an MFN-based system.[31] But should in its absence developing countries go in for hasty structural adjustment as a consequence of adopting policies of trade liberalization? There are in this regard a number of ethical and political issues as well that have not received adequate consideration.

ii. Ethical and Political Objections

First, in calling for structural adjustment through trade liberalization, free trade theorists tend to treat individuals and local communities as mere means to an end?[32] Even where adjustment assistance is provided, the question remains whether it takes care of the social and cultural loss to individuals and local communities. Kant exhorted that 'so act that you use humanity, whether in your person or in the person of any other, always at the same time as an end, never merely as a means'.[33] Murphy and Nagel therefore legitimately ask, 'whether it is right to change the rules midway through people's lives'?[34] To be sure, the means and ends issue is implicated both when the tool of protection is used as when it is removed; protectionist policies also have moral consequences. But trade liberalization has a more certain and immediate impact on human rights and therefore cannot be ignored despite its apparent status quo bias. For as Fernandez and Rodrik note, the status quo bias is the result of 'uncertainty about who the

---

28. Khor (n 15 above).

29. N Kumar and KP Gallagher, 'Relevance of "Policy Space" for Development: Implications for Multilateral Trade Negotiations' (2007) RIS Discussion Paper 120, 1-26, 4 <http://www.ris.org.in/dp120_pap.pdf>.

30. Bhagwati (n 19 above) 90.

31. B Hoekman, 'Expanding WTO membership and Heterogeneous Interests', (2005) 4 WT Rev 401, 404.

32. P Alston, 'Resisting the Merger and Acquisition of Human Rights by Trade Law: A Reply to Petersmann' (2002) 13 EJIL 815.

33. D Palmeter, 'A Note on the Ethics of Free Trade' (2005) 4 WT Rev 449, 459.

34. Murphy and Nagel go on to note: 'Even though no one may be entitled to any particular bundle of resources in the abstract sense, a plausible norm of political morality has it that we are entitled to enjoy what we had reason to believe would be the consequences of our choices under the prevailing institutional arrangement'. Cited in ibid 451.

individual winners and losers from a policy change might be'.[35] In these circumstances, the welfare of those negatively impacted by free trade policies cannot be sacrificed.

Second, feminist trade theory has in recent years highlighted the fact that mainstream trade theory has been 'gender-blind'.[36] Where in a rare instance gender has been taken into account, the methodology and empirical evidence used to show that free trade contributes to gender equality has been questioned.[37] The understanding of feminist trade theory coincides with the popular view that free trade contributes to gender inequality and highlights the need for looking at gender indicators for monitoring trade agreements.[38]

Third, free trade skeptics distinguish between harm caused to individuals and local communities by fellow nationals as against those caused by strangers. As Kemp points out, 'individuals often think beyond their own narrow self-interest when considering government economic policies in areas such as trade. However, this altruism may extend only to conationals, rather than to everyone affected by these government decisions'.[39] This is not an entirely irrational response. The reason why harm caused by a foreigner is viewed with greater disapproval is that the goal of distributive justice is still confined to the nation state and the idea of *global* distributive justice hotly contested (even in the era of accelerated globalization).[40] The classic Hull view that 'one could not expect to get something for nothing', and that 'reciprocity was the key' even when economic theory suggests that unilateral tariff reductions are advantageous is simply an acceptance of this reality.[41] In other words, where developing countries are concerned, the framing moral calculus for free trade is how much fellow nationals gain from international trade as against strangers. Given the fact of unequal power and resources, this moral calculus is however not to the point where developed countries are concerned.

Fourth, while free trade theory uses the idea of special interests to emphasize the benefits of accepting GATT/WTO obligations, it proceeds to make other recommendations (eg, with regard to adjustment assistance) on the assumption

---

35. Cited in S Kemp, 'Psychology and opposition to free trade' (2007) 6 WT Rev 25, 31.
36. D Elson, C Grown and N Cagatay, 'Mainstream, heterodox and feminist trade theory' in I Stavern and others (eds), *The Feminist Economics of Trade* (2007) 33, 36.
37. Ibid 37–41; E Kongar, 'Importing equality or exporting jobs? Competition and gender wage and employment differentials in US manufacturing' in ibid 215.
38. On gender indicators to monitor trade indicators, see I Van Stavern, 'Gender indicators for monitoring trade indicators' in I Stavern and others (eds), ibid 257.
39. Kemp (n 35 above) 35.
40. J. Gathii, 'International Justice and the Trading Regime' (2007) 19 EmILRev 1407; JP Trachtman, 'Welcome to Cosmopolis, World of Boundless Opportunity' (2006) 39 CornILJ 477; BS Chimni, 'A Just World Under Law: A View from the South' (2007) 22, AUIL Rev 199, 212.
41. Dam (n 16 above) 86.

that the State is a neutral actor possessing autonomy from dominant interest groups. But if the extent of autonomy is misjudged or exaggerated, the State may not heed the concerns of the poor and marginal groups negatively affected by trade liberalization. Trade-led growth rates do not, it is widely accepted, automatically translate into welfare for the poor. For this to happen, appropriate laws and institutions have to be put in place.[42] In other words, simply stating that 'x' is the rational response in situation 'y' is not very helpful. Trade theorists may legitimately argue that they can do no more than indicate what these are. On the other hand, free trade skeptics are well within their rights to point out that since state policies are determined by dominant social classes, the appropriate legal and institutional framework to benefit the poor may never be created. In countries where the working class/peasant movement is weak, it may not be able to restrain the State from undertaking trade liberalization to the disadvantage of subaltern groups. Indeed, the inability of the organized worker/peasant movement to mobilize opposition explains recent trade liberalization in countries like India. In short, free trade theory relies on political assumptions that do not withstand close scrutiny.

iii. Nature and Character of GATT/WTO

Likewise free trade theorists rely on questionable assumptions about the nature and character of GATT/WTO. *First*, free trade theory yields a set of abstract propositions that do not take into account the manner in which its recommendations are negotiated and embodied in legal texts. This process is seen as the domain of international politics. But the popular support or opposition to free trade is often a function of how its principles are negotiated and codified in legal regimes. Free trade skeptics draw attention in this regard to the undemocratic nature of the trade negotiation process that led to the creation of the WTO and characterize all subsequent negotiations.[43]

Second, the rules embodied in GATT/WTO have always favored the developed world. The developed countries, for instance, have taken more than 60 years for undertaking structural adjustment of inefficient industry. As Hudec pointed out, the GATT incorporated 'a very large number of exceptions written for the benefit of developed country producers'.[44] These included the right to use quantitative import restrictions on agricultural imports and export subsidies. Equally, the 'escape clause' seemed to testify to a developed country view that trade protection could "help" weak industries. Further, as Hudec went on to note, exports of advanced developing countries were faced with discriminatory protection whenever these were 'uncomfortably successful' in the markets of developed countries. Such protection often assumed 'the form of export-restraint arrangements

---

42. Bhagwati (n 16 above) 260.
43. Chimni (n 13 above), 13ff.
44. Hudec (n 1 above).

negotiated "outside" the framework of GATT norms, rules and procedures'.[45] In the textile sector, new trade restrictions were constantly put in place to limit the competitive exports from developing countries, ending only with the Agreement on Textiles and Clothing (ATC).[46] The policy space historically available to the developed countries to undertake slow structural adjustment is today denied by GATT/WTO rules to developing countries.

Third, free trade skeptics are concerned about the linkages between trade and nontrade issues like environment and labor standards being established. Here the popular view is no different from that of trade theorists. Thus, for example, Bhagwati notes in his book *Free Trade Today* that these nontrade issues 'are more potent and potentially lethal to free trade'.[47] He views it as 'dangerous rhetoric' to suggest that unequal environmental and labor standards amounts to unfair trade.[48] But attempts at establishing these linkages continue at various levels. It also did not deter the WTO Appellate Body in the *Shrimp Turtle II* case to decide that in the final analysis (ie, subject to certain procedural preconditions being met), unilateral trade measures could be used to deny market access to exports of developing countries.[49] Reference may also be made to the near consensus that the WTO Agreement on TRIPS has little to do with trade and negatively affects the welfare of the peoples of the developing countries. In these circumstances, it is not difficult to understand the popular opposition to the idea of 'free trade'. This is true, especially because the results of the Uruguay Round of Trade Negotiations were adopted through the 'single undertaking' mechanism that removed the possibility of developing countries not accepting extra trade obligations. The 'single undertaking' mechanism is also the basis on which the Doha Round is now being negotiated.

Fourth, free trade skeptics point to the manner in which legal obligations relating to free trade are interpreted; developed-country protectionism is often smuggled in through the interpretative route. This is especially so in the case of WTO agreements because indeterminacy happens to be their defining feature. Broadly speaking, there are five categories of indeterminacy that typify

---

45. Hudec (n 1 above) 15.
46. See Trebilcock and Howse (n 15 above) 472. In this light, one has to agree with Trebilcock and Howse that
    although it is fashionable to blame leftist theories of development economics and the influence of Soviet bloc central planning approaches for the protectionist follies of the developing world in this epoch (ie, GATT era) the treatment of developing countries in the Western-dominated global trading order made inward-oriented policies easy, while it set up obstacles to export-led growth.
47. Bhagwati (n 19 above) 47.
48. Bhagwati (n 19 above) 57.
49. BS Chimni, 'WTO and Environment: The Legitimization of Unilateral Trade Sanctions' (2002), 37 Econ & Pol Weekly 133; BS Chimni, 'WTO and Environment: The *Shrimp-Turtle* and *EC-Hormone* cases', (2000) 35 Econ & Pol Weekly 1752.

WTO agreements. These include indeterminacy (i) relating to the object and purpose of WTO agreements; (ii) arising from linguistic ambiguities and unanticipated gaps in the text (iii) resulting from the fact that the legal texts are written in very general terms and then applied to complex factual situations, (iv) arising from the inability to reach closure during negotiations on particular issues; and (v) stemming from the inapplicability of the formal doctrine of precedent. These categories of indeterminacy are to be resolved using international rules of interpretation (customary rules of public international law) that are in turn to be interpreted. The result is that sufficient space is created for interpretations that favor dominant trading interests. Gathii has shown how WTO norms are incorporated 'into US law only to the extent that international trade norms are consistent with US policy considerations.'[50] Illustrating this in the context of Article 17.6(ii) of the ADA, Gathii notes that 'international legal minimalism is facilitated by the plasticity or the possibility of ascribing multiple permissible interpretations of US and international antidumping rules and their interrelationship'.[51] Therefore, 'rather than constraining US sovereignty, international anti-dumping rules seem to promote US power and influence'.[52] The WTO dispute settlement bodies also tend to accept those interpretations that have the support of powerful trading nations (eg, the *Shrimp Turtle* case cited earlier).

To sum up, it is time to ask what do these difficulties/criticisms add up to? While these certainly do not make a case against free trade or for protectionism, the popular sources of trade skepticism do suggest the limits of free trade theory and the need to give it a contextual interpretation. But it may be said that there is little new in this claim inasmuch as advocates of free trade admit the need for some contextual interpretation. The contention is that these difficulties/criticisms cumulatively make a case for *strong* contextual interpretation of the idea of free trade. Such an approach would allow developing countries *greater flexibility* to determine the *timing* and *extent* of trade liberalization in the matrix of prevailing local conditions. It would incorporate the critical insight that trade regimes are, above all, the function of international power relations. Adam Smith himself recognized, it is worth noting in this regard the deleterious role of power in international commerce in observing that such commerce was 'the most fertile source of discord and animosity' and hoped that greater equality between states would lead to making it 'a bond of union and friendship'.[53]

---

50. Gathii (n 26 above) 3.
51. Ibid 5.
52. Ibid 11.
53. S Muthu, 'Adam Smith's Critique of International Trading Companies: Theorizing "Globalization" in the Age of Enlightenment' (2008) 56 Pol Theory 185, 207.

C. BEYOND GATT

In the ongoing Doha Round of Trade Negotiations, the policy flexibility desired by developing countries is being denied by the powerful bloc of western industrialized nations. Their proposals on NAMA and GATS further erode the policy space of developing countries. In the instance of GATS this section takes issue with the Trachtman view that the Hudec thesis on accepting GATT/WTO disciplines can be extended to GATS. Finally, this section considers the proposal advanced by several scholars on the need for an external mechanism that would help convert the "enabling clause" into an "enabling mechanism". The problem in this case is that it may not be easy to establish an international mechanism that has the trust of both the developed and developing countries. In the circumstances, the question is whether the traditional form of S&D treatment is entirely inappropriate?

i. NAMA

The developing countries are today being asked to make major concessions in the ongoing NAMA Negotiations that may result in the codification of a reverse S&D rule or a 'more than full reciprocity' instead of 'less than full reciprocity' principle agreed to for the Doha Round of Trade Negotiations.[54] The Hong Kong Ministerial meeting of December 2005 accepted a Swiss formula that calls for tariff reductions on each product which represents a 'significant departure' from the past practice of reducing only the average of industrial tariff.[55] This means that the developing countries would lose flexibility to 'spread the average over the whole range of tariffs' in keeping with their development goals.[56] It thereby removes the discretion of the policy maker at the product level.[57]

Calculations showed that the developing countries would be making deeper cuts than the developed countries, a far cry from the 'less than reciprocity' principle.[58] In this context, Chang compares the situation of the United States

---

54. Paragraph 16 of the Doha Ministerial Declaration states that the negotiations on NAMA shall take fully into account the special needs and interests of developing countries and least developed countries. WTO, 'Doha WTO Ministerial 2001: Ministerial Declaration' (20 November 2001) WT/MIN (01)/DEC/1.

55. BL Das, 'Dangers in the Dark Alleys'' (2007) 42 Econ & Pol Weekly 627–29.

56. Ibid.

57. J Francois, W Marti, and V Manole, 'Formula Approaches to Liberalizing Trade in Goods: Efficiency and Market Access Considerations' in SJ Evenett and BM Hoekman (eds) (n 8 above) 89. Moreover, 'the Swiss formula connects the initial and final tariffs in such a way that adoption of a lower coefficient results in greater tariff reduction', Das (n 55 above) 629.

58. Chang notes that under the circumstances, 'it is wrong to say that these countries are being less than fully reciprocal, even if they are making less cuts in proportional terms than are the developed countries. In the smoke and mirrors of the Doha Round, the reality

in the late nineteenth until the middle of the twentieth century with that of India:

> When the USA accorded over 40% average tariff protection to its industries in the late 19th century, its per capita income in PPP terms was already about 3/4 that of Britain ($2,599 vs. $3,511 in 1875). And this was when the "natural protection" accorded by distance, which was especially important for the USA, was considerably higher than today.... Compared to this, the 71% trade-weighted average tariff rate that India used to have just before the WTO agreement, despite the fact that its per capita income in PPP terms is only about 1/15 that of the US, makes the country look like a champion of free trade. Following the WTO agreement, India cut its trade weighted average tariff to 32%, bringing it down to the level below which the US average tariff rate never sank between the end of the Civil War and World War II.[59]

India has since brought down its trade weighted average tariff further through unilateral and multilateral tariff cuts. The developing countries have therefore rightly argued:

> Whilst many developing countries have continued to undertake unilateral liberalization beyond their WTO Uruguay Round commitments and reform their industrial sectors, a significant part of their production and employment remain in sensitive sectors, and further liberalization of these sensitive sectors would have to be preceded by carefully managed adjustment policies.[60]

It is not as if developing countries have not been willing to provide more NAMA. But the Group of 11 in June 2006 expressed the legitimate concern that[61]

> ... developed countries are offering a (tariff) reduction of only 20% to 30%. In sharp contrast, in this development Round, developing country Members are being asked to undertake tariff reductions of 60% to 70%. This inverts the mandate of "less than full reciprocity in reduction commitments" by developing countries.[62]

---

for many developing countries is closer to "more-than-full reciprocity"'. Chang (n 14 above) 95.

59. Ibid 47.

60. WTO, 'Reclaiming Development in the WTO Doha Development Round: Submission by Argentina, Brazil, India, Indonesia, Namibia, Pakistan, the Philippines, South Africa, and Venezuela to the Committee on Trade and Development' (1 December 2005) WT/COMTD/W/145 3.

61. The Group of 11 countries are Argentina, Bolivarian Republic of Venezuela, Brazil, Egypt, India, Indonesia, Namibia, Pakistan, Philippines, South Africa, and Tunisia.

62. WTO, 'Negotiating Group on Market Access Communication from the NAMA 11 Group of Developing Country' (6 July 2006) TN/MA/W/79.

But rather than attend to the concerns of developing countries, the February 8, 2008 draft of the chairman of NAMA Negotiations has suggested modalities that perhaps make matters worse.[63] Speaking for the Group of 11, South Africa stressed that what should have been proposed is the negotiation architecture and not the level of ambitions relating to the two key elements of coefficients and flexibilities.[64] Trade Unions from the Group of 11 and other developing countries have expressed their concern about the impact of the new proposals on employment and industrial development and opposed them.[65] Independent analysis confirms that 'the latest draft modalities do not address the core concerns of a large number of developing countries'.[66] Subsequent texts (the May 2008 proposals) have also been found problematic and criticized by developing countries.[67] On the other hand, the developed world, as Hudec had noted, 'seem committed to the practice of imposing new restrictions that limit developing country exports once they begin to cause discomfort and none of the legal strategies currently being advocated appears capable of changing this situation'. Add to this the use of a number of nontariff barriers, including antidumping and strenuous technical regulations, against goods from developing countries, and the problem becomes acute.[68]

ii. Services

In so far as GATS Negotiations are concerned, a key issue is whether the response of developing countries should be based on a different premise from that of

---

63. WTO, 'Draft Modalities for Non-Agricultural Market Access, Negotiating Group on Market Access' (8 February 2008) TN/MA/W/103.

64. M Khor, 'Different responses to issue of Chair's NAMA options' (19 March 2008) <http://www.twnside.org.sg/title2/wto.info/twninfo20080320.htm>.

65. K Raja, 'Trade Unions Voice Opposition to WTO's revised NAMA text' (2008) <http://www.twnside.org.sg/title2/wto.info/twninfo20080220.htm>.

66. P Kumar, and A Kaushik, 'Chair's Draft NAMA Modalities: Against the Core Mandate of Less than Reciprocity' (2008) <http://www.cuts-citee.org/pdf/A-Critical-Note-on-NAMA-Draft-Modalities.pdf >.

67. M Khor, 'Developed and Developing Countries Clash over NAMA Text' (29 May 2008) <http://www.twnside.org.sg/title2/wto.info/twninfo20080531.htm>; South Centre, 'Comments to the Second Revision of the WTO NAMA Draft Modalities' (May 2008) TN/MA/W/103/Rev.1 <http://www.southcentre.org/index.php?option=com_docman&task=cat_view&gid=45&Itemid=69>.

68. WTO (n 60 above) 3.
'Developed countries have largely become highly competitive in the industrial sector and will need to make relatively insignificant adjustments in this Round. However, many developed countries still maintain high tariffs, tariff peaks and tariff escalation on products of interest to developing countries. In addition a range of non-tariff barriers, including strenuous technical regulations and excessive anti-dumping measures, are frequently utilized by developed countries to disrupt developing country exports and potential to export their products to these markets'.

GATT? Or, to put it differently, is there a need to distinguish between unilateral liberalization of the services sector and liberalization under GATS? The answer to both the questions is perhaps a partial 'Yes'.

There is a need to distinguish between unilateral liberalization and GATS liberalization because of three kinds of uncertainties that characterize GATS commitments. These uncertainties relate to (i) the scope and nature of GATS obligations, (ii) the trade impact of GATS commitments, and (iii) the difficulties in modifying or withdrawing GATS commitments.[69] First, GATS is not clear as to the scope of exclusion from the definition of "services" of 'services supplied in the exercise of governmental authority' which is defined as 'any service which is supplied neither on a commercial basis nor in competition with one or more service suppliers'. Thus, to take an extreme example, would the simple fact that public and private service suppliers coexist mean that public services are provided in competition 'with one or more service suppliers'? There is also some anxiety about how issues related to subsidies, treatment of monopolies and domestic regulation, will eventually be handled.[70] Second, the benefits that will accrue from the acceptance of greater WTO discipline are uncertain. As Trachtman concedes in the context of Article VI and disciplines on domestic regulation, 'the general disciplines that exist today are somewhat asymmetric in the wrong direction: they seem to discipline new regulation more strongly than existing regulation, and so may be expected to have a greater restrictive effect on developing countries'.[71]

Finally, given the sensitivity of some service sectors like education and health, there is the issue of inability to recover policy space lost if this proves necessary. In the absence of sufficient information and analysis, there may be unforeseen consequences of undertaking specific commitments.[72] Under the GATS text, certain preconditions (vide Article XXI) have to be met before any commitment

---

69. VJ Anthony, 'Navigating between the Poles: Unpacking the Debate on the Implications for Development of GATS Obligations relating to Health and Education Services' in E Petersmann (ed), *Reforming the World Trading System* (2005) 167, 192.

70. P Agarwal, 'Higher Education Services in India and Trade Liberalization' in R Chanda (ed), *Trade in Services & India: Prospects and Strategies* (2006) 299, 343, and 345.

71. JP Trachtman, 'Negotiations on Domestic Regulation and Trade in Services (GATS Article VI): A Legal Analysis of Selected Current Issues' in Petersmann (n 69 above) 205, 206.

72. 'A significant challenge for many developing countries is the absence of adequate capacity to assess the costs and benefits of GATS commitments in health and education and to conceive and implement an appropriate regulatory regime capable of ensuring that the benefits of trade liberalization are attained in a manner consistent with the achievement of a range of objectives informing government policy related to these areas'. JA Van Duzer, 'Navigating between the Poles: Unpacking the Debate on the Implications for Development of GATS Obligations relating to Health and Education Services' in Petersmann (n 69 above) 167, 202.

in the schedule can be withdrawn or modified. Arguably these together render undertaken commitments almost irreversible. First, three years must have elapsed from the date on which that commitment entered into force.[73] Second, at the request of an affected member, the modifying member 'shall enter into negotiations with a view to reaching agreement on any necessary compensatory adjustment'. Third, the compensatory adjustment must be maintained on an MFN basis.

In sum, since the consequences of opening up certain service sectors are not fully known and in the absence of a dumping and safeguards provisions like in the GATT text, undertaking GATS commitment may have a negative welfare impact. Therefore, cautious liberalization may be the appropriate response.[74] This does not, of course, prevent unilateral liberalization.[75] Take the case of India. Significant changes have taken place in the domestic policy regime in services in the belief that liberalization would facilitate development.[76] There has been substantial liberalization in transport, telecommunications, and financial services.[77] At the multilateral level, also, India submitted a revised offer in August 2005.[78] India has 'signaled that it was willing to remove commercial presence

---

73. A notice of three months has also to be given to modify or withdraw a commitment to the Council for Trade in Services.

74. It must certainly be accompanied by strengthening of the public health and education systems. N Singh, 'Services-led industrialization in India: Prospects and Challenges' in *Industrial Development for the 21st Century: Sustainable Development Perspectives* (New York: UN 2007) 235, 256.

75. In the case of India the present position is described in a consultation paper thus:
.... hundred per cent FDI (foreign direct investment) in higher education services on automatic route is allowed in India. Also, foreign participation through twinning, collaboration, franchising, and subsidiaries is permitted. India has received requests from several countries like Australia, Brazil, Japan, New Zealand, Norway, Singapore, and the US.
The same paper states that civil society 'fears and reservations seem to be somewhat overstated'. Department of Commerce, India, 'A Consultation Paper on Higher Education in India and GATS: An Opportunity' (2006) 17 <http://commerce.nic.in/trade/international_trade_tis_gaitis.asp>.

76. The share of service sector in India's GDP 'has been rising consistently over the years, with an average share of 52% between 2000-01 and 2005-06 ... During the 1990s, India had the highest growth of service exports among all economies, and during the 2000–05 period, its services exports grew at an average annual growth rate of 33% ... India's exports of IT and IT-enabled services have grown from $4 billion in 2000 to around $24 billion in 2006'. R Chanda, 'Introduction and Overview' in Chanda (n 70 above) 1, 2; A Mattoo and RM Stern, 'India and the Multilateral Trading System Post-Doha: Defensive or Proactive?' in A Mattoo and RM Stern (eds), *India and the WTO* (2003) 327.

77. Ibid 347–49.

78. Chanda (n 76 above) 5.

restrictions in some key areas that it had already committed. Eleven sectors and 94 sub-sectors were covered in the revised offer as opposed to seven sectors and 47 sub-sectors in the initial conditional offer. The change in stance reflected a new strategy on the part of India—of being more forthcoming in the services negotiations'.[79] But it may not be prudent to go beyond the revised offer, at least to further open up crucial social sectors like education and health.[80] In the case of both, the problems include commercialization and commodification with implications for equitable access and quality.[81] In short, the response to GATS should be based on a different premise because unlike in the case of trade in goods, it is not certain as to when, in which sectors, and to what extent a country should liberalize. The need for such policy flexibility is explicitly incorporated in Article XIX of GATS.[82]

However, the decision of the Hong Kong Ministerial Conference goes against the letter and spirit of Article XIX and the Doha Development Agenda. First, the Hong Kong Declaration has 'fixed the base levels for liberalization across the board in all sectors'.[83] Thus, in Mode 3 it calls for (i) commitments on enhanced levels of foreign equity participation, (ii) removal or substantial reduction of economic needs tests, and (iii) commitments allowing greater flexibility on the types of legal entity permitted. In other modes, the proposals called for developing countries to bind existing levels of actual liberalization and then commit to

---

79. Ibid.

80. For India's revised offer on higher education services, see Agarwal, (n 67 above) 349 or <http://commerce.nic.in>.

81. Agarwal (n 70 above) 343–45; KM Gopakumar and N Syam, 'Health Services Liberalization in India' in Chanda (n 70 above) 249, 261–63. It may be noted that Agarwal, after reviewing the objections to the opening up of the higher education sector concludes: 'Both the apprehensions associated with the liberalization of higher education services and India's export potential in higher education services are overstated. These are not based on facts and objective analysis. The debate is often driven by baseless sensitivities', ibid 357.

82. Article XIX (1) on "Negotiation of Specific Commitments" *inter alia* states that negotiations 'shall take place with a view to promoting the interests of all participants on a mutually advantageous basis and to securing an overall balance of rights and obligations'. Article XIX (2) states:

The process of liberalization shall take place with due respect for national policy objectives and the level of development of individual Members, both overall and in individual sectors. There shall be appropriate flexibility for individual developing country Members for opening fewer sectors, liberalizing fewer types of transactions, progressively extending market access in line with their development situation and, when making access to their markets available to foreign service suppliers, attaching to such conditions aimed at achieving the objectives referred to in Article IV entitled "Increased Participation of Developing Countries".

83. Das (n 55 above) 629.

liberalize further.⁸⁴ In these circumstances, policy space may be lost, and the outcome may not represent an overall balance of rights and obligations.

Second, the developing countries have not received a favorable response on Mode 4 requests. This is despite the fact that according to one study, '. . .an increase in developed countries' quotas on the inward movement of temporary workers equivalent to 3 per cent of their work forces would generate an estimated increase in world welfare of over $150 billion per annum'.⁸⁵. Subsequent to the Hong Kong Ministerial meeting, a plurilateral request by India and a group of countries has called for new and/or improved market access commitments in Mode 4 categories delinked from commercial presence. It is to be seen if a positive response is forthcoming. In sum, according to Action Aid,

> The Ministerial Declaration on services is anti-development, anti-poor and favors transnational corporations. The text will force developing countries to liberalize sectors which they don't want to, binds countries to increase foreign equity levels, focuses on commercial presence, replaces the bilateral request-offer approach with a plurilateral process, targets sectors under a sectoral approach that are of export interest to rich countries, takes away the right to regulate, and contradicts the GATS negotiating guidelines and Doha mandate. This text will increase poverty, deny people's rights to basic services, expand the role of corporations and shrink the role of the state.⁸⁶

Even if this were just rhetoric, it would be advisable for developing countries to not rapidly open up social sectors like the education and health sectors as this may have far-reaching implications. Recent developments show that the developing countries await firm developments with regard to the negotiations on agriculture and NAMA and the new offers in the service sectors from developed countries before agreeing to adopt a new text on services negotiations.⁸⁷

iii. The Special and Differential Treatment Principle

It is time to turn to the Hudec thesis that developing countries are better off not placing reliance on the S&D principle. At present it is estimated that there are 155 S&D provisions in WTO. The Doha Round has seen more proposals advanced.

---

84. Khor (n 15 above) 15. Further, the European Union on 28 October 2005 proposed that developing countries be required 'to improve their commitments or make new ones in 57% of the services sub-sectors. Other proposals are that developing countries would be required to bind in the GATS their present level of liberalization in the various sectors, and then to extend the level of liberalization through new GATS commitments'. Das, ibid.

85. WTO (n 60 above) 4.

86. T Rice and M Talpurl, *A Development Analysis of the WTO Hong Kong Declaration* (2006).

87. M Khor, 'WTO Services talks caught in webs of "horizontal process" and blame game' <http://www.twnside.org.sg/title2/wto.info/twninfo20080309.htm>.

These have been classified by one writer under five categories: (i) dispensation from obligations; (ii) financial support and technical assistance; (iii) preferential market access; (iv) incentives for transfer of technology; and (v) result-oriented, purposive provisions (eg, rapid and sustained growth of export earnings).[88] Hudec was not necessarily against S&D concepts like infant industry protection. But as Trubek and Cottrell point out, he was skeptical

> whether developing countries could effectively *implement* them. He saw three obstacles to making such protection work for the general good. The first was the limited ability of governments to pick the right winners. The second was that even potentially efficient industries may lose their competitive edge due to the subsidies protection gives them. And the third—and most important—is that once such protective policies are adopted, the pressure to protect inefficient as well as efficient industries, will be too great to overcome. For that reason he thought it best for developing country governments to nail themselves to the mast of reciprocity rather than seek special and differential treatment.[89]

In a recent analysis of the standard arguments in favor of S&D treatment, Keck and Low conclude in the manner of Hudec that S&D provisions are difficult to support as these are politicized and blunt instruments that are insufficiently discriminating between development objectives and protectionism and between different sets of developing countries.[90] Others, including Keck and Low, lament the absence of empirical work on whether S&D treatment promotes development.[91] But there appears to be, it is believed, enough evidence to conclude that

---

88. T Cottier, 'From Progressive Liberalization to Progressive Regulation in WTO Law' (2006) 9 JIEL 779, 787.

89. DM Trubek and PM Cottrell, 'Robert Hudec and the Theory of International Economic Law: The Law of Global Space' (in this volume).

90. A Keck and P Low, 'Special and Differential Treatment in the WTO: Why, When, and How?' in SJ Evenett and B M Hoekman (eds) (n 8 above) 147. The five arguments that they identify are: SDT is an acquired political right; countries should enjoy privileged access to the markets of their trading partners, particularly the developed countries; developing countries should have the right to restrict imports to a greater degree than developed countries; developing countries should be allowed additional freedom to subsidize exports; and developing countries should be allowed flexibility with respect to the application of certain WTO rules or be allowed to postpone the application of rules. Ibid 152–53.

91. 'Economic theory tells us that S&D treatment may or may not foster development; therefore, the question is ultimately an empirical one. Unfortunately, there is very little quantitative work that has been done regarding how S&D treatment has actually affected the economic performance of DCs. A recent study by Oezden and Reinhardt found perverse effects of GSP, retarding the integration of countries eligible into the world trading system:

> While empirical studies are far from complete, it is increasingly recognized that existing and well-established legal strategies, addressing regulatory problems of DCs

the case for preferential arrangements is overstated.[92] Therefore, arguably there is a need for a new regulatory approach.

But what will be the essential features of this new approach? Cottier usefully summarizes for us some of the new thinking on S&D treatment:

> Hoekman, Michalopolous, and Winter suggest that current country groupings be renegotiated. They contend that an 'LDC+' group would, by and large, capture those countries in actual need of S&D treatment. Prowse suggests country-specific 'audits' that would determine a tailored package of temporal exemptions and technical assistance for each developing WTO member. While these approaches seek for refined country groupings, Stevens [...] suggested ... to determine the application of S&D treatment on the basis of thresholds specific to the application of specific rules, based on relevant economic factors and criteria. This approach was assessed by Keck and Low..... In their view, 'S&D treatment provisions should be defined to the maximum extent possible in terms of economic needs that automatically identify the beneficiary Members' .... Hoekman summarized suggestions made for a new approach to S&D treatment focusing on implementation of rules: (i) acceptance of the principle of 'policy space' implying flexibility for all DCs to implement rules 'as long as this does not impose significant negative (pecuniary) spillovers'; (ii) a country-specific approach rendering implementation commensurate with national policy priorities; (iii) an agreement-specific approach involving *ex ante* criteria that allow countries to opt out of the application of rules for a limited period of time; and finally (iv) a simple rule-of-thumb approach that allows DCs to opt out from what he calls 'resource-intensive' agreements. According to him, all these avenues share in common recourse to economic criteria in order to determine the applicability of (resource-intensive) rules.[93]

Cottier himself suggests, in the vein of Hoekman and others, that the S&D idea needs to move beyond transitional periods. It should involve 'the idea of applying single and uniform rules in a manner that different levels of social and economic development are taken into account *as a matter inherent to the rule itself...*'.[94] Thus, 'progressive regulation responds to phasing in of obligations, rather than defining opting out and exceptions'.[95]

---

and LDCs, are failing in bringing about the results aspired: consideration of developmental needs, competitiveness, and progressive integration into the world trading system, combined with enhanced market access in industrialized markets'.
See Cottier (n 88 above) 791.
92. Keck and Low (n 90 above) 157–59, 181.
93. Cottier (n 88 above) 791–92.
94. Ibid 794. Emphasis added.
95. Ibid.

In his contribution to this volume, Trachtman also proposes an external mechanism that 'would provide careful and independent analysis of the justification for derogation from all WTO obligations, including but not limited to the GATT itself'.[96] The assigned institution would 'evaluate proposed derogations to determine their consistency with the development needs of the proposing state. Measures consistent with development needs would be approved and accepted despite any inconsistency with other WTO obligations'.[97] The Trachtman proposal is in accord with the Hoekman suggestion to 'shift away from the traditional 'Enabling Clause' approach based on exceptions for developing countries towards an 'Enabling Mechanism' that actively assists developing country governments to attain their trade-related objectives'.[98] Trachtman thus has no objection to promoting infant-industry protection if it is done under international supervision. The international mechanism would go to ensure that infant-industry protection is not used as a tool of long-term protection. The presence of the international mechanism would also help meet the Hudec concern that developing country governments cannot be trusted to decide on the basis of objective criteria the question as to which industry deserves protection and for how long.[99]

The diplomatic challenge lies in working out the details of the independent mechanism acceptable to both developed and developing countries. But can an external agency make an objective assessment of the local conditions in relation to the goal of development? Can there be an external agency that operates outside the domain of power of dominant social forces and states? Will such an agency be in a better situation than democratically elected governments to suggest an appropriate policy measure? These are the difficult questions. For a consensus to be secured, perhaps it is best that the external agency have only an advisory capacity with the developing country in question having the final say. The advantage of an advisory opinion will be the delegitimization of unjustifiable measures of protection.

---

96. Trachtman (n 9 above).
97. Ibid.
98. B Hoekman, 'Expanding WTO membership and Heterogeneous Interests' (2005) 4 WT Rev 401, 405.
99. Cottier also agrees with the standpoint of Hudec:
Even if the goals of more precise and operational rules on S&D treatment can be attained, the result is likely to reflect experiences of the past. S&D treatment provisions have remained without much impact in accommodating real needs of DCs —a finding already made by Professor Hudec in his seminal work published in 1987. There is little hope that they may deploy what they have missed to achieve in the past since the term S&D treatment became part of the vocabulary of international trade regulation. At best, the outcome will be mixed, if not harmful, to social and economic development, at least in a longer term perspective.
See Cottier (n 88 above) 788.

In the meantime, despite the danger of their misuse by governments for protectionist ends, the developing countries have no choice but to rely on S&D provisions to secure greater policy space. It deserves mention that many S&D provisions are couched in soft law language. It would help if the developed countries accept binding obligations in such instances.

D. CONCLUSION

In considering the validity of the Hudec thesis that developing countries should, 'in their own economic interest' respond with a fuller commitment to GATT/WTO law, a key issue is how the historical, economic, ethical, and political elements that intersect in GATT/WTO are interpreted. In this regard, reviewing popular sources of free trade skepticism, it has been argued, first, that the peoples of developing countries believe that the official history of international trade is overly sanguine about the role free trade has played in the development of western industrialized countries. Second, it is felt that free trade theory has neglected a range of ethical and political factors; its abstractions are not always sensitive to the concerns of real people divided on class, gender, and race lines. In sum, free trade skeptics distinguish between the theory and practice of free trade and contest the epistemological basis of the abstractions advanced by free trade theorists.

The case of free trade skeptics is strengthened by the experience of developing countries under the GATT/WTO regime. First, the empirical evidence of the advantages of accepting GATT/WTO disciplines is inconclusive. Second, the economic success of countries like India and China tends to support the case of free trade skeptics as recent liberalization has come about after 'high levels of trade protection'.[100] There is thus merit in the Rodrik view that the emphasis should be on the need for 'policy diversity, for selective and modest reforms, and for experimentation'.[101] Third, even if the benefits of S&D provisions are inconclusive, there is no reason for the developed countries to insist on 'a more than reciprocity position' in the Doha "Development" Round Negotiations. Such an outcome, following the unbalanced outcome of the Uruguay Round of Trade Negotiations, is unacceptable in the ongoing NAMA and services negotiations. The fact that developing countries have deployed "new forms of collective action" (eg, G-20 and G-11) grounded in cognitive and institutional adaptation through reflecting on their failure in the Uruguay Round of Trade Negotiations means that it will not be easy to ignore the concerns of developing countries.[102]

---

100. Rodrik (n 18 above).
101. Ibid.
102. A Hurrell and A Narlikar 'A New Politics of Confrontation? Brazil and India in Multilateral Trade Negotiations' (2006) 20 GSoc 415.

3. DYSFUNCTION, DIVERSION, AND THE DEBATE OVER PREFERENCES
(How) do Preferential Trade Policies Work?

JEFFREY L DUNOFF*

A. Introduction 45
B. The History of an Idea 47
C. Evaluating Preferences: Economics or Politics? 50
    I. Do Preferences Work? An Economic Approach 51
    II. How Do Preferences Work? A Political Economy Approach 56
D. *Developing Countries*' Methodological Commitments 59
    I. Hudec's Dark Vision 60
    II. Utilizing Econometrics and Political Economy: Toward a Progressive Research Agenda 61
        Do preference schemes lead to PTAs? 62
        Do preference programs reinforce protectionism in developing states? 65
        Is the debate over preferences a diversion? 67
E. The Hidden Costs of *Developing Countries*' Rhetorical Strategy 68
F. Conclusion 72

A. INTRODUCTION

Robert Hudec embodied a rare combination of scholarly qualities. He possessed an insider's knowledge of the trade system's diplomatic history and a scholar's understanding of GATT's complex jurisprudence. Hudec's interests spanned the wide range of international trade law; he made influential contributions on topics as diverse as the liberalization of trade in agricultural products, the shifting jurisprudential meaning of "national treatment," and the myriad functions of dispute settlement. In addition, he blended a pragmatic and deeply practical wisdom with a vivid and engaging writing style. For all of these reasons, Robert Hudec is widely–and properly–recognized as one of the most important trade scholars of our times.

All of Hudec's considerable strengths are evident in *Developing Countries in the GATT System* (*Developing Countries*).[1] The book is elegantly written, thoroughly

---

* Visiting Senior Research Scholar, Law & Public Affairs Program and Visiting Professor, Woodrow Wilson School, Princeton University; Charles Klein Professor of Law & Government and Director, Institute for International Law & Public Policy, Temple University Beasley School of Law. I am grateful to Joel Trachtman and Frank Garcia for thoughtful comments on an earlier draft and to the Clifford Scott Green Chair and Research Fund in Law for generous financial support.

1. RE Hudec, *Developing Countries in the GATT Legal System* (Aldershot: Gower 1987).

researched, and gracefully analytical. Moreover, despite the passage of two decades, the text's descriptive and normative analyses remain valuable—although surely contestable—as many of the contributions to this volume suggest.

Developing Countries makes at least two important contributions to the trade literature. First, the text provides an authoritative history of the debate over preferential treatment for developing states.[2] Second, *Developing Countries* offers an influential analysis of the effects of preferences. Hudec rejects the conventional wisdom that preferential treatment disserves developing states because a policy of reciprocity would produce greater concessions from developed states. He argues that, given the economic disparities between developed and developing states, reciprocity by developing states is unlikely to produce greater access to developed state markets. Instead, Hudec argues that a policy of reciprocity can help developing state governments resist local demands for protection and hence pursue more rational economic policies.

This analysis leads to a more provocative claim. Hudec argues that the economic performance of developing states has more to do with their own trade policies than with the trade policies pursued by developed states. Hence, he suggests that developing states should view the trade system less as a mechanism for changing developed state policy and more as a mechanism for reforming their own economic policies.

Developing Countries details the arguments for and against preferential treatment in clear, accessible prose and sets out an original and important position in this contentious policy debate. Nevertheless, the text's claims are necessarily limited by the methodological approaches Hudec adopts, the theory of trade politics he employs, and the ontology of international system that he draws upon. Of course, alternative approaches to the study of preferences are available, and Hudec's arguments can be usefully compared with the scholarship on preferences that uses other methodologies, particularly econometrics. One purpose of this essay is to explore what we know about preferences and how we know it. This essay also seeks to explore whether juxtaposing alternative methodological approaches can suggest a progressive research agenda designed to enhance our understandings of how preferences work and, in particular, their effects on developing states.

To do so, this paper proceeds as follows. Following this introduction, Part B will summarize the historical narrative that Hudec provides in the first part of *Developing Countries*. Part C turns from description to analysis. I briefly

---

2. Preferential treatment, also sometimes called nonreciprocal or "S&D" treatment, consists of a set of rights and privileges that apply to developing states but not developed states. Although this treatment can take many forms, for the most part these provisions are intended to (1) grant developing states more favorable access to developed state markets and/or (2) grant developing states freedom from some of the disciplines imposed by trade norms, thereby increasing the policy discretion they enjoy regarding foreign access to their own domestic markets.

summarize the enormous literature on the economic effects of preferences on developing states, as well as Hudec's innovative arguments concerning the political effects of preferences. In Part D, I explore in greater detail the assumptions and orientation underlying Hudec's methodological commitments in *Developing Countries*. As described more fully below, this orientation is rooted in a deeply pessimistic view of domestic politics and international institutions. I juxtapose Hudec's understanding of trade politics with recent empirical literature to suggest several novel lines of inquiry regarding the effects of preferences. In Part E, I return to Hudec's methodological commitments and rhetorical style. I argue that *Developing Countries* is theoretically more sophisticated than it purports to be, offer a few possible reasons why the book sells itself short as a scholarly work, and describe some of the costs of doing so. A brief conclusion follows.

B. THE HISTORY OF AN IDEA

Developing Countries opens with an account of a debate that, from the inception of the multilateral trade system, has been as prominent as it has been divisive: Should the trade regime provide differential treatment to developing states, given that trading nations are at widely different levels of social and economic development? Or are uniform, nondiscriminatory rules more appropriate? Hudec argues that, in addressing this question, the framers of the GATT system were entering uncharted territory. Although the destructive trade wars and protectionism of the 1930s gave GATT's drafters much relevant experience with respect to tariffs, quotas, and the like, there was little relevant experience regarding the role of developing states in a multilateral trade system.

The United States, a prime mover in the early negotiations, sought a nondiscriminatory system that had no special rules for developing states.[3] The Europeans, in contrast, sought to maintain their historical systems of preferences for colonial areas. Both positions reflected national interests. As the world's dominant economy, the United States believed that it had the most to gain from open world markets. The Europeans believed that market interventions were necessary to assist developing states; this position was entirely consistent with the position that European states should be able to extend preferential treatment to each other to boost postwar reconstruction. Developing states sought resource transfers, freedom from trade rules, tariff preferences, and nonreciprocity. Hudec suggests that these positions grew out of developing states' colonial experience in which they saw colonial powers attempt to maximize economic gains by controlling trade and suppressing economic competition. In addition, developing

---

3. This is not to suggest that the United States was unaware of the special issues posed by developing states. Rather, it argued that the needs of developing states should be addressed in other fora, such as the United Nations and World Bank. Hudec (n 1 above) 8–9.

states were acutely aware of recent developed state practice, including the United Kingdom's turn away from free trade policies and the United States' enactment of Smoot-Hawley tariffs.[4]

Initiating a pattern that would continue over time, no single party's view ultimately prevailed, and the negotiations 'ended, as they had begun, with no basic consensus on the trade-policy rules that should apply to developing countries'.[5] As a result, the original GATT contained many terms that reflected parts of various parties' positions. Thus, for example, the text contained infant-industry and balance-of-payments provisions for developing states, although not the preferential access to developed states markets that developing states sought.

Perhaps more important, practice during these early years enshrined a 'fundamental . . .contradiction' into the trade regime. The United States purported to insist on 'reciprocity', ie, that any reductions it made in trade barriers should be paid for—or reciprocated—by reductions in trade barriers by other states. Hudec argues that the US 'fixation with reciprocity' was rooted in a mercantilist view of international trade.[6] The implicit theory underlying this view is that exports are good and imports are bad, and that states make 'concessions' in lowering trade barriers to obtain similar 'concessions' from trading partners. Of course, if reducing one's own trade barriers is understood to be a 'cost', then it follows that maintaining (or raising) barriers will be understood to be a benefit. Hudec argues that by implicitly acknowledging the legitimacy of developing state demands for differential treatment at the outset, the United States, in effect, shifted the basis for all future debate from 'whether' preferential treatment was appropriate to 'how much' assistance to give: '(o)nce it had been conceded, as a matter of principle, that legal freedom constitutes "help" to developing states, the future was virtually fixed'.[7]

Developing Countries details the ensuing developments decade-by-decade. The GATT's first decade saw the 'fuller and now almost enthusiastic endorsement of the idea that legal freedom "helps" developing countries' at a 1954–55 Review Session.[8] Moreover, Hudec observes, events during this decade demonstrated that once a negotiation begins, all parties have to be prepared to 'give' something, and that 'the easiest concession (for developed states) to "give" is a little more legal freedom'.[9] During this period, '(t)he declining rigor of GATT legal discipline toward developing countries produced a rather curious legal policy. The substance withered, but the form remained'.[10]

---

4. Ibid 12.
5. Ibid 13.
6. Ibid 17.
7. Ibid 18.
8. Ibid 28.
9. Ibid 28.
10. Ibid 30.

In 1958, an influential GATT report directed attention to the link between disappointing developing state export earnings and developed state trade barriers. As a result, developing countries began to focus less on securing exceptions for their own policies and more on obtaining preferential access to developed state markets. Hudec's account of the extension of preferences to developing states over the next several decades is, in many respects, a story of form without substance. Time and again, developed states agreed to texts that seemed to promise preferential treatment to developing states, but these instruments often said less than they appeared to and frequently delivered less than they promised. Thus, for example, in 1979, GATT parties agreed to the Enabling Clause,[11] permitting certain forms of preferential treatment; characteristically, this text used language that appeared to be "legalistic" and hence produced the 'illusion of greater commitment' but actually 'contained no definable legal obligations'.[12] Thus, this much-debated language 'added nothing to the existing legal relationship between developed and developing countries'.[13]

The story of the Enabling Clause encapsulates, in many ways, the politics of preferences at the GATT. Over time, developing states repeatedly demanded new and different forms of preferential treatment, and developed states would generally resist these pleas. Eventually, a compromise would result that recognized in principle the legitimacy of preferences, but that imposed little by way of legal obligation and often produced little economic effect. Hudec summarizes the 'pattern' that emerged:

> . . . (A)s experience with this tactic [of demanding preferential treatment] grew, it could be seen that results would continue to be very slow in coming. . . . The absence of any real progress led to a continual search for additional forms of activity that would give the appearance of movement. The GATT became very skillful in creating such appearances, primarily by erecting new procedural mountains and them climbing them. The GATT's work evolved into a slow and patient form of bureaucratic slogging—unending meetings, detailed studies of trade flows and trade barriers and repeated declarations in increasingly urgent but never-quite-binding language.[14]

---

11. The formal name for the Enabling Clause is the "Decision on Differential and More Favourable Treatment, Reciprocity and Fuller Participation of Developing Countries". Adopted in November 1979, it includes a number of provisions permitting GATT contracting parties to grant differential and more favorable treatment to developing states, notwithstanding the nondiscrimination requirement found in GATT Article I. It thus authorizes, most notably, trade concessions granted to developing states under various GSP schemes.

12. Hudec (n 1 above) 56.

13. Ibid.

14. Ibid 44–45.

The Uruguay Round marked a shift in emphasis. The Round's "single undertaking" produced a largely uniform system of rights and obligations. Hence, WTO texts reduced the scope of special exceptions from GATT disciplines available to developing states. Moreover, just as the range and reach of legal obligations increased, the new Dispute Settlement Understanding rendered these obligations judicially enforceable. Taken together, these changes reduced developing states' policy flexibility.

Notably, the concept of S&D treatment did not disappear in the Uruguay Round. While developing states assumed the same obligations as developed states, they had additional time to implement these obligations. Thus, the new agreements moved from a nonreciprocal approach to obligations to a nonreciprocal approach to implementation. In the post-Uruguay Round period, however, developing states experienced capacity constraints and other obstacles that rendered implementation difficult or disproportionately costly. As a result, developing states demanded greater amounts of time to meet certain obligations. In the Doha Declaration, WTO members agreed to review special and differential obligations to strengthen them and make them more precise and operational.[15] However, efforts to do so have, to date, borne little fruit.

Hudec's history is rather sobering. By his account, trading states devoted substantial diplomatic attention over many years to the treatment of developing states. These efforts generated an inconclusive political debate that in turn produced ambiguous legal texts. However, this history does not address a key question: do preferential trade policies work? Hudec provides one approach to this question in the second part of *Developing Countries*; as we shall see, recent empirical research can supplement Hudec's account and suggest new avenues for research into the efficacy of preferential trade policies.

C. EVALUATING PREFERENCES: ECONOMICS OR POLITICS?

The second part of *Developing Countries* turns from historical narrative to evaluation: What is the impact of special and differential trade policies? Does the granting of preferential access to developed state markets boost developing state exports? More generally,

> (i)s the legal policy of . . . providing preferences to developing countries in the best interest of the developing countries themselves, or would developing countries achieve better results under a legal policy based on . . . reciprocity and non-discrimination?[16]

---

15. WTO, 'Doha WTO Ministerial 2001: Ministerial Declaration' (14 November 2001) WT/MIN(01)/DEC/1, para 44.

16. Hudec (n 1 above) 127.

These sound like empirical questions, and a substantial literature purports to provide empirical answers to these questions. However, *Developing Countries* does not draw appreciably upon this literature.[17] To be sure, much of the literature has been published after *Developing Countries* was first released. However, the decision not to survey the available empirical literature is somewhat surprising given that all relevant actors in the preferences debate agree on the goal of providing greater economic benefits to developing states; the central point of contention is whether preferences, in fact, advance this objective.[18]

Rather than undertake an empirical evaluation, Hudec engages in an unexpected analytical move; part II of *Developing Countries* evaluates the effect of preferences through a political economy lens. In particular, Hudec examines whether preferences make it more or less difficult for states to pursue liberal economic policies. Because both economic and political economy approaches can enrich our understanding of the effect of preferences, I briefly review below the empirical literature on preferences that *Developing Countries* does not address, and then summarize Hudec's political economy arguments. As we shall see, each line of analysis provides ample reason to doubt the utility of preferential treatment.

i. Do Preferences Work? An Economic Approach

A substantial literature examines the empirical effects of preferences. Although no consensus emerges from this large body of scholarship, it is fair to say that much of this literature is deeply skeptical about the effects of preferences. In particular, the weight of the econometric and simulation analysis performed to date suggests that preferential schemes are underinclusive and underutilized, that the benefits generated by preferential schemes are limited and narrowly focused, and that preferences have done disappointingly little to promote economic development in beneficiary states. As the limitations of preference programs have been ably discussed elsewhere, I briefly summarize the arguments below.

One factor that significantly reduces the value of preferential schemes is the widespread exclusion of goods from sectors in which developing states enjoy comparative advantage from preference schemes. For example, labor-intensive industries provide developing states a base for industrialization and participation in the world economy. But many developed state preference programs exclude precisely these sectors from deep preferences. Particularly controversial examples of limitations on economically significant goods include the strict

---

17. Indeed, the text explicitly disclaims any intent to engage the empirical literature in a sustained manner, stating that '(i)t is not the purpose of this study to examine this [empirical literature] in any depth'. Ibid 128. Thus, although the text references the empirical literature from time to time, it does not analyze this literature in any sustained fashion.

18. Eg, ibid 152–53.

limitations on imports of sugar—which accounts for more than half of all foreign exchange earnings for some Caribbean states—from the US Caribbean Basin Initiative (CBI),[19] the exclusion of tuna, leather and footwear products, petroleum products and apparel from the US Andean Trade Preferences Act,[20] and highly complex rules regarding apparel found in the US African Growth and Opportunity Act.

Many preferential programs have a number of other features that limit their reach. For example, many preference schemes incorporate the concept of graduation, whereby beneficiary states lose preferential treatment when exports reach a certain value[21] or when a state reaches a certain level of economic development.[22] As states successfully export certain goods, or are dropped entirely from preferential programs, they may be left with overcapacity and a production structure that does not reflect comparative advantage.[23] Moreover, the US and EU GSP programs also contain safeguards clauses that permit preferences to be suspended for certain products or states if those imports cause real or potential injury to domestic producers.

In addition, most preference programs are legislated to last a certain number of years and must then be reauthorized. Reauthorization is, of course, never guaranteed, and has at times occurred on a retroactive basis following expiration of the program. For example, the US GSP program has been renewed nine times since its inception in 1974; eight of these renewals have been after periods of expiration ranging in length from two to fifteen months. All of these features

---

19. The Caribbean Basin Trade Partnership Act is an extension of CBI; notably the bill extends eligibility for preferential tariff treatment to a number of sensitive products, including apparel and petroleum and petroleum products.

20. As amended by the Andean Trade Promotion and Drug Eradication Program, preferences were extended to these goods, subject to restrictive rules of origin.

21. Thus, under the US GSP program, goods lose their eligibility for preferential treatment when they exceed a specified amount—$130 million in 2007, an amount that increases by $5 million every year—or when a beneficiary country captures more than 50 percent of market share for imports of a particular good. Not surprisingly, research reveals that these "competitive need limitations" primarily benefit US import-competing firms rather than firms in beneficiary states. Eg, J Devault 'Competitive Need Limits and the US Generalized System of Preferences' (1996) 14 Cont Econ Pol 58.

22. Thus, for example, a number of states have been "graduated" from the US' GSP program, including Singapore, Hong Kong, Taiwan, Korea, Malaysia, Mexico, and Botswana. In addition, states can also be removed from preference programs for political reasons. For example, the Central African Republic, Eritrea, Cote d' Ivoire, and Mauritania were removed from AGOA following political events such as coups and failures to implement democratic reforms.

23. A Keck and P Low, 'Special and Differential Treatment in the WTO: Why, When and How?' in S Evenett and B Hoekman (eds), *Economic Development and Multilateral Trade Cooperation* (London and Washington, DC: Palgrave Macmillan, CEPR and World Bank, 2005).

introduce substantial commercial uncertainties and hence lower the incentives to invest in eligible sectors. Simply put, investors and importing firms attracted by preferences have reduced incentives to invest in or source from beneficiary states when the status of the preferences is in doubt.

Moreover, a number of factors tend to reduce developing states' ability to take advantage of the preferences that are potentially available. Perhaps most important, complex rules of origin and relatively high administrative costs result in significant underutilization of available preferences.[24] In 1999, for example, only one-third of imports to the European Union (EU) which were eligible for preferences actually entered the EU with reduced tariffs, largely due to complex and restrictive rules of origin;[25] during the same year, excluding minerals, only 4 percent of dutiable imports into the United States from developing countries received preferential treatment.[26] A more recent study found that the share of eligible exports to the European Union that requested GSP treatment was only 6 percent.[27] Similarly, for the United States' GSP program, the utilization rate of many tariff lines is zero, and the average for all lines is 25 percent.[28] Conversely, liberalization of restrictive rules of origin can produce significant results, as changes to the African Growth and Opportunity Act (AGOA) and Canada's GSP program demonstrate.[29]

---

24. Rules of origin set out the conditions that a product must satisfy to be considered as originating from a beneficiary state. The classic work on rules of origin in preference programs is J Herin, 'Rules of Origin and Differences between Tariff Levels in EFTA and in the EC' (1986) EFTA Occasional Paper No 13. For more recent research, eg, US International Trade Commission, *The Economic Effects of Significant US Import Restraints: Fifth Update* (USITC Publication 3906 2007); P Augier, M Gasiorek and C Lai-Tong, 'The Impact of Rules of Origin in Trade Flows' in O Cadot and others (eds), *The Origin of Goods: Rules of Origin in Regional Trade Agreements* (London: CEPR/IADC/Oxford University Press, 2005). Also, J Anson and others, 'Assessing the Costs of Rules of Origin in North-South PTAs with an Application to NAFTA' (2003) CEPR Discussion Paper No 2476.

25. P Brenton and M Manchin, 'Making EU Trade Agreements Work: The Role of Rules of Origin' (2003) 26 W Econ 755, 757.

26. Ibid.

27. M Manchin, 'Preference Utilisation and Tariff Reduction in EU Imports from ACP Countries' (2006) 29 W Econ 1243, 1246. Manchin also reports that ACP states utilized Cotonou preferences (which are generally better than GSP preferences) close to 50 percent of the time. Another study found that utilization rates for preferences granted by Canada, the European Union, Japan and the United States are 61, 31, 46, and 67 percent respectively. WTO, 'Market Access Issues Related to Products of Export Interest Originating from Least-Developed Countries' WT/COMTD/LDC/W/31 (Geneva: WTO, 2003).

28. D Lederman and C Özden, 'US Trade Preferences: All are Not Created Equal' (2004) Central Bank of Chile Working Paper No 280.

29. A Mattoo, D Roy and A Subramanian, 'The Africa Growth and Opportunity Act and its Rules of Origin: Generosity Undermined?' (2003) 26 W Econ 829; D Audet,

Finally, the gains that are generated by preferential tariff schemes tend to be narrowly concentrated.[30] Consider the United States' AGOA program. In 2003, approximately 33 sub-Saharan African states were eligible for preferential treatment under AGOA. However, three states—Nigeria, South Africa, and Gabon—accounted for over 86 percent of total AGOA imports. Benefits were similarly highly concentrated in a few economic sectors. In 2003, energy-related products represented 79.5 percent of US purchases from sub-Saharan states; the second largest sector, textiles and apparel, accounted for 8.5 percent of US imports.[31] Moreover, within the apparel sector, the seven sub-Saharan states that accounted for 99 percent of exports to the United States before AGOA also captured 99 percent of exports after AGOA was enacted.[32] Similar results obtain for other preferential schemes; as a general matter 'the top ten beneficiaries generally occupy a share of between 80 and 90 percent of total imports receiving preferences under any individual scheme'.[33] Even more troubling, an emerging literature suggests that a substantial share of the 'benefits' generated by preferential market access may accrue to importers rather than firms in the beneficiary state.[34]

In the aggregate, the features identified above have significantly reduced the economic and developmental impacts of preferential programs. Although it is difficult to calculate empirical estimates of trade effects, a number of econometric studies shed light on the aggregate economic effects of GSP schemes. Many of these empirical studies suggest that that GSP has produced at best a 'modest' increase in beneficiary state exports, with some of these gains resulting from trade diversion rather than trade creation.[35]

'Smooth as Silk? A First Look at the Post MFA Textiles and Clothing Landscape' (2007) 10 JIEL 267.

30. UNCTAD, 'Trade Preferences for LDCs: An Early Assessment of Benefits and Possible Improvements,' UNCTAD/ITCD/TSB/2003/8 (Geneva: UNCTAD, 2004). See also D Brown, 'General Equilibrium Effects of the US Generalized System of Preferences' (1987) 54 Sth Econ J 27, 47.

31. US International Trade Commission, *US Trade and Investment with Sub-Saharan Africa: Fifth Annual Report* (USITC Publication 3741, 2004).

32. M Olarreaga and C Özden, 'AGOA and Apparel: Who Captures the Tariff Rent in the Presence of Preferential Market Access?' (2005) 28 W Econ 63. On the other hand, these states enjoyed dramatic increases in their exports to the United States following AGOA's enactment. Ibid 67.

33. Keck and Low (n 25 above).

34. Eg M Olarreaga and C Özden (n 34 above).

35. C MacPhee and V Oguledo, 'The trade effects of the US Generalized System of Preferences' (1991) 19 Atl Econ J 19; D Brown, 'Trade and Welfare Effects of the European Schemes of the Generalized System of Preferences' (1989) 37 Econ Dev & C 757; J Whalley, 'Non-Discriminatory Discrimination: Special and Differential Treatment under the GATT for Developing Countries' (1990) 100 Economic J 1318; A Sapir and L Lundberg, 'The US

Moreover, a number of more recent studies find that GSP is associated with negative economic effects. For example, Özden and Reinhardt find that the United States GSP is not associated with an increase in trade.[36] A more recent study found that in the absence of GATT/WTO membership or a regional trade agreement (RTA), preference programs increase trade between states by 41 percent; however, if states have one of these other trade relationships, then the granting of preferences appears to benefit the importing state and harm the exporting state.[37] Similar counterintuitive results were reached in a recent study using quite different data and econometric techniques.[38] Hence, the general consensus is that the economic effects of preference programs have been, at best, disappointing; a more pessimistic account concluded that '(b)eyond some relative success stories, the picture is dismal'.[39]

To be sure, the studies summarized above should not be understood as conclusive arguments against preferential schemes. First, empirically identifying the effects of preferences is extraordinarily difficult, as researchers must separate out the specific impacts of preferences as opposed to other factors.[40] In addition, the studies do not always carefully separate out the effects of different preference schemes; for example, studies that focus the effect of GSP programs may be seriously misleading as, over time, GSP programs have been supplemented by a variety of programs affording more preferential treatment, such as the Caribbean Basin Initiative (CBI), AGOA, and everything but arms (EBA).[41] Moreover, the literature here is vast, and no consensus emerges. While a majority

---

Generalized System of Preferences and its Impacts' in A Kruger and R Baldwin (eds), *The Structure and Evolution of US Trade Policy* (Cambridge: NBER/AMA, 1984) 191.

36. C Özden and E Reinhardt, 'The Perversity of Preferences: GSP and Developing Country Trade Policies, 1976–2000' (2005) 78 JDE 1.

37. J Golstein, D Rivers and M Tomz, 'Institutions in International Relations: Understanding the Effects of the GATT and the WTO on World Trade' (2007) 61 Int'l Org 37. The authors characterize this finding as 'implausible' and as a 'mystery left to be solved'.

38. Eg, B Herz and M Wagner, 'Do the World Trade Organization and the Generalized System of Preferences foster bilateral trade?' (2007) Universitat Bayreuth Diskussions papier 01-07 ('We find a significantly negative effect of the Generalized System of Preferences of around -16% on bilateral trade . . . .').

39. UNCTAD (n 32 above).

40. For example, it is difficult for empirical analysis to address the so-called endogeneity effect. Imagine that the US extended preferential tariff treatment to goods from a particular developing state just as that state was emerging from a protracted civil war. It would be empirically quite difficult to determine how much of a hypothetical boost in exports would be related to reduced tariffs and how much to the end of the fighting.

41. For example, a more useful, albeit more complex, approach is to look at the size, utilization, and value of all nonreciprocal trade preference programs. For one such effort, see J Dean and J Wainio, 'Quantifying the Value of US Tariff Preferences for Developing Countries' (2006) Policy Research Working Paper No 3977.

of published studies suggest that preferences have limited—or even negative—economic effects, other studies, using different assumptions and methodologies, find more positive results.[42]

Finally, the disappointing effects of preference schemes can be understood more as an argument for their reform than an argument for their elimination. That is, the studies summarized above can be understood as a powerful critique of preference schemes *as they are currently designed and implemented*, as opposed to a critique of their underlying logic. Empirical research suggests that liberalizing product coverage and rules of origin, for example, can substantially increase developing state exports. Similarly, where preferences are stable and secure, trade and investment have increased.[43] Moreover, recent scholarship suggests a number of ways that preference programs can be refined to provide greater benefits to developing states.[44]

ii. How Do Preferences Work? A Political Economy Approach

As noted above, *Developing Countries* does not attempt to review or analyze the substantial empirical literature on preferences. Nevertheless, Hudec's conclusions are broadly consistent with those reached in the empirical literature: preferential treatment can provide, at best, marginal benefits, and may be counterproductive, particularly for developing states that wish to open their economies to the benefits of global trade.[45]

---

42. Ibid; G Frazer and J Van Biesebroeck, 'Trade Growth under the African Growth and Opportunity Act' (2007) University of Toronto Department of Economics Working Paper No 289 (finding that AGOA has had 'a large and robust impact' on African exports to the US); C Stevens and J Kennan, *Comparative study of G8 preferential access schemes for Africa* (2004).

43. J Dean, 'Do Preferential Trade Agreements Promote Growth: An Evaluation of the Caribbean Basin Economic Recovery Act' (2002) USITC Office of Economics Working Paper No. 2002-07-A.

44. For recent and thoughtful efforts to prompt a debate over reform along these lines, see Keck and Low (n 23 above); P Kleen and S Page, 'Special and Differential Treatment of Developing Countries in the World Trade Organization' (2004) Report for the Ministry of Foreign Affairs, Sweden; C Melamed, *Doing Development at the World Trade Organization: the Doha Round and special and differential treatment* (IDS 2003); T Oyejide, 'Special and Differential Treatment', in B Hoekman and others (eds), *Development, Trade and the WTO: A Handbook* (Washington, DC: World Bank, 2002).

45. In this respect, *Developing Countries* can be located within a larger literature that elaborates various critiques of preferential treatment that have been raised repeatedly in the policy literature. Eg, G Patterson, 'Would Tariff Preferences Help Economic Development?' (1965) 76 Lloyds Bank Rev 18; H Johnson, *Economic Policies Toward Less Developed Countries* (Washington: Brookings, 1967). An influential contemporaneous report setting out the case in favor of preferences is UNCTAD, *Towards a New Trade Policy for Development: Report by the Secretary General of United Nations Conference on Trade and Development* (New York: UN, 1964).

Hudec's skepticism about preferences is rooted in his understanding of the 'practical realities' of GATT's impact on domestic policy making.[46] He explains that trade liberalization hurts some firms and individuals, and that these actors will produce a 'normal, permanent and quite vigorous' opposition to trade liberalization.[47] Hence, governments will inevitably experience a 'built-in political opposition to liberal trade policy'.[48] This opposition will be in more or less continuous conflict with the various forces that favor liberalization, including those with direct interests in lowering trade barriers, such as importers and consumers; those with more diffuse interests in the general conditions of international trade, such as financial intermediaries and foreign investors; and those committed to liberal economic policies for economic or political reasons.

The role of GATT/WTO obligations is to 'augment the political power' of the broad set of interests that support trade liberalization. It does so by providing legal and policy arguments to government officials and others who seek to overcome the inevitable forces of protectionism[49] and by helping to mobilize export-oriented groups to countervail the influence of import-sensitive constituencies. Thus, Hudec employs, without using the term, a "liberal" understanding of the domestic determinants of a state's international policy and a "second image reversed" model of how international law can empower or disempower various domestic constituencies.[50]

---

46. Hudec (n 1 above) 129.
47. Ibid 160.
48. Ibid 161.
49. Hudec identifies four specific ways that GATT/WTO legal obligations can do so:
   (i) the desire to honor international obligations can be sufficient to drive government positions, as governments seek to avoid unlawful policies that can produce 'unpleasant and damaging public controversy';
   (ii) international obligations provide a useful public justification for decisions taken on other, including less popular, reasons;
   (iii) international legal norms provide a concise way of defining policy for public officials;
   (iv) international obligations signal publics not to expect or rely upon trade-distorting measures. Ibid 162–63.
50. For more on liberal theories of international law and international relations, see, eg, AM Slaughter, 'A Liberal Theory of International Law' (2000) 94 ASIL Proceedings 240; A Moravcsik, 'Taking Preferences Seriously: A Liberal Theory of International Politics' (1997) 51 Int'l Org 513; AM Slaughter, 'Liberal International Relations Theory and International Economic Law' (1995) 10 AUJIL & Pol 717. For more on second image reversed theories of international law and international relations, eg, P Gourevitch, 'The Second Image Reversed: The International Sources of Domestic Politics' (1978) 32 Int'l Org 881. See also R Keohane and H Milner (eds), *Internationalization and Domestic Politics* (Cambridge: Cambridge University Press 1996); X Dai, 'Why Comply? The Domestic Constituency Mechanism' (2005) 59 Int'l Org 363.

How do preferences change the political dynamics in developing states? Preference schemes provide developing state exports with preferential access to developed state markets, without asking developing states to 'pay' for this increased access through tariff reductions. This alters the political dynamic in developing states, as export interests will now have little incentive to lobby their governments to reduce tariffs. Hence, although protectionist interests will continue to lobby developing states, these governments will experience reduced pressure from those that favor liberal policies. These governments will therefore face fewer incentives to liberalize and will be more likely to pursue protectionist policies. As a result, Hudec concludes that developed state preference schemes 'can provide no assistance [to the liberalization project] and [are] probably a political impediment'.[51]

For developing states that wish to pursue interventionist policies on the grounds that under certain circumstances these policies enhance economic welfare,[52] the picture is a bit more nuanced. Here, in principle, a policy of non-reciprocity may be desirable, as greater freedom from GATT disciplines can produce economic gains. The problem is in distinguishing the economically useful forms of government intervention from those that are welfare-reducing.

Given the predictable pressures from protectionist interests, and his dim view of state capabilities, Hudec doubts the ability of developing state governments to appropriately draw this distinction.[53] He argues that 'developing country governments following active interventionist policies are going to need all the help they can get in order to contain [protectionist] forces'—and that GATT disciplines are one potentially important source of help.[54] Hence, Hudec concludes that whether

---

51. Hudec (n 1 above) 163.

52. Hudec reviews the circumstances under which interventionist policies may be welfare enhancing, including in the nurturing of infant industries. Eg, ibid 144–151; 171–72.

53. Ibid 167–68. On the other hand, developing states often claim that they are in the best position to decide whether and when to adopt interventionist policies and should be able to do so free of GATT disciplines. They also claim that since some interventions are economically useful, a presumption that pro-export lobbies should prevail over import-sensitive lobbies in developing state domestic politics is unwarranted. Developing states would presumably reject Hudec's likely response—that liberalized markets are more likely to produce economic growth—as inconsistent with their experience.

Some empirical research undertaken after original publication of *Developing Countries* lends support to Hudec's argument. Eg, B Hoekman, C Michalopoulos and L Winters, 'Special and Differential Treatment of Developing Countries in the WTO: Moving Forward after Cancún' (2004) 27 W Econ 481; S Lall, 'Selective Policies for Export Promotion: Lessons from the Asian Tigers' in G Helleiner (ed), *Non-Traditional Export Promotion in Africa—Experience and Issues* (Helsinki, New York: Palgrave 2002) 23; A Panagariya, 'Evaluating the Case for Export Subsidies'' (2000) World Bank Policy Research Working Paper No 2276. I am grateful to Frank Garcia for elaborating these arguments.

54. Hudec (n 1 above) 164.

a developing state government wishes to pursue a liberal or an interventionist economic policy, preferences disserve developing state interests.

D. *DEVELOPING COUNTRIES'* METHODOLOGICAL COMMITMENTS

Having surveyed the arguments in *Developing Countries*, it is useful to review the text's methodological orientation. As noted above, the book opens with a systematic analysis of the historical debate over whether developing states should receive preferential treatment. Hudec's historical narrative reads, for the most part, as a straightforward realist account of international trade relations.[55] Thus, Hudec focuses on states that pursue what they understand to be their political and economic interests in the international trade regime. To do so, states exercise diplomatic and economic leverage, and the agreements they reach represent a messy compromise among conflicting national interests.

Developing Countries' second part, which engages in a political economy analysis, has a rather different theoretical and methodological orientation. Here the focus turns from relations among states to interactions among interest groups and bureaucracies. However, Hudec's analysis moves well beyond the familiar public choice insight that, due to collective action problems, well-organized special interests can capture domestic law-making processes.[56] In addition, Hudec describes how international legal norms can empower or disempower various domestic constituencies and therefore impact domestic politics.

It is possible to conclude that the methodological and theoretical orientations of the first part of *Developing Countries* are in unacknowledged tension with the theoretical approach adopted in the second part of the text. However, for current purposes it is more fruitful to understand the methodological frameworks used in both parts of the book as resting upon Hudec's rather bleak understanding of political actors and political institutions. Indeed, the inconclusive nature of the negotiations over preferential treatment and the disappointing, if not counterproductive, effects of preferential policies are entirely consistent with the larger

---

55. To be sure, Hudec's account is more nuanced than this necessarily brief summary may suggest. Thus, for example, he recognizes the influence of ideas on international relations, eg, ibid 57–59 (developed states underestimate power and significance of nonbinding principles) and that international law can play an important constraining role in international relations. However, for the most part, the historical account in part I of *Developing Countries* focuses on states and their interests.

56. EE Schattschneider, *Politics, Pressures, and the Tariff: a Study of Free Private Enterprise in Pressure Politics, as Shown in the 1929–1930 Revision of the Tariff* (New York: Prentice-Hall 1935) (documenting the logrolling phenomenon under the notorious Smoot-Hawley Tariff Act of 1930); P Gourevitch, 'Domestic Politics and International Relations' in W Carlsnaes, T Risse and B Simmons (eds), *Handbook of International Relations* (London: Sage Publications 2002).

narrative that informs *Developing Countries*. As explained more fully below, it is only a slight exaggeration to characterize the dominant images that the book conveys of the trade system and the states that comprise it as dysfunction, hypocrisy, and contradiction.

i. Hudec's Dark Vision

Virtually every actor and every policy that comes under Hudec's discriminating gaze is seen as, at best, ineffective and at worst, counterproductive. Domestic governments are repeatedly pictured as weak and hypocritical. Thus, for example, the original US position in postwar trade negotiations was 'full of internal contradictions', because at the same time as it argued against preferences and for nondiscrimination as a matter of principle, it insisted on trade-distorting exceptions for itself, such as the ability to impose quotas on agricultural imports.[57] Moreover, continued US support for these and other exceptions is a 'contradiction' that has been 'a constant in GATT's legal history and is as true today as it was in 1947'.[58]

Elsewhere, Hudec generalizes this critique to encompass virtually all governments. For example, Hudec states that developed state critiques of illiberal developing state trade policies are a 'sham', and he provocatively claims that 'many developed countries are really quite happy with the absence of legal discipline over developing countries because it gives them an excuse for the illegal trade barriers they themselves are imposing'.[59] He colorfully describes many of the ways that developed state governments mask the 'inadequacy of the(ir) performance' in the realm of trade policy, including by their ability to 'rearrang(e) the numbers until they provide maximum trade gains'.[60] Developing states, as well, seek the 'easy way out' and try 'to satisfy as many domestic political interests as possible,' even if such policies impose welfare costs on the state's population.[61]

International efforts fare little better. As noted above, *Developing Countries* details nearly six decades of international negotiations that prove unable to resolve underlying tensions over preferences. Moreover, although the trading nations are unable to reach substantive agreement, they can and do repeatedly agree to produce much legal form without substance. Hudec is scornful of the enormous amount of energy and attention spent in GATT's time-consuming but

---

57. Hudec (note 1 above) 16. The legacy of GATT's treatment of agriculture is explored in Tracey Epps and Michael Trebilcock's contribution to this volume. T Epps and M Trebilcock, 'Special and Differential Treatment in Agricultural Trade' in Chapter 13 of this collection.
58. Ibid 16.
59. Ibid 135.
60. Ibid 165.
61. Ibid 230.

fruitless negotiations, never-ending meetings, and useless bureaucratic squabbling, characterizing these efforts as 'tedious, repetitive and often absurd'.[62]

Developing Countries implicitly suggests that the entire enterprise of creating an international body designed to reduce state interference with international trade is potentially self-defeating. Hudec notes the paradox involved in constructing an international trade regime:

> It is possible that the design of the [international trade system] may itself have encouraged a preference for market-distorting solutions. The [trade regime] represented a new idea in international economic affairs—the idea that the governments of the world, by acting together in concerted rule-making activity, could shape the international trade environment in which their economies would operate. Although the sponsors of this 'architectonic' enterprise were actually seeking to diminish government activity in the market place, rule-making institutions tend to encourage just the opposite instincts—the urge to improve on nature by writing rules about how it should function. The existence of the institution tends to affirm the efficacy of the work it does.[63]

For current purposes, it is not necessary to determine whether the realist orientation Hudec adopts in the first part of *Developing Countries* is more or less accurate than the liberal approach employed in the second part of the book, or whether his dark view of state actors is exaggerated or accurate. Rather, the goal here is to unmask Hudec's methodological commitments, to juxtapose them with the tools of the econometric analysis discussed above, and to examine whether and how a research agenda that employs both methodologies might enrich our understanding of preferences and their effects upon developing states. I now turn to this task.

ii. Utilizing Econometrics and Political Economy: Toward a Progressive Research Agenda

Hudec's emphasis on political economy and dark vision of politics and institutions, combined with the empirical research summarized above, suggest the

---

62. Ibid 45.

63. Ibid 12. Ironically, the only entities that do not appear to suffer from these forms of dysfunction are the protectionist interests who are able to successfully pursue policies that disserve the interests of their fellow citizens. In contrast to the other actors that appear in *Developing Countries*, these rent-seeking interests seem well-organized, purposive, and all-too-successful. Of course, given the problems that plague decision-making in all other institutions, it is not clear why rent-seeking firms and industries will not also, at times, pursue counterproductive strategies. Nor does Hudec address why, even if protectionist interests attempt to pursue their interests in a rational manner, they will not suffer from incomplete information and bounded rationality, or from problems of corruption, fraud, and malfeasance, like other institutions.

outlines of a progressive research agenda.[64] What insights might be gained by juxtaposing *Developing Countries'* dark vision of politics with the econometric research exploring the empirical effect of preferential trade polices? Can utilizing political economy and econometric analysis reveal any hidden costs—or benefits—associated with the enactment and administration of preferential tariff policies?

A full exploration of these questions is well beyond the scope of this brief essay. However, by way of example, I sketch out below three lines of inquiry that may reveal important and underappreciated effects of preferential trade policies. Thus, for example, utilizing both political economy and econometric analysis could shed light on (i) whether the proliferation of preferential tariff programs has contributed to the proliferation of bilateral and regional trade agreements and, if so, whether these agreements promote or hinder developing state interests; (ii) whether the proliferation of preferential tariff programs produces greater protectionism in developing states and, if so, whether preference schemes can be refined to avoid this result; and (iii) whether the debate over preferences has served, in part, to divert attention from policies more likely to promote developing state growth and, if so, whether the trade regime can encourage developing states to pursue more successful economic policies.

Do preference schemes lead to PTAs? Trading nations have entered into a frenzy of bilateral and regional trade agreements in recent years; indeed, more preferential trade agreements (PTAs) were created during the WTO's first decade than during GATT's five decades. Moreover, unlike in the past, many recent bilateral and regional free trade agreements have been between developed and developing countries. Although a growing literature attempts to explain the causes and consequences of the proliferation of PTAs,[65] virtually no empirical scholarship examines whether there is a link between preferential trade schemes

---

64. By 'progressive' I do not mean to suggest a particular political orientation as much as research methodology that seeks to generate predictions, and then prove or disprove these predictions with data, to generate a coherent research agenda. For more the idea of a progressive research agenda, eg, I Lakatos, J Worrall and G Currie (eds), *The Methodology of Scientific Research Programmes* (Cambridge: Cambridge University Press, 1980); I Lakatos, 'Falsification and the Methodology of Scientific Research Programmes' in I Lakatos and A Musgrave (eds), *Criticism and the Growth of Knowledge* (Cambridge: Cambridge University Press, 1970).

65. Eg, R Fiorentino, L Verdeja and C Toqueboeuf, 'The Changing Landscape of Regional Trade Agreements: 2006 Update' (2007) WTO Discussion Paper No 12; JA Crawford and R Fiorentino, 'The Changing Landscape of Regional Trade Agreements' (2005) WTO Discussion Paper No 8; J Whalley, 'Recent Regional Agreements: Why So Many, So Fast, So Different and Where are They Headed?' (2006) CIGI Working Paper No 9.

and preferential trade agreements.⁶⁶ In particular, academics have not explored whether the design of preference schemes contributes to the proliferation of PTAs.

A causal relationship is quite plausible, particularly if one adopts the realist perspective Hudec uses in the first part of *Developing Countries*, where states are concerned about relative gains. As noted above, preferential trade schemes are inherently unstable in several respects. For example, developed states have virtually unlimited discretion to add or subtract countries and goods from their preference programs. Moreover, as developing states grow their economies and become more effective exporters, they are "graduated" from preference programs. To address these risks, developing states might seek to enter into PTAs with developed states. The rationale for doing so would be relatively straightforward: in contrast to preference schemes; PTAs are reciprocal agreements and cannot be unilaterally changed.

This relatively simple hypothesis suggests a rich research agenda. For example, empirical research could explore the factors that induce developing states to enter into trade agreements with developed states. Do they fear the loss of preferential access to developed state markets by being excluded from GSP schemes? Do developing states seek PTAs when they see developed states negotiating PTAs with other developing countries or when competitors obtain preferential market access? In short, do developing states use PTAs an insurance policy against being placed at a competitive disadvantage through discriminatory policies?

This potential link between preference schemes and PTAs is important because the rise of PTAs may disserve developing state interests. First, recent experience suggests that, in practice, many of the problems associated with preference schemes—such as trade diversion, product exclusions, and complex rules of origin—are largely replicated in PTAs.⁶⁷ Moreover, many PTAs are highly comprehensive in coverage. Notably, in recent years the inclusion of issues beyond the WTO's ambit has been especially marked in PTAs among developed and developing economies.⁶⁸ For example, at the 2004 WTO Ministerial

---

66. The terminology for these trade agreements can be confusing. For current purposes, I wish to contrast the WTO agreements, on the one hand, and all bilateral, regional, and plurilateral trade agreements of a preferential nature, on the other hand. The traditional umbrella term used for this latter group of agreements is 'regional trade agreements'. However, increasingly these agreements are entered into by states that are not geographic neighbors. Hence, I will usually refer to these agreements as PTAs rather than use the traditional term of regional trade agreements.

67. WTO, *The Future of the WTO: Addressing Institutional Challenges in the New Millennium*, Report by the Consultative Board to the Director-General Supachai Panitchpakdi (Geneva: WTO, 2004).

68. Eg, World Bank, *Global Economic Prospects 2005: Trade, Regionalism and Development* (Washington: IBRD/World Bank, 2005).

Conference in Cancun, developing states were able to exclude the so-called 'Singapore Issues' of trade facilitation, investment, government procurement, and competition from the negotiating agenda. However, these issues are addressed in many recent PTAs between developing and developed country partners.[69] Similarly, the United States is able to address issues that developing states can keep out of WTO negotiations, like labor and environment, in its PTAs with developing states.

Finally, there is substantial evidence that developed states' ability to address WTO-plus issues in PTAs with developing states has reduced developed states' willingness to reduce tariffs on a multilateral basis. Empirical research suggests that both EU and US reductions in MFN tariffs for PTA products during the Uruguay Round were on average only about one-half of the reduction for similar products that did not receive preferences.[70] To the extent that US and EU preference schemes require cooperation in labor, environment, drug enforcement, immigration, and other issues, we might understand the extension of preferential trade access as payment for cooperation. This implies 'that a reduction in MFN tariffs that lowers the preferential margin will be resisted by both the country that receives preferences and the country that grants them'[71]; more broadly, it implies that the current round of PTAs between developing and developed states are stumbling blocks rather than building blocks to multilateral liberalization.[72] And substantial research suggests that multilateral liberalization would benefit developing states more than preferential liberalization.[73]

These arguments point toward a series of substantial, albeit indirect, hidden costs associated with preference programs. However, there are a number of claims embedded in these arguments that would benefit from empirical research. The studies cited above examine the effect of PTAs on US and EU tariff rates; future studies could extend this inquiry to other states that grant preferences, such as Canada and Japan, to see if similar results obtain. Moreover, the studies

---

69. Examples of FTAs between developed and developing countries including all or some of the Singapore issues include: EC-South Africa, EFTA-Chile, US-Morocco, US-Jordan, and Thailand-Australia. FTA Negotiations between EC-Mercosur and US-Andean countries, among others, also contemplate the inclusion of these issues.

70. N Limão, 'Preferential Trade Agreements as Stumbling Blocks for Multilateral Trade Liberalization: Evidence for the US' (2006) 96 AE Rev 896; B Karacaovali and N Limão, 'The Clash of Liberalizations: Preferential versus Multilateral Trade Liberalization in the European Union' (2005) World Bank Policy Research Working Paper No 3493.

71. N Limão and M Olarreaga, 'Trade Preferences to Small Developing Countries and the Welfare Costs of Lost Multilateral Liberalization' (2006) 20 WB Econ Rev 217.

72. Ibid.

73. Ibid; G Harrison, T Rutherford and D Tarr, 'Rules of Thumb for Evaluating Preferential Trading Arrangements: Evidence from Computable General Equilibrium Assessments' (2003) 40(121) Cuadernos de Economía 460.

cited above focus on tariffs; future studies could explore whether PTAs affect market access through nontariff barriers.

In addition, future research could address related lines of inquiry. For example, how do PTAs affect states that are not part of the PTA? If, as suggested above, the European Union liberalizes less on an MFN basis because of its PTAs, might that lead, say, New Zealand or Brazil to reciprocate by reducing their MFN tariffs less than they would otherwise be willing to?[74] If so, that would mean that PTAs might generate important adverse spillover effects in other developed states that negatively impact developing states.

Inquiries like these call for econometric analysis. However, even if econometric studies reveal various indirect effects of preferences, these studies would ultimately call for a political economy explanation for precisely how PTAs effect multilateral liberalization. Hence, inquiries like these are illustrative of how econometric and political economy explanations can be mutually reinforcing and can illuminate the unexplored relationship between preference programs and PTAs.

Do preference programs reinforce protectionism in developing states? As noted above, Hudec argues that preferences are unlikely to assist developing states who wish to pursue liberalized trade policies. Scholars have just begun to test this claim empirically. A 2005 study by Özden and Reinhardt examined 154 developing states and found that states dropped from the United States' GSP program subsequently adopted lower trade barriers than those states that remained eligible for the program.[75] This result is entirely consistent with *Developing Countries'* argument. Hudec suggests that developing states' ability to enjoy preferential access to developed state markets will reduce the incentives that beneficiary state exporters have to lobby for trade liberalization. As a result, the policy process will be dominated by import-sensitive groups, and governments will be more likely to respond to their pleas.

This apparent confirmation of Hudec's insight by empirical research suggests several areas of further inquiry. For example, the Özden/Reinhardt study looks only at states that participate in the US GSP program. Future studies might examine the effects of participation in various other preference schemes to determine whether some have greater effects on beneficiary states than others; similarly, as preference schemes differ in their details, it may be fruitful to examine how different types of programs influence the balance between protectionist and liberalizing forces within beneficiary states.

Moreover, the Özden/Reinhardt study examines available data on aggregate trade openness; future studies might focus less on degrees of openness and

---

74. N Limão, 'Preferential vs. multilateral trade liberalization: evidence and open questions' (2006) 5 WT Rev 155, 171.

75. C Özden and E Reinhardt, 'The perversity of preferences: GSP and developing country trade policies, 1976-2000' (2005) 78 JDE 1.

more on levels of economic performance. Do reduced tariffs lead to increased GDP? Does liberalization produce increased levels of investment? Is increased openness associated with improved quality of life indicators?[76] Perhaps more important, future studies should attempt to identify the actual political economy mechanisms that produce the effects Özden and Reinhardt identify. These studies might suggest ways to fine-tune preference programs to avoid the 'perverse' effects they seem to have on developing states.

A related and underexplored area of inquiry relates to the effects of preference programs that include various forms of conditionality. For example, following the Appellate Body report in the *GSP* dispute, the European Union revised its GSP program. The new program extends additional tariff preferences to developing states that commit to ratify and implement a number of human rights and good governance conventions.[77] United States preference programs similarly condition certain preferences on various types of domestic reforms in beneficiary states, particularly by requiring that workers' rights be protected. As discussed below, an emerging school of thought argues that these types of domestic legal reforms are important determinants of economic performance. Moreover, the comparative politics literature has long debated the political institutional determinants of liberal trade policy.[78] The existence of multiple preference schemes that require different types of domestic reforms offer a valuable means to test the hypotheses developed in these literatures.

Moreover, these preference schemes allow empirical investigation of another one of Hudec's claims. Hudec's analysis suggests that sustainable domestic reform in developing states cannot be kept in place out of fear of losing access to developed state markets. Instead, to be sustainable, domestic reforms must produce noticeable economic gains. Empirical research could examine whether reforms enacted to satisfy preference schemes contribute to economic growth and whether or not these reforms survive following withdraw of preferences. As with other efforts to extend the Özden/Reinhardt study, the goal here would be

---

76. This approach to development is reflected in, for example, the UNDP's annual Human Development Report. This approach is associated with the writings of Amartya Sen and Martha Nussbaum. Eg, M Nussbaum, *Women and Human Development: The Capabilities Approach* (Cambridge: Cambridge University Press 2002); A Sen, *Democracy as Freedom* (New York: Anchor 1999).

77. European Union Council, 'Council Regulation (EC) 980/2005 applying a scheme of generalized tariff preferences' (2005) OJ L169/1.

78. SD Erlich, 'Access to Protection: Domestic Institutions and Trade Policy in Democracies' (2007) 61 Int'l Org 571; WJ Henisz and ED Mansfield, 'Votes and Vetoes: The Political Determinants of Commercial Openness' (2006) 50 Int'l SQ 189; HV Milner and K Kubota, 'Why the Move to Free Trade? Democracy and Trade Policy in the Developing Countries' (2005) 50 Int'l Org 107; GM Grossman and E Helpman, 'A Protectionist Bias in Majoritarian Politics' (2005) 120 QJE 1239; M Olson, 'Dictatorship, democracy, and development' (1993) 87 A Pol Sci Rev 567.

to identify whether conditionality has "perverse" effects on developing state economies and, if so, how to fine-tune preference programs to avoid such effects in the future.

Is the debate over preferences a diversion? Finally, there is an important dysfunctionality that *Developing Countries* does not explicitly address: the dysfunctionality of the debate over preferences itself. As the first part of *Developing Countries* illustrates, developing state demands 'for greater market access (became) the first issue on the agenda' during the GATT's early years,[79] and has remained at or near the center of the trade policy agenda ever since. The contrast between the political salience of preferences and their disappointing economic results raises an intriguing puzzle: if preferential treatment generates limited economic benefits and renders the pursuit of sensible economic policies more difficult, why do developing states continue to advocate for these programs?

Perhaps another of Hudec's observations in *Developing Countries* may shed light on this puzzle. Despite—or perhaps because of—his deep engagement with the trade system, Hudec was acutely aware of the limits of trade law and policy. Indeed, he emphasizes that the economic performance of a developing state is influenced more by its domestic policies than by developed state trade policy; he writes that 'a government's own trade-policy decisions are the most important determinant of its own economic welfare'.[80] Recent empirical studies lend support to the claim that export performance correlates with economic reforms in the exporting country.[81] This claim fits into a larger literature—mostly produced after *Developing Countries* was first published—arguing that development has less to do with preferential access to rich state markets than with, for example, various features of the domestic domain such as meaningful political representation, individual liberties, independent judiciaries, the rule of law, and other aspects of institutional and legal infrastructure.[82]

This research suggests that the primary responsibility for the disappointing economic performance of many developing states lies primarily with developing state governments rather than with developed state tariff or subsidy policies.

---

79. Hudec (n 1 above) 41.

80. Ibid at 159.

81. UNCTAD, *The African Growth and Opportunity Act: A Preliminary Assessment*, UNCTAD/ITCD/TSB/2003/1 (New York: UN 2003).

82. An influential body of political economy scholarship focuses upon domestic institutions. Eg, D Rodrik and others, 'Institutions Rule: The Primary of Institutions Over Geography and Integration in Economic Development' (2004) 9 JEcon Growth 131; D Acemoglu and others, 'The Colonial Origins of Comparative Development: An Empirical Investigation' (2001) 91 AE Rev 1369; R Hall and C Jones, 'Why Do Some Countries Produce So Much More Output per Worker than Others' (1999) 114 QJE 83. Many of the arguments in this literature regarding the importance of domestic institutions build upon the pioneering work of Douglass North. Eg, D North, *Institutions, Institutional Change and Economic Performance* (Cambridge: Cambridge University Press 1990).

These arguments also raise the question of whether the lengthy and contentious debate over preferences has diverted diplomatic and scholarly attention to an issue of decidedly secondary importance and hence obscured more important issues related to domestic reform in developing states.[83] Ironically, although much effort has been devoted to measuring the economic effects of preferences, no scholarly attention has been paid to the opportunity costs associated with this misdirection of diplomatic and political efforts. But current knowledge regarding successful development strategies raises the question of whether this diversion of energies and attention represents a hidden cost of the debate over preferences.

I imagine that Robert Hudec would not be shocked by the suggestion that governments engage in diversionary tactics to deflect attention from their own shortcomings. This claim would dovetail with his observations about the hypocrisy and ineptitude of government officials. And it would be perfectly consistent with the time-honored state practice of scapegoating foreign actors to divert attention from their own shortcomings. Nor would Hudec be taken aback by a claim that the international trade system aided and abetted this diversionary tactic. As we have seen, he was a fierce critic of the ineffectual and often counterproductive nature of GATT processes and politics.

Of course, it would be presumptuous to suggest that this means that Hudec would endorse the type of analysis set out above. Although I know Robert Hudec only through his work and the recollections of friends and colleagues, I'd like to think that he would appreciate this effort to "transcend the ostensible" regarding the debate over preferences and to use his methodological orientation and underlying assumptions about the nature of states and the trade system to identify a research agenda that might illuminate some hidden dimensions of the debate over preferential treatment for developing states.

E. THE HIDDEN COSTS OF *DEVELOPING COUNTRIES'* RHETORICAL STRATEGY

Developing Countries succeeds in offering profound insights for trade specialists while remaining accessible for lay readers and justifiably is considered one of the classics of trade scholarship. For current purposes, however, the book may be as interesting for what it does not say as for what it does say. Indeed, in several important respects, the text—ambitious as it is—sells itself short. *Developing Countries* presents itself as providing a straightforward account of the tensions

---

83. To be sure, this literature does not exclude the possibility that the relative importance of domestic policy exists precisely because existing preference policies have been poorly designed and unevenly applied. Eg, F Garcia, 'Beyond Special and Differential Treatment' (2004) 27 BCICL Rev 291.

between developed and developing states over preferential treatment and offering a pragmatic and realistic critique of current thinking about trade policy. The book is relentlessly instrumental in tone and approach and can easily be taken as an example of Hudec's oft-noted 'realistic, functional, fact-focused and anti-conceptual way of thinking'.[84]

And yet, of course, the book presupposes a rather complex set of positive assumptions about the way the world works. Indeed, it could hardly be otherwise. Any instrumental approach to international law necessarily rests upon a series of assumptions about the principal actors in the trade system—these actors' motivations and capacities, and the constraints imposed by the international system itself.[85]

For example, *Developing Countries* implicitly utilizes an extremely sophisticated vision of the role and limits of international law, including international trade law. The text includes important but underdeveloped insights about the nature of international dispute resolution, an implicit theory of the mechanisms that induce compliance with international norms, and important observations regarding the function and role of soft law.[86] In brief, *Developing Countries* assumes a rather complex account of the ways that international law does and does not affect state behavior and is a text of enormous theoretical interest and sophistication. As a result, *Developing Countries* is a much richer and theoretically ambitious undertaking than it lets on. Although it is refreshing to encounter a text that does not try to oversell itself, it is worth considering whether there are hidden costs to Hudec's undersell.

---

84. D Palmeter, 'Robert E. Hudec—A Practitioner's Appreciation' (2003) 37 JWT 703, 705. See also J Trachtman, 'Robert Hudec and the Vocation of International Trade Law' (2003) 6 JIEL 742. ('Hudec was impatient with most legal theory'.)

85. Of course, instrumental approaches are not the only, or necessarily the best, approaches to international law. For example, some approach international law as a deontological quest for justice. Eg, J Thompson, *Justice and World Order: A Philosophical Inquiry* (London: Routledge, 1992). Frank Garcia's contribution to this volume is informed by a deontological approach. F Garcia, 'The Bank and the Poor: Justice, Bretton Woods Institutions and the Problem of Inequality', in Chapter 18 of this collection. Garcia's contribution builds upon his earlier work on justice in the trade system. F Garcia, *Trade, Inequality and Justice: Toward a Liberal Theory of Just Trade* (New York: Transnational, 2003).

86. Hudec explored many of these themes in a number of important works, including 'Adjudication of International Trade Disputes' (1978) Trade Policy Research Centre, Thames Essay No 16; 'Reforming GATT Adjudication Procedures: The Lessons of the DISC Case' (1988) 72 Minn L Rev 1443; 'The New WTO Dispute Settlement Procedure: An Overview of the First Three Years' (1999) 8 Minn JGT 1; 'Broadening the Scope of Remedies in WTO Dispute Settlement, in F Weiss (ed), *Improving WTO Dispute Settlement Procedures—Issues and Lessons from the Practice of other International Courts and Tribunals* (London: Cameron May, 2000) 345; 'The Adequacy of WTO Dispute Settlement Remedies: A Developing Country Perspective' in B Hoekman and others (eds), *Development, Trade and the WTO* (Washington DC: World Bank 2002).

To approach this issue, it is useful to consider what has changed in the two decades since *Developing Countries* first appeared. The trade regime has, of course, seen substantial institutional and doctrinal changes, including the creation of the WTO, the expansion of trade disciplines into new areas such as intellectual property and services, and the establishment of the WTO's strengthened dispute settlement system. Moreover, when Hudec's text was first released, the GATT was a relatively obscure institution. During its first several decades, the GATT operated as a 'club' where a relatively small number of diplomats and economists from like-minded states worked quietly to make trade policy without significant public input or oversight.[87]

Simply put, when Hudec wrote *Developing Countries*, the trade regime was practically unknown outside a small group of trade cognoscenti, 'globalization' had not yet entered the public lexicon, and trade negotiations and agreements rarely captured media or public attention.

The current landscape could hardly be more different. Today, international trade is at the heart of debates over globalization, the WTO is widely understood to be a central pillar of the emerging international economy, and international trade law is one of the most important and highly developed fields of international law. The WTO is no longer an obscure body but rather a highly visible and controversial component of an emerging regime of global economic governance. Moreover, the current trade regime is no longer preoccupied with sleepy topics like tariffs and quotas; instead it has become a central battleground for contentious issues like developing state access to affordable medicines and the locus of transnational conflicts pitting trade against nontrade values.

Changes in the academic study of international trade have been no less dramatic. Trade law was a marginalized and underdeveloped discipline when *Developing Countries* was first issued. Articles on trade rarely appeared in international law journals,[88] let alone flagship general topic law reviews,[89] and many of the peer-reviewed journals that now help to define the field had not yet been

---

87. R Keohane and J Nye, 'The Club Model of Multilateral Cooperation and the World Trade Organization: Problems of Democratic Legitimacy', in RP Porter and others (eds), *Efficiency, Equality, and Legitimacy: The Multilateral Trading System at the Millennium* (Washington DC: Brookings 2001) 264. See also JHH Weiler, 'The Rule of Lawyers and the Ethos of Diplomats: Reflections on the Internal and External Legitimacy of Dispute Settlement, in ibid 334; R Howse, 'From Politics to Technocracy—and Back Again: The Fate of the Multilateral Trading Regime' (2002) 96 AJIL 94.

88. On the relative marginalization of international trade law in a leading US journal, DF Vagts, 'International Economic Law and the American Journal of International Law' (2006) 100 AJIL 769; D Bederman, 'Appraising a Century of Scholarship in the American Journal of International Law' (2006) 100 AJIL 20.

89. Indeed, it appears that the first article in an American law review on countervailing and antidumping duties was not published until 1958. P Ehrenhaft, 'Memories of the Supreme Court in the 1961 Term' (2004) 13 Minn JGT 215, 220 n 7.

established.⁹⁰ International trade was not taught at many law schools, and very few US law schools had full-time faculty who specialized in trade law. As a result, despite its substantial strengths, *Developing Countries* was likely of interest only to a relatively small number of international trade practitioners and scholars when it was first released.

Today, courses in international trade have become a fixture in numerous law schools, economics departments, public policy schools, and international relations departments; a growing number of monographs, essay collections, and journals address trade issues; and conferences and symposia on international trade are now common. The trade regime is an increasingly important object of study in several academic disciplines; specialists in international relations (IR), international political economy, and international economics devote substantial attention to the trade system and address questions of great interest to trade lawyers such as the optimal design of the trade system, the nature and effects of WTO dispute settlement, and the function of contingent protection.

The influence of these various disciplines upon each other has been enormous; it is no exaggeration to suggest that virtually all serious students of the trade regime today necessarily draw upon insights from disciplines that neighbor their own.⁹¹ Perhaps if Robert Hudec was alive today and producing an updated edition of his classic text, he would substantially draw on these literatures. Doing so would enrich *Developing Countries* in at least two respects.

First, insights from these cognate literatures could enhance *Developing Countries'* arguments. For example, the lively debate in IR circles over the impact of security-related concerns on trade cooperation might inform *Developing Countries'* reflections on why the United States originally choose to pursue a GATT with larger membership but shallower commitments and why the United States later shifted course and insisted that the Uruguay Round be a single undertaking.⁹² Perhaps more important, Hudec sets forth a controversial claim about the relative importance of developing states' domestic policy as opposed to preferential access to developed state markets. As noted above, I take this claim to be one of the text's central ideas and hence I believe that *Developing Countries*

---

90. The first edition of the *Journal of World Trade* was published in 1967. Other leading journals are even more recent. For example, the *Journal of International Economic Law* was first published in 1998, and the *World Trade Review* was first published in 2001.

91. Ironically, Hudec himself organized one of the earliest interdisciplinary projects examining trade law. J Bhagwati and R Hudec (eds), *Fair Trade and Harmonization: Prerequisites for Free Trade?* (Cambridge: MIT Press 1996). The American Law Institute's publication of annual volumes that analyze WTO case law is a more recent initiative along these lines. Eg, H Horn and P Mavroidis (eds), *The WTO Case Law of 2003* (Cambridge: Cambridge University Press 2006).

92. R Steinberg, 'In the Shadow of Law or Power? Consensus-Based Bargaining and Outcomes in the GATT/WTO' (2002) 56 Int'l Org 339.

would be a stronger work if it tested this claim against the substantial literature that addresses the domestic determinants of economic growth.

Of course, Hudec's jargon-free writing is one of the virtues of *Developing Countries*, and I am not suggesting that his text would be improved by a detailed engagement with each of the theoretical literatures mentioned above. But reference to these larger bodies of scholarship could provide support for many of Hudec's arguments, help identify the limits of these arguments, and help locate those arguments within a rich set of scholarly literatures.

Second, locating *Developing Countries'* arguments within their larger scholarly contexts would facilitate dialogue with a broader academic audience. Consider, for example, Hudec's work on dispute settlement. This groundbreaking scholarship helped inspire a generation of empirical research by political scientists into GATT and WTO dispute settlement.[93] Hudec's work did so, in part, because it presented data and evidence about trade disputes in a way that political scientists could easily understand and utilize.

Developing Countries should likewise be of interest to a broad and interdisciplinary audience; in addition to international trade law scholars, the topics *Developing Countries* addresses are of interest to a wide variety of international lawyers, international political economy scholars, economists, and students of international development and international relations. Locating the broader questions raised by *Developing Countries* in the context of various scholarly literatures it implicates would make the book both more accessible and appealing to a wide variety of readers from different disciplines. Doing so would render *Developing Countries'* important insights more salient to a broader audience of readers.

F. CONCLUSION

Preferential treatment for developing states has been a defining feature of the multilateral trade system since its inception. However, as *Developing Countries* reminds us, preferential treatment was neither inevitable nor uncontroversial. *Developing Countries* masterfully reviews the history of this controversy and will serve as an authoritative guide to the historical, political, and normative dimensions of the debate over preferential treatment for developing states. For these reasons, all those interested in international trade should welcome the opportunity to revisit *Developing Countries*.

---

93. Eg, M Bush and E Reinhardt, 'Testing International Trade Law: Empirical Studies of GATT/WTO Dispute Settlement' in D Kennedy and J Southwick (eds), *The Political Economy of International Trade Law: Essays in Honor of Robert E. Hudec* (Cambridge: Cambridge University Press 2002) 457.

As the essays in this volume illustrate, *Developing Countries* contains insights and arguments that can inform a rich research agenda. Drawing on an empirical literature that largely postdates the initial release of *Developing Countries*, I have tried to suggest some additional lines of inquiry inspired by Hudec's arguments, including (i) whether the proliferation of preferential tariff programs has inadvertently contributed to the proliferation of bilateral and regional trade agreements, and, if so, whether these agreements disserve developing state interests; (ii) whether preferential schemes hinder developing states' ability to liberalize; and (iii) whether the debate over preferences diverts focus from policies more likely to promote developing state growth.

In sum, *Developing Countries* clearly details the arguments for and against preferential treatment and offers an influential critique of preferences. Moreover, as detailed above, *Developing Countries* is a theoretically sophisticated text that contains more than meets the eye. In particular, Hudec's arguments, combined with recent empirical work, suggests a research agenda designed to uncover whether there are hidden costs—or hidden benefits—associated with the debate over preferential treatment for developing states.

4. TRADE AND DEVELOPMENT
Systemic Lessons from WTO Experience with Implementation, Trade Facilitation, and Aid for Trade

J MICHAEL FINGER

A. Introduction 76
B. The Story of the Uruguay Round 76
    I. Well-Developed Politics 79
    II. Underdeveloped Economics 80
C. The Results of 1987 81
D. Robert Hudec's Recommendations 82
E. Active Non-mercantilist-Developing Country Participation in the Uruguay Round 83
    I. Motivation for Developing Countries 83
    II. Result 84
F. Mercantilism Strikes Back: Evaluating the Uruguay Round Outcome 86
    I. The Unbalanced Outcome 87
    II. The Implementation Problem 89
G. WTO Response 90
H. Implementation 91
    I. Special and Differential Treatment 92
I. Aid for Trade Comes Forward—and Recedes 94
J. Trade Facilitation Enters the Agenda 95
    I. Identifying Concrete Implementation Needs/Support 96
    II. Assistance Mechanics of the Proposals 98
    III. W142 Differences 99
        Mandatory provisions (if any) 99
        Optional provisions 99
        Obligations on donors to provide assistance 99
    IV. Problems 100
K. Conclusions 101
    I. Special and Differential Treatment 101
    II. Implementation 102
    III. Aid for Trade 102
    IV. Trade Facilitation 102
    V. Support for Developing Country Liberalization 103
    VI. Déjà vu—All Over Again 103

Robert Hudec's analysis of developing countries in the GATT system led him to conclude that the identity of developing countries in the system was almost entirely a matter of their demanding nonreciprocal and preferential treatment, and developed countries responding grudgingly to those demands. The relationship, he concluded, had been politically ineffective either to discipline-developed country restrictions against developing countries or to support liberalization within them. He also demonstrated that as a legal matter it was impossible to transform such a relationship into a generic obligation. Moreover, Hudec was pessimistic about the relationship breaking away from the struggle over non-reciprocal and preferential treatment. He saw a dark destiny, but his expression of despair offered a glimmer of hope. 'There are those who believe that the GATT has become so committed to the current policy that the only way to change it would be to start a new organization'.[1]

We did start a new organization. Has the WTO achieved what Robert Hudec hoped a new organization might?

A. INTRODUCTION

In the Uruguay Round, developing countries behaved as full partners rather than as supplicants in the system. This step forward has, however, been reversed by outrageous mismanagement of the hangover of the Uruguay Round—the 'implementation problem' and the 'imbalance' of the Uruguay Round outcome. That is the story I will tell. In telling it, I will first summarize Hudec's analysis of the GATT's first four decades—how we got to the Uruguay Round. I then review the Uruguay Round and since. I conclude that from the perspective of the GATT/WTO system supporting development and poverty reduction, we are back where we were in 1987, or worse.

B. THE STORY OF THE URUGUAY ROUND

Perhaps the key insight of Robert Hudec's study of developing countries in the GATT system is not that he saw the GATT as a relationship among the developed countries but between developed and developing countries.

The GATT began as part of the plan among post-World War II western leaders to establish a safer and more stable (Western) world than they had inherited. Linking the major countries into a web of commerce and shared prosperity would help to free them from the power diplomacy and the every-second-generation cycle of war in which European-based civilization had been trapped.

Developing countries at the International Trade Organization (ITO) and GATT Negotiations demanded a commitment from developed countries to provide significant resource transfers. They also wanted freedom from the general idea of discipline that the arrangements were trying to impose on others. In the latter regard, their position was hardly different from that of developed countries acting individually.

---

1. R Hudec, *Developing Countries in the GATT Legal System* (Aldershot: Gower, for the Trade Policy Research Center, 1987) 230.

Why then, Hudec asks, did the system increasingly leave developing countries outside of the momentum toward liberalization that the developed countries built among themselves and exempt them from the general, though imperfect, sense of discipline that the GATT system evolved?[2]

In his answer to that question, Hudec emphasizes the sense of ethics that the system embodied. As high politics, the GATT was collective action: *individual sacrifice for the common good*. As low politics it was mercantilism—the benefit was access to foreign markets, but this had to be paid for by giving access to one's own. From either perspective, the individual members had to give; the domestic economics and the domestic politics of the vision was indeed, 'individual sacrifice'. A point that Hudec emphasizes is that to Western society in an arrangement such as this—individual sacrifice for the common good—one cannot ask the lesser/poorer members to contribute equally with the stronger/eminent/richer.

The virtue of import restrictions and the sacrifice of giving them up was driven home by the developed countries' insisting on the right to retain some of theirs. Europeans were more sympathetic to the infant-industry (and reconstruction) argument for protection than were US leaders, but the US position on discipline had its own exceptions (eg, quantitative restrictions on agricultural imports, the escape clause, and antidumping provisions).

> This theoretical contradiction was fundamental. In an avowedly welfare relationship, where the needy have a recognized claim to unilateral payments, the strong cannot make a principled demand for liberal trade policies by the needy when, in the same breath, they define trade liberalization as a "payment."[3]

---

2. An early indication of the place of developing countries in the system was the formality with which the legal relationship was addressed. By the mid-1950s, a large share of GATT's developed as well as of its developing contracting parties had balance-of-payments measures in place, and legal review was as rigorous for developing countries as for developed ones. The difference was that developed countries were pressed to remove such measures—through the reviews and also through other relationships such as the IMF and the Organization for European Economic Cooperation. Hudec notes, '(t)he developing country reviews became increasingly pro forma as their balance of payments problems remained drearily the same. Waivers for surcharges were routinely given.' Ibid 30. He continues, '(w)ith developing countries, where there is no common underlying discipline, legal form is all there is to the relationship. Setting aside the formalities . . . they [developed and developing countries] would have nothing else to say to each other'. Ibid 32. In contrast, a 'diplomat's jurisprudence' among developed countries avoided clear legal decisions so as to allow developed country governments to adjust toward shared objectives in ways that their understandings of domestic politics indicated would be most effective. R Hudec, 'The GATT Legal System: A Diplomat's Jurisprudence' (1970) 4 JWTL 615–65. Reprinted in RE Hudec, *Essays on the Nature of International Trade Law* (London: Cameron May 1999) 17–76.

3. Hudec (n 1 above) 17.

Hudec elaborates the point with two reminders: (a) Western governments generally prefer taxes graduated by income over head taxes and (b) the accepted unfairness of laws that treat unequals equally, a point made by Anatole France's suggesting a law that would prohibit the rich as well as the poor from sleeping under bridges.

The developing countries could hardly be expected to sacrifice for the refabrication of the Western system. In the old regime, they had been hardly more than prizes over which the imperial powers fought and reservoirs of soldiers impressed into imperial armies.

Why then—if developing countries asked for resource transfers as well as for license to maintain trade restrictions—did their payoff not come in the form of resource transfers?

First, the coin of the GATT was legal discipline; at GATT there had to be a payoff in this coin. As Hudec explains, '(t)here were welfare concessions to be made in other areas, but diplomats at one meeting always want to bring home some achievement of their own'.[4]

Among the links between developed and developing countries, the GATT Negotiations were the most visible and celebrated. The GATT Rounds were named for presidents (one was), and World Bank lending programs have never been so adorned. No developing country government could have pointed to its World Bank or other aid portfolio to moderate the shame of having given in at GATT.

Among developed countries, the relationship was a shared vision expressed in many ways, the GATT process being only one. Between developed and developing countries, the relationship was limited to the legalities of the rules; hence freedom from these legalities and from the mercantilist demands for reciprocity became the medium of exchange. Within GATT's first decade, pressure waned on developing countries to give concessions in the tariff negotiations; rules that regulated restrictions by developing countries were relaxed. '(F)rom about 1958 onwards, developing countries seized the initiative and persuaded the GATT to concentrate on the behavior of developed countries towards them, rather than on their own behavior'.[5]

Finally—and this is where Hudec's political incorrectness comes forward—developing country leadership as well as developed country leadership bought into the scam.

> The policy of nonreciprocity has flourished primarily because for both sides it has been **the path of least resistance**. It has been **the easy way out** for the governments of developing countries because it has given them a free hand to satisfy as many domestic political interests as possible. It has been the easy way out for the Group of 77 as a whole because it has offered an undemanding

---

4. Hudec (n 1 above) 16.
5. Hudec (n 1 above) 32.

policy on which they can most easily achieve solidarity. It has also been the easy way out for diplomats from developing countries because it has allowed them to maintain the posture of vigorous representation without ever having to ask home governments to take difficult decisions. Finally, and perhaps most important, it has been the easy way out for the governments of developed countries and their diplomats. Relaxation of legal discipline has always been the cost-free answer—the concession that developed countries could make without having to go through the unpleasant business of asking legislatures for real trade liberalization (or real resources). Like penny gin, it was an inexpensive way to keep the peace by pandering to the other side's worst instincts.[6] (emphasis added)

i. Well-Developed Politics

How did things come to this? Parts of Hudec's explanation are the Cold War rivalry for developing countries' loyalties and the United Nations providing a voice for the right of developing countries to nonreciprocal and preferential treatment, eg, in the Declaration of a New International Economic Order and the Charter of Economic Rights and Duties of States. The United Nations Conference on Trade and Development (UNCTAD), created in 1964, became a trade-specific venue for competition with GATT for developing country loyalties. 'By the early 1960s, GATT relations between developed and developing countries had become almost entirely centered on competition with UNCTAD'.[7]

The influence of UNCTAD was substantial, eg, its framework for presentation of the Tokyo Round outcome was followed by the GATT Secretariat in its report on the Kennedy Round results.[8]

Many GATT statements, eg, the 1958 Action Program, GATT Part IV added in 1965, and the GATT framework agreements of 1979, repeated the acceptance of nonreciprocal and preferential treatment as the GATT policy toward developing countries. At the 1964 Kennedy Round Negotiations first appeared the language, 'the contribution of the less-developed countries to the overall objective of trade liberalization should be considered in the light of the development and trade needs of these countries'.[9] This language acknowledged developing countries as part of the undertaking—they would make a contribution—and thus countered the creeping realization that developing countries were not party to the GATT vision. It imposed, however, no substance on what that contribution

---

6. Hudec (n 1 above) 230–31.
7. Hudec (n 1 above) 39.
8. In JM Finger 'Development Economics and the General Agreement on Tariffs and Trade' in J deMelo and A Sapir (eds), *Trade Theory and Economic Reform: Essays in Honor of Béla Balassa* (1991) 203–23, I concluded that as a soccer match the score then stood at UNCTAD 2, GATT 0; the second being an own-goal.
9. Cited by Hudec (n 1 above) 45.

would be.[10] In practice, it was minimal, eg, India's contribution to the Kennedy Round was its acceptance of the reduction of its preference margin when United Kingdom MFN rates were reduced.[11]

In the 1960s, 37 developing countries joined 28 of them under special procedures for newly independent territories (Article XXVI.r(c)), that exempted them from having to negotiate concessions in order to enter.[12]

ii. Underdeveloped Economics

'Gains from trade', as economists understand it, was hardly part of postwar Western leaders' conception of what trade policy was about. President Franklin Roosevelt's economic advisors saw trade policy's role as preventing imports from interfering with domestic recovery programs and UK leadership saw a large role for economic planning in the postwar world.[13] As the United Nations—particularly UNCTAD—gave increasing voice to the developing countries' argument, the United States never elaborated a protrade development view; it had no economics brief to support developing country trade liberalization. For reasons of Cold War competition as well as altruism, the United States was sympathetic to the developing countries.

As Japan and then other Asian countries used trade as a development vehicle, a number of studies, eg, those organized by Bela Balassa; Little, Scitovsky and Scott; Anne Krueger; Jagdish Bhagwati; and Jergen Donges documented this success and elaborated the case for developing countries to reduce their own trade restrictions.[14] This codification of successful trade experiences of developing countries was not, however, taken up in the trade discussion at GATT.

---

10. As old institutionalists understand, institution formation depends on more than the constellation of forces that influence them; it depends on repetitions that eventually settle into a groove that is convenient for all sides. When I worked in the US Treasury Department in the 1970s, usually on matters in which we disagreed with the US State Department, we insisted that the State Department's motto was, "When we have found a formula that avoids the issue, we can all agree".

11. Hudec (n 1 above) 45.

12. Hudec (n 1 above) Chapter 3.

13. C Hull, *The Memoirs of Cordell Hull* (London: Hodder and Stoughton, 1948) 81. Hull at Parts 1 and 2 describes Secretary of State Cordell Hull's struggle with Roosevelt's economic advisors over Hull's attempt to convince the president to support the Reciprocal Trade Agreements program. Kock contrasts US and UK economic ideologies at the time. K Kock, *International Trade Policy and the GATT 1947–1967* (Stockholm: Almquist and Wiksell, 1969) Chapter 1.

14. B Balassa and Associates, *The Structure of Protection in Developing Countries* (Baltimore: Johns Hopkins University Press 1971), IMD Little, T Scitovsky and MF Scott, *Industry and Trade in Some Developing Countries: A Comparative Study* (London and New York: Oxford University Press for the Development Center of the Organization for Economic Cooperation and Development, 1970); J Bhagwati, *Anatomy and Consequences of Exchange Control Regimes* (Cambridge: Ballinger, 1978); and JB Donges, 'A Comparative

At GATT, nonreciprocal and preferential treatment continued to define the trade-development issue; debate was confined to how much of it developed countries would offer. Was insisting on it a good strategy or receiving it a good result? These questions were not in play.[15]

The GATT response to the Haberler Report of 1958[16] was an earlier indication that the GATT was about the behavior of developed countries and not that of developing ones. The report concluded that existing arrangements were relatively unfavorable to primary producing countries, but it also concluded that progress depends on both developing and developed countries reducing their restrictions. The action program that followed took up only the need for change in developed country policies.[17]

C. THE RESULTS OF 1987

The most obvious result is that reformers in developing countries did not receive the support that international law obligation has brought to developed country reformers.[18] A second result Hudec brings out is that the GATT process has not, on the other hand, created an international law obligation on the developed countries to provide nonreciprocal and preferential treatment to developing countries.

> The number of quasi-commitments has already persuaded many legal scholars to characterize the welfare concept (nonreciprocal and preferential treatment) as a sort of quasi-law, using various labels such as 'soft law,' 'legal principle,' 'law-in-the-making,' and 'obligation of good faith'. In the author's view, however, this is as far as the legal force of the welfare obligation can ever go.[19]

Survey of Industrialization Policies in Fifteen Semi-Industrial Countries' (1976) Weltwirtschaftliches Archiv. Band 112 (Heft 4) 626–59.

15. I have documented these points previously (n 8 above).

16. Campos and others, *Trends in International Trade* (GATT 1958).

17. I document this point previously (n 8 above). The report is often cited for supporting only the case for developed country action; eg, Wikipedia states that 'Haberler's report seems to prefigure the report written by Prebisch for UNCTAD in 1964'. Wikipedia, 'Gottfried Haberler' at <http://en.wikipedia.org/wiki/Gottfried_Haberler> (accessed 26 April 2007).

18. In recent days, the phrase 'developing country ownership' has entered the litany of international development. If Robert Hudec were to ponder the phrase, he might point out that 'ownership' is not something the GATT system extols, rather it is something that the system manipulates. Ownership of trade policy in developed countries has been wrested from protection-seekers, the GATT system has not supported the same manipulation in developing countries.

19. Hudec (n 1 above) 186–87.

Hudec quotes in support a UN review of the development of such legal principles.[20] He also examines the form that the 'have versus have-not obligation' has taken in national laws and points out that

> The examples of redistributive justice found in national tax and welfare laws do not...create citizen-to-citizen rights and duties. They are always structured as public law; the extra duties of the rich (for example, paying higher taxes) are owed to the sovereign rather than to particular deserving claimants; the rights of the deserving poor (for example, rights to welfare payments) are recognized as an obligation owed by the sovereign, rather than by any individual taxpayer.[21]

Contemporary law does not work that way, but Hudec points out that feudal law 'was able to enforce status-defined rights and duties'.[22] Because there is no sovereign in the international system, the idea of creating a legal obligation/right to nonreciprocal and preferential treatment is not in the cards.

Even so, the repetition of demands and acknowledgments might have some effect—influence actions by the developed countries without going so far as to regulate them. An alternative interpretation would be that such repetition of demands followed by rhetorical response can perpetuate the lack of a substantive response.[23] Even if it is effective, the process is browbeating, not jurisprudence.

D. ROBERT HUDEC'S RECOMMENDATIONS

Hudec's analysis brought him to conclude that: 'developing countries are wrong to think of GATT legal policy primarily in terms of its impact on the behavior of developed countries and instead should start paying careful attention to its impact on their own trade-policy decisions'.[24]

He recommended that the GATT system abandon 'nonreciprocal and preferential treatment' as the foundation of developing countries' place in the GATT: 'the contracting parties should instead establish a regime of developing country legal obligations that would provide support for governments of developing countries in opposing unwanted protectionist policies at home'.[25]

---

20. Hudec (n 1 above) 105.
21. Hudec (n 1 above) 187.
22. Hudec (n 1 above) 187.
23. To paraphrase a Henny Youngman joke, developing country sympathizers have been satisfied to bait the trap with a picture of a cheese and have responded enthusiastically to the capture of a picture of a mouse.
24. Hudec (n 1 above) 229.
25. Hudec (n 1 above) 229.

As to protecting themselves from rogue behavior by developed countries, the motive force the agreement captured was reciprocity; its central controlling device was nondiscrimination: '(t)he MFN obligation is the only solid foundation on which effective legal protection of the interests of developing countries can ever be built'.[26]

Hudec was aware of the difficulty of implementing these recommendations. Nondiscrimination is abstract and impersonal; discrimination is sympathetic case-by-case and immediate. Besides, in the mercantilist ethic, nondiscrimination misassigns blame, eg, if safeguard action responding mostly to increased imports from China had to be applied to all exporters.

Though pessimistic, Hudec did see the possibility that a new organization could make a difference. I turn now to the Uruguay Round and since.

E. ACTIVE NON-MERCANTILIST-DEVELOPING COUNTRY PARTICIPATION IN THE URUGUAY ROUND

Through the Tokyo Round, developing country participation in multilateral trade negotiations had been either passive or defensive. At the Uruguay Round, things were different. Many developing countries were in the midst of extensive economic reforms; trade liberalization was an integral part of these programs; and already in the run-up to the Round, developing countries took an active role.[27]

i. Motivation for Developing Countries

The rationale behind these reforms differed from the rationale that had motivated developed country liberalization under the GATT. (Section B above) The Asian example enjoyed increasing influence, and it was heavily proselytized by the Bretton Woods institutions and others in the 1980s. Key concepts in this view of trade restrictions were 'domestic resource cost' and 'effective protection.' Domestic resource cost measured the amount of resources needed to produce importable goods at home rather than importing them in exchange for the country's exportables. Effective protection brought forward how a country's import restrictions on inputs raised the cost of its exportables. Both concepts thus highlight the burden a country's import restrictions place on its own people and industries.

Another aspect of the change of attitude can be described politely as import substitution fatigue. 'Developing country leaders increasingly realized that import substitution strategies were running into decreasing returns' is the diplomatic

---

26. Hudec (n 1 above) 223.
27. Narlikar reports the participation of developing countries in reaching agreement to undertake the Uruguay Round. A Narlikar, "Café au Lait Diplomacy" in B Hoekman, A Mattoo and P English (eds), *Development, Trade and the WTO: A Handbook* (Washington, DC: World Bank, 2002) 488–90.

expression—though the accumulated inventory of trade policies and practices in many countries hardly deserved the label 'strategy'. As Bela Balassa pointed out in the preface of his study of developing country trade policies:

> [T]he existing system of protection in many developing countries can be described as the historical result of actions taken at different times and for different reasons. These actions have been in response to the particular circumstances of the situation, and have often been conditioned by the demands of special interest groups. The authorities have generally assumed a permissive attitude toward requests for protection and failed to inquire into the impact of the measures applied on other industries and on the allocation of resources in the national economy . . .[28]

Reform was more accurately described as cleaning house than as changing strategy.

An additional factor, again undiplomatically expressed, was that some developing country leaders had had enough of taking a supplicant position in international affairs. No matter how emotionally that supplicant position was rationalized by Raúl Prebisch and others, blaming developing countries' second-class status on someone else had to be preceded by acceptance that they were second class. For some developing country leaders, the abasement of the latter came to outweigh the solace offered by the former.

Moreover—a point brought out by Sylvia Ostry—economic reform had become *de rigueur*. The 1980s debt crisis and the fall of the Berlin Wall triggered 'a major transformation in the economic policy paradigm. Economic reforms— deregulation, privatization, liberalization—were seen as essential elements for launching and sustaining growth'.[29]

ii. Result

At the Uruguay Round, developing countries accepted bindings on most of their tariff lines, Table 1 reports the percentages of bound imports to be nearly the same for developing countries as for developed ones. The tariff cuts reported in the table were largely bindings of unilateral reductions that were part of countries' reform programs. These figures understate the reduction of developing country applied rates; they measure reductions from previously applied rates only to the bound rates notified at the Uruguay Round. Many developing countries notified 'ceiling bindings' higher than their post-Uruguay Round

---

28. B Balassa and Associates, *The Structure of Protection in Developing Countries* (Baltimore, Md: Johns Hopkins University Press, 1971) xv.

29. S Ostry, 'The Uruguay Round North-South Grand Bargain: Implications for Future Negotiations' in DM Kennedy and JD Southwick (eds), *The Political Economy of International Trade Law: Essays in Honor of Robert E. Hudec* (Cambridge and New York: Cambridge University Press, 2000) 285–300, 286.

TABLE 1. URUGUAY ROUND TARIFF CONCESSIONS GIVEN AND RECEIVED—ALL MERCHANDISE

	Bindings		Tariff Reductions	
	Pre-UR	Post-UR	Percent of Imports	Depth of Cut[a] $(dT/(1+T)*100$
Tariff Concessions Given	(percent of 1989 imports)			
Developed countries	80	89	30	1.0
Developing countries	30	81	29	2.3
Tariff Concessions Received[b]	(percent of 1989 exports)			
Developed countries	77	91	36	1.4
Developing countries	64	78	28	1.0

Source: Finger and Schuknecht (2001, Table 1).
Notes:
[a] The formula measures the percentage by which the tariff cut will reduce the import price—takes into account, eg, that a reduction by one-half of a 40 percent tariff has a bigger trade impact than a reduction by one-half of a 10 percent tariff.
[b] The figures for concessions received are the mirror image of those for concessions given. For bindings, the figures measure the percentage of exports that enter, where they are imported, and at bound rates. For tariff cuts, the figure is an average of the reductions made on exports where they are imported.

applied rates. Table 2 shows that while post-Uruguay Round bound rates averaged over 25 percent, applied rates averaged some 12 percentage points less.

The Uruguay Round Agreements were, of course, a single undertaking. Every country that chose to become a member of the new organization, the WTO, accepted all of the obligations of the agreements (except for plurilateral agreements such as the Government Procurement Agreement) as well as its notified tariff bindings. These bindings, along with acceptance of international discipline over safeguards, antidumping, etc., helped developing country leaders with the management of trade liberalization and served to lock it in against future backsliding[30], but as noted above, the reciprocal exchange of mercantilist

---

30. Case-by-case backsliding rather than a shift of economic philosophy had several times before undermined significant trade liberalizations by Latin American countries. Thus the discipline international rules could bring to the application of safeguards and other trade remedies was important. These disciplines, of course, do not apply if tariffs are not bound, so it is not possible to say that such disciplines over trade were more important to Latin American liberalization than tariff bindings. Finger and Nogués bring together the experiences of Argentina, Brazil, Chile, Colombia, Costa Rica, México, and

TABLE 2. POST-URUGUAY ROUND TARIFF RATES—ALL MERCHANDISE

	Bound Rate, Average Ad Valorem	Applied Rate, Average Ad Valorem
Developed countries	3.5	2.6
Developing countries	25.5	13.3
All	6.5	4.3

Source: Finger and Schuknecht (2001, Table 3).

'concessions' provided less of the motivation for developing country liberalization than it had for the earlier developed country liberalization.[31]

F. MERCANTILISM STRIKES BACK: EVALUATING THE URUGUAY ROUND OUTCOME

In the GATT/WTO system, reciprocity is more than motivation. It is also an accepted standard.[32] It is no surprise then that the Uruguay Round's gains and losses for developing countries and for developed ones have been prodigiously compared. The 'grand bargain'[33] struck at the Uruguay Round was that the developing countries would take on significant commitments in new areas such as

---

Perú. JM Finger and JJ Nogués (eds), *Safeguards and Antidumping in Latin American Trade Liberalization* (Palgrave-Macmillan and the World Bank, 2006).

31. Finger and Schuknecht report for a sample of countries for which data were available that bindings at the Uruguay Round reduced few developing country rates below the rates established in their unilateral liberalizations. See Table 2. Though the GATT's Integrated Data Base (from which the figures above were calculated) generally took 1988 or 1989 as the 'pre Uruguay Round' year for tariff data, the question of developing countries receiving 'credit' for their unilateral liberalizations was handled by allowing developing countries to submit to the GATT's figures for tariff rates from an earlier year, if their unilateral liberalizations had begun earlier. JM Finger and L Schuknecht, 'Market Access Advances and Retreats: The Uruguay Round and Beyond' in B Hoekman and W Martin (eds), *Developing Countries and the WTO* (Blackwell, 2001) 251–308. Also available as World Bank Policy Research Working Paper No. 2232, November 1999. (Of course, the legal obligation that countries took on was the bound rates they notified, not a percentage reduction.)

32. Reciprocity, like nondiscrimination, is a GATT/WTO principle. Reciprocity however is not a 'rule', an 'unbalanced' negotiated agreement cannot be contested in the dispute settlement process.

33. The label was first applied by Sylvia Ostry in 2000. Ostry (n 29 above).

intellectual property and services where developed country enterprises saw opportunities for expanding international sales.[34] The developed countries, in exchange, would open up in areas of particular export interest to developing countries: agriculture and textiles/clothing.

i. The Unbalanced Outcome

There soon emerged a concern that the basic GATT/WTO ethic of reciprocity had been violated—developing Members had given more than they got. The dominant expression of this imbalance focused on what developing Members received. The newly tariffied schedules of protection of agriculture proved to be hardly less restrictive than the hodgepodge of nontariff measures they replaced.[35] Developed Members removed all MFA-sanctioned quantitative restrictions on imports of textiles and clothing but mostly at the end of a ten-year phase-in period. The agreement also permitted 'special safeguards' in case of particular disruption. In mercantilist terms, what developing countries gave was due immediately; what they received would be in the future; or, in the case of agriculture, remained to be negotiated.

Earlier rounds had been in large part tariff negotiations. For these, evaluation in mercantilist terms—concessions given versus received—did not misstate the relative gain for one country versus another. All concessions were in a common currency—tariff reductions. In real economics, concessions 'given' provide a net economic benefit to the giver as well as to the receiver; the bias introduced by treating concessions as costs would be to understate the benefits to each country. Hence it was not likely that a country would accept an agreement from which, to that country, its costs exceeded its benefits. Indeed, that in real economics there were no losers from what was agreed may have contributed to the GATT

---

34. Few developing countries had signed the Tokyo Round codes, hence obligations in the areas these codes regulated, eg, customs valuation, import licensing, and technical standards, were also 'new' for developing countries.

35. Again, the legal obligations were the schedules of rates that Members notified, not the percentage cuts specified in a 'modalities paper' that specified that developed Members would reduce rates by an average of 36 percent over six years, developing Members by an average of 24 percent over ten years. General Agreement on Tariffs and Trade 'Modalities for the Establishment of Specific Binding Commitments Under the Reform Program' (1993) MTN.GNG/MA/W/24. Not only was the base years for the determination of tariff equivalents chosen so as to give large values, from the perspective of maintaining high rates of protection, the arithmetic applied was generous. The phrase 'dirty tariffication' came into the literature. Hathaway and Ingco document these points. D Hathaway and M Ingco, 'Agricultural Liberalization and the Uruguay Round' in W Martin and LA Winters (eds), *The Uruguay Round and Developing Countries* (Cambridge: Cambridge University Press, 1996) 30–9.

tradition of applying only a soft and often nonquantitative 'diplomat's economics' to the subject matter.[36]

The Uruguay Round outcome was more complex. Some of the 'concessions given' were indeed costs, in real economics as well as in mercantilist economics. As to what developing countries gave, the real economics of TRIPS dominates the economics of the Uruguay Round Agreements. For the United States and other intellectual property providers, the value of the claims TRIPS generates is several times larger than the gain to them from all the merchandise trade liberalization agreed, including the liberalization of their own restrictions.[37] For countries that mostly use intellectual property established in other countries, the TRIPS-generated obligation to pay is several times larger than the gains they will enjoy from all countries' Uruguay Round merchandise trade liberalization.[38]

In addition, TRIPS' gains for intellectual property owners are protected by 'the law'; its alleged benefits to intellectual property users are not. If intellectual property-using countries do not pay royalties, the governments of intellectual property owners can take them to trial at the WTO. If, however, the increased foreign investment econometrically predicted to follow from higher levels of intellectual property protection is not realized, intellectual property-using countries cannot sue the econometrician.

As to the economics of the Multi-Fiber Arrangement (MFA), eliminating quantitative restrictions on imports of textiles and clothing was a gain of market access but also a loss of quota rents. Indeed, computations of the impact indicate that the elimination of quota rents is the larger part. Many developing countries are net losers; developed countries are winners.[39] (Figure 1) And, as the afterglow

---

36. The 'diplomat's economics' parallels the 'diplomat's jurisprudence' that served the system well in its early decades. Hudec (n 2 above). Though the GATT in time shifted to a jurist's jurisprudence, it is still trying to operate with the inadequate diplomat's economics. R Hudec, 'The New WTO Dispute Settlement Procedure: An Overview of the First Three Years' (1999) 18(1) Minn JGT 1–53.

37. An element in the economic success of intellectual property owners was that they led the international community to see the issue as morality rather than economics; combating 'piracy' rather than the costs and benefits to each country of the proposed agreement. Before TRIPS, intellectual property was strictly a matter of national definition. The 'pirates' were in violation of neither international nor the relevant national standards, their own.

38. Eg, for the United States, the gains are 13 times larger. For China, the obligation to pay for intellectual property is five times larger than the benefits from Uruguay Round merchandise trade liberalization by all countries. Finger provides details. JM Finger, 'The Doha Agenda and Development: A View from the Uruguay Round', Manila, Asian Development Bank; 2002, <http://www.adb.org/Economics/pdf/doha/Finger_paper.pdf>.

39. This economics was well-known before the Uruguay Round was completed. For example, Hufbauer and Elliott calculated that 83 percent of the cost of trade protection in the United States was from quantitative restrictions on imports of textiles and clothing; of that cost 71 percent was the quota rent (excess of price above cost) and only 29 percent

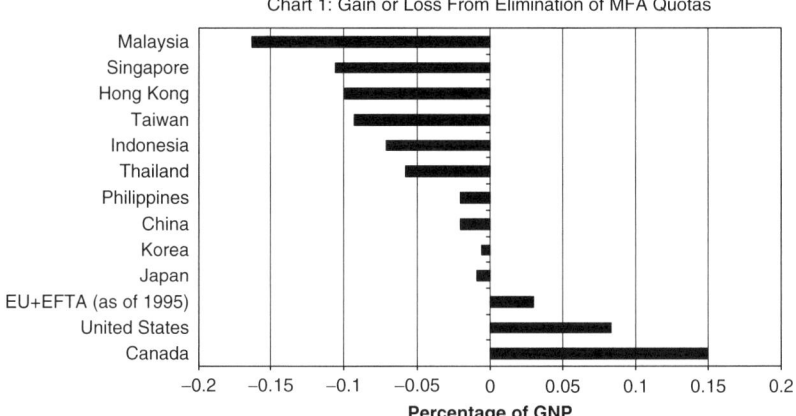

FIGURE 1. GAIN OR LOSS FROM ELIMINATION OF MFA QUOTAS
Source: Brown et al. (2001, Table 1)

of the diplomatic victory has dimmed, smaller exporters have come to fear that with the elimination of MFA quotas on powerful exporters such as India and China, they will be driven from developed-country markets.[40]

ii. The Implementation Problem

'The implementation problem' was another concern that arose as Members began to appreciate the implications of the Uruguay Round Agreements. What the North gave in the Uruguay Round bargain was traditional market access; reduction of import restrictions; plus, in agriculture, reduction of export subsidies

---

were the efficiency losses from misallocation of resources. GC Hufbauer and KA Elliott, *Measuring the Cost of Protection in the United States* (Washington, DC: Institute for International Economics, 1994) Table 1.7.

40. Finger and Nogués speculate on why developing countries accepted such an unbalanced agreement. JM Finger and JJ Nogués, 'The Unbalanced Uruguay Round Outcome: The New Areas in Future WTO Negotiations' (2002) 25(3) W Econ 321–40. Also available as (2001) World Bank Policy Research Working Paper No. 2732. The reasons we brought forward were: (a) The GATT tradition of applying a soft, 'diplomat's economics'—Sylvia Ostry emphasizes that the Uruguay Round Agreements were imprecisely understood when they were accepted; in new areas such as services few developing countries even collected statistics for their trade or domestic production. (b) The diplomatic appeal of charter membership in an organization the international community had struggled for 50 years to establish; developing country GATT delegations were often from foreign ministries, developed country delegations more closely linked with commercial interests. (c) They were between a rock and a hard place. Creating the new organization was accompanied by members' withdrawing from the GATT. Creating a new, 'GATT 1994' was part of the WTO package. Any country not a WTO Member would have at best pre-1947 rights vis-à-vis its trading partners; eg, would have faced the Smoot-Hawley tariff in the United States.

and production subsidies. While the politics of agreeing to tariff reductions is difficult, implementing such an agreement provides no particular challenge. New tariff schedules are printed and distributed to customs houses.

What the South gave in the 'new areas' was different. World Trade Organization obligations in services, intellectual property, technical, and sanitary standards, etc., took a form different from that of traditional agreements to reduce or eliminate barriers. They require that countries' regulations be harmonized to a common standard; eg, every WTO Member must apply the same standard for defining and protecting intellectual property and vigorously apply that standard to foreign-owned property. The standards were more or less those already in place in developed countries.

Implementation of such obligations by developing countries would demand significant investment in facilities, equipment, staff, training, etc. Comparison of these agreements with development project experience revealed that the amount was significant—more than a year's development budget in many of the poorer WTO Members. It also revealed that the demands of the agreements—taken in large part from current practice in the more advanced economies—are not always good development advice. The expenditures demanded often are not those that maximize the trade impact, much less the development or poverty reduction impact of the resources.[41] The latter part of the implementation problem was eventually generalized into the 'one-size-fits-all' issue.

Several of the Uruguay Round Agreements do take up the provision of implementation assistance but only in a hortatory manner. Developing Members accepted bound obligations to implement in exchange for unbound obligations to provide assistance.

G. WTO RESPONSE

As early as 1999 (when her paper was written), Sylvia Ostry noted 'broad consensus among the Southern countries that the Uruguay Round Agreement was asymmetrical and must be "rebalanced" before any new negotiations were launched'.[42] Acceptance of the label 'Doha Development Agenda' by the entire WTO membership indicated general acceptance that the system owed something to developing countries.

As to the specifics of the WTO response, 'rebalancing' has not become a named part of the WTO work program. Developing countries have renewed their insistence on special and differential treatment, and there have been fervent

---

41. JM Finger and P Schuler. 'Implementation of Uruguay Round Commitments: the Development Challenge', in B Hoekman and W Martin (eds), *Developing Countries and the WTO* (Blackwell, 2001) 115–30.

42. Ostry (n 34 above) 287.

expressions of support both within and without the WTO. *Special and differential treatment* is again a prominent part of the work program.

Each WTO higher-level decision since the Uruguay Round has taken up implementation. In the work program, however, 'implementation' is a false label; the WTO work program on implementation has included, from its inception, nothing more than the traditional elements of *'special and differential treatment'*.

A third part of the WTO response has been an extended discussion of 'aid for trade' involving elements of special and differential treatment and of implementation. Of the topics on the Doha agenda, the trade facilitation negotiations have involved the most focused discussion of both implementation and of aid for trade.

H. IMPLEMENTATION

World Trade Organization Ministers, in the Doha Declaration, which opened the new round of negotiations, stated that they 'attach the utmost importance to the implementation-related issues and concerns'.[43] Indeed, the Ministers also released at Doha an additional Decision on Implementation-Related Issues and Concerns.[44]

As to how the WTO might take on the implementation problem, Rubens Ricupero, while Secretary-General of UNCTAD, had made an important suggestion: proposals should include an implementation audit that would identify the specific investments needed to meet new obligations so that any agreement could include bound commitments to provide the needed support.[45] Such audits would do more than identify the implementation costs. They would face up to the reality of the one-size-fits-all issue, and they would carry the implementation issue into the domain of project identification and design where the challenge to introduce the dimensions of time and place into multilateral rules would have to be faced.

---

43. World Trade Organization, 'Ministerial Conference Fourth Session, Doha, 9–14 November 2001 Ministerial Declaration' (20 November 2001) WT/MIN(01)/DEC/1 para 12.

44. World Trade Organization, 'Ministerial Conference Fourth Session, Doha, 9–14 November 2001 Implementation-Related Issues And Concerns' (20 November 2001) WT/MIN(01)/17.

45. R Ricupero, 'Integration of Developing Countries into the Multilateral Trading System' in J Bhagwati and M Hirsch (eds), *The Uruguay Round and Beyond: Essays in Honor of Arthur Dunkel* (Ann Arbor: University of Michigan Press, 1999) 9–36. R Ricupero, 'A Development Round: Converting Rhetoric Into Substance' Paper presented at John F. Kennedy School of Government Harvard University Cambridge, Massachusetts, Symposium on Efficiency, Equity and Legitimacy: The Multilateral Trading System at the Millennium, 1–2 June 2000.

The Doha Ministerial Decision on Implementation ignored Ricupero's suggestion. Ministers did not call for identification of the resources developing countries would need to meet WTO implementation requirements—and perhaps expand trade capacities more generally. They specified that wherever there was a specific negotiating mandate, 'the relevant implementation issues shall be addressed under that mandate' but provided no guidance as to how implementation would be approached. Indeed, ministers provided no work program at all on implementation, only a work program on special and differential treatment—'we endorse the work program on special and differential treatment set out in the Decision on Implementation[46]—a work program on special and differential treatment falsely labeled a Decision on Implementation. As WTO ministers structured the new round, 'implementation' was completely absorbed by traditional 'special and differential treatment'; they did not recognize its unique challenges. (The matter of making assistance an obligation or tying developing country obligations to implementation assistance, I take up again in the sections on aid for trade and trade facilitation.)

i. Special and Differential Treatment

World Trade Organization ministers, in the Doha Declaration of 2001, signaled a return of attention to special and differential treatment. They called for a review of special and differential treatment provisions 'with a view to strengthening them and making them more precise'; they also took note of a proposal from a group of developing countries for a framework agreement on special and differential treatment.[47]

Table 3 summarizes the elements in the Work Program.

The proposed framework agreement[48] would

- make special and differential treatment mandatory and legally binding;
- mandate an evaluation of the 'development dimension' of any future agreement, ie, the facts as to how the agreement would facilitate attainment of development targets such as the Millennium Development Goals;
- mandate an implementation audit;
- allow 'industrial policy' by developing countries;
- allow any developing Member to opt out of any new agreement—no Single Undertaking.

---

46. WTO (n 44 above) para 12.
47. WTO (n 44 above) para 44.
48. World Trade Organization, 'Proposal for a Framework Agreement on Special and Differential Treatment' (19 September 2001) WT/GC/W/442 submitted by Cuba, Dominican Republic, Honduras, India, Indonesia, Kenya, Malaysia, Pakistan, Sri Lanka, Tanzania, Uganda, and Zimbabwe.

TABLE 3. DOHA WORK PROGRAM ON SPECIAL AND DIFFERENTIAL TREATMENT: TABULATION OF CONTENT BY SUBJECT

Subject	Number of items
Use or extension of special and differential treatment provisions	16
• less discipline on developing country policies	9
• more favorable access for developing country exports	7
Lengthen phase-in or phase-out (eg, sanitary phytosanitary regulations, export subsidies)	10
Review to clarify certain points of the antidumping, subsidies, and TRIPS agreements	8
Technical assistance	1046
• to participate in the WTO or standards-related international bodies	
• to implement WTO obligations	
Reminder that Members have a legal obligation under TRIPS Article 66.2 to provide incentives for their enterprises and for institutions to promote and encourage technology transfer to least-developed countries	1
Total	37

Source: Tabulated from WTO (2001b) MINISTERIAL CONFERENCE, Fourth Session, Doha, 9–14 November 2001, Implementation-Related Issues And Concerns, WT/MIN(01)/17, 20 November 2001

The 2004 Work Program[49] reaffirmed that special and differential treatment was an integral part of the WTO system: it noted progress in and called for completion of the review called for in the Doha Declaration. It did not add to the scope of special and differential treatment specified there.

The work program agreed at Hong Kong in December 2005 continued the emphasis on issues of interest to developing countries. As to how these issues are perceived, the phrase 'special and differential treatment' appears 23 times in the 45-page Declaration (including the annexes). By comparison, 'liberalize' or 'liberalization' appears 9 times.

There is, however, nothing in this work program that was not part of the traditional GATT approach to developing countries. We are back to where the GATT system was after its first decade. All these elements were in the 'work program' when Robert Hudec concluded 20 years ago that insistence on special and differential treatment was politically ineffective either to control developed

---

49. World Trade Organization, 'Doha Work Program: Decision Adopted by the General Council on 1 August 2004' (2 August 2004) WT/L/579.

country discrimination against developing countries or to support liberalization within developing ones. He also demonstrated that as a legal matter, it was impossible to transform such elements into generic obligation.

I. AID FOR TRADE COMES FORWARD—AND RECEDES

The Hong Kong Declaration[50] brought forward a new emphasis on assistance; the word 'assistance' appears in the declaration 34 times. It also broadened considerably the scope of assistance under consideration. 'Aid for Trade should aim to help developing countries, particularly least-developed countries (LDCs), to build the supply-side capacity and trade-related infrastructure that they need to assist them to implement and benefit from WTO Agreements and more broadly to expand their trade'.[51]

The same paragraph invites the WTO director-general to 'create a task force that shall provide recommendations on how to operationalize Aid for Trade'.

At the basic level of negotiations, bringing forward aid for trade created the possibility that market-access concessions by developing countries would buy additional aid—or aid might buy additional market-access concessions from developing countries. This rationale has been widely rejected as part of the Doha Negotiations; it however remains a lurking element in other rationales.[52]

More broadly, the concern for aid for trade has both factual and analytical grounding. As matters of fact, many developing countries have not been taken up in the global economic expansion of the second half of the twentieth century. They have not exploited the opening of developed country markets as, say, the Asian tigers have and in many liberalization has not been followed by growth.

Analytically, trade experts now argue that without complementary reforms, trade liberalization would not work its magic. Complementary reforms would include

- trade facilitation; eg, customs reform and control of bribery to lower the cost of moving goods and services across borders;
- investments in business infrastructure such as telecommunications, in up-to-date enterprise capacities;

---

50. World Trade Organization, 'Ministerial Conference 6th Session Hong Kong, 13–18 December 2005, Doha Work Programe: Draft Ministerial Declaration, Revision Document' (18 December 2005) WT/MIN(05)/W/3/Rev.2.

51. Ibid at para 57.

52. One popular argument behind the unwillingness of developing countries to give access to their markets in exchange for aid is that they have already paid—the Uruguay Round imbalance. Another is that without aid to build capacity, improved access to developed country markets has no value—no development impact.

- mastery of the tools of modern commerce such as standards and trademarks.

The WTO Task Force on Aid for Trade came after Ricupero's suggestion for implementation audits and after several proposals had been tabled to create 'platforms' through which WTO legal obligations to implement and to provide assistance could be forged and linked. (These are taken up in Section I.) The Task Force Recommendations—endorsed by the General Council on 10 October 2006—mention neither implementation audits nor such platforms; ie, it rejects such WTO involvement.

The Task Force recommended an exclusively bureaucratic role for the WTO. In its list of 13 'major challenges/gaps', 12 are administrative matters such as mainstreaming, linking mechanisms, monitoring, coordination, and coherence. Resources for infrastructure and enterprise capacities rank no better than second-to-last on the list. Its flagship recommendation is an annual debate on aid for trade in the WTO General Council. This debate is to be supported by a published global review of aid for trade by a new WTO monitoring body. The global report would draw on aid-for-trade reports from recipient countries (the Organisation for Economic Co-operation and Development ((OECD)/WTO database lists 174); donor countries (the OECD/WTO database lists 27 plus the European Union); regional entities (the WTO Web page lists 33 regional agreements) international agencies (The WTO/OECD database lists 26); and the private sector. A bonanza for consultants, nothing for development.

J. TRADE FACILITATION ENTERS THE AGENDA

The negotiations on trade facilitation had to take on squarely the challenge to find a way to link developing country acceptance of new obligations to developed country obligations to provide assistance. As to how this topic entered the WTO Negotiations, the Doha Ministerial Declaration announced an agreement to undertake preliminary work on four new subjects for possible multilateral agreements: investment, competition policy, government procurement, and trade facilitation. These, like the 'new issues' of the Uruguay Round, are topics where implementation-related issues and concerns would be important. They would be taken up as negotiating issues only if the Members at a future meeting reached explicit consensus to do so.

The next WTO Ministerial Meeting, Cancun 2003, ended without agreement, but the WTO General Council did, in July 2004, agree to a new work program. The 2004 WTO Work Program[53] includes an agreement to commence negotiations

---

53. WTO (n 50 above).

on trade facilitation; its annex on trade facilitation limits these negotiations to 'clarify and improve relevant aspects of Articles V, VIII, and X of GATT 1994'.[54] Paragraph 5 of this annex commits developed Members to ensure adequate assistance during the negotiations—so that developing and least developed countries can 'fully participate in and benefit from the negotiations'. Who is responsible for assistance on implementation is not specified. Paragraph 6, in passive voice, states that 'Support and assistance should also be provided' to help with implementation of commitments.[55]

Perhaps the tightest link relates to 'commitments whose implementation would require support for infrastructure development.' Here, 'developed-country Members will make every effort to ensure support,' but 'where required support and assistance for such infrastructure is not forthcoming, and where a developing or least-developed Member continues to lack the necessary capacity, implementation will not be required'.[56] The most tightly drawn link is a negative one, not a positive one.

Trade facilitation brought forward a number of submissions, the most recent WTO Secretariat tabulation of proposals[57] covers some 150 pages. The submissions include national experience papers describing reforms undertaken, proposed measures to improve and clarify the GATT articles covered by the negotiating mandate; suggestions for enhancing assistance on trade facilitation; and thoughts on the practical application of the principle of special and differential treatment.

The content of a WTO agreement raises several issues: what constitutes good practice; how a WTO agreement might help to accelerate the installation of such practices; and particularly, how the obligation to provide assistance might be linked to new obligations on trade facilitation policies and practices. Several aspects of the situation in trade facilitation indicate that a WTO agreement could usefully support development.

i. Identifying Concrete Implementation Needs/Support

Trade facilitation is a subject area in which there is minimal disagreement as to the usefulness of reforms. Differences that have surfaced at the Doha Negotiations are almost entirely about how to link new obligations to the provision of assistance

---

54. These articles take up *Freedom of Transit, Fees and Formalities connected with Importation and Exportation*, and *Publication and Administration of Trade Regulations*.

55. The July 2004 Work Program furthered also the shift of WTO attention toward dealing with the implementation requirements of future negotiations rather than resolving those created by the Uruguay Round Agreements. The Work Program devotes only eight lines in a 778 line document to "those elements of the Work Program which do not involve negotiations" (para 1.h)

56. Para. 6.

57. WTO, 'Negotiating Group on Trade Facilitation WTO Negotiations on Trade Facilitation: Compilation OF Members' Proposals' (11 August 2006) TN/TF/W/43/Rev.10.

by developed Members, not about the substance of what constitutes good trade facilitation practice.

Initial proposals on how to deal with the implementation problem—how to incorporate assistance into WTO mechanisms—were institutionally ambitious. The European Union, for example (TN/TF/W/46), proposed that the WTO and other organizations (the World Bank, World Customs Organization (WCO), UNCTAD, OECD, regional development banks, etc.) establish and operate a 'platform' for international cooperation and coordination on the provision of technical assistance and capacity building for trade facilitation. Its tasks would include

- taking stock of trade facilitation needs in relation to the provisions/ obligations emerging from the negotiations;
- helping to identify if and what kind of technical assistance and support for capacity building would be needed to support implementation, over what time frame, by each developing Member.

A United States communication seemed to reflect Ricupero's suggestion that implementation audits be conducted before an agreement was reached.

> The unique situation of each individual Member regarding implementation of the proposed commitment could be addressed early in the negotiations through the use of diagnostic tools providing an assessment of specific needs, which can lead to appropriate and workable transition periods combined with assistance targeted at individual situations.[58]

In May 2006, the African Group[59] submitted a communication that elaborated from a development perspective the elements and principles that a WTO trade facilitation agreement should embody: (a) obligations and assistance should be tailored to the circumstances of individual Members, (b) national development objectives would have priority, (c) obligations and assistance should be linked and equally obligated, and (d) the agreement would be outside the WTO dispute settlement process.

A parallel communication from a group of Latin American countries[60] put forward an outline for a mechanism to manage the assistance-obligation linkage for developing Members. The process would include four phases: (i) capacity

---

58. TN/TF/W/13, Section V.
59. African Group (All African members of the WTO, currently 41 countries): Angola, Benin, Botswana, Burkina Faso, Burundi, Cameroon, Central African Republic, Chad, Congo, Congo (Democratic Republic), Côte d'Ivoire, Djibouti, Egypt, Gabon, The Gambia, Ghana, Guinea, Guinea Bissau, Kenya, Lesotho, Madagascar, Malawi, Mali, Mauritania, Mauritius, Morocco, Mozambique, Namibia, Niger, Nigeria, Rwanda, Senegal, Sierra Leone, South Africa, Swaziland, Tanzania, Togo, Tunisia, Uganda, Zambia, Zimbabwe. TN/TF/W/95. 19 May 2006.
60. Chile, Dominican Republic, Ecuador, Guatemala, Honduras, Mexico, Nicaragua, Paraguay and Uruguay; TN/TF/W/81, 3 April 2006.

self-assessment, (ii) notification, (iii) capacity development, and (iv) confirmation of capacity acquisition and compliance with the obligation. A Trade Facilitation Register within the WTO Secretariat would handle notifications sent by Members and publish them on the Members' Web site on the WTO Internet portal.

The African Group and Latin American communications were followed in July 2006 by two textual proposals. One of these was sponsored by the 'Core Group' of developing Members,[61] the other by a group that included both developing and developed Members.[62] Following their document symbols in the WTO archives, I will refer to the Core Group proposal as W142, the other as W137.

ii. Assistance Mechanics of the Proposals

The basics of the two proposals are similar. The following outlines the procedure W137 provides; after that I will explain how W142 differs. Under both, a trade facilitation agreement would include a list of trade facilitation provisions or requirements, eg, publication of customs rules, application of risk-management techniques, and application of procedures for audit after release of goods. Assistance would be managed as follows:

1. Self-assessment: After the signing of a trade facilitation agreement, each developing Member (including transition economies) may undertake a self-assessment; ie, will assess its own needs and capacities in regard to the trade facilitation agreement's substantive provisions. (At its own discretion, a developing Member might request assistance from other Members or international organizations such as the WCO.)
2. Capacity building plans: Following the self-assessments, each developing Member may prepare a plan for acquiring the capacity needed to meet the pending obligations of the agreement.
3. Notification: Before the entry-into-force date of the agreement:[63]
    A. Each developing Member will notify the WTO of the provisions for which it needs additional time (limited to [N] years) and assistance before accepting these provisions as obligations.

---

61. Bangladesh, Botswana, Cuba, Egypt, India, Indonesia, Jamaica, Kenya, Malaysia, Mauritius, Namibia, Nepal, Nigeria, Philippines, Rwanda, Tanzania, Trinidad & Tobago, Uganda, Venezuela, Zambia, and Zimbabwe; TN/TF/W/142, 21 July 2006. WTO, 'Negotiating Group on Trade Facilitation, Communication from the Core Group of Developing Countries on Trade Facilitation, Proposal on Implementation Mechanism for Special and Differential Treatment(S&D) and Technical Assistance and Capacity Building (TACB) Support' (31 July 2006) TN/TF/W/142.

62. Chile, Colombia, Costa Rica, Dominican Republic, Ecuador, Guatemala, Honduras, Mexico, Nicaragua, Paraguay, Peru, Uruguay, China, Japan, Kyrgyz Republic, Pakistan, Sri Lanka, Armenia, European Communities, Georgia, Moldova, Switzerland, and Canada; TN/TF/W/142, 31 July 2006. Ibid.

63. As to the time that might apply, the Uruguay Round Negotiations were completed 15 December 1993, the Agreements entered into force 1 January 1995.

B. All provisions not so notified become obligations at the entry in force date of the trade facilitation agreement.[64]
  4. Developed Members provide assistance: Developed Members are obligated to provide assistance, on request and under mutually agreed terms, with the needs assessments and with the preparation of capacity-building plans.
  5. A provision becomes an obligation after:
     A. the Developing Member notifies it has acquired the necessary capacity or
     B. six months after expiration of the extended implementation period (notified as per line 3, above).

iii. W142 Differences

W142 provides the same general outline of procedure: self-assessment, preparation of capacity building plans, notification, etc. However, W142 allows for some (or perhaps all) substantive provisions to be optional for developing Members; ie, a developing Member may decline to accept any or all of these as obligations.

Mandatory provisions (if any). For these, a developing Member would follow the same steps as they would under W137—it may choose to notify a capacity building plan and an extended implementation deadline for any of these.

Optional provisions. A developing Member may request additional implementation time and assistance with capacity building for any or all of these. For any of these for which an assistance package is agreed and notified, procedure and obligation follow the same steps as for W137.[65]

Obligations on donors to provide assistance. Developed Members are obligated to provide assistance on request with the self-assessments, preparation, and implementation of the capacity building plans. This differs from W137 in that (a) the phrase 'under mutually agreed terms' is not included and (b) the obligation extends to implementation of the capacity building plans.

---

64. If, as foreseen, a trade facilitation agreement was part of the Doha package, the entry-into-force date of the trade facilitation agreement would be the entry-into-force of the Doha single undertaking.

65. W142 proposes also a list of "best endeavor" standards. These do not become obligations even if a developing Member requests and receives capacity-building assistance. The obligation on donor Members to provide implementation assistance does not apply. One possible reason for such a list would be to provide an extended or forward-looking blueprint for trade facilitation measures. The WTO is not, however, the agency on which the international community depends for such; other international conventions and organizations, eg, the World Customs Organization, the Kyoto Convention, do this. Moreover, any county can already request assistance from a bilateral or a multilateral agency for help with installation and management of such standards—without WTO 'permission'. The category then seems to be superfluous.

iv. Problems

A major problem with both of these alternatives is that their "bureaucratics" will not work.

First, both proposals ask more of 'needs assessment' than it can deliver. To link obligation to implement and obligation to provide assistance, the capacity needed to meet the agreement's performance standards must be identified *ex ante*—with sufficient precision that borrowers and donors will enter into contractual relationships.[66]

In development agency practice, self-assessment does not provide such legal instruments. Self-assessment is the initial step in a cooperative process (among donor, beneficiary, and implementing organizations) that leads to project and loan documents—legal instruments. The intermediate steps include not only project identification and design; they also include environmental, social, and financial assessments—all subject to public notice requirements so that stakeholders who wish to may participate.

For the relationship of a donor and a recipient country to be productive, the two parties must develop a sense of trust and a shared view of how the donor will help the countries toward its development targets. Legal documents will ultimately define what the donor will provide and what the recipient will do with these resources, but the process of developing trust and a shared view requires considerably more time and effort than does the preparation and execution of these documents.

W142 might seem to override the imprecision of the assessments and eliminate the delays for project preparation and assessments. It would obligate donor Members to provide the assistance the self-assessments identify. For donor Members, accepting this obligation would be the equivalent of signing

---

66. WTO-related needs assessments have been undertaken since the Integrated Framework was initiated in 1997. The most recent of these, the WB-IMF-WCO needs assessment study, was described as it began as 'The Cost of Implementation Studies'; it adds a modicum of reality to the trade facilitation assistance discussion but hardly the precision on which a government would want to accept the legal obligation that a WTO agreement would involve—or a donor would want to commit to providing assistance. World Bank International Trade Department, *Needs, Priorities and Costs Associated with Technical Assistance and Capacity Building for Implementation of a WTO Trade Facilitation Agreement: A Comparative Study Based on Six Developing Countries*, (November 2006) Working Paper November 2006. This report, like the Integrated Framework needs assessments, passes that responsibility to the as-yet unspecified persons/platforms who would conduct the self-assessments on the basis of which developing Member would notify the obligations they accepted, donor Members would accept the obligation to provide the assistance specified in those motivations. As professional work, the flaw of the paper is not the imprecision of its estimates. It is the suggestion that further work would refine them to the level that the proposals demand.

a check—the receiver is free to fill in later the amount. Such is far beyond any delegation's negotiating authority, and if put into the WTO by legal slight of hand, would be unenforceable.

If a trade facilitation agreement is part of a single undertaking, negotiators could not avoid the aid commitments becoming part of the overall bargaining—in economics, the equivalent of developing countries auctioning off market access for cash.

A second problem is that there is no process for rationing. The arrangements proposed would bring forward pressure on the WTO to provide assistance but no process for rationing available assistance among competing demands. In this context, the recent OECD/Development Assistance Committee (DAC) report[67] notes that the WTO definition of 'developing countries' includes many countries that do not receive assistance from either bilateral or multilateral donors. Furthermore, self-assessment—as a process for bringing forward requests for assistance—may increase the size of each country's request and increase the attractiveness of such requests as an alternative to using its own resources.

The problem of 'Saying NO!' would be intensified by the fact that some of the poorer countries have already made significant investments of their own money (including money from local businesses) in improved border facilities. The OECD/DAC report describes such improvements in Ghana, Malaysia, Mauritius, Mozambique, Senegal, and Thailand.[68] Only the laggards would be in a position to demand assistance.

The hope of many who propose WTO involvement with assistance is to have the opportunity to say **Yes!** to developing country requests. The reality is that they would be in a position in which they would often have to say **No!**

The bottom line: as legal obligation the provisions for assistance from developed Members are hardly worth the paper they are printed on. Robert Hudec told us 20 years ago that such a legalism was impossible. We should have believed him.

K. CONCLUSIONS

i. Special and Differential Treatment

The Doha consideration of special and differential treatment has added nothing to the discussion that was not there in 1987. Hudec demonstrated to my satisfaction that this was ineffective politics and that it asked for impossible law. What Hudec

---

67. Organization for Economic Cooperation and Development/DAC, 'Making Technical Assistance and Capacity Building for Trade Facilitation Effective and Operational' (15 December 2006) DCD/DAC(2006) 49.

68. Ibid para. 32.

concluded analytically 20 years ago, another generation of negotiators has proven empirically—trying every possible way to make special and differential treatment for developing countries a legal obligation, arriving each time at a dead end. I have nothing to add.

ii. Implementation

The implementation problem challenged the GATT/WTO system to deal substantively with an economics more complex that what had been adequate for tariff negotiations. The Doha treatment of implementation, however, has fallen flat on its face before this challenge. It has defined implementation as identical with special and differential treatment, hence the conclusion above—Hudec's of 1987, applies.

iii. Aid for Trade

The Aid for Trade Task Force recommendations amount to a conclusion that the WTO will have only a bureaucratic role here.[69] To Pascal Lamy's subsequent report of WTO 'progress and momentum' on aid for trade,[70] I would ask, 'What part of "No!" do you not understand'?

iv. Trade Facilitation

It is unfortunate that the Doha discussion of trade facilitation has been blocked by an attempt to do the impossible: make legally obligatory the provision of assistance to developing Members by developed. Here was an opportunity for a WTO agreement to be useful—an agreement that would help policy managers in developing countries as well as in developed to overcome domestic resistance to reforms that would advance the national economic interest.

There is a solid basis for international cooperation on trade facilitation, extensive knowledge of what works, and experience applying that knowledge productively in developing countries. The relevant experience of the WTO dispute settlement process has been constructive—managing the application of the WTO SPS and TBT agreements, which involve the incorporation into WTO obligations of standards established by other international organizations or conventions.[71]

The record shows solid support in developed Members' assistance programs for trade facilitation in developing countries and solid support for such from commercial constituencies in developing and in developed Members. Trying to

---

69. 'Contribute coherence and clarity' is the politically correct phrasing.

70. Lamy, Pascal, "Statement to WTO General Council 10 October 2006" at <http://www.wto.org/english/news_e/news06_e/gc_10oct06_e.htm> (accessed 10 May 2007).

71. I treat these matters in detail in JM Finger, 'Trade Facilitation: The Role of a WTO Agreement' Manuscript, 12 March 2007 (available on request, michael.finger@comcast.net).

force the extensive international cooperation that is already taking place into a legal straightjacket would more likely compromise the existing trust and appreciation of shared benefits rather than bring forward additional money.[72]

v. Support for Developing Country Liberalization

In the Uruguay Round, developing country leaders used the GATT/WTO system to lock in place trade liberalization that they had pressed for on the basis of its domestic impact rather than on the basis of it being the only way to win access to foreign markets. That spirit has ebbed; the ascendance anew of special and differential treatment has to a considerable degree discredited that generation of leaders. We are back to the GATT/WTO system being a buttress for resistance to developing country liberalization and for insisting that the key to developing countries using trade as an effective instrument for development and poverty reduction is how they are treated by developed countries.

vi. Déjà vu—All Over Again

Sixteen years ago when I looked at how the GATT had adjusted to accumulating knowledge of how trade can support development, I concluded that when we—negotiators and analysts—put on our GATT hats, we put on also our GATT minds.[73] I repeat that conclusion today and add that the WTO has brought no change of our millinery.

---

72. Philip Schuler and I are responsible for the phrase 'bound obligations exchanged for unbound promises of assistance', but we did not recommend making assistance a legal obligation. While I have here and elsewhere cited Rubens Ricupero for recommending implementation audits, Rubens was aware of the impossibility of applying WTO legality here. His recommendation was part of his argument against the WTO entering into such areas. If you actually tried to do it, you would learn that it cannot be done.

73. Finger (n 8 above).

5. ASYMMETRY IN THE URUGUAY ROUND AND IN THE DOHA ROUND

SYLVIA OSTRY*

A. Introduction 105
B. Asymmetry 106
C. Conclusion 108

A. INTRODUCTION

As we know, the Uruguay Round resulted in a fundamental transformation of the multilateral trading system. Unfortunately, I called it a 'Grand Bargain', but that phrase was intended as an ironic remark. I said later in that paper that it was not a Grand Bargain but instead a Bum Deal. Looking back, I think one of the most important contemporary issues is how little we understood the implications of what we had agreed to at Punta Del Este.

When evaluating important government actions, the unintended consequences are more important than the objectives. The unintended consequences of the Uruguay Round were quite phenomenal. Those of us that were involved in the beginning in the effort to try to get the Round going really did not fully understand. I can remember that when I arrived at the meeting in Punta, one of the Americans, who will remain unnamed, said, '(l)ast night, our President had dinner with (blank) and was told that the single most important issue in the world trading system was piracy and we had to stop it'. I burst out laughing, and I said, 'Oh, c'mon! Queen Elizabeth knighted Francis Drake because he was such a superb pirate!' I was then told that I had better take this issue seriously because it was very important. They were right and I was, of course, totally wrong.

The notion that only the southern countries did not understand what was going on was quite false. Those of us that had been involved throughout could not anticipate how complex the new system would be and what effects on North-South relations would result from the Bum Deal.

---

* Distinguished Research Fellow, Munk Centre for International Studies, University of Toronto. This speech was given at a Panel on Robert Hudec's work at the University of Minnesota, Minnesota on 25 May 2007. I, like everyone else who participated in this conference, want to emphasize how much I admired Robert Hudec and how honored I am to be involved in this discussion. As we all must feel, I am deeply regretful that he is no longer with us. It is bearing his example in mind that this essay focuses on an issue that was of so much concern to him, the role of developing countries in the WTO system.

B. ASYMMETRY

One of the issues that I did not see, and that is of considerable importance and of moral significance in the Uruguay Round, is something that I think deserves much more analysis than it has had thus far. I call it asymmetry, and I want to say a little about it and its significance as one of the transformations that was created by the Uruguay Round.

A number of case studies by the World Bank demonstrate both the capacity deficit in poor countries and the heavy costs of implementation. There was very little participation by the African countries in the Uruguay Round because of both the lack of personnel in Geneva delegations and the lack of coordination and expertise at home. The situation in Geneva has not improved very much. There is still serious weakness in *domestic* coordination mechanisms among a number of ministries; this institutional deficiency is not confined to the poorest countries but affects many developing and transition economies as well. Finally, there is little, if any, coordination between Geneva and the home country. A former delegate noted, '(d)uring the entire duration of the Uruguay Round our Geneva-based WTO team received *two* instructions from our capital'.

The disappointing results of the Uruguay Round in agriculture have ensured that it remains at the centre of the Doha agenda. But what is equally important and far less studied is the impact of the SPS Agreement. Case studies from the World Bank provide incredible examples of the imposition of new standards for alleged (minor) health reasons that cut African exports of nuts and grains by 60 percent. The poor countries play no role in the setting of international standards such as the Codex Alimentarius because they simply cannot participate, lacking both monetary and human resources. Thus, standards developed by a limited number of countries can get the status of international ones.

The situation is likely to worsen as developed countries increase regulation for high valued-added products and as large multinational buyers increasingly dominate the retail market. 'Walmartization' of standards may be the new wave and the small and medium enterprises (SMEs) in poor countries, lacking information about export markets, are unable to compete. The gap between domestic and international regulation is widening. The need to reform agriculture by moving up the value-added scale would require major changes in institutional infrastructure. The cost would be high, and the poor countries do not have the resources. Similar problems exist in the TBT Agreement covering trade in goods. While both the TBT and SPS Agreements were supposed to provide technical assistance, this has been inadequate,and in any case, significant infrastructure investment is required.

Another example of system asymmetry deserves mention. The Round created the WTO and its Dispute Settlement Understanding (DSU), which was the jewel in the crown of the new and transformed multilateral trading system. For the first time, institutional constraints on the powerful had been achieved on trade issues through international law. Ideally, the playing field should have been leveled as poorer states had as much legal authority as the more powerful states. Did this increased legalization of the system offset asymmetry? Not exactly, alas.

I cannot get too detailed, but I think there has been enough analysis at least to point out that the new legal order has not affected the poorest countries. It is not possible to get data on a number of legal experts in their Geneva missions or their domestic ministries. One can safely assume that the numbers are very small or even nonexistent. And there has been no participation as complainant or respondent by any of the poor African countries.

One reason is very clear and simple—lack of money. The absence of government legal services either at home or in Geneva would require hiring lawyers, which is far too expensive. The Advisory Centre on WTO Law, established in December 1999 and entered into force in July 2001, was a welcome development. It is funded mainly by European governments and Canada. While welcome, most observers would likely argue that more is needed, especially in enhancing capabilities in economic research. The role of sophisticated econometric research and economic evidence in WTO dispute settlement is another example of the asymmetry issue.

But the cost side of the cost-benefit model for dispute participation often includes more than money or legal service subsidies. Political costs brought by political threats of a reduction in development aid or the removal of trade preference by other countries may also be powerful deterrents to initiating a WTO dispute.

In this ironic situation, the issue of asymmetry is reinforced by the highly sophisticated and advanced legal system that the United States established. In fact, although I was no longer in the government at that time, I was involved with the discussions because it was Canada that put forth the proposal for the WTO. It was, of course, the United States that was concerned in strengthening the dispute settlement system and had some real skepticism about the legal quality of the GATT, and now the WTO. In the end, the unintended consequence was that the most complex and sophisticated institution established in the post-World War II system had the most advanced and sophisticated legal system in the history of international law but did not have any executive or legislative capacity. I used to call the WTO a 'Mercedes-Benz without gas', but most observers were not amused.

I have simply provided some examples of the impact of the enormous complexity of the trading system created by the Uruguay Round. There has not been adequate study of this, and I am hoping that it will be examined more and more. Unlike in the GATT, there is a requirement for advanced and sophisticated knowledge due to the complexity. Complexity requires knowledge, and knowledge enhances power. The strong are stronger in the WTO because of their store of knowledge. The weak are weaker because of their poverty of knowledge. The term 'poverty trap' should be replaced with the term 'knowledge trap', but that is another story.

Most important in my view in the issue of asymmetry is the fundamental question of equity in the WTO. The endless discussion on S&D does not get to the pressing issue of equity. Hudec was right that this issue is fundamental to the legitimacy of the organization. But equity is not capable of being dealt with as a legal question. The question of equity is a moral question for the global system. Again, I am sure that we will have some discussion and disagree on this. But, if there was an attempt to think through the nature of the institution, there might have been the creation of a forum that did not create rules but allowed for discussion and debate. Issues like equity could be discussed. While such a forum did exist, it was dissolved at the end of the 1980s. If that had been discussed and a different kind of institution was created, we would have been able to look at this issue not simply as a legal one.

That is why I think it is trivial to deal with asymmetry as simply an implementation issue. Cooperation between the WTO and World Bank or regional banks could deal with the question of capacity building in a very fundamental sense. One example is the Integrated Framework, although I'm told that it is still not working very well. The Integrated Framework involved the WTO, the World Bank, the International Money Fund (IMF), UNCTAD, United Nations Development Programme (UNDP), and the International Trade Centre (ITC), as well as a number of bilateral donors. Although it may need some reforming and certainly something similar to a joint venture could be developed, the purpose is to launch a project as part of a process of international coherence. That is the issue which was certainly part of the Uruguay Round which did not amount to anything of importance. When I was involved in this, exchange rates and international cooperation and trade were the major foci. Now I think we must agree that the key issue is development. To say that the WTO should not involve itself in development issues is irrelevant. It is involved in all issues involving growth and development.

In many of the discussions on the issues of poor countries, the emphasis is on market access. Market access without infrastructure capability is not market entry. This has come out in a number of countries in Latin America, among others. I know that most of my friends feel that I am being extremely naive to accept the idea that development was key in getting the Doha Round going. I was chastised and told that all the symbolic words and rhetoric were just a normal negotiating side payment.

C. CONCLUSION

What is clear now in my view is that there is a new geography, and a major shift of the balance of power is on route with no consensus in sight.

I want to make one final point. Several years later, I was reading an article about the Uruguay Round, and there was a quote from one of the negotiators from the South. It was, '(w)ell, we got agriculture, they got TRIPS'. If I only could have met him, I would have said, '(b)ut you did not get agriculture, they got TRIPS'. So perhaps I should find another term besides the Bum Deal as it was not even a Bum Deal at all.

6. DEVELOPING COUNTRIES, THE DOHA ROUND, PREFERENCES, AND THE RIGHT TO REGULATE

JOEL P TRACHTMAN

> A. S&D Treatment 113
> B. Beyond Market Opening 116

In *Developing Countries in the GATT Legal System*, Robert Hudec argued against preferential and nonreciprocal treatment for developing countries. He did so on the basis of a nuanced combination of economic, political, and legal analysis that showed that this treatment would not benefit developing countries. It is a testament to Hudec's work that his analytical insights seem fresh today, over 20 years later. However, the WTO, established in 1995, is a more complex enterprise than the GATT that Hudec discussed, and the world has changed since Hudec first wrote *Developing Countries*. The rise of Brazil, China, and India, among other developing countries, has changed the power constellation in international trade.

Hudec's analysis was informed by an acute understanding of politics and of the public choice insight that even though trade liberalization as a general matter is individually and collectively rational for states, governments both in developed and developing countries are not sufficiently motivated to pursue it. He saw legally prescribed reciprocity as the incremental motivating force behind compliance, supporting domestic forces that favor liberalization.

Hudec recognized, but discounted, political and legal forces that some thought would bring liberalization in developed countries in favor of developing countries, without reciprocation by them. These political forces are based on growing concern for poverty in developing countries. These forces seem to be growing in strength today, but Hudec's analysis suggests that it would be risky to rely on these forces to induce liberalization by developed countries in goods and services of interest to developing countries. The legal forces, in the form of arguments for a customary international law rule, argued for by the proponents in the 1970s and 1980s of the 'New International Economic Order', have disappointed and dissipated. The new international economic order seems to have lost force soon after Hudec's book, largely for the reasons he anticipated. Moreover, Hudec showed that the legal rules advocated by the new international economic order were of questionable utility in improving the lot of developing countries.

Given that most developing countries (China, India, and a few others may be important exceptions) are unlikely to wield significant market power—to have effects on world prices—in most products, they would be unlikely to capture terms of trade benefits from protection. If they were able to select industries for protection accurately, developing countries might benefit from selective protection of infant industries until these industries become able to compete on world markets.

Like many others, Hudec was skeptical of the ability of developing country governments (and all other governments) to make these choices and to deny protection to industries that have little hope of attaining globally competitive efficiency. However, he felt that selective legal obligation—tariff schedules; restrictions on quotas and other balance of payments measures; and today, services commitments—would assist developing country governments in resisting calls for protection from these hopeless industries. This conundrum is at the core of Hudec's approach.

Hudec's original 1987 work, of course, only addressed GATT and did not address the WTO, which was formed in 1995. Significantly, his analysis does not apply directly to TRIPS or TRIMS commitments or perhaps to certain subsidies commitments. However, it would seem to apply to GATS liberalization commitments.

One reading of *Developing Countries'* work might see it as supportive of the trade component of the Washington Consensus: the prescription to developing countries to liberalize.[1] However, this reading, while partially quite accurate, would miss important nuance. Hudec did not propose his own economic theory but rather took the economic theories of others as assumptions and worked out their consequences for legal policy. He found that even assuming that some infant-industry protection or subsidization is good for developing countries, some legal commitments would also be good. The trick is in the discrimination: who discriminates and how?

Hudec assumed that the developing country governments themselves would discriminate between good and bad protection and would use international law as a tool by which to bind themselves, or more accurately, by which to plead to domestic lobbies that they are bound. Where commitments are made, and where they seem inconsistent with development goals of developing countries, what is to be done? Hudec was attracted to the GATT Article XVIII mechanism of multilateral review and chronicled its rise and fall as an effective mechanism for discriminating between valid and invalid protection.

Hudec's 1987 book, in the light of subsequent developments, including the Uruguay Round and the breakdown of the Washington Consensus, raises the

---

1. While this prescription has been criticized and has been subject to important empirical challenge, the weight of evidence appears to support it. LA Winters, N McCulloch, and A McKay, 'Trade Liberalization and Poverty: The Evidence So Far' (2004) 42 JELit 72–115. More recently, see D. Rodrik, *One Economics, Many Recipes* (Princeton: Princeton University Press, 2007) chapter 8; A Estevadeordal and AM Taylor, 'Is the Washington Consensus Dead? Growth, Openness, and the Great Liberalization, 1970s–2000s', (August 2008) NBER Working Paper No. W14264.

following questions: Which obligations should not be imposed on/accepted by developing countries? Which obligations should be imposed on/accepted by developing countries? How and when should these latter obligations be contingently relaxed?

The Washington Consensus continued to erode after the conclusion of the Uruguay Round.[2] In fact, something of a backlash against the Washington Consensus took place. Part of this backlash included a return to arguments for infant-industry protection as a basis for export-led growth. While there seems to be wide agreement among economists that infant-industry protection in developing countries is not *necessarily* adverse to development, there are significant questions about the choice of industries for protection, the duration and magnitude of protection, and the effects of protection on reciprocal negotiations for liberalization. Importantly, even the backlash has not included a reversion to import substitution as a strategy for growth. Of course, an import substitution strategy would be aligned with maintenance of high import barriers, which would require a negotiating position of nonreciprocity if developed country import barriers are to be reduced.

The GATT 1947 obligations that developing countries incurred did not significantly restrict their development policy. Developing countries had few obligations to liberalize, could use balance of payments exceptions to protect domestic markets, and had few other obligations. This changed in the Uruguay Round, with increased tariff and other commitments, reduced access to balance of payments exceptions, greater additional obligations, and stronger dispute settlement.

A. S&D TREATMENT

In connection with the DDA, there are important initiatives toward intensifying special and differential treatment for developing countries: these initiatives propose increasing the preferences available to developing countries and reducing the commitments applicable to them.

Hudec's work suggested that preferences, at least as heretofore structured under the GSP, would do little to help developing countries in the real world. Ever the realist, Hudec expected these preferences to be granted with strings attached or to develop strings over time: he did not expect the developed world to give something for nothing. While there may be greater political impetus in developed countries to assist developing ones, it will be difficult to translate this impetus into useful preferences. Hudec also anticipated that these preferences would be granted in ways that resulted in trade diversion hurting other developing

---

2. See N Birdsall and A De La Torre, *Washington Contentious: Economic Policies for Social Equity in Latin America* (Washington DC: Carnegie Endowment for Peace, 2001); JE Stiglitz, *Globalization And Its Discontents* (New York: W. W. Norton & Company, 2002).

countries rather than trade creation putting the adjustment burden on developed countries. At the 2005 Hong Kong Ministerial meeting, ministers agreed to provide duty-free and quota-free access for products from least-developed countries. This action accords with Hudec's prediction that preferential treatment would devolve into multiple tiers of preferential treatment. Finally, he understood that these preferences would be unstable, making them poor lures for investment, which is the critical factor in development.

Hoekman, Michalopoulos and Winters find that MFN liberalization of trade in goods and services that are of export interest to developing countries would be superior in global welfare terms to more selective preferences.[3] This is a critical point and argues that developing countries should not be placated by preferences but should demand MFN liberalization in areas where they hold actual or potential advantage. This certainly includes trade in unskilled and semiskilled services under Mode 4 of GATS, and even more broadly suggests less reticence to put immigration on the table.

Hudec suggested that reducing the commitments applicable to developing countries might not be helpful to their development. This is more than paternalism; it is based on a political economy perspective that understands that domestic import-competing producer interests are likely to be more influential than domestic consumer interests. Reciprocity is expected to co-opt domestic export producer interests to add their voice to that of the consumers in order to counter the force of the domestic import-competing producers.

Nevertheless, part of the DDA includes making operational a set of provisions on special and differential treatment. In the Doha Declaration, member governments agree to review all special and differential treatment provisions in order to strengthen them and make them more precise.[4] This goal stands in contrast to the broad, hortatory, and ultimately unenforceable 'requirements' of the New International Economic Order (NIEO). The Declaration (combined with the Decision on Implementation-Related Issues and Concerns) calls on the WTO Committee on Trade and Development to identify which existing special and differential treatment provisions are mandatory and to consider the implications of making mandatory those that are currently not binding.

However, as Hudec noted, few special and differential treatment provisions arising from prior negotiations are binding. Moreover, even formally binding provisions must be evaluated in order to determine their legal effect. While the nonreciprocity principle seems formally binding, it has had limited effect in terms of obtaining concessions for developing countries without reciprocation. The Doha Mandate calls for 'less than full reciprocity' on the part of developing

---

3. B Hoekman, C Michalopoulos and LA Winter, 'Special and Differential Treatment of Developing Countries in the WTO: Moving Forward After Cancún' (2004) 27(4) W Econ 481–506.

4. Paragraph 44 of the 2001 Doha Ministerial Declaration.

countries in connection with market access for nonagricultural products. This seems to be a retreat from a principle of nonreciprocity.

Furthermore, Faizel Ismail, the former head of the South African Delegation to the WTO, argued that S&D treatment 'should not be confused with the broader development dimension of the trading system nor become a substitute for it'.[5] Indeed, there seems to be a good case against S&D treatment, at least in the core areas of MFN, national treatment, the prohibition on quantitative restrictions, tariff bindings, and reciprocal negotiations.[6] One critical part of the broader development dimension of the trading system, as mentioned above, is MFN tariff reductions and reductions in developed country subsidies with respect to goods that developing countries have the capacity to produce efficiently. In terms of the Doha Negotiations, there is a direct correlation between countries requesting further special and differential treatment and those receiving nonreciprocal market access under various preference arrangements.

Between 1980 and 2005, the United States established some arrangements for 'better than GSP' treatment in geographically selected areas: the Caribbean Basin Initiative and later the Caribbean Basin Economic Partnership, the Andean Trade Preferences Act and later the Andean Trade Promotion and Drug Eradication Act, and the African Growth and Opportunity Act. Although these programs themselves have significant limitations and are often less preferential than regional trade arrangements such as NAFTA, they generally provide treatment superior to that available under GSP. The EC provides 'better than GSP' treatment under its Cotonou Convention. The EC also has the 'Everything but Arms' initiative for least-developed countries. Many of these programs use rather restrictive rules of origin that both have distorting effects and impose significant costs of compliance. These rules of origin may have distorting effects similar to those caused by trade related investment measures.[7] Furthermore, without suitable infrastructure and vertically integrated industries and with stringent (and costly) SPS Agreement requirements, many LDCs are not able to fully take advantage of the preferential market access.

An important rejection of discriminatory preferences came in 2004, when the WTO Appellate Body, in the *EC-Tariff Preferences* case, addressed the scope of permissible conditionality—reciprocity—that may be applied in connection with GSP programs under WTO law. India complained against the EC regarding the conditions under which the EC accords tariff preferences to developing countries.

---

5. Faizel Ismail, 'A Development Perspective on the WTO July 2004 General Council Decision' (2005) 8 JIEL 377, 379.

6. Bernard Hoekman, 'Operationalizing the Concept of Policy Space in the WTO: Beyond Special and Differential Treatment' (2005) 8 JIEL 405, 409.

7. See B Hoekman and C Ozden, 'Trade Preferences and Differential Treatment of Developing Countries: A Selective Survey' (April 2005) World Bank Policy Research Working Paper 3566.

The Appellate Body found that the requirement in the Enabling Clause for non-discriminatory treatment does not require formally identical treatment but requires identical treatment of similarly situated beneficiaries. The distinction among beneficiaries must 'respond positively' to the needs of developing countries. Thus, demands for reciprocity by developed countries in the form of policy concessions in exchange for GSP treatment are sharply constrained. The scope of this constraint will no doubt be tested in the future.

B. BEYOND MARKET OPENING

Hudec's perspective was developed with GATT market-opening obligations in mind. As suggested earlier, it is important to distinguish among types of obligations:

- Category 1: goods and services liberalization. The first category, and the one on which Hudec focused his analysis, is obligations to liberalize trade in goods by removing quantitative restrictions and by reducing tariffs. Although liberalization in trade in services is different and different service sectors might be treated differently depending on whether they are infrastructural or consumer services, many types of services liberalization can be treated as analogous to goods liberalization. Some types of services liberalization, such as Mode 4 services liberalization involving movement of natural persons to perform services, may provide substantial benefits to developing countries in particular service sectors. Other types of services liberalization, such as Mode 3 commercial presence, are akin to investment liberalization addressed in Category 4.
- Category 2: standards liberalization. The second category, implicating the "right to regulate" prudentially, is regulation of standards for manufactured goods and sanitary and phytosanitary standards for agricultural goods. This type of liberalization, in the form of disciplines on importing country product standards, is an adjunct to liberalization of explicit protection through restrictions on quotas and tariff bindings. This may assist developing countries, but it is also costly for developing countries to comply with required procedures. Furthermore, it leaves in place much of developed country product standards which may be costly for developing country firms to meet.
- Category 3: intellectual property rights. There is some argument that intellectual property rights protections, at least in some fields such as drugs that cure tropical diseases, might be useful to developing countries. However, it seems clear that as a whole, the increased protection of intellectual property rights required of developing countries by the TRIPS component of the Uruguay Round bargain resulted in welfare losses to

developing countries. This welfare loss is to be distinguished from the presumed welfare gains that developing countries are generally expected to realize from Category 1 obligations—liberalization.
- Category 4: investment measures. While there have been initiatives to include a full panoply of investment liberalization and protection within the WTO, these have not been successful. The existing rules in TRIMS are extensions of GATT obligations prohibiting requirements of local inputs and restrictions on importation of inputs as conditions for investment. We also include in Category 4 investment liberalization requirements in services pursuant to Mode 3 of the GATS.
- Category 5: subsidies, including export subsidies and import substitution subsidies. Under the CVD Agreement, the GATT prohibition on export subsidies is extended to import substitution subsidies and is applicable to developing countries (but not to LDCs).

In economic, political, and legal analysis, each of these categories should be considered separately. It complicates and muddies analysis to recognize that the Uruguay Round, like the Doha Round, is a package deal. Of course, package deals may involve tradeoffs between components such that it is unrealistic to evaluate any component individually. However, we must at least begin by analyzing the components individually before we can synthesize an overall perspective.

To repeat, Hudec's main work focused on Category 1 measures relating to goods. This is because at the time he wrote *Developing Countries*, GATT was only concerned with goods and largely concerned with Category 1 measures. In order to consider the role of developing countries in the WTO legal system, it is necessary to extend Hudec's analysis to address Categories 2, 3, 4, and 5. It is also useful to examine Hudec's analysis of Category 1 in light of some of the developments since 1987.

One of the main questions that has been articulated since 1987 concerns the 'right to regulate'. While this is not a legal right *per se*, it expresses the concern that states retain a certain measure of autonomy in order to carry out important functions. The field of regulation can be divided into two parts. First is regulation that might be termed "prudential," relating to health, safety, consumer protection, or other similar goals and addressing information asymmetries or externalities. This type of regulation concerns developing countries as exporters or as market entrants where developed countries might apply regulation that intentionally or unintentionally restricts market access for developing countries or imposes implementation costs on developing countries. Second is regulation that might be termed 'economic', designed to manage the economy in order to promote economic growth. This type of regulation might include subsidies, tariffs, quotas, and foreign exchange control. WTO law restricts certain actions in this second group, and we will focus below on this second group.

It is perhaps facile to say that the main commitments in Category 1 relating to liberalization leave room for economic regulation. In connection with goods, developing countries, like other countries, make the commitments for tariff reduction that they negotiate. Their negotiation should be informed by their overall economic policy. To what extent are developing countries making commitments that are too great—that are inconsistent with their economic growth strategy? Of course, developing countries, like other WTO members, are generally prohibited to impose quotas under Article 11 of GATT although they may be eligible for balance-of-payments exceptions. But quotas are a particularly wasteful form of protection, and there is little reason to protect the right to regulate through *de jure* quotas.

Hudec concluded that it would be a good thing for developing countries to accept market-opening obligations of the Category 1 type. He did so on the basis that even assuming that some protection is economically beneficial, not all protection would be beneficial. Therefore, and because governments find it difficult to resist claims for protection, developing country governments would need external support to resist the less desirable claims for protection.

According to Hudec's model, this is the critical function of WTO law. However, Hudec left unanswered several questions. First, he did not explain how commitments could be made in the first place if domestic industry lobbied for protection. Second, he did not explain why commitments would be made in the 'right' sectors. Third, Hudec did not explain why the incremental leverage against protectionism that WTO law would provide would be enough to prevail. The first question can be answered by appeal to the possible existence of an inconsistency in interests across time. Perhaps the protectionist interests would not yet have arisen at the time the commitments are entered into or are at that time weak enough to be subjected to commitments at little political cost. The second question can be answered in a positive way only by referring to the ability of government to discriminate accurately between good and bad protection. The third question can only be answered in marginalist terms: the compliance pressure of the WTO legal system would add to the incentives for compliance and in marginal cases would determine compliance.

Hudec's model also could not anticipate the significant amount of unilateral liberalization effected by developing countries since 1987. Much of this liberalization did not take place in a formal reciprocal context although it is possible that it constituted asynchronous reciprocity or was motivated by the desire to have a reciprocal threat to use to hold open foreign markets.

Perhaps time inconsistency explains the importance of Article XVIII to Hudec as what we might term a 'development safeguard' mechanism.[8] Article XIX of

---

8. See WTO, '1979 Decision on Safeguard Action for Development Purposes' (1980) 26 BISD 209–210 (providing a facility for special safeguards in order to address development needs).

GATT, the general safeguards provision, does not provide any special privileges to developing countries. However, it does address the problem of time inconsistency where commitments give rise to unforeseen increases in imports. Article XIX itself requires compensation in another sector although the Uruguay Round Safeguards Agreement delays the obligation to provide compensation.

Article XVIII could provide a broader tool, more easily available to developing countries, by which to obtain contingent relaxation of commitments. Article XIX requires proof of unforeseen circumstances, causation by increased imports, and serious injury or threat of serious injury to a domestic industry. It does not readily lend itself to infant-industry protection.

But as Hudec points out, Article XVIII has disappointed in a variety of ways, at various times. At some times, it has been too readily available, licensing all defections from commitments. With carte blanche under Article XVIII, or more broadly under Part IV of GATT, developing country commitments would mean little, either to trade partners or to domestic governments seeking arguments by which to resist domestic industries seeking protection. The purpose of Article XVIII, as envisioned in 1955 when the current version was established, is appealing today:

> The general concept of the new Article is that economic development is consistent with the objectives of the General Agreement and that the raising of the general standards of living of the underdeveloped countries which should be the result of economic development will facilitate the attainment of the objectives of the Agreement. In that sense, the new text represents a new and more positive approach to the problem of economic development and to the ways and means of reconciling the requirements of economic development with the obligations undertaken under the General Agreement regarding the conduct of commercial policy. Article XVIII:B became the principal provision used, as it did not require prior authorization—it allows unilateral protective action. However, even Article XVIII:B has not withstood the move away from import substitution and the establishment of the WTO. Most countries that were using Article XVIII:B have now unilaterally ceased application, while India was forced to cease application through litigation.

In the years after the conclusion of the Uruguay Round, there were some instances in which states asked whether the GATT-era practices relating to developing countries were really intended to end, countering clear legal text with diplomatic practice, and perhaps intent. This was the thrust of India's position in the *India—Quantitative Restrictions* case in which India argued for continuity of the lax approach to developing country access to balance-of-payments exceptions that was followed under GATT. The Appellate Body in this case upheld the clear meaning of the Uruguay Round Understanding on Balance of Payments, subjecting member state claims of exceptions under Articles XII or XVIII to judicial scrutiny. Prior to the advent of the WTO, these claims were sometimes subjected to panel evaluation, but developing countries had become accustomed to undisciplined access to these exceptions.

The Appellate Body saw no conflict or redundancy between the competence of the BOP Committee and the General Council and the competence of WTO panels but considered that panels should take into account the deliberations and conclusions of these "political" bodies.[9] It concluded that the dispute settlement provisions of the WTO can be invoked with respect to any matters relating to balance-of-payments restrictions.

In subsequent Doha Round Negotiations, some developing countries have called for a decision to specify that only the BOP Committee would have authority to examine the justification of balance-of-payments measures.

However, in order to discriminate more accurately, in terms of economic development rather than in terms of domestic political power in the protecting country, it seems desirable to restructure and reinvigorate an Article XVIII:B- type mechanism. Ideally, such a mechanism would provide careful and independent analysis of the justification for derogation from all WTO obligations, including but not limited to the GATT itself.[10]

At present, the WTO itself probably lacks the institutional capacity to engage in the type of detailed analysis that would be required. Under current rules and arrangements, the WTO relies to a significant extent on analysis by the IMF of balance of payments ramifications of derogations from WTO commitments under Article XVIII:B. This type of arrangement could be extended to deal more explicitly with development policy and other organizations, such as the World Bank, could be involved.[11] The goal would be to evaluate proposed derogations to determine their consistency with the development needs of the proposing state. Measures consistent with development needs would be approved and accepted despite any inconsistency with other WTO obligations. This mechanism would formalize and constrain the developing countries' position of the 1970s that Part IV provides a blanket 'exception' for measures taken to promote development.

Of course, if approval resulted in adverse effects on exporters from developed states, such a mechanism could reduce the ability to form coalitions within developed states in favor of reciprocal liberalization. So a broad development exception, even if carefully targeted, would have costs in terms of the potential for MFN liberalization by developing countries.

---

9. WTO, *Appellate Body Report, India—Quantitative Restrictions on Imports of Agricultural, Textile and Industrial Products ("India—Quantitative Restrictions")* (22 September 1999) WT/DS90/AB/R paras 103–104.

10. See B Hoekman and others (n 3 above) pp. 481–506 (calling for a 'country-specific approach that would make implementation of new rules a function of national priorities').

11. See J. Michael Finger, *The Doha Agenda and Development: A View from the Uruguay Round* (Manila: Asian Development Bank, 2002).

Such a mechanism could be applied wholesale to Category 1 obligations in much the same way that Article XVIII:B was intended to operate. In order for it to be useful, however, such a mechanism must apply in a way that developing countries can trust it to be available to allow appropriate derogations and that developed countries can trust it to disallow inappropriate derogations. So it must be depoliticized, and it will also take some time to develop a 'jurisprudence' that would make derogations predictable.

An alternative might rely on the concept of Article XVIII:C, relating to infant industries. The real development concern today is not so much balance of payments as contemplated by Article XVIII:B. Rather, the real concern is fostering the growth of industry in developing countries. For a variety of reasons, including the requirement of compensation, Article XVIII:C has only been used by Bangladesh.

Of course, the concept of Article XVIII:C is that of import substitution, at least in the sense that it is premised on the idea that by blocking imports of competing goods, a local industry may be fostered. The import substitution concept was discredited by the Washington Consensus, but one might argue alternatively that the Article XVIII:C concept is not limited to import substitution but expects that after a period of domestic dominance, the protected local industry will become capable of competing in global markets, including in an unprotected domestic market. This concept would find some support in the Washington Consensus but leaves unanswered three questions: (i) are protected markets or competitive markets more conducive to the growth of global competitors, (ii) how can governments select and foster domestic industries that will develop into global competitors under protection, and (iii) how can protected industries be weaned from protection? Although it is not clear that developed country governments or international organizations have better tools with which to answer these questions than developing country governments, Hudec suggested that national governments could not be trusted to make these decisions well. Therefore, some contingent derogation mechanism—some international supervision—might be useful to constrain national governments and give them a basis on which to reject protection in some cases.

With respect to Category 2 obligations, it is not clear how much help a contingent derogation mechanism can provide. A contingent derogation mechanism might allow developing countries to apply standards without doing all of the scientific or other work necessary to justify them. It might thus reduce the costs of implementation of WTO procedural requirements. However, it cannot do much to reduce the costs of ensuring the compliance of developing country products with developed country standards. Here, the main problem is not the development impact of SPS Agreement constraints on developing countries but the failure of the SPS Agreement to address the cost to developing countries of complying with SPS measures implemented by developed countries. Agricultural exports are a main source of earnings for developing countries, and these exports can be blocked by SPS measures. The question of proportionality might be raised: do the health benefits in the developed country importing state justify the costs of compliance imposed on the developing country exporting state? The SPS Agreement leaves much room for a developed country to impose this type of cost on developing countries despite the 'necessity' requirement of Article 2.2.

It is important to note that this latter type of cost pre-dated the SPS Agreement, and that the SPS Agreement did not exacerbate this cost but provided an enhanced basis for developing countries, and others, to challenge protectionist SPS measures. The question is whether the SPS Agreement did enough to restrain the imposition of costs on developing countries.

Article 9 of the SPS Agreement is an example of a rather imprecise facility that could, if applied, relieve some of this potential burden of compliance by developing country producers with developed country SPS standards. It provides for technical assistance by developed countries to developing countries to assist in compliance. It may be appropriate, more specifically, to require developed countries as they implement new standards, to provide technical assistance to appropriate developing countries to ensure that compliance does not inappropriately burden the developing country suppliers of regulated goods. Articles 10.2 and 10.3 of the SPS Agreement and 12.8 of the TBT Agreement are examples of aspirational provisions intended to relieve some of this potential burden on developing countries through transition periods.

With respect to Category 3 obligations, contingent derogation may or may not be appropriate. It has become clear that derogation from the specific obligations of TRIPS will often be appropriate for developing countries from a poverty reduction perspective. One way to legitimate and justify this derogation would be to establish a process for examination of proposed derogations. However, developing countries may view this type of incremental case-by-case derogation as too slow, unwieldy, and unpredictable, while developed country constituencies may be unwilling to relinquish gains made under TRIPS. It may be more appropriate to negotiate broader, generally applicable, reductions of TRIPS obligations.

The issue of TRIPS and essential medicines is a good example of the frequent result of negotiations between developed countries and developing ones: the developed countries are successful at securing harder legal rights, while the developing countries obtain softer, less realizable, exceptions or principles based on their concerns. In subsequent formal legal proceedings, the developed countries will have the upper hand. However, in political and public relations fora, it is difficult for the developed countries to press their advantage.

As developing countries began to appreciate the costs of compliance with the patent protection requirements of TRIPS, especially with respect to essential medicines such as AIDS drugs, they examined the TRIPS Agreement seeking sources of legal authority to abrogate some of the patent protection requirements otherwise applicable. Several provisions of TRIPS provide possible exceptions or flexibility. For example, Articles 7 and 8 of TRIPS assert aspirations for social welfare and a balance of rights and obligations as well as flexibility to protect public health, with an important proviso that measures must be consistent with the rest of the TRIPS Agreement. These provisions have not been made operational in litigation, but their language has been used as a reference in negotiations and in the public relations battle.

TRIPS was intended to curtail the practice of compulsory licensing whereby governments license production using a patented technology without the permission of the owner of the patent. Article 31 of TRIPS establishes a number of limitations. Perhaps the most important limitation, as it turned out, was the requirement under Article 31(f) that compulsory licensing be effected 'predominantly for the supply of the domestic market'. This limitation operates to make it difficult for smaller or less advanced developing countries to utilize the compulsory licensing flexibility that does exist where they lack domestic manufacturing capabilities. In the Doha Negotiations, the greatest focus on negotiations has been on permitting manufacturing under compulsory licenses for foreign developing country markets.

While the Doha Declaration on the TRIPS Agreement and Public Health made certain clarifications regarding what constitutes a national emergency or other circumstances of extreme urgency, permitting compulsory licensing without prior negotiation with the patent holder, and making statements to the effect that TRIPS *should* allow action to protect public health, it made only one formal change to WTO law. In accordance with the Declaration, member states later agreed to give the least developed countries an additional ten-year transition period with respect to patent protection of medicines.

At the Hong Kong Ministerial in 2005, ministers agreed to make permanent the 'Paragraph 6 Solution', whereby countries without suitable infrastructure could import medicines from third parties.[12] The decision makes it easier for developing countries to obtain less expensive generic versions of patented medicines by relaxing the application of Article 31(f) of the TRIPS Agreement that would otherwise hinder exports of pharmaceuticals manufactured under compulsory licenses to countries unable to produce them.

Category 4 obligations as they exist today involve only a limited range of TRIMS measures, including in particular local content requirements, but excluding export performance requirements. While local content requirements may be part of an *import substitution* or infant-industry program, they are unlikely to be core elements of a development policy. Local content requirements imposed as a condition for investment approval act as a burden on investment, which is a critical factor in development. They also serve as a burden on domestic production,

---

12. *See* Fredrick Abbott, 'The Doha Declaration on the TRIPS Agreement and Public Health: Lighting a Dark Corner at the WTO' (2002) 5 JIEL 469–505.

which is prevented from sourcing inputs from the most efficient supplier.[13] So, while a contingent derogation mechanism could be devised to permit certain TRIMS measures, the measures that are currently prohibited are unlikely to make a good case for derogation.

Category 5 obligations present difficult questions from a development standpoint. There is certainly wide agreement that developed country agricultural subsidies may cause harm to farmers in developing countries, and while developed country agricultural subsidies may help poor farmers in some locations and consumers who rely on subsidized food, one important area of reform of the WTO is reduction of developed country agricultural subsidies. Some argue that restrictions on subsidization constrain the right of developing countries to engage in economic regulation for growth. The experience of the East Asian economies from 1960 to 2000 suggests that subsidies to promote certain types of technology and information management may be important to growth.[14] But WTO law does not generally restrict nonagricultural domestic subsidies except where they may cause serious prejudice and to the extent that these subsidies are not to specific industries or groups of industries, they are not actionable. The SCM Agreement provides exceptions for least-developed countries, and certain other countries, from its prohibition of export subsidies. However, from a welfare standpoint, it appears unlikely that export subsidies harm other states or help the granting state. On the other hand, there may be strategic circumstances in which an export subsidy may allow producers from one country to compete effectively against producers of another (nonsubsidizing) country.

As with SPS measures, perhaps the bigger issue for developing countries is not in terms of their domestic subsidies but in terms of the subsidies of developed countries. Much of the concern here relates to agricultural subsidies. Cotton is a good example.

Cotton became an iconic agricultural issue in the lead-up to the Cancun ministerial. In May 2003, the West and Central African states of Benin, Burkina Faso, Chad, and Mali made a proposal for reduction of developed country agricultural subsidies in cotton.[15] These states argued that their cotton producers are efficient, but that their cotton industries declined due to high levels of subsidies in the United States and European Communities that depress world cotton prices. They sought reduction of these subsidies and cash compensation to provide

---

13. *See* A Keck and P Low, 'Special and Differential Treatment in the WTO: Why, When and How?' WTO Economic Research and Statistics Division, Staff Working Paper ERSD-2004-03 (May 2004).

14. McCulloch, Neil, L. Alan Winters and Xavier Cirera, *Trade Liberalization and Poverty: A Handbook* (London: CEPR, 2001) 157.

15. WTO, 'WTO Negotiations on Agriculture, Poverty Reduction: Sectoral Initiative in Favour of Cotton' (16 May 2003) WTO TN/AG/GEN/4.

livelihoods to their displaced cotton farmers until the subsidies are eliminated. In a move to salvage the Cancun negotiations, the United States and European Communities agreed to establish a subcommittee on cotton.

The cotton negotiations highlight the link between trade distortion, on the one hand, and development prospects and livelihoods, on the other. They also highlight the need for an integrated approach to help developing countries take advantage of the potential gains under Doha that would involve not only the WTO but also multilateral and bilateral development agencies. Broader efforts involving proposals to enhance the Integrated Framework[16] attempt to address the need for a more cohesive trade and development policy.

At the Hong Kong Ministerial meeting at the end of 2005, developed countries agreed to remove all export subsidies on cotton and to provide duty-free and quota-free access to exports of cotton from least-developed countries. They also agreed on the negotiating objective that trade distorting domestic subsidies for cotton production would be reduced more ambitiously than under whatever general formula is agreed for domestic subsidies in agriculture generally.

The above analysis of different types of WTO obligations suggests some variations of treatment. The core perspective of these suggestions is development-favorable, with development as the primary goal of policy. However, this perspective is not necessarily deferential to developing country governments (just as it would not be deferential to developed country governments). While it responds to the African Group proposal that 'notwithstanding any provisions of any WTO Agreement, [LDCs] shall not be required to implement or comply with obligations that are prejudicial to their individual development needs . . . . ',[17] it does not leave to the LDCs or to other developing countries the unconstrained flexibility to determine what is and is not prejudicial to development needs. It responds in a more precise and institutionally nuanced manner. In some contexts, it provides blanket exceptions, but in others it relies on specific case-based analysis and multilateral control of policy. This multilateral control is to be based not on

---

16. The "Integrated Framework" was established in 1997 to coordinate the work of the IMF, the International Trade Center, United Nations Conference on Trade and Development, United Nations Development Programme, the World Bank, and the World Trade Organization to address trade related assistance and capacity building needs in least-developed countries. The Integrated Framework is designed to address poverty issues by helping to ensure that trade related assistance needs are included in national development plans. The idea is to examine how particular least-developed countries may address constraints to trade and sectors of export potential and plan to integrate into the trading system. The Integrated Framework, valuable though it is, is a modest start toward coherence in this field and operates at the level of national policy, rather than substantial redistribution.

17. WTO, 'Proposal by the Africa Group' TN/CTD/W/3/REV.2.

political deliberation but on expert analysis regarding development policy. Within the Category 1 context, it recognizes that it is useful for developing countries to be able to bind themselves to liberalize. Development policy-based exceptions, subject to multilateral control, seem reasonable. Here, the differential treatment should be for developed countries to liberalize in the goods and services that are of export interest to developing countries.[18]

---

18. B Hoekman and others. (n 3 above).

PART TWO

INSTITUTIONAL CAPACITY AND DISPUTE SETTLEMENT

7. ROBERT HUDEC AND THE THEORY OF INTERNATIONAL ECONOMIC LAW
The Law of Global Space

DAVID M TRUBEK AND M PATRICK COTTRELL*

A. Introduction 129
B. The Legalization of 'Global Space' 130
C. Outline of the Chapter 131
D. Functions and Features of Law in Global Space 132
    I. Standards Not Rules 134
    II. Networks 134
    III. Decentered Deliberation and Negotiation 134
    IV. Multilevel Coordination 134
    V. Substance versus Procedure 134
    VI. Soft and Hard Law 134
E. Hudec on Governance Issues 135
F. Global Legal Space and the Future of Governance 142
    I. Proposals to Reform the WTO 143
    II. The WTO: Communication and Facilitation through Councils and Committees 146
    III. Hybrid Governance in the European Union 148
G. Conclusion 150

A. INTRODUCTION

Robert Hudec's work on trade law not only helped create and guide the field, it also made a contribution to the general theory of law in a globalized world economy. While Hudec's contribution to trade law is well-known and fully documented in this volume and elsewhere, there has been less attention to the broader relevance of his work. In his struggle to understand trade law in action, he worked out a framework of analysis that has implications for many areas of international law and can be used to illuminate a wide variety of issues. In this chapter we outline some general principles about the role of law in the world economy, show how Hudec anticipated them in his work on trade, and demonstrate how these principles can help us deal with contemporary issues in international economic law. We show that Hudec's general analysis can still be used

---

* Senior Fellow, Center for World Affairs and the Global Economy (WAGE) and Voss-Bascom Professor of Law Emeritus, University of Wisconsin, Madison and Assistant Professor, Linfield College, respectively.

to deal with current issues in the area of trade and development, in the operation of councils and committees in the WTO and their potential for opening more policy space for developing countries, and even for understanding the role of law in the EU.

B. THE LEGALIZATION OF 'GLOBAL SPACE'

Much recent discussion of governance beyond the level of the nation state has drawn attention to 'legalization' or the tendency to bring more and more aspects of international life into the ambit of law-like processes.[1] The legalization discussion has looked at the growing importance of rules governing the behavior of many actors, from states to private parties, in more and more areas of international life. Attention has been given to the rules, processes to interpret and apply the rules, and questions of compliance. Nowhere has this development been more pronounced than in the area of trade. The replacement of the GATT by the WTO has been heralded as a move from a diplomatic approach to the governance of trade to a legal regime, which includes binding rules and a court-like system for authoritative interpretation of the rules.

While no one would question the importance of legalization, it would be a mistake to think that this trend has totally transformed global governance in trade or in any other aspect of world society. Indeed, concentration on legalization may deflect attention from the full complexity of the 'new world order', to quote Anne Marie Slaughter, obscuring the continued importance of other modes of governance, the variety of mechanisms by which they can affect outcomes, and their interrelationship with more strictly juridical approaches.[2] Consequently, one of the foremost challenges facing legal theory is to confront the diversity and density of 'global space'. Because global space involves states, supranational and international agencies, multilevel arrangements, great diversity of circumstances, and complex coordination issues, law may play different roles than it does in domestic settings.

---

1. See, for example, the special issue of Int'l Org (2000) on 'The Legalization of World Politics'.
2. For example, if one looks at the emerging literature on "new governance" in the European Union and elsewhere, one finds a more nuanced understanding of these complexities and relationships. See, for example, the special issue of the Col JEL (2007) on 'Narrowing the Gap? Law and New Approaches to Governance in the European Union'. See also C Sabel and J Zeitlin, 'Learning from Difference: The New Architecture of Experimentalist Governance' (May 2007), European Governance Working Paper, EUROGOV No. C-07-02; J Scott and D Trubek, 'Mind the Gap: Law and New Approaches to Governance in the European Union' (2002) 8 EL Rev 1–18; and D Trubek and L Trubek, 'New Governance and Legal Regulation: Complementarity, Rivalry, and Transformation' (2007) 13 Col JEL 540–64.

As a result of globalization, international regimes of one type or another are playing a growing role in the regulation of affairs. International institutions like the WTO reach deeply into national legal orders as do supranational bodies like the EU. We are presented with a proliferation of regulatory approaches and instruments with legal or law-like characteristics creating a new phenomenon we might call the 'law of global space'.

This new phenomenon challenges our received understandings of law. Because some of the law of global space is set out in treaties, it bears some resemblance to traditional public international law. But because it may have direct impact on subnational bodies and private actors and because it may emanate from arenas that include some degree of popular participation, it often has features not normally associated with public international law. The law of global space, like national regulatory law, may specify detailed rules for behavior and provide sanctions for noncompliance. But it also may rely on very broad standards, collective deliberation over norm elaboration, and voluntary adherence to agreed-upon standards. Where classical theories of law saw international law and municipal law as distinct legal orders, the very purpose of much of the law of global space is to bring them together.

The result has been a vigorous debate about the nature, functions, and effectiveness of law in international regimes like the WTO and supranational institutions like the EU. Scholars have drawn attention to many of the features to be found in the law of global space and argued about their importance and desirability. To be sure, many of the developments highlighted in the debate over law in global space have their counterparts in debates about the changing nature and role of law at the national level, and arguments could be made that there is a general move away from classical legal conceptions. However, this not the place to debate such issues: our task is to outline the characteristics thought most salient to the law of global space.

C. OUTLINE OF THE CHAPTER

Our purpose in this chapter is threefold. First, we sketch a preliminary vision of the role of law in global space. This requires both an examination of law's functions and law's features. What role do we think law is or should be playing in the regulation of transborder phenomena? What tools have or could be used to carry out those functions? Traditional legal theory tends to see law as combining three functions: communication, facilitation, and coercion. But in order to theorize about the role of law of global space, it is necessary to separate the three functions and ask how they relate to one another. Traditional theory stresses the importance of such features as clear and predictable rules backed by sanctions and administered by specialized staff. In contrast, in global space we may see much more use of open-ended, nonbinding standards managed through transnational public/private networks.

Second, we look to the early work of Robert Hudec to help us think about how these functions and features operate and interact. In several articles written before the emergence of the WTO, Hudec articulated a nuanced view of the role of law in the trade regime that prefigures contemporary understandings of the multifaceted role that law plays in global regulation.[3]

Finally, we draw on Hudec's insights to raise questions about the present and future of law in global governance. In so doing, we consider how these insights might apply to more recent developments in trade law, including proposals to reform trade law to make it more supportive of the goals of developing nations as well in other areas of international economic law.

D. FUNCTIONS AND FEATURES OF LAW IN GLOBAL SPACE

When we speak of the law of global space, we refer to the use of various authoritative processes that affect transactions that cross national borders. While these processes bear some resemblance to law at the national level and in some cases operate in similar ways, in many cases they are performing functions and employing features that are fundamentally different from their municipal counterparts.[4]

Law at any level can perform various functions. These include communication, facilitation, and coercion. Law as communication sets forth standards for behavior, whether it is of individuals, organizations, or states. Law as facilitation creates arenas in which individuals or groups may seek to set rules for their interaction or solutions to common problems. Law as coercion provides sanctions for noncompliance with authoritative standards or mutually agreed-upon rules.

In the typical municipal regulatory scheme, standards and coercion go together. Detailed rules are elaborated by legislatures and agencies and sanctions provided for noncompliance. Similarly, facilitation and coercion can go together if penalties are provided for breach of the contracts that result from private ordering.

---

3. Parts of this chapter are inspired by D Trubek's remarks, 'Transcending the Ostensible: Some Reflections on Bob Hudec as Friend and Scholar' (May 2007) which will be reprinted in a forthcoming issue of Minn JIL.

4. This discussion draws on Trubek and Trubek (n 2 above); D Trubek, P Cottrell and M Nance, 'Soft Law, Hard Law and EU Integration' in G de Búrca and J Scott (eds), *Law and New Governance in the EU and US* (Hart Publishing, 2006); D Trubek and L Trubek, 'Hard and Soft Law in the Construction of Social Europe: the Role of the Open Method of Coordination' (2005) 11 ELJ 343–64. For a somewhat similar perspective, see C Knill and A Lenschow, 'Compliance, Competition and Communication: Different Approaches of European Governance and their Impact on National Institutions' (2005) JCMS 43, 583–606.

All this can be found in the law of global space: here we can sometimes see communication, facilitation, and coercion fused. For example, the EU legal system is based on agreements that have been worked out by the Member States and recorded in treaties, regulations, and directives. These establish standards for the behavior of states and nonstate actors and in some cases, sanctions are available for noncompliance. We could look at the WTO the same way. International treaties like GATT and GATS establish standards, and the dispute settlement system legitimates sanctioning of actions that are GATT inconsistent.

While the law of global space can perform all three functions, it is much more likely to be based on communication and facilitation than it is on coercion. Especially to the extent that legal orders like the EU and the WTO are designed to affect the behavior of states, not individuals and organizations, they must deal with the reality of the state as an actor, the complexity of global life, and the limits of the international legal order.

Legal fictions to the contrary notwithstanding, states are not unitary actors. Rather, their behavior is determined by the complex interplay of the state and civil society. Efforts to impose international standards on states must take account of this complexity. Sometimes this is best done by the use of specific rules to which sanctions are attached, but in other cases it may be best to deploy very open-ended standards which allow the participating state to work out details voluntarily. In those cases, communication and facilitation are best delinked from coercion.

A second defining characteristic of global space is diversity and complexity. To the extent that the law of global space seeks to bring out some degree of uniformity across borders, it must confront the great variation in the social systems and legal orders of the world's 190-plus nation states. To be effective, the law must not only allow the participants great leeway in defining the standards they will have to live with in order to avoid interference with embedded systems of national organization; it should not demand more convergence than is necessary to achieve fundamental goals. Also, because of the complexities and uncertainties in global space, law may seek to foster diversity and experimentation in order to promote the search for 'best practices'.

A third aspect of global space is the relative weakness of international systems of coercion in the face of national resistance. The range of sanctions available to back-up international standards is limited so that coercion is less available in the law of global space than it is in many aspects of municipal law. And even when sanctions are applied, they do not necessarily have the coercive power required to bring about conformity with legal norms.

In the theory of law in global space, we can therefore accept that law can communicate without either facilitating or coercing, and law can both communicate and facilitate without also coercing, but it is rare that law can be coercive if it does not also communicate or facilitate. For in the law of global space, pure coercive capabilities are weak and 'compliance' unlikely unless the affected parties accept and internalize the norms being applied. For that to happen, law must have performed communicative and facilitative functions.

Because the functions of law in global space differ from those of municipal law, it is no surprise to see that global institutions employ features that, while they may have counterparts in municipal law, are much more developed in global arenas. If one looks at the literature, we can see at least six such features:

i. Standards Not Rules
Although in municipal law much of law constitutes a set of relatively detailed rules knowable in advance, in the law of global space more emphasis is placed on broad and open-ended standards whose full meaning and impact must be worked out through multilevel, deliberative, and probably consensual means.

ii. Networks
In our conventional understanding of municipal law, the source of law is the legislature and its implementation the task of formally constituted bureaucracies. But in the law of global space, much of the task of norm elaboration occurs through the work of formal and informal networks that may include public officials, private actors, and technical experts.

iii. Decentered Deliberation and Negotiation
All types of law are formed by deliberation and negotiation. But in classical models, this occurs at the legislative level so that once the norms are promulgated they can, at least in theory, be imposed by authoritative and coercive means. In the law of global space, however, we see often it is understood that deliberation and negotiation will occur at all stages of the legal process.

iv. Multilevel Coordination
Received notions of law see it as a unitary command, issuing from a single identifiable sovereign. But the law of global space often involves the coordination of multiple levels of governance from the global to the strictly local.

v. Substance versus Procedure
Classical theories of law stress the importance of substantive norms, with procedure seen as simply a tool for ensuring compliance with these norms. But in the debates about the law of global space, more and more emphasis is placed on the procedural role law can play in the development and elaboration of broad standards and the coordination of multiple levels of governance.

vi. Soft and Hard Law
Hand in hand with tendencies to proceduralization, we see the increasing use of 'soft' or nonbinding norms. To the extent that the function of law in global space is to promote coordination rather than impose standards, and to the extent that

multilevel coordination works best when decisions are consensual, the use of soft guidance rather than hard standards becomes more important.

Each of these emerging features of the law of global space underscores the increased importance of communicative and facilitative aspects of law. Standards leave room for negotiation and diversity, networks promote communication and multilevel coordination, and proceduralism encourages the emergence of consensual norms and adaptability.

E. HUDEC ON GOVERNANCE ISSUES

Robert Hudec's discussion of trade law anticipated these developments. Hudec came to trade law after a period of practical work for the US government and maintained close contacts to GATT and its operations throughout his career. To explain the working of what be observed as he followed trade law 'in action', he had to disaggregate the three functions specified above and show that trade law could communicate and facilitate even when it was unable to coerce.

Hudec wrote his early work in an era when there was less transnational interaction than we see today. But his pragmatic insights proved to be prescient, particularly in terms of his treatment of three issues: (1) why diplomats may draft detailed rules but then include very broad exceptions, (2) why detailed trade rules may be preferable to open-ended bargaining even if the rules cannot be strictly enforced, and (3) why legal processes may advance substantive goals even when the legal standards are vague.

In his seminal essay, 'The GATT Legal System: A Diplomat's Jurisprudence', Hudec began by noting an apparent paradox between the style of the GATT agreement itself and the way that its parties went about enforcing it. On one hand, the substantive obligations of the GATT resembled a tax code in that they 'form a long, complex, and carefully drafted instrument which is on the whole fairly rigorous in its demands'.[5] On the other, the GATT's enforcement apparatus presented 'a front of ambiguity and uncertainty' that seemed "altogether at odds with the lawyerlike precision of the code".[6] The legal decisions produced through the enforcement mechanisms of the GATT tended to be 'deliberately obscure, often leaving it unclear whether there has even been a legal ruling at all'.[7] In light of this paradox, Hudec took a step back to ponder the very nature of legal obligations—how they were understood; what purposes they served; and most important, how they were meant to be used in practice.

---

5. R Hudec, 'The GATT Legal System: A Diplomat's Jurisprudence' (1970) reprinted in R Hudec, *Essays on the Nature of International Trade Law* (London: Cameron May, 1999) 17.
6. Ibid 17.
7. Ibid 17.

In so doing, Hudec saw beyond the doctrinal surface of trade law to find other forces at work. He viewed detailed rules and hard legal mechanisms as part of a bigger picture in which law and politics are intertwined. He resisted the temptation to transpose assumptions about municipal law onto international legal arrangements. He saw that the combination of substantive norms and a very open-ended legal process was better equipped to accommodate the diversity of interests among states, the variety of domestic pressures they face, and the shifting nature of regulatory politics.

> The key to understanding the GATT legal system is to recognize that GATT's law has been designed and operated as an instrument of diplomacy. Although the GATT legal system has many points in common with domestic models, the thing which sets it apart from others is the overriding concern for 'flexibility'—the insistence that the law's coercive pressures be applied in a controlled fashion which allows room for maneuver at every stage of the process. To achieve this flexibility, the GATT has developed forms and techniques which work to suppress the law's natural instinct for final decisions. Adjudication, and to some extent even legislation, are not the terminal events one is accustomed to look for in more conventional legal systems. They are, rather, stages of a continuous process in which there is usually more than one answer in the air at any one time, and in which no answers are really final until the results are in—and even then one may not be sure.[8]

In many ways, Robert Hudec was a lawyer's lawyer. In his research, he carefully delineated the rules that made up the substance and design of the GATT. But he also saw the importance of process and flexibility in the GATT legal system once the rules were established. For Hudec, these characteristics kept the diplomatic machinery moving and often proved capable of harnessing whatever basis for consensus existed at the time, despite the welter of rules that constituted the GATT framework. Although Hudec recognized that trade diplomacy began with the formal legal structures outlined by the substantive rules of GATT, he also knew that *which* rules received emphasis would 'vary greatly according to the prevailing community sentiment'.[9] Nevertheless, he appeared to believe that the ability of a legal system to capture the community sentiment was significant in its own right because it served as an important precondition for progress.

Hudec argued that 'the flexible sort of legal process found in the GATT has a capacity for creative development which is quite surprising for an

---

8. Ibid 75.
9. Ibid 76.

international institution.'[10] Through a discussion of the *Belgian Family Allowances* case, he showed how

> the techniques used to soften the application of established rules happens also to be a perfect mechanism for advancing and testing more novel propositions of law. And likewise, the tradition of treating all legal obligations as less-than-absolute mechanisms makes it much easier for governments to accept, and to use, something new. In short, however cautious and restricted the initial commitment by governments, there is some possibility of growth.[11]

These arguments are strikingly similar to those advocated by proponents of experimental forms of 'new governance' in contemporary times.

Almost four decades ago, Hudec saw a flexible legal process that tracks well with the emphasis on standards, soft law, and multilevel deliberation we see today. He found evidence in the evolution of the ITO into the GATT and in the application of GATT procedures that law often functions more to facilitate settlement through bargaining rather than setting a firm rule that everybody has to comply with. But he also saw the need for balance between traditional legal perspectives and the alternative forms of governance so prominent in the contemporary law of global space.

In a second early work, 'GATT or GABB? The Future Design of the General Agreement on Tariffs and Trade', Hudec pondered the role of substantive rules in international trade policy. At the time, he felt that the GATT as he had come to know it was in danger. 'Unless governments decide, fairly soon, to make a major effort to save the old GATT code', he argued, 'the pressures of a changing world will leave no choice but to commit the major part of GATT's work to GABB-type procedures'.[12] By GABB, Hudec meant a General Agreement on Better Bargaining—a hypothetical institution devoid of substantive rules.

> The question to be addressed is whether a code of substantive rules contributes to the success of [GATT] procedures . . . The major difference is that GABB procedures would not be directed toward formal judgment about previously defined normative standards, but would seek to produce a satisfactory result through consultation in which all the relevant social and economic factors would be considered in depth. One hesitates to say that GABB procedures reject all forms of normative judgment, for even in negotiations both sides will strive to marshal the community's normative sentiments as a tool of persuasion. But GABB would reject prior standards, trusting instead to the analysis of causes and consequences to reveal whatever normative judgments are appropriate.[13]

---

10. Ibid 76.
11. Ibid 76.
12. R Hudec, 'GATT or GABB? The Future Design of the General Agreement on Tariffs and Trade' (1971) reprinted in R Hudec (n 5 above) 79.
13. Ibid 109.

However, Hudec saw this as a mistake. He argued that 'conciliation' procedures alone would not work as effectively as the more rule-oriented GATT.

> The principal difficulty with the GABB approach is that it assumes a much greater degree of cooperation from the object government than usually exists... The object government may try to find reasons for not discussing the matter at all. It may try to draw out and divert what discussion there is by insisting on consideration of as many other things as possible. And it may, as a final defense, take whatever plausible position there is in defense of its action and hold that position to impasse.

In this cleverly constructed counterfactual argument, Hudec seemed to make the case that substantive rules prevented the abuse of a diplomat's jurisprudence. 'By rejecting not only the means but also the objective of imposing any more systematic normative framework on its procedures', he wrote, 'GABB puts itself at the mercy of any government practicing this all-too-well developed art'. In this sense, Hudec appeared to advocate 'bargaining in the shadow of the law' idea in which substantive rules functions more to facilitate settlement than setting out final and hard prescriptions requiring and receiving strict compliance.[14]

Hudec recognized that there were disadvantages to relying on substantive rules. Anticipating later scholarship, he understood that traditional forms of top down, command and control regulation could be too rigid to accommodate diversity and achieve the compromise required to adapt to exogenous shocks and exigent circumstances that would inevitably confront the legal framework over time. He asked whether '... the tendency to approach trade problems in terms of wooden rules may not blind the participants to the possibility of exceptional circumstances, as well as the general need to consider compromise'. But this was not a reason to eschew rules altogether. Contrary to some critics, Hudec argued that 'GATT practice has generally vindicated this expectation. Then as now, special circumstances were invariably argued as the excuse for such deviations, and the decisions permitting them were justified in these terms'.[15]

Hudec also observed that actors tended to rely on hard law only as a last resort. And when hard legal mechanisms had been utilized, they produced legal decisions and precedents that were sufficiently ambiguous as to facilitate a continued process deliberation among relevant actors. 'Formal legal rulings have seldom been sought before the parties are in evident deadlock. The rulings themselves have usually been expressed in terms that are soft and tentative, and have almost invariably been accompanied by an invitation to continue negotiations.'[16]

---

14. For the seminal treatment of bargaining in the shadow of the law, see R Mnookin and L Kornhauser, 'Bargaining in the Shadow of the Law: The Case of Divorce' (1979) 88 Yale LJ 950–77.

15. Hudec (n 12 above) 114.

16. Ibid 115.

Also addressed by Hudec is what he called '. . . the increasingly common argument that introduction of legal claims will 'poison the atmosphere' in a way which reduces the possibility of favorable action by the object government'. Unlike domestic models of enforcement, coercive compliance on the world stage is much more difficult to achieve, particularly by the more powerful actors. The imposition of 'hard' legal mechanisms such as formal adjudication, one could argue, would impinge upon the perceived sovereignty of a given state in a way that would cause them to disengage diplomatically from the legal process. But Hudec, showing his legalist side, did not see this happening in the case of the WTO/GATT. 'The short answer is,' he wrote, 'that the poison seems not have been noticed very much during the years when lawsuits were very common. To be sure, legal rulings cause some discomfort. That is one of their purposes. The word "poison" simply means that, for some reason, governments no longer consider the discomfort owing'.

Robert Hudec was a legalist in the sense that he saw a role for rules in the trade regime and world order more generally. But he was a pragmatic and qualified legalist, and he maintained his faith in rules in large measure because, in our terms, he emphasized the facilitative and communicative rather than coercive elements of the law. He saw that both general standards and detailed rules sometimes can play an important but not necessarily decisive role in a complex normative process. He showed how actors deploy rules in varied ways and how they may buttress them with other sources of power and persuasion.

Finally, Hudec recognized that the norms of trade law were part of a larger whole. In another one of his well-known essays, 'Transcending the Ostensible: Some Reflections on the Nature of Litigation Between Governments', Hudec illustrated through a discussion of subsidy code litigation during the Tokyo Round how legal processes may advance substantive goals even when the legal standards are vague. Although the subsidy code negotiations did not produce any real groundbreaking substantive results, for Hudec it highlighted subtle functions of the international legal process at work.

> If the story of the Subsidies Code teaches any lesson, it is to underline just how useful and inviting the overselling of international legal instruments can be. It solves problems for any number of participants in the political process. Consequently, one should be ready to find, in almost any particular structure of international obligations, a significant number of what might be called paper obligations—apparent engagements which do not in fact reflect any real consensus or commitment. And when one finds the tendency to create paper obligations coupled with the tendency to write more rigorous litigation rules, one can expect to find dramatic legal failures.[17]

---

17. R Hudec, 'Transcending the Ostensible: Some Reflections on the Nature of Litigation between Governments' (1987) reprinted in Hudec (n 5 above) 128.

For Hudec, the legal process at times could allow actors to 'temporize', to maintain the political momentum toward the eventual strengthening of legal norms without the precise (and potentially more controversial) legal rules. He had a vision of trade law as a governance system designed to harmonize and control the behavior of states. He saw that states are not unitary actors but made up of competing interests and tendencies. He saw that there are things that you can keep states from doing, but there are times when it is an error to try to constrain them too much. And he saw that detailed rules had a role to play in managing this regime but that other tools were needed as well. He showed it is often important to use broad standards that would permit flexibility and allow exceptions that would avoid irresolvable impasses. Hudec suggested that to understand trade law, one has to look for latent as well as manifest functions, and he illustrated this brilliantly by analyses of several trade disputes.

In many ways, Hudec's early work anticipated several aspects of the law of global space that we see today. In each of the cases discussed above, Hudec stresses that either rules or mandatory processes can communicate norms and facilitate internalization of the norms even though the likelihood of strong coercive measures is low. When these communicative and facilitative functions of the legal process are operating, legal standards are more likely to take hold; when they are not or they are blocked, it complicates the ability of the legal arrangement to achieve its goals.

The emphasis on communicative and facilitative functions of the law appear to track well with the so-called 'managerial approach' first articulated by Chayes and Chayes, which draws upon social constructivist insights to understand compliance with legal norms. For them, legally binding agreements and institutions promote interactive processes such as justification, deliberation, and persuasion, which establish and reinforce norms that actors use to pattern their behavior.[18] It follows from this logic that the more these legal norms become internalized, the more compliance becomes automatic.[19] Enforcement mechanisms have little

---

18. A Chayes and A Chayes, *The New Sovereignty: Compliance with International Regulatory Agreements* (Cambridge: Harvard University Press, 1998) 8. See also H Koh, 'Why do Nations Obey International Law?' (1997) 106 Yale LJ 2599–659. Koh, while broadly sympathetic to the managerial approach, critiques Chayes and Chayes for under-specifying the social processes that underpin the will to obey international law.

19. Conversely, the sources of noncompliance derive from three factors: the ambiguity and indeterminacy of treaty language, capacity limitations of states, and uncontrollable social or economic changes. Because of the intense negotiation process required to develop consensus (or 'least common denominator') between states on a given agreement, treaties are often ambiguously worded by design. Once in force, agreements are open to a wide degree of interpretation, which makes it difficult to determine noncompliance. Indeed, states might have different understandings of what the treaty means. In addition, states might not have the internal capacity to comply to the same degree as other states (because

to no role in facilitating compliance because of difficulties in pinning down a violation of an agreement, the costs of imposing coercive punishment, and risks in jeopardizing future cooperation. In sum, given the increased interdependence in the global environment and the intricate web of international regimes, inducing compliance through management, which emphasizes the communicative and facilitative functions of the law, is both preferable to and more effective than through coercion.[20]

While the managerialist arguments are extremely insightful, it may be a mistake to dismiss the coercive function of the law out of hand. Consider Hudec's 1987 critique of the role of developing countries in the GATT legal system. He argued that the efforts of developing countries to get special and differential treatment in GATT were a mistake, in significant part, because the very freedoms they sought made it harder for developing country governments to resist pressures to protect inefficient industries. In Hudec's words:

> A government's own trade-policy decisions are the most important determinant of its economic welfare. It is here that the GATT's legal policy can make its most important contribution to developing country welfare—or do the greatest harm ... the GATT's current policy [ie, of relieving developing countries from many trade disciplines] is harming developing countries more than helping them, even under the assumption that developing countries can be helped by infant industry policies.[21]

What led Hudec to make this argument? The key mechanism for change (and adopting the 'real' MFN prescription) would be the use of GATT and its coercive elements to make it easier for leaders in developing countries to resist pressures for inefficient forms of protection. However, the preferential treatment afforded to developing countries in the GATT system undermined these incentives.

---

of varying technical, scientific, or enforcement mechanisms, for example), though this is normally known *ex ante*. Finally, if a regime is to operate effectively over time, it must adapt to the transitory social, economic, and security conditions that affect the provisions of the agreement. The considerable lag time it usually takes to develop and implement appropriate revisions creates an environment conducive to noncompliance. A Chayes and A Chayes. 'On Compliance' (1993) Int'l Org 47, 175–206. On norms and political change, see M Finnemore and K Sikkink, 'International Norm Dynamics and Political Change' (1998) 55 Int'l Org 887–917.

20. For a critique of the managerial approach centered on the importance of enforcement, see G Downs, D Rocke and P Barsoom. 'Is the Good News about Compliance Good News about Cooperation?' (1996) Int'l Org 50, 379–406.

21. R Hudec, *Developing Countries in the GATT Legal System* (Aldershot: Gower, 1987) 159–60.

> The distinctive character of the current policy is not that it permits import protection, but that it makes no real effort to limit or to control such protection. Instead of providing politicians and officials with ground to oppose trade barriers, the GATT's current policy constitutes and authoritative blessing for them ... The whole point of the non-reciprocity doctrine is to protect developing-country export markets from any negative effects caused by protectionism at home. To the extent that it is successful, the non-reciprocity doctrine tends to remove the major incentive that export industries have ... for opposing protectionist policies at home ... The overall effect of the GATT's current policy, then is to intensify the political forces pressing politicians to use import protection as a solution to most problems.[22]

Without incentives—material and otherwise—to change their behavior, states are far less likely to comply with aspirant legal norms. The absence of such incentives in turn undermines the communicative and facilitative processes of the law that promote norm internalization and allow politicians the ability to 'temporize' in order to sustain momentum necessary to achieve substantive goals.

Hudec's perspective might therefore be more closely aligned with that of Harold Koh, who argues, 'The managerial model ... succeeds not just because of the power of discourse, but also because of the possibility of or "shadow of" sanctions, however remote that prospect might be'.[23] Moreover, Hudec would likely be sympathetic to Koh's argument regarding the need to theorize the transnational legal processes—interaction, interpretation, and internalization—by which domestic political structures eventually incorporate constraining norms. The exemptions afforded to developing countries in the GATT legal system, in Hudec's view, inhibited these processes in a way that undermined the potential for progress.

F. GLOBAL LEGAL SPACE AND THE FUTURE OF GOVERNANCE

A glance at some current issues in transnational law show the continued relevance of the functional analysis underlying Hudec's insights, and his instincts concerning the need for a complex system that employs communication, facilitation, and coercion in varying degrees and circumstances. In this section, we take up three contemporary issues and suggest ways in which Hudec's insights have continued relevance. The cases include but are not limited to trade matters. In this section we look at (a) proposals to reform the WTO to make it more supportive of development, (b) the operation of committees and councils in the WTO, and (c) the role of framework directives in the EU.

---

22. Ibid 170.
23. Koh (n 18 above) 2640.

i. Proposals to Reform the WTO

In recent years, a number of economists have raised questions concerning the impact of the WTO on developing countries and suggested the need for reform. While these experts understand the value of an open trading system for developing countries, they question whether strict adherence to all current WTO rules and disciplines is in the best interest of developing nations. Thus, they propose reforms that would allow developing countries more leeway in their relationship to the world economy.

A leading figure in this group is Harvard economist Dani Rodrik. In a chapter entitled 'The Global Governance of Trade as if Development Really Matters', Rodrik analyzes the relationship between free trade and development and comes to the conclusion that rapid and complete liberalization and strict adherence to various trade-related rules may not be in the best interest of developing countries. While he recognizes the importance of global rules, he calls for reform of trade law to give developing countries more policy space. In the essay, Rodrik asserts: '. . . a sound . . . architecture has to combine international harmonization and standard setting with generalized exit schemes, opt-outs, and escape clauses'.[24]

Rodrik's view of the importance of flexibility in application of trade rules comes from his view of the development process. He believes that institutions matter for development and that the key to rapid growth lies in the creation and maintenance of appropriate institutions. This means that he shares with most economists the view that *institution-building* is essential for development. Where he deviates from the mainstream, however, is in his views about how nations acquire effective institutions.

While many in the development field think that it is possible to derive an institutional blueprint from the experience of developed countries and use it to guide institutional development in the Global South, Rodrik rejects this idea and questions the effectiveness of externally guided change. Rather, he thinks that there are many viable forms of institutions and many routes toward their creation. For him, the optimal set of institutions and the best path toward them will require experimentation, innovation, and mechanisms capable of accommodating the local conditions and traditions of each developing country. He thinks that some of the fastest growing economies in the world, such as China, achieved this result by following paths that differ from the standard prescriptions and could have conflicted with some aspects of current trade law.

Rodrik's views on the need for flexibility in the trade regime rests on the importance of heterodoxy in development strategies and the risk that uniform application of international standards will stifle needed experimentation and preclude potentially desirable policies. But that does not mean that he opposes any

---

24. D Rodrik, *One Economics, Many Recipes: Globalization, Institutions, and Economic Growth* (Princeton: Princeton University Press, 2008) 196.

uniformity in trade law. Quite the contrary, he thinks global rules are important to ensure sound functioning of the global market, just as he thinks the law is important for domestic markets. Indeed, his belief in the importance of rules is one reason he favors flexibility. Thus he states that '(b)uilding opt-outs into the rules generally does better than the alternatives, which are either not to have rules or to have rules that are frequently flouted'.[25]

And Rodrik observes that the rules are more likely to be effective if they encourage convergence on a voluntary basis.[26]

While Rodrik makes no reference to Hudec (or any other trade lawyer) in his discussion, his view of the importance of combining universal rules with various forms of flexibility echo Hudec's analysis in important ways. Rodrik, like Hudec, believes in a rules-based global trading system. And, like Hudec, he understands that such a system cannot operate in a rigid manner, and that it must rely on communication and facilitation more than coercion. So both favor a complex combination of rules and ways to soften or defer the impact of the rules. Both want to include formal exceptions and opt-outs although Hudec also stresses the role of informal processes that can temper the strict application of the rules.

However, while it seems clear that at a general level Rodrik and Hudec agree on the need for some flexibility to be built into the architecture for the trade regime, they could be seen as disagreeing on the goals such flexibility should serve. In his 1987 book, Hudec argued that it was better for developing countries to be subject to MFN disciplines than to be free of reciprocal obligations. He concluded that on balance it was more in their interest to be bound by the obligation to open their markets than it was to enjoy the freedom to protect domestic industries on economic development grounds. But that freedom is one of the changes Rodrik argues for since one of his goals is to allow developing countries to be able to shield domestic producers from import competition while maintaining access to developed country markets.

We believe that these two positions can be reconciled, and that Hudec's deep understanding of the relationship between trade law and trade politics can help us flesh out Rodrik's proposals. While no one can say what Hudec would think about a proposal he never saw, there is evidence that he would have shared Rodrik's policy views and reason to believe we can use his insights on the relationship between trade law and politics to improve on the procedural suggestions sketched in Rodrik's chapter.

The first thing to establish is Hudec's position on infant-industry protection and the value of allowing such an exception. Like Rodrik, Hudec accepted the

---

25. Ibid 205.
26. Ibid.

case for such protection as a *theoretical* matter.²⁷ He saw that markets could 'fail' in such cases and recognized that if governments protected industries that would in the long run become globally competitive, it could enhance overall welfare. While admitting that such policies could promote development, Hudec questioned whether developing countries could effectively *implement* them. He saw three obstacles to making such protection work for the general good. The first was the limited ability of governments to pick the right winners. The second was that even potentially efficient industries may lose their competitive edge due to the subsidies protection gives them. And the third—and most important—is that once such protective policies are adopted, the pressure to protect inefficient as well as efficient industries will be too great to overcome.²⁸ For that reason, he thought it best for developing country governments to nail themselves to the mast of reciprocity rather than seek S&D treatment.

Rodrik understands that governments, like markets, may 'fail' and is aware of the risks that infant-industry protection could be inefficient. But he thinks that such government failure can be avoided and has two arguments to counter Hudec's pessimism about governmental capacity. First, Rodrik is able to point out that countries like Japan, Korea, Taiwan, and China effectively managed these policies, shielding industries behind protectionist walls initially but ensuring they would become globally competitive. Full information on the 'Asian miracle' was not available at the time that Hudec wrote his book, but now the role of protection in that story has been well-documented.

Second, Rodrik believes that there are procedures that can be implemented to ensure that the kinds of government failures Hudec feared can be overcome. Rodrik wants to change the trade rules to allow opt-outs from reciprocal obligations for a variety of reasons including developmental priorities.²⁹ But he would condition this privilege on proof that the policies in question were adopted through an open and transparent process in which all affected parties would be required to participate, and the decision maker enjoined to '. . . ensure that protectionist measures that benefit a small segment of industry at large cost to society would not have much chance of success'.³⁰

Hudec, like Rodrik, saw that there might be a way to build procedures into trade law that would ensure that infant-industry policies could be pursued without the risk of their being captured by inefficient domestic producers. He suggested that instead of being completely free of trade disciplines, developing countries might accept them subject to requests for a waiver under GATT Article XVIII.³¹

---

27. He stated that "The theoretical case for intervention is certainly a respectable one". Hudec (n 23 above) 147.
28. Hudec (n 21 above) 147–48.
29. Rodrik (n 24 above) 230–31.
30. Ibid 231.
31. Hudec (n 21 above) 231.

Such a process, if properly designed, could provide the discipline necessary to avoid misuse of the protectionist measures for development while allowing legitimate use for developmental goals.

While neither Hudec nor Rodrik developed a full-blown procedural proposal, it seems to us that Hudec's detailed analysis of the barriers to effective use of a developmental exception could illuminate any effort to flesh out Rodrik's suggestions. Thus, any effective procedure would have to ensure that the government has determined that there is a strong case that the results of its policy will be efficient in the long run, that the protected industry has strong incentives to become globally competitive without continued subsidy, and that mechanisms are in place to offset any disproportionate political power that might be exercised by inefficient domestic industries.

ii. The WTO: Communication and Facilitation through Councils and Committees

One of Hudec's core insights was that trade law needed to employ complex mechanisms and procedures designed to create closure when possible but only when some degree of real consensus exists. An example of just this type of mechanism can be found in some of the processes that operate within the WTO. While most scholarly attention with respect to governance in the WTO these days is focused on legal rules and formal litigation, in fact the WTO also includes less well-known processes that serve communicative and facilitative purposes. Like the EU, the WTO faces a tremendous challenge in balancing the diversity and complexity of the governed. Reaching decisions by consensus among some 150 members, with their diverse interests and cultures, can be extremely difficult. Therefore, it is not surprising that we can find alternative mechanisms performing communicative and facilitative functions similar to those that Hudec discovered in an earlier era of the trade regime. The resulting flexibility and the opportunity these mechanisms provide for dialogue and deliberation could be of substantial benefit to developing countries as they seek to carve out more policy space within the trade regime.

Take, for example, the operation of the councils that operate under the WTO umbrella. For each major trade area—goods, TRIPS, and services—a corollary council (eg, Goods Council) exists, which is responsible for the workings of the WTO agreements dealing with its respective areas of trade. Each council consists of all WTO members, reports to the General Council (the primary governing organ of the WTO), and contains subsidiary committees, which are further specialized in focus. These committees deal largely with tensions between national regulatory orders and international norms, practices, and standards. The committee process is soft, flexible, and open-ended, but operates in conjunction with the substantive rules that constitute the WTO framework.

The Services Council and its subsidiary committees provide interactive forums whereby member states and other actors can exchange information, seek clarification for and justify actions, and discuss their respective experiences.[32] In addition, these committees often engage in processes of norm elaboration. When a particular ambiguity in a legal provision exists or a new service arises and it is not clear whether and how existing law applies to it, issues related to the application of legal norms can be brought before the committee for discussion. In each of these senses, the committees provide institutional space in which routinized practices of communication and facilitation can occur. They are involved in the construction and dissemination of knowledge about the services economy. The body of knowledge, in turn, helps to provide a common foundation for discursive interaction and the formation of substantive consensus at the committee level and beyond.[33]

A second example of mechanisms designed primarily for communication and facilitation in the WTO system might be the SPS Agreement and the corresponding WTO committee. The SPS Agreement deals primarily with food safety and animal and plant health standards. It attempts simultaneously to help member states protect their consumers against known dangers and potential hazards related to animal, plant, and human health while 'avoiding the use of health and safety regulations as protectionism in disguise.[34] The SPS Agreement relies heavily on the communicative and facilitative functions of the law. According to the WTO Web site,

> The WTO's SPS Agreement encourages member countries to use standards set by international organizations . . . but it also allows countries to set their own standards. These standards can be higher than the internationally agreed ones, but the agreement says they should be based on scientific evidence, should not discriminate between countries, and should not be a disguised restriction to trade.[35]

An SPS committee consisting of Member States operates as a forum in which members can raise "specific trade concerns", monitor the harmonization of activities of the standard-setting international organizations, and elaborate upon

---

32. A Member might, for instance, make a presentation to the Committee on their experience with liberalization and regulatory reform in the financial services sector. This presentation then provides the basis for subsequent discussion, elaboration, questioning, and sharing of related experiences from other Members and nonstate actors such as international organizations. Written responses to many of the questions are later circulated, and the dialogue continues at subsequent meetings. A Lang and J Scott, 'The Hidden World of WTO Governance: Law and Constitutionalism in the WTO', unpublished manuscript.

33. This discussion in based on Lang and Scott (n 34 above).

34. WTO website <http://www.wto.org/english/thewto_e/minist_e/min99_e/english/about_e/08sps_e.htm>.

35. Ibid. Relevant standards include those set out by the FAO-WHO codex alimentarius. See also <http://www.wto.org/english/thewto_e/whatis_e/tif_e/agrm4_e.htm>.

the open-ended norms laid out in the agreement.[36] If necessary, however, 'the WTO "courts" [can give] shape and meaning to the requirements laid down. In so doing, they are performing the important function of determining the scope of Member State regulatory autonomy in important and sensitive areas, including in relation to food safety.'[37]

It seems that the WTO is working toward processes and policies that allow substantial diversity while protecting core international values and standards. To strike this balance, it relies heavily on the communicative and facilitative functions of law. These functions allow member states the flexibility to, in Hudec's words, temporize, but also promote the social and dialogical processes by which the cognitive consensus that underpins substantive rules is formed. The WTO committee system also falls back on a hard legal framework that provides the boundaries in which action is judged and, if necessary, coercive pressures exercised. As Hudec predicted, this hybrid combination of soft processes and hard rules encourages bargaining in the shadow of the law and allows flexibility in the application of general norms. It may be possible for developing countries to use these processes to secure some of the policy space that Rodrik and others think is necessary to ensure that trade law truly serves development.

iii. Hybrid Governance in the European Union

Not only does Hudec's approach to the law of global space help us deal with new issues in trade law: it also can be useful in other areas of international economic law. Hudec has taught us that it is often important to combine communication, facilitation, and coercion in global space. We can see such a constellation is the EU's use of 'hybrids' in which new forms of governance and more traditional legal approaches are combined to create a system that includes both communication and facilitation and, in some limiting cases, coercion. An excellent example can be found in the EU's Water Framework Directive (WFD).[38] The WFD is an ambitious piece of legislation that launched an innovative approach to maintaining and improving water quality throughout the EU. Designed to replace a series of centralized and traditional command and control directives that dealt separately with groundwater, surface water, drinking water, and so forth, the WFD mixes classic top-down regulatory modes and legally binding requirements with decentralized, bottom-up, participatory and deliberative processes; iterative planning; horizontal networks; stakeholder participation; information pooling; sharing of best practices; and nonbinding guidance.

---

36. See Lang and Scott (n 32 above).
37. Lang and Scott (n 34 above).
38. EC, Council Directive 2000/60/EC, 2000 OJ (L 327). Note that this discussion is drawn heavily from Trubek and Trubek 2007 (n 4 above). See also J Holder and J Scott, 'Law and Environmental Governance in the European Union' in G de Búrca and J Scott (eds), *Law and New Governance in the EU and US* (Hart Publishing, 2006).

The WFD emerged from a long process that involved a complex interaction among the EU Commission, Parliament, and Council. The resulting document includes broad standards and objectives as well as specific requirements. Member States are required to avoid any deterioration of water status and achieve "good water status" within a defined time frame. They are required to take measures "with the aim of achieving good water status", but the measures are described in rather general terms and the Directive does not define precisely what 'good water status' means.[39] While an Annex provides guidance for determination of what constitutes 'good' status for different types of water, it does not set final, uniform, and technically verifiable standards—that work is left to further work by the Commission and Member State authorities in the implementation phase.[40]

It is important to note that the WFD includes detailed rules as well as open-ended standards and employs binding legal obligations as well as nonbinding guidance and peer review. The system for classifying water status is open ended. The general concept of good water status is not fully defined in the Directive or the Annex. Rather, the Directive indicates that specific, harmonized, and binding standards for 'good' status are a long-term goal to be reached though subsequent processes and horizontal collaboration. But the WFD also contains some specific requirements of the type found in classic EU directives. The Water Framework Directive requires that countries adopt a strategy of integrated management based on all waters within each river basin and create river basin authorities by a specific date. It specifies that Member States promulgate a series of measures that deal with various types of waters and risks initiated.

In this regard, the WFD emphasizes the communicative and facilitative aspects of law, while maintaining the coercive elements necessary to provide the incentives to comply. By allowing as much national diversity as possible while holding Member States to measurable results in the long run, by tapping into the expertise of 27 Member States, by ensuring widespread public participation, and by facilitating information pooling and peer review, the WFD creates the potential for better environmental law and more effective management of water quality. Although the WFD process is still underway and much more needs to be done before the structures and measures it mandates are fully operational, and while we lack the detailed empirical evidence needed to determine if the system really will achieve all its ambitious goals, the WFD, nonetheless, stands as a strong example of how the functions of law in global space might fit together.

---

39. EC, Council Dir 2000/60/EC, art 4.
40. EC, Council Dir 2000/60/EC, annex V.

G. CONCLUSION

Over 30 years ago, Robert Hudec began to construct a vision for the role of law in the trade regime. He built it empirically from his deep knowledge of how things work and his understanding of both the value and the limits of law. Through close observation, he saw behavior that did not square with traditional conceptions of the law nor with what proponents of a regime devoid of substantive rules would predict. He viewed the roles and functions of the GATT legal framework in ways that most others did not. He saw how law could communicate, facilitate, and coerce. And he appreciated how these functions might sometimes work separately and sometimes work together. This vision is still with us. It will continue to live when all the specific rules and trade disputes he wrote about are long forgotten.

Of course, it would be too much to argue that Hudec had developed a full-blown theory that would account for all the features and functions of the contemporary law of global space. He did not spell out a systematic model to account for the relations between legal constraint and unregulated spaces, hard and soft law, detailed rules and open-ended standards, litigation and negotiation, or authority and dialogue. Although we might say he was a constructivist *avant la lettre*, he did not fully anticipate recent developments in the theories of global governance and law. Hudec did not fully incorporate the lessons of network analysis, the managerial approach, or multilevel governance theory. He wrote before the rise of 'new governance' or experimentalist theories of law which suggest that law at all levels from the municipal to the international may be undergoing transformation. There is plenty of work left to be done. But Hudec built a solid foundation on which all of us and future generations can build.

8. WINNERS AND LOSERS IN THE PANEL STAGE OF THE WTO DISPUTE SETTLEMENT SYSTEM

BERNARD HOEKMAN, HENRIK HORN AND
PETROS C MAVROIDIS[*]

A. Introduction 151
B. The Data 154
C. A Broad Characterization of the Distribution of Claims 155
    I. The Distribution of Bilateral Disputes Across Groups 156
    II. The Distribution of Claims Across Groups 156
    III. The Distribution of Claims Across Provisions/Agreements 158
D. A Broad Characterization of the Distribution of Outcomes 160
E. Concluding Remarks 163

A. INTRODUCTION

Most research on the role of developing countries in the WTO Dispute Settlement (DS) system has focused on their propensity to participate as complainants, respondents, and third parties. Much of this line of research has sought to examine claims that developing countries are underrepresented as complainants and/or overrepresented as respondents in the DS system. Several reasons have been suggested why such biases are likely. For instance, developing countries may lack economic/legal capacity to defend their rights; or 'power' considerations might play a role (fear of issue linkage). Alternatively, market size considerations may play a role, with the limited scope for credibly threatening retaliation acting as a disincentive to bring cases.[1] The research along these lines has looked for

---

[*] Of the World Bank, Washington and CEPR, London; Research Institute of Industrial Economics (IFN), Stockholm and Bruegel, Brussels and CEPR, London; and Columbia Law School, New York, University of Neuchâtel, CEPR, London respectively. We are very grateful to our discussant Richard Steinberg and to Chad Bown, Marc Busch, and Bill Davey for helpful comments on the conference version of this paper. We are also indebted to Ivan Crowley and Martin Olsson for excellent research assistance and to Pehr-Johan Norbäck and Fredrik Hesselborn for help with the dataset. Horn and Mavroidis gratefully acknowledge financial support from the World Bank and Horn also from the Marianne and Marcus Wallenberg Foundation. The views expressed are personal and should not be attributed to the World Bank.

[1]. There is also research arguing that there are good reasons why one would expect to see developing countries *under*-represented as respondents in the DS system, reflecting the fact that the small size of markets acts as a disincentive for trading partners to bring cases—the expected 'rate of return' is too low.

circumstantial evidence in terms of biased participation or operation of the DS system.

If the above-type of allegations are well-founded, it can be argued that reduced participation does not capture the full damage done to developing countries. The same factors that deter developing countries from participating as complainants in the first place may also cause disadvantages in those cases where developing countries do participate. Lack of legal resources may adversely affect the quality of the legal argumentation by developing countries. Very little systematic evidence exists beyond the pioneering work of Hudec[2]—at least as far as we are aware—on whether developing countries, when they actually *do* participate in the DS system, fare better or worse than richer countries. The purpose of this paper is to take a first small step in enhancing our knowledge on this subject by *examining whether the outcomes with regard to legal claims differ between developing and developed countries*.

This paper employs a dataset describing various aspects of the DS system that have been compiled under a World Bank project (hereinafter, the dataset) to take a first cut at exploring what the experience to date suggests regarding this question.[3] The objective underpinning the assembly of the dataset was to systematically compile information on various aspects of the DS system, in order, *inter alia*, to facilitate assessment of its implications for developing countries. The dataset contains a large number of variables that reflect various aspects of developing country participation in disputes, as well as the procedural aspects of disputes. The most recent version covers all 351 WTO disputes initiated through the official filing of a *Request for Consultations* at the WTO, from January 1, 1995 until December 31, 2006. For these disputes, the dataset covers exhaustively all stages of dispute settlement proceedings, from the moment when consultations are requested, to the eventual implementation of the panel/Appellate Body (AB) rulings (or, if not yet finalized, the last stage of the DS process that has been officially reported). The dataset contains several hundred variables, providing information on various aspects of the legal procedure. Horn and Mavroidis describe the structure of the dataset,[4] and they provide some descriptive statistics employing the data.[5]

---

2. RE Hudec, *Enforcing International Trade Law: The Evolution of the Modern GATT Legal System* (Salem, NH: Butterworth Legal Publishers, 1993).

3. The dataset can be freely accessed and downloaded at The World Bank, 'WTO Dispute Settlement Database' <http://www.worldbank.org/trade/wtodisputes> accessed 17 August 2008.

4. H Horn and PC Mavroidis, 'The WTO Dispute Settlement System Data Set: User's Guide' <http://www.worldbank.org/trade/wtodisputes> accessed 17 August 2008.

5. H Horn and PC Mavroidis, 'The WTO Dispute Settlement System Data Set: Some Descriptive Statistics' <http://www.worldbank.org/trade/wtodisputes>.

The dataset contains information on the legal claims made in each dispute, as well as a rough classification as to whether each specific claim was accepted or not by the panel/AB. In this paper we use these data to examine whether there are any systematic differences between developing and developed countries in terms of the outcomes of cases at the panel stage. The approach we take to classify outcomes is straightforward: we simply count the share of claims made by complainants in each case that was upheld by the panel. While this tells us nothing about the relative economic importance of different claims to the complainants, it does allow us to explore whether there are substantial differences across country groups in terms of one objective measure of the outcomes of DS cases, and this is what we are interested in. More generally, an analysis of number of claims made by countries is of interest in its own right—to our knowledge this has not been the subject of analysis to date in the literature.

A problem with our unit of account in assessing outcomes is that some measures (and thus some claims) will be more important than others to the claimants. Our approach does not provide any insight into this very important practical dimension of dispute cases. However, it is very difficult, if not impossible, for researchers to determine from the data on a DS case what 'really mattered' and what did not. Indeed, in some situations being found to have violated a WTO agreement or commitment may actually be the preferred outcome for a respondent: eg, if a government sees this as helpful in pursuing a policy reform that is opposed by a powerful domestic constituency. For instance, it has been suggested to us that the Chilean alcoholic beverage dispute is a case in point. What should be meant by 'winning' such a dispute, and how should the analyst be able to correctly classify the outcome?

This problem also affects the approach taken by Hudec, who focused on whether respondents comply.[6] Hudec argued that the appropriate measure of the outcome of a DS case is the policy result of a dispute, that is, whether the case lead to the implementation of policy changes by the 'losing' party. While this has the advantage of being an objective measure that is comparable across cases, it is not necessarily a good measure of the outcome of a dispute. Indeed, there is no obvious 'appropriate' measure of outcomes of DS cases. Even if the variable of interest is held to be implementation, this can occur on either substantive or procedural grounds. If a complainant loses on all substantive claims but nonetheless wins the case on the grounds of lack of notification, the respondent will be requested to notify. But this is unlikely to make much of a difference in practice, even if the respondent would comply with 100 percent. More generally, as already mentioned, 'losers' may actually perceive that they have won, eg, if this helps the government concerned pursue policies that it thinks are beneficial but were impeded by domestic political economy constraints. Or the objective may

---

6. Hudec (n 2 above).

simply have been to raise the political profile of a policy matter, perhaps as part of a strategy to place the subject on the agenda of a negotiating round. Although obviously important, implementation as the benchmark is not necessarily the most appropriate indicator of outcomes, given the absence of information regarding the 'true' underlying objectives of the parties to a dispute. While our focus in this paper is narrower than the one advocated by Hudec, it is arguably a useful complement to the approach he pioneered. The number of claims can be readily observed and measured—there is no need for subjective assessments or interpretation by observers: the number of claims made in a dispute is simply a datum.

The analysis in the paper is limited to an initial exploration of the data with a view to identifying more precise hypotheses for future research, both qualitative and quantitative, that can be pursued using the database. The data on number of claims made by different groups of countries across different types of policy areas/WTO disciplines throw up many questions regarding the determinants of the expected payoffs of alternative legal strategies and the observed behavior of WTO Members—including whether to bring a dispute, whether to participate in one as a co-complainant, the importance of the identity of co-complainants, the number of claims to bring—and the factors that affect the rulings of WTO panels/AB (eg, nationality of panelists, role of legal representation, and legal precedent).

B. THE DATA

The focus of our analysis is on *bilateral disputes*, where the term *bilateral* refers to a dyad of WTO Members (complainant, defendant). A bilateral dispute might contain more than one legal claim. Multiple complaints (for instance, DS27, *EC—Bananas III*, where four WTO Members challenged the consistency of EC practices), are disaggregated into a number of bilateral disputes equal to the number of complainants involved.[7] The 'unit of account' that is the center of attention in the analysis are *legal claims* as defined in the WTO case law on Art. 6.2 DSU: a legal claim comprises a factual matter and the legal provision that it allegedly violates.

Our interest is in the outcomes of the cases. The universe of outcomes that form our dataset comprises the findings of WTO adjudicating bodies as they appear in the Conclusions and Recommendations Section of each report. We classify outcomes into three groups: (1) claims where the complainant prevailed, (2) claims where the defendant prevailed, and (3) a residual group of claims

---

7. So far, there has never been a case before a WTO panel where more than one defendant has been involved.

where the outcome is unclear. While in principle a panel should either find for or against a claim by a complainant, practice has made inclusion of this third category a necessity. One reason is that claims may not be addressed by a panel as result of the exercise of judicial economy. Outcomes also may not correspond to specific claims initiated by the complainant: this is the case where a panel, for instance, reviews, on its own initiative, its competence to adjudicate a particular claim.[8] Insofar as they are reported, we also map intermediate findings—those that *might* have a bearing on the final finding (that is, the finding on the claim as presented by the complainant) but which are distinct from final findings—into the third category.

In this paper, WTO Members are classified into four groups: G2—the EC[9] and the United States; IND—15 other industrialized countries, including three high-income WTO Members that are (self-)classified as developing in the WTO (Hong Kong, South Korea, and Singapore), DEV—developing countries other than LDCs; and LDC—the group of least-developed countries. The exact classification is described in Appendix 1. The LDC group comprises the countries that the United Nations has defined to be least developed. All OECD countries are mapped to IND, as are all current EC members in the period before they acceded to the EC. The DEV group consists of all other countries.

C. A BROAD CHARACTERIZATION OF THE DISTRIBUTION OF CLAIMS

We use information on all bilateral disputes between 1995 and 2006 in which a panel was formed and issued a report, and in which at least one legal claim was made. There are in total 144 such bilateral disputes.[10]

---

8. WTO adjudicating bodies have, according to standing case-law under Art. 6.2 DSU, the competence to unilaterally review their competence to adjudicate a dispute and are not, consequently, *necessarily* bound by the content of a request for establishment of a panel as submitted by the complainant.

9. We follow the evolution of the EC membership in the sense that up to January 1, 2004, EC is EC-15; after that date, EC-25; and as of January 1, 2007, it is EC-27.

10. The difference between the 351 formal disputes brought between 1996 and 2006 and the 144 that are the focus of this paper reflects cases that were settled, dropped, or remain pending. The consultation process and more generally the role and effectiveness of the DS system in getting WTO members to settle cases 'out of court' is an important and relatively neglected dimension of the WTO process. In this paper, as is true of most of the literature, the focus is on those cases that went to the panel stage. See, eg, Davey for a discussion of the effectiveness of consultations. W Davey, 'Evaluating WTO Dispute Settlement: What Results Have Been Achieved Through Consultations and Implementation of Panel Reports?' (2005) University of Illinois College of Law Research Paper 5–19.

TABLE 1. DISTRIBUTION OF THE NUMBER OF BILATERAL DISPUTES BY GROUP PAIRING

		Respondent			
		G2	IND	DEV	TOT
Complainant	G2	20	22	13	55
	IND	35	5	7	47
	DEV	33	4	5	42
	TOT	88	31	25	144

i. The Distribution of Bilateral Disputes Across Groups

Table 1 provides a classification of these disputes across the various groups of complainants and respondents. As is often remarked, LDCs are completely absent, reflecting the fact that the few instances where they have participated in the DS system, the cases have not gone beyond the consultations stage. The shares of the three groups as complainants in the bilateral disputes are fairly evenly distributed: G2 accounts for slightly more (55 cases or 38 percent) than IND (33 percent) and DEV (29 percent). The role of G2 as a respondent is much more highly concentrated: the EC or United States are respondents in 88 of the disputes (61 percent of all cases), compared to 22 percent for IND and 17 percent for DEV. Noteworthy is that G2 countries are involved on one or the other side in 85 percent of the bilateral disputes in the dataset. Both IND and DEV mainly target G2 when acting as complainants—presumably reflecting the fact that these are the two largest markets in the world—while the G2 spread their complaints more evenly across each other and the two other groups.

It should be noted that although the DEV group encompasses 74 countries, only 18 have brought a case. Of these 18 countries, Brazil and India account for more than half of the total number of bilateral disputes brought by DEV (Appendixes 6 and 7).

ii. The Distribution of Claims Across Groups

As noted above, the unit of account used in this study is a 'legal claim'. The 144 bilateral disputes in the dataset involved a total of 2,369 claims. A total of 301 different legal grounds are quoted according to the dataset. The majority of cases have a limited number of claims—between 1 and 15—but a few have over 80 (Figure 1). The mode is two claims. Table 2 provides a breakdown of these claims across the three groups of Members. A first striking feature is that the IND group accounts for 1089 of the 2,369 claims, or almost half (46 percent) of all the claims that have been made during the first 12 years the WTO DS system was operational. This contrasts with IND's 33 percent share of the 144 bilateral disputes in the dataset. Thus, in this crude sense IND is overrepresented (they include more claims per bilateral dispute than any other group). DEV accounts

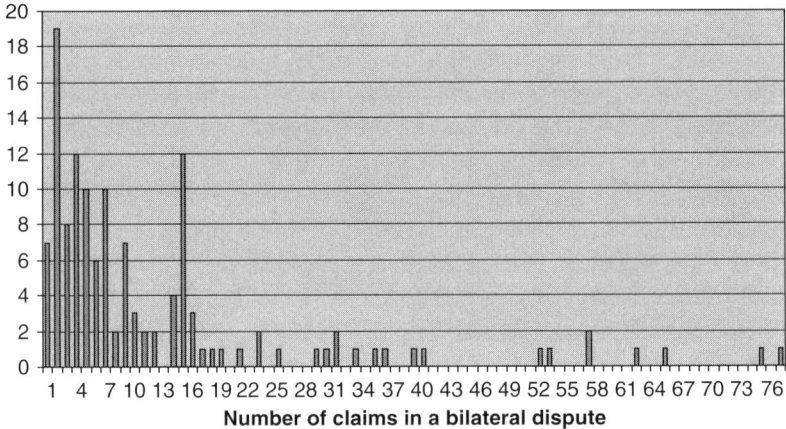

FIGURE 1. DISTRIBUTION OF NUMBER OF CLAIMS IN THE 144 BILATERAL DISPUTES

for 27 percent of all claims, which is closely in line with their 29 percent share of all bilateral disputes. Consequently, G2 is 'underrepresented', accounting for only 27 percent of all claims, while acting as complainants in 38 percent of all bilateral disputes. An interesting question, therefore, is why the G2 on average—across all the disputes in which they have been complainants—make fewer claims than DEV and IND.

The claims by all three groups, but in particular by IND, are heavily skewed toward G2 as a respondent. While acting as a respondent in 61 percent of the bilateral disputes in the dataset, they are the targets of 78 percent of all claims. The situation is the opposite for developing countries: they are respondents in 17 percent of the bilateral disputes but only confront 9 percent of the claims. The role of G2 as a complainant against DEV is very modest compared with those of IND and DEV: G2 only accounts for 23 percent of the claims against DEV, while IND accounts for 38 percent and DEV for 39 percent.

TABLE 2. DISTRIBUTION OF NUMBER OF LEGAL CLAIMS BY GROUP PAIRING

		Respondent			
		G2	IND	DEV	TOT
Complainant	G2	380	201	48	629
	IND	971	37	81	1089
	DEV	489	79	83	651
	TOT	1,840	317	212	2369

TABLE 3. AVERAGE NUMBER OF CLAIMS WITHIN EACH GROUP PAIRING

		Respondent		
		G2	IND	DEV
Complainant	G2	19	9.14	3.7
	IND	27.7	7.4	11.6
	DEV	14.8	19.8	16.6

There are two rather different ways to view the burden imposed by the DS system on DEV. If judged from the point of view of the number of bilateral disputes in which they have to put up a legal defense, 17.4 percent of the bilateral disputes are directed at DEV. On the other hand, if the burden is measured by the number of legal claims that need to be refuted, 8.9 percent of all claims are against DEV. Table 3 provides another way to characterize activity with regard to legal claims. It depicts the average number of claims for each pair (complainant group, respondent group). There is significant variation, both for each complainant group across respondents, and for each respondent group across complainants. At the lower end, a G2 complaint against a DEV country on average involves 3.7 claims, while an IND complaint against a G2 country on average comprises almost 28 claims. This pattern presumably reflects a complicated interaction between trade patterns, features of the various agreements under which the trade takes place, and all other factors going into the decision on legal strategy.

iii. The Distribution of Claims Across Provisions/Agreements

The majority of claims made in the disputes relate to the three contingent protection-related disciplines of the WTO: the agreements on anti-dumping (AD), subsidies and countervailing measures (SCM), and safeguards (SG) (Table 4; detailed information on the number of claims by WTO provision and country grouping is given in Appendices 2-5). This is not surprising, given that in absolute terms the case law on these three instruments constitute almost 25 percent of all disputes. In part, this is simply a reflection of the significant increase in the use of these three instruments (see Table 5). The high share of SG claims is somewhat misleading in that they do not imply these types of cases have come to be an important share of all DS. The high number of claims instead reflects similar (identical) cases being brought by multiple WTO members. More specifically, the US steel safeguard cases alone (DS248–54, 258–59) represent almost 80 percent of the total number of SG claims made. This compares to the 15 percent share of the United States in the total number of safeguard actions imposed during the 1995–2005 period.[11]

---

11. The United States launched ten safeguard investigations during this period.

A similar point can be made in respect of disputes concerning the use of sanitary and phytosanitary (SPS) measures. Of the 286 claims made in respect of the SPS Agreement, over 90 percent pertain to three related cases: the *EC—Approval and Marketing of Biotech Products* disputes (DS 291/292/293). Another factor that may explain why the majority of claims occur for these three instruments is the fact that detailed procedural requirements are laid out for actions under each to be WTO-compliant. Many of these requirements are not expressed in precise language. A number of AD disputes concern Art. 12, which calls for the investigating authorities to publish the essence of their findings. However, it does not spell out exactly what must be published.[12]

TABLE 4. THE DISTRIBUTION OF CLAIMS ACROSS AGREEMENTS/WTO PROVISIONS

Provision/Agreement	No of Claims
Anti-dumping (AD)	615
Agreement on Textiles and Clothing (ATC)	13
Agreement on Agriculture (AA)	46
DSU:3.7	16
GATS	30
GATT:II	23
GATT:III	88
GATT:VI	69
GATT:X	46
GATT:XI	19
GATT:XIII	10
GATT:XIX	69
GATT:XX	25
Subsidies and Countervailing Measures (SCM)	269
Safeguards (SG)	580
Sanitary & Phytosanitary Measures (SPS)	285
Technical Barriers to Trade (TBT)	14
TRIPs	61
WTO:XVI.4	30

---

12. While one may expect that if specific provisions have been interpreted in a consistent manner by panels/AB. these should give rise to fewer disputes than for provisions where the case law has not been uniform, this hypothesis remains to be tested. In practice it is not straightforward to identify a benchmark for establishing which provisions have been interpreted in a uniform manner, and which have not.

TABLE 5. USE OF THE WTO AGREEMENTS ON SAFEGUARDS AND ANTI-DUMPING, 1995–2005[13]

	Number of Safeguard Investigations Initiated	Number of Definitive Safeguard Measures Imposed	Number of Anti-dumping Investigations Initiated	Number of Definitive Anti-dumping Measures Imposed
Developing/transition economy members	120	59	1,687	1,126
Developed economies	25	11	1,225	696

Source: Bown

D. A BROAD CHARACTERIZATION OF THE DISTRIBUTION OF OUTCOMES

We next turn to the reaction by panels to the 2,369 legal claims recorded in our dataset. As described above, the outcomes are coded using three categories: win, loss, or unclear. Table 6 gives the number of successful claims for each pair of complainant and respondent, as well as totals for the various categories.[14]

Of interest here is the average number of successful claims. This can be calculated in different ways. One is to simply divide the total number of successful claims ('wins') for a given group by the total number of claims made by the

TABLE 6. TOTAL NUMBER OF SUCCESSFUL CLAIMS BY GROUP PAIRING

		Respondent			
		G2	IND	DEV	TOT
Complainant	G2	237	127	43	407
	IND	538	35	41	614
	DEV	300	18	58	376
	TOT	1,075	180	142	1,397

---

13. CP Bown, 'Global Anti-dumping Database' (September 2006) World Bank and Brandeis University <http://people.brandeis.edu/~cbown/global_ad/> accessed 15 August 2008.

14. Detailed data by dispute is presented in Appendix 6.

TABLE 7. SHARE OF SUCCESSFUL CLAIMS BASED ON THE SUM OF ALL CLAIMS BY GROUP PAIR (%)

		Respondent			
		G2	IND	DEV	TOT
Complainant	G2	62.4	63.2	89.6	64.7
	IND	55.4	94.6	50.6	56.4
	DEV	61.3	22.8	69.9	57.8
	TOT	58.4	56.8	67.0	59.0

group for a specific pairing. Data on this measure are reported in Table 7. It is striking that when comparing the three groups' overall success rates, they are remarkably similar: when acting as complainants, G2, IND, and DEV win between 56 percent and 65 percent of the claims they advance, when calculated as a share of all the claims each group makes (Table 7). Similarly, the complainant on average wins 56–67 percent of all claims regardless of whether it is directed vis-à-vis G2, IND, or DEV.

Although shares of successful claims are similar across many group pairs, Table 7 also reveals a significant variability across several complainant-respondent constellations. In particular, DEV countries have been much less successful against IND countries than they have been against the G2 or other DEV countries. However, the 22.8 percent success rate is to a significant degree explained by the large number of claims in DS 312 *Korea—Certain Paper*, where Indonesia acted as complainant. It thus, probably, suffers from selection bias. But DEV have also been less successful in two of the other three bilateral disputes they have had against IND. The other 'outliers' in terms of success rates are IND against other IND countries and G2 versus DEV—in both instances registering around a 90 percent success rate. These numbers indicate that the cases brought were directed toward rather clear-cut violations of the relevant WTO disciplines.

Table 8 provides an alternative picture of the average success rates of claims. In order to compile it, we first calculate the fraction of claims that are successful for each dispute and then compute the average of these fractions. This method, in a certain sense, takes greater account of the variability across disputes of success rates.[15] The picture emerging from Table 8 appears to be rather similar to the one provided by Table 7. Again, the overall success rates of the three groups

---

15. To see the difference between the two methodologies, consider the following example. Let there be two disputes A and B for some complainant-respondent pairing. In A there was one claim, and it was accepted, and in B there were two claims, one of which was accepted. One view of this is to say for this pairing, there were a total of three claims and two of these where successful so the average success rate is two-thirds—this is how Table 6 is constructed. An alternative would be to do as in Table 7, and say that the success

162 DEVELOPING COUNTRIES IN THE WTO LEGAL SYSTEM

TABLE 8. AVERAGE PERCENTAGE SUCCESSFUL CLAIMS BY GROUP PAIRINGS BASED ON SUCCESS RATES FOR EACH BILATERAL DISPUTE

		Respondent			
		G2	IND	DEV	TOT
Complainant	G2	68.7	70.8	94.1	77.9
	IND	53.9	95.6	72.7	74.1
	DEV	76	43.5	59.8	59.8
	TOT	66.2	70	75.5	70.6

when acting as complainants are comparable, while there are greater differences across the bilateral disputes where each of the three groups acted as a respondent. In particular, 66 percent of all disputes against G2 succeeded, while the corresponding number for disputes against DEV is 75.5 percent.

A natural question is whether the number of claims that are made affects the success rate. For instance, it might be thought that a large number of claims reflects a careful examination of the legal situations, or alternatively, careless litigation. Figure 2 provides some information on this. An alternative hypothesis is that a large number of claims will lead the courts to use judicial economy or to not adjudicate for other reasons. Figure 3 shows evidence compatible with such an argument. As can be seen, there is a clear tendency that with larger number of claims, an increasing fraction is not being adjudicated. It is also noteworthy, however, that 119 out of the 144 bilateral disputes, (over 80 percent of cases) record no instance of non-adjudication.

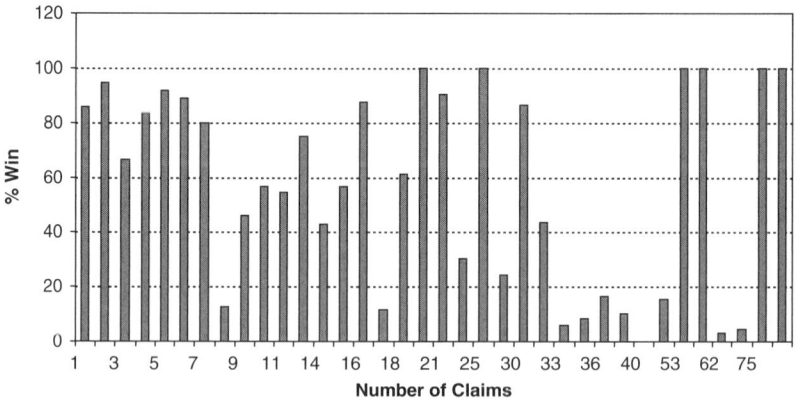

FIGURE 2. AVERAGE SUCCESS RATE OVER ALL BILATERAL DISPUTES

---

rate was 1 in dispute A and .5 in dispute B, so the average success rate is $(1 + .5)/2$ or three-fourths.

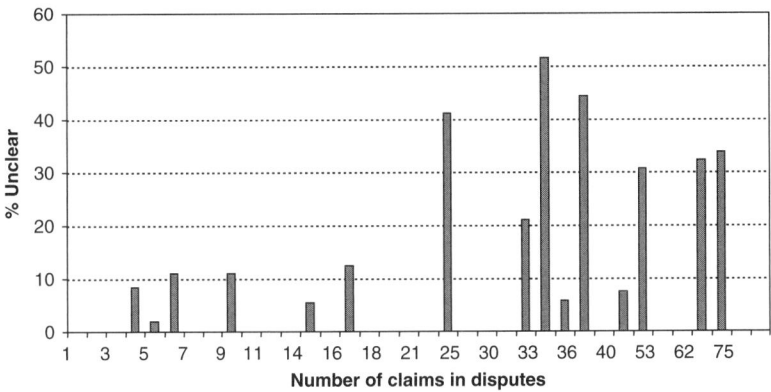

FIGURE 3. AVERAGE RATE OF NONADJUDICATED CLAIMS OVER ALL BILATERAL DISPUTES

Another relevant question is whether success rates vary across types of disputes. Table 9 reports for each WTO agreement the number of claims that are won, lost, and unclear, as well as the percentage distribution for each type of outcome for claims under the agreement. Across WTO disciplines, the largest number of claims made in the DS system during 1995–2006 referred to the AD, GATT, SG, SPS, and SCM agreements (in declining order). The average 'win rate' across all claims and agreements is 59 percent. Claims under AD have among the lowest win rates (30 percent), while win rates for claims under the SCM and SPS agreements are also below the average, at 44 percent and 51 percent. The SG is *sui generis* in that the US steel cases dominate this category—they account for 447 of the 580 SG claims (77 percent). Thus, of the agreements that have generated a large numbers of claims in the aggregate, only one—GATT—is generally associated with a high share of 'wins' (68 percent). What underlies this disparity requires further research; possible explanations are that GATT articles are well-understood, with an extensive case law that predates the formation of the WTO, and that they are relatively broad and unambiguous to interpret (eg, disciplines such as national treatment, tariff bindings, MFN). Whatever the reason, there appears to be less certainty/clarity for claimants and/or the panels when it comes to assessing claims pertaining to the AD, SCM, and SPS agreements.

E. CONCLUDING REMARKS

This paper has presented and discussed one dimension of a new, comprehensive dataset on WTO dispute settlement—the number of claims made in cases and the extent to which they are accepted by panels. The data reveal that on the

TABLE 9. OUTCOME OF CLAIMS IN BILATERAL DISPUTES FOR VARIOUS AGREEMENTS

Agreement	Data	Outcome			Total
		Win	Lose	Unclear	
AD	Number of claims	183	329	103	615
	Row percent	30	53	17	100
ATC	Number of claims	12	1	0	13
	Row percent	92	8	0	100
AA	Number of claims	43	2	1	46
	Row percent	93	4	2	100
DSU	Number of claims	9	4	3	16
	Row percent	56	25	19	100
Enabling Clause	Number of claims	1	0	0	1
	Row percent	100	0	0	100
GATS	Number of claims	23	5	2	30
	Row percent	77	17	7	100
GATT	Number of claims	257	88	36	381
	Row percent	68	23	9	100
GPA	Number of claims	0	1	0	1
	Row percent	0	100	0	100
Import Licensing	Number of claims	6	2	0	8
	Row percent	75	25	0	100
Rules of Origin	Number of claims	0	8	0	8
	Row percent	0	100	0	100
Ref Paper(GATS)	Number of claims	2	1	0	2
	Row percent	67	33	0	100
SCM	Number of claims	118	112	39	269
	Row percent	44	42	14	100
SG	Number of claims	560	14	6	580
	Row percent	97	2	1	100
SPS	Number of claims	145	55	85	285
	Row percent	51	19	30	100
TBT	Number of claims	1	2	11	14
	Row percent	7	14	79	100
TRIMS	Number of claims	5	2	0	7
	Row percent	71	29	0	100
TRIPS	Number of claims	17	30	14	61
	Row percent	28	49	23	100
WTO	Number of claims	15	10	5	30
	Row percent	50	33	17	100
Total	Number of claims	1398	666	305	2369
	Row percent	59	28	13	100

one hand there is very substantial variation across types of disputes (the WTO agreements that are invoked) and types of countries—with lower income countries (DEV) tending to put forward a significantly greater number of claims than higher income WTO members. But the data on the other hand suggest that the rate of success in WTO DS cases—if measured by the share of claims 'won'—is broadly similar across industrialized and developing countries, despite the differences in 'capacity' and 'administrative sophistication' that presumably exist across the groups, in particular DEV relative to IND and G2. This is somewhat counterintuitive in that it goes against the literature which places a lot of emphasis on the importance of embedded, institutional expertise as a factor that importantly influences the outcome in WTO litigation.

While capacity constraints of various types certainly may constrain the use of the DS system—ie, result in fewer cases being brought by DEV members—the data suggest that *conditional* on a case being brought that results in the formation of a DS panel, the success rate as measured by share of claims 'won' is similar. As things stand, absent additional research on these questions, the data do not support the argument that the DEV group is disadvantaged because they cannot display expertise comparable to that of G2 and IND. Understanding the reasons for this finding requires further research but may well reflect the fact that the countries in the DEV group that make most use of the DS system are generally either large or middle-income. Thus, the participation constraint for these countries may be much less than it is for lower-income countries. In addition, initiatives such as the Advisory Centre on WTO Law (ACWL) should have helped to level the playing field with regard to access to legal expertise for smaller and poorer countries.

An interesting question for which we know fewer potential explanations is why we observe such large differences in the number of claims across complainant-respondent groupings. The type of case/dispute clearly plays a role: Anti-dumping, SCM, and SPS all have high numbers of claims. All three agreements are rather technical and impose numerous disciplines that can—and do—give rise to violation claims. Understanding this dimension of the DS caseload is a subject on which further research is needed, in particular the extent to which it can explain the large discrepancy in the average number of claims brought by countries with different levels of per capita incomes. Even if the number of claims brought is just one, perhaps minor, dimension of the DS system, we believe that additional analysis of the determinants of the pattern of claims revealed by the dataset could generate useful insights into the behavior/strategy of countries. Possible hypotheses that could be explored in empirical analysis using the database include the following:

(a) Is legal capacity not an issue because panels are quite intrusive and can make up for deficient arguments? How effective has been the use of discovery powers by panels?

(b) Is it the case that legal expertise is not that costly and/or readily available (eg, as a result of the ACWL) and that even WTO Members with limited institutional expertise can easily outsource/obtain it?
(c) Is it the case that the picture emerging from the claims data is, in a way, flawed, since WTO Members with *very* limited administrative expertise do not participate as complainants in the first place? The argument to explore here would be whether those participating in WTO panel adjudication share a minimum level of internal government/administrative expertise that is required for successful litigation.
(d) Do the chances for a developing country to succeed with a claim depend on the identity of the respondent?
(e) Do the chances for a developing country to succeed with a claim depend on the number of complainants in a case, or whether a major trading power is a co-complainant?

Appendix 1: Classification of WTO Members

G2
EC
US

LDCs
Angola
Bangladesh
Benin
Burkina Faso
Burundi
Cambodia
Central African Rep
Chad
Dem. Rep. Congo
Djibouti
Gambia
Guinea
Guinea-Bissau
Haiti
Lesotho
Madagascar
Malawi
Maldives
Mali
Mauritania
Mozambique
Myanmar
Nepal
Niger
Rwanda
Senegal
Sierra Leone
Solomon Islands
Togo
Uganda
Zambia

Industrialized (IND)
Australia
Canada
Croatia
Hong Kong–China
Iceland
Israel
Japan
Korea
Liechtenstein
Mexico
New Zealand
Norway
Singapore
Switzerland
Turkey

Developing (DEV)
Albania
Antigua and Barbuda
Argentina
Armenia
Bahrain
Barbados
Belize
Bolivia
Botswana
Brazil
Brunei Darussalam
Cameroon
Chile
China
Colombia
Congo
Costa Rica
Côte d'Ivoire
Cuba
Dominica
Dominican Republic
Ecuador
Egypt
El Salvador
Fiji
FYR Macedonia
Gabon
Georgia
Ghana
Grenada
Guatemala
Guyana
Honduras
India
Indonesia
Jamaica
Jordan
Kenya
Kuwait
Kyrgyz Republic
Macao—China
Malaysia
Mauritius
Moldova
Mongolia
Morocco
Namibia
Nicaragua
Nigeria
Oman
Pakistan
Panama
Papua New Guinea
Paraguay
Peru
Philippines
Qatar
Saint Kitts and Nevis
Saint Lucia
Saint Vincent & the Grenadines
Saudi Arabia
South Africa

Developing (DEV)
(continued)
Sri Lanka
Suriname
Swaziland
Chinese Taipei
Tanzania
Thailand
Trinidad and Tobago
Tunisia
United Arab Emirates
Uruguay
Venezuela
Zimbabwe

Appendix 2: Detailed Description of Number of Claims per Provision

Provision	No of Claims	Provision	No of Claims	Provision	No of Claims
AD:1	18	AD:3.4	24	AD:9.4	1
AD:10.1	2	AD:3.5	22	AD:9.5	2
AD:10.2	1	AD:3.6	2	AD:AnnI.2	1
AD:10.4	1	AD:3.7	4	AD:AnnI.7	1
AD:10.6	2	AD:3.7i	1	AD:AnnII	4
AD:10.7	2	AD:3.8	2	AD:AnnII.1	1
AD:11	2	AD:4	1	AD:AnnII.3	4
AD:11.1	8	AD:4.1	4	AD:AnnII.5	2
AD:11.2	7	AD:5.1	1	AD:AnnII.6	7
AD:11.3	19	AD:5.2	3	AD:AnnII.7	4
AD:12.1	4	AD:5.3	6	ATC:2	1
AD:12.1.1	1	AD:5.4	12	ATC:2.4	2
AD:12.1.1iv	1	AD:5.5	4	ATC:6	2
AD:12.2	6	AD:5.6	2	ATC:6.10	1
AD:12.2.2	4	AD:5.7	1	ATC:6.2	3
AD:12.3	2	AD:5.8	12	ATC:6.4	3
AD:15	14	AD:6	1	ATC:6.6d	1
AD:17.6i	1	AD:6.1	3	AoA	1
AD:18	1	AD:6.1.1	2	AoA:10.1	2
AD:18.1	12	AD:6.1.2	4	AoA:3.1a	1
AD:18.3	2	AD:6.1.3	1	AoA:3.1b	1
AD:18.4	23	AD:6.10	5	AoA:3.2	4
AD:2	5	AD:6.2	9	AoA:3.3	7
AD:2.1	6	AD:6.4	9	AoA:4.2	4
AD:2.2	3	AD:6.5	2	AoA:5.1b	1
AD:2.2.1	1	AD:6.5.1	1	AoA:6	2
AD:2.2.1.1	1	AD:6.6	2	AoA:7.2a	2
AD:2.2.2	4	AD:6.7	2	AoA:8	8
AD:2.4	29	AD:6.8	15	AoA:9.1a	7
AD:2.4.1	4	AD:6.9	8	AoA:9.1c	5
AD:2.4.2	16	AD:7.4	1	AoA:9.1d	1
AD:2.6	1	AD:8.3	10	DSU:21.5	1
AD:3.1	32	AD:9.1	2	DSU:22.6	1
AD:3.2	21	AD:9.2	3	DSU:23.1	4
AD:3.3	7	AD:9.3	11	DSU:23.2a	4

170 DEVELOPING COUNTRIES IN THE WTO LEGAL SYSTEM

Provision	No of Claims	Provision	No of Claims	Provision	No of Claims
DSU:23.2b	1	GATT:VI.6a	1	ROO:2c	3
DSU:23.2c	4	GATT:VIII	2	ROO:2d	2
DSU:3.7	1	GATT:X	1	Reference Paper(1.1)	1
EnC:2a	1	GATT:X.1	2		
GATS: Telecom Annex	2, 5a	GATT:X.2	2	Reference Paper(2.2b)	2
		GATT:X.3	8		
GATS: Telecom,55	2	GATT:X.3a	33	SCM:1	4
GATS:II	7	GATT:XI	9	SCM:1.1	3
GATS:V	2	GATT:XI.1	8	SCM:1.1a	2
GATS:VI.1	1	GATT:XIII	2	SCM:1.1b	2
GATS:VI.3	1	GATT:XIII.1	6	SCM:1.2	1
GATS:XI	1	GATT:XIII.2	1	SCM:10	16
GATS:XIV	1	GATT:XIII.2a	1	SCM:11.4	11
GATS:XIV.a	1	GATT:XIX	4	SCM:12	1
GATS:XIV.c	1	GATT:XIX.1	52	SCM:12.6	1
GATS:XVI.1	1	GATT:XIX.1a	13	SCM:14	10
GATS:XVI.2	1	GATT:XV.9a	1	SCM:14.d	2
GATS:XVII	9	GATT:XVII.1	1	SCM:14d	1
GATT:6.1.3	1	GATT:XVII.1a	3	SCM:15.1	1
GATT:I	9	GATT:XVII.1b	1	SCM:15.2	3
GATT:I.1	9	GATT:XVIII.11	1	SCM:15.4	2
GATT:II	4	GATT:XVIII.B	1	SCM:15.5	2
GATT:II.1	3	GATT:XX	6	SCM:17.1b	1
GATT:II.1(a)	1	GATT:XX.b	3	SCM:17.2	1
GATT:II.1(b)	2	GATT:XX.d	14	SCM:17.3	1
GATT:II.1a	4	GATT:XX.g	2	SCM:17.4	1
GATT:II.1b	9	GATT:XXIII.1b	2	SCM:17.5	1
GATT:III	2	GATT:XXIV	2	SCM:18.3	10
GATT:III.2	25	GPA:XXII.2	1	SCM:19	2
GATT:III.4	44	Illustrative List (TRIMS)	1	SCM:19.1	5
GATT:III.8b	1			SCM:19.4	12
GATT:VI	5	ILA:1	1	SCM:2	3
GATT:VI.1	12	ILA:1.2	5	SCM:2.1	1
GATT:VI.2	26	ILA:1.4a	1	SCM:2.1c	1
GATT:VI.3	17	ILA:3	1	SCM:2.4	1
GATT:VI.4	2	ROO:2b	3	SCM:20.6	2

Provision	No of Claims	Provision	No of Claims	Provision	No of Claims
SCM:21	2	SG:2	4	SPS:5.7	2
SCM:21.1	5	SG:2.1	192	SPS:7	1
SCM:21.2	1	SG:3	1	SPS:AnnB.1	1
SCM:21.3	7	SG:3.1	160	TBT:2.1	1
SCM:22.3	1	SG:3.2	1	TBT:2.2	1
SCM:27.4	1	SG:4	5	TBT:2.4	1
SCM:28.2	4	SG:4.1a	1	TRIMS:2	6
SCM:3	1	SG:4.1b	6	TRIPS:13	2
SCM:3.1a	24	SG:4.1c	5	TRIPS:33	1
SCM:3.1b	3	SG:4.2	74	TRIPS:70.1	1
SCM:3.2	8	SG:4.2a	8	TRIPS:70.2	1
SCM:32.1	19	SG:4.2b	74	TRIPs:1.1	1
SCM:32.5	14	SG:4.2c	3	TRIPs:15.1	1
SCM:4	1	SG:5	3	TRIPs:16.1	4
SCM:4.10	10	SG:5.1	3	TRIPs:2.1	12
SCM:5c	2	SG:7.1	1	TRIPs:20	1
SCM:7	1	SG:8.1	2	TRIPs:22.2	1
SCM:7.9	10	SG:9.1	1	TRIPs:49	1
SCM:AnnI	1	SPS3.1	1	TRIPs:63.1	1
SG:11	1	SPS:2.2	5	TRIPs:63.2	1
SG:12.1	2	SPS:2.3	1	TRIPs:65.1	1
SG:12.1a	1	SPS:3.1	1	TRIPs:70.8a	2
SG:12.1b	1	SPS:3.3	2	TRIPs:70.9	2
SG:12.1c	1	SPS:5.1	4	TRIPs:9.1	2
SG:12.2	2	SPS:5.5	3	WTO:XVI.4	30
SG:12.3	5	SPS:5.6	4		

Appendix 3: Detailed Description of Number of Claims per Provision with G2 Complainants

Provision	No of Claims	Provision	No of Claims
SG:2.1	26	GATT:I	5
GATT:III.4	24	GATT:XI	5
SG:3.1	23	SCM:14	5
GATT:III.2	20	AD:5.8	4
GATT:X.3a	19	SCM:19.4	4
GATT:XIX.1	11	SCM:21.1	4
SG:4.2	10	SCM:3.1a	4
WTO:XVI.4	10	SG:12.3	4
SG:4.2b	9	TRIMS:2	4
GATT:VI.2	8	AD:11.1	3
GATT:XX.d	8	AD:11.2	3
AD:1	7	AD:3.1	3
AD:18.4	7	AD:3.2	3
AD:2.4	7	DSU:23.1	3
GATT:VI.1	7	DSU:23.2a	3
SCM:10	7	DSU:23.2c	3
SCM:21.3	7	GATT:II.1	3
AD:2.4.2	6	GATT:XI.1	3
AD:9.3	6	SCM:32.5	3
TRIPs:2.1	6	SG:4	3

Appendix 4: Detailed Description of Number of Claims per Provision with IND Complainants

Provision	No of Claims	Provision	No of Claims
SG:2.1	123	SCM:19.4	8
SG:3.1	102	AD:2.4.2	7
SG:4.2	50	AD:18.1	6
SG:4.2b	49	AD:2.1	6
GATT:XIX.1	31	AD:3.3	6
AD:11.3	18	AD:5.8	6
AD:3.1	15	AD:6.2	6
WTO:XVI.4	15	SCM:32.5	6
AD:2.4	14	TRIPs:2.1	6
GATT:III.4	14	AD:2	5
AD:3.5	13	AD:5.4	5
SCM:32.1	13	AD:AnnII.6	5
AD:3.4	12	GATT:VI.1	5
AD:18.4	11	GATT:X.3	5
GATT:VI.3	11	SCM:11.4	5
AD:3.2	10	SCM:14	5
GATT:VI.2	10	SG:4.1c	5
SCM:10	9	AD:11.1	4
AD:1	8	AD:15	4
GATT:X.3a	8	AD:6.8	4

Appendix 5: Detailed Description of Number of Claims by DEV per Provision

Provision	No of Claims	Provision	No of Claims
SG:2.1	52	GATT:III.4	6
SG:3.1	40	GATT:X.3a	6
SG:4.2b	20	AD:18.1	5
SG:4.2	19	AD:18.4	5
SCM:3.1a	18	AD:8.3	5
AD:3.1	14	AoA:8	5
AD:3.4	11	GATT:VI.3	5
AD:6.8	10	GATT:XI.1	5
GATT:XIX.1	10	SCM:11.4	5
AD:15	9	SCM:18.3	5
GATT:XIX.1a	9	SCM:32.1	5
AD:2.4	8	SCM:32.5	5
AD:3.2	8	SCM:4.10	5
AD:6.4	8	SCM:7.9	5
GATT:VI.2	8	WTO:XVI.4	5
SCM:3.2	8	AD:12.2	4
AD:3.5	7	GATT:XX	4
AD:5.4	6	SG:4.2a	4
AD:6.9	6	AD:1	3
GATT:II.1b	6	AD:12.2.2	3

Appendix 6: The Outcomes of Claims Made in the Bilateral Disputes

DS No	Title of Abb	Complainant	Defendant	No of Win	No of Lose	No of Unclear	Tot no Claims
2	US – Gasoline	Venezuela	US	4	0	0	4
4	US – Gasoline	Brazil	US	4	0	0	4
8	Japan – Alcoholic Beverages II	EC	Japan	2	0	0	2
10	Japan – Alcoholic Beverages II	Canada	Japan	2	0	0	2
11	Japan – Alcoholic Beverages II	US	Japan	2	0	0	2
18	Australia - Salmon	Canada	Australia	5	0	0	5
22	Brazil – Desiccated Coconut	Philippines	Brazil	0	0	4	4
24	US – Underwear	Costa Rica	US	6	0	0	6
26	EC – Hormones (US)	US	EC	4	0	2	6
27	EC – Bananas III	Ecuador	EC	7	0	0	7
27	EC – Bananas III	Guatemala	EC	3	0	0	7
27	EC – Bananas III	Honduras	EC	7	0	0	7
27	EC – Bananas III	Mexico	EC	7	0	0	7
27	EC – Bananas III	US	EC	7	0	0	7
31	Canada – Periodicals	US	Canada	4	1	0	5
33	US – Wool Shirts and Blouses	India	US	2	0	0	2
34	Turkey – Textiles	India	Turkey	3	0	0	3
44	Japan – Film	US	Japan	0	3	0	3
46	Brazil – Aircraft	Canada	Brazil	5	0	0	5

DS No	Title of Abb	Complainant	Defendant	No of Win	No of Lose	No of Unclear	Tot no Claims
48	EC – Hormones (Canada)	Canada	EC	4	0	2	6
50	India – Patents (US)	US	India	4	0	0	4
54	Indonesia – Autos	EC	Indonesia	4	1	0	5
55	Indonesia – Autos	Japan	Indonesia	3	1	0	4
56	Argentina – Textiles and Apparel	US	Argentina	2	0	0	2
58	US – Shrimp	India	US	2	0	0	2
58	US – Shrimp	Malaysia	US	2	0	0	2
58	US – Shrimp	Pakistan	US	2	0	0	2
58	US – Shrimp	Thailand	US	2	0	0	2
59	Indonesia – Autos	US	Indonesia	3	4	0	7
60	Guatemala – Cement I	Mexico	Guatemala	2	0	0	2
62	EC – Computer Equipment	US	EC	1	0	0	1
64	Indonesia – Autos	Japan	Indonesia	3	1	0	4
67	EC – Computer Equipment	US	UK	1	0	0	1
68	EC – Computer Equipment	US	Ireland	1	0	0	1
69	EC – Poultry	Brazil	EC	2	6	0	8
70	Canada – Aircraft	Brazil	Canada	4	10	0	14
75	Korea – Alcoholic Beverages	EC	Korea	2	0	0	2
76	Japan – Agricultural Products II	US	Japan	5	0	0	5
79	India – Patents (EC)	EC	India	2	0	0	2
84	Korea – Alcoholic Beverages	US	Korea	2	0	0	2

87	Chile – Alcoholic Beverages	EC	Chile	2	0	2
90	India – Quantitative Restrictions	US	India	4	0	4
98	Korea – Dairy	EC	Korea	3	6	9
99	US – DRAMS	Korea	US	1	0	1
103	Canada – Dairy	US	Canada	6	0	6
108	US – FSC	EC	US	4	0 1	5
110	Chile – Alcoholic Beverages	EC	Chile	2	0	2
113	Canada – Dairy	New Zealand	Canada	5	0	5
114	Canada – Pharmaceutical Patents	EC	Canada	1	2	3
121	Argentina – Footwear (EC)	EC	Argentina	2	0	2
122	Thailand – H-Beams	Poland	Thailand	6	6	12
126	Australia – Automotive Leather II	US	Australia	2	1	3
132	Mexico – Corn Syrup	US	Mexico	10	5	15
135	EC – Asbestos	Canada	EC	1	2	3
136	US – 1916 Act (EC)	EC	US	6	0	6
138	US – Lead and Bismuth II	EC	US	1	0	1
139	Canada – Autos	Japan	Canada	7	2	9
141	EC – Bed Linen	India	EC	3	8	11
142	Canada – Autos	EC	Canada	7	2	9
152	US – Section 301 Trade Act	EC	US	0	9	9
155	Argentina – Hides and Leather	EC	Argentina	5	0	5
156	Guatemala – Cement II	Mexico	Guatemala	19	0	19
160	US – Section 110(5) Copyright Act	EC	US	2	2	4
161	Korea – Various Measures on Beef	US	Korea	16	0	16
162	US – 1916 Act (Japan)	Japan	US	10	0	10
163	Korea – Procurement	US	Korea	0	1	1

182 DEVELOPING COUNTRIES IN THE WTO LEGAL SYSTEM

DS No	Title of Abb	Complainant	Defendant	No of Win	No of Lose	No of Unclear	Tot no Claims
165	US – Certain EC Products	EC	US	12	0	0	12
166	US – Wheat Gluten	EC	US	8	3	3	14
169	Korea – Various Measures on Beef	Australia	Korea	16	0	0	16
170	Canada – Patent Term	US	Canada	3	0	0	3
175	India – Autos	US	India	4	0	0	4
176	US – Section 211 Appropriations Act	EC	US	2	13	0	15
177	US – Lamb	New Zealand	US	6	1	0	7
178	US – Lamb	Australia	US	6	1	0	7
179	US – Stainless Steel	Korea	US	4	6	0	10
184	US – Hot-Rolled Steel	Japan	US	7	22	0	29
189	Argentina – Ceramic Tiles	EC	Argentina	5	0	0	5
192	US – Cotton Yarn	Pakistan	US	4	1	0	5
194	US – Export Restraints	Canada	US	0	2	0	2
202	US – Line Pipe	Korea	US	26	4	0	30
204	Mexico – Telecoms	US	Mexico	4	3	0	7
206	US – Steel Plate	India	US	2	5	0	7
207	Chile – Price Band System	Argentina	Chile	19	2	0	21
211	Egypt – Steel Rebar	Turkey	Egypt	3	30	2	35
212	US – Countervailing Measures	EC	US	25	0	0	25
213	US – Carbon Steel	EC	US	5	4	0	9

217	US – Offset Act (Byrd Amendment)	Australia	US	9	6	0	15
217	US – Offset Act (Byrd Amendment)	Brazil	US	9	6	0	15
217	US – Offset Act (Byrd Amendment)	Chile	US	9	6	0	15
217	US – Offset Act (Byrd Amendment)	EC	US	9	6	0	15
217	US – Offset Act (Byrd Amendment)	India	US	9	6	0	15
217	US – Offset Act (Byrd Amendment)	Indonesia	US	9	6	0	15
217	US – Offset Act (Byrd Amendment)	Japan	US	9	6	0	15
217	US – Offset Act (Byrd Amendment)	Korea	US	9	6	0	15
217	US – Offset Act (Byrd Amendment)	Thailand	US	9	6	0	15
219	EC – Tube and Pipe Fittings	Brazil	EC	4	35	0	39
221	US - Section 129(c)(1) URAA	Canada	US	0	14	0	14
222	Canada – Aircraft Credits and Guarantees	Brazil	Canada	3	7	0	10
231	EC – Sardines	Peru	EC	1	0	0	1
234	US – Offset Act (Byrd Amendment)	Canada	US	9	6	0	15
236	US – Softwood Lumber III	Canada	US	11	5	7	23
238	Argentina – Preserved Peaches	Chile	Argentina	10	0	6	16
241	Argentina – Poultry Anti-dumping Duties	Brazil	Argentina	20	9	2	31
243	US – Textiles Rules of Origin	India	US	0	8	0	8
244	US – Corrosion-Resistant Steel Sunset Review	Japan	US	0	37	3	40
245	Japan – Apples	US	Japan	3	0	0	3
246	EC – Tariff Preferences	India	EC	3	0	0	3
248	US – Steel Safeguards	EC	US	75	0	0	75
249	US – Steel Safeguards	Japan	US	57	0	0	57

DS No	Title of Abb	Complainant	Defendant	No of Win	No of Lose	No of Unclear	Tot no Claims
251	US – Steel Safeguards	Korea	US	57	0	0	57
252	US – Steel Safeguards	China	US	77	0	0	77
253	US – Steel Safeguards	Switzerland	US	77	0	0	77
254	US – Steel Safeguards	Norway	US	77	0	0	77
257	US – Softwood Lumber IV	Canada	US	7	13	11	31
258	US – Steel Safeguards	New Zealand	US	77	0	0	77
259	US – Steel Safeguards	Brazil	US	53	0	0	53
265	EC – Export Subsidies on Sugar	Australia	EC	4	0	0	4
266	EC – Export Subsidies on Sugar	Brazil	EC	4	0	0	4
267	US – Upland Cotton	Brazil	US	12	2	0	14
269	EC – Chicken Cuts	Brazil	EC	2	0	0	2
276	Canada – Wheat Exports and Grain Imports	US	Canada	11	7	0	18
282	US – AD Measures on Oil Country Tubular Goods	Mexico	US	2	14	17	33
283	EC – Export Subsidies on Sugar	Thailand	EC	4	0	0	4
285	US – Gambling Services	Antigua and Barbuda	US	5	2	2	9
286	EC – Chicken Cuts	Thailand	EC	2	0	0	2

290	EC – Trademarks and Geographical Indications	Australia	EC	6	14	16	36
294	US – Zeroing	EC	US	3	40	22	65
296	US – Countervailing Duty Investigation on DRAMs	Korea	US	3	8	12	23
301	EC – Commercial Vessels	Korea	EC	2	2	5	9
302	Dominican Republic – Import and Sale of Cigarettes	Honduras	Dominican Republic	9	2	0	11
308	Mexico – Taxes on Soft Drinks	US	Mexico	6	0	0	6
312	Korea – Certain Paper	Indonesia	Korea	8	28	16	52
315	EC – Selected Customs Matters	US	EC	2	15	0	17
322	US – Zeroing	Japan	US	2	40	20	62

Appendix 7: Percentage Win and Total Number of Claims by Complainant-Respondent Pair

COMPLAINANT	RESPONDENT																	
	Argentina	Australia	Brazil	Canada	Chile	Dominican Republic	EC	Egypt	Guatemala	India	Indonesia	Japan	Korea	Mexico	Thailand	Turkey	US	Total
Antigua and Barbuda																	56	56
																	9	9
Argentina					90													90
					21													21
Australia							58						100				73	72
							40						16				22	78
Brazil	65			29			59										86	64
	31			24			53										86	194
Canada		100	100				50					100					26	53
		5	5				9					2					85	106
Chile	63																60	61
	16																15	31
China																	100	100
																	77	77

188 DEVELOPING COUNTRIES IN THE WTO LEGAL SYSTEM

	RESPONDENT																	
COMPLAINANT	Argentina	Australia	Brazil	Canada	Chile	Dominican Republic	EC	Egypt	Guatemala	India	Indonesia	Japan	Korea	Mexico	Thailand	Turkey	US	Total
Costa Rica																	100	100
																	6	6
EC	100			56	100					100	80	100	67				63	74
	12			12	4					2	5	2	11				255	303
Ecuador							100											100
							7											7
Guatemala							100											100
							7											7
Honduras						82	7											91
						11												18
India	100						64									100	58	64
							14									3	34	51
Indonesia												75	15				60	38
												9	15				52	67
Japan				78													48	57
				9													213	231

Winners and Losers in the Panel Stage of the WTO

Country									
Korea				22 / 9				67 / 67	60 / 136
Malaysia									145 / 100
Mexico		100 / 5		100 / 7					100 / 2
New Zealand									2 / 6
Norway									77 / 33
Pakistan									61 / 93
Peru				100 / 1					95 / 84
Philippines		0 / 4							89 / 100
Poland						50 / 12			100 / 77
Switzerland				100 / 6					77 / 90
Thailand				80 / 33	9 / 35		100 / 12	43 / 7	90 / 7
Turkey								75 / 13	23 / 100
US	100 / 2	67 / 3	85 / 32					75 / 19 / 28	9 / 35 / 79 / 149

190 DEVELOPING COUNTRIES IN THE WTO LEGAL SYSTEM

COMPLAINANT	RESPONDENT																	
	Argentina	Australia	Brazil	Canada	Chile	Dominican Republic	EC	Egypt	Guatemala	India	Indonesia	Japan	Korea	Mexico	Thailand	Turkey	US	Total
Venezuela																	100	100
																	4	4
Average % win	88	83	50	69	97	82	74	9	100	100	68	83	64	75	50	100	65	71
Total no of claims	61	8	9	82	25	11	193	35	21	14	21	17	98	28	12	3	1254	1892

9. ACCESS TO JUSTICE IN THE WTO
A Case for a Small-Claims Procedure?

HÅKAN NORDSTRÖM AND GREGORY SHAFFER*

A. Introduction 192
B. The Case for a Small-Claims Procedure 197
    I. Trade Stakes 198
    II. Litigation Costs and Internal Expertise 203
    III. Alternative WTO Dispute Settlement Mechanisms 209
C. Small-Claims Procedures 214
    I. The National Context 214
    II. The EU Regional Context 217
    III. Small Claims in International Dispute Settlement 218
D. Adaptation of a Small-Claims Procedure to the WTO Context 221
    I. Definition of a 'Small Claim' in the WTO Context 223
    II. Who Could Bring a Small Claim Under the Procedure? 227
    III. No Precedential Effect and Cap on Remedies 230
    IV. Institutional Issues: Panels, Appeals, and Procedures 236
    V. Creation for a Trial Period 239
E. Conclusion 239

The current dispute settlement system of the WTO creates a particular challenge for WTO Members with limited exports because litigation costs are more or less independent of the commercial stakes involved in a dispute. Small Members with small trade stakes may therefore find it too costly to pursue legitimate claims. Reviewing the aims and practices of small-claims procedures at the national and supranational level, we analyze whether a similar institution

---

* Håkan Nordström is the chief economist of the National Board of Trade, the central administrative body in Sweden dealing with foreign trade and trade policy. He formerly was an economist in the research division of the WTO secretariat. Gregory Shaffer is the Melvin C. Steen Professor of Law, University of Minnesota Law School. He is also Senior Research Fellow for the International Centre on Trade and Sustainable Development (ICTSD) for its project on the WTO dispute settlement system and developing countries (see <http://www.ictsd.org/issarea/dsu/index.htm> for a description). The views expressed in this chapter are those of the authors and should not be attributed to the Swedish government or ICTSD. We wish to thank Matt Fortin and Kyle Shamberg for their research assistance and ICTSD for its support. We also wish to thank Chad Bown, William Davey, Brett Frischman, Donald McRae, Niall Meagher, Joost Pauwelyn, Alan Sykes, Joel Trachtman, Spencer Waller, and two anonymous reviewers for their comments, as well as participants at a workshop at the WTO in Geneva and a conference at the University of Minnesota in June 2007.

could be introduced at the WTO. While a strong empirical case can be made for such an innovation, the legal and political challenges should not be underestimated. As an initial step, we make a *prima facie* case that the current dispute settlement system effectively discriminates against small claims and hence owners of small claims, and thus, in particular, against least-developed countries, small-island economies, and low-income developing countries. This empirical task is carried out in Part B. In Part C we explain what small-claims procedures are at the national level, what purpose they serve, how they are organized in different jurisdictions involving alternative design features, and what challenges they have faced. Part D explores the issues raised by adding a small-claims procedure in the WTO context and indicates specific design features that could address them.

A. INTRODUCTION

The law and legal system of the WTO are in principle blind to the commercial stakes involved in a dispute between its Members. As laid down by the DSU, '(t)he prompt settlement of situations in which a Member considers that *any benefits* accruing to it directly or indirectly under the covered agreements are being impaired by measures taken by another Member is *essential* to the effective functioning of the WTO and the maintenance of a proper balance between the rights and obligations of Members' (emphasis added).[1] The law makes no formal distinction between a claim of $1 million and a claim of $1 billion. In practice, however, it may be difficult to enforce a $1 million claim because of the substantial resource commitments involved in a legal dispute. Under the current dispute settlement system, it can take up to three years to litigate a dispute, cost more than one-half of $1 million in legal fees, and require a significant time commitment from government officials who may already be severely underresourced. Moreover, all this could be for naught because there is no assurance that a ruling will be affirmative or that the respondent will comply in a manner that leads to market access. Small claims are therefore unlikely to be pursued unless some important principle is at stake.

This is all as it should be, some would argue. If there were no implicit 'user fees', the dispute settlement system would implode. It has to cost something to keep out nuisance cases of insignificant value. Perhaps this is what the drafters had in mind when they, in one of the first articles of the DSU, wrote: 'Before bringing a case, a Member shall exercise its judgment as to whether action under these procedures would be fruitful'.[2]

---

1. '*Understanding on Rules and Procedures Governing the Settlement of Disputes*, 15 April 1994, *Marrakesh Agreement Establishing the World Trade Organization*, Annex 2, Article 3.3.
2. DSU Article 3.7.

The latter interpretation is not without problems, however. What is insignificant for some Member states is highly significant to others. A million dollars in forgone export revenue may not matter much for the European Union or the United States; it would only be a few seconds worth of exports. For small developing countries like Burundi, Gambia, and Guinea-Bissau, on the other hand, $1 million corresponds to about 1.45 percent of annual exports, or put in relationship to national income, between 0.17 and 0.42 percent of gross domestic product (GDP). Forgone export revenue of this magnitude would not be a small order for them.

What is 'small' is thus a relative concept. Yet the WTO Dispute Settlement (DS) system does not take into account the inherent variation in exports across the WTO's membership. A case worth $1 million is treated in the very same way (at least formally)[3] as a case worth $1 billion. The timetable is the same, the submission requirements are the same, the standard of proof is the same, the appeal procedures are the same; *everything* is the same unless the parties opt for the alternative resolution mechanisms offered by the DSU, including mediation and arbitration, or the 1966 fast-track procedures for cases brought by developing countries against developed ones. The alternative tracks of mediation and arbitration have only been used twice, suggesting that they are poor substitutes for the regular panel process. A major problem with these alternatives is that both parties, including the respondent, must approve the use of mediation or arbitration, and the use of such procedures may conflict with the longer term strategic interests of respondents. By never yielding a case without a legal battle and never granting simplified procedures, respondents can develop a reputation for being tough and costly to take on, which will discourage price-sensitive complainants to take legal action. As regards the 1966 fast-track procedures, they have never been used since the WTO's creation in 1995, arguably because shorter time lines are not practical unless the complexity of the current dispute settlement process is reduced. Shorter time lines can place developing country Members at an even greater disadvantage. We further address parties' experiences with these options in Section B(iii).

In sum, where the procedures are the same while stakes differ, the system is not neutral to size. Notionally equal litigation rules provide unequal opportunities for WTO Members. Small trading nations are effectively constrained from being able to use the legal system to the full extent, constituting, in practice, a form of in-built discrimination.

---

3. Insiders in WTO litigation have stated to us that where the WTO director general and secretariat influence or determine the panel selection process, a large (eg, the billion dollar case) will get much 'better' panelists than the small (eg, million dollar) one, and that the bigger case will be assigned to more senior secretariat staff. They state that this can affect the quality of panel reports. Correspondence and discussions with Gregory Shaffer, June and December 2007.

TABLE 1. THE RELATIVE IMPORTANCE OF $1 MILLION OF EXPORTS (2003)

Rang	Member	Share of export (%)	Share of GDP (%)
1	Burundi	1,47	0,17
2	Gambia	1,45	0,27
3	Guinea Bissau	1,43	0,42
4	Solomon Islands	1,01	0,41
5	Rwanda	0,86	0,06
6	Dominica	0,84	0,38
7	Djibouti	0,80	0,16
8	Central African Republic	0,79	0,09
9	Saint Kitts and Nevis	0,66	0,27
10	Sierra Leone	0,63	0,09
11	Saint Vincent and the Grenadines	0,60	0,27
12	Grenada	0,57	0,27
13	Mauritania	0,28	0,09
14	Burkina Faso	0,27	0,03
15	Belize	0,27	0,11
16	Saint Lucia	0,26	0,14
17	Niger	0,24	0,04
18	Antigua and Barbuda	0,22	0,15
19	Haiti	0,22	0,03
20	Lesotho	0,19	0,09
21	Malawi	0,18	0,05
22	Maldives	0,17	0,14
23	Chad	0,15	0,04
24	Guinea	0,15	0,03
25	Togo	0,15	0,06
...	...	...	...
145	Canada	0,000318	0,000117
146	China	0,000206	0,000071
147	Japan	0,000183	0,000023
148	United States of America	0,000099	0,000009
149	EU25*	0,000025	0,000009

Own calculations based on data from the WTO and UNSTAT.

* Including intra-EU25 export.

One solution to this dilemma is to reduce the system's 'user fees' for smaller trading nations. This can be done in four principal ways, which could serve as alternatives or complements to each other. These choices can involve use of a public prosecutor, legal aid, stronger remedies, a streamlined procedure for small claims, or a combination of them, in each case changing the calculation of the costs and benefits of pursuing a case. The *first* way is to create a WTO public prosecutor with objectives and powers similar to those of the European Commission within the EU legal system.[4] The public prosecutor would have the right and obligation to initiate legal proceedings against governments in the general interest of upholding the treaties.[5]

A *second* way is to provide greater legal aid, for example, by offering Members legal counsel funded out of the regular WTO budget or a designated legal aid fund. The political feasibility of this route appears constrained, however. It is not just or even primarily the cost that raises a problem—it is the use of the funds. The EU may have no interest in contributing to a legal aid fund that would enable resource-constrained countries to challenge its sensitive policies such as the Common Agricultural Policy (CAP). The US government would likewise face stiff opposition from organized labor and import-competing industries at home if it contributes to a fund that would be used to challenge US antidumping policies. In Japan, it would be tantamount to political hara-kiri to contribute funds to foreign governments with an interest in prying open the Japanese market for rice and other culturally sensitive commodities. Indeed, neither the European Union,[6] nor the United States nor Japan has contributed to the funds of the *independent* Advisory Centre on WTO Law (ACWL), which is the only provider of subsidized legal assistance at present, an alternative or complement which we will review further. At the same time, we would not entirely rule out the feasibility of an in-house legal aid fund. It has proven possible to create a trust to fund legal assistance for developing countries who are parties before the International Court of Justice, subject to defined criteria.[7]

A *third* option is to increase the benefits of bringing a case, instead of reducing the costs of dispute settlement, through reforming WTO remedies. If cash remedies were adopted and enforced, they could be used by a Member to help cover

---

4. Weiler, in contrast, maintains that if the secretariat is to play an independent role in the dispute settlement system, it should do so more transparently by publishing its legal opinions, much as the Advocate General does before the European Court of Justice, so that the parties may respond to them. That proposal, however, would not assist smaller trading nations with the cost of enforcing their rights. See JHH Weiler, 'The Rule of Lawyers and the Ethos of Diplomats: Reflections on the Internal and External Legitimacy of WTO Dispute Settlement' (2001) 25 JWT 191–207.

5. To the extent that one accepts the concept of 'efficient breach', then it is desirable to let parties settle a dispute without interference of a WTO public prosecutor. This debate, however, is not relevant to the analysis of a small claims procedure's desirability.

6. Some individual member states of the European Union have however contributed to the funds of the ACWL, including Denmark, Finland, Ireland, Italy, Netherlands, Sweden, and the United Kingdom. Apart from Italy, the contributors belong to the free trade block in the community, known collectively as the 'northern liberals.'

7. ME O'Connell, 'International Legal Aid: The Secretary General's Trust Fund to Assist States in the Settlement of Disputes Through the International Court of Justice' in Mark Janis (ed), *International Courts in the Twenty-First Century* (1992) and PHF Bekker, 'International Legal Aid in Practice: The ICJ Trust Fund' (1993) 87 AJIL 659–68.

the cost of attorneys, potentially leading to more filings. Cash remedies would also create incentives for entrepreneurial attorneys, particularly if wrongdoers would have to compensate for the damage already incurred (ie, through retrospective remedies),[8] facilitating the bundling of smaller Members' claims in a manner roughly analogous to a 'class action'. Even more controversially, the WTO could provide for fee-shifting in all or some subset of cases so that a losing respondent would pay the complainant's legal fees.[9] There are costs and benefits to such alternative approaches, which have been explored elsewhere, and we do not address them further in this chapter.[10]

A *fourth option* explored in this chapter is to introduce simplified and less costly litigation procedures for "small claims" pursuant to defined criteria that we address. As in domestic systems, it can be more socially efficient to reduce procedural complexity for small claims than to promote legal aid where the cost of litigation would exceed its social value. Indeed, that is a primary rationale for the small-claims procedural alternative.[11] It is not possible to draw a direct parallel between small-claims procedures at the national level and a corresponding institution at the international level. The parallel lies more in the underlying philosophy (a recognition that disadvantaged members of society face particular difficulties to access the judicial system) than in the institutional and political context. In the WTO context, the disadvantaged can be viewed either as poorer states within an 'international community of states' (the traditional international law perspective) or as private parties who are indirectly represented by states within the WTO and who are disadvantaged because they have small stakes. These private parties are even more disadvantaged when they have small stakes and reside in poor states, both because their stakes are not pooled within a larger collectivity and because the collectivity that represents them exercises less clout on the international stage.

---

8. Current WTO remedies appear to be only prospective in effect for most claims although the rules are not entirely clear on this point and panels in some GATT antidumping cases, and one WTO subsidy case have suggested the contrary.

9. See eg, US Equal Access to Justice Act, 5 USC 504 (2000); 28 USC 2412(d)(a) (2000). Some US consumer statutes also provide for minimum specified damages to facilitate the bringing of private enforcement actions. See eg, Motor Vehicle Information and Cost Savings Act (2000) (providing for minimum damages of $1,500 for civil actions by private persons); and Truth in Lending Act of 1968, 15 USC. § 1640(a)(2)(A) (2000) (providing for minimum damages of $100 or $200 depending on the nature of the underlying consumer transaction). State consumer protection statutes also provide consumers with incentives to bring private actions. See J Sovern, 'Protecting Privacy with Deceptive Trade Practices Legislation' (2001) 69 Ford L Rev 1305–50. ('statutes often provide for a bonus for successful consumer plaintiffs in the form of one or more of multiple damages, punitive damages, and statutory minimum damages').

10. G Shaffer, "How to make the WTO Dispute Settlement System Work for Developing Countries: Some Proactive Developing Country Strategies," *Towards A Development-Supportive Dispute Settlement System in the WTO* 5 (ICTSD Resource Paper) (2003).

11. In the law and economics literature, the balance sought is between the direct costs of litigation and the indirect costs of judicial error, points that we address in Part C.

The challenge is thus to find an appropriate model (or alternative mechanism) for a small-claims procedure adapted to the WTO context. Indeed, can we define a 'small claim' in a meaningful way in a context where government policies are being disputed? Can such disputes ever be "small" no matter the monetary value? And can we expect a government to honor a ruling by an international small-claims panel with no possibility of appeal now that the Appellate Body exists? Many observers may answer negatively so that we have to think creatively if this institution is to be adapted to the WTO context.

The primary aim of this chapter is to *spur* a policy discussion on the appropriateness of a small-claims procedure in the WTO context, subject to different design criteria. We recognize the serious challenges (and have our own serious doubts, in particular, regarding the obstacles from a political economy perspective). The challenges are particularly great given the path-dependent nature of institutions. Commentators on and users of the DSU are accustomed to the current rules and may be wary of the risk of any significant reforms—first, 'to do no harm', as the saying goes.[12] Yet if the system is not functioning for a party, as arguably is the case for smaller Members and their constituents, then there is also a downside risk of doing nothing. What is ultimately at stake is the legitimacy of the WTO if only a subset of the Members can make profitable use of the dispute settlement system. We therefore think it is worthwhile to discuss various options, including innovative ones like a small-claims procedure.

Although we have no pretension of providing a definitive answer or model for such an institution, we offer a structured analysis of the challenges posed and of possible institutional responses to them. As an initial step, we make a *prima facie* case that the current DS system effectively discriminates against small claims and hence owners of small claims, and thus, in particular, against least-developed countries, small-island economies, and low income developing countries. This empirical task is carried out in Part B. Part C examines experiences with small-claims procedures domestically and supranationally, including (quite recently) within the EU. In Part D, we assess the issues raised by adding a small-claims procedure in the WTO context, and we propose specific design features that would address them. Part E concludes.

B. THE CASE FOR A SMALL-CLAIMS PROCEDURE

The case for a small-claims procedure rests on three premises that we examine sequentially. First, trade stakes vary across the Members of the WTO. Second, claims involving smaller trade stakes are not sufficiently offset by smaller litigation costs or a reduced need for domestic WTO legal expertise. Third, the

---

12. See WTO, 'The Future of the WTO: Addressing institutional challenges in the new millennium: Report of the Consultative Board to the Director-General Supachai Panitchpakdi' (Geneva: WTO, 2004) 51 para 214.

alternative means to facilitate access to the DSU, and in particular the alternative dispute resolution tracks now provided by the DSU, do not substitute for a small-claims procedure.

i. Trade Stakes

At the aggregate level of trade, the first premise is true almost by definition. Trade varies systematically with the size of the country. Figure 1 shows the strong correlation in data between aggregate trade and economic size measured by a WTO Member's GDP. It includes data for all WTO Members for 2003, apart from Liechtenstein. The European Union is treated as a single market. On average, a one percentage difference in GDP between two Member states is associated with a 0.97 percent difference in aggregate exports.[13] Only a few WTO Members fall outside the picture (as shown by the low spread around the fitted line and the high R2 value).

Of course, trade disputes normally do not concern everything that is exported by a nation but only the export of a specific product to a specific market, such as the export of bananas to the EU.[14] Any evidence of *de facto* discrimination against smaller trading nations because of smaller aggregate trade values must therefore be verified at the disaggregated level of trade. After all, small trading nations could be large suppliers of particular products (oil, bananas, cotton, etc.) to particular markets (eg, to neighboring countries: Mexico to the United States is a case in point) and hence be equally motivated to defend their market access under the DSU wherever it matters for that country. It is just that the number of products and markets in which they have a strong interest is much smaller, which is one reason why small economies are less active litigants overall.[15]

In order to investigate the market situation at disaggregated levels of trade, we have extracted the 2003 trade matrix for each Member state at the 4-digit level of the Harmonised Commodity Description and Coding System (HS).[16] At this level of trade, the 1966 revision of the HS defines 1,241 product 'headings'.

---

13. Note that the scales on the horizontal and vertical axes are in logarithms. That is, each notch is ten times larger than the notch before it.

14. An example of an exception is the dispute between the European Union and the United States over the alleged export subsidies provided by the US Foreign Sales Corporation legislation. The European Union maintained that these export subsidies (tax breaks on exports) put EU firms at a competitive disadvantage vis-à-vis US firms across product sectors and markets.

15. Horn H Horn, P Mavroidis and H Nordström, 'Is the Use of the WTO Dispute Settlement System Biased?' (1999) Center for Economic Policy Research Discussion Paper No. 2340 and J Francois and H Horn, *Trading Profiles and Developing Country Participation in the WTO Dispute Settlement System* (ICTSD, 2008).

16. The data is extracted from United Nations Commodity Trade Statistics Database (COMTRAD), accessed through the World Integrated Trade Solution (WITS) portal. The export statistics for nonreporting countries are 'mirrored' from the import statistics of

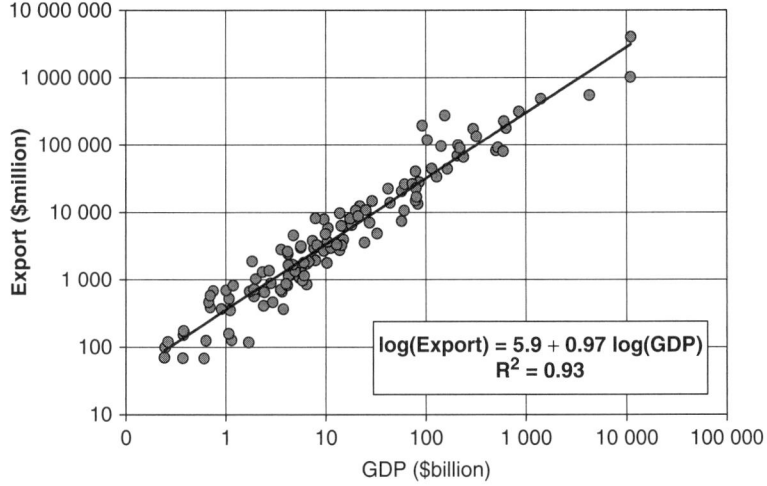

FIGURE 1. CORRELATION BETWEEN TOTAL EXPORT AND GDP

Cotton, sugar, bananas, coffee, and milk are examples of agricultural product headings. Ships, airplanes, cars, trucks, and electronic printed circuits are examples of product headings under the industrial chapters of the HS nomenclature. Many trade disputes concern this level of trade. However, a dispute can in principle cover anything from all trade to an individual tariff line. It depends on the scope of the disputed policy measure.

The total number of data points in our dataset is close to 19 million observations, comprised of the following: 124 WTO Members (the EU is treated as a single market) times 123 potential trading partners times 1,241 potential product headings. Only 5 percent of the potential export records are positive, however. Most countries export only a subset of the product range to a subset of the Member markets. It is only the largest members of the WTO that have an export interest in respect of most products and markets. A Member's export diversity is calculated as the number of entries in the matrix with positive trade (entries below $1,000 are discarded, that is, treated as zeros). For example, a country that exports 100 product headings to an average of ten partners receives a diversity index of 1,000. The actual export diversity ranges from 70 for Saint Kitts and Nevis to 96,011 for the EU, with an average of 7,300. The theoretical maximum is 123 partners times 1,241 product headings, equal to 152,643 positive records in the trade matrix. When the result is plotted in Figure 2, we find strong evidence that larger countries export a greater variety of products to a greater variety of markets. The data for individual countries is reported in Table 1.

---

reporting countries. The trade between nonreporting countries is not included since neither side of the transaction reports any trade data to the UN (or WTO for that matter).

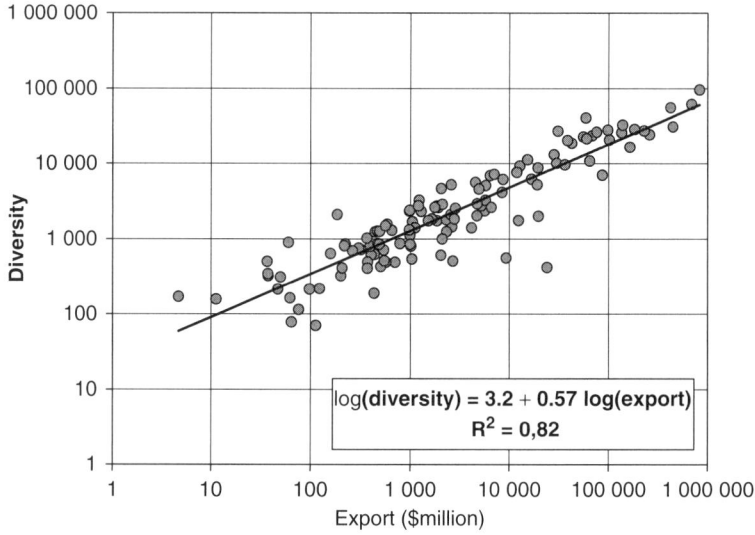

FIGURE 2. TOTAL EXPORT VS. DIVERSITY OF EXPORTS

The relationship between total exports and the diversity of exports is log-linear with a slope coefficient of 0.57.[17] That is, a WTO Member that exports twice as much as another Member state is on average 57 percent more diversified across products and markets. A large proportion of the variation in total exports can thus be attributed to the variation in a Member's export diversity. However, and this is an important argument for a small-claims procedure in the WTO, 43 percent of the variation in aggregate exports can be attributed to variations in sales per exported product. Larger countries have, as a general rule, larger commercial stakes in absolute terms *also* at the product level of trade.

This finding could be a fallacy of composition, however. If large countries specialize in big-ticket items (manufactures) and small countries in small-ticket items (agricultural products), we will observe a higher average trade stake for large countries even if the trade stakes are identical in the product range that overlap. The most neutral way of making a comparison is to go product-by-product and market-by-market. That is, if we compare sales of individual products to individual markets, can we still establish that the stakes vary with the size of the country?

The answer is in the affirmative, as shown in the statistical analysis below. We use a so-called fixed-effect panel model where each panel is comprised of the countries that export a certain product heading to a certain market. The dataset includes 124,333 panels in total with an average of 7.2 exporters per panel.[18]

---

17. The standard deviation is 0.024 and the t-value is 23.7.
18. The potential number of panels is 1,241×124 = 153,884. However, in about 20 percent of the cases, there is no recorded trade.

TABLE 2. THE RELATION BETWEEN BILATERAL EXPORTS AT THE 4-DIGIT HS LEVEL AND THE SIZE OF THE EXPORTING NATION

	(1)	(2)	(3)
Log(Aggregate export)	0.557*		
	(0.0014)		
Log(GDP)		0.498*	
		(0.0012)	
Log(Population)			0.510*
			(0.0014)
Log(Per capita income)			0.474*
			(0.0018)
R2 within	0.171	0.178	0.179

* Significant at the 1 percent level.

If the size of the supplying country were irrelevant for trade at the four-digit product level, none of our measures of size would have any explanatory power. This is not the case. A country that exports twice as much as another country at the aggregate level of trade tends to export 55.7 percent more of those products that overlap in the export portfolio. The result is similar if we measure size in terms of GDP.

Our dataset also allows us to investigate how dependent each country is on small export lots, and, in this indirect way, to investigate its sensitivity to high litigation costs (including the cost of maintaining internal personnel experienced with the DSU's complexities). Specifically, if we let the computer search through each country's export matrix at the four-digit level, how many entries fall below the given threshold of litigation costs, and what share of exports do they make up in total? The underlying idea is that rights regarding "small" export lots may not be profitable to defend under the current DS system which treats all claims equally, regardless of their value. Let us first consider a threshold of litigation costs equal to $1 million. The result is plotted against total exports in Figure 3. (The results are similar if instead plotted against GDP.)

The scattered plot shows that export lots below $1 million fall with the size of the country in a nonlinear fashion and approach zero for countries with total exports of more than $100 billion. Two Members stick out as being extremely sensitive to high litigation costs (including demands on internally developed expertise) because of the predominance of small export lots: 100 percent of Gambia's exports of goods falls below the $1 million mark and Djibouti is not far behind at 90.7 percent.[19] Five Caribbean countries (Dominica, Saint Vincent and the Grenadines, Barbados, Grenada, and Saint Lucia) also depend on a large

---

19. Services are not included in the analysis because of the shortage of data.

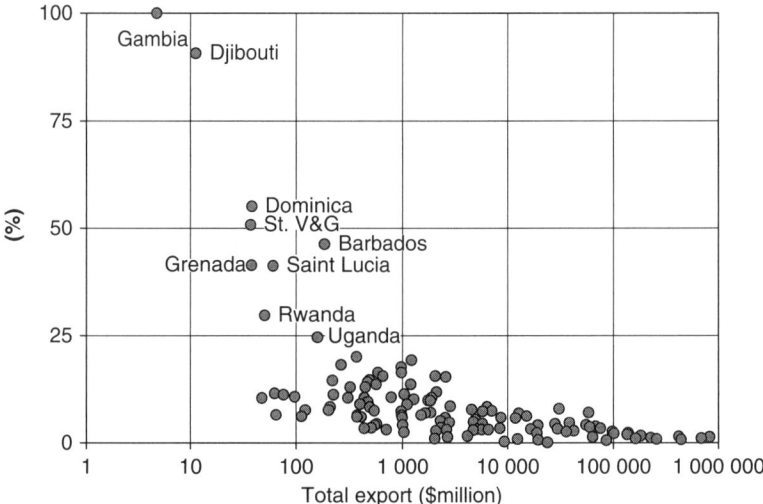

FIGURE 3. SHARE OF EXPORT BELOW $1 MILLION

number of small export lots that may not be worthwhile defending at the WTO under the current procedures.

If the true threshold for profitable use of the DSU is $10 million, many more WTO members are effectively shut out from using the system. Virtually all LDCs and small-island economies are at risk of being without legal protection because they may not be able to recoup the legal expenses and other costs of a

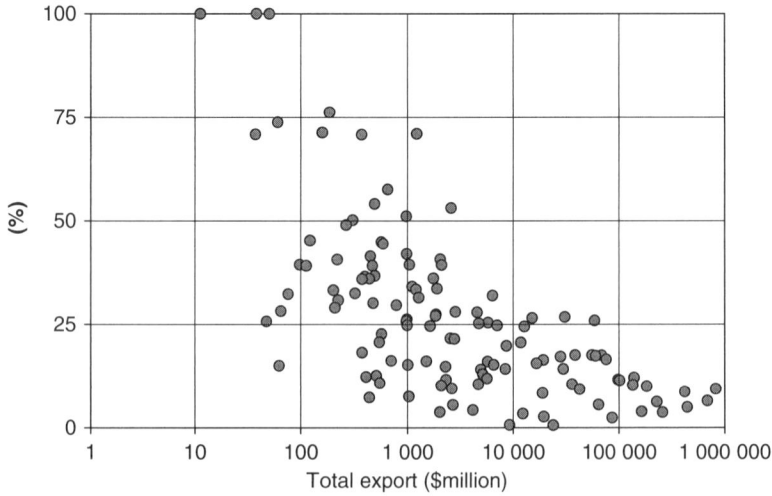

FIGURE 4. SHARE OF EXPORT BELOW $10 MILLION

successful trade dispute.[20] The situation for individual WTO Members is reported in Annex 1.

In sum, smaller trading nations have smaller trade stakes both at the aggregate and disaggregated levels of trade. We therefore have good reasons to believe that they are more sensitive to costly dispute settlement proceedings than larger trading nations.

ii. Litigation Costs and Internal Expertise

The fact that smaller trading nations have smaller trade stakes overall and at the individual product level would not cause any particular problem from the point of view of dispute settlement if it were correspondingly cheaper to litigate small cases, is a point that we address in this section.

WTO Members face three primary types of costs in determining whether to bring a case. The first is the direct out-of-pocket cost for hiring outside legal counsel. The second is that of hiring and dedicating government personnel with expertise to oversee and provide necessary support in the bringing of a complaint. The third is the opportunity cost of expending scarce government resources and personnel time for this particular use as opposed to other social priorities, which in turn also affects a Member's perception of the cost. Because poorer countries have scarcer resources and perhaps more immediate economic and social priorities, they are particularly likely to perceive WTO legal costs to be significant, especially where the future benefits are uncertain.

To bring a complaint within the increasingly complex WTO legal system is *not* simply a matter of outsourcing a file to legal counsel. A WTO Member first needs the internal capacity to select, monitor, and coordinate with outside legal counsel, including for the development of the factual basis for a claim. World Trade Organization case law has been increasingly demanding on litigants in this respect.[21] Second, a WTO Member must make a political decision whether to invest in a WTO case or some other government priority. The aggregate amount of litigation costs arising from DSU procedures is thus clearly a factor. While many commentators may contend that WTO litigation costs are really not that significant of a factor, our discussions with representatives from lesser developed countries suggest that they are certainly perceived to be a restraining factor.[22] They are more likely to be perceived by lesser developed countries

---

20. There are also the costs of internal bureaucratic support as well as political costs (if legal actions are viewed as a hostile act), which need to be factored into any cost-benefit analysis. See G Shaffer, 'The Challenges of WTO Law: Strategies for Developing Country Adaptation' (2006) 5 WT Rev 177–98.

21. We confirmed this aspect in extensive interviewing of WTO Members, as well as of representatives of the ACWL and of private law firms handling WTO cases.

22. This perception was confirmed in dozens of interviews that Shaffer conducted with representatives of poorer developing countries over the past five years, funded in part by

to be high not only because the prospective future benefits from bringing a WTO complaint are smaller on account of the smaller stakes, but also because these countries face more immediate priorities that must be met with limited government budgets so that they are less likely to invest in a longer term legal process whose outcome is uncertain where the legal process is particularly complex and costly.

The costs of dispute settlement would be reduced if the WTO provided meaningful legal aid. But the WTO does not have the budget or the mandate to do so. The WTO agreements rather impose a rather strict *impartiality constraint* on the WTO Secretariat, and the WTO's budget for the provision of more *general* legal counsel to Members is limited. The prospect of a legal aid fund for the hiring of outside lawyers appears constrained because it is not in the interest of key member states and because the WTO is operated on a consensus basis.

Developing countries can seek assistance from the *independent* ACWL which provides legal assistance at discounted rates.[23] The ACWL is currently the best option for the poorest WTO Members today and will likely remain so. Yet the existence of the ACWL does not in itself undermine the need to assess the rationale for adding a small-claims procedure for a number of reasons. First, the ACWL has limited staff and thus is limited in its ability to handle all matters potentially referred to it. Second, although ACWL's assistance represents a form of subsidised legal aid, it is not free.[24] At some threshold, the demands of the process are much more likely to affect the decision of a poor country to bring a complaint. Third, legal aid and a small-claims procedure can be complementary. The legal aid provided (whether through ACWL or otherwise) will be more efficiently used if procedures are designed appropriately for small claims. Fourth, the current system's procedures also require considerable internal work at the national level, which is not practicable for many poorer Members. These demands exist even when outside counsel is used. A small-claims procedure would reduce the demands on poorer developing countries' bureaucracies

---

a grant from the National Science Foundation Law and Social Science Program, NSF Grant Award ID 0351078, and with assistance from ICTSD.

23. Under the annexes to the agreement establishing the Centre, developing countries are divided into three categories: A, B, and C, with least-developed countries (as defined by UN rules) constituting a fourth category. As of October 2007, hourly rates for the Centre's members for WTO litigation support were set at $200 for category A countries, $150 for category B countries and $100 for category C countries. Least-developed countries hourly rates are set at $25. Nonmember developing country rates are set at $350 for category A countries, $300 for category B countries, and $250 for category C countries. See The Agreement Establishing the Advisory Centre on WTO Law, Annex II, Nov. 13, 1999 <http://www.acwl.ch/Docs/ACWLAgreementEnglish.htm>.

24. The ACWL provides free legal opinions to ACWL members about WTO legal questions (including regarding their own proposed measures), but not free services for handling a case before the DSU.

because the procedural demands on the litigants would be simpler than under the normal procedures.

Turning to the cost of legal counsel on the private market, we have some information, although it is incomplete. Law firms do not publicly state what they bill their clients, and fees depend on the complexity of the case and how far the case goes before a settlement is reached. A case that goes the full three-year course with appeal and subsequent contestation over the respondent's implementation of the decision may cost millions of dollars. The unofficial record is the *Japan-Photographic Film* case where the legal fees for each side are reported to have topped $10 million for each party,[25] although this amount is likely being exceeded by a wide margin in the US-EU dispute over aircraft subsidies respectively granted to Airbus and Boeing.

One way of conservatively 'estimating' the cost of legal counsel is to multiply the estimated commercial rates charged by private law firms with the indicative time budget applied by the ACWL vis-à-vis its developing country clients. The hourly rate charged by top-notch law firms in Brussels and Washington, D.C. is somewhere in the range of $350 to $750 (or more). The higher rates apply to senior lawyers and the partners of the law firm. Let's assume for the sake of this example that the average rate is $500 per hour, excluding other expenses, such as for travel or where outside economic consultants are needed. The time budget published by the ACWL is conservative according to the director of the ACWL, Frieder Roessler, and private counsel handling WTO cases. The ACWL staff, we understand, typically devotes two-to-three times as many hours to a case as they actually bill their clients. Private law firms cannot be expected to waive costs in the same fashion since they are for-profit businesses, and they typically spend many more hours than listed in the ACWL's estimated time budget.[26] They spend more time preparing in order to enhance the prospects of a legal victory and bolster their reputation, including among high-paying clients in the private sector. Accordingly, we scale up the conservative ACWL time budget by a factor of 2.5, which is the estimated underreported preparatory time for the ACWL staff. The results of these back-of-the-envelope calculations are presented in Table 3.

Factors that affect the cost include the complexity of the case from both a factual and legal point of view and how far the case proceeds before a settlement is reached. Under these back-of-the-envelope calculations, a case of average complexity would cost $100,000 if it ends after the initial consultations because the parties have settled or the complaint is otherwise withdrawn. If the case advanced

---

25. See G Shaffer, *Defending Interests: Public-Private Partnerships in WTO Litigation* (2003).

26. Shaffer interview with private legal counsel working on WTO matters, Geneva, May 2007. As indicated earlier, some pro bono assistance is available, but it is by no means guaranteed.

TABLE 3. "ESTIMATED" LITIGATION COST

Degree of complexity

Time budget (hours)	Low	Medium	High
Total	643	1110	1765
Consultations	108	200	318
Panel	358	640	1028
Appeal	178	270	420
Estimated costs at $500 per hour			
Total	321 250	555 000	882 500
Consultations	53 750	100 000	158 750
Panel	178 750	320 000	513 750
Appeal	88 750	135 000	210 000

Source: ACWL home page and own calculations.

to the panel stage, it would cost another $320,000. And if the panel decision were appealed, the bill would rise by another $135,000. The total cost would then top one-half of $1 million. To the extent that a party uses the ACWL, the costs would be reduced but can still be considerable.

One particular problem for a complainant concerned about legal costs is that the total amount (as well as the prospective benefits) cannot be assessed beforehand since they depend on the actions of the other party. If the respondent decides not to settle and the case goes to a panel, the price will increase. If the respondent decides to appeal the ruling, the price will increase further. If the parties choose to litigate over compliance, the price continues to rise. If the respondent does not comply with a ruling, then the entire litigation could be for naught.[27] This possibility only adds to the underlying uncertainty that the complainant might not prevail legally, even if the case looks promising. World Trade Organization Members that have smaller government budgets allocated for legal affairs, and in particular smaller developing countries that need to weigh other immediate priorities, will perceive the legal fees and associated uncertainties to be considerable, especially where there is no guarantee that the case will lead to a positive outcome. The dual uncertainty of possibly losing a case and of the respondent not complying with an affirmative ruling can discourage governments from filing a complaint.

---

27. It is not unusual that a case goes the full course. The European Union, for example, would seem almost systematically to appeal cases even if an appeal rarely changes the substantive outcome of a case, which suggests a strategic motivation (at least in part to scare price-sensitive litigants).

Nonetheless, a small-claims procedure would be needed less if small cases (in commercial terms) are less costly to litigate under the current system because they are less complex from a factual and legal perspective—that is, if costs and stakes move in tandem. Casual empiricism suggests that some high stakes cases cost more to litigate, indeed much more. The *Airbus-Boeing (US-EU)* dispute, for example, involves teams of lawyers and economists lined up on each side to gather factual evidence and prepare legal arguments. There appears to be little limit to spending money in such a high profile, multibillion dollar case involving state-supported multinational companies.

Such casual empiricism however, says little about the *inherent* relationship between litigation costs (including internal personnel time) and commercial stakes. What it tells us is that governments and their private clients are less fussy about the billable hours when the stakes are high. Yet there is no rule that factual and/or legal issues are *inherently* more complex in cases that concern a billion dollars rather than a million. It may be true in some cases and untrue in others. Indeed, one could make the opposite case by referring to the relatively simpler rules that apply to most manufactured imports compared with agricultural imports, in spite of the fact that the former tend to involve larger values. Some of the most complex and controversial trade law issues involve relatively small commodities in value terms, such as bananas, sugar, rice, and cotton.

Even if one believes that small cases in commercial terms are inherently cheaper to prepare than large cases (which we doubt), the issue remains whether the offset is complete. If answered in the affirmative, both sides of the cost-benefit equation would move in tandem, maintaining the neutrality of the DS system with respect to size. But this result is not plausible because of the fixed costs of bringing a case. Jurisprudence must be reviewed and assessed and a factual dossier developed. The consultations, the panel process, and the appeals process follow a certain track regardless of the value of the case. The complainant must have internal staff that follows the case and provides support to outside counsel, in particular for the factual dossier. That staff also needs to be of a sufficiently high bureaucratic status that it receives the necessary political support for the case in the capital. Countries with high stakes that are repeat players before the WTO dispute settlement system are more likely to have such officials, benefiting from economies of scope.[28] The result of DS procedures is to create a threshold effect that effectively discriminates against small claims and countries that have them, even though such small claims are relatively large in relation to those countries' small economies.

---

28. Although the ACWL is a repeat player that can assist smaller countries, once again, it needs active support from the WTO Member that it is representing, including regarding the factual basis and political support for a claim.

This conclusion is indirectly supported by the empirical research undertaken by Chad Bown.[29] The starting point of Bown's research is that many disputes involve policies having a multilateral reach. Any country with a trade interest in the product(s) affected by the disputed measure *could* have filed the complaint.[30] In fact, if the incentives to file *were* identical, as would be the case if stakes and costs moved in tandem, we should not see any relationship to size in the filing data. All potential litigants would be equally likely to file and the actual filing pattern would be a random draw. But this is not what the data shows. Quite the contrary, the decision to file is *systematically* related to export stakes, legal capacities, and other variables that enter the cost-benefit analysis.[31] Bown's findings suggest very strongly that the DS system is not neutral to size.

Our data compilation, using a less sophisticated method but in the same spirit, provides further evidence to this effect. Based on the product coverage reported in the Dispute Settlement Data Set assembled by Horn & Mavroidis for the World Bank,[32] we have extracted the covered trade data from COMTRADE in the year preceding the dispute. Our database covers 190 disputes between 1995 and mid-2004.[33] The results corroborate Bown's findings. In 38 percent of the cases, the country with the highest export stake in the covered products filed the complaint. In a further 17 percent, the second largest supplier filed. And in three cases out of four, the complainant(s) were among the top five suppliers. The likelihood that this pattern is random and independent of the commercial stakes is virtually nil. Figure 5 shows the relationship between the distribution of filings and the rank of the exporter in the defendant's market for the covered products.

Where a country can 'piggyback' on another WTO Member's filings, it can benefit, and even 'free ride'. Yet small countries then become dependent on circumstance. In certain cases they will benefit as a side effect of another Member's litigation; in others they will not. Where a large country does not export the product, or has different interests in regard to the product or is able to negotiate

---

29. CP Bown, 'Participation in WTO Dispute Settlement: Complainants, Interested Parties and Free Riders' (2005) 19(2) WB Econ Rev 287–310.

30. In fact, almost any Member of the WTO can file. The Appellate Body established in the *European Communities–Bananas III* case that an active trade interest is not a prerequisite. (The European Union was trying to remove the United States from the case with the argument that the United States had no direct trade interests in bananas). It suffices that a member has a potential trade interest or a "systemic interest" in the issues concerned.

31. As regarding the impact of legal capacity, see also M Busch, E Reinhardt and G Shaffer, 'Does Legal Capacity Matter?' (2008) ICTSD Working Paper <http://papers.ssrn.com/sol3/papers.cfm?abstract_id=1091435>.

32. H Horn and P Mavroidis, 'The WTO Dispute Settlement System 1995–2004: Some Descriptive Statistics' (2006) World Bank.

33. For about a third of the disputes we have no trade data, either because the dispute concerned services and intellectual property rights for which trade data is scant or because the coverage of the dispute was not reported in the H&M database.

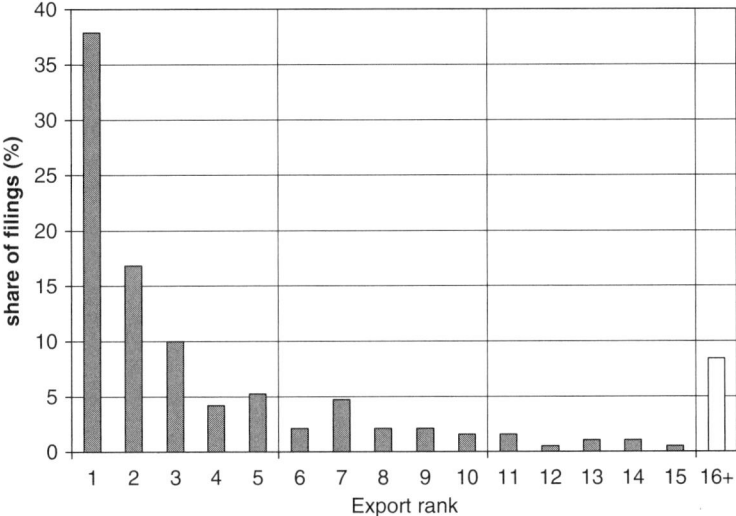

FIGURE 5. THE FILING DISTRIBUTION (1995 TO MID 2004)

a settlement regarding the dispute that defends its interests but not that of the small country, the idea of 'piggybacking' and 'free riding' provides little less solace. In fact, most trade disputes are settled without WTO litigation but in the shadow of potential litigation.[34] There is no assurance that these settlements extend the same benefits to other exporters of the same product (although they in principle should because of the most-favored-nation obligation), especially where parties settle a dispute outside of the WTO system without any complaint being filed.

In sum, the evidence strongly suggests that the DS system is not neutral to size. Exporters with the highest export stakes are more likely to file a complaint. In a truly neutral system, the individual stakes should not matter, and neutrality among trading nations is the stated ambition of the DSU, as laid down in DSU Article 3.3 which we cited at the start.

iii. Alternative WTO Dispute Settlement Mechanisms

The final issue we need to address before we have established a *prima facie* case for considering a small-claims procedure in the WTO is that the DSU does not

---

34. Even where parties file WTO complaints, most complaints are settled without litigation. See M Busch and E Reinhardt, 'Bargaining in the Shadow of the Law: Early Settlement in GATT/WTO Disputes' (2000) (24) Ford ILJ 158 158–59; CC Parlin, 'Operation of Consultations, Deterrence, and Mediation' (2000) 31 L & Pol Int'l Bus 565 567–69. If we include potential claims that are settled without an actual filing, the figure increases.

already offer an alternative that has a similar impact of reducing costs for Members with small trade stakes. In fact, the DSU *does* offer a number of alternative tracks that at least in principle could be suitable for cases of less value.

First, the DSU encourages parties to resolve their disputes amicably using the instruments of good offices, conciliation, or mediation.[35] Under good offices, the institution provides primarily logistical support to the parties to resolve their dispute. With conciliation, a third party also directly participates in the discussions and negotiations between the parties. In a mediation, the mediator not only contributes to the discussions and negotiations but also may propose a solution. The parties, however, are not obligated to accept the proposal.

Second, the DSU provides for arbitration upon agreement of the parties, with the arbitrator's decision being binding.[36] Arbitration is a potentially more expeditious procedure than the normal panel process. It may also be a less costly one since it would not be subject to appeal (although its cost-effectiveness is not guaranteed since international arbitrations can be costly). In WTO arbitration, as in international commercial arbitration generally, the parties 'agree to abide by the arbitration award'.[37] Enforcement could therefore be less of an issue, which advantages smaller players.

These alternative tracks are only available, however, *if both sides agree to use them*. We have no data regarding whether mediation or arbitration has been requested by one party and refused by the other. What we know is that there has only been one joint request to the WTO director-general for mediation, which was submitted by the Philippines, Thailand, and the European Communities in the particular context of the launching of the Doha Round of Trade Negotiations and the granting of a ten-year waiver for the preferential agreement between the EC and Asia-Pacific-Caribbean countries (the EC-ACP Agreement).[38] Similarly, arbitration under Article 25 has never been used as an alternative to the regular panel process although there has been one arbitration again agreed in the context of the waiver granted for the EC-ACP preferential agreement.[39] Finally, parties

---

35. See DSU Article 5.
36. See DSU Article 25.
37. See DSU Article 25, para 3. Par.a 4 of Article 25, however, states that DSU Article 22 "shall apply *mutatis mutandis* to arbitration awards, and Article 22 includes provisions on the "suspension of concessions" in the event of noncompliance.
38. WTO, 'Request for Mediation by the Philippines, Thailand and the European Communities' (16 October 2002) WT/GC/66.
39. The only recorded use of Article 25 arbitration so far is the arbitration of the level of nullification or impairment in *United States–Section 110(5)(B) of the US Copyright Act*, a dispute between the European Union and the United States. In addition, as part of the waiver granted for the EC-ACP Cotonou preferential arrangement, the European Union agreed that banana exporting countries that do not benefit from such preferences could seek arbitration if they do not agree with the tariffs that the European Union proposed to replace its quota system for bananas. See *ACP-EC Partnership Agreement*

have, to our knowledge, only once (recently) used the good offices of the WTO director-general,[40] although they have used good offices under the Agreement on SPS Agreement three times (using the chair and secretariat of the SPS Committee).[41]

We can only speculate why these alternative procedures are not used more frequently. One likely explanation is that the stronger party in a bilateral dispute is not interested in agreeing to procedures that could put the other side on a more equal footing. The possibility of raising the price for the other side by not yielding without a full-scale legal battle could induce the weaker party into a settlement on favorable terms or discourage the case from being submitted in the first place. Why yield this advantage by agreeing to a less-demanding mediation or arbitration? Defendants may, in addition, prefer to litigate WTO disputes under the full procedures for internal political reasons so that they can respond to their domestic constituencies protected by the trade measure that they have done everything possible to defend it but now must comply with the legal ruling. Complainants, in contrast, may find that using good offices or mediation would only facilitate respondent's ability to prolong the maintenance of an illegal trade barrier. Finally, there is no defined procedure for these alternatives so that the parties would need to define the procedure each time on an *ad hoc* basis. Such *ad hoc* negotiations over procedures can be quite long and, as a result, undermine the very idea of a more 'expeditious' and less costly alternative.[42]

The *third and final* option is for a party to invoke the accelerated procedures provided by the GATT Decision of 5 April 1966,[43] which has now been incorporated into the WTO.[44] This option is only available for developing country

---

Arbitration (Banana Tariffs Arbitration), WT/L/616 (1 August 2005) (Brazil, Colombia, Costa Rica, Ecuador, Guatemala, Honduras, Nicaragua, Panama, and Venezuela/European Communities), as well as the *Second ACP-EC Partnership Agreement Arbitration*, WT/L/625 (27 October 2005), involving the same parties.

40. See WTO, 'Request for Consultations by Colombia, European Communities— Regime for the Importation of Bananas' (26 March 2007) WT/DS361/1. The 'good offices'process commenced in December 2007. We thank an anonymous reviewer for noting this development.

41. Two of the three referrals resulted in a settlement. The International Plant Protection Commission and the World Organization for Animal Health (OIE') also offer informal dispute settlement procedures relating to sanitary and phytosanitary measures. Shaffer interview with WTO secretariat member assigned to the SPS committee, June 12, 2007, Geneva.

42. The term 'expeditious' is used in DSU Article 25.1.

43. WTO, 'Decision of 5 April 1966 on procedures under Article XXIII' in BISD 14S/18.

44. The Decision of 5 April 1966 procedures are incorporated into the WTO via Article 3, Paragraph 12 of the Dispute Settlement Understanding, which provides:

Notwithstanding paragraph 11, if a complaint based on any of the covered agreements is brought by a developing country Member against a developed country Member, the

complainants against developed country respondents. Although mutual consent is not required, this accelerated procedure was applied only once by a panel during the GATT era (whose decision was blocked by the respondent and thus never adopted), and it has yet to be used under the WTO.[45] The explanation provided on the WTO home page for developing countries' decision not to use the procedure is that 'developing country Members tend to prefer to have more time to prepare their submissions'.[46] Indeed, litigation in the WTO has become a *very* demanding exercise. The legal submissions typically exceed 100 pages and include frequent references to previous WTO jurisprudence. These submissions are demanding to prepare even for an experienced law firm (if a Member can afford it). Shorter time frames will not be a viable option for developing countries unless the demands on the parties are reduced correspondingly, especially for poor developing countries that are not repeat players and thus have significantly less experience with WTO law and jurisprudence. Although a developing country could prepare its initial submission before filing its complaint,

---

complaining party shall have the right to invoke, as an alternative to the provisions contained in Articles 4, 5, 6 and 12 of this Understanding, the corresponding provisions of the Decision of 5 April 1966 (BISD 14S/18), except that where the Panel considers that the time-frame provided for in paragraph 7 of that Decision is insufficient to provide its report and with the agreement of the complaining party, that time-frame may be extended. To the extent that there is a difference between the rules and procedures of Articles 4, 5, 6 and 12 and the corresponding rules and procedures of the Decision, the latter shall prevail.

See WTO, 'Understanding on Rules and Procedures Governing the Settlement of Disputes, Marrakesh Agreement Establishing the World Trade Organization, Annex 2' in *The Legal Texts: The Results Of The Uruguay Round Of Multilateral Trade Negotiations* (Geneva: WTO, 1999).

45. The 1966 procedures were invoked under the GATT by Israel in 1972, by Chile in 1977, by India in 1980, and by Mexico in 1987, but the time frames were never applied because the cases were settled (or in the case of Mexico, consolidated with other complaints). See R Hudec, *Developing Countries in the GATT Legal System* (Aldershot: Gower, 1987) 66–67; and WTO, *GATT Analtyic Index: Guide to GATT Law and Practice, Vol. 2* (Geneva: WTO, 1995) 765. The procedures were applied, however, in the 1993 bananas case. See Panel Report, *EEC— Member States' Import Regime for Bananas*, WT/DS32/R (3 June 1993). The European Union, however, blocked adoption of the report. See MS Dunne III, 'Redefining Power Orientation: A Reassessment of Jackson's Paradigm in Light of Asymmetries of Power, Negotiation and Compliance in the GATT/WTO Dispute Settlement System' (2002) 34(1) L & Pol Int'l Bus 277 295–96. The GATT Analytical Index also notes two times in which paragraphs 1–3 of the 1966 procedures were invoked by Brazil, respectively made in 1987 and 1993, and does not mention the complaint by Israel in 1972. See WTO, *GATT Analytic Index: Guide to GATT Law and Practice, Vol. 2* (Geneva: WTO, 1995) 765 765–66. Paragraphs 1–3 include use of the 'good offices' of the director-general.

46. See <http://www.wto.org/english/tratop_e/dispu_e/disp_settlement_cbt_e/c11s2p1_e.htm>.

it still would have reduced time for its second submission in response to the respondent's arguments, as well as for its preparation for oral hearings and any questions raised by a panel to which it must respond. Moreover, the shorter time lines under the 1966 procedure would apply only at the panel stage, and not to Appellate Body review, nor before proceedings before implementation panels and compliance panels, so that they should have little impact on total litigation costs, including in terms of personnel time.[47] The creation of multiple levels of appeal and review has made the 1966 procedures less relevant.

Before moving on to address the design of a small-claims procedure, we note one important development in the Doha Negotiations. A broad array of developed and developing country Members have proposed the addition of a new facilitative mechanism for the resolution of market-access disputes that do not involve agricultural matters. Under their joint 2007 proposal, a new WTO mediation procedure would be created to address nontariff barriers to trade (other than to agricultural trade) pursuant to which a Member may identify a barrier and request the initiation of a mediation procedure.[48] Under the proposal, the other party should 'accord sympathetic consideration' to that request, but it would retain the discretion to block the procedure's commencement. If the procedure were initiated, a 'facilitator', who would typically be the chairman or vice chairman of the relevant WTO committee within the Council for the Trade of Goods, would hear the parties' concerns and perspectives. The facilitator could 'offer advice and propose solutions for the parties' consideration taking into account the information presented by the parties'. The facilitator would do so within a set period of time, with 60 days being proposed in brackets. The facilitator would then write a factual report to the relevant WTO committee, summarizing the measure in question, the procedure followed, and any mutually agreed solution. We would welcome the addition of such a defined mediation procedure, which would address many of the concerns raised in this chapter.

---

47. It is sometimes maintained that developing country complainants prefer to use the normal procedures for status reasons–that is, they wish to be perceived as full-fledged members. This argument has never been tested, and at some point, alleged status concerns need to be weighed against other factors, especially in light of the fact that the vast majority of WTO Members have never participated in the DSU as a complainant. In any case, the existence of multiple levels of appeal in the WTO has made the 1966 procedures less relevant from a cost-benefit perspective.

48. See WTO, 'Market Access for Non-Agricultural Products: Non-Tariff Barriers—Proposal on Procedures for the Facilitation of Solutions to NTBs, Communication from the African Group, Canada, European Communities, LDC Group, NAMA-11 Group of Developing Countries, New Zealand, Norway, Pakistan and Switzerland' (23 July 2007) TN/MA/W/88. For an overview of the earlier process that led to this 2007 proposal, see Issue Brief, 'A New Facilitative Mechanism at the WTO to Address Non-Tariff Measures: Issues for Consideration,' CIEL (August 2006).

Even were it adopted,[49] however, there would arguably still be a need for a small-claims procedure to address matters that are blocked from being heard under the procedure, are not settled through it, or are not covered by it (such as those concerning agricultural trade).

C. SMALL-CLAIMS PROCEDURES

Before turning to an assessment of a small-claims procedure in the WTO context, we briefly examine domestic and supranational experiences with such a procedure.[50] In this Part C, we explain what small-claims procedures are at the national level, what purpose they serve, how they are organized in different jurisdictions involving alternative design features, and what challenges they have faced. We also discuss the recent creation in the EU of a transnational European Small Claims Procedure, which represents a new initiative at the supranational level in this area, as well as the use of small-claims procedures in international arbitration.

i. The National Context

Most advanced national legal systems include special procedures for small claims that otherwise would be too costly to pursue.[51] The primary purpose of these procedures is to provide greater access to justice to those persons and for those situations where the normal civil justice system is too costly and time-consuming.

Small-claims courts in the United States originated in the first two decades of the last century as part of a legal realist reform movement which maintained

---

49. The United States and Japan have questioned whether it is needed. See CIEL Issue Brief, at 3.

50. Cf. D McRae, 'What is the Future of WTO Dispute Settlement?' (2004) 7 JIEL 3–10 ('domestic law experience in forms of dispute resolution developed as an alternative or supplement to litigation needs careful consideration').

51. This presentation draws from the following sources, among others: B Zucker and M Her, 'The People's Court Examined: A Legal and Empirical Analysis of the Small Claims Court System' (2003) 37 U San Fran L Rev 315–50; J Baldwin, 'Small Claims Courts' in *Legal Systems of the World: A Political, Social, and Cultural Encyclopedia, Vol 4* (2002); J Ruhnka, S Weller and J Martin, *Small Claims Courts: A National Examination* (1978); A Best and others, 'Peace, Wealth, Happiness, and Small Claims Courts: A Case Study' (1994) 21 Ford Urb LJ 343–79; and R Lempert and J Sanders, *An Invitation to Law and Social Science* (1986). See also B Yngvesson and P Hennessey, 'Small Claims, Complex Disputes: a Review of the Small Claims Literature' (1975) 9 L & Soc Rev 219–74; and A Sarat, 'Alternatives in Dispute Processing: Litigation in a Small Claims Court' (1976) 10 L & Soc Rev 339–75.

that the formal legal system failed to respond to the needs of most citizens.[52] Reformers believed that the regular civil justice system's complexities and technicalities made it virtually impossible for average citizens to use it. They hoped that a small-claims procedure would enable wage earners and small businessmen to use the courts to collect wages and accounts that they were owed.[53] In the 1960s and following decades, with the rise of the consumer movement and demands for 'access to justice', there was a renewed push for facilitating access to the legal system. Advocates of small-claims procedures again maintained that regular civil court procedures were too cumbersome for small cases, resulting in unreasonable delay and expense and the requirement of a lawyer for parties to find their way through the system's complex procedural requirements. Advocates wished to reduce legal costs and delay by reducing filing fees, simplifying pleadings, eliminating procedural steps, and eliminating the need for litigants to hire a lawyer. They contended that citizens would look more favorably on the legal system were they provided greater access to it. Indeed, some observers maintain that a particular benefit of small-claims procedures is that claimants believe that they have been able to have access to the courts and participate effectively in proceedings where otherwise they would not, affecting their perceptions of the legal system.

Small-claims procedures are typically provided for a defined category of claims before a division of an existing lower court of general jurisdiction, be it a municipal, county, or district court, although there is great variation among jurisdictions. United States courts, for example, provide small-claims proceedings for civil claims that can be satisfied by money damages up to a specified dollar amount. They sometimes exclude from small-claims procedures certain categories of claims, regardless of the amount sought, such as libel and slander actions, on the theory that these actions are quasi-criminal and are too serious to entrust to an informal procedure. The United States has also created small-claims procedures for some public law claims at the federal level, as before the US Tax Court.[54]

Some jurisdictions have prohibited commercial enterprises from using small-claims procedures because these parties tend to be better resourced and experienced users of litigation so that they have less need for such procedures.[55] In Europe, for example, Ireland's small-claims procedure is limited to consumer complaints,

---

52. See Lempert and Sanders ibid. (citing the work of Roscoe Pound).

53. See Ruhnka and others (n 51 above) 1. See also S Elwell and C Carlson, 'The Iowa Small Claims Court: An Empirical Analysis' (1990) 75 Iowa L Rev 433–34; JC Turner and JA McGee, 'Small Claims Reform: A Means of Expanding Access to the American Civil Justice System' (2000) 5 UDC L Rev 177–78; Best and others (note 51 above) 346–47.

54. WC Whitford, 'The Small-Case Procedure of the United States Tax Court: A Small Claims Court that Works' (1984) 9 Am Bar Found Res J 797–828.

55. Baldwin (n 51 above).

while that for England and Wales allows businesses to use it.[56] Rather than shut their doors to businesses and collection agencies, some jurisdictions limit the number of claims that any one individual or entity may file within a specified time period.[57] Most jurisdictions, however, appear to offer these procedures without quantitative limitation to businesses as well as individuals.[58]

Although the adversary process is largely retained in small-claims procedures in the sense that each side to a dispute is responsible for presenting the arguments and facts in its favor, trial procedures and rules of evidence are more informal and left largely to the discretion of the trial judge. The judge can play a more active role at trial, assisting litigants in bringing out relevant facts and clarifying the legal issues involved. Court clerks can also provide some basic services to the parties, such as assisting with the filing of the complaint forms and providing advice on what types of proof are needed at trial and how to subpoena supporting witnesses when needed. To facilitate use of these procedures, the state of California has created a Small Claims Legal Advisor Program.[59]

While small-claims courts have broadened the access to justice for ordinary people and small businesses, they have not always lived up to expectations. Ruhnka et al note the following concerns, although they find that at least some of these concerns are overstated:

- 'Where business plaintiffs are permitted in small-claims court they tend to dominate the caseload of these courts, and they usually sue individual (nonbusiness) defendants;
- Plaintiffs almost always win and defendants almost always lose in small-claims court (with the implication being that the process is somehow arrayed against defendants or the type of people who are often defendants);
- Where lawyers are used at trial they are most often used by business plaintiffs against unrepresented individual defendants (which further disadvantages defendants);
- Small-claims trials are often rushed, which tends to disadvantage inexperienced defendants;
- Many litigants, particularly unrepresented individuals and small businessmen, are unable to subsequently collect their small-claims judgments;
- Many small claims can be factually or legally complex and they may not be adequately dealt with in an informal proceeding;

---

56. P Cortes, 'Does the Proposed European Procedure Enhance the Resolution of Small Claims?' (2007) <http://papers.ssrn.com/sol3/papers.cfm?abstract_id=983527> 1–4.
57. Ibid 3.
58. See Ruhnka and others (n 51 above) 41–48.
59. Turner and McGee (n 53 above).

- Role conflict problems may arise when judges attempt to mediate or settle claims instead of deciding them outright'.[60]

Overall, most small-claims procedures, at least in the United States, have retained many characteristics of the formal system. Lawyers can be present in most jurisdictions (although some restrict their use),[61] and judges retain much of their traditional role. As Lempert and Sanders write, "most small claims courts [have been] simplified versions of traditional dispute decision courts using adversarial processes to reach binary decisions".[62] The forum remains a primarily adjudicative (and not mediative) one. Many of the points addressed above may be relevant in considering whether to create a small-claims procedure adapted to the WTO context, and if so, how to design it. We imagine that a WTO small-claims procedure would largely remain a simplified version of the DSU procedures, with some adaptations that we address in Part D.

ii. The EU Regional Context

European Member States have their own versions of small-claims procedures. What is particularly noteworthy in Europe, however, is the move to create for the first time a small-claims procedure at the supranational level. In July 2007, the EU created a new European Small Claims Procedure.[63] It covers cross-border claims of up to 2,000 euros, other than certain categories of claims, such as for defamation. It will go into effect in all EU Member States in January 2009 except for Denmark, which opted out.

In its initial proposal, the Commission made the following observations as way of background to the needs of introducing European Small Claims Procedures, many of which are relevant to our concerns:

> Costs, delay and vexation of judicial proceedings do not necessarily decrease proportionally with the amount of the claim. On the contrary, the smaller the

---

60. Ruhnka and others (n 51 above) 5–6. Judges may, for example, identify more with those of a similar social class (landlords over tenants) or gender (men in divorce proceedings). As for the first concern noted by Runkha, an empirical study of the small-claims courts in Colorado showed that 'the number of claims of businesses against individuals was relatively low compared to the number of claims filed by businesses against other businesses'. Best and others (n 51 above) 357.

61. While most US states allow litigants to be represented by attorneys, some jurisdictions either prohibit attorney representation or restrict their use. For example, Michigan prohibits attorneys from taking part in small-claims litigation except on the attorney's own behalf, Mich Comp Laws § 600.8408(1) (2007); Oregon allows attorneys only with the court's consent, Or Rev Stat § 46.415(4) (2007); and Montana allows a party to be represented by an attorney only if all the parties are represented by attorneys, Mont Code Ann § 25-35-505(2) (2007).

62. Lempert and Sanders (n 51 above) 246.

63. See Regulation (EC) 861/2007 of 11 July 2007 of the European Parliament and of the Council of 11 July 2007 establishing a European Small Claims Procedure, 2007 OJ (L 199) 1.

claim is, the more the weight of these obstacles increases. This has led to the creation of simplified civil procedures for Small Claims in many Member States. At the same time, the potential number of cross-border disputes is rising as a consequence of the increasing use of the EC Treaty rights of free movement of persons, goods and services. The obstacles to obtaining a fast and inexpensive judgment are clearly intensified in a cross-border context. It will often be necessary to hire two lawyers, there are additional translation and interpretation costs and miscellaneous other factors such as extra travel costs of litigants, witnesses, lawyers etc. Potential problems are not limited to disputes between individuals. Also the owners of small businesses may face difficulties when they want to pursue their claims in another Member State. But as a consequence of the lack of a procedure which is 'proportional' to the value of the litigation, the obstacles that the creditor is likely to encounter might make it questionable whether judicial recourse is economically sensible. The expense of obtaining a judgment, in particular against a defendant in another Member State, is often disproportionate to the amount of the claim involved. Many creditors, faced with the expense of the proceedings, and daunted by the practical difficulties that are likely to ensue, abandon any hope of obtaining what they believe is rightfully theirs.[64]

The arguments made by the Commission parallel those made in Section B, with the key difference being that WTO law is not directly applicable to private subjects (at least not in the EU, United States, and most other jurisdictions) in the same way as under the EC Treaty. It is therefore not possible for businesses to file a complaint before a national court arguing that a regulation violates a WTO provision. Moreover, it is only governments that have standing at the WTO. The EU's recent creation of a European Small Claims Procedure (involving a civil procedure to be used by persons) is therefore not directly applicable to the WTO context (involving an international procedure to be used by states). It is nevertheless interesting because it recognizes the need for small-claims procedures at the supranational level as well.

iii. Small Claims in International Dispute Settlement

Finally, we briefly turn to two precedents for the handling of small claims against states at the international level: the Iran-US Claims Tribunal and the United Nations Compensation Commission (UNCC), respectively, involving claims against Iran following the Iranian revolution and against Iraq following its invasion of Kuwait. The context for these claims was quite distinct, as there were close to 4,000 claims before the Iran-US Claims Tribunal and over two million

---

64. See Commission of the European Communities, Proposal for a Regulation of the European Parliament and of the Council establishing a European Small Claims Procedure, COM (2005) 87 final (15 March 2005) (initial Commission proposal), at article 2.1.1.

claims before the UN Compensation Commission.⁶⁵ However, we note the mechanisms used in these cases since they involved claims against states at the international level in which small claims were treated distinctly.

As part of the settlement of the hostage crisis in 1981 following the Iranian revolution, the United States and Iran entered into a Claims Settlement Declaration (CSD) which established the Iran-US Claims Tribunal in the Hague.⁶⁶ The CSD created separate mechanisms for the handling of small and larger claims. While claimants would directly represent themselves at their own expense for claims that were equal or greater than $250,000, claims less than this amount were to be presented by the claimant's government on the claimant's behalf.⁶⁷ Although neither the CSD nor the tribunal created procedural rules for expediting small claims,⁶⁸ 'a procedure evolved whereby, for small claims, the United States initially filed very brief Statements of Claim, which were then augmented with Supplemental Statements of Claim as particular cases were scheduled for further consideration by the Tribunal'.⁶⁹ By August 1989, however, the tribunal had decided only 36 of the 2,795 small claims that had been filed,⁷⁰ allegedly on account of noncooperation of the Iranian arbitrators and the tribunal's determination to address the larger claims first.⁷¹ Responding to the delay,

---

65. See D Caron, 'The United States Compensation Commission for Claims Arising out of the 1991 Gulf War: the "Arising Prior to" Decision', (2005) 14(2) Flor St UJTL Pol 309–34.

66. Declaration of the Government of the Democratic and Popular Republic of Algeria Concerning the Settlement of Claims by the Government of the United States of America and the Government of the Islamic Republic of Iran, Jan. 19, 1981, 20 I.L.M. 223 [hereinafter Claims Settlement Declaration].

67. Id., art. III, ¶ 3.

68. *Alcan Aluminum Ltd. v. Ircable Corp.*, 2 Iran-US Cl Trib Rep. 294, 301 (1983) (Mosk, J. concurring) ('The Tribunal Rules lack some of the modern or innovative case-resolution techniques. There are no explicit provisions for joinder or consolidation of cases; for coordination of cases; for intervention; for representative or class claims; for the application of a decision in one case to other cases; for the elimination of unnecessary pleadings; for meaningful discovery; for the use of special masters; or for the elimination of various formal procedures for claims of less than $250,000, which are presented by the Governments under Article III, paragraph 3, of the Claims Settlement Declaration... The Tribunal can, of course, without formal rule, utilize many of these devices to expedite cases... in practice, however, even these are rarely or inadequately used'.)

69. *Int'l Telephone & Telegraph Corp. v. Iran*, Case No. 11045, July 7, 1989 (Holtzmann, J. concurring).

70. Dep't of State File No. P90 0111-1911/1912. Another 72 small claims had been settled, which settlements were approved by the tribunal.

71. Powell A. Moore, Assistant Secretary of State for Legislative and Intergovernmental Affairs, responding to a request from Senator Barry Goldwater for information regarding the progress of a constituent's small claim against Iran, July 28, 1983. In fact, "[t]he small claims are particularly irritating to Iran because many of the claimants have dual Iranian-American

the US Congress passed legislation in 1985 that gave the Foreign Claims Settlement Commission (FCSC) jurisdiction to adjudicate claims by US nationals in the event Iran and the United States entered into a lump-sum settlement agreement of the small claims.[72] Iran and the United States reached a settlement agreement on May 13, 1990, pursuant to which the United States withdrew the small claims from the tribunal in return for a lump-sum payment from Iran.[73] The United States then referred these claims to the FCSC for adjudication, which finished processing them in February 1995.[74]

The UNCC likewise adopted a distinct means for handling small claims arising from Iraq's invasion of Kuwait in 1990. As one commentator writes:

> (a)s for the functioning of the UNCC, it is remarkable that its very first decision, adopted symbolically enough on the anniversary of Iraq's invasion, gave precedence to the processing of claims by individuals not exceeding US $100,000, as opposed to claims by corporations and governments. The political intent of the UNCC, to offer a very different model to that of the US-Iran Claims Tribunal, is evident here, and was strengthened in 1994 by Decision No. 17 of the UNCC according to which all claims in categories A, B and C would receive a minimum compensation of US $2,500 each, before starting with the payments for category D, E and F claims.[75]

The first phase of minimum payments was completed in July 1999, and the Commission continued to prioritize the smaller claims of individuals until completing its work on them.[76]

We mention the work of these bodies because they represent attempts to address the distinct situation of small claims at the international level. In each case, they involve a separate handling of small claims brought by private parties against a state.

---

citizenship or are former citizens of Iran. The Iranian Government and the Iranian judges insist that such people are not entitled to remuneration from the tribunal". Pear 1990.

72. Title V, Foreign Relations Authorization Act, Fiscal Years 1986 and 1987, Pub. L. No. 99–93, 99 Stat. 405, 437 (50 USC § 1701 note).

73. Settlement Agreement in Claims of Less than $250,000, Case No. 86 and Case No. B38, 25 Iran-US Cl Trib Rep. 327, Article III, ¶ (v) (1990). See also *Abrahim-Youri v. United States*, 139 F.3d 1462, 1464 (DC Cir 1997).

74. *Abrahim-Youri v. United States*, 139 F.3d 1462, 1464 (DC Cir 1997).

75. A Gattini, 'The UN Compensation Commission: Old Rules, New Procedures on War Reparations' (2002) 13 EJIL 161 166–67.

76. UNCC Governing Council, Press Release for the Closing of the Thirty-Second Session, June 24, 1999; as well as the Commission's Web site at <http://www2.unog.ch/uncc/>.

D. ADAPTATION OF A SMALL-CLAIMS PROCEDURE TO THE WTO CONTEXT

As we emphasised in the introduction, it is not possible to make a direct parallel between small-claims procedures at the national level and a corresponding institution at the international level. The parallel lies more in the underlying philosophy than in the institutional and political context. The challenge is to find a model with appropriate design features for the WTO context.

Some of the issues that need careful analysis are:

- What is a 'small claim' in the WTO context?
- Should a small-claims proceeding be available to all WTO Members? Or should it be available only to poorer developing countries, and if so, which ones? Should it be available against all respondents?
- Should small-claims rulings have the same precedential value as regular panel reports? Or no precedential value at all?
- Should different remedies be preferred, such as cash compensation in the event of noncompliance?
- How could procedures be streamlined to save costs?
- What body would hear these claims? The same kind of *ad hoc* panels that hear regular cases? A new "small-claims body" with professional judges? A new permanent panel body?
- Should appeals be permitted, eliminated, or only made available by petition to the Appellate Body?

Our primary aim in this Part D is to stimulate policy debate by offering a structured analysis of these issues and of possible institutional responses to them. We nonetheless propose specific design features that we believe should be included in order to facilitate the policy discussion.

There clearly are challenges if institutional innovations developed at the national level are to be transposed to a setting where governments dispute alleged violations of an international agreement. The *first* characteristic to recognize is the predominantly *government-to-government* character of WTO law and the WTO dispute settlement process. Disputes in the WTO are formally between governments and not between private parties as in civil proceedings in the national and EU contexts.[77]

---

77. Behind these disputes, we often find a frustrated business that is losing market access because of a defendant government measure, such as an antidumping duty, an import quota, or an alleged discriminatory tax or regulation. If the issue is important enough from a commercial perspective, the business *may* be able to convince the home government to bring a complaint to the WTO on its behalf. The government, however, would typically ask for convincing evidence since it is politically embarrassing to take another government to an international proceeding without a strong case. See Shaffer

Second, the subject of the disputes is very different. What is being challenged at the WTO is the law or government practice itself. A WTO dispute settlement panel must address whether a provision of a national law or administrative practice violates a WTO Agreement. If the panel finds a violation, the government must change its law or administrative practice or be subject to retaliatory measures in an equivalent amount.[78] The process of compliance or other settlement takes time. If the respondent complies, it must modify its law or regulatory practice in accordance with its internal legislative and administrative procedures.

Third, WTO law is complex and often open to interpretation. WTO disputes do not involve the processing of simple matters such as the collection of unpaid debts but rather the interpretation and application of complex treaties. These treaties have been negotiated among over 100 governments that do not typically agree on the meaning of each provision. The art of international negotiations includes creative drafting that allows all parties to sign but that can leave significant ambiguities. Given the very nature of language, moreover, terms are often subject to interpretations with quite different implications. Interpretive issues are thus central to the dispute settlement process. Article 3.2 of the DSU correspondingly states the following regarding the mandate for the WTO dispute settlement process as follows:

> The Members recognize that it [the dispute settlement system] serves to preserve the rights and obligations of Members under the covered agreements, and *to clarify the existing provisions of those agreements in accordance with customary rules of interpretation of public international law*. Recommendations and rulings of the DSB cannot add to or diminish the rights and obligations provided in the covered agreements (emphasis added).

In cases when the law is not clearly drafted and when precedents have not yet been established, some observers may consider a small-claims procedure to be inappropriate. This objection is particularly valid if there were an expectation that

---

(n 25 above); G Shaffer, 'What's New in EU Dispute Settlement? Judicialization, Public-Private Networks and the WTO Legal Order' (2006) 13(6) JE Pub Pol 832–50; and G Shaffer, MR Sanchez and B Rosenberg, 'The Trials of Winning at the WTO: What Lies Behind Brazil's Success' (2008) 40(2) Corn ILJ.

78. Regarding the choice of a respondent to comply or be subject to retaliation, cf JH Jackson, 'Editorial Comment: The WTO Dispute Settlement Understanding – Misunderstandings on the Nature of Legal Obligation' (1997) 91 AJIL 60–64; J Bello, 'Editorial Comment: The WTO Dispute Settlement Understanding: Less Is More' (1996) 90 AJIL 416–18; W Schwartz and A Sykes, 'The Economic Structure of Renegotiation and Dispute Resolution in the World Trade Organization' (2002) 31 J Leg Stu 179–204 (maintaining that the WTO dispute settlement system can be viewed as facilitating efficient breach of a WTO agreement, where the remedy is not full compliance but rather the withdrawal of equivalent trade concessions); and J Trachtman, 'The WTO Cathedral' (2007) 43 Stan JIL 127–67 (on liability vs. property rules in the WTO context).

the respondent must comply with a ruling following a small-claims procedure (constituting a remedy of specific performance) as opposed to an alternative remedy. It can be argued that if a Member must change its law or regulatory practice, then that Member should be able to defend its measures before a full legal proceeding. However, there would be a stronger rationale for making a small-claims procedure available for all complaints if alternative remedies are made available, including monetary compensation in lieu of compliance and if there is a prospect of some Appellate Body oversight, which we examine below.

In light of these characteristics of the WTO system, we address the key institutional design issues that will arise if a small-claims procedure is to be adapted to the WTO context. They are: (i) the definition of a small claim; (ii) whether the procedure should be available to all parties or only a subset of parties; (iii) the precedential effect of a small-claims procedure; (iv) the remedies available; (v) the ways in which the procedure should be streamlined to reduce costs; (vi) the possibility of using a specialized panel body; and (vii) the availability of appellate review, possibly limited to review by petition to the Appellate Body which would have the discretionary authority to grant it.

i. Definition of a 'Small Claim' in the WTO Context

The key threshold issue that negotiators would need to address is the category of cases that would be admissible in a WTO small-claims proceeding. We present two criteria in this section for consideration (monetary value and the existence of precedent) and one criterion in the next section (the identity of the complainant and/or respondent). The first criterion for using the procedure would be the *monetary value of the claim*. Based on our analysis in Part B, a threshold amount *could* be in the range of $1 to $10 million dollars, for example. The small-claims procedure would only be available for claims up to such a defined amount, which would be negotiated by WTO Members.

Since small-claims procedures must be simple to serve their purpose, one would want a simple means to assess the complaint's value. Some commentators may contend that it would be extremely difficult to determine this value. Indeed, in an analogous context, it has been notoriously difficult for arbitrators to establish the level of "nullification or impairment" in order to determine the amount of permissible retaliation where a respondent has not complied with a panel decision.[79] One simple solution would be to accept the value of the complaint at face value for purposes of determining the procedure's availability. If the complainant declared that the value was less than or equal to the defined threshold, then the small-claims procedure could be used. Alternatively, the respondent could be granted the right to contest this valuation but subject to

---

79. See T Sebastian, 'World Trade Organization Remedies and the Assessment of Proportionality: Equivalence and Appropriateness' (2007) 47 Harv ILJ 337 342–43.

significant constraints. A demanding burden of proof could be allocated to the respondent in such a way that the complaint would proceed unless the panel found that the complaint's value clearly exceeded the threshold.

The rules for the small-claims procedure could be structured so that the complainant would not have an incentive to use it abusively. For example, if panel decisions in small-claims procedures were to have no precedential value, then the complainant would lack an incentive to use the procedure for systemic reasons. In addition, if the remedy in the event of a respondent's noncompliance with a ruling were capped at the threshold amount, then a complainant would not have an incentive to use the procedure for high-value claims. Were the respondent not to comply with a decision in a small-claims procedure, the remedy could be retaliation in the form of a withdrawal of equivalent concessions in an amount capped by the threshold or the payment of monetary damages subject to such maximum amount. If the complainant believed that the value of its complaint exceeded this amount, then it should use the normal panel process.

A second potential criterion (which we raise as an option but about which we retain some scepticism) could be that *sufficiently well-established precedent* must apply to the issue in question, as determined by the panel. The small-claims procedure would thus not be applied to novel issues but rather to more routine ones where clear precedent already existed. In this way, only the regular panel system would 'clarify the existing provisions of (WTO) agreements in accordance with customary rules of interpretation of public international law' pursuant to DSU Article 3.2. Using this criterion, the set of admissible cases might not be large initially, but as WTO jurisprudence develops over time, the coverage would grow and hence the usefulness of a small-claims procedure.

United States federal and state rules of appellate procedure provide an analogue to this criterion when the courts apply a form of truncated procedure when they find that precedent is settled. The Federal Rules of Appellate Procedure require oral arguments to be heard in every case unless a panel of three judges unanimously agrees that oral argument is unnecessary for any of three reasons, one of which is that 'the dispositive issue or issues have been authoritatively decided.'[80] By allowing courts to dispense with oral arguments in simple cases

---

80. Fed R App P 34(a)(2); see also DC Cir Handbook of Practice and Internal Procedures, XI(C)(2). A number of appellate courts in the United States use staff attorneys to review appeals that have been briefed by the parties to identify the basic legal issues involved and rank the overall degree of difficulty. In the Ninth Circuit, appeals that raise relatively few issues and which are governed by well-established law are designated as 'screening cases'. Each screening case is assigned to a research staff attorney who presents the merits of the case to a rotating panel of three judges. The panel reviews the briefs and record as necessary. If the panel unanimously agrees that oral argument is unnecessary, then it adopts and files a decision prepared by the staff attorney in advance, modified as the panel sees fit. The Ninth Circuit disposes of over 100 cases a month through this process.

involving settled principles of law, the rule saves judicial and private litigants' resources. Similar mechanisms exist in US state court appellate systems.[81] We do not mention this domestic mechanism to suggest that oral argument should be eliminated in a WTO small-claims panel proceeding but rather to show how the existence of precedent has been a criterion in domestic court systems for adopting a more streamlined and less costly procedure.

To give an example of the potential application of this criterion in the WTO context, the WTO Appellate Body has established that the practice of 'zeroing' under national antidumping regulations violates the Anti-Dumping Agreement. As a result, when national officials calculate a dumping margin, they must account for all transactions in order to make a 'fair comparison' between prices charged in the importing country and in the home country (or a deemed equivalent) and not just those transactions in which dumping occurred.[82] Should new zeroing claims be filed that fall within the monetary threshold, a small-claims panel could hear them since jurisprudence on zeroing has been sufficiently established.

If the criterion were included, any complaint involving a matter that did not fall under clear precedent would instead be referred to the regular panel system. The first task for a small-claims panel would thus be to rule on the claim's admissibility in terms of whether sufficiently clear precedent existed. This issue could be addressed either in a preliminary hearing with the parties or be subject to an

---

See JC Wallace, 'Improving the Appellate Process Worldwide Through Maximizing Judicial Resources' (2005) 38 Vand JTL 187 196–99.

81. The state of Illinois, for example, allows its appellate courts to dispose of appeals with a summary order in a number of situations, including when 'the disposition is clearly controlled by case law precedent, statute, or rules of court,' or 'the issues involve no more than an application of well-settled rules to recurring fact situations.' Ill Sup Ct R. 23(c). See also Ks Sup Ct R 7.041 ('In any case in which it appears that a prior controlling appellate decision is dispositive of the appeal, the court may summarily affirm or reverse, citing in its order of summary disposition this rule and the controlling decision.'); Fla R App P 9.315 ('After service of the initial brief in appeals under Rule 9.110, 9.130, or 9.140, or after service of the answer brief if a cross-appeal has been filed, the court may summarily affirm the order to be reviewed if the court finds that no preliminary basis for reversal has been demonstrated'.); and La Ct App Unif R 2-16.2; Neb Sup Ct & Ct App R 7.

82. Under zeroing, an authority takes account of only those transactions in which dumping is found to have occurred and not all transactions. As a result of such 'zeroing', the average dumping margin and the antidumping duty are higher. See WTO Appellate Body Report, *European Communities—Anti-Dumping Duties on Imports of Cotton-Type Bed Linen from India*, WT/DS141/AB/R (1 March 2001); WTO Appellate Body Report, *United States—Laws, Regulations, and Methodology for Calculating Dumping Margins (Zeroing)*, WT/DS294/AB/R (18 April 2006); WTO Appellate Body Report, United States—*Measures Relating to Zeroing and Sunset Reviews*, WT/DS322/AB/R (9 January 2007); and WTO Appellate Body Report, *United States Final Anti-Dumping Measures on Stainless Steel From Mexico*, WT/DS344/AB/R (30 April 2008).

understanding that the case could be transferred to the regular panel system at any time when the panelists learn more about it. An additional option (which we mention with reservation because of the delays that it could trigger) would be the creation of a preliminary reference system pursuant to which a small-claims panel could ask the Appellate Body specific questions for clarification of WTO law. The Appellate Body could then respond to the legal question in a manner analogous to the way that the European Court of Justice responds to questions posed by national courts regarding the interpretation of EC law.[83]

Many observers (especially lawyers) will contend that it is easy to challenge the clarity of precedent as applied to different factual situations. As regards the example of zeroing, panelists might have to determine how to apply WTO law to address a distinct factual scenario or in relation to a different method of antidumping calculation deployed by antidumping officials that has a similar effect but takes a different form.[84] To the extent that the issue of 'clear precedent' were to be litigated, this procedural innovation could result in increased delay and costs for the bringing of 'small claims'. In the United States, the meaning and application of precedent is intensively litigated, with circuit courts of appeal and members of the Supreme Court often disagreeing.

Although we reserve definitive judgment on inclusion of this criterion in the WTO context, we have laid out both how it could work and the arguments against it. We note, in addition, other design features that can address the central concern at stake, which is the litigation of novel issues having systemic implications regarding national laws and practices without full-scale judicial review. We examine in sections D(iii) and D(iv) below how WTO members could address this concern while maintaining the procedure's relatively streamlined nature through three other institutional design features—the provision of a limited form of appellate review of small-claims panel decisions based on a petition (as in a writ of *certiorari)*; a clarification that small-claims panel decisions will have no precedential effect; and the possible tailoring of the remedy for

---

83. We thank Don McRae for indicating this additional option in his comments to us. The Members would then have the additional option of determining whether these appellate body rulings would constitute precedent for future cases (see discussion of precedent in small claims procedures in Section D (iii) below). We have no problem with these appellate body rulings constituting precedent since they are different in nature than those of a small-claims panel in a streamlined proceeding where parties have no guaranteed right of appeal. However, Members could decide otherwise in light of the streamlined procedure and to retain consistency in respect of the precedential value of decisions made under it. One final option would be to limit the precedential effect of these rulings to claims filed under the small claims system. Again, see Sction D (iii) on the issue of precedent.

84. In fact, WTO jurisprudence on zeroing has taken an incremental approach. See CP Bown and AO Sykes, 'United States—Final Dumping Determination on Softwood Lumber from Canada, and United States Softwood Lumber from Canada: Recourse to Article 21.5 of the DSU by Canada (Softwood V)' (2008) (on file).

noncompliance to include (as an option available to the complainant) the payment of cash compensation, subject to a small-claims cap.

ii. Who Could Bring a Small Claim Under the Procedure?

A next major issue would be who could use the small-claims procedure. Just as some national jurisdictions have provided that commercial enterprises cannot use a small-claims procedure because they are more likely to be able to use the regular legal system, use of a small-claims procedure in the WTO context could be limited to a defined category of WTO Members.

Whether to constrain the procedure's use in this way would reflect the rationale for the procedure and, in particular, whether the predominant rationale is to provide access to complainants with small-trade stakes, or to facilitate the hearing of small-claims generally. If the rationale were to open WTO dispute settlement for all claims of a smaller value, then the procedure should be open to all Members. If the rationale, in contrast, were to facilitate access to WTO dispute settlement for countries with smaller-trade stakes because the regular procedure under the DSU has not been tailored to their needs and they otherwise will be largely excluded from bringing claims under it, then access to the procedure could be limited to these Members.

In Part A, we noted two arguments relevant to the creation of a small-claims procedure. On the one hand, it is argued that there should be implicit 'user fees' for the WTO dispute settlement system so that it does not implode from extensive litigation. It has to cost something to keep out nuisance cases of insignificant value. On the other hand, we noted that what constitutes a small claim is a relative concept for WTO Members. Where Members' trade stakes radically differ and DSU procedures are the same for all claims, the system is not neutral to size. Small trading nations are effectively constrained from being able to use the legal system, constituting, in practice, a form of in-built discrimination. Thus, a competing rationale for adoption of a small-claims procedure focuses on the situation of the complainant as opposed to the size of the claim.

A small-claims procedure could certainly be open to all WTO Members. Since private constituencies are typically behind WTO complaints and are certainly affected by them, all of those constituencies would thus have relatively greater (indirect) access to the system, regardless of their location. There are arguments for and against making a small-claims procedure available to all WTO Members. On the one hand, it can be contended that reserving the procedure to only a category of WTO members would formally create *de jure* inequality within the system, as opposed to the *de facto* inequality that exists under the current system. Reserving use of the procedure to a category of Members would inevitably involve an arbitrary cutoff. It may be politically more difficult to create a procedure available to only some WTO Members, especially where the most powerful Members would be excluded from using it.

On the other hand, there are arguments in favor of limiting access to the procedure to certain WTO Members. First, there is already a historic precedent in the 1966 procedures which remain available only to developing country Members. This precedent suggests that the procedure could be designed in a politically acceptable way [85] although, as we have seen, the alternative of the 1966 procedures does not fit well within the DSU context. Second, a small-claims procedure open to all WTO Members could, in practice, exacerbate asymmetries within the system. Since larger developed countries are repeat users of the system for larger claims and thus already have developed internal governmental infrastructure and know-how for making use of the system, they could be the primary users of a small-claims procedure as well if it is open to all Members. In this way, adoption of a WTO small-claims procedure could replicate the experience in some national civil systems in which small-claims procedures have been used predominantly by wealthier and more knowledgeable creditors and landlords (repeat players) against more vulnerable parties.[86] Interestingly, one Geneva-based insider responded to us that if 'developed countries became primary users of a small-claims procedure, the process would fairly quickly get overlawyered and would simply incorporate/repeat the resource imbalances of the current process, to the detriment of small countries'.[87] In practice, a small-claims procedure open to all Members could be primarily used by the United States and EU to collect patent and copyright royalties that they claim have not been paid on account of violations of the TRIPS Agreement. Developing country Members may thus be wary of adopting it.

A design feature could be considered that both opens the procedure to all WTO Members and attempts to ensure that large Members do not monopolize its use (as well as to ensure that the system does not implode from excessive litigation). The DSU could limit the number of times any single Member can use the small-claims procedure in a given time period, such as a calendar year. A similar feature has been used in some national jurisdictions.[88]

If a small-claims procedure is adopted for only a set of Members as an "*S&D treatment*" provision on behalf of those with small-trade stakes, then that set of Members would need to be defined. One option would be to make the procedure available for all developing countries, as with the 1966 procedures, but this option would likely be undesirable (and politically infeasible) because some developing countries have relatively high aggregate stakes because of the size of their economies, with Brazil, China, and India being the most prominent examples. Moreover, WTO Members self-designate whether they are to be considered

---

85. For example, a small claims procedure reserved for use by a defined category of developing country Members could be part of a larger negotiated package.
86. But cf. Runkha et al (n 51 above) 41–48.
87. Correspondence with Gregory Shaffer, 5 December 2007.
88. Runkha et al (n 51 above) 3.

'developing countries', subject to challenge by another Member, which could result in considerable contestation.

Another option would limit use of the procedure to a set of developing country Members, such as the "least-developed countries" since this category is already a term whose definition is accepted, linked to per capita income, and related development criteria. There are currently 50 least-developed countries, 32 of which are WTO Members. As indicated by Tables 1 and Figures 3 and 4, these countries generally have the lowest average trade stakes and thus are in particular need of such a procedure. This list, moreover, could be expanded to cover other developing countries, such as small-island economies and low-income developing countries pursuant to defined criteria. World Trade Organization Members agreed to an expanded list of beneficiaries of an S&D treatment provision in the CVD Agreement, which exempts 20 developing countries (in addition to the "least developed") from the agreement's prohibition on export subsidies so long as their per capita gross national product (GNP) remains less than $1,000 per year.[89] The ACWL also offers a potential model in its use of two proxies for a country's development status to determine the applicable legal fees charged for its services—a country's per capita income and its share of global trade. Similar criteria could be used for determining the beneficiaries of a WTO small-claims procedure.

Finally, if Members maintain that it would be unfair to make the procedure one-sided—in the sense that Members who could be subject to the procedure as respondents could not use it as complainants—then *it could be agreed that those benefiting from access to the small-claims procedure can only bring claims against each other*. That is, if the defined group of beneficiaries were all developing countries, then a complaint under the small-claims procedure could only be brought against another developing country. Similarly, if it were agreed that only a set of developing countries (based on their share of world trade and per capita income) could bring claims under the procedure, then use of the procedure could be limited to claims against that same set of developing countries. In this way, there would be no inequality among those having access to the procedure as complainants and those subject to it as respondents, while providing a new procedural alternative under the DSU which is better tailored for smaller countries. The prospects of creating the procedure from a political economy perspective would also accordingly be increased. If Members with larger trade stakes are generally satisfied with current DSU procedures and Members with small stakes are not, then this alternative may be the easiest way to proceed politically.

There is a serious drawback to this option, however, from the perspective of Members with small trading stakes. These Members' largest export markets are

---

89. See *Agreement on Subsidies and Countervailing Measures*, Apr. 15, 1994, *Marrakesh Agreement Establishing the World Trade Organization*, Article 27.2(a) and Annex VII.

typically countries with the largest economies, especially those relatively nearby.[90] The EU is the largest market for Members from Africa and the United States for Members from Latin America. The potential value of the small-claims procedure would be significantly diminished for those countries that most need it were they unable to use it against larger Members.[91] Thus, on the one hand, from the perspective of *realpolitik*, the United States, European Union, and Japan would more likely accept the addition of a small-claims procedure available only for use by the smaller Members against each other. They would more likely accept this alternative to legal aid because the procedure would not be used against them. On the other hand, such an institutional design choice would significantly curtail the procedure's benefit for Members with smaller trading stakes.

iii. No Precedential Effect and Cap on Remedies

The small-claims procedure could be structured to assuage concerns that it might be abused, such as where claims of minor monetary value are brought that can have major systemic repercussions without being subject to full judicial oversight. One could imagine a US multinational company funding a law firm to work for a small developing country to bring a complaint under a small-claims procedure, as opposed to lobbying its own government to bring that same complaint in which case the small-claims cap would be vastly exceeded. Whether (and which) private party might be behind a case is not of formal legal concern to WTO panelists. Use of a small-claims procedure is, however, of systemic concern for the WTO system. More generally, some observers may contend that more litigation facilitated by a small-claims procedure could spur political contention that is simply not worth the cost to the system in light of the 'small stakes' of the claim. This concern may particularly arise when politically sensitive government policies are challenged. We have endeavored in this Part D to raise design features that respond, at least in part, to these concerns. *We address three design features that would limit incentives for abuse of the procedure, two in this section and a third feature in the following one. The first two address the issues of precedent and remedy. The third addresses that of appellate review.*

---

90. We have calculated the share of developing country exports going to the following developed country WTO Members (European Union, United States, Canada, Japan, Norway, Iceland, Australia, New Zealand, and Switzerland), using our 2003 database. It was 62.2 percent.

91. It can be argued that smaller developing countries tend to benefit from tariff preferences in large developed country markets, which creates a disincentive for their use of the dispute settlement system. See, eg, H Nottage, 'Trade and Development' in D Bethlehem and others (eds), *Oxford Handbook of International Trade Law* (2008). While this is true, the value of the tariff preferences is declining over time on account of increased liberalization, and in many cases bound tariff rates are not at issue in dispute settlement, as in subsidies, antidumping, and SPS cases.

In national settings, small-claims procedures typically do not create legal precedents for cases before the regular civil justice system.[92] Some jurisdictions explicitly provide that judgments in small-claims proceedings do not constitute precedent,[93] while others reach this result through other means, such as by not publishing the decisions.[94] In our view, a key feature of a WTO small-claims procedure is that decisions under it would likewise have no precedential effect. Thus, a primary distinction of a WTO small-claims proceeding would be that only panels operating under the regular system would 'clarify the existing provisions of [WTO] agreements'. The DSU could state explicitly that an adopted panel decision from a small-claims procedure shall have no relevance for future cases and cannot be cited in any subsequent small-claims or other DSU proceeding.[95]

---

92. WMC Weidemaier, 'Arbitration and the Individuation Critique' (2007) 49 Ari L Rev 69–78 ('Nor do small claims courts typically publish their decisions or create precedent'.); G Yang, 'Can-Spam: A First Step to No-Spam' (2004) 4(1) Chi-Kent JIP 1–44 (decisions of small claims courts 'carry very little value as precedents'); FE Zollers, 'Alternative Dispute Resolution and Product Liability Reform' (1988) 26 Am Bus LJ 479 490 ('The procedures within small claims courts are very informal, and the decision of the court has no precedential effect').

93. See, eg, Model State Administrative Tax Court Act § 13(h) ("A judgment of the Small Claims Division shall not be considered as precedent in any other case, hearing or proceeding."); 18 C.F.R. § 1308.35(e) (Tennessee Valley Authority decisions in appeals involving small claims have no precedential effect); 10 C.F.R. § 1023.120, Rule 13(f) (decisions of the Department of Energy's Board of Contract Appeals in appeals of small claims judgments have no value as precedent for future cases).

94. Even where not directly prescribed by rule, limitations on the appealability of small-claims judgments may have the same effect. See, eg, Model State Administrative Tax Court Act § 13(h) ("A judgment of the Small Claims Division shall be conclusive upon all parties and may not be appealed"). Even where appealable, a small-claims action brought in a court of limited jurisdiction or otherwise outside of the regular civil court system may not be allowed to the reach the intermediate appellate level. For example, California allows a judgment of the small-claims court to be appealed to the superior court, a court of general jurisdiction. Ca. Civ. Proc. Code § 116.710(b). The superior court's judgment on appeal is final and unappealable to the state court of appeals. § 116.780(a). In any event, opinions in small-claims cases are rarely published, further limiting the use of a small-claims judgments as authority. See J Sovern, 'The Jewel of Their Souls: Preventing Identity Theft Fraud Through Loss Allocation Rules' (2003) 64 UPitt L Rev 343–76 (noting that a published opinion is 'an unusual step for a small claims case').

95. There is precedent for this option in some national jurisdictions. For example, the procedural rules of some US appellate courts at the appellate level formerly provided that unpublished appellate court opinions could not be cited in future decisions, and many US state courts continue to prohibit the citation of unpublished opinions. Although this situation changed at the federal level in 2006 with the adoption of Federal Rule of Appellate Procedure 32.1, federal appellate courts still do not consider unpublished decisions to constitute binding precedent. Since the vast majority of US federal appellate opinions are not published, most in fact have little to no precedential value, even though the US system

They would thus contrast with decisions under the regular system, which the Appellate Body recognizes as creating "legitimate expectations" for parties in future cases and which it cites prolifically in practice, and which commentators have found to constitute a form of *de facto stare decisis*.[96]

Some observers may criticize the potential formalization of a 'two-tier system' of justice in which precedent is only created under the regular panel procedure and not in small-claims cases brought by small trading nations. However, a developing country complainant to which the small-claims procedure is available could always use the normal panel process, and it could weigh the value of potentially setting precedent through litigation against the additional litigation costs. In other words, small trading nations would still retain the autonomy to choose which procedure to use in a given context based on the nature of the claim. Small trading nations constitute the vast majority of the WTO's membership and most of them have never used the DSU, which is a major rationale for creating a small-claims procedure. The procedure could be a point of entry for

---

otherwise adopts a rule of *stare decisis*. See SR Barnett, 'No-Citation Rules Under Siege: A Battlefield Report and Analysis' (2003) 5 J App Pract & Pro 473 481; JO Cooper, 'Citability and the Nature of Precedent in the Courts of Appeals' (2002) 35 Ind L Rev 423–32; and D Greenwald, 'The Censorial Judiciary' (2002) 35 UC Davis L Rev 1133 1135. The DSU could similarly provide that small-claims panel decisions shall not be published, but we would oppose this alternative out of concerns over the transparency of the WTO process to the broader public. Although many international arbitral awards are confidential, there is growing concern with transparency. The decisions in the two *European Communities–Banana Tariff Arbitrations*, as well as the arbitration over the level of nullification and impairment in the *US-Copyright* case, were published and made available through the WTO Web site. See H Nottage and J Bohanes, 'Arbitration as an alternative to litigation in the WTO: observations in the light of the 2005 Banana Tariff Arbitrations' in Taniguchi, Yanovich and Bohanes (eds), *The WTO in the Twenty-first Century: Dispute Settlement, Negotiations, and Regionalism in Asia* (2007) 212, 221.

96. See generally R Bhala, 'The Precedent Setters: De Facto Stare Decisis in WTO Adjudication' (1999) 9(1) Flor St UJTL Pol 849–82 (speaking of "a myth that the doctrine of stare decisis does not exist or operate in WTO adjudication"); and R Bhala, *International Trade Law: Theory and Practice* (2nd ed, 2001) 240. The Appellate Body has spoken of panel reports in terms of creating "legitimate expectations". See, eg, WT/DS8, *Japan—Taxes on Alcoholic Beverages*. As one panel stated, "following the Appellate Body's conclusions in earlier disputes is not only appropriate, but is what would be expected from panels, especially where the issues are the same". See, eg, See WTO Panel Report, *United States—Antidumping Measure on Shrimp from Ecuador*, WT/DS335/R (20 February 2007) para. 7.37. See also WTO Appellate Body Report, *United States Import Prohibition of Certain Shrimp and Shrimp Products* WT/DS58/AB/RW (22 October 22 2001) para. 107–09 ('Nor are we surprised that the Panel made frequent references to our Report in United States—Shrimp. Indeed, we would have expected the Panel to do so. The Panel had, necessarily, to consider our views on this subject, as we had overruled certain aspects of the findings of the original panel on this issue and, more important, had provided interpretative guidance for future panels, such as the Panel in this case').

them so that they can become more familiar with the DSU without being subject to the demands of full-fledged DSU procedures from the start. In this way, it could facilitate bottoms-up capacity-building.

Second, to further constrain the systemic implications of a complaint in a small-claims procedure (and thus help ensure that a small claim is indeed 'small'), the DSU could explicitly provide that the respondent, in lieu of compliance with a panel ruling from a small-claims procedure, could either be subject to retaliation in an amount equivalent to the harm caused or provide compensation (whether financial or in the form of additional market access) up to the value of the complaint. Both alternatives, in fact, are already provided in DSU Article 22 for the normal panel procedure as 'temporary measures available', although they are rarely used.[97] The remedy in both cases would be subject to a cap, which would be the maximum amount for bringing a complaint under the procedure, although we would favor the DSU to provide that, for ongoing market-access violations, the payment would remain due on an ongoing annual basis so long as the respondent has not complied.[98] In that case, a respondent would not simply pay a single check to get out of an ongoing market-access violation, once and for all.

Although the second alternative of a cash remedy is permitted under the DSU, this remedy must be agreed between the parties to the dispute. In contrast, WTO Members could agree in the provisions establishing a small-claims procedure that they will pay monetary compensation if they do not agree to comply with an adopted small-claims panel ruling. Of course, the WTO does not have police powers to enforce such payment. However, since the maximum amount of payment would be limited by the definition of a small claim, then it may be easier to agree to (and comply with) such a remedy in this context.

Use of this remedy could correspondingly reduce the costs of using the DSU for small trading nations, which is an additional reason for its consideration. To the extent that countries would pay damages as determined by the panel (up to the small-claims maximum amount, which again could be paid annually until compliance), then there would be no need for arbitration over the 'reasonable period of time' for implementing the decision, nor for arbitration over whether

---

97. Moreover, and Article 22 explicitly provides that neither of these alternatives (of compensation or suspension of concessions) 'is preferred to full implementation of a recommendation to bring a measure into conformity with the covered agreements' (ie, to compliance).

98. That is, if violation is an ongoing one (such as an ongoing ban on imports), and not a one-shot measure (such as a specific one-time subsidy), payment could be due on an ongoing basis until the respondent complied with the ruling. In such case, a given amount of trade would be determined to be affected on an annual basis (up to the small claims cap), which amount would be due unless compliance occurred or additional market access were granted in an equivalent amount.

the respondent has actually complied with it. Payment would simply be due within a defined period of time. In addition, a small trading country would be more assured that it would receive some form of compensation and thus greater certainty as to whether bringing a complaint is worthwhile. This change would, in sum, reduce the time, cost, and uncertainty of bringing a WTO complaint.

Some commentators may contend that the express provision of a cash remedy would undermine the normative pull for compliance under the current DSU, resulting in a reduction of the welfare benefits from trade liberalisation. Compliance, however, could remain the preferred remedy as provided in DSU Article 22.1.[99] Indeed, a Member may well prefer to comply with a ruling rather than pay damages out of its treasury, which is why we have not seen grants of compensation under the current system except in two cases—once in the *Japan-Alcoholic Beverages* case (involving a temporary reduction of specific tariffs) as a temporary measure in exchange for an extension of the implementation period[100] and once in the *US-Copyright* case (involving a financial transfer) in a matter that remains ongoing.[101]

---

99. Article 22.1 provides: 'Compensation and the suspension of concessions or other obligations are temporary measures available in the event that the recommendations and rulings are not implemented within a reasonable period of time. However, neither compensation nor the suspension of concessions or other obligations is preferred to full implementation of a recommendation to bring a measure into conformity with the covered agreements'.

100. See Communication from Japan, *Mutually Acceptable Solutions on Modalities for Implementation*, on US Complaint concerning Japan—Taxes on Alcoholic Beverages, WT/DS8/19 (12 January 1998).

101. See B O'Connor and M Djordjevic, 'Practical Aspects of Monetary Compensation: The US—Copyright Case' (2005) 8 JIEL 127–42 ('The mutually satisfactory temporary arrangement was notified to the WTO on 26 June 2003. According to the notification, the US was to make a lump-sum payment in the amount of $3,300,000 to a fund, to be set up by the performing rights societies in the European Communities for the provision of general assistance to their members and the promotion of authors' rights. The temporary arrangement is to last until December 2004. Before the actual payment could be made, the US Congress needed to approve an appropriation order, authorizing payment in accordance with the EC-US arrangement. The US Congress approved such an appropriation order in June 2003. According to this order, the payment was to be issued to the European Communities. However, in early September 2003, the payment was made directly to a private fund established by the European Grouping of Societies of Authors and Composers (GESAC). There is no public record of why GESAC was chosen. Shortly after receipt of the moneys, GESAC informed the European Commission of the objectives of the fund and the arrangements taken for its management. A GESAC press release, issued on 5 September 2003, indicates that the moneys would be used to combat piracy on the Internet and to support actions for copyright in the European Communities and the United States. The details of the fund or its distribution are not publicly available'). The European Union and Ecuador may have negotiated a side deal where a form of compensation was paid to Ecuador to refrain from challenging a settlement of the *EC-Bananas*

As we noted in Part A, the existence of a cash remedy could facilitate the pooling of claims, led by an entrepreneurial attorney, in a manner roughly analogous to a class action. Some observers might find this result to be beneficial because Members with small trade stakes (and, indirectly, constituencies within them) would more likely be represented and thus be able to defend (and have defended) their interests before the WTO legal system. Others might find it to be problematic, both because of the effect on compliance (with large Members possibly 'buying out' of compliance) and because the amount of a cash remedy could rise significantly with a pooling of claims. In that case, the payment of a cash remedy could remain voluntary as currently under the DSU.

In any event, where a Member determines that it prefers not to comply with a ruling, we believe that it should be permitted either to pay compensation (whether financial or through granting additional market access) or be subject to a withdrawal of concessions in an equivalent amount in lieu of compliance. Such an outcome is supported both by normative concerns over democratic choice in regulatory policy and theoretical law-and-economic concerns regarding 'efficient breaches' of agreements. Under the theory of efficient breach, where the value to a respondent of being able to breach an obligation is greater than the value to a complainant of compliance, then the respondent should be permitted not to comply with the obligation provided that the respondent compensates the complainant for the harm (whether in terms of monetary compensation or retaliation through suspension by the complainant of concessions of an equivalent amount).[102] Parties may have broader normative reasons to retain a particular regulatory policy that fails to meet WTO requirements, such as US concerns over animal welfare, as reflected in the *US-Shrimp-Turtle* dispute and European concerns over genetically modified foods, as reflected in the *EC-Agricultural Biotechnology* case. WTO Director-General Pascal Lamy has referred to this situation in terms of a Member's 'collective preferences' for regulation.[103]

This being said, if noncompliance becomes an acceptable choice for respondents, it could largely eliminate the incentive to bring a complaint under the small-claims procedure *unless* the alternative remedy is sufficiently attractive.

---

case, although no formal settlement was provided to the WTO Dispute Settlement Body. We do not know whether this occurred in other cases, but since most WTO cases involve complex bilateral negotiations following the judicial ruling, it is surely possible that other forms of compensation have been exchanged.

102. See, eg, Schwartz and Sykes (n 78 above).

103. See Pascal Lamy, EU Trade Commissioner, The Emergence of Collective Preferences in International Trade: Implications for Regulating Globalization, Address at Conference on Collective preferences and global governance [sic]: what future for the multilateral trading system (15 September 2004) (transcript available at <http://europa.eu.int/comm/archives/commission_1999_2004/lamy/speeches_articles/spla242_en.htm>; see also S Charnovitz, 'An Analysis of Pascal Lamy's Proposal on Collective Preferences' (2005) 8 JIEL 449–72.

For a complainant with a small claim, holding a right to withdraw concessions of an equivalent value will typically be a poor substitute for compliance from both an economic and a political perspective. First, withdrawing concessions may be economically counterproductive for the complainant since it would prejudice its own consumers, domestic importers, and domestic producers using imported products. Second, the rationale for providing a right of retaliation is to enable the complainant to place political pressure on the respondent to comply with a ruling, not for the complainant to receive 'compensation'. Members bringing claims involving small stakes (especially those Members that have small markets) may exercise little political leverage over the respondent, thus undermining the value of bringing and winning a case.

We thus must find a design feature that addresses two competing concerns. On the one hand, we have argued that noncompliance should be an acceptable option since it would be unreasonable to require a government to change a law or administrative practice without the protection of full WTO procedural rights. On the other hand, the current mechanism of suspending concessions is particularly unsuitable for small claims brought by Members with small trade stakes. Relying on it as a remedy would reduce the procedure's relevance. There is, however, a way to address these dual concerns. The rules for a small-claims procedure could prescribe compensation as the remedy if the respondent does not comply and the *complainant* so requests. If a respondent failed to comply with a ruling, it could provide compensation either through granting additional market access to the complainant of an equivalent value, subject to the usual most-favored nation obligation, or monetary compensation. The option of withdrawing equivalent concessions would thus remain at the complainant's discretion, but it would not be favored. Finally, in considering this option, we recall that most WTO matters (as most GATT matters in the past) settle, so that an additional rationale for this (formal) alternative remedy would be its facilitation of fair settlements. In sum, we believe that, in the context of a small claim procedure, the rules should be structured so that compensation would be the preferred alternative remedy to a suspension of concessions where the respondent does not comply.

iv. Institutional Issues: Panels, Appeals, and Procedures

World Trade Organization Members would also have to determine the distinct procedures for small claims, the make-up of the body that would hear the claims, and whether the rulings of a small-claims panel would be subject to appeal before the WTO Appellate Body. Since the central idea behind the procedure is to reduce the cost of bringing a WTO complaint, we need to consider how the time period and procedural demands could be reduced in comparison with those under the current system. William Davey has already noted how the normal panel process could be expedited by eliminating the need for a second meeting of the Dispute Settlement Body before establishing a panel, by establishing a permanent panel body, by modifying and adhering to the standard times for submissions and hearings, and by eliminating the interim review procedure.[104] Even if these reforms are not adopted for the normal panel procedure, they could be adopted for small claims. In addition, a small-claims procedure could consist of only one filing by each side and one oral hearing, instead of two, again reducing the time and costs. One could also consider limiting the number of pages in submissions, as is done in national jurisdictions, in order to force the parties to focus their arguments and thus reduce the demands on the judicial process, as well as on each other. (One reason why the ACWL is able to hold down the costs for its clients, it maintains, is precisely because it focuses on the key aspects of the dispute and leaves out secondary arguments that it believes are unlikely to impress a panel. Despite the ACWL's more minimalist approach, it has a good track record.) Moreover, it appears that most domestic courts, at least in the United States and Europe, impose page or word limits on legal submissions.[105] Since a small-claims panel decision would not create precedent, the decision could also be shorter and more to the point, saving time both in the writing of the decision and in its translation into the WTO's official languages. In a number of ways, the resulting small-claims procedure would resemble the procedures under the GATT, following the 1979 reforms, yet be automatic (on account of the reverse consensus rule) and be limited to a defined set of claims in terms of their value.[106]

---

104. WJ Davey, 'Expediting the Panel Process in WTO Dispute Settlement' in Janow and others (eds), *WTO: Governance, Dispute Settlement and Developing Countries* (2008).

105. For example, principal briefs submitted to US federal appellate courts may not exceed 30 pages in length or 15 pages in the case of reply briefs. Fed R App P 32(a)(7)(A). The US Supreme Court prescribes word limitations for 13 types of documents submitted to the Court, ranging from 3,000 words for Petitions for Rehearing to 15,000 words for Briefs on the Merits. US Sup Ct R 33(g). Limitations also exist at the federal trial court level. The US District Court for the Northern District of California, for example, limits briefs and memoranda filed with the court to twenty-25, while the United States District Court for the Northern District of Illinois limits submissions to 15 pages without prior approval of the court. ND Cal Civ R 7-4(b); and ND Ill Civ R 7.1. Similarly, the Court of First Instance of the European Communities limits submissions to between 15 and 50 pages depending on the circumstances. Court of First Instance, Practice Directions to Parties, 2007 OJ (L 232) 7, 8 (EC). The European Court of Justice, more by way of entreaty than steadfast rule, observes that '[i]t is the Court's experience that, save in exceptional circumstances, effective pleadings need not exceed 10 or 15 pages and replies, rejoinders and responses can be limited to 5 to 10 pages', Court of Justice, Practice Directions Relating to Direct Actions and Appeals, 2004 OJ (L 361) 15, 19 (EC).

106. See, eg, R Hudec, *Enforcing International Trade Law: The Evolution of the Modern GATT Legal System* (2003) 53–57 (on the Tokyo Round Agreements on Dispute Settlement). The most important difference is that the formation of the panel and the adoption of a panel ruling would be almost automatic on account of the 'reverse consensus' rule under the DSU pursuant to which a panel will be formed and a panel decision adopted unless the Members decide by consensus not to create the panel, or not to adopt the ruling.

We would also opt for a permanent body of standing panelists to hear these claims in place of the current WTO system of *ad hoc* panels. This shift could be part of a larger DSU reform in which a panelist body is created for all WTO disputes.[107] If a proposal for a standing pool of panelists were accepted by WTO members, then there would be no need to create a special body for small claims since the same body could hear claims under both procedures. Many small-claims courts are organized this way in the national context.

In our view, this organization would be preferable for two reasons. First, the primary rational for a permanent panel body is that it would save time and expense. The constitution of panels has become a cumbersome exercise that may take months because of disagreements between the parties. In the majority of cases (and around three-fourths of them in the 2004–2006 period), the WTO director-general has been asked to intervene and appoint the panel, using his mandate under DSU Article 8.7. To use the same selection procedures for a small-claims procedure would undermine the purpose of creating a more cost-effective, timely alternative for Members with small claims. Second, if the procedure's use were limited to cases where there is clear precedent (the second criterion discussed in section D(i)), then a panel would have to determine whether the procedure applies in a given case. It would then be even more important to have panelists knowledgeable of WTO precedent. Even were the procedure not subject to such a criterion involving precedent, we believe that it would be advisable to use experienced panelists, especially since a panel decision in a small-claims procedure might not be subject to appeal before the Appellate Body.

Time and costs could be further saved were WTO Members to agree that panel decisions in small-claims proceedings would not be subject to automatic appeal before the Appellate Body. In this way, a WTO small-claims procedure would reflect national practice, in which appeals in small-claims procedures are often discouraged through procedural mechanisms or, where permitted, are rare. Permitting automatic appeals increases the time and costs of bringing a complaint and thus partly defeats the purpose of a small-claims procedure. An appeals process could, however, still be available to ensure the system's coherence and reduce the potential for judicial error resulting from streamlined procedures. The DSU could permit a party to petition the Appellate Body to grant judicial review (as in a writ of *certiorari*). The Appellate Body could grant petitions on an exceptional basis if it believed that the small-claims panel had no

---

107. See, eg, Communication from the European Communities, Contribution of the European Communities and its Member States to the improvement and clarification of the WTO Dispute Settlement Understanding, TN/DS/W/38 (23 January 2003). See also WJ Davey, 'The Case for a WTO Permanent Panel Body' (2003) 6(1) JIEL 177–86. Another option would be to include former Appellate Body members for these panels, similar to the way that retired judges are used in national systems in alternative dispute resolution mechanisms, including in small-claims procedures.

jurisdiction, that its ruling was erroneous as a matter of law, or that the case raised novel issues of systemic importance that the Appellate Body should address. The WTO system would, in this way, include a third safeguard against abusive use of a small-claims procedure and help retain the system's overall coherence.[108]

Finally, we note that a particular advantage of a small-claims procedure over the current WTO alternative of arbitration is that the procedure would be defined in advance as part of a revised DSU (possibly as an annex to the DSU). It thus would not need to be determined each time on an *ad hoc* basis. Over time, the procedure could be viewed as a 'normal' process for small claims as opposed to an exceptional one.

v. Creation for a Trial Period

A final option in creating a WTO small-claims procedure is to adopt it on a trial basis for a period of time, such as a five-year period. After the initial trial period, the small-claims procedure could either be automatically renewed or automatically discontinued, or modified, unless otherwise agreed by a consensus of those Members to whom it applies. If the procedure is initially made available only to a set of WTO Members (as potential complainants and respondents), then only that set of Members might vote on renewal, discontinuation, or modification (provided the revised procedure would continue to apply only to them). If, however, Members desired to expand or limit availability of the procedure to a different set of Members, then the overall membership would determine whether to so expand or limit its availability and modify its rules accordingly. In any case, through the initial trial period, WTO Members would learn from experience so as to determine whether a small-claims procedure should be an ongoing feature of the DSU, and if so, how best to adapt it.

E. CONCLUSION

In this chapter, we have established a *prima facie* case for the creation of a small-claims procedure in the WTO based on three premises. First, we have shown how trade stakes vary among WTO Members. Second, we have shown how claims involving smaller trade stakes are not offset by smaller litigation costs or a reduced need for domestic WTO legal expertise. Third, we have shown how the alternative dispute resolution tracks provided by the DSU do not substitute for a

---

108. For example, one could imagine two complainants bringing a similar complaint, one involving a 'small claim', and the other a claim that exceeds the defined amount. In such situation, either the DSU could grant a small claims panel the authority to refer the 'small claims' complaint to the normal panel process, or the Appellate Body could review the small-claims decision pursuant to a petition for *certiorari* in order to ensure consistency.

small-claims procedure. We have thus demonstrated how the current system is not neutral to size but favors those WTO Members with large trade stakes. The addition of a small-claims procedure would reduce the cost of using the WTO dispute settlement system for Members with small trade stakes.[109] Depending on its design, it could enhance the system's equity and efficiency without inflicting greater net political costs on government officials from a political economy perspective.

Yet just because there is a case for creating a small-claims procedure does not mean that one is appropriate in the WTO context. Any international claim against a government measure is arguably not 'small', regardless of the amount at stake. Maintaining orderly international economic relations can be a delicate matter so that any significant change of the relatively successful WTO dispute settlement system should be approached with caution. We have thus noted design features that could be considered to ensure the system's overall coherence and to prevent the abuse of a small-claims procedure.[110]

If a small-claims procedure is to be considered, it should have the following key features. First, procedures should be streamlined, and we have noted some procedural steps under the current system that could be eliminated in order to reduce costs. In many ways, the small-claims procedure would resemble the procedures under the GATT, following the 1979 reforms, yet be automatic (as under the current DSU) and be limited to a defined set of claims in terms of their value. Second, the small-claims procedure would not replace current procedures but would simply be an alternative option for those bringing small claims. Third, panel rulings under the procedure should have no precedential effect. Fourth, remedies should include an attractive alternative to compliance, such as the provision of compensation (financial or in the form of market access), subject to the defined cap for the procedure's use. Fifth, there should be a permanent body to hear these complaints. Sixth, appellate review should only be available by petition (as in a writ of *certiorari*) in order to control for judicial error and systemic coherence. Finally, we note that if WTO Members consider adopting such a procedure, they

---

109. We, of course, cannot guarantee that small developing country Members would use a small claims procedure, especially where they believe that they face political costs in initiating a WTO claim. However, we believe that a clearly defined small claims procedure would be *much* more attractive for them for the reasons that we have examined in Part B.

110. We recognize that many of these design features, such as those regarding remedies and the creation of a permanent panel, have been addressed by Members in their ongoing review of the DSU. We know that the adoption of these design features faces severe challenges generally. Our primary purpose, nonetheless, is to identify alternative features as to how a small-claims procedure could be shaped to meet systemic concerns, while addressing how these alternatives might be received from a political economy perspective. For some observers, one advantage of adopting these design features in a small-claims procedure would be to gain experience as to how these features operate in practice, on a trial basis.

could experiment with it on a trial basis for a set period of time, subject to renewal or modification. In this way, they could learn from their experience with it.

A central issue that Members would have to address would be whether the procedure should be open to all WTO Members or to only a set of Members with small trade stakes. One's response to this issue depends on the rationale for the procedure—whether it is to facilitate the bringing of small claims generally or to facilitate use of WTO dispute settlement by Members with small trade stakes. In the latter case, the small-claims procedure could be reserved for a defined set of developing countries as a matter *of S&D treatment*. In that case, however, a new issue would arise—would Members that cannot use the procedure themselves have to respond to complaints under it? Some observers may contend that rights and obligations should be in parallel: If a Member is not permitted to initiate a complaint under a procedure, it should also not have to respond to one. Although this point has some validity, governments have accepted S&D treatment provisions in many other cases both at the WTO level and within many of their own domestic jurisdictions for small claims. Moreover, if use of the small-claims procedure were available only against the same defined set of Members having small trading stakes, then the procedure's value would be much diminished. Countries with small economies trade primarily with Members having large ones.

The creation of a small-claims procedure in the WTO context would have to be given careful consideration before its adoption. We believe that its addition with the design features that we have indicated would have a net positive effect on Members' social welfare, assessed both in terms of fairness and efficiency. These design features should also enhance its acceptance politically. A central motivation for adding a small-claims procedure is to make the WTO system more equitable for those with small trade stakes. This innovation, we believe, would enhance the legitimacy of the dispute settlement system and indirectly of the WTO system at large. If developing countries sense that they have a fairer chance of enforcing market-access concessions in their favor or receiving due compensation, then they should engage more actively in trade negotiations. This engagement would benefit all Members.

Appendix 1: Trade Data

	Export ($million)	HS4	Markets	Diversity	Export < $1m	Export < $10m
Europe and Central Asia						
Albania	433	446	25	620	10,6	36
Armenia	539	357	36	708	7,6	20,7
Bulgaria	6368	1024	105	6899	8,4	31,9
Croatia	4708	952	88	2931	4,9	25,2
EU25	826939	1240	122	96011	1,4	9,4
Georgia	262	392	40	695	18,2	49
Iceland	2308	418	58	1247	3,5	11,6
Israel	29731	961	115	10060	3,3	14,2
Kyrgyz Republic	370	229	29	405	6,1	18,2
Liechtenstein	NA	NA	NA	NA	NA	NA
Macedonia	1044	658	48	1682	11,4	39,4
Moldova	365	501	34	1018	20,1	70,8
Norway	63880	1093	118	10843	1,4	5,6
Romania	16649	1022	108	6193	3,2	15,6
Switzerland	98258	1201	122	28018	2,6	11,6
Turkey	38387	1127	120	20352	4,7	17,6
North America						
Canada	256069	1228	122	24379	0,9	3,7
United States of America	688009	1234	122	61855	1,1	6,5
East Asia and Pacific						
Australia	55416	1198	120	22668	4,2	17,6
Brunei Darussalam	4136	527	35	1403	1,6	4,3
Cambodia	2075	316	63	995	2,8	10,2
China	418786	1220	122	55750	1,5	8,7
Chinese Taipei	138602	1164	122	32594	2,3	12,1
Fiji	443	425	48	1239	13	41,4
Hong Kong	226710	1155	117	27259	1,2	6,3
Indonesia	59780	1211	121	21542	3,7	17,4
Japan	444195	1206	122	30878	0,8	5
Korea, Republic of	181653	1166	121	28579	1,7	10
Macao	2536	655	53	2099	5,9	21,6
Malaysia	101510	1164	120	20762	2,2	11,4
Mongolia	567	257	32	490	4,4	22,7
Myanmar	2764	517	61	1835	4,8	21,5
New Zealand	15174	1064	118	11190	6,3	26,5

	Export ($million)	HS4	Markets	Diversity	Export < $1m	Export < $10m
Papua New Guinea	996	356	39	845	6	24,8
Philippines	35994	920	109	9653	2,6	10,5
Singapore	135138	1179	85	25911	2	10,3
Solomon Islands	122	130	30	217	7,7	45,3
Thailand	75381	1151	122	26413	3,4	16,5
South Asia						
Bangladesh	5639	469	91	2344	3,1	11,9
India	58512	1222	122	40631	7,1	25,9
Maldives	113	20	19	70	6,2	39,1
Nepal	651	442	48	1297	15,6	57,6
Pakistan	11898	804	114	7624	5,8	20,6
Sri Lanka	4528	817	112	5595	7,8	27,9
Middle East and North Africa						
Bahrain	1849	552	54	1738	7,1	27,4
Djibouti	11,2	124	28	157	90,7	100
Egypt	7045	1019	90	7187	7,5	24,7
Jordan	1894	615	83	2601	10,6	33,6
Kuwait	19513	650	65	2000	0,7	2,7
Morocco	8444	827	101	4152	3,4	14,2
Oman	2826	572	77	2535	8,6	28
Qatar	12415	522	67	1754	0,9	3,4
Saudi Arabia	86185	1026	86	6999	0,6	2,4
Tunisia	6544	740	85	2626	3,1	15,2
United Arab Emirates	42321	1178	85	18518	2,8	9,3
Sub-Saharan Africa						
Angola	9304	288	46	556	0,3	0,7
Benin	394	445	42	793	9,1	36,5
Botswana	2016	340	28	606	1	3,8
Burkina Faso	318	291	41	719	13	32,5
Burundi	62,5	91	29	163	11,6	15
Cameroon	2608	582	69	1449	3,1	9,5
Central African Republic	64,8	49	20	78	6,6	28,2
Chad	97,5	151	38	213	10,8	39,4
Congo	2671	275	60	509	1,4	5,5
Côte d'Ivoire	4673	659	63	2024	3	10,5
Democratic Rep of the Congo	1036	308	48	542	2,5	7,6
Gabon	303	295	58	756	10,6	50,2
Gambia	4,8	114	24	169	100	100
Ghana	2286	605	81	1800	5,2	14,8
Guinea	702	283	56	488	3,1	16,2

	Export ($million)	HS4	Markets	Diversity	Export < $1m	Export < $10m
Guinea Bissau	76,2	95	18	114	11,3	32,3
Kenya	2035	956	109	4634	15,6	40,7
Lesotho	433	131	24	188	3,4	7,3
Madagascar	471	391	55	868	9,6	30,1
Malawi	488	428	73	1257	8,4	36,7
Mali	222	418	62	852	11,3	30,8
Mauritania	505	225	51	428	3,5	12,6
Mauritius	1838	745	87	2723	9,9	27
Mozambique	1011	420	56	805	4,2	15,2
Namibia	1280	939	63	2320	10,2	31,4
Niger	207	219	33	409	8,4	29
Nigeria	23833	195	52	420	0,1	0,6
Rwanda	50,2	144	35	310	29,7	100
Senegal	982	597	55	2382	16,4	42
Sierra Leone	217	455	49	811	14,6	40,6
South Africa	30682	1212	117	27037	8	26,8
Swaziland, Kingdom of	562	518	69	1490	13,7	44,9
Tanzania	1203	700	87	2751	13,7	33,4
Togo	485	327	66	846	14,7	54,1
Uganda	158	282	49	638	24,6	71,3
Zambia	977	555	52	1319	7,4	25,8
Zimbabwe	1753	854	61	2625	10	36,1
Latin America and the Caribbean						
Antigua and Barbuda	404	334	45	608	6,1	12,3
Argentina	28014	1102	112	13118	4,4	17,2
Barbados	184	539	68	2093	46,3	76,2
Belize	200	176	31	322	7,7	33,2
Bolivia	1638	550	57	1835	7	24,6
Brazil	68173	1166	121	23668	3,8	17,5
Chile	19325	1013	98	8794	4,1	16,4
Colombia	12774	1030	102	9224	6,9	24,5
Costa Rica	5762	870	82	5093	7,4	25,4
Cuba	988	464	72	1122	6,5	26,2
Dominica	37,8	130	18	321	55,1	100
Dominican Republic	5147	729	68	2736	3,2	13
Ecuador	5719	693	76	3260	4,5	16
El Salvador	1223	805	56	3266	19,3	71
Grenada	37,6	178	24	342	41,4	100
Guatemala	2573	968	76	5212	15,4	53,1
Guyana	464	421	63	1264	14,2	39,1
Haiti	371	238	48	493	6,5	35,9

	Export ($million)	HS4	Markets	Diversity	Export < $1m	Export < $10m
Honduras	976	696	65	2336	17,7	51,1
Jamaica	1506	507	70	1733	6,5	16,1
Mexico	163494	1185	96	16556	1	3,9
Nicaragua	585	561	41	1559	16,4	44,5
Panama	785	228	43	864	10,7	29,6
Paraguay	1110	384	73	1400	9	34,1
Peru	8635	913	98	6127	5,9	19,8
Saint Kitts and Nevis	47,3	148	17	213	10,5	25,7
Saint Lucia	60,5	337	32	891	41,3	73,8
St. Vincent and the Grenadines	36,9	222	17	500	50,8	70,9
Suriname	545	304	53	511	4,1	10,8
Trinidad and Tobago	4916	771	75	4562	5,5	14,1
Uruguay	2092	644	91	2874	11,9	39,3
Venezuela	18963	879	85	5232	2,3	8,4

10. WITH A LITTLE HELP FROM OUR FRIENDS?
Developing Country Complaints and Third-Party Participation

MARC L BUSCH AND ERIC REINHARDT[*]

A. Introduction 247
B. Third Parties at the WTO 249
C. Hypotheses and Findings 252
    I. Hypotheses 253
    II. Data and Model 255
    III. Findings 257
D. Developing Countries and Third Parties 258

A. INTRODUCTION

In advance of filing for a compliance panel in the latest round of *Bananas III* litigation, Ecuador surprised many observers by asking for consultations with the EC. Indeed, by most accounts, this request was both unnecessary and unprecedented.[1] More interesting still, Ecuador revised its request two weeks later to make a single change: it wanted to pursue consultations with the EC under GATT Article XXII rather than under GATT Article XXIII.[2] The reason for this was simple: Ecuador hoped that by holding consultations under GATT Article XXII, it might attract *third parties*[3] to its side, and in doing so, improve the odds that Europe would negotiate a resolution to this dispute. Statistically speaking,

---

[*] School of Foreign Service, Georgetown University, mlb66@georgetown.edu and Department of Political Science, Emory University, erein@emory.edu, respectively. This paper was prepared for presentation at the conference on 'Developing Countries in the WTO Legal System', University of Minnesota Law School, May 24–26, 2007.

1. 'US Participates in WTO Banana Consultations with Ecuador, EU' *Inside US Trade* (22 December 2006).

2. WTO Document WT/DS27/65/Rev.1.

3. The WTO, like international law more generally, does not offer an explicit definition of third parties. See Christine Chinkin, *Third Parties in International Law* (Oxford: Clarendon, 1993) 7. Instead, it contrasts third (or 'other') parties with the complainant(s) and defendant and permits these members to 'reserve rights', a status that means they can directly participate in dispute proceedings, as we detail below. The key is not to confuse third parties with *cocomplainants* (ie, members who join the complaint as fellow plaintiffs) or with *amicus curiae* participants (ie, 'friend of the court' submissions by *non*governmental organizations), whose role and effects on dispute settlement outcomes are qualitatively distinct.

Ecuador was right on the first count but greatly mistaken on the second. In particular, developing country complaints *do* attract more third parties, but these third parties *undermine* the prospects for reaching a mutually agreed solution. This paper explains why and discusses what might be done to minimize the negative impact of third parties on effective use of dispute settlement by developing countries.

Third parties participate in the majority of WTO disputes and typically outnumber the complainant(s) and defendant (i.e., the 'main litigants') by a substantial margin. The DSU extends them the right to give testimony before panels and the Appellate Body (AB) such that they have a voice in the proceedings. Not surprisingly, the conventional wisdom is that third parties influence verdicts by offering a broader perspective on a dispute.[4] For example, Alan Rosas suggests that third-party testimony prevents panels and the AB from becoming too narrowly focused on the main litigants' claims.[5] James McCall Smith concurs, insisting that third-party testimony is taken as an important signal of the wider membership's preferences, resulting in rulings that are in keeping with these interests.[6] We find, moreover, that this conventional wisdom holds up to statistical scrutiny: the more procomplainant third parties, the more likely a panel or the AB is to render a procomplainant verdict.[7]

There is, however, a crucial twist in this story that matters for developing countries, in particular: before third parties exert any influence on the direction of rulings, they dramatically lower the chances that the case ends in *early settlement*, which we define as trade-liberalizing agreements negotiated before a panel rules. Our argument is that third parties, as a *participatory audience*, raise the main litigants' bargaining costs. As David Stasavage explains it, third parties, like any audience, can incite negotiators to posture, making them 'more reluctant to retreat from initially stated positions', even where a deal might otherwise be struck.[8] But moreover, because third parties are able to participate in the proceedings, there is the added risk that, as James Sebenius observes, 'the more parties (and issues), the higher the costs, the longer the time, and the greater the

---

4. C Carmody, 'Of Substantial Interest: Third Parties Under GATT' (1997) 18 Mich JIL 615; Z Lanye, 'The Effects of the WTO Dispute Settlement Panel and Appellate Body Reports' (2003) 17(1) Temple Int'l & Comp LJ 235; DW Layton and JO Miranda, 'Advocacy before World Trade Organization Dispute Settlement Panels in Trade Remedy Cases' (2003) 37 (1) JWT 95–96.

5. A Rosas, 'Joinder of Parties and Third Party Intervention in WTO Dispute Settlement' in F Weiss (ed), *Improving WTO Dispute Settlement Procedures: Issues & Lessons from the Practice of Other International Courts & Tribunals* (London: Cameron May 2000).

6. JM Smith, 'WTO Dispute Settlement: The Politics of Procedure in Appellate Body Rulings' (2003) 2(1) WT Rev.

7. ML Busch and E Reinhardt, 'Three's a Crowd: Third Parties and WTO Dispute Settlement' (2006) 58(3) W Pol 446–77.

8. D Stasavage, 'Open-Door or Closed-Door? Transparency in Domestic and International Bargaining' (2004) 58(4) Int'l Org 682.

informational requirements for negotiated settlement'.[9] In line with these expectations, we find that third parties do, in fact, influence rulings but only because they *first* undermine early settlement. This is especially problematic for developing countries since poor complainants tend to file against large-market defendants—as in *Bananas III*—and these cases attract a greater number of third parties, making it harder to reach a negotiated solution.

Two possible objections might be raised at this point. The first is that our causal explanation is backward, since it might be, instead, that harder cases attract more third parties—not that third parties make cases harder to settle. And second, even if our causal explanation is correct, early settlement is not the only goal of WTO litigation. As we will show, the first objection is easy to put to rest since we directly test for endogeneity bias and clearly find that third parties independently make negotiations more difficult, *not* that more difficult cases attract third parties. As for the second objection, there is no denying that, at times, complainants may prefer to win a legal verdict rather than settle early, and third parties can be of some help in this regard. Yet, as we show elsewhere, the challenge is that the fullest concessions on trade liberalization and market access are had by settling early, and rich complainants realize far more early settlement than do poor ones. In fact, developed—but *not* developing countries—have won greater concessions at the WTO than under GATT precisely because they are more likely to settle early, not because they win more rulings (they do not) or gain better compliance with the rulings that they win (they do not).[10] In short, early settlement *is* what distinguishes the records of rich versus poor complainants at the WTO, and third parties are the key to this puzzle. Playing on the title of our paper, developing countries would do better *without* a little help from their (third-party) friends.

This paper proceeds as follows. First, we discuss what the DSU allows by way of third-party participation. Second, we elaborate our hypothesis on how third parties shape rulings, conditional on the fact that they first undermine early settlement, and then turn to our findings. Third, we look at the evidence concerning third-party participation in cases filed by poor complainants and conclude by examining the various proposals for reforming third-party rights under the DSU and how these might bear on developing countries, in particular.

B. THIRD PARTIES AT THE WTO

Members join disputes as third parties for a variety of reasons. Chad Bown finds that countries with sizable exports to the disputed market that are affected only

---

9. JK Sebenius, 'Negotiation Arithmetic: Adding and Subtracting Issues and Parties' (1983) 37(2) Int'l Org 308. See also B Koremenos, C Lipson and D Snidal, 'The Rational Design of International Institutions' (2001) 55(4) Int'l Org 782.

10. ML Busch and E Reinhardt, 'Developing Countries and GATT/WTO Dispute Settlement' (2003) 37(4) JWT 719–35.

indirectly by the defendant's policy, in *market share* rather than volume terms, are likely to become third parties, while countries with large exports, the volume of which is directly affected by the disputed policy, are more likely to become cocomplainants.[11] There also exists a 'learning-by-watching' incentive to file for third-party rights, inasmuch as Members, and developing countries, more specifically, can benefit simply by observing the proceedings firsthand. Related to this, we would add that a lack of transparency concerning the terms of early settlement motivates governments to participate as third parties, the logic being that they can better monitor concessions offered, and protect their interests. What, then, do third parties do?

At first blush, the WTO's provisions for third parties are simple enough. DSU 10 permits them to offer both written and oral testimony before panels during the first of two rounds of litigation, and DSU 17 ensures that the same third parties reserving rights at the panel stage have similar access to proceedings before the AB in the event that a verdict is appealed, which happens roughly 70 percent of the time.

And yet things are not quite as simple as they seem. This is because third parties almost always get involved in disputes long *before* the DSU formally designates them as such: namely, in consultations. Indeed, DSU 4.11 allows Members 'other' than the main litigants to be joined in consultations, paving the way for what we call *informal* third parties. In truth, though, the two are one and the same; in our data set of 507 instances of third-party participation in disputes through 2002, fully 99 percent started in consultations. In other words, nearly every formal third party began as an informal one.[12] In this sense, it is little wonder that, in proposing reforms of the DSU, Members have spent a good deal of effort debating third-party rights in *consultations*.[13]

It is at this point that observers usually respond that while third parties may be interested in a case, the main litigants can *choose* to allow them to participate or not. There is something to this but not much. Starting with consultations, the first potential obstacle is DSU 4.11, which stipulates that to be joined, informal third parties must have a 'substantial trade interest' in the dispute. This entry barrier is meant to give the main litigants more latitude to negotiate a resolution

---

11. CP Bown, 'Participation in WTO Dispute Settlement: Complainants, Interested Parties and Free Riders,' (2005) 19(2) WB Econ Rev.

12. Moreover, each of these four exceptions effectively proves the rule. For example, Thailand's intervention on the side of the complainants in the *EC—Bananas* dispute (DS158), while initiated only after the panel was established, was also rapidly withdrawn. In the other three instances, the governments in question attempted to join consultations but had their requests to do so denied; however, they later submitted briefs as official third parties at the panel stage (eg, Thailand and the Philippines in *Turkey—Textile and Clothing Products*, DS34, and the European Communities in *Korea—Government Procurement*, DS163).

13. See WTO Document TN/DS/W/36.

by excluding 'other' Members with no real economic stake in the outcome. And yet through 2002, few requests to be joined in consultations have been rejected; of the 507 instances of third-party participation in our data set, only 19 were declined. Of those that were, moreover, many were just refiled when the case was subsequently brought before a panel, given that at this stage, the DSU requires only a 'substantial interest', rather than a substantial *trade* interest, the former being defined more broadly than just a commercial stake.

That said, in addition to or instead of a substantial trade interest, a Member can also claim a 'systemic interest' to be joined in consultations. Indeed, systemic interests are often raised when disputes are likely to hinge on the interpretation of untested or politically charged WTO texts, for example, or where domestic legislation is challenged. In this sense, a systemic interest is *not* just a substitute for the lack of substantial trade interest but a signal that third parties plan to raise broader—and potentially more axiomatic—issues. Along these lines, China, Japan, and Taiwan cited systemic *and* substantial trade interests in a dispute over oil tubular goods even though all three, as sizeable producers of these products, had much at stake commercially. They chose to claim systemic interests, however, because they had more fundamental concerns about the dispute, as suggested by the 48 pages dedicated to their submissions in the final panel report.[14] More generally, in cases targeting measures that do *not* specifically apply to any identifiable good and thus could *not* attract other Members with a substantial trade interest, we find that third parties are no more likely to claim a systemic interest than in cases where the measure in dispute does bear on an identifiable good. This lends considerable weight to the view that claims of systemic interests are signals of a third party's intent to participate fully in the dispute and not simply substitutes for a substantial trade interest. To be sure, even the exceptions prove the rule: when the US rejected Japan's request to be joined in consultations on the grounds that it had no substantial trade interest, Japan responded that its commercial interests included 'systemic' concerns.[15]

A second potential hurdle to third-party participation concerns the specific article under which the complainant requests consultations with the defendant. This, after all, is why Ecuador chose to revise its first request for consultations with the EC in advance of a compliance panel in *Bananas III*. Here, the issue is whether, along with DSU 4, the complainant invokes GATT XXII:1 or GATT XXIII:1. Since GATT XXIII, in general, provides for *bilateral* dispute settlement, the intuition is that a complainant will request consultations under this article if it wants to exclude third parties, but invoke GATT XXII:1 if, like Ecuador, it wants to attract them.[16] Empirically, the relationship is far from clear-cut: roughly

---

14. WTO Document DS282.
15. WTO Document DS200/12.
16. See A Porges, 'Settling WTO Disputes: What Do Litigation Models Tell Us?' (2003) 19 Ohio St J DR 158.

half of all WTO complaints start with GATT XXIII:1 consultations, and half of these attract third parties. The practical difference between the two articles has nothing whatsoever to do with third parties per se but rather with the complainant's *ex ante* intention of 'paneling' its dispute; in the GATT years, those cases brought under GATT XXIII:1 were 40 percent more likely to go before a panel.[17] That said, it is true that GATT XXII:1 consultations *do* attract more third parties, but the point is that, as we show below, even controlling for which article consultations are held under, third parties still undermine early settlement.

The final potential obstacle is found in DSU 10, which says that third parties must have a substantial interest in the dispute. This, of course, is a lower entry barrier than the one found in DSU 4, which requires a substantial trade interest. Much like in consultations, a defendant could choose to block a third party on the grounds that it lacks the relevant interest, though at the risk that this rejected third party would, in turn, simply file as a cocomplainant. Regardless, the fact is that empirically, third parties are seldom resisted. This gives us license to ask whether third parties really matter? On this, there is no doubt.

C. HYPOTHESES AND FINDINGS

The conventional wisdom says that third parties help shape panel and AB rulings because these are strategic actors. Just as Geoffrey Garrett, Daniel Keleman, and Heiner Schulz insist that it is no longer controversial to ascribe strategic decision making to the European Court of Justice (ECJ),[18] few if any WTO observers doubt that political expediency guides panels and the AB in rendering decisions.[19] The tension, as Smith explains it with respect to the AB, is to balance the need to render legally consistent decisions with a desire to increase the likelihood of compliance. Here, compliance is not just a function of whether the defendant will abide by the ruling but how the membership, as a whole, will receive it. Smith, like Rosas,[20] identifies a key opportunity for third parties in this regard, observing that the AB has sought their participation 'to gain access to valuable information regarding the views of the broader WTO membership'.[21]

---

17. ML Busch, 'Democracy, Consultation, and the Paneling of Disputes Under GATT' (2000) 44(4) J ConR.

18. G Garrett, RD Keleman and H Schulz, 'The European Court of Justice, National Governments, and Legal Integration in the European Union' (1998) 52(1) Int'l Org 152.

19. F Weiss, 'Third Parties in GATT/WTO Dispute Settlement Proceedings,' in E Denters and N Schrijver (eds), *Reflections on International Law from the Low Countries* (Netherlands: Kluwer Law, 1998); N Covelli, 'Member Intervention in World Trade Organization Dispute Settlement Proceedings After *EC—Sardines*: The Rules, Jurisprudence, and Controversy' (2003) 37(3) JWT.

20. Rosas (n 5 above).

21. Smith (n 6 above) 75, 85.

Even a cursory glance at WTO panel reports seems to bear out these expectations. In *Chile—Alcoholic Beverages*, the panel explained that it had rejected one of the defendant's legal arguments because the EC, '*as well as third parties*, objected that such a notion was absurd', nodding to the import of their intervention in this dispute.[22] In *Canada—Aircraft*, the United States' third-party testimony was deemed to be so germane to the case that the panel refused to let it be withdrawn, not least because the panel 'had asked the parties to submit comments *on specific aspects of the US submissions*'.[23] More telling still, in *Canada—Patents*, the panel decided not to rule on a key question of law, explaining that it did not want to adjudicate 'a normative policy issue that is still obviously a matter of *unresolved political debate*', a conclusion it reached in large measure because of the participation of third parties in the case.[24] The question, however, is whether these examples are representative? Taken at face value, they are not. To see why, let us turn to our argument.

i. Hypotheses

Our argument is *not* that this conventional wisdom is wrong but that it misses all the real action. One of the most axiomatic tenets of bargaining theory is that more parties to a dispute make negotiations increasingly difficult. Add this to the fact that third parties almost always participate in consultations, and it becomes hard to imagine that whatever impact they are having on dispute settlement is not unfolding long before a panel is even requested. We hypothesize that third parties increase the main litigant's bargaining costs in two complementary ways. First, third parties, as an audience, make negotiations more *transparent*, which is likely to motivate the protagonists to posture. James Fearon argues that audiences inspire states to dig in their heel, and that when it comes to signaling resolve in this way (i.e., by raising 'audience costs'), they seldom bluff.[25] Tim Groseclose and Nolan McCarty also show that third parties can induce posturing and, as a result, deadlock negotiations, even when the parties are fully informed about each other's preferences.[26] As one former trade lawyer explains, this is why '(p)rivacy for the negotiating process can be essential. . .'.[27]

Second, as an audience that can actually participate in the dispute, third parties are not only likely to induce posturing by the main litigants but influence the content of what they argue about. As Bill Davey points out, third parties can

---

22. WTO Document DS87, para 7.136. Emphasis added.
23. WTO Document DS70, para 7.47, n 4 above (emphasis added).
24. WTO Document DS114/R, para 7.82 (emphasis added).
25. J Fearon, 'Signaling Foreign Policy Interests: Tying Hands Versus Sinking Costs' (1997) 41(1) J ConR.
26. T Groseclose and N McCarty, 'The Politics of Blame: Bargaining Before an Audience', (2001) 45(1) Am J Pol Sci.
27. Porges (n 17 above), 176.

interpret cases in ways that may be at odds with the complainant's and defendant's positions and thus prove distracting.[28] Jeff Waincymer agrees, observing that while third parties are not supposed to raise claims of their own, they can nonetheless draw attention to other arguments that fit within the terms of reference but which the complainant and defendant had not introduced or—worse still—do not favor.[29] Along these lines, the Dominican Republic complained that Honduras had been prodded by third parties to expand the terms of reference in a dispute over cigarettes, insisting that '(i)t was not until the first meeting of the Panel that Honduras suddenly included all of the products in the complaint, taking the idea from the written submissions of certain third parties'.[30] Similarly, the United States insisted in the online gambling dispute that "Antigua and the third parties are expending a great deal of rhetorical energy in an effort to seek to modify the text of the US Schedule through dispute settlement'.[31] The involvement of third parties in consultations poses similar risks in that they may desire a settlement that the main litigants find unacceptable or introduce new issues to be resolved which might put a settlement out of reach.

Finally, third parties may also raise systemic legal questions about a dispute, further circumscribing the grounds on which the main litigants might negotiate. In particular, third parties might have little commercial stake in changing a specific measure(s) but prefer, instead, a broader legal decision that bears on their own policies or the policies of those against whom they might file future disputes.[32] If the main litigants believe that the outcome of their dispute is likely to cast a long shadow, they are likely to become further entrenched, thereby reducing the opportunity for early settlement.

Accordingly, we hypothesize that third-party participation makes early settlement *less* likely and, by extension, increases the likelihood of a panel ruling. We further argue that both of these consequences should be especially likely when a third party raises systemic issues. Taken together, this means that any test of the conventional wisdom (i.e., that third parties affect the direction of a ruling) must be conditional on the fact that they undermine early settlement, thus

---

28. William Davey warns, in particular, against the recommendation that panels and the AB be required to address all the points raised by third parties, since this "could potentially lead to abuse where a third party views the case completely differently than the parties . . . ." See W Davey, 'The WTO Dispute Settlement Mechanism' (2003) University of Illinois: Illinois Public Law and Legal Theory Research Papers Series No. 03-08 15.

29. J Waincymer, *WTO Litigation: Procedural Aspects of Formal Dispute Settlement* (London: Cameron May, 2002) 339. See also Smith (n 6 above) 85.

30. WTO Document DS302/R, para 4.351.

31. WTO Document DS285.

32. As Porges astutely observes, "In the absence of a stakeholder with a financial interest in early settlement, the government may have no incentive to have a bargaining position oriented toward settlement." See Porges (n 17 above) 155.

making rulings more likely in the first place. We conduct one of the first tests of this sort.

ii. Data and Model

To test our hypotheses, we compiled a data set of 202 WTO disputes filed through 2002 for which litigation had concluded as of January 2004. Our coding procedures are discussed elsewhere;[33] here we briefly describe the data and review our results.

Of the 202 disputes in our data set, a panel was established in 99 (49 percent). Our main interest is in how third parties affect early settlement, and in this regard it is interesting to note that the defendant offered liberalizing concessions before a ruling was issued (either in consultations or at the panel stage) in 40 percent of the 120 cases where we can code the policy outcome.[34] Of the 99 panel proceedings, a ruling was issued in 65 cases, of which 39 favored the complainant, net of any appeal. Third parties participated in 64 percent of the cases in our data set, averaging 3.9 per dispute. In all, 61 different Members are counted among these third parties. True, the economic superpowers frequently are well-represented; the United States was a third party in 43 cases (of the 86 in which it was *not* one of the main litigants); the EC in 52 (of 120), and Japan in 52 (of 183). Other frequent third parties include Australia, Brazil, Canada, Chile, India, Korea, Mexico, Norway, and Switzerland. That said, developing countries account for 52 percent of all third parties, whereas they tally for only 36 percent of all complainants. In this light, if a Member has any experience with WTO dispute settlement, chances are it is as a third party.

We constructed three variables to look at third-party participation: a dummy variable (i.e., whether or not a third party participated); a count (i.e., how many participated); and an index of their economic significance, which weights the participating third parties by their GDP in relation to the defendant (this is 0 if the dispute attracts no third parties). A fourth variable accounts for which side a third party took in a dispute to help determine if they bear on the direction of rulings; we coded this as either procomplainant, prodefendant, or mixed, based on their submission to the WTO. In our data set, 66 percent of all third parties intervene in support of the complainant, 27 percent for the defendant, and 7 percent offer mixed testimony.

We also constructed a variable to test whether early settlement is especially more difficult when third parties cite systemic interests in their submissions, literally using this term (which makes our coding very straightforward). In our data set, third parties invoke systemic interests 40 percent of the time, again

---

33. Busch and Reinhardt (n 7 above).
34. The data on policy outcomes in these cases are taken from Busch and Reinhardt (n 10 above).

suggesting that such claims are not simply filling in where arguments about a substantial trade interest fall short.

To round out our model, we added several other variables that are expected to influence the prospects for settlement or the issuance and/or direction of a ruling.[35] These include: (1) a dummy for US-EC cases, given the belief that transatlantic disputes are different for a variety of reasons, ranging from the volume of trade at stake to the resources these members can invest in litigation, including over fundamental questions of law;[36] (2) the log of the complainant's and defendant's GDP, to control for their market power;[37] (3) the number of complainants (the average is 1.3), to ensure that our findings concerning third parties are not attributable, instead, to the multiplicity of complainants in a given case; (4) whether the complainant requested consultations under GATT XXII:1, which is the article chosen in about half of all WTO disputes; (5) whether the complainant alleged a *nonviolation* offense, since these charges are more vague and may thus greatly complicate negotiations;[38] (6) whether the contested measure discriminates against some, but not all, Members as these likely run afoul of the WTO's most axiomatic principles (such as GATT I and GATT III); (7) the legal complexity of the case, proxied by the number of distinct treaty articles cited in the complaint,[39] as these may be harder for the complainant to argue coherently and effectively, and are generally viewed as being less meritorious;[40] and (8) five case-specific attributes, including: dummies for agricultural disputes; politically sensitive disputes (i.e., those concerned with national security, environmental regulations, sanitary and phytosanitary rules, cultural protection, and policies falling under the jurisdiction of subnational authorities in federal states); the volume of trade at stake, or, if no trade volume is at stake, we code it as a nonmerchandise dispute; and last, the stakes for (potential) third

---

35. For more information about sources and coding of these variables, see Busch and Reinhardt (n 7 above).

36. See, for example, the contributions to E Petersmann and MA Pollack (eds), *Transatlantic Economic Disputes: The EU, the US, and the WTO* (Oxford: Oxford University Press, 2003).

37. These are calculated for the year the complaint was first filed, using constant (1995) US dollars, from the World Bank's *World Development Indicators*.

38. D Palmeter and PC Mavroidis, *Dispute Settlement in the World Trade Organization: Practice and Procedure* (2nd ed, Cambridge: Cambridge University Press, 2004) 164.

39. Specifically, as cited in the complainant's request for consultations and, where applicable, request(s) for a panel. *Number of Articles Cited* ranges from 1 to 39, averaging 7, in our data set.

40. See MA Bailey, B Kamoie and F Maltzman, 'Signals from the Tenth Justice: The Political Role of the Solicitor General in Supreme Court Decision Making' (2005) 49(1) Am J Pol Sci 79; RS Solberg and L Ray, 'Capacity, Attitudes, and Case Attributes: The Differential Success of the States before the United States Courts of Appeals (2005) 5(2) St Pol Q 155–56, 159.

parties, which is the share of imports into the disputed market for the affected product, in the year prior to the complaint, supplied by countries other than the main litigants.[41]

iii. Findings

The data bear out our two hypotheses: third parties sharply lower the odds of early settlement, and any impact they have on the direction of rulings is conditional on the fact that they first make it more likely that disputes go the legal distance to a ruling. Consider the prospects for early settlement. For the average case (i.e., holding all other variables at their sample means) with no third-party involvement, and thus no possibility of systemic interests being raised, the predicted probability of early settlement is a reasonably high 69 percent. If we then take this same case, but add third parties, still with no systemic issues raised, the predicted probability of early settlement drops precipitously to 31 percent. If we then add the complication of third parties citing systemic interests, the predicted probability of early settlement plummets to a mere 4 percent—a remote prospect at best. By comparison, again holding all other variables at their sample means, the predicted probability of early settlement is 16 percent for politically sensitive cases and 40 percent for those cases that are not politically sensitive. In short, third-party participation is *the* single most important influence on early settlement in our model.

Moreover, these findings are robust; they hold for all three coding variants of our third-party variable and are not merely an artifact of frequent third-party participation by the United States and the EC, a dummy for which is not even statistically significant when included in our model. In addition, these results hold up if we recode the outcome variable to distinguish *partial* from full concessions in defining early settlement and are not sensitive to the inclusion of variables that strongly predict third-party participation, notably the share of the contested market held by economies other than the main litigants, and—to a lesser extent—whether the complainant requested consultations under GATT XXII:1.

The strongest predictor, however, is this *nondisputant market share* variable. In fact, going from its sample minimum to maximum and holding all other variables at their sample means, nondisputant market share increases the predicted number of third parties from 1.2 to 2.8. That is, third parties get involved when they supply a large percent share of the disputed market's imports of the affected product. Because this variable can influence early settlement only through third parties but is not itself correlated with early settlement, it serves as an ideal 'instrumental variable' which we can use to test directly for endogeneity bias.

---

41. It takes on a value of 100 for disputes not naming a specific merchandise product(s).

In doing so, we find that the process causing third-party intervention is independent of that driving early settlement and thus that our primary finding—that third parties reduce the prospects for reaching a negotiation solution prior to ruling—*cannot* be attributed to endogeneity bias.[42]

What about ruling *direction*? First, we ran a model that ignored our hypothesized selection effect, using the 65 cases in which rulings were issued. The results were starkly at odds with the conventional wisdom; the model failed to reject the null hypothesis that its variables' coefficients were collectively zero. We then ran a model that explicitly incorporated our hypothesized selection effect, with the issuance of a ruling as its first stage and the direction of the ruling as its second. In other words, the model asks about ruling direction conditional on their being a ruling in the first place, which we hypothesize to be the result of third parties participating because they undermine early settlement. The model tells us that there is, indeed, selection bias; third parties and systemic increase the odds of a ruling and controlling for this, procomplainant third parties increase the odds of a procomplainant ruling. The substantive effects are impressive: for an average case, the marginal probability of a procomplainant ruling is just 6 percent if there are no third parties, but this rises to 29 percent if only procomplainant third parties intervene, and to 55 percent if those parties also raise systemic issues. Yet it drops back to 33 percent if we add prodefendant third parties to the mix.

We also find evidence that nonviolation charges and the number of articles cited bear on the direction of rulings. With all other variables at their sample means, the marginal probability of a procomplainant ruling is 45 percent if the complaint makes no nonviolation claim and cites only one article. But if this complainant alleges a nonviolation infraction and cites ten articles (which is *not* an extreme value), its odds of prevailing fall to 3 percent.

In sum, our findings support the conventional wisdom, but this is only because we model for the fact that, before third parties have any influence on rulings, they undermine early settlement.

D. DEVELOPING COUNTRIES AND THIRD PARTIES

While third parties pose obstacles for complainants in general, the problem is only compounded for developing countries. This is because poor complainants typically challenge large-market defendants, and these cases attract more third parties, resulting in less early settlement. As Andrew Guzman and Beth Simmons conjecture, poor complainants are likely to target bigger economies since, net

---

42. For a detailed discussion of this instrumental variable approach, see Busch and Reinhardt (n 7 above).

the costs of litigation, the expected payoff from defeating these defendants is greater.[43] While we do not disagree with this intuition, our concern is that by filing these disputes, developing countries end up contending with about 60 percent more third parties than the average complainant and thus are far less likely to win concessions in advance of a ruling. Since early settlement is *the* source of the gap in concessions secured by rich versus poor complainants,[44] this is arguably *the* most important problem that developing countries face when litigating at the WTO.

To put this in perspective, recall that the average dispute attracts 3.9 third parties, lowering the odds of early settlement by more than half (from 69 percent to 31 percent), and this assuming that none cites a systemic interest. By way of comparison, the average developing country complaint attracts 6.15 third parties, enough to virtually foreclose any opportunity of achieving early settlement. Figure 1 speaks to this, plotting the number of third parties per dispute against instances of early settlement. The key here is the precipitous decline in negotiated solutions when more than five third parties participate, setting a tipping point that is *below* the developing country average. Most telling, in this regard, is that of the 11 disputes that attracted more than five third parties, only one ended in early settlement. With this tipping point in mind, it is interesting to note that Ecuador's consultations with the EC drew 18.

These findings are all the more striking when considering that many of the attributes of cases filed by developing countries are associated with *more* early settlement. In marked contrast to their wealthy counterparts, poor complainants tend *not* to file disputes that are politically sensitive,[45] concern agriculture, call into question domestic legislation, or challenge broad legal principles, all of which reduce the odds of reaching a negotiated solution. In fact, not only are developing country cases more focused on tangible commerce but implicate *less* trade; whereas poor complainants, on average, contest product-specific measures on $447 million in trade (1995 prices), the comparable figure for developed countries is $1.2 billion (1995 prices). This suggests that, if anything, poor complainants litigate disputes that ought to be easier to settle early.

Add to this that developing country cases are (at least) as meritorious as those of developed countries, and it becomes clear that third parties are the reason poor complainants fail to realize early settlement. The competing explanation would be that poor complainants bring legally weak cases, and that, as a result, defendants have little incentive to settle early, preferring, instead, to be vindicated

---

43. AT Guzman and BA Simmons, 'Power Plays and Capacity Constraints: The Selection of Defendants in WTO Disputes' (2005) 34 J Leg Stu 557–98.

44. Busch and Reinhardt (n 10 above).

45. I.e., those concerned with national security, environmental regulations, sanitary and phytosanitary rules, cultural protection, and policies falling under the jurisdiction of subnational authorities in federal states.

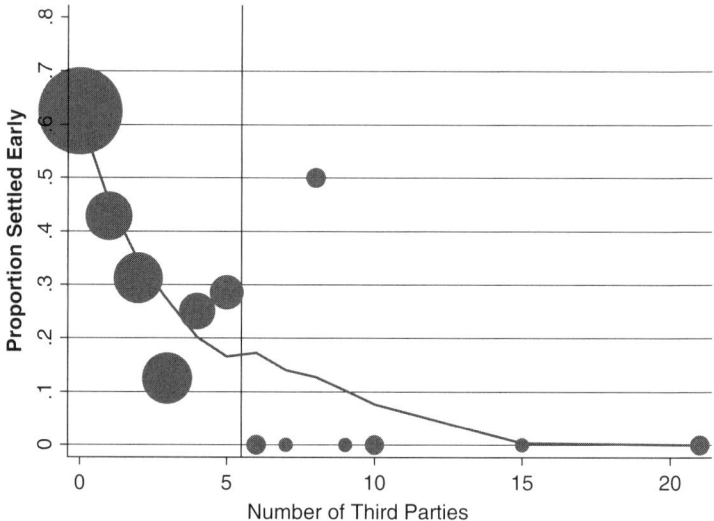

FIGURE 1. PROPORTION OF COMPLAINTS SETTLED EARLY, BY NUMBER OF THIRD PARTIES (N =120).[1]

[1] Note: the size of the circles is proportional to the number of cases having the stipulated number of third parties.

by a panel. On the one hand, developing countries cite about 50 percent more articles in their complaints, which, as we explained, is suggestive of weaker legal merits. On the other hand, they make far fewer nonviolation claims than rich complainants (3 versus 13 percent), which, as we also explained, do vastly more to undermine early settlement than the number of articles cited. In short, differences in the legal merits of cases brought by rich versus poor complainants are doubtful to shed much light on the gap in early settlement.

While this rightly puts the spotlight back on third parties, some might ask whether our focus on early settlement is misguided. After all, our results indicate that third parties can help complainants win at trial, and this, more than early settlement, may be valued by developing countries. Our response is in two parts. First, the influence of third parties on rulings largely washes out when they offer mixed testimony, or when some side with the complainant and others with the defendant. This is not surprising; if panels and the AB are politically astute and take third-party testimony as a signal of the wider membership's preferences, divisions among them ought to be expected to limit the impact of their input. Of the 18 third parties reserving rights in Ecuador's consultations with the EC, about half shared interests with the defendant.

Second, and more important, a legal ruling is *not* a guarantee that the defendant will grant concessions. On the contrary, our research shows that, regardless of how panels or the AB decide a case, rulings are associated with *fewer* concessions. Indeed, in our study of the concessions had by developed and developing countries under the GATT and WTO, variables for procomplainant, mixed, and prodefendant rulings are all negatively signed and, at least for the latter two, statistically significant.[46] Much the same is true in our study of US-EC disputes, where all three rulings variables are negatively signed, statistically significant, and substantively important: prodefendant rulings lower the odds of concessions by 63 percent, mixed rulings by 43 percent, and even procomplainant rulings by 25 percent.[47] Our point is this: concessions are far more likely to be had through early settlement than by winning a ruling, and while third parties *might* better the chances of the latter (assuming they all side with the complainant), they are *guaranteed* to undermine the former.

If this argument is hard to accept, it is only because it runs counter to all received wisdom on third parties. To be sure, it has long been taken as an article of faith that third parties help, rather than hinder, complainants. Ecuador is no exception in this regard; in a proposal for reforming DSU 21 that foreshadows its strategy in *Bananas III*, Ecuador not only calls for consultations in the lead-up to a compliance panel but for 'an adequate opportunity' for any third party 'to express its views'.[48] Following through on its own proposal, Ecuador went looking for third-party input by filing for GATT XXII consultations, the aim being to motivate the EC to settle early in the face of wider political pressure. In particular, Ecuador was purportedly looking to negotiate a €130/ton tariff, a figure lower than Europe's current €176/ton tariff, but markedly higher than the €33/ton tariff Ecuador estimates would fulfill the 'total market-access' criterion set out by the WTO.[49] With 18 third parties participating in its dispute, however, the odds were stacked against Ecuador realizing early settlement in consultations. Since many of these third parties side with the EC,[50] moreover, their potential to influence a procomplainant ruling is likely to be small.

Many developing countries share this view that third-party participation should be encouraged, including in consultations. Jamaica proposes, for example, that the requirement for joining consultations should be a substantial interest, not a substantial *trade* interest (in which case it proposes 'enhanced status' as a third party); that a written record of consultations be given to the panel; that the main litigants not be allowed to reject third-party participation; and that

---

46. Busch and Reinhardt, (n 10 above) 728.
47. ML Busch and E Reinhardt, 'Transatlantic Trade Conflicts and GATT/WTO Dispute Settlement' in E Petersmann and MA Pollack (eds), *Transatlantic Economic Disputes: The EU, the US, and the WTO* (Oxford: Oxford University Press, 2003) 475.
48. WTO Document TN/DS/W/33, p. 3 (emphasis added).
49. "Ecuador Unpeels new Chapter in Banana Dispute With EU" *ICTSD Bridges Weekly Trade News Digest* 10 (39) 2006.
50. WTO Document WT/DS27/78.

panels be required to consider third-party views on issues not necessarily raised by the main litigants.[51] Jordan concurs on the need for unfettered third-party participation,[52] as does the African Group, which insists that developing countries, in particular, should 'not be required to demonstrate a *trade or economic interest*' to join as a third party, and that they should be allowed to testify during all rounds of litigation.[53] Along these same lines, Costa Rica calls for more third-party access to 'all the substantial meetings' and, provocatively, for more 'consideration to the arguments' of third parties in panel reports.[54]

Other developing countries are not convinced. A group led by Taiwan stands out in this regard, arguing for the substantial trade interest criterion to 'ensure that the necessary space and simplicity for the disputing parties is retained in the consultation stage', in light of the fact that 'consultation is an important method of settling trade disputes'. The group goes on to warn against requiring panel reports to dwell on third-party submissions as these may often prove to be orthogonal to the issues raised by the main litigants.[55] We could not agree more.

First, we favor the requirement that third parties notify a substantial *trade* interest to be joined in consultations. This will go some distance in balancing the need for access with the desire to give the main litigants more latitude to negotiate. In fact, we see merit in having third parties explain their reasons for wanting to participate, as this will help the main litigants better anticipate their input and evaluate whether to accept their requests to be joined. At the same time, we agree with the chairman's draft text on DSU reform that the main litigants should provide reasons for denying these requests, if simply to prevent others from registering as third parties on the suspicion that something is amiss.

Second, we concur with several developing countries that the main parties should report the details of any early settlement to the DSB ex post.[56] Given that many third parties request to be joined in consultations in order to keep apprised of any deal struck, this might temper interest in reserving rights *ex ante* and thus result in more early settlement. This same logic is at work in Japan's proposal that submissions be shared with *all* Members so that this information can be used to help interpret decisions and be used by others in deciding whether to file their own disputes.[57] A report to the DSB on the terms of any early settlement would accomplish the same goal, not least for those Members denied access to consultations, for whom filing a case is their only recourse. In this sense, greater

---

51. See WTO Document TN/DS/W/21, pp 1–3; and WTO Document TN/DS/W/44, p. 1.
52. TN/DS/W/43, p 5.
53. WTO Document TN/DS/W/15, p 4.
54. WTO Document TN/DS/W/12/Rev.1, p 1.
55. WTO Document TN/DS/W/25, p 3.
56. WTO Document TN/DS/W/18, para 2.
57. WTO Document TN/DS/W/22, para 4.

transparency after the fact may reduce the need for Members to reserve third-party rights in the first place.

That said, we oppose proposals to increase transparency *during* consultations. In particular, we are especially troubled by calls for a written record of these negotiations, as Jamaica has suggested,[58] since this would only lessen the incentive to make concessions, fearful that offers might be interpreted as an omission of noncompliance.[59] The key is that, as Canada explains it, public scrutiny of consultations 'could undermine Members' ability to reach negotiated solutions to disputes',[60] raising the domestic political costs of negotiating a deal that might not be popular at home.[61] Since this is precisely what third parties do internationally, the same logic would argue against increasing transparency (indirectly) through stronger third-party rights.

---

58. WTO Document TN/DS/W/21, p 1.
59. AF Daughety and JF Reinganum, 'Keeping Society in the Dark: On Admissibility of Pretrial Negotiations as Evidence in Court' (1995) 26(2) *Rand Journal of Economics* 203–221; Davey (above n 28).
60. WTO Document TN/DS/W/41, par. 6.
61. Busch (above n 18).

11. MFN AND THE THIRD-PARTY ECONOMIC INTERESTS OF DEVELOPING COUNTRIES IN GATT/WTO DISPUTE SETTLEMENT

CHAD P BOWN[*]

A. Introduction 266
B. Economic Reasons for Third-Party Interest 270
    I. Disputes Alleging Respondent Engaged in Excessive Import Protection 272
        Third-country exporters of the disputed product 272
        Third-country importers of the disputed product 274
    II. Disputes Alleging Respondent Engaged in Excessive Export Promotion 275
        Third-country exporters of the disputed product 275
        Third-country importers of the disputed product 275
    III. Disputes Alleging Respondent Engaged in Excessive Export Restrictions 276
        Third-country exporters of the disputed product 276
        Third-country importers of the disputed product 277
C. Empirical Analysis: Import Liberalization and the Impact on Developing Third-Country Exporters 277
    I. Formal Third Party Interventions vs. Implicitly Interested Third Parties 278
    II. Data Analysis—the Underlying 'Bilateral' Trade Dispute 279
        The importance of the discriminatory nature of the initial allegation 281
        Trade liberalization and economic success in the bilateral disputes 281
    III. Identifying the Developing Third-Country Exporters in the Trade Dispute 281
    IV. The Economic Performance of Developing Third-Country Exporters 282
        How many developing third countries also increase exports? 282
        How large are the increases in developing third-country exports? 286
        Does being a GATT/WTO member matter for MFN in this setting? 287
    V. Summary and Interpretation of Empirical Results 287
D. Conclusions, Extensions, and Policy Implications 288

---

[*] Department of Economics and International Business School, MS021, Brandeis University, Waltham, MA 02454-9110, USA tel: +1.781.736.4823, fax: +1.781.736.2269, e-mail: cbown@brandeis.edu, web: http://www.brandeis.edu/~cbown/. The author gratefully acknowledges financial support through a Mazer Award and Perlmutter Fellowship at Brandeis University. Thanks for helpful comments to Rachel McCulloch, Bernard Hoekman, William Davey, Chantal Thomas, and participants at the Developing Countries in the WTO Legal System Conference at the University of Minnesota Law School. Jassa Chawla provided outstanding research assistance. All remaining errors are my own.

A. INTRODUCTION

There is clear evidence that developing countries have been increasing their participation in the world trading system and also the dispute settlement processes of the GATT/WTO. There have already been more disputes with developing country complainants and respondents initiated since the WTO's 1995 inception than there were during the entire 1947–1994 GATT period. Some of this increase merely reflects the growth of developing country membership; nevertheless, the increase in complainant activity is consistent with the idea that some barriers to the initiation of disputes have been reduced. Furthermore, the increase in respondent activity suggests that some developing countries have increased their market-access commitments to a level that trading partners increasingly find such commitments valuable enough to spend resources to defend them.

Equally and increasingly important to any developing countries' economic success achieved by acting as complainants in WTO disputes in order to enforce their export market access may be the *indirect* impact of the dispute settlement process on their trading interests. Given the recent growth in imports and exports to and from developing countries, an increase in the frequency of DSU litigation activity over products in which developing countries trade implies that they are increasingly affected by the outcome of *other* countries' disputes in which they are neither complainant nor respondent. For every two-country (complainant/respondent) WTO dispute, there may be dozens of developing countries which also trade in the disputed product and which are thus potentially affected by the dispute's economic resolution. Despite the potential for this impact to be quite important economically and politically, there is relatively little in the formal research literature examining this complex issue.[1] This chapter

---

1. There is some related work in the formal empirical research literature on the DSU. An empirical examination of determinants of third-country exporters' decisions of whether to formally participate in disputes related to their market-access interest is CP Bown, 'Participation in WTO Dispute Settlement: Complainants, Interested Parties and Free Riders' (2005) 19 WB Econ Rev 287. The empirical analysis below examining whether the outcome of economically successful bilateral disputes is also extended to third-country exports relies heavily on CP Bown, 'Trade Policy under the GATT/WTO: Empirical Evidence of the Equal Treatment Rule' (2004) 37 Can JEcon 678. Finally, other authors analyze the impact of third parties on the formal DSU process itself, presenting evidence that allowing (or even encouraging) the formal role of third parties is not costless, as third parties are empirically associated with disputes that are less likely to be settled early and more likely to proceed to a panel ruling—see ML Busch and E Reinhardt, 'Three's a Crowd: Third Parties and WTO Dispute Settlement' (2006) 58 W Pol 446, as well as ML Busch and E Reinhardt, 'With a Little Help From Our Friends? Developing Country Complaints and Third Party Participation" in Chapter 10 of this collection. The main difference in the respective approaches is that the analysis here focuses on *economic* outcomes as measured via trade flows.

focuses on this indirect or 'third-party' interest of developing countries in WTO trade disputes over market access.

A contributing explanation for the lack of research on third-party performance in formal dispute settlement is that there is no 'one-size-fits-all' metric for assessment. How a dispute's 'successful' resolution is likely to affect economically third countries depends on a number of interrelated factors, even abstracting from the important political question of whether respondents actually comply with DSU rulings. For example, is the third country an exporter or importer of the product at issue in the dispute? Are the complainant and/or respondent countries 'large' in the sense that their changes in market access will have externality implications via changes in world prices? Is the market access issue under dispute one of import or export policy? If export policy, is it excessive export restriction or promotion (eg, subsidies)? If import policy, was the GATT/WTO violation applied on a discriminatory (leading to implicit preferences for some third countries) or nondiscriminatory basis? Given the possibility of such divergent economic interests, the first task of this chapter is to clarify and categorize the various potential third-party interests that a developing country could expect to face in a trade dispute.[2]

The *EC–Sugar Regime* case is a particularly illustrative example of a WTO dispute in which the legal-economic resolution is expected to create divergent economic effects on many developing countries that are neither the complainant nor respondent but which face an economic interest in the dispute as a third party.[3] If a large economy like the EC complies with the WTO legal ruling by reducing its domestic support for sugar, economic theory predicts a resulting increase in the world price of sugar, allowing for enhanced exports for developing countries that are competitive exporters in the global marketplace. On the other hand, the same withdrawal of the European supply of sugar from global markets and increase in world price is likely to *reduce* imports and welfare of some net sugar importing countries as the losses to adversely affected consumers (eg, food processors) are not sufficiently offset by gains to any domestic producers. Finally, part of the EC's WTO-inconsistent policy in this dispute involved an additional scheme of preferential import market access to sugar producers in African, Caribbean, and Pacific (ACP) countries. Such WTO members have a third-party interest because they are likely to face a reduction in exports via the loss of discriminatory access to the EC market.

The first task of this chapter is thus to characterize and categorize the variety of economic interests facing developing countries in different types of trade disputes.

---

2. We do not address the issue of WTO members formally intervening in a dispute if they do not have a trading interest in the product under dispute.

3. *EC–Sugar Regime* combine the disputes brought by Australia (WT/DS265), Brazil (WT/DS266), and Thailand (WT/DS283). For a discussion of the economics in the dispute, see BM Hoekman and R Howse, 'EC Sugar' (2008) 7 WT Rev 149.

We turn to the predictions of basic economic theory under the assumption of large countries disputing over the use of commercial policies that, because of the WTO dispute settlement process, are in the process of being restored to MFN treatment. We use this framework to identify third-party concerns and expected changes in market access resulting from respondent compliance to challenges to various types of WTO-inconsistent policies.[4] As suggested by reference to even just one dispute, ie, *EC–Sugar Regime*, in some instances a developing country's overall third-party interest derives from expected net gains from the dispute's resolution, and in others its interest derives from expected net losses. We examine these issues and the *within*-country distributional consequences as well.

After we characterize the many economic reasons why WTO members may have a third-party interest in a trade dispute, we introduce a data-driven analysis and examine one class of trade disputes and developing countries with a particular third-party perspective. This analysis builds upon the more formal framework focusing specifically on trade disputes alleging that the respondent has implemented too little market access (ie, failed to sufficiently liberalize imports) relative to its GATT/WTO commitments.[5] We identify in the data a set of interested developing third countries that all export the disputed product to the respondent, like the complainant in the dispute. We then analyze these countries' economic performance to examine whether there is evidence of respondent countries abiding by MFN in this one particular class of trade disputes.

Why begin an analysis of developing countries as third parties via such an empirical exercise? First, many of the disputes involving excessive import protection relate to sectors in which developing countries have a substantial exporting interest (eg, agriculture, textiles), even when a developing country is not a complainant or respondent in the dispute. Furthermore, there are theoretical arguments that the dispute settlement process is biased both toward and against the interests of developing countries. The claims that the GATT/WTO reliance on retaliation threats to balance concessions, the concerns for extra-WTO retaliation via withdrawn preferential access or bilateral assistance, and the need for a country to have substantial resources and legal capacity to operate effectively within the dispute settlement process suggest that the process is biased against developing country interests.[6] On the other hand, there are many areas of the

---

4. For an economic analysis of the role of the WTO and its principles for affecting market access, see K Bagwell and RW Staiger, *The Economics of the World Trading System* (2002).

5. See CP Bown, 'Trade Policy under the GATT/WTO: Empirical Evidence of the Equal Treatment Rule' (2004) 37 Can J Econ 678.

6. In addition to the research described in fn 1, see also CP Bown, 'Developing Countries as Plaintiffs and Defendants in GATT/WTO Trade Disputes' (2004) 27 W Econ 59; CP Bown, 'On the Economic Success of GATT/WTO Dispute Settlement' (2004) 86 Rev Econ Stats 811; CP Bown, 'Trade Remedies and World Trade Organization

DSU that explicitly require disputing parties to give special consideration to the interests of developing countries.[7] Article 21:2 states that '(p)articular attention should be paid to matters affecting the interests of developing country Members with respect to measures which have been subject to dispute settlement". Given theoretical arguments of bias both against and in favor of developing countries, ultimately the question of any bias is an empirical one.[8]

While this chapter only begins to analyze developing country third-party interests in WTO dispute settlement, there are a number of arguments to suggest that there are policy implications requiring a focus of substantial additional research. First, economists have argued that there are fundamental, efficiency-enhancing properties to trade agreements having an MFN rule.[9] Thus, from an institutional perspective, it is important to begin to empirically evaluate whether countries are abiding by MFN under the WTO in dispute settlement in practice, or whether it is being ignored here just like in many other areas of the agreement.

Second, from a policy perspective, an emerging area of research has called into question the ability of developing countries to sufficiently engage in the WTO's resource-intensive dispute settlement system—either as complainants

---

Dispute Settlement: Why Are So Few Challenged?' (2005) 34 J Leg Stu 515; CP Bown and BM Hoekman, 'WTO Dispute Settlement and the Missing Developing Country Cases: Engaging the Private Sector' (2005) 8 JIEL 861; CP Bown and BM Hoekman, 'Developing Countries and Enforcement of Trade Agreements: Why Dispute Settlement Is Not Enough' (2008) 42 JWT 177; H Horn, PC Mavroidis and H Nordström, 'Is the Use of the WTO Dispute Settlement System Biased?' in PC Mavroidis and A Sykes (eds), *The WTO and International Trade Law/Dispute Settlement* (2005); G Shaffer and H Nordström, 'Access to Justice in the World Trade Organization: The Case for a Small Claims Procedure?' (forthcoming); WT Rev, ML Busch and E Reinhardt 'Developing Countries and GATT/WTO Dispute Settlement', (2003) 37 JWT 719; and G Shaffer, 'The Challenges of WTO Law: Strategies for Developing Country Adaptation', (2006) 5 WT Rev 177. The underlying data on GATT trade disputes that is the focus of a number of these earlier chapters derives, in part, from the substantial data collection efforts of RE Hudec, *Enforcing International Trade Law: The Evolution of the Modern GATT Legal System* (1991).

7. See DSU Articles 3:12; 4:10; 8:10; 12:10 and 11; 21:7 and 8; 24; and 27:2 in addition to Article 21:2. For a discussion on the various rules on special and differential treatment afforded to developing countries under the DSU, see ME Footer, 'Developing Country Practice in the Matter of WTO Dispute Settlement' (2001) 35 JWT 55.

8. We do not intend to compare and contrast the performance of developing countries versus industrialized countries. Our focus is whether developing countries are receiving more or less trade than they should expect to receive, given the relevant rules (eg, MFN) of the GATT/WTO system. For example, we address the following empirical question for a certain class of trade disputes: Given that the complainant in the average successful bilateral dispute increases disputed sector exports to the respondent by 36 percent, how large is the average increase in developing third-country exports in the disputed sector to the respondent? Is this consistent with expectations of a functioning MFN rule?

9. See K Bagwell and RW Staiger, *The Economics of the World Trading System* (2002).

or respondents. Our analysis raises an additional potential concern. Whenever a complainant/respondent trade dispute introduces substantial economic 'shocks' into third countries—eg, induced by changes in world prices caused by a change in market access resulting from the resolution of the dispute—the existence of such international externalities suggests a role for enhancing institutional transparency beyond what is solely in the interest of the two disputing (complainant/respondent) parties. Regardless of whether the dispute's resolution imposes on the third country a positive (increased exports or imports) or negative (decreased exports or imports) externality, there may be an efficiency rationale for enhancing the transparency of dispute resolution to allow those affected in third countries as much time as possible to both economically and politically adjust to the new conditions and implications for market access. We return to a discussion of this issue in the conclusion.

The rest of this chapter proceeds as follows. Section B documents the various economic reasons why a country may have an economic third-party interest in a formal GATT/WTO dispute. In Section C we take a sample of data of disputes involving allegations of excessive import protection, and we provide an economic assessment of the developing, third-country liberalization gains associated with bilateral, complainant liberalization gains from the respondent. Section D then concludes.

B. ECONOMIC REASONS FOR THIRD-PARTY INTEREST

In this section we review the primary economic reasons why a country has a third-party interest in a GATT/WTO trade dispute. The basic third-party interests are easiest to understand if we first identify the types of underlying bilateral (complainant/respondent) trade disputes that we have in mind.[10] To focus on third-party economic interests, we characterize a trade dispute as falling into one of three basic categories: (1) allegations of excessive import protection of a product by the respondent through tariff or nontariff measures; (2) allegations of excessive export promotion of a product by the respondent, typically due to domestic support policies such as subsidies; and (3) allegations of excessive export restrictions by the respondent. Within each class of disputes, there is the potential for multiple third-party interests and perspectives for a given

---

10. We omit from the analysis more general disputes that focus on a country's overall treatment of exports or imports and where the allegation is not product- or industry-specific. For example, we do not consider disputes such as *US—The Cuban Liberty and Democratic Solidarity Act* (DS38); *US—Tax Treatment for "Foreign Sales Corporations"* (DS108); and *US—Sections 301-310 of the Trade Act of 1974* (DS152). We also do not consider cases where a third country may be interested in a dispute for legal or systemic reasons, eg, because it has a policy in place similar to the respondent policy under investigation.

developing country. We detail each category of dispute and each third-party perspective explicitly below and with reference to Figures 1 through 3. In these figures 'R' represents the respondent, 'C' represents the complainant, 'T' represents the interested third country, and, where necessary, 'ROW' represents the rest of the world, for a typical dispute.

We focus on the perspective of the third country, its economic interests within a particular category of disputes, and how this relates to the economic success of the dispute settlement process. Before we move on to our formal analysis, it is important to define what we mean by the economic interests of a given country or the economic success of the dispute settlement process. With respect to a country's economic interests, we appeal to the results of standard economic models of international trade and compare policies (and the economic outcomes of the dispute settlement process) based on how they affect a country's overall national welfare.[11] Within our discussion of the economic interests of a country, we will, however, explicitly consider the income redistribution that accompanies a particular trade policy change. This also allows us to understand the motivations of a country that is influenced not only by the concern for maximizing national welfare but which is also confronted with domestic sectors or interest groups with a particularly strong political presence.

For the purpose of this chapter, we define an 'economically successful' outcome to a trade dispute as the respondent removing any policies that affect trade in a way that is inconsistent with its GATT/WTO obligations. We thus focus here on the ability of the process to eliminate policies that either explicitly violate GATT/WTO rules or nullify and impair the benefits that trading partners expect to receive through concessions negotiated with the respondent in an earlier negotiating round. The primary implication of our narrow definition of an economically successful outcome is that we treat the negotiated market-access concessions as a (nonrenegotiable) standard. This is not an innocuous implication, as one could well argue that a dispute that concludes with countries renegotiating and balancing concessions (eg, through complainant retaliation) may be 'legally successful' because it led to the resolution of a dispute in accordance with GATT/WTO rules and the respondent 'compensating' the complainant, even though the market-access standard was not met. We do not treat such an outcome as an economic success because it did not lead to the respondent satisfying its market-access obligations and liberalizing trade.[12]

---

11. Formally, our basic perspective is to treat the third country as a small price-taking country, trading in perfectly competitive markets. The respondent and complainant countries are assumed 'large' so that their market-access policy changes affect world prices and impose externalities on our third countries of interest.

12. While our approach is primarily motivated for reasons of data availability, it may also be motivated from the perspective of economic efficiency. An outcome that results in the respondent failing to liberalize and the complainant retaliating introduces inefficiencies

Furthermore, with regard to our empirical assessment in Section C, it is important to note that we do not have comprehensive data on trade policy adjustments. Therefore, our empirical approach is to *infer* whether a particular respondent policy has been changed in accordance with its GATT/WTO obligations. To do this, we use trade data to assess whether trade flows in the disputed sector are being affected in a way that is consistent with the policy's change. Furthermore, given that we also do not have data on the size of the negotiated concession, we also not comment on whether a country is fully compliant with its obligations. Rather, as an initial investigation into this question, we limit ourselves to a discussion of whether the respondent's trade in the disputed sector is moving (increasing or decreasing) in the direction that we expect, given the nature of the allegation, the country's obligations, and the rules of the GATT/WTO system. We also compare the sizes of these trade flows for complainant countries versus interested third countries.[13]

i. Disputes Alleging Respondent Engaged in Excessive Import Protection

First consider Figure 1, which illustrates a typical dispute alleging that the respondent has provided excessive protection and limited market access to imports, relative to its GATT/WTO commitments. In such a dispute, an interested third country may also be an exporter of the disputed product to the respondent (case a), or it may be an importer of the disputed product like the respondent (case b).

Third-country exporters of the disputed product Look at Figure 1a, where the third country also exports the product that the respondent has been accused of restricting. Suppose further that the respondent country's violation leading to the trade dispute was a discriminatory policy which favored one set of third-country exporters at the expense of the complainant country and another potential set of third-country exporters. An example would be the *EC–Banana Regime* dispute, where the claim was that exporters from the African, Caribbean, and Pacific (ACP) countries received preferential access to the EC market at the expense of complainant countries such as Ecuador, Guatemala, Honduras, Mexico, and the United States.[14] The EC was also accused of giving Costa Rica,

---

into the system, relative to the liberal trade outcome without retaliation. In order to assess the economic success of a dispute that ended with a rebalancing of concessions, we would also require information on how the third countries would be affected (if at all) by the complainant's implementation of retaliation.

13. A more rigorous analysis would also control for other factors likely to affect product-level trade flows such as other demand determinants, cost shocks, etc. See Bown (n 5 above).

14. *EC–Banana Regime* refers to disputes DS27; Panama later joined the dispute as a complainant (DS105) after its 1997 accession to the WTO. ACP countries that formally intervened as third parties in this dispute included Belize, Cameroon, Côte d'Ivoire,

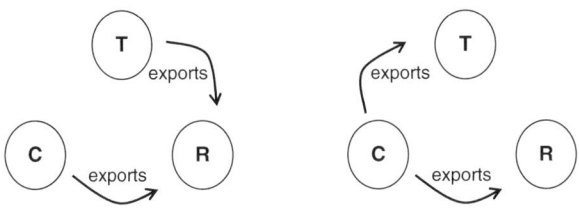

a. Third-country exporter   b. Third-country importer

FIGURE 1. THIRD-COUNTRY INTERESTS IN TRADE DISPUTES INVOLVING AN ALLEGATION OF EXCESSIVE IMPORT PROTECTION BY THE RESPONDENT

Colombia, Venezuela, and Nicaragua preferential access to its import market through the 1994 Framework Agreement that settled an earlier GATT dispute involving bananas in which these countries were complainants. Nevertheless, in *EC–Banana Regime* there were likely other interested third countries who were not given preferential access to the EC market and thus find themselves facing circumstance similar to the complainants in the case. In an analysis of the 6-digit data (HS category 080300) of other countries that export bananas to the EC, Brazil fits the profile of such a third-country banana exporter.[15]

Therefore, in Figure 1a, there are potentially two distinct sets of third-country exporting interests—exporting countries that benefited from any initial discrimination by the respondent and exporting countries that were harmed (like the complainants) by the initial restrictive trade policy, whether it was discriminatory or applied on an MFN basis. We expect an EC policy change that complies with the GATT/WTO MFN principle and the dispute settlement panel's ruling in this dispute to have opposing economic impacts on the two different sets of third-country exporters. Banana exports to the EC from the ACP third countries should fall if those producers were not as competitive as the complainant and other third-country banana exporters. On the other hand, banana exports to the EC from other (non-ACP, non-Framework Agreement) third-country exporters, such as Brazil, should rise. Therefore, predicting whether a third country's exports should rise or fall with a dispute's bilaterally successful outcome and the respondent implementing its market-access commitments in a means consistent with the MFN rule requires prior knowledge of whether a given interested third country was a beneficiary or a victim of the respondent's initial discriminatory trade policy.

Dominica, the Dominican Republic, Ghana, Grenada, Jamaica, Saint Lucia, Saint Vincent and the Grenadines, Senegal, and Suriname.

15. While Brazil may not be a substantial supplier of bananas, the value of its banana exports to the EC in 1999 was higher than that of Ghana, an ACP country that formally intervened as an interested third party in the dispute.

Third-country importers of the disputed product Next consider Figure 1b, where the third country is now an import market that is also served by the complainant, as opposed to a rival exporter. In this case, the excessive protection by the respondent may be *deflecting* exports from the complainant toward the third country's market.[16] On economic welfare grounds, such a policy improves the welfare of the third country's consumers through access to lower prices and more products. However, the trade deflection-induced increase in third-country imports resulting from the respondent's protection may be detrimental to a particularly sensitive and politically powerful domestic industry that competes with the diverted products. Nevertheless, the policy is likely to make the third country's national welfare higher, even if the third country is also a producer of the product, as the gains to consumers in this case typically outweigh the economic losses to import-competing producers.

This is one potential concern of the *US–Steel Safeguards* dispute brought to the DSU after United States imposition of temporary import restrictions on steel in March 2002.[17] In these disputes, a steel-importing third country may be concerned that the steel exports deflected from the US market due to the safeguard measure will end up in its import market, thus hurting the third country's domestic steel producers.[18] However, if a third country were concerned only with its economic interests as measured through overall national welfare, such an importing country would enjoy net benefits from the deflected, cheaper steel. We would then expect it to be dissatisfied with any resolution to the bilateral dispute which restored complainant exports to the respondent and thus reduced the flows of deflected steel that the third country had previously enjoyed. Thus, whether a third-country net importer of steel prefers an outcome where the respondent liberalizes as opposed to not liberalizing is determined by the political significance of the third country's domestic, import-competing (steel) industry

---

16. See CP Bown and MA Crowley, 'Trade Deflection and Trade Depression' (2007) 72 J Int'l Econ 176.

17. *US–Definitive Safeguard Measures on Imports of Certain Steel Products* cases (DS248, DS249, DS251, DS252, DS253, DS254, DS258, DS259, hereafter *US–Steel Safeguards*). Complainants were the European Communities, Japan, Korea, China, Switzerland, Norway, New Zealand, and Brazil, respectively.

18. One response to the US steel safeguards measure imposed in March 2002 was a "policy surge" as other WTO Members imposed new safeguard measures of their own on imports of steel. Between March 2002 and October 2003 Chile, China, Czech Republic, the European Communities, Hungary, Poland, and Venezuela applied at least provisional safeguard measures on imports of steel, while Bulgaria and Canada initiated safeguard investigations that did not result in the imposition of definitive measures on steel. Presumably these actions were designed to do more than simply retaliate against the United States, but also to halt the surge in steel imports deflected from the US market through a resort to similar acts of temporary protection.

relative to the weight that the country places on the larger consumer gains that would be enjoyed through access to imports of cheaper steel.

ii. Disputes Alleging Respondent Engaged in Excessive Export Promotion

Figure 2 details a second set of disputes, where the allegation is that the respondent's policy has excessively promoted exports, usually through a subsidy that is inconsistent with its GATT/WTO obligations. For simplicity, we have illustrated the complainant as a rival exporting country that also exports the same products to the rest of the world (ROW).[19]

Third-country exporters of the disputed product Consider Figure 2, where the third country is also a rival exporter of the same product as the respondent. Here the third country aligns itself with the interests of the complainant—it would also like to see the subsidy to the respondent's exporters dismantled, thus decreasing the artificial competitive advantage of the respondent's exporters relative to its own. An example of this would be a third-country exporter in the cases brought by the Brazil against alleged US subsidies of cotton, ie, *US–Upland Cotton* (DS267). Benin, a developing country with substantial exporting interests in the cotton products that were allegedly subsidized by the US government, formally intervened in this case as an interested third party, presumably to represent the concerns of its cotton exporters that compete with US products on the world market.

Third-country importers of the disputed product Next consider Figure 2b, where the third country is now a consumer/importer of the exports that are being subsidized by the respondent, rather than a rival exporter. Much like the results in Figure 1a, a standard economic analysis reveals that, when measured in terms of overall national welfare, the third country actually benefits from the excessive trade that results from the respondent's policy. The third country's consumers have greater access to cheap imports that have been subsidized by the respondent, and therefore the third country prefers that the respondent *not* be forced to remove its export promoting policy.[20]

An example of such a dispute is *EC–Measures Affecting the Exportation of Processed Cheese* (DS104), where the United States accused the EC of offering

---

19. Alternatively, the complainant could be an importing country with a politically powerful domestic industry competing with the respondent's subsidized exporters. The implications of our analysis on the typical third country would be unchanged. We represent the complainant as a rival exporter because a dispute is its only legal recourse, whereas an importing country could also levy a countervailing duty against the respondent's exporters as an alternative means of addressing the subsidy.

20. For an economic interpretation of the agricultural subsidies restrictions under the GATT/WTO and the prisoner's dilemma problem, see K Bagwell and RW Staiger, 'Strategic Trade, Competitive Industries and Agricultural Trade Disputes' (2001) 13 Econ & Pol 113.

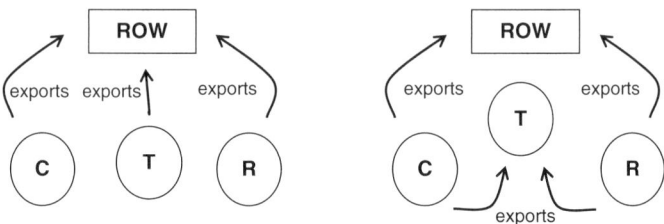

a. Third-country exporter   b. Third-country importer

FIGURE 2. THIRD-COUNTRY INTERESTS IN TRADE DISPUTES INVOLVING AN ALLEGATION OF EXCESSIVE EXPORT PROMOTION BY THE RESPONDENT

export subsidies to producers of processed cheeses in violation of provisions of the Agreement on Agriculture and the Agreement on Subsidies and Countervailing Measures. Japan, which is primarily a consumer/importer of processed cheeses, formally intervened in the case as an interested third party, noting that EC exports accounted for roughly 77 percent of the Japanese total processed cheese import market.[21] While there have been relatively few trade disputes concerning excessive export promotion when compared to the number of disputes alleging excessive import protection, there are likely to be many more of these cases in the future if agriculture and fisheries subsidies become subject to greater WTO discipline. An important area for future research is the economic impact of the reduction of export promotion policies on agricultural consuming/importing countries, including many such developing countries in Africa.

iii. Disputes Alleging Respondent Engaged in Excessive Export Restrictions

Next is Figure 3, which illustrates a final category of trade disputes in which countries interfere with GATT/WTO rules and their obligations by excessively restricting exports. The complainant country in this scenario is an importing country, and the respondent is an exporter.

Third-country exporters of the disputed product In Figure 3a, the third country is an exporter of the disputed product, similar to the respondent in the case. While such disputes are fairly infrequent, two examples include *Pakistan–Export Measures Affecting Hides and Skins* (DS107) and *India–Measures Affecting Export of Certain Commodities* (DS120). In both cases, the EC accused the respondent of inducing a shortage by restricting exports of certain raw hides and skins. A third country that also produced and exported the kinds of hides and skins that had been restricted by these two countries would benefit from any respondent

---

21. On the other hand, Australia and Canada, two other countries with substantial exporting interests in processed cheeses and thus aligned with the US complainant's export interests, also formally intervened in this particular dispute as interested third parties. They would fit the third-country profile of Figure 2a.

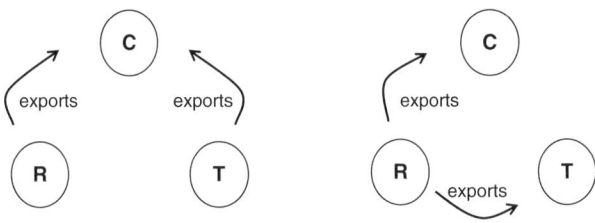

FIGURE 3. THIRD-COUNTRY INTERESTS IN TRADE DISPUTES INVOLVING AN ALLEGATION OF EXCESSIVE EXPORT RESTRICTIONS BY THE RESPONDENT

policies that restricted exports, as this restriction increases the scarcity value of the third-country exporter's product as well. While no third countries formally intervened in these particular disputes, those that also had substantial exports of raw hides and skins of bovine and equine animals (HS category 4101) to the EC in 1997 included developing countries such as South Africa, Brazil, and Venezuela.

Third-country importers of the disputed product Finally, consider Figure 3b, where the third country is now an importer of the product that the respondent is restricting. Take again as our example the Pakistan or India disputes discussed in the last section. A third country that was an importer of raw hides and skins as opposed to an exporter would find itself aligned with the EC's interests. An outcome to the dispute that led to the end of respondent export restrictions would allow for a more plentiful and cheaper supply of raw hides and skins, thus benefiting the third country's consumers of the product as well as those consumers in the EC.

C. EMPIRICAL ANALYSIS: IMPORT LIBERALIZATION AND THE IMPACT ON DEVELOPING THIRD-COUNTRY EXPORTERS

As we have suggested in Section B, the interests of the third country in trade disputes—ie, whether it faces a positive or negative economic shock overall, as well as distributional implications *within* the third country—depend both on the nature of the disputed policy and the importing or exporting role of the third country. In this section of the chapter, we focus on a set of disputes with the structure of Figure 1a, ie, where the third country exports the same product as the complainant in a dispute over allegations of excessive import protection.

A relatively neglected area of research is an empirical assessment of whether the DSU process is having an economic impact on third countries—and in particular, developing countries—that coincides with the basic predictions of the last section. Ultimately this research must begin to examine the distributional consequences of DSU-induced shocks within these third countries. Nevertheless, as a first pass at the data, we examine the economic resolution of such disputes by focusing on the impact of the dispute's negotiated outcome via the trade flows from developing third-country exporters.

i. Formal Third Party Interventions vs. Implicitly Interested Third Parties

For the purpose of our empirical exercise, it is important to clarify exactly what we mean by third parties in these disputes. First, the indirect impact on a developing country's trade can be made 'explicit' when that country formally notifies the GATT/WTO of its desire to intervene as an interested third party in a formal dispute.[22] However, in order to get a true gauge of the indirect impact of dispute settlement negotiations on third countries, it is also important to analyze the impact on 'implicitly' affected countries that are concerned due to a trading interest in the products at issue in the disputed sector. The identity of implicitly affected countries that do not formally intervene can thus only be obtained by analyzing the respondent and complainant country's trade in the case's disputed sector. In this section we provide a brief discussion of some data on the frequency with which developing countries are explicitly and implicitly interested as third parties in formal trade disputes.

Table 1 illustrates examples of trade disputes over the 1990–1998 period in which large numbers of developing countries have signaled their *explicit* interest by formally intervening in a trade dispute. Not surprisingly, the *EC–Banana Regime* disputes involved many explicitly interested developing third countries, in addition to the substantial number of developing country complainants. There are many other examples in Table 1 of disputes in which numerous developing countries intervened as third parties, including the *US–Shrimp* (DS58, DS61) dispute, which also had multiple (India, Malaysia, Pakistan, Thailand, and the Philippines) developing country complainants.

Nevertheless, Table 2 presents data on a sample of formal disputes with large numbers of *implicitly* interested developing third countries, ie, ones that also export the disputed product to the respondent country. Such countries are thus likely to have their own trade affected by the dispute's resolution if the respondent applies the equal treatment (MFN) rule when it liberalizes imports as a result of dispute settlement negotiations. A comparison of Tables 1 and 2 yields results that are not surprising: large numbers of explicitly and implicitly interested developing third countries tend to be associated with disputes where the respondent has a large import market (eg, United States, EC) and the disputed

---

22. For example, a WTO Member country is permitted to intervene formally as a third party under Article 10 of the DSU when it has a 'substantial interest' in the dispute's proceedings. For the 1995–1998 period, developing countries comprised more than one-third of all formal third-party interventions to the DSU. Data compiled by the author and obtained from trade dispute documents obtained from the WTO's Web site, www.wto.org.

TABLE 1. GATT/WTO TRADE DISPUTES WITH LARGE NUMBERS OF DEVELOPING COUNTRIES INTERVENING AS INTERESTED THIRD PARTIES, 1990–1998

Dispute Name (WTO Number or GATT Year)	Number of Formally Intervening, Developing Third Countries
EC–Banana Regime (DS27)	24
EC–Banana Regime (GATT 1991)	17
US–Tuna I (GATT 1990)	13
US–Shrimp (DS58, DS61)	8
US–Section 301-310 of 1974 Trade Act (DS152)	8
Canada–Patent Protection of Pharmaceuticals (DS114)	7
Turkey–Textiles (DS29)	6
US–Textiles (DS151)	6
US–Tuna II (GATT 1992)	5
EC–Coffee (DS154)	4
Argentina–Footwear Safeguards (DS121)	4

Source: Estimates compiled by the author from dispute settlement documents available from the WTO's Web site, http://www.wto.org/.

product is a traditional developing country export (eg, agriculture, textiles, and other primary commodities).

In the next section we present a more extensive analysis of the economic data associated with developing third-country exporters in these GATT/WTO disputes in order to investigate their economic performance.

ii. Data Analysis—the Underlying 'Bilateral' Trade Dispute

For our data-driven analysis, we consider a set of 88 bilateral (complainant/respondent) GATT/WTO trade disputes initiated and completed between 1990–1998 in which the respondent was legitimately accused of offering too little import market access to the complainant.[23] The typical dispute thus fits the profile of Figure 1a. Our first step is to aggregate multiple complainant disputes or simultaneous disputes involving a common respondent and disputed product and different complainants. As we are interested in the perspective of third-country exporters

---

23. Information on trade disputes is derived from WTO, Analytical Index: Guide to GATT Law and Practice, Vols. 1 and 2 (1995); and WTO, Panel Reports under the MTN Agreements and Arrangements (Tokyo Round Codes) of 1979, (1997) on file with the author. See also the WTO's on-line source Web site, www.wto.org. A case is subsequently 'legitimate' for the purpose of our empirical exercise if it was reported that the respondent made a policy change relating to the dispute or the panel requested the respondent to bring its policies into conformity with GATT/WTO rules.

TABLE 2. EXAMPLES OF GATT/WTO TRADE DISPUTES WITH LARGE NUMBERS OF IMPLICITLY* INTERESTED DEVELOPING THIRD COUNTRIES** IN A SAMPLE OF CASES INITIATED AND COMPLETED BETWEEN 1990–1998

Dispute Name (WTO number or GATT year)	Number of Implicitly Interested, Developing Third Countries
EC–Oilseeds (GATT 1993)	80
US–Cotton and Man-Made Underwear (DS24)	54
EC–Unbleached Cotton Fabrics (DS140)	50
EC–Wood of Conifers (DS137)	42
US–Woven Wool Shirts and Blouses (DS33)	43
US–Women's and Girls' Wool Coats (DS32)	43
Japan–Leather (DS147)	34
US–Alcoholic and Malt Beverages (GATT 1991)	31
US–Tobacco (GATT 1993)	28
US–Textiles and Apparel Products (DS85)	26
EC–Grains (DS13)	25
EC–Banana Regime (GATT 1992)	24
US–Shrimp (DS58, DS61)	24

Notes: * Implicitly interested third country is revealed by the UNCTAD/TRAINS data as also sending the disputed HS 6-digit exports to the respondent country during the period of the dispute. **Includes both GATT contracting parties, WTO members and noncontracting parties and nonmembers.

to the respondent in the disputed sector, this aggregation technique ensures that we do not have redundant third-country observations in the data. This approach leaves us with a set of 52 underlying cases to which we refer as 'bilateral' disputes, where the economic performance of the representative complainant in our data is based on the aggregate performance of the underlying complainants in any common disputes.[24]

We focus on the developing third country's exports of the disputed product to the respondent. In particular, we ask whether the economic success of bilateral (complainant/respondent) liberalization at the conclusion of dispute settlement negotiations is associated with respondent liberalization of disputed sector imports from developing third-country exporters. Specifically, we consider the growth in third-country exports to the respondent between the year of the dispute's initiation and one year after the dispute's resolution. We define the year of

---

24. For example, we aggregate the complainants of the *US–Shrimp* disputes (DS58 and DS61), and bilateral performance of the complainant would be the overall growth in US imports of shrimp from India, Malaysia, Thailand, Pakistan, and the Philippines.

the dispute's resolution to be the last year that there was correspondence between either the GATT/WTO and the complainant or respondent regarding the case.

The importance of the discriminatory nature of the initial allegation Another important question in the 52 bilateral disputes is the nature of the initial allegation made against the respondent in the underlying case. In our sample of disputes, 14 were claims of illicit use of antidumping or countervailing measures (AD/CVM) which discriminate only against the country facing the measure, ie, the complainant in the dispute. Another 17 cases (or in 31 of the disputes in total) alleged discrimination through some violation of Article I, ie, where it was possible for the discrimination to negatively affect additional (third) countries beyond the complainant(s) in the dispute.

These distinctions are important, given that the GATT/WTO dispute resolution process is subject to the MFN principle. In disputes where the respondent has been accused of discrimination across trading partners, we not only expect to observe less frequent and smaller liberalization extended to third countries, but third countries may face a reduction in exports as their implicit preferential access is removed.

Trade liberalization and economic success in the bilateral disputes In much of the data analysis that follows, we also limit ourselves to a further subset of bilateral disputes that we have described as being 'economically successful', from the bilateral (complainant/respondent) perspective, where our measure of bilateral success is an increase in the complainant country's exports of the disputed product to the respondent. One motive for narrowing the focus to this subset of disputes is that a respondent may be more likely to follow the MFN rule and extend liberalization to third-country exporters given that it liberalizes with respect to the complainant.

How many of these 52 disputes are bilaterally successful in terms of our economic definition? In the sample of 52 disputes, 26 result in the complainant increasing its exports to the respondent, while in 26 cases complainant exports fail to increase. Of the 26 disputes that the trade data determine to have been bilaterally successful, 5 involved claims of illicit AD/CVM and 13 involved some claim of discrimination through an Article I violation. We would thus expect to find less liberalization extended to third-country exporters in these cases, relative to the disputes where there was no initial allegation of discrimination. We investigate this question below. Finally, of the 26 disputes that the trade data determine to have been bilaterally unsuccessful, 9 involved claims of illicit AD/CVM while 18 involved some claim of discrimination through an Article I violation.

iii. Identifying the Developing Third-Country Exporters in the Trade Dispute

It is important to reiterate that, in analyzing the economic performance of developing third-country exporters, we do not restrict ourselves to consideration of only those developing third countries that formally intervene in the dispute settlement process. Rather, we analyze the trade impact on all developing third countries that the data reveal as having a trading interest in the disputed sector of the respondent—both the countries that explicitly intervene and the countries that are only implicitly revealed through an analysis of the trade data.[25] In fact, one empirical question that we are interested in is whether developing third-country exporters that explicitly reveal themselves by formally intervening in the dispute settlement proceedings are more successful, in terms of the trade liberalization gains, than are third countries that are only implicitly revealed by the data.

How many implicitly interested third countries are there in one of these disputes? In 7 of the 52 bilateral disputes, there are no developing third-country exporters of the disputed product to the respondent country. In the 45 bilateral disputes with at least one developing third-country exporter, the average number of implicitly interested developing third countries at the time of the dispute is 19.07, the median is 14, and the high is 80.

iv. The Economic Performance of Developing Third-Country Exporters

How many developing third countries also increase exports? How do developing third-country exporters perform in bilaterally successful GATT/WTO trade disputes? Do their exports of the disputed product to the respondent increase when exports from the complainant increase? Consider the data presented in the top half of Table 3, where from our subsample of 26 bilaterally successful cases, we are able to identify 449 implicitly interested developing third countries that also export the disputed product to the respondent. Our first result is that, of these 449 third-country exporters, 293 countries (or 65 percent) also saw their exports to the respondent increase.

Recall from our discussion of Figure 1a, however, that if the respondent's initial violation was discriminatory in nature, then we should not necessarily expect exports from all third countries to increase when exports from the complainant increase, given that some third countries actually benefited (through an 'artificial' increase in their exports) from the initial act of discrimination. We thus expect a larger percentage of implicitly interested third countries' exports to rise in the disputes where the initial violation by the respondent was nondiscriminatory in nature.

It is difficult to judge the severity of the initial discrimination merely by investigating the allegation presented in the case. Nevertheless, we attempt to address the issue here by using two different criterion to characterize the initial violations

---

25. Note that we use the HS 6-digit import data available from UNCTAD/TRAINS, the most disaggregated data available for the countries and years needed for the empirical analysis. This data is often more aggregated than the products at issue in the dispute, which may be defined at even the 10-digit level—thus we do introduce some amount of measurement error by having to resort to UNCTAD data, which are more aggregated but also more comprehensive in terms of country coverage.

TABLE 3. DEVELOPING COUNTRY PERFORMANCE AS IMPLICITLY INTERESTED THIRD PARTIES IN A SAMPLE OF GATT/WTO TRADE DISPUTES INITIATED AND COMPLETED BETWEEN 1990–1998*

	Overall	Observations Resulting in Increased Third-country Exports	Observations Not Resulting in Increased Third-country Exports
Total observations derived from bilaterally successful** complainant/respondent negotiations	449	293	156
Observations where initial complainant allegation did not include AD/CVM by the respondent	417	278	139
Observations where initial complainant allegation did not include violation of Article I	292	198	94
Observations where third country has explicitly intervened in the dispute	9	6	3
Total observations derived from bilaterally unsuccessful** complainant/respondent negotiations	225	94	131
Observations where initial complainant allegation did not include AD/CVM by the respondent	146	73	73
Observations where initial complainant allegation did not include violation of Article I	68	34	34
Observations where third country has explicitly intervened in the dispute	17	8	9

Notes: Estimates compiled by the author.
* Only includes third countries that are GATT contracting parties or WTO Members at the time of the dispute. ** Successful indicates a case that led to bilateral trade liberalization gains in the 6-digit HS product under dispute extended from the respondent to the complainant.

and whether they were discriminatory versus nondiscriminatory. First, we use only those observations where allegations did *not* involve the respondent discriminating by imposing an AD/CVM against the complainant. In the cases that fall into this (non-AD/CVM violation) *nondiscrimination* category, 278 out of 417 (67 percent) developing third-country observations showed an increase in exports. While not shown in the table, this implies that, of the remaining 32 developing third-country observations involving an initial respondent discriminating through violation of the rules on AD/CVM, only 15 (47 percent) developing third countries saw their exports increase with the complainant. This is evidence that liberalization is extended to more countries in disputes where the initial violation is nondiscriminatory as opposed to discriminatory. Furthermore, this is consistent with respondents following the principle of equity embodied in the MFN rule.

However, respondent country violations could involve discrimination through means other than the imposition of AD/CVM. Thus, as a second method of characterization, we include a broader set of discriminatory violations, including both AD/CVM violations and other complainant allegations that the respondent has violated Article I.[26] In the third row of Table 3 we consider the performance of developing third countries in the alternative (non-Article I violation) nondiscrimination category. Here we find that 198 of the 292 (68 percent) implicitly interested developing third-country exporters saw their exports increase.[27] This too is higher than the ratio of the comparison category of third-country observations derived from discriminatory, Article I violations. Only 95 out 157 (61 percent) implicitly interested developing third-country exporters saw their exports increase in the discriminatory cases. This provides additional, albeit slightly weaker evidence that respondents are following the MFN rule toward exports from developing third countries.

Finally, in the fourth row of data on the top half of Table 3, we present information on the export performance of developing third countries that intervene formally by identifying themselves to the GATT/WTO as an explicitly interested third party. Of the nine countries that intervened formally, six of them showed an increase in exports to the respondent's disputed market. As this ratio is quite similar to the third-country success ratios presented in the other rows, it does not appear from this presentation of the data that a third country that intervenes formally is any more likely to have its exports to the respondent increase than would a third-country exporter that did not intervene formally. Consider next the

---

26. For example, if it were in our dataset, the *EC–Bananas III* dispute would fall into this second, broader category of discrimination through an Article I violation, but it would not fall into the first category since it was not an AD/CVM violation.

27. We have also broken down the results illustrated in Table 3 by GATT era and WTO era disputes, and there is little difference across institutional time periods. Thus to conserve space, we omit that comparison here.

graphic evidence of Figure 4, in which we break down the developing third-country exporters by region. Our results appear fairly consistent across regions of the world as well—the evidence is that roughly two out of three developing third-country exporters also see their exports to the respondent country increase when complainant country exports to the respondent increase.

One additional check on our results can be made by appealing to the lower half of Table 3. There we document the export performance of developing third countries in disputes that were not bilaterally successful, ie, that did not result in the respondent increasing imports from the complainant country. In the nondiscrimination subsample of observations, we again use our two categories and present results in the second and third rows of the lower half of the table. In each nondiscrimination subsample, exactly one-half of the implicitly interested developing third countries see exports increase: 73 out of 146 for the non-AD/CVM violations and 34 out of 68 for the non-Article I violations. These 50 percent ratios are much better than the success ratios of third-country exporters in the corresponding disputes involving discrimination allegations: only 21 out of 79 (27 percent) AD/CVM violation observations were successful; and 60 out of 157 (38 percent) Article I violation observations were successful. Again, as we would expect, more developing third-country exporters receive liberalization in disputes where the initial violation was not discriminatory relative to the discrimination disputes.

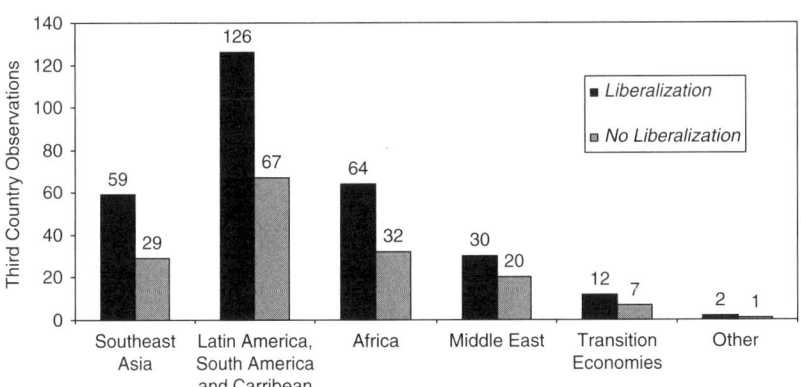

FIGURE 4. DEVELOPING THIRD-COUNTRY* PERFORMANCE IN A SAMPLE OF 26 GATT/WTO TRADE DISPUTES THAT WERE BILATERALLY SUCCESSFUL,** 1990–1998

* Only includes third countries that are GATT contracting parties or WTO members at the time of the dispute.
** Bilateral success is defined as the complainant receiving a positive increase in HS 6-digit imports in the respondent's disputed sector between the year of the beginning of the dispute and one year after the dispute's conclusion.

Source: Estimates compiled by the author.

How large are the increases in developing third-country exports? In the previous section, we documented evidence that when complainant exports of the disputed product increase, the exports of roughly two out of three implicitly affected developing third countries increase as well. The follow-up to this question is: how large are the developing third-country gains from trade liberalization? While two-thirds of developing third countries are also increasing their exports to the respondent, are those increases small relative to what the complainant in the dispute is receiving?

To address this question, we turn to the results presented in the first two columns of Table 4. We compare statistics on the size of the increase in exports experienced by developing third-country exporters, relative to the complainant exporter, in the subsample of bilaterally successful cases. If we look at the average for the entire subsample, presented in the first row, the complainant increases exports at a substantially higher average rate than do developing third-country exporters (36 percent versus 28 percent). However, once we separate the observations based on the discriminatory nature of the initial respondent violation, the numbers for developing third countries appear much better. If

TABLE 4. DEVELOPING COUNTRY PERFORMANCE AS IMPLICITLY INTERESTED THIRD COUNTRIES IN A SAMPLE OF BILATERALLY SUCCESSFUL* GATT/WTO TRADE DISPUTES, 1990–1998

	Mean (median) respondent import growth from the complainant in the disputed sector...	Mean (median) respondent import growth from the implicitly interested developing third country in the disputed sector...		
		Overall	GATT/WTO Members only	GATT/WTO non-Members only
...in all such disputes	36.3% (28.8%)	28.0% (26.8%)	27.4% (27.8%)	30.6% (25.1%)
...in *non*-Article I allegation disputes only	39.7% (38.0%)	37.6% (30.7%)	36.6% (32.2%)	41.9% (29.7%)
...in Article I allegation disputes only	32.8% (21.7%)	11.5% (17.9%)	10.3% (15.2%)	15.2% (22.9%)
...in *non*-AD/CVM violation disputes only	33.4% (21.7%)	29.3% (28.6%)	29.4% (29.3%)	29.1% (24.8%)
...in AD/CVM violation disputes only	48.2%** (37.0%)	10.0% (7.2%)	1.5% (−10.2%)	64.2%** (67.3%)

Notes: * Successful indicates a case that led to bilateral trade liberalization gains in the 6-digit HS product under dispute extended from the respondent to the complainant.
** Data based on only 5 observations.
Source: Estimates compiled by the author.

nondiscrimination is characterized as the respondent not violating the rules on AD/CVM, the average increase in exports is still larger for the complainant, but the difference across the two groups is now much smaller (33 percent versus 29 percent). This is also the case if the nondiscrimination is measured as not violating Article I (40 percent versus 38 percent).

Perhaps most striking are the cases that did allege *some* degree of discrimination on the part of the respondent in the initial dispute. We do not expect to observe a substantial increase in developing third-country exports in these disputes, given that the initial GATT/WTO violation may have either directly benefited them or at least not harmed them. Indeed, we would not be surprised to observe a *decline* in third-country exports in such cases as implicit preferences are removed. As expected, in both categories of discriminatory disputes, the average increase in exports by the developing third-country exporter is substantially smaller than the average increase for the complainant: 10 percent versus 48 percent for the AD/CVM violations and 12 percent versus 33 percent for the more general Article I violations.

Does being a GATT/WTO member matter for MFN in this setting? A final question that we consider is whether there is evidence that, by itself, membership in the GATT/WTO system matters for this context.[28] Do developing countries that are members of the GATT/WTO system experience better third-country export performance than developing country nonmembers in the outcome of dispute settlement negotiations? Is there any evidence from this sample of data that respondent countries discriminate between members and nonmembers?

We address these questions by comparing the data in the last two columns of Table 4. If respondents were systematically favoring developing country exporters that were GATT/WTO members to the detriment of nonmembers, we would expect all of the statistics in the third column of data for the GATT/WTO members to be larger than for the non-Member data in the fourth column. Clearly there is no systematic evidence that this has been the case. If anything, non-Members may be experiencing a slightly larger increase in exports to the respondent on average than are GATT/WTO members.[29]

v. Summary and Interpretation of Empirical Results

At a broad level, we present evidence from a particular class of trade disputes that MFN under the dispute settlement provisions of the GATT/WTO is working as expected. In trade disputes where the respondent's initial GATT/WTO-inconsistent policy was discriminatory, we expect fewer third countries to

---

28. For ease of exposition, we refer to countries as being 'Members' of the GATT, even though they were technically 'Contracting Parties'.

29. We do not put too much faith in the size (64 percent and 67 percent) of the non-Member export growth results for the AD/CVM violation disputes presented in the very last row in Table 4, as the statistics were derived from only 5 observations.

receive liberalization, relative to disputes where the initial allegation was that the respondent imposed a 'nondiscriminatory' policy of import protection in violation of its GATT/WTO obligations. The expected pattern has been documented in Table 3. Furthermore, in trade disputes where the respondent discriminated initially, we expect developing third-country exporters to receive less additional import market access, relative to disputes where the initial allegation was that the respondent imposed a 'nondiscriminatory' policy of import protection that violated its GATT/WTO obligations. This has been documented in Table 4.

Our results are particularly important given the concerns raised by the theoretical research of other economists.[30] Other economists have argued that in multilateral trade agreements, subsets of countries have an incentive to form coalitions and renegotiate terms of market access to their own benefit but at the expense of third countries that are not party to the negotiations. They term this the problem of 'bilateral opportunism', but they also use economic theory to show how the GATT/WTO rules of reciprocity, MFN, and the ability of third countries to file future nonviolation complaints can help to control this problem.

As this applies to our setting, one might fear that bilateral dispute settlement negotiations between the respondent and complainant could lead to bilaterally opportunistic or discriminatory behavior. The dispute settlement negotiations could facilitate a collusive outcome, where the respondent provides the complainant with increased market access at the expense of all other developing third-country exporters, whose own trade would fall. We find no evidence of bilaterally opportunistic or discriminatory behavior against developing third countries in this sample of data on the trading outcomes of dispute settlement negotiations.[31]

D. CONCLUSIONS, EXTENSIONS, AND POLICY IMPLICATIONS

In this chapter, we have reviewed the different externality explanations for why a developing country has a third-party economic interest in a formal GATT/WTO trade dispute over market access. We then focused on a particular class of trade disputes, those in which the respondent was alleged to have offered excessive import protection relative to its GATT/WTO market-access commitments. Within a sample of this class of disputes taking place over the 1990–1998 period, we investigated a dataset of developing countries that we define as being implicitly

---

30. See K Bagwell and RW Staiger 'Multilateral Trade Negotiations, Bilateral Opportunism and the Rules of GATT/WTO' (2004) 63 J Int'l Econ 1.

31. The empirical results reported here are also consistent with Bown (n 5 above), which uses a larger sample of developing and nondeveloping third-country data and controls for other factors that may affect the respondent's disputed sector import growth using formal econometric techniques.

interested as a third party through their own exports interests to the respondent country in the disputed sector. Finally, in assessing disputes in which the initial respondent violation was nondiscriminatory, we present some evidence that liberalization gains extended to the complainant have also been extended to third-country exporters, which is consistent with a functioning principle of equity embodied in the MFN rule. In disputes that conclude with the complainant receiving an increase in market access to the respondent, roughly two out of three developing third countries also see their exports to the respondent increase, and the average rate of increase of these exports is only slightly less than the average increase experienced by the complainant. While the empirical analysis presented here focuses only on a comparison of averages and counts of data, it is consistent with more formal econometric results reported in other research.[32]

We should also note some additional caveats to our conclusions. First, the brief empirical analysis also concentrates on a fairly short-run economic result. It may take longer than simply one year after the dispute's conclusion for the full trade liberalization gains of all cases to materialize. This may understate our results, for example, if market-access gains to third-country exporters follow subsequent to trade liberalization gains that are extended to complainants. Second, we consider a fairly limited number of disputes and only a certain class of GATT/WTO violations. While a starting part, this analysis is but a starting point for an area that requires much more systematic empirical analysis.

Not only is it important to obtain a better understanding of the economic impact of the GATT/WTO dispute settlement process on developing country interests in cases in which they are complainants and respondents, but it is increasingly critical to analyze the externality impact of *others'* disputes on developing country economic interests as third parties. We have identified various ways in which the economic interests of developing third countries are affected, depending on the nature of the dispute and their importing or exporting role. Future research should address the other classes of disputes from the third-party perspective that we have identified in Figures 1 through 3, in order to get a truer assessment of the overall economic impact of the dispute settlement process. Finally, it would also be of great interest to have a deeper sense of what is happening *within* these developing third countries beyond what is simply happening to trade flows. What are the distribution consequences of these—sometimes positive, sometimes negative—externalities? How are production, employment, wages, and the distribution of income being affected?

Finally, from a policy perspective, we once again highlight the critical need for transparency when it comes to formal DSU litigation activity. Our breakdown of the varied third party interests in Section B reveals a complex web of externalities being imposed on the nonprimary (ie, noncomplainant/nonrespondent) litigants

---

32. Bown (n 5 above).

in trade dispute activity. For example, *realizing* the positive externality of enhanced, nondiscriminatory market access that results from a trade dispute may require industries undertake substantial new investment. On the other hand, for the third countries that face a negative externality, their governments may need new domestic policies so as to enhance the facilitation of resources out of a shrinking industry (the result of preference erosion) and into newly expanding sectors elsewhere in the economy. Finally, for disputes in which there are significant negative externality losers at the country-wide level, there may be equity arguments for compensation to the losers via some sort of international transfer. At a minimum, transparency in the DSU process can enhance the likelihood that national governments implement the necessary *complementary* policies to best respond to the externalities generated by the outcomes of trade disputes.

12. ECONOMIC DEVELOPMENT AND THE WORLD TRADE ORGANIZATION
Proposal for the Agreement on Development Facilitation and the Council for Trade and Development in the WTO

YONG-SHIK LEE*

A. Introduction: Trade and Development 292
B. Current Development-Assistance Provisions and the Organizational Apparatus of the WTO 294
    I. Current Provisions 294
        Article XVIII 295
        GATT Articles XXXVI–XXXVIII 296
        The Enabling Clause 298
        S&D provisions 298
    II. The Current Organizational Apparatus in the WTO 299
    III. Case for the Council for Trade and Development and the Agreement on Development Facilitation 301
C. The Elements of the ADF and the Role of the New Council 303
    I. Possible Elements of the ADF 303
        Setting procedures to monitor and enforce commitments under Part IV of GATT 303
        S&D provisions 304
        Adjustment to tariff bindings 306
        Subsidy treatment 308

---

* University of Sydney Law School. Professor Y.S. Lee is the founding editor-in-chief of the *Law and Development Review* (www.bepress.com/ldr) and associate editor of the *Journal of World Trade*. He has authored a number of articles and several volumes of books on international economic law and economic development, including *Reclaiming Development in the World Trading System* (Cambridge University Press, 2006), *Safeguard Measures in World Trade: The Legal Analysis* (2nd ed, Kluwer Law International, 2005), and *Economic Development Through World Trade: A Developing World Perspective* (Kluwer Law International, 2008). Professor Lee is also former legal counsel for the Ministry of Foreign Affairs and Trade, Korea. Correspondences to the author; fax: 440-919-7416; e-mail: wtogeneva @hotmail.com. This paper has been prepared for the May 2007 ASIL conference on WTO and developing countries. Older versions of this paper have been published in *Asper Review of International Business and Trade Law* (2006) and in Y.S. Lee (ed), *Economic Development Through World Trade: A Developing World Perspective* (Kluwer Law International, 2008).

　　　　　　The suspension of antidumping measures, TRIMS Agreement,
　　　　　　　and TRIPS Agreement 310
　　　　　　Extension of special treatment for LDCs 316
　　II. The Role of the Council for Trade and Development 316
　　　　　　Development-assistance policy implementation 317
　　　　　　Regulatory monitoring 317
　　　　　　Instituting and supervising committees 318
　D. Conclusion—Development Assistance from Rhetoric to Action 318

A. INTRODUCTION: TRADE AND DEVELOPMENT

The facilitation of economic development has become an essential issue in the discussion of world trade today.[1] The increased participation of developing countries in the world trading system, comprising currently two-thirds of the WTO membership, has brought more attention to the issue of trade and development in recent years.[2] This issue has become an important agenda in the WTO; the WTO Agreement[3] sets out the facilitation of development as its objective,[4] and the first WTO Ministerial Conference addressed the importance of integrating developing countries in the multilateral trading system by assisting with their economic development.[5] The Doha Round also includes a development agenda (DDA) that addresses key issues of trade and development, such as debt and finance, trade and transfer of technology, technical cooperation and capacity building, LDCs, and S&D treatment.[6]

---

1. Y.S. Lee, *Reclaiming Development in the World Trading System* (New York: Cambridge University Press, 2006), which discusses the impact of the current regulatory framework for international trade on economic development.

2. The participation of developing countries in the world trading system began in the previous GATT regime. RE Hudec, *Developing Countries in the GATT Legal System* (London, Trade Policy Research Centre, 1987) for a discussion of how GATT as an institution came to accommodate the increasing involvement of developing countries in the world trading system.

3. Agreement Establishing the World Trade Organization (15 April 1994), <http://www.wto.org/english/docs_e/legal_e/04-wto.pdf>.

4. Its preamble provides in relevant part, '*Recognizing* further that there is need for positive efforts designed to ensure that developing countries, and especially the least developed among them, secure a share in the growth in international trade commensurate with the needs of their economic development.' Ibid [emphasis in original].

5. To facilitate this integration, '. . . the WTO Agreement embodies provisions conferring differential and more favorable treatment for developing countries, including special attention to the particular situation of least-developed countries'. WTO, 'Singapore Ministerial Declaration' (18 December 1996); WTO Doc. WT/MIN(96)/DEC para 13.

6. WTO, 'Ministerial Declaration' (20 November 2001) WTO Doc. WT/MIN(01)/DEC/1.

With the majority of the world population in poverty (mostly in developing countries), relieving this human tragedy is one of the most pressing issues of our time.[7] The only long-term solution to this problem is the economic development of developing countries; this will create economies capable of providing higher standards of living to these populations. Trade can play an essential role in the facilitation of economic development.[8] A group of developing countries in East Asia, namely the newly industrializing (now industrialized) countries (NICs) such as South Korea, Taiwan, Hong Kong, and Singapore achieved splendid economic development within a few decades using active export facilitation. The NICs have brought themselves out of poverty through successful economic development.[9] Export facilitation, being an essential part of the development strategy, needs to be supported by the WTO.

The regulatory framework for international trade currently represented by the WTO affects the ability of developing countries to adopt trade related development policies.[10] The author examined in his previous works how the current regulatory framework for international trade facilitates the economic development of

---

7. In 2000, the United Nations estimated that over half the world's population (six billion people) live under substantial deprivation, surviving on income equivalent to $2 or less per day. To address the question of poverty, the United Nations set the "Millennium Development Goals" (MDG) with several development objectives. United Nations, 'UN Millennium Development Goals' <http://www.un.org/millenniumgoals>.

8. A large body of literature discusses the contribution of trade to development including: World Trade Organization, 'The High Level Symposium on Trade and Development' (March 1999) *Focus* 6–9; J Riedel, 'Trade as the Engine of Growth in Developing Countries, Revisited' (1984) 94 (373) Econ J 56–73; LE Westphal, 'Industrial Policy in an Export-Propelled Economy: Lessons From South Korea's Experience' (1990) 4(3) J Econ Pers 41–59; R Nurkse, *Patterns of Trade and Development* (New York: Oxford University Press, 1959); R Nurkse (ed), *Problems of Capital Formation in Underdeveloped Countries* (New York: Oxford University Press, 1967); K Krishna, A Ozyildirim and NR Swanson, 'Trade, Investment, and Growth: Nexus, Analysis, and Prognosis' (December 1998) NBER Working Paper No. 6861; JA Frankel and D Romer, 'Trade and Growth: An Empirical Investigation' (March 1996) NBER Working Paper No. 5476; D Salvatore and T Hatcher, 'Inward Oriented and Outward Oriented Trade Strategies' (1991) 27(3) J Dev Stu 7–25.

9. These four economies have achieved rapid economic development since the 1960s. Between 1961 and 1996, South Korea's gross domestic product (GDP) increased by an average of 9.80 percent per annum, Hong Kong by 9.58 percent, Taiwan by 10.21 percent, and Singapore by 9.95 percent. The growth of exports from the NICs, fueled by their rapid industrial growth, was phenomenal during their development. For instance, during 1980–1990, exports from South Korea, Taiwan, Hong Kong, and Singapore grew at the average annual rates of 12.0 percent, 8.9 percent, 14.4 percent, and 10.0 percent respectively.

10. For instance, the prohibition of export and import-substitution subsidies under the current subsidy rules deprives developing countries of the ability to adopt these subsidies for the purpose of development. For further discussions see Lee (n 1 above) ch 3.

developing countries.[11] This examination revealed the inadequacy of the current system. The author, therefore, proposed alternative provisions intended to facilitate economic development, including Development-Facilitation Tariff (DFT) and Development-Facilitation Subsidy (DFS). He also briefly reasoned the need for a new regulatory treatment of development facilitation, tentatively called the 'Agreement on Development Facilitation' (ADF), as well as the necessity to create a new body within the WTO to oversee trade and development issues, namely 'the Council for Trade and Development' (the Development Council).[12] This chapter, reiterating the need for the ADF and the Development Council, provides a more detailed account of the possible elements of the ADF, including DFT and DFS and the role of the proposed Council.

Section B discusses the current development-assistance provisions and organizational apparatus in the WTO and examines their effectiveness in facilitating development. Based on this examination, a case for the Development Council and ADF is made. Section C explores the possible elements of the ADF and the role of the Development Council. Further, this section addresses the need for the Development Policy Review Mechanism (DPRM). Finally, Section D provides a conclusion based on the forgoing discussion.

The Doha Round was suspended in July 2006 for the next several months because, in part, of the significant dissatisfaction by developing countries about the current and proposed trade concessions as well as the level of the proposed elimination of agricultural subsidies by major developed countries, including the United States and European Union. Developing countries have felt that the process of the Doha Round did not live up to its promise of the 'development round'. The continued impasse of the multilateral trading negotiations will threaten the future of the WTO, and fundamental reform in WTO disciplines in favor of economic development of developing countries is necessary to ensure continued participation of both developing and developed countries in the WTO. The proposals in this article have been put forward to aid in this effort.

B. CURRENT DEVELOPMENT-ASSISTANCE PROVISIONS AND THE ORGANIZATIONAL APPARATUS OF THE WTO[13]

i. Current Provisions

The major development-assistance provisions include GATT Articles XVIII, XXXVI– XXXVIII, the 'Enabling Clause', and the special and differential provisions (S&D provisions) in various WTO agreements.

---

11. Lee (n 1 above). See also Y.S. Lee, 'Facilitating Development in the World Trading System: A Proposal for Development Facilitation Tariff and Development Facilitating Subsidy' (2004) 38(6) JWT 935–54.

12. Lee (n 1 above) ch 2.

13. Much of Section B is based on Lee (n 1 above) ch 2.

Article XVIII Article XVIII of GATT, entitled 'Governmental Assistance to Economic Development',[14] facilitates the establishment of industries by authorizing relevant trade measures. Paragraph 2 provides:

> The contracting parties recognize further that it may be necessary for those contracting parties [contracting parties the economies of which can only support low standards of living and are in the early stages of development], in order to implement programmes and policies of economic development designed to raise the general standard of living of their people, to take protective or other measures affecting imports, and that such measures are justified in so far as they facilitate the attainment of the objectives of this Agreement. They agree, therefore, that those contracting parties should enjoy additional facilities to enable them (a) to maintain sufficient flexibility in their tariff structure to be able to grant the tariff protection *required for the establishment of a particular industry* and (b) to apply quantitative restrictions for balance of payment purposes in a manner which takes full account of the continued high level of demand for imports likely to be generated by their programmes of economic development. [Explanation and emphasis added.]

This Article supports the infant-industry promotion policy,[15] which uses tariff protection to promote domestic industries in the early stages of development. Article XVIII allows developing countries to establish a particular industry by authorizing them to maintain a flexible tariff structure (eg, increase tariff rates by modifying the Schedule of Concessions). This flexibility enables developing countries to grant tariff protection for infant industries. Article XVIII also acknowledges the need for trade measures for balance-of-payments (BOP) purposes.[16]

Reciprocity is required for a modification of the Schedule of Concessions to facilitate an industry; the modifying WTO Member is required to negotiate with other Members with which the relevant concession was initially negotiated having a substantial interest (paragraph 7(a) of Section A). Therefore, this modification under Article XVIII may require a compensatory measure by the modifying Member to reach agreement with other Members. If an agreement is not reached

---

14. General Agreement on Tariffs and Trade (30 October 1947) (entered into force 1 January 1948), 58 U.N.T.S. 187 <http://www.wto.org/english/docs_e/legal_e/gatt47_e.pdf>.

15. Friedrich List (1789–1846) is widely known as the father of infant-industry promotion, which was proposed in his famous work, *The National System of Political Economy*.

16. Section B of Article XVIII authorizes balance-of-payments (BOP) measures for development purposes. Paragraph 8 of the Article provides, 'The contracting parties recognize that contracting parties coming within the scope of paragraph 4(a) of this Article [ie, developing countries in the early stages of development] tend, when they are in rapid process of development, to experience balance-of-payment difficulties arising mainly from efforts to expand their internal markets as well as from the instability in their terms of trade.' GATT (n 14 above) (explanation added).

within 60 days after the WTO is notified of the modification, the Member may still unilaterally modify the concession in question. This can occur only on the condition that the WTO finds that the compensatory adjustment offered by the modifying Member is adequate and that every effort was made to reach an agreement.[17] In addition, the modifying Member must give effect to the compensatory adjustment at the same time as the modification.[18] However, if the WTO finds that the compensatory adjustment offer is not adequate, other Members with a substantial interest are free to adopt retaliatory measures by modifying or withdrawing substantially equivalent concessions against the modifying Member.[19] The Article XXVIII general modification process is also analogous to that provided under Article XVIII, but the former process can only be initiated every three-year period or in special circumstances which, arguably, may also include the need for economic development.

Article XVIII relaxes the requirement of binding concessions under Article II and authorizes developing country Members to modify their Schedule of Concessions to facilitate an infant industry. However, the requirement of consultations and negotiations may cause considerable delays in implementing trade measures for development purposes. The requirement of reciprocal concessions (compensation) may also impose a burden on the economy of the modifying developing country. While the effectiveness of infant-industry facilitation policies has been questioned in economic circles, the cases of recent development history indicate that the facilitation of industry by government has contributed to successful economic development.[20] The case for infant-industry promotion is examined in the discussion of adjustment to tariff bindings for development purposes.[21] Thus, the provisions of Article XVIII can play a positive role in assisting economic development, but the requirements of negotiations and compensation may diminish the effectiveness.

GATT Articles XXXVI–XXXVIII Part IV of GATT (Articles XXXVI–XXXVIII) entitled 'Trade and Development'. provides another set of provisions attempting to assist economic development. The provisions in GATT Articles XXXVI–XXXVIII set out an array of measures, commitments, and collaborations on the part of developed countries and the WTO in support of economic development.

Article XXXVI[22] addresses the vital role of export earnings in economic development, possible authorization of special measures to promote trade and development, the need for more favorable and acceptable conditions of access to world markets for primary products (on which many developing countries depend),

---

17. GATT ibid, article XVIII, para 7(b).
18. Ibid.
19. Ibid.
20. For more discussion on this point, see Lee (n 1 above) ch 3.
21. See section B(i) below.
22. GATT (n 14 above) article XXXVI.

the need to diversify the economic structure in developing countries and to avoid excessive dependence on the export of primary products, and the important relationship between trade and financial assistance to development.[23] The Article also clarifies that there should be no expectation of reciprocity by developed countries for commitments made by them in trade negotiations to reduce or remove tariffs and other trade barriers for developing Members.[24]

Article XXXVII[25] elaborates developed country Members' commitment to assist developing countries with economic development. Methods include:

- according high priority to the reduction and elimination of import barriers to products of particular export interest to developing country Members;
- refraining from introducing or increasing import barriers to such products;[26]
- according high priority to the reduction and elimination of policies specifically applicable to primary products wholly or mainly produced in developing countries, which hamper the growth of consumption of those products.[27]

Developed country Members are also required to make efforts to maintain trade margins for developing countries at equitable levels when a government directly or indirectly determines the resale price of products wholly or mainly produced in developing country Members.[28] They are also obligated to adopt measures providing a greater scope for the development of imports from those developing countries.[29] Special regard is to be given to the trade interests of developing countries in the application of trade measures against imports (paragraph 3). Article XXXVIII[30] provides for joint action and calls for an institutional effort by the WTO to assist with the development of developing countries.

Critics have argued that the provisions of Article XXXVI–XXXVIII are declaratory rather than obligatory since they are not enforced by effective sanctions.

---

23. Ibid.
24. Ibid. para 8.
25. GATT (n 14 above) article XXXVII. Also with respect to this commitment, para 1 of Article XXXVII provides in relevant part: "The developed contracting parties shall to the fullest extent possible—that is, except when compelling reasons, which may include legal reasons, make it impossible—give effect to the following provisions". This provision allows developed countries to avoid this commitment by, for instance, legislating for import restraints from developing countries.
26. Ibid para 1(b).
27. Ibid para 1(c). .
28. Ibid, para 3(a).
29. Ibid, para 3(b).
30. Ibid, article XXXVIII.

Hudec explained that Part IV of the GATT includes 'principles, but not law'.[31] Article XXXVII excuses developed country Members from the various commitments set out in the Article for 'compelling reasons', thus further weakening the effectiveness of these provisions.[32] These compelling reasons may include domestic legal obligations; therefore, developed countries may avoid their 'commitments' by legislating against them. Thus, it is doubtful that the commitments under Articles XXXVI–XXXVIII have actually affected the policies of developed countries in any significant way to accord more favorable treatment to developing countries.

The Enabling Clause A set of policy statements made in the GATT Decision on 28 November 1979, in favor of developing country Members referred to as the Enabling Clause, also provides development- assistance provisions.[33] This Enabling Clause approves the GSP and the exchange of preferences among developing country Members.[34] It also provides for differential and preferential treatment for developing countries with respect to nontariff measures[35] as well as special treatment for LDCs.[36] The Enabling Clause also states that developed countries should not expect reciprocity for the commitments made by them in trade concessions[37] and should exercise utmost restraint in seeking concessions from the LDCs.[38] As in the case of Articles XXXVI—XXXVIII discussed earlier, the Enabling Clause is not mandatory in that there is no effective sanction against a violation of these commitments. The Enabling Clause *enables* developed countries to provide preference for developing countries, but it does not *obligate* them to do so.

S&D provisions There are other provisions in the GATT/WTO disciplines, the majority of which are found in the Uruguay Round Agreements, which provide special and differential treatment in favor of developing countries.[39] These provisions relax current discipline requirements for the benefit of developing countries, require protection of the interests of developing countries, or give

---

31. Hudec (n 2 above) 59. Hudec explained that Part IV was mostly aspirational. Hudec (n 2 above) 56–59.
32. GATT (n 14 above) article XXXVII, para 1.
33. GATT, *Differential and More Favourable Treatment, Reciprocity and Fuller Participation on Developing Countries*, GATT C.P. Nov. L/4903, 26th Supp. B.I.S.D. (1980) 203.
34. Ibid, para 2(a).
35. Ibid, para 2(b).
36. Ibid, para 2(d).
37. Ibid, para 5.
38. Ibid, para 6.
39. One hundred and forty-five such provisions are scattered throughout several WTO agreements, understandings, and GATT articles. Twenty-two are applied exclusively to LDCs. For a review of the special and differential treatment provisions in the WTO, see *Implementation of Special and Differential Treatment Provisions in WTO Agreements and Decisions—Note by Secretariat*, WTO Doc. WT/COMTD/W/77 (25 October 2000).

more compliance time for developing countries (transitional period). Currently, however, this S&D treatment is not sufficient to meet the development needs of developing countries for several reasons.

First, protection is often not sufficient. For instance, Article 9.1 of the Safeguards Agreement requires the exemption of imports originating in a developing country from safeguards where the portion of such imports does not exceed 3 percent, provided that the collective share of imports from all such developing country Members (under 3 percent) accounts for not more than 9 percent.[40] Article 9.2 of the Safeguards Agreement also allows developing country Members to apply safeguards for an additional two years beyond the maximum duration and to reapply safeguards to the same product after shortened intervals.[41] Critics have argued that the ceilings (the individual 3 percent and collective 9 percent) are too tight, and the small extensions are not very helpful for developing countries.[42] Similarly, these provisions do not relieve developing countries of the requirements of WTO disciplines in any significant way or give substantial protection in the areas where their trade interests are significantly affected, such as tariff bindings, subsidies, and antidumping rules.[43]

The transition period, provided as a preference for developing countries, is not very helpful either—the S&D treatment will expire after a stipulated period for transition, while the need of development that may justify the S&D treatment may remain. Where permanent exceptions are given, the number of beneficiary developing countries is often too limited, eg, where exemptions are allowed in subsidy rules to permit export subsidies, only a handful of LDCs benefit from this exemption on a permanent basis.[44] In addition, current S&D treatment does not provide differentiated treatment to developing countries of widely different development status other than LDCs. A recent study has pointed out the need for greater differentiation in S&D treatment.[45]

ii. The Current Organizational Apparatus in the WTO

The major organizational body that concerns trade and development within the WTO is the Committee on Trade and Development (CTD). The CTD is established under the General Council with a mandate to handle issues on trade

---

40. Agreement on Safeguards <www.wto.org/english/docs_e/legal_e/25-safeg.pdf>.
41. Ibid
42. JS Mah, 'Injury and Causation in the WTO Agreement on Safeguards' (2001) 4(3) JWIP 380–82.
43. Thus, the author proposed regulatory reforms in these areas. Lee, Reclaiming Development in the World Trading System (n 1 above).
44. For instance, only LDCs are exempted from the prohibition of export subsidies. See section C(i) below for a relevant discussion.
45. M Hart and B Dymond, 'Special and Differential Treatment and the Doha "Development" Round' (2003) 37(2) JWT 409.

and development. Its mandate is also to address related issues such as implementation of preferential provisions for developing countries, guidelines for technical cooperation, increased participation of developing countries in the trading system, LDCs, notifications of GSP programs, and preferential trade arrangements among developing countries.

Current WTO assistance to developing countries focuses on capacity-building. In this area, the WTO offers assistance through its Training and Technical Cooperation Institute. Assistance includes providing regular training sessions on trade policy in Geneva, organizing approximately 400 technical cooperation activities annually, including seminars and workshops in various countries and courses in Geneva, and offering legal assistance to some developing countries.[46] These capacity-building activities are undoubtedly helpful to developing countries, but the scope of assistance is rather limited as the focus is on technical capacity-building. The WTO needs to consider other essential areas concerning trade and development, such as technology transfer, financial mechanism, and debt relief.

The CTD does not have the mandate to address these other essential issues and thus, developing countries have requested discussion of these issues at the WTO level. The need for a new round to address a development agenda has resonated widely. The 2004 Report on the implementation of the United Nation Millennium Declaration emphasized the responsibility of developed countries to meet development goals, stating specifically that developed countries must fulfill their responsibilities 'by increasing and improving development assistance, concluding a new development-oriented trade round, embracing wider and deeper debt relief and fostering technology transfer'.[47] In response to this demand, the new round includes a series of development issues in its agenda (DDA). In addition, the DDA established two working groups: 'Trade, Debt and Finance' and 'Trade and Transfer of Technology'.[48] The CTD met in special sessions to handle work under the DDA.

---

46. For legal assistance, 32 WTO governments created an Advisory Centre on WTO Law in 2001. Its Members consist of countries contributing funding and those receiving legal advice. Least-developed countries are automatically eligible for advice, while other developing countries and transition economies have to be fee-paying Members. For further information see <www.wto.org>. In addition, The WTO Reference Centre program was also initiated in 1997 with the objective of creating a network of computerized information centers in LDC and developing countries. The International Trade Centre, a joint body with UNCTAD, also helps developing countries to expand export and to improve their import operations.

47. *Implementation of the United Nations Millennium Declaration*, UN 59th Sess., UN Doc. A/59/282 (2004), para 43.

48. The DDA address issues of trade, debt, and finance; trade and transfer of technology; technical cooperation and capacity building; LDCs; and special and differential treatment. WTO, *Ministerial Declaration*, (20 November 2001) WT/MIN(01)/DEC/1.

iii. Case for the Council for Trade and Development and the Agreement on Development Facilitation

The current problem with WTO provisions and the organizational structure concerning trade and development is that these provisions are not very effective, as discussed above, and that the current organizational apparatus is rather insufficient to address complex and long-term development issues on trade and development.[49] The mandate of the CTD is limited and the WTO's activities to assist developing countries also have been rather limited in scope. The problem of ineffectiveness and insufficiency can be answered by elevating the existing Committee to full Council status, thus strengthening the organizational apparatus and by establishing a separate Agreement on Development Facilitation (ADF).

With respect to the suggested organizational reform, the need for such an elevation can be explained by comparison with the treatment of trade related aspects of intellectual property rights promoted by developed countries. While trade and development issues concern the vast majority of WTO Members, a relatively limited number of countries promoted intellectual property rights in the Uruguay Round negotiations. Nonetheless, the importance of intellectual property rights was emphasized during the negotiations, and the full Council, not a Committee, as well as a separate agreement (TRIPS Agreement) were established to address complex and long-term intellectual property issues in the WTO.[50]

As mentioned, trade and development issues concern a vast number of developing countries, and there is consensus in the WTO that these issues should be addressed within the WTO. The DDA reflects this consensus, and the Doha Round is called 'the development round'. If these trade and development issues, which concern the majority of WTO membership, are considered as important as TRIPS, which was promoted by a smaller number of developed countries, it is fair and proper that trade and development issues be accorded the same institutional attention and weight by elevating the present Committee to full Council status. This proposed institutional reform would help resolve the doubt that trade and development issues have not received due attention and have been set aside.[51]

The suggested elevation will not only make a statement recognizing the essential importance of development issues but also meet practical needs. The practical

---

49. The current organizational apparatus consists of the CTD and the Subcommittee on LDCs aided by the Training and Technical Cooperation Institute under the WTO secretariat.

50. The Council for Trade Related Aspects of Intellectual Property Rights is organized under Article IV of the WTO Agreement (n 3 above).

51. WTO, International Institute for Sustainable Development, *Report of the WTO's High-Level Symposium on Trade and Development* (17–18 March 1999) <http://www.wto.org/english/tratop_e/devel_e/summhl_e.htm>.

needs include the replacement of present working groups with separate committees. World Trade Organization working groups have been established to address important trade and development issues such as trade, debt and finance, and trade and technology transfer. These issues are complex and require continued attention within the WTO. Separate committees, rather than limited subcommittees, will be necessary to incorporate these important issues as a working agenda in the WTO. To oversee the effective operation of these committees, a separate Council would need to be established within the WTO. In addition, individual developing countries face unique problems resulting from increased participation in the WTO and securing full benefits of WTO membership. Therefore, an additional committee is necessary to bring adequate institutional attention to these problems and to assist with the needs of developing countries more effectively on an individual country basis. The current Advisory Centre on WTO Law[52] may be expanded and report to this committee.

In summary, the lack of due organizational status and the resulting appearance of insufficient institutional attention to development issues have created a widespread perception that the WTO represents the interests of developed countries and multinational corporations rather than those of its majority Members—developing countries. One way to resolve this issue is to elevate the current body in charge of development issues to Council level. Instituting a new Council could also serve important functions that the current CTD is not mandated to serve. Such functions could include a better organizational apparatus to deal with specific complex and long-term issues of development. Such new Council will have a wider mandate to implement all necessary measures to promote trade and development and a capacity to address essential development issues that concern the majority of WTO Members.

As previously discussed, the ineffectiveness of the current WTO provisions assisting development is an issue. For instance, relevant GATT provisions such as Articles XVIII and XXXVI-XXXVIII have become ineffective and obsolete. Yet, unlike other areas, the Uruguay Round did not elaborate on these GATT Articles and did not set out more effective and enforceable agreements. Provisions offering S&D treatment are scattered throughout the GATT/WTO disciplines without any coherent regulatory standard, and developed countries have shown reluctance in extending these provisions. To address trade and development issues more effectively and consistently, consideration should be given to the establishment of a coherent set of rules in the form of a separate agreement within the WTO disciplines.

What regulatory elements should be included in the ADF? The ADF may develop specific legal obligations as well as monitor its implementation to increase the enforceability of developed countries' commitments under Part IV

---

52. See n 46 above.

of GATT. This is not unlike other Uruguay Round agreements that expand and elaborate on GATT provisions, turning them into more specific, enforceable obligations. The ADF may also provide coherent and differentiated standards to apply S&D treatment to developing country Members. In addition, the author examined the inconsistency of current WTO disciplines in relation to the development interests of developing countries. It was proposed that reforms of the regulatory disciplines were necessary in areas relevant to development, such as tariff bindings, subsidies, antidumping measures, safeguards, agriculture, trade related investment measures (TRIMS, TRIPS, and GATS).[53] Some of these proposed reforms can also be incorporated in the ADF, as will be discussed in the following section; however, these elements do not comprise an exhaustive list. The scope and contents of the ADF need to be further analyzed and discussed, taking into account the progress made in the current discussion of the DDA.

If the suggested elements in the following section are to be included in the ADF, the ADF may require separate status within Annex 1 of the WTO Agreement, as the provisions of the ADF would affect the TRIPS Agreement and the Multilateral Agreements on Trade in Goods. In addition to facilitating development, the ADF, by providing a coherent and permanent regulatory structure on trade development (unlike temporary and limited S&D treatment), would make a statement that development issues are considered as essential as other issues promoted by developed countries, thereby demonstrating that development issues are no longer only a subject of elaborate rhetoric.

C. THE ELEMENTS OF THE ADF AND THE ROLE OF THE NEW COUNCIL

i. Possible Elements of the ADF[54]

Setting procedures to monitor and enforce commitments under Part IV of GATT GATT Articles XXXVI–XXXVIII are the major provisions that attempt to assist the economic development of developing countries; however, we discussed, these provisions are largely declaratory and do not create enforceable obligations. The ineffectiveness of these provisions is, in part, the result of an ineffective monitoring and enforcement system. Thus, setting procedures to monitor and enforce specific commitments by developed country Members may increase their effectiveness. One way to do this is to obligate developed country Members and participating developing country Members to report periodically on their specific commitments under these provisions and consult with the WTO on the implementation of these commitments. The Council for Trade and Development, proposed, can oversee this procedure.

---

53. See Lee (n 1 above) and also Lee (n 11 above).
54. The contents of Section C(i) incorporate regulatory reforms proposed by the author in his book, *Reclaiming Development in the World Trading System* (n 1 above).

This report, provisionally named Trade-Related Development Assistance Report, or TDAR, may itemize the commitments listed under Article XXXVII[55] and require every developed country Member to list its specific economic and trade measures that would implement commitments under each item. Developed country Members should also be required to list any laws, practices, and policies that are inconsistent with these commitments and consult with the Council to resolve the problem. A time table can be agreed upon between the developed country Member and the Council, setting out for the removal or change of any offending practices. The broad exemption that currently excuses developed country Members from commitments under Article XXXVII for any compelling reason, including legal reasons,[56] should be removed as it allows Members to disregard these commitments simply by legislating against them.

Developed country Members should also be required to report to the Council on a regular basis on the implementation of relevant measures under the itemized commitments, as well as on any undertaking to remove or change inconsistent policies, laws, and practices. The Council should review these reports, consult with the Members for any violation of their commitments, and adopt measures, if necessary, to ensure their compliance. Any interested Member should be allowed to report a violation of these commitments to the Council. The Council should then examine the incident and determine whether there has been a violation. If it determines a violation occurred, the Council may also adopt necessary measures to secure compliance, including the authorization of trade sanctions. This combination of monitoring, consultation, and enforcement measures, as well as the ability to set the procedures in the ADF should increase the regulatory force of Article XXXVII. Last, the ADF may also establish procedures to set out specific joint actions to be undertaken by the WTO under Article XXXVIII and report implementation of these actions on a regular basis. The Council and other institutions, with which the WTO has collaborated under this Article, may prepare these reports jointly.

S&D provisions Provisions offering S&D treatment to developing countries are scattered throughout various WTO disciplines without any coherent regulatory standards, ie, standards that regulate the underlying principle providing S&D treatment and determine which developing country Members benefit from this preferential treatment. Under the current system, the developing country status is self-declaratory, and the absence of definition for developing country Members seems to create regulatory ambiguity. In addition, the current system provides the same level of S&D treatment to developing country Members with widely different levels of development status and economic need for S&D treatment. A recent study emphasizes the need for greater differentiation in

---

55. For the discussion of these commitments see Section B(i) above.
56. See n 14 above.

S&D treatment.[57] The ADF should provide a definition for a developing country Member and also differentiate S&D treatment for developing country Members to enhance the clarity and rationality of the system.

What standard can be adopted to determine developing country status? Individual income levels can be considered. The World Bank uses gross national income (GNI) per capita to categorize nations into different income groups.[58] This economic indicator can be used as a primary determinant for the development status.[59] Methods for differentiating S&D treatment for different developing country Members should also be sought, and the subcategorization of the developed country Members, such as the one used by the World Bank, can be adopted for such differentiation. Article 9.2 of the Agreement on Safeguards authorizes a longer duration of a safeguard measure to be applied by a developing country Member.[60] This additional duration can be differentiated in accordance with the developed status of the particular developing country Member (perhaps extended for poorer developing countries and shortened for richer ones) identified by the subcategorization discussed earlier.

Achieving regulatory coherency for S&D treatment also requires establishing reasoned principles for providing this treatment. It is not clear if such coherent principles exist because provisions offering S&D treatment arose out of political compromises among developed and developing country Members. Developed country Members were rather reluctant to provide extensive S&D treatment, while developing country Members insisted on it. Some types of S&D treatment simply buy developing country Members more time to comply with WTO obligations, while others provide permanent preferential treatment.[61] The tendency of trying to limit preferential treatment to developing country Members seems to continue, as reflected in a statement made by a prominent speaker at the 1999

---

57. See n 45 above. Hudec considered that differentiation among developing countries would distablize the trading system. Hudec (n 2 above). However, a well-formulated differentiation for differential treatment as proposed in the Development-Facilitation Tariff and Development-Facilitation Subsidy below is not expected to cause instability in the system.

58. As of May 2007, the World Bank made this classification according to its 2005 statistics: low-income group ($875 or less per capita), lower-middle-income group (between $875 and $3,465 per capita), upper-middle-income group (between $3,466 and $10,725), and high-income group ($10,726 or above) <http://www.worldbank.org>.

59. The above threshold for the high-income group can be used to create a presumption of the developed country status. If a Member claims the developing country status despite its per capita GNI level above this threshold, due to other factors that indicate a low level of social development or an excessive economic dependency on the production of primary products (eg, oil), the Member should be allowed to counter the presumption of the developed country status.

60. Safeguard Agreement (n 40 above).

61. See n 39 above.

WTO High-Level Symposium on Trade and Development advising developing countries to avoid a push for renewed S&D treatment.[62]

The reluctance on the part of developed country Members to provide extensive S&D treatment may represent their preference for 'one rule for all nations'. In other words, eventually one rule should apply to all trading nations, both developed and developing, and S&D treatment that offers temporary preference should not be extended in time. In addition, S&D treatment that offers a permanent preference to a limited number of developing country Members, such as LDCs, should not be expanded to benefit more developing country Members. It would be necessary to reconsider whether this one-rule policy is justifiable. If the development needs of developing country Members justify preferential treatment in the first place, then this treatment *should not expire* until they attain developed status, and therefore, this one-rule policy is not tenable from the perspective of economic development.[63] The proposed regulatory reforms suggest that preferential treatment be extended to all developing country Members in many areas of trade, as will soon be discussed.

Adjustment to tariff bindings[64] The GATT/WTO system requires Members to maintain their commitments on import concessions in the form of tariff bindings stipulated in the Schedule of Concessions.[65] While this principle provides essential stability to the international trading system, the tariff commitments remove the ability of developing countries to use trade protection to facilitate their industries in the early stages of development (infant industries). There is considerable debate on the validity of infant-industry promotion policies. Nonetheless, a recent study recognizes that fundamental economic restructuring seldom takes place in the absence of governmental intervention,[66] and the case for state-supported industrial facilitation has already been made in some literature.[67] Regardless of the debate, a developing country should be allowed to choose policies that are best suited for its own development, fully considering the ramifications of the proposed tariff increases. If it finally determines that its industrial promotion policy demands tariff increases, its previous import commitments should not tie its hands. The provisions of GATT Article XVIII allow modification of the schedule to aid the facilitation of infant industries, but these provisions require Members to undergo potentially time-consuming and complicated negotiations with other interested Members prior to the application of higher tariffs.

---

62. C. Fred Bergsten (main speaker), *Report 1999* (n 51 above).
63. See also (n 1 above).
64. The proposal to adjust binding concessions to facilitate development was first made in Facilitating Development (n 11 above).
65. GATT (n 14 above) article II.
66. Dani Rodrik, 'Industrial Policy for the Twenty-First Century' (September 2004) paper prepared for UNIDO 15.
67. Lee (n 11 above) 938–39.

Thus, more flexible treatment should be available to developing countries with respect to binding concessions authorizing additional tariffs beyond their scheduled commitments to facilitate industries for economic development.[68]

This additional tariff applied for the purpose of infant-industry promotion can be called the Development-Facilitation Tariff or DFT.[69] In brief, the DFT allows a developing country to apply tariff rates above the scheduled commitments unilaterally when the country can demonstrate a development need for such a tariff with a concrete plan for industrial facilitation. The application of a DFT should require procedural safeguards to minimize the possibility of abuse. Safeguards could include a formal investigation and hearing requirement, notices to other interested Members, consultations, and a maximum duration for its application. The maximum applicable rate of the DFT should also be systematically differentiated according to the development stage of a particular developing country, as determined by the level of its per capita income. For example, the maximum DFT rate applicable by wealthier developing countries should be lower than that of a less affluent developing country, measured by per capita income.[70]

Some may argue that the introduction of DFTs in the world trading system will undermine the import concessions made by developing countries and disrupt the balance of concessions achieved through trade negotiations. While these concessions are important, the need for economic development should be given priority. The impact of DFTs on world trade will be rather limited since around two-thirds of world trade is conducted among developed economies and, therefore, not subject to DFT applications.[71] In addition, due to demands by developed countries with more powerful economies, developing countries with limited negotiating power are often compelled to make concessions in multilateral negotiations

---

68. Arguably, the need for tariff protection should have been contemplated by developing countries when they agreed to specific tariff bindings in the multilateral trade negotiations. Nonetheless, their economic needs and national goals may have changed following political shifts (eg, election of a new government, end of a dictatorship, etc.), and therefore, development initiatives may begin long after the conclusion of trade negotiations. If so, the developing country should not be prohibited from offering trade protection to its infant industry because of its previous import commitments, and it should be allowed to do so without prolonging negotiations and the burden of compensations or threat of retaliations.

69. Lee (n 11 above), for the details of the proposed DFT.

70. There will likely be some concern that this liberal treatment may lead to rampant protectionism by developing countries without either a genuine need or a constructive plan for infant-industry promotion. The procedural safeguards introduced above counter this possibility of abuse.

71. Developing countries' share of world merchandise exports was 36 percent in 2006. World Trade Organization, "World Trade 2006, Prospects for 2007", Press Release /472 <http://www.wto.org/english/news_e/pres07_e/pr472_e.htm>.

beyond the levels that they are prepared to offer/accept.[72] Consequently, where there are clear development plans that demand import protection, it would be fair to allow import restraints to meet development needs.[73]

Subsidy treatment Another essential element of industrial promotion policies for economic development is a government subsidy. Strategically planned government subsidization has contributed to the successful development of some developing countries such as South Korea. Under the SCM Agreement, export subsidies and import-substitution subsidies are prohibited as they have adverse effects on international trade.[74] In addition, a subsidy is 'actionable' when certain conditions are met.[75] Countervailing duties (CVDs), which are additional tariffs imposed on imports to offset the effect of subsidies,[76] are also an applicable remedy where subsidization causes or threatens material injury to an established domestic industry or materially retards the establishment of one.[77]

Current WTO subsidy provisions prohibiting export subsidies and import-substitution subsidies, as well as those authorizing countervailing measures against actionable subsidies,[78] reduce the key ability of developing countries to

---

72. For developing countries and trade negotiations, see Anne Krueger, 'The Developing Countries and the Next Round of Multilateral Trade Negotiations' (1999) 22 (7) W Econ 909–32.

73. Joel Trachtman opined that additional multilateral supervision of access to DFT and other derogations would be valuable. See Joel P. Trachtman, 'The WTO and Development Policy in China and India' (11 August 2006) paper presented at National University of Singapore International Symposium on China, India, and International Economic Law.

74. Agreement on Subsidies and Countervailing Measures (15 April 1994) LT/UR/A-1A/9 <www.wto.org/english/docs_e/legal_e/24-scm.pdf>. Annex I of the *SCM Agreement* includes the illustrative list of prohibited export subsidies.

75. These conditions are: i) the subsidy is specifically limited to an enterprise or group of enterprises, an industrial sector or group of industries, or a designed geographic region within the jurisdiction of the granting authority (specificity requirement); and ii) the subsidy causes adverse effects to the interests of other Members. Adverse effects include a) injury (material injury) to the domestic industry of the importing country, b) nullification or impairment of benefits of bound tariff rates, or c) serious prejudice to the domestic industry. Subsidies and Countervailing Measures Agreement (SCM), ibid, articles. 2 and 5.

76. Part V of the SCM Agreement (articles 10–23) provides for substantive and procedural rules for the application of countervailing duties. According to article 18, exporters can also avoid countervailing duties by undertaking to increase their export prices (price undertaking). This price undertaking is voluntary on the part of the exporters, and the importing country may consider the acceptance of the undertaking impractical, for instance, where the number of actual or potential exporters is too great. (SCM Agreement, Ibid.)

77. GATT (n 14 above) article VI, para 6.

78. See notes 74 and 75 above.

provide support to promote their industries in the early stages of development.[79] Infant industries in developing economies often need export markets due to a limited domestic market. Government support is called upon to improve their competitiveness in the foreign market, as well as in their own. The SCM Agreement recognizes this and affirms, *'subsidies may play an important role in economic development programmes of developing country Members'*.[80] The SCM Agreement also provides certain special and differential treatment to developing countries, ie, LDC Members are not prohibited from applying export subsidies,[81] and other developing countries are permitted to apply export subsidies for a period of eight years from the date of entry into force of the WTO Agreement in 1995, which has already expired.[82] These prohibited or otherwise actionable subsidies should be allowed for developing countries if they demonstrate a need for such subsidies with a concrete development plan. This subsidy that is specially authorized to facilitate development can be labeled Development-Facilitation Subsidy or DFS.

As in the case of the DFT, procedural safeguards should be provided to minimize the abuse of DFS applications. The maximum applicable DFS rate should also be differentiated in accordance with the per capita income level of a developing country proposing to apply a DFS, as the development need would be greater for poorer developing countries. A question may arise as to whether the availability of a DFS would lead to a subsidy race among developing countries, thus diminishing the effect of the subsidy for the industrial promotion of individual developing countries and causing only a distortion of resources. The answer is that a developing country should be trusted with its own best judgment as to whether subsidization would be necessary. Many economic and political factors would affect a government decision to grant a subsidy, and a prudent government will consider the existence and even the possibility of similar subsidies that may be applied by competing countries in the future. A developing country will subsidize those export industries that it believes have the best potential of success, and the possibility of these competing subsidies will be part of that equation. A possible collective action problem may or may not occur, and the point of this proposal is to give a policy option for a developing country.

---

79. It has been observed that the current subsidy rules have made 'a significant dent in the ability of developing countries to employ intelligently-designed industrial policies'. Rodrik, (note 66 above) 34–35. Note that today's developed countries provided extensive subsidies during their development stages, which would have been either prohibited or actionable under the SCM. H Chang, *Kicking Away the Ladder: Development Strategy in Historical Perspective* (London, Anthem Press, 2002), ch 2.

80. SCM Agreement (n 74 above) article 27.1 (emphasis added).

81. SCM Agreement, ibid, article 27.2(a). This preference ceases to apply to any of these LDC Members when it reaches $1,000 GNP per capita. SCM Agreement, Ibid, Annex VII.

82. SCM Agreement, ibid, article 27.2(b).

The suspension of antidumping measures, TRIMS Agreement, and TRIPS Agreement Elements of the ADF may also include suspension of antidumping (AD) measures and the TRIMS and TRIPS Agreements in favor of developing countries.[83] Antidumping actions[84] that are applied against 'dumped imports' in the form of increased tariffs are the most frequently applied import measures in the world today. As of June 2005, there were as many as 1,291 AD actions reported to be in force.[85] Exports from developing countries have been the primary target of AD actions. Between July 2004 and June 2005, over half of the 209 AD investigations targeted imports from developing countries.[86] Considering that total exports from developing countries are less than half the exports from developed countries,[87] a substantially higher rate of exports from developing countries has been targeted for AD actions.

Most economists doubt that solid economic justifications exist for antidumping measures. Also, inherent complexity and arbitrariness in the determination of dumping[88] have created a breeding ground for abuse of AD actions.[89]

---

83. An argument may be made that these elements can be included in the corresponding agreements and not in the ADF. Their regulatory placement requires further discussion. In this paper, these elements are introduced to discuss their substantive merits.

84. For the specific determination of dumping margins and the imposition and collection of antidumping duties, see WTO, The WTO Agreement on Implementation of Article VI of the General Agreement on Tariffs and Trade 1994, articles. 6.10 and 9 <www.wto.org/english/docs_e/legal_e/19-adp.pdf>.[hereinafter "Antidumping Practices Agreement" or "ADP Agreement"]. Price undertakings are also allowed as in the application of CVD actions. *Supra* note 76; ADP Agreement, article 8. For the origin of antidumping measures, see Congressional Budget Office, *How the GATT Affects Antidumping and Countervailing-duty Policy* (1994), p. 18. Antidumping actions include both antidumping duties and price undertakings.

85. WTO, *Annual Report 2006*, 31 <http://www.wto.org>,.

86. Ibid.

87. WTO, 'World Trade 2006, Prospects for 2007' (n 71 above).

88. A dumping is defined as the sale at a price under 'normal value' that needs to be first determined. Anti-Dumping Practices Agreement (n 84 above) article 2.1. The complexity and arbitrariness in the determination of normal value are easily seen: *eg*, there may not be a single home market price to compare, and the complex adjusted average may have to be calculated to come up with a reference home price; the home country may not completely be a market economy (eg, 'transitional economy'), and therefore, the home price may not represent the true market price; or the product in question may not even be sold in the home market or too few of it is sold to be the basis of a valid home price. In all these cases, the price needs to be 'constructed' by an evaluation of cost (constructed cost) plus reasonable profit. Finding the 'export price' that is necessary to determine the existence of dumping by comparison with the home price can be equally complex since a number of adjustments to the transaction price may be necessary to keep the comparison with the home price fair. These adjustments may include complex calculations involving numerous items such as warranty services, advertising costs, etc. Lee (n 1 above) ch 4.

89. Depending upon a specific methodology adopted to calculate costs and average prices, the result can be vastly different, not to mention that the measure of "reasonable

National authorities can adopt a methodology that will yield the least desirable result for exporters[90] and then come up with a finding of dumping.[91] Depending upon their choice of methodology and calculation, the authorities will also be able to find different dumping margins.[92] This arbitrariness in the current AD rules and its significant adverse effect on trade have led to the inclusion of AD rules in the new Doha Round agenda, with a possibility for rule modifications.[93] Nonetheless, it is unlikely that the inherent arbitrariness in determining dumping could be reduced to a satisfactory level.[94]

Antidumping measures cause a critical problem to trade of developing countries. The competitiveness of their product is normally based on low prices, reflecting lower labor costs. Developing countries should be allowed to exploit this advantage to achieve economic development through international trade. Antidumping measures targeting inexpensive products have been major impediments to the exports of developing countries.[95] Although a lower price alone is not a sufficient ground for the application of AD measures,[96] the current provisions permitting the 'construction' of costs and reference prices make it

---

profit" can also vary. A recent study has revealed that in the case of the United States, the vast majority of national AD practices do not even actually identify either price discrimination or sales below cost. B Lindsey, 'The US Antidumping Law: Rhetoric versus Reality' (16 August 1999) Cato Institute Trade Policy Analysis No. 7 <http://www.cato.org/pub_display.php?pub_id=3650>.

90. Article 2 of the ADP Agreement authorizes such leeway in the determination of dumping. ADP Agreement (n 84 above).

91. Although the provisions of the ADP Agreement attempt to provide disciplines on AD actions, 'in common parlance, it is usual to designate all low-cost imports as dumped imports.' International Trade Centre UNCTAD/WTO & Commonwealth Secretariat, *Business Guide to the Uruguay Round* (Geneva, ITC/CS, 1995), p 181.

92. ADP Agreement (n 84 above).

93. WTO, *Ministerial Declaration*, WT/MIN(01)/DEC/1 (20 November 2001), para 28. Reform proposals have been made to reduce the abuse and arbitrariness in the application of AD measures. See B Lindsey and D Ikenson, Reforming the Antidumping Agreement: A Road Map for WTO Negotiations, Cato Institute Trade Policy Analysis No. 21 (11 December 2002) <www.cato.org/pub_display.php?pub_id=3636>.

94. It is because the very attempt to determine the 'normalcy' of a price in a market economy, in which prices are determined by market forces and not by any normative rules, is inherently arbitrary no matter what standard is applied. It was pointed out that '[t]he primary justification for the antidumping law is really more political than economic. The guiding precept is *legitimacy* rather than *efficiency*' (emphasis in original). B Lindsey (n 89 above) 3.

95. See n 91 above.

96. It is required that dumping *causes* or *threatens* material injury to the domestic industry for the application of an AD measure. GATT, *supra* note 14, article VI, para 6. Unlike the serious injury standard required for the application of a safeguard measure (Agreement on Safeguards, n 40 above, article 4), the threshold for material injury is not considered high.

relatively easy for national authorities to find dumping and apply AD measures against exports from developing countries. Yale economist TN Srinivasan has characterized antidumping as the equivalent of a 'nuclear weapon in the armory of trade policy', and suggested removing it at the 1999 WTO High-Level Symposium on Trade and Development.[97] Indeed, considering the economic needs of developing countries, AD measures should not be applicable to their trade in general. Safeguard measures[98] can respond to the predatory dumping that results in the displacement of domestic products, which may be the only justification for antidumping rules.[99]

Another area that has significant relevance to the economic development and trade of developing countries is foreign investment. Foreign direct investment (FDI) may provide developing countries with resources necessary for the development that these countries typically lack, including financial capital, technological resources, production facilities, and managerial expertise. Foreign direct investment also offers employment opportunities for local populations. In accepting FDI, the host developing countries may be inclined to set a series of conditions to steer FDI to maximize its contribution to their development objectives. For example, to facilitate export industries, these governments may adopt investment measures requiring foreign investors to export a certain portion of products produced in the host country. Investment measures may have significant implications on trade. If the host country adopts investment measures requiring foreign investment to export a certain portion of their products in an attempt to promote exports and reduce competition with other domestic producers, this foreign company may be compelled to export more than it would otherwise have. Similarly, if investment measures require foreign investments to purchase domestic products, this may reduce the importation of these products from other countries that it may have imported from in the absence of such measures. The TRIMS Agreement[100] attempts to regulate certain investment measures that affect trade, namely, those that are inconsistent with Articles III and XI of GATT.[101]

As mentioned, TRIMS are often adopted in pursuing development objectives. Although there was some doubt as to the industrial promotion effects of TRIMS,[102] they may nevertheless play an important role in industrial promotion

---

97. *Report 1999* (n 50 above).

98. Article 2.1 of the Agreement on Safeguards sets out the general requirement for the application of a safeguard measure. See n 40 above.

99. For more discussion, see Y.S. Lee, *Safeguard Measures in World Trade: The Legal Analysis*, (2nd ed, Kluwer Law International, 2005) ch 14.2.

100. Agreement on Trade Related Investment Measures (TRIMS) <http://www.wto.org/English/docs_e/legal_e/18-trims.pdf>.

101. GATT (n 14 above) articles III and XI.

102. The criticism includes: TRIMS are economically inefficient since investment terms are controlled by investment measures rather than by market forces; the governments of the hosting countries may abuse TRIMS politically, for instance, to serve the

since they can help facilitate infant domestic industries by promoting exports and encouraging the use of domestic products. Note that all of today's developed countries also adopted investment measures to meet their development objectives during their own development.[103] The TRIMS Agreement seems to mainly target the investment regulations of developing countries, but there seems to be no clear need for such multilateral control on investment. Major investors are often in a position to negotiate the terms of their investment with the host developing country. In addition, nearly 2,500 bilateral investment treaties (BITs) around the world already require national treatment in favor of foreign investors and prohibit a wider range of TRIMS than those restrained by the TRIMS Agreement. If a developing country is ready to give up certain TRIMS, it will do so bilaterally or unilaterally, even without any treaty obligations. However, if a developing country considers the adoption of TRIMS as necessary to meet its development objectives, then mandatory trade rules should not prohibit their adoption. Therefore, the multilateral control on TRIMS needs to be lifted generally in favor of developing countries.[104]

Last, the application of the TRIPS Agreement to developing countries should be reconsidered. Advanced knowledge, such as new technology and production techniques, is essential to facilitating industries. Historically, the ability to copy technologies developed in advanced countries has been one of the most essential elements in determining the ability of developing countries to catch up.[105] Today, developed countries attempt to prevent the unauthorized use of advanced

---

interests of select producers that are not necessarily relevant to the needs for development; and the restrictive terms of TRIMS may also discourage investors from making investments in developing countries adopting these measures and thereby deprive the host developing countries of the opportunities to benefit from the investment that can provide necessary resources for their development. This criticism about TRIMS is in line with the objections to state industrial promotion discussed earlier. See also Lee (n 1 above) ch 3.1.

103. H Chang and D Green, *The Northern WTO Agenda on Investment: Do As We Say, Not As We Did* (South Centre/CAFOD, June 2003) 33. TRIMS can be either effective or countereffective to the development interest of a given developing country depending upon the economic conditions and the development stage which the individual developing country is in. For instance, an imposition of a local content requirement may be unnecessary and economically inefficient at a time when the domestic industry can compete with imports. On the other hand, this particular investment measure may be useful and facilitate domestic infant industries in the initial stages of development where domestic industries require some protection. This suggests that TRIMS can be a means to facilitate development.

104. Reflecting this concern, 12 countries proposed to change the text of the TRIMS Agreement to make commitments under the Agreement optional and not mandatory. WTO, *Preparations for the 1999 Ministerial Conference*, WTO Doc. WT/GC/W/354 (1999).

105. RR Nelson, 'The Changing Institutional Requirements for Technological and Economic Catch Up' (2004) Paper presented at the Danish Research Unit for Industrial

technology by assigning a propriety right called an intellectual property right (IPR). Thus, the enforcement of IPRs affects the ability of developing countries to acquire advanced technology for the purpose of development. The introduction of the TRIPS Agreement in trade disciplines is one of the important attempts to enforce IPRs around the world.

The introduction of the TRIPS Agreement was an ambitious undertaking in the Uruguay Round.[106] This Agreement, comprised of 73 articles in 7 parts, is one of the most extensive provisions in the WTO Agreement. It establishes mandatory standards for the protection of various IPRs, including copyrights, trademarks, geographical indications, industrial designs, patents, and layout-designs of integrated circuits, providing substantial minimum terms of protection (eg, 50 years for copyright, 20 years for patent, and indefinite renewal of trademark with a minimum of 7 years for each registration).[107] In addition to providing effective enforcement procedures under their own laws,[108] the TRIPS Agreement also requires Members to apply national treatment and the MFN treatment to protect foreign IPRs.[109] Rules of other major IPR conventions are also incorporated by reference in the relevant provisions of the TRIPS Agreement.[110]

The adoption of the TRIPS Agreement as part of trade disciplines raises important concerns. First, the TRIPS Agreement attempts to establish a regulatory regime to protect IPRs within all WTO Members. This includes those Members whose economic and social developments do not yet embrace the concept of IPRs and whose judicial systems have not yet developed sufficiently to recognize and enforce IPRs.[111] It is doubtful that the imposition of an economic and legal system, such as an IPR regime, should be the role of trade disciplines. Their role should be limited to remedying trade injury resulting from IPR violations where such injury has been demonstrated. The adoption of the TRIPS Agreement in the WTO, primarily for the effectiveness of enforcement, is not a desirable precedent.

Dynamics (DRUID) Summer Conference 2004 to Industrial Dynamics, Innovation and Development <http://www.druid.dk/conferences/summer2004/papers/ds2004-280.pdf>.

106. Agreement on Trade Related Aspects of Intellectual Property Rights (TRIPS) <www.wto.org/English/docs_e/legal_e/27-trips.pdf>.

107. Ibid

108. Ibid, article 41.

109. Ibid, articles 3–4.

110. The Paris Convention (1967), the Berne Convention (1971), the Rome Convention (1961), and the Treaty on Intellectual Property in Respect of Integrated Circuits (1989) are incorporated by reference. TRIPS, ibid, Article 1.

111. A historical study shows that IPRs began to be recognized and protected when considerable economic and social developments had taken place. Chang (n 79 above) 83–85.

The imposition of an IPR regime may prematurely set economic and legal barriers to acquiring advanced technology for development.[112] This concern is amplified because the current TRIPS provisions require long durations of IPR protections.[113] One may argue that the protection of IPRs provides an incentive for creations and innovations that may contribute to economic development, but in today's world where technological gaps between developed and developing countries are wider than ever, developing countries cannot close this gap by relying on their own 'creativity' alone.[114] They need access to advance knowledge and technology. In this respect, developing countries today are at a considerably larger disadvantage than those of the past as no international IPR regime was imposed on them or certainly not to the extent imposed by the TRIPS Agreement today.

While the trade effect of IPR violations may need to be addressed, the imposition of an IPR regime clearly and unnecessarily impedes the development interest of developing countries. However, the need to acquire advance knowledge and technology on the part of developing countries does not mean that developed countries have to give up their IPR interests entirely. Alternative provisions that enable developed countries to apply trade sanctions where they demonstrate that a violation of their IPR has led to significant injury to their trade but not provisions that attempt to establish a uniform IPR regime throughout the world is one consideration.[115] In the meantime, the provisions of the TRIPS Agreement should be

---

112. In addition, concern was raised that the compliance requirement of the TRIPS Agreement will impose a considerable financial burden on developing countries, particularly LDCs. According to a study, implementing the TRIPS obligations would require "the least developed countries to invest in buildings, equipment, training, and so forth that would cost each of them $150 million—for many of the least developed countries this represents a full year's development budget". JM Finger, 'The WTO's Special Burden on Less Developed Countries' (2000) 19(3) Cato J 425.

113. TRIPS (n 106 above).

114. On the other hand, if a developing country considers that the extensive protection of IPRs is in their own interest, this country, rather than the WTO, should be trusted to set its own standards for protection under their own laws and regulations. Lee (n 1 above) ch 5.

115. The general exceptions of Article XX already allow trade sanctions to protect IPRs. What seems necessary is to set detailed rules for the substantive and procedural requirements for the application of a trade measure to remedy injury cased by an IPR violation. A Member should be authorized to apply trade measures only where a violation of its IPRs *causes injury* to its domestic industry through trade. An injury test, such as the one found in Article 4.2(a) of the Agreement on Safeguards, should be required to ensure that the measure is applied based on a reasonable assessment of injury caused by IPR violations and not on an arbitrary determination by national authorities. This way, developed countries will be able to protect their own IPR interests by applying their own laws as well as the rules of relevant international IPR conventions, without imposing regulatory burden on developing countries such as the one currently imposed by the TRIPS Agreement. Lee (n 1 above) ch 5.

suspended in favor of developing countries to the extent that it imposes on these countries the establishment of an IPR regime that they are not even ready for.

Extension of special treatment for LDCs Some developed countries have offered preferential treatment to LDCs greater than that provided under the existing GSP scheme. The European Union has introduced the 'Everything But Arms' (EBA) initiative, offering duty-free and quota-free treatment to products currently exported by LDCs.[116] Other countries, such as the United States and Canada, offer similar preferential treatment to LDCs, although less comprehensive and more limited in scope than the EBA initiative.[117] Considering the dire economic need of LDCs, an EBA-type of duty-free and quota-free treatment to the trade of LDCs needs to be implemented by all developed countries and participating developing countries in the WTO. While implementing this initiative in favor of LDCs, a transitional period can be established for the complete removal of trade barriers to sensitive products.[118] Members would also have to ensure that nontariff measures do not undermine the trade benefit of these preferences for LDCs.[119]

ii. The Role of the Council for Trade and Development

The remainder of this section considers the role of the Council for Trade and Development proposed earlier. The primary objective of the new Council is to set a development agenda and promote development interests in the trading system. Its role can include:

i) promotion of a development agenda and implementation of trade related development-assistance policies,
ii) regulatory monitoring concerning development,
iii) instituting and supervising development-assistance activities, including those of committees.

---

116. For an initial evaluation of the EBA initiative, see P Brenton, 'Integrating the Least Developed Countries into the World Trading System: The Current Impact of European Union Preferences Under "Everything But Arms"' (2003) 37(3) JWT 623–26.

117. For instance, the United States has implemented the *Africa Growth and Opportunity Act* which offers improved access to certain African, but not Asian, LDCs. Ibid, 644–45.

118. In the EBA initiative, trade liberalization is complete except for three products: fresh bananas, rice, and sugar, where tariffs will be gradually reduced to zero (in 2006 for bananas and 2009 for rice and sugar). Duty-free tariff quotas for rice and sugar will be increased annually. Ibid, 625.

119. It has been observed that nontariff measures, as well as stringent rules of origin, continue to limit exports from LDCs significantly. S Inama, 'Market Access for LDCs: Issues to Be Addressed' (2002) 36(1) JWT 115. Applications of administered protection, such as antidumping measures, countervailing duties, and safeguards, can also diminish the beneficial effect of preference for LDCs.

Development-assistance policy implementation The Council should create a regulatory environment in the trading system that allows and facilitates the implementation of effective development policies by developing country Members. In doing so, the Council should identify problems and gaps in the current trading system in facilitating development and accordingly set a trade and development agenda on a regular basis. This agenda may be discussed at the Ministerial Conferences and trade negotiation rounds to develop a more development-supportive regulatory system and modify relevant rules when necessary. In promoting a trade and development agenda, the Council should cooperate with relevant international bodies such as the United Nations Committee on Trade and Development (UNCTAD) and the United Nations Industrial Development Organisation (UNIDO). Through such cooperation, the trade and development agenda set by the WTO would be promoted more effectively and consistently throughout the world.

In addition, a mechanism should be devised for developed country Members and participating developing country Members to file a mandatory Trade-Related Development Assistance Report (TDAR) on a regular basis. It would report those Members' activities that are relevant to the compliance with the trade and development agenda set by the Council. The Council should receive and examine TDARs on a regular basis and consult with relevant Members to discuss their development-assistance activities. The Council and developed country Members may agree on specific commitments to be fulfilled by the developed country Members to promote the trade and development agenda, and the Council may further examine, within a certain time period, whether these commitments are being met.

The point of this proposal is to have an independent Council to set a relevant trade and development agenda on a regular basis and, through the reporting mechanism, impose specific commitments on each developed and participating developing country Member to assist with development. The enforceability of these commitments may be questioned as the WTO may not always be able to apply effective sanctions against violating Members. The authorization of retaliatory measures may not be an effective sanction if developing countries do not have leverage against the violating developed country Member. Nonetheless, Council's activities to identify the relevant trade and development agenda and to identify and monitor Members' specific obligations in the trading system will still nevertheless promote development interests. Since the implementation of the WTO, Members have largely complied with the specific obligations imposed by the WTO, even without the threat of sanctions.

Regulatory monitoring The Council should also monitor compliance of development assistance WTO provisions, including the existing S&D provisions, GATT Articles XXXVI–XXXVIII, and the provisions of the suggested ADF. Part of these monitoring elements can be incorporated in the aforementioned TDAR. Violations of these provisions should be reported to the Council if the violations are detrimental to the trade interests of developing country Members. The Council should subsequently consult with the violating Member to seek a resolution. The commitments of developed country Members in GATT Articles XXXII can be monitored by the TDAR. Compliance with these commitments may require a broader policy adjustment by the developed country Member, which may necessitate the monitoring by the Council. The Council should publish an annual report on the compliance status of these development-assistance provisions and provide monitoring of any systematic compliance failure. The Council should include such a problem in the trade and development agenda for possible rule modification.

Instituting and supervising committees The Council should institute standing or ad hoc committees to address specific issues of trade and development that require long-term attention, such as technological transfer between developed and developing country Members. There should be at least one committee specifically devoted to the problems of LDCs and another to assist with building capacities of developing countries to participate fully in the trading system and realize the benefits. Assistance should be provided to developing country Members involved in costly and time-consuming trade disputes, and the current WTO Advisory Center[120] should be expanded to offer assistance to every developing country Member in need of assistance with respect to the panel or Appellate Body proceedings. Consideration should be given as to whether it would serve the need of developing country Members to assign the function of the existing WTO Advisory Center to a committee under the Council for Trade and Development.

D. CONCLUSION—DEVELOPMENT ASSISTANCE FROM RHETORIC TO ACTION

To facilitate development effectively in trade disciplines, it is important to examine the current institutional apparatus and regulatory structure of development-assistance provisions in the WTO. The current Committee on Trade and Development and the development-assistance provisions scattered throughout the GATT/WTO disciplines are not sufficient to meet this objective. Regulatory and organizational reforms are thus necessary to effectively meet the development agenda and implement development-assistance policies. This reform should include the elevation of the CTD to the new Council on Trade and Development and the establishment of a coherent body of rules that facilitate development (ADF).

The proposed expansion of the current organizational apparatus means an expansion of staff and an increase in resources available to assist developing countries. As of 2007, the current WTO budget of 7 million Swiss francs (roughly

---

120. See n 46 above.

$5.8 million) for technical cooperation and training would be inadequate to meet this proposal. Financial assistance from some Members has allowed trade ministers and representatives from developing countries to participate in WTO meetings and negotiations. The financial assistance necessary to enable participation of developing countries should not be left to the generosity of individual Members but should be provided systematically by the WTO. The WTO Advisory Center on WTO Law should also be supported by the WTO budget. The WTO budget allocation to the activities and functions of trade and development should be significantly increased to meet these needs.

Logistics need to be improved to address the needs arising from the limited financial and human resources of developing countries. The scarcity of these resources often prevents developing countries from participating in the trade organization fully, so WTO meetings and negotiation schedules should also be set to allow maximum participation of developing countries.[121] The use of modern technology, such as web technology, should be adopted to increase participation of developing countries, which cannot afford to station experts in Geneva to participate in these meetings without having to travel to Geneva from their home countries. The lack of participation by developing countries in WTO processes has been often pointed out as a reason for the poor representation of the interests of developing countries; thus ways to relieve these difficulties, such as the proposals made above, should be sought.

The monitoring and enforcement mechanism of the development-assistance provisions and policies should also be devised. The requirement of a Trade-Related Development Assistance Report can be considered. Developed country Members should be required to make this Report regularly, subject to review by the Council for Trade and Development. Willing developing country Members may also participate in the reporting process on a voluntary basis. This Report requirement will be consistent with the objectives of development facilitation manifested in Part IV of GATT. The proposed organizational and regulatory reform, as well as this suggested improvement of practical logistics, would help to turn what many have doubted as merely 'rhetoric for development assistance' into real and effective actions to assist developing countries.

---

121. Renato Ruggiero, the former general-director of the WTO, acknowledged that some developing and least-developed countries had difficulty in participating fully in the organization, mainly due to too many meetings. He believed that it was an objective problem, but not the result of a deliberate policy of exclusion. *Report 1999* (n 51 above).

PART THREE
SUBSTANTIVE CHALLENGES

13. SPECIAL AND DIFFERENTIAL TREATMENT IN AGRICULTURAL TRADE
Breaking the Impasse

TRACEY D EPPS AND MICHAEL J TREBILCOCK*

A. Introduction 323
B. From Geneva to Uruguay 326
C. Agreement on Agriculture (AOA) 334
D. The Doha Development Round 341
  I. What is at Stake for Developing Countries? 341
  II. The Doha Development Round Agenda 344
  III. Negotiating Positions 345
E. Breaking the Impasse? 351
F. Conclusion 362

A. INTRODUCTION

We have frankly exhausted all other avenues and the prospect of failure is, as a consequence, now so familiar to us that it can almost present itself seductively to us as our friend. (Ambassador Crawford Falconer, Chairman of the Committee on Agriculture, Special Session, Revised Draft Modalities for Agriculture, August 2007)

In his 1987 book, *Developing Countries in the GATT Legal System*, Robert Hudec wrote that both critics and supporters of the GATT's policies toward developing countries speak of the same ultimate goal—the maximum possible improvement in the economic welfare of developing countries.[1] Hudec also wrote of the difficulties in achieving this goal due to the fact that none of the legal strategies then available to developing countries appeared to offer much help in improving the behavior of developed countries toward them. In particular, he was skeptical that special and differential treatment (SDT), as it had

---

* Lecturer, Faculty of Law, University of Otago, New Zealand; and University Professor, Faculty of Law, University of Toronto, Canada, respectively. We are indebted to Dr Brett Williams, University of Sydney Law School and Chantal Thomas, University of Minnesota Law School, for helpful comments on an earlier draft.
1. R Hudec, *Developing Countries in the GATT Legal System* (London: Gower, 1987) 131.

come to be understood, offered much prospect for improving the welfare of developing countries:

> Consequently the first major recommendation of this study is that developing countries should redirect their long-term objectives to the strengthening of GATT's most-favored-nation obligation in all respects. Developing countries should stop spending diplomatic capital trying to enlarge preferences under the Enabling Clause and, instead, should accept the progressive dilution of GSP and other preference systems through MFN tariff reduction and should allow the current GSP initiative to languish. . . .
>
> [This conclusion points] to the second major recommendation of this study— that GATT's legal policy toward developing countries should change and . . . the contracting parties should instead establish a regime of developing country legal obligations that would provide support for governments of developing countries in opposing unwanted protectionist policies at home. Such a change would involve setting aside both the principle of nonreciprocity and the principle of preferential treatment.[2]

It has become increasingly apparent that not only have the Uruguay Round Agreements largely failed to ameliorate the state of affairs described by Hudec in 1987,[3] but that in the agricultural sector, they may have actually impacted adversely on developing countries.[4] Today, the international trading community is faced with the question not only of what policies would better serve developing countries but of what is realistic in the current geopolitical environment.

The goal of improving the economic welfare of developing countries is uppermost in the rhetoric of today's trade liberalization agenda. The Doha Declaration speaks of the promotion of economic development and the alleviation of poverty and states that Members shall make 'positive efforts designed to ensure that developing countries, and especially the least-developed among them, secure a share in the growth of world trade commensurate with the needs of their economic development'.[5]

---

2. Hudec, ibid 228–29.

3. See generally B Hoekman, 'Operationalizing the Concept of Policy Space in the WTO: Beyond Special and Differential Treatment' (2005) 8 JIEL 2 405; B Hoekman, C Michalopoulos and LA Winters, 'Special and Differential Treatment of Developing Countries in the WTO: Moving Forward After Cancun' (2004) 24 W Econ 4 481; and M Pangestu, 'Special and Differential Treatment in the Millennium: Special for Whom and How Different?' (2000) 23(9) W Econ 1285.

4. See generally, United Nations Development Programme, *Making Global Trade Work for People* (London and Sterling, Virginia: Earthscan Publications Limited, 2003). UNDP finds, for example, (at 132) that the Philippines experienced its first agricultural trade deficits since the 1970s in the six years following the 1994 Uruguay Round agreements, and that the Agreement on Agriculture played a key role in this process. See also MD Ingco and JD Nash, 'Agriculture and the WTO—Creating a Trading System for Development' (Washington, DC: The World Bank & Oxford University Press 2004).

5. WTO, 'Doha WTO Ministerial 2001: Ministerial Declaration' WT/MIN(01)/DEC/1.

Indeed, in launching the current round of multilateral negotiations in 2001, delegates officially characterized it as the 'Doha Development Round'. Yet while consensus can be reached on the goal, questions remain as to whether there is a genuine commitment on the part of developed countries to its operationalization. As former US Trade Representative Charlene Barshefsky stated: 'there may have been the broad "intention" on the part of the wealthy nations to make this a development round, but their ability to execute has always, in important respects, been absent—something clear from the outset, rhetoric aside'.[6]

As noted above, since the 1950s, the GATT/WTO has sought to address inequitable distribution of wealth among its Members and integrate developing countries more fully into the world trading system through a policy of what has come to be known as SDT. As we will discuss in more detail, there are three broad limbs of SDT which apply to agriculture as well as other sectors. On the *import* side, SDT has traditionally entailed the policy freedom of developing countries to protect their domestic industries for either balance-of-payment or infant-industry reasons. By implication, this has meant that on the *export* side, developing countries could not be expected to provide concessions to developed countries in return for access to their markets. Thus, the second ('export') limb revolved around the idea of nonreciprocal trade concessions and preferences granted by rich countries to developing countries. With implementation of the Uruguay Round 'single undertaking' and its associated obligations, the import side of SDT also came to include longer transitional periods for implementation. In addition, a third limb was established, that of encouraging developed countries to provide technical assistance to developing countries in various areas. Much has been written as to the merits, or otherwise, of SDT. Given doubts of the kind expressed by Hudec in 1987 as to whether SDT measures actually serve the needs of developing countries, the question arises as to whether developing countries would be better served by abandoning the SDT agenda in favor of stronger involvement in setting multilateral trade rules.[7]

Nowhere does this question have greater salience than in the negotiations on trade in agriculture, which for many developing countries have become the focal point of the Doha Development Round. Difficulties of integration faced by developing countries are particularly acute in the agricultural sector, where developed countries continue to protect their markets, leaving developing countries struggling to participate successfully in world markets. Compounding this situation is the importance of the agricultural sector in the economies of developing countries. Described as the primary engine of economic growth in low-income

---

6. D Altman, 'Managing Globalization: Q&A with Charlene Barshefsky', International Herald Tribune Blog <http://blogs.iht.com/tribtalk/business/globalization/?p=342> (date accessed: 20 May 2008).

7. MF Jensen, 'African Demands for Special and Differential Treatment in the Doha Round: An Assessment and Analysis' (2007) 25(1) Dev Pol Rev 91, 92.

countries, it is responsible on average for 24 percent of GDP in low-income developing countries.[8] It also plays a significant role in middle-income developing countries, where, although it accounts for less than 10 percent of GDP, it accounts on average for one-quarter of total employment.[9] While there is debate over the precise extent to which liberalization of agricultural markets will contribute to growth of the sector in developing countries, there is a strong consensus that the outcome of the Doha Round Negotiations in agriculture is critical for developing countries.

Special and Differential Treatment (SDT) has thus emerged as a key issue in the agricultural talks of the Doha Round Negotiations. Developed and developing countries have been unable to agree on a mutually satisfactory way forward. This paper will review the role of SDT policies in agricultural trade and will explore the possibilities for an approach that takes account both of political realities and the ultimate goal of economic improvement for developing countries. Section B reviews the historical development of SDT policies, while Section C pays particular attention to agriculture in the Uruguay Round and considers whether such policies have achieved what developing countries hoped they would. Section D explores what is at stake for developing countries in the Doha Development Round and examines the arguments relating to SDT policies in the agricultural sector. Finally, Section E considers possibilities for a way forward that takes account of the goal of SDT policies as they have been conceived by developing countries, as well as the interests of developed countries and the *realpolitik* of trade negotiations.

B. FROM GENEVA TO URUGUAY

As noted in the Introduction, prior to the Uruguay Round, SDT measures fell into two categories: those relating to *imports* (policy flexibility) and those relating to *exports* (enhanced and preferential nonreciprocal market access). With the implementation of the Uruguay Round Agreements, they took on the added dimension of technical assistance, at least for the issues that were the subject of the new agreements such as the SPS Agreement and the TRIPS Agreement. Here, we look at the development of these measures from the birth of GATT in 1947 through to the conclusion of the Uruguay Round in 1994.

The GATT was established in 1947 with 23 signatories, including 11 developing countries. Despite such a significant proportion of developing country Members, the Agreement did not initially recognize them as a group and made no special provision for their benefit. However, by the 1950s, developing

---

8. MD Ingco and JD Nash, 'Agriculture and the WTO—Creating a Trading System for Development' (Washington DC: The World Bank & Oxford University Press, 2004) 2.
9. Ibid.

countries had begun to raise concerns and identify the challenges that they faced in international trade.[10] They argued that it was not realistic to expect them to compete on a level playing field with industrialized countries and that free trade would only entrench the legacy of colonialism and dependence on primary commodities.[11] Their case for SDT was thus in part based upon notions of fairness and equality and the belief that trade policies which maximize welfare in the currently rich industrialized countries may not be the same as those which do the most to promote development in the poorest countries.[12]

Developing countries made their case for infant-industry protection based on the theory that they had inherited truncated economies from their former colonial powers that rendered them little more than hewers of wood and drawers of water (or sources of natural resources). They saw industrialization as a way out of dependence on primary commodities and thus sought to shift resources from the traditional agricultural sector, where the marginal product of labor was thought often to be close to zero, to the industrial sector.[13] However, they argued that this could only be achieved if infant-domestic industries were protected from low-cost producers already established in the international market. They also noted that many currently rich industrialized countries had deployed such policies earlier in their economic development. They thus argued for inclusion in the GATT of provisions that would enable them to protect their infant industries. Developing countries also saw the ability to impose import restrictions as crucial to addressing often chronic balance-of-payment problems. Related to these economic rationales for SDT was the notion that developing countries would face disproportionately high adjustment costs from trade liberalization which they would have difficulty mitigating, given low levels of education, poor infrastructure, weakly developed financial markets, and often weak social safety nets. It is important to note that at this time, developing countries were for the most part focused on expanding their industrial sectors and did not view agriculture as a sector with potential to contribute toward economic growth and development. The economic rationales advanced for SDT were therefore based predominantly around its potential to protect industry.

---

10. The following description of the history of SDT relies in large part on the succinct overview provided by Hunter Nottage: H Nottage, 'Trade and Competition in the WTO: Pondering the Applicability of Special and Differential Treatment' (2003) 6(1) JIEL 23, 24.

11. E Acorn, *Learning from Experience: Special and Differential Treatment in the World Trade Organization* (Toronto: University of Toronto, 2006) 6 (on file with the authors).

12. JE Stiglitz and A Charlton, *Fair Trade For All: How Trade Can Promote Development* (New York: Oxford University Press, 2005) 88.

13. For intellectual histories of development theories, see M Todaro, 'Classic Theories of Development: A Comparative Analysis' in *Economic Development* (9th edn, Addison-Wesley-Longman, 2006) and HW Arndt, *Economic Development: The History of an Idea* (University of Chicago Press, 1987).

This push by developing countries led to the redrafting of Article XVIII (Government Assistance to Economic Development) at the 1954–1955 GATT Review Session. The redrafted Article specifically addressed developing countries through provisions relating to *imports*. They provided developing countries with policy space and flexibility by allowing them to, *inter alia*, derogate from scheduled tariff commitments in order to promote the establishment of a particular industry (Article XVIII, Section A); use quantitative restrictions for balance-of-payment purposes (Article XVIII, Section B); along with other measures to promote certain industries (Article XVIII, Section C). In addition, the Members amended two other provisions to make allowances for developing countries: Article XVI.4 allowed the use of export subsidies for manufactured goods, while Article XXVIII*bis* permitted more flexibility in modifying tariff commitments.

Developed countries continued to push for greater recognition in the GATT and in 1964 at the conclusion of the Kennedy Round, the Members addressed the *export* side of SDT by adopting Part IV of the GATT. Part IV specifically addressed 'Trade and Development' and encouraged developed countries to recognize the importance of market access for developing countries. Most important, however, Part IV formalized the principle of 'nonreciprocity'. Article XXXVI.8 exempted developing countries from having to make reciprocal tariff concessions, stating that 'the developed contracting parties do not expect reciprocity for commitments made by them in trade negotiations to reduce or remove tariffs and other barriers to trade of less-developed contracting parties'.

The significance of the nonreciprocity principle must be understood in the context of mercantilist assumptions which hold that countries stand to benefit from expanding exports because exports create larger markets for a country's own producers and more employment for their workers. Conversely, countries are thought to lose when they increase imports because this will lead to a smaller market share for their own producers, leading to smaller profits and less employment. In 1987, Hudec argued that while this concept had been largely discredited among economists,[14] it continued to be influential in political and business circles.[15] He noted that governments had a tendency to justify reduction of trade barriers in mercantilist terms by placing strong emphasis on reciprocity, showing that reduction of trade barriers at home (increased imports) will be matched by a similar reduction abroad (increased exports).[16] That reciprocity was, and still remains, a key feature of the world trading regime is highlighted in the

---

14. Note, however, that K Bagwell and R Staiger, *The Economics of the World Trading System* (Cambridge, Mass: MIT Press, 2002), have recently argued that reciprocity internalizes Prisoners' Dilemma terms of trade externalities among larger economies from trade protection.

15. Hudec (n 1 above) 143.

16. Ibid.

Preambles to both the GATT[17] and the Marrakesh Agreement Establishing the World Trade Organization. The latter refers to the Members' desire to enter into 'reciprocal and mutually advantageous arrangements'. Seen in this context, it becomes apparent that the principle of nonreciprocity is not one that developed countries will accept lightly. As we will discuss further, developing countries' insistence on the continuation and even strengthening of the principle does not sit well with governments of industrialized countries who must justify trade liberalization policies to their domestic constituencies.

The *export* side of SDT was strengthened on the basis of the nonreciprocity principle during the Tokyo Round in the 1970s. The 'Differential and More Favourable Treatment, Reciprocity and Fuller Participation of Developing Countries' framework agreement (the 'Enabling Clause') adopted in 1979 following a temporary MFN waiver adopted in 1971 created a permanent legal basis for preferential tariff treatment to exports from developing countries accorded under the Generalized Scheme of Preferences (GSP)[18] as well as greater flexibility in the formation of preferential trade regimes between developing countries. The Enabling Clause also introduced the concept of special treatment for least-developed countries (LDCs). Provision for preferential access arrangements was based primarily on the assumption that such arrangements could produce economic benefits for developing countries.[19] The assumption is based in part on the argument that, unlike infant-industry protection, the use of preferences allows for extranational economies of scale, at least to the extent that the major competitors preventing the realization of economies of scale in the short run are located outside the countries enjoying preferential access.[20]

There are limits to the use of preferential trading arrangements, however, including supply-side constraints such as lack of physical infrastructure, education, well-functioning financial markets, and modern technologies, which mean that a number of developing countries simply do not have the ability to take advantage of market openings, even where they exist.[21] Despite these constraints, there has been significant interest in preferential trading arrangements both

---

17. As Finger observes, at the time the original GATT was signed, the good that trade economists see in trade policy was not of sufficient political weight to force changes in domestic programs of any importance. JM Finger, 'A diplomat's economics: reciprocity in the Uruguay Round Negotiations' (2005) 4(1) WT Rev 27, 28.

18. The GSP was implemented under the auspices of UNCTAD in 1971: Resolution 21(II) of the Second UNCTAD Conference, in UNCTAD, Proceedings of the Conference of 1968, Report and Annexes (United Nations, TD/97).

19. Hudec (n 1 above) 151.

20. The Danish Institute for International Studies & The Food and Resource Economics Institute, 'Special and Differential Treatment and Differentiation between Developing Countries in the WTO' (2005) The Danish Institute for International Studies & The Food and Resource Economics Institute 6.

21. Ibid 9.

politically and in the academic and policy literature.[22] Indeed, preferential-access measures have gained impetus in recent years, with the European Union and United States both taking steps to improve preference schemes for African countries, via the United States' African Growth and Opportunity Act[23] and the European Union's Everything But Arms (EBA) Regulation.[24]

Early on, economists began to question the assumptions regarding infant-industry protection and preferential access. Research in the 1970s suggested that the policies in place were failing to achieve their goals,[25] and some even suggested that these policies were actually hindering the growth of developing countries. Several studies suggested that infant-industry protection was both inefficient as a means to achieve industrialization and development and was often accompanied by a rise in rent-seeking behavior and corruption in government administration. It was suggested that trade barriers designed to protect infant industries created disincentives to export as protection distorted relative prices in favor of import competing production. Thus, many infant industries remained inefficient and failed to become competitive exporters.[26] Balassa found that protectionist policies had hurt developing countries by encouraging industrialization at the expense of agriculture, leading to increased levels of rural poverty, worsened income distribution, reduced domestic savings, increased unemployment, and a lower rate of capital utilization.[27] In parallel with these findings, economic research began to highlight the value to developing countries of open trade policies, for example, by contrasting the growth experiences

---

22. See, for example, S Page and P Kleen, 'Special and Differential Treatment of Developing countries in the World Trade Organization' (Report commissioned by the Secretariat for the Expert Group on Development Issues, 2005).

23. Signed into law on May 18, 2000 as Title 1 of the Trade and Development Act of 2000.

24. EBA grants duty-free access to imports of all products from LDCs, except arms and ammunitions. It was adopted in February 2001 by Regulation (EC) 416/2001 and was later incorporated into GSP Council Regulation (EC) No. 2501/2001.

25. M Pangestu, 'Special and Differential Treatment in the Millennium: Special for Whom and How Different?' (2000) 23(9) W Econ 1285, 1295.

26. See, for example I Little, T Sctivosky and M Scott, *Industry and Trade in Some Developing Countries* (London: Oxford University Press, 1970); B Balassa, *The Structure of Protection in Developing Countries* (Baltimore: John Hopkins University Press, 1971); J Bhagwati, *Foreign Trade Regimes and Economic Development: Anatomy and Consequences of Exchange Control Regimes* (New York: National Bureau of Economic Research, 1978); AO Krueger, *Liberalization Attempts and Consequences* (New York: National Bureau of Economic Research, 1978); and C Michalopoulos, *The Role of Special and Differential Treatment for Developing Countries in GATT and the World Trade Organization* (Washington, DC: The World Bank, 2000) 11.

27. B Balassa ibid.

of rapidly growing and outward-oriented East Asian economies with low growth in many other inward-oriented developing economies.[28]

By the 1980s, many developing countries themselves were questioning the effectiveness and value of SDT, the results of which had proven to be disappointing. In addition to evidence that industries protected by high tariffs were not internationally competitive,[29] there was also evidence that trade and exchange controls were not as efficient in addressing balance-of-payment problems as fiscal and monetary instruments.[30] In addition to these factors, developing countries were experiencing serious market access problems. The nonreciprocity principle did not appear to be helping developing countries make inroads into industrialized countries' markets. As Trachtman argues, those who are not required to reciprocate often find that few concessions are accorded to them.[31] As he notes, the products of export interest to developing countries often differ from those of interest to other countries, and thus are not included in the give-and-take of negotiations over concessions. The evidence reflects these concerns. By the 1980s, tariff escalation was substantial, hindering the entry of developing countries into world-processed goods markets. Rather, there is evidence that the opposite occurred, with the share of developing countries in world exports of processed agricultural products decreasing from 27 percent in 1981–1990 to 25 percent in 1991–2000. For LDCs, the share in processed agricultural exports fell from 0.7 to 0.3 percent over this period.[32] In addition, developing countries were negatively affected by the use of contingent protection measures by developed countries, including antidumping duties, countervailing measures, and 'grey-area measures' such as voluntary export restraints.[33]

Preferences were not proving to be as useful as developing countries had envisaged. First, the benefits of the preferences seemed to be concentrated on the more advanced developing countries which needed them the least. Studies have found that GSP schemes have only had minimal benefits for

---

28. See discussion in D Irwin, 'Trade and Development: A Review of the Debate' (2003), Yale Center for the Study of Globalization, Background Papers Prepared for the UN Millennium Project International Task Force on Trade); M Noland and H Pack, *Industrial Policy in an Era of Globalization: Lessons from Asia* (Institute for International Economics, March 2003).

29. M Pangestu, 'Special and Differential Treatment in the Millennium: Special for Whom and How Different?' (2000) 23(9) W Econ 1285, 1289.

30. See generally J Bhagwati, *Anatomy and Consequences of Exchange Control Regimes* (New York: National Bureau of Economic Research, 1978).

31. J Trachtman, 'Legal Aspects of a Poverty Agenda at the WTO: Trade Law and 'Global Apartheid'' (2003) 6 JIEL 1, 3, 11.

32. N Elamin and H Khaira, 'Tariff Escalation in Agricultural Commodity Markets' (Food and Agriculture Organization (FAO), Rome 2003) 102.

33. H Nottage, 'Trade and Competition in the WTO: Pondering the Applicability of Special and Differential Treatment' (2003) 6(1) JIEL 23, 28.

developing countries.[34] A 1987 study found that four beneficiaries—Brazil, Hong Kong, Korea, and Taiwan—derived more than 50 percent of all GSP benefits.[35] Second, GSP market-access preferences were becoming less beneficial in any event as margins of preference were eroded through successive negotiating rounds which reduced MFN tariff levels. Preferences were also less secure since they were increasingly being tied to the level of economic development and countries with higher incomes were being 'graduated' out of the programs. They were also increasingly subject to conditions such as human and labor rights, especially in sensitive areas such as agricultural products. Donor countries can also withdraw preferences if the imports become too competitive with domestic producers. The United States, for example, will withdraw GSP preferences if imports of the item exceed $115 million or account for 50 percent or more of annual imports of the item.[36] Nontariff barriers and rules of origin also dilute the value of GSP preferences; the European Union, for example, maintains strict rules of origin that inhibit developing countries' ability to produce goods at the lowest possible cost.[37]

A further problem with preferences is that they cause trade diversion from nonpreference recipient developing countries to the preference recipients. Where the diversion is from countries who could produce the products in question at a lower cost, this can lead to a decrease in world prices for the product and a terms-of-trade loss for nonrecipient countries that export the same product. Thus, while they may benefit some countries in the short term, they are unlikely to benefit developing countries overall and may create inducements to distort comparative advantage which puts the preference recipients at risk in the long term if and when preferences are withdrawn.[38]

These problems with SDT were particularly pronounced in the agricultural sector which remained essentially excluded from GATT commitments. In 1955, the United States had obtained a waiver of its GATT Article XI obligations with respect to a variety of agricultural products, including sugar, peanuts, and dairy products. While not obtaining a formal waiver, the European Union had either blocked the adoption of, or refused to implement, panel decisions that threatened

---

34. See, for example, G Karsenty and S Laird, 'The Generalized System of Preferences: A Quantitative Assessment of the Direct Trade Effects and of Policy Options' (1987) UNCTAD Discussion Paper 18.

35. Ibid.

36. GB Grossman and AO. Sykes, 'A Preference for Development: The Law and Economics of GSP' (2005) 4 WT Rev 41 at 61.

37. P Brenton and M Manchin, 'Making EU Trade Agreements Work: The Role of Rules of Origin' (2003) 26 W Econ 755.

38. GB Grossman and AO Sykes, 'A Preference for Development: The Law and Economics of GSP' (2005) 4 WT Rev 41, 61.

its Common Agricultural Policy.[39] As Josling, Tangermann, and Warley note, developing countries were faced with the 'double jeopardy' of virtually closed OECD markets alongside subsidized European competition in their domestic and third-country markets.[40]

At the same time as developing countries began to question the effectiveness of SDT, many began to reconsider what trade policies would be appropriate to development. In the early 1980s, a fall in commodity prices forced countries who were dependent on commodity exports to consider diversification strategies. Combined with increased competition in world markets, this pushed some countries to become more competitive, including liberalizing their trade regimes to increase competition in domestic markets.[41] However, some developing countries remained committed to policies of import substitution, causing a divide in what had previously been a fairly homogeneous negotiating bloc. By the time the Uruguay Round Negotiations began, it was not clear whether there was a consensus among developing countries on whether SDT was any longer considered a priority.[42] Reflecting Hudec's views, Gibbs writes that some developing countries referred to SDT as 'ideological baggage' from the past, or a 'crutch' which was no longer required and had to be discarded if countries wanted to become competitive in world markets.[43] While still seeking maintenance of preferential access arrangements, negotiators from developing countries who had developed an export-led growth strategy focused much of their effort on obtaining better market access and strengthened rules with respect to measures such as voluntary export restraints, the use of antidumping and countervailing duties, lower MFN tariffs for products of interest to developing countries, tariff escalation, and the ineffectiveness of GATT disciplines on agricultural trade.[44]

---

39. MJ Trebilcock and R Howse, *The Regulation of International Trade* (3rd edn, London and New York: Routledge, 2005) 322.

40. T Josling, S Tangermann and TK Warley, *Agriculture in the GATT* (London: St Martin's, 1996) 402.

41. M Pangestu, 'Special and Differential Treatment in the Millennium: Special for Whom and How Different?' (2000) 23 W Econ 9, 1285, 1290. Pangestu notes that while some of these reforms were initiated under World Bank Structural Adjustment loans, others were undertaken on a unilateral basis.

42. The Danish Institute for International Studies & The Food and Resource Economics Institute, 'Special and Differential Treatment and Differentiation between Developing Countries in the WTO' (The Danish Institute for International Studies & The Food and Resource Economics Institute, Copenhagen & Frederiksberg, 2005) viii.

43. M Gibbs, 'Special and Differential Treatment in the Context of Globalization', Note presented at the G15 Symposium on Special and Differential Treatment in the WTO Agreements (New Delhi, 10 December 1998). Cited in Pangestu (n 39 above) 1291.

44. H Nottage, 'Trade and Competition in the WTO: Pondering the Applicability of Special and Differential Treatment' (2003) 6(1) JIEL 23, 28. Ibid 1290.

C. AGREEMENT ON AGRICULTURE (AOA)

While SDT had fallen out of favor somewhat by the launch of the Uruguay Round Negotiations, it remained enough of an imperative for developing countries that the Agreements resulting from that Round contain a large number of SDT provisions. However, the focus of these provisions shifted away from the traditional notion of treating developing countries as exceptional, to an attempt to further their integration into the world trading system.[45] This was sought to be achieved through asking developing countries to take on the same substantive rights and obligations as developed countries and was consistent with the nature of the negotiations as a single undertaking which meant developing countries either had to accept the full package of agreements or none at all. Special and Differential Treatment provisions were intended to assist in the integration process. Thus, the Uruguay Round Agreements introduced, on the *import* side, provisions giving developing countries extended time periods to comply with various obligations. In addition, they added a new layer of SDT provisions aimed to assist developing countries adjust to the liberalization required of them by having developed countries provide them with technical assistance. The Agreements also provided specifically for LDCs. The AOA reflects this approach as discussed below.

On the *export* side, the AOA aims to increase trade opportunities for developing countries through increased *market access*. The Preamble states the goal of 'providing for greater improvement of opportunities and terms of access for agricultural products of particular interest to [developing countries], including the fullest liberalization of trade in tropical agricultural products . . . and for products of particular importance to the diversification of production from the growing of illicit narcotic crops'.

The evidence available shows that despite these commitments, developing countries continue to face a number of trade related impediments in expanding production and returns in their agricultural sectors. Despite the AOA requirements to reduce tariffs, many rich countries maintain extremely high tariff rates on agricultural products. First, the base rates resulting from the tariffication exercise in converting quotas into tariffs were extremely high in OECD countries. Second, the requirement to reduce tariffs by 36 percent on a simple average basis, with a minimum reduction of 15 percent, allowed developed countries to minimize reductions in sensitive products, many of which are products of export interest to developing countries, for example, sugar, fruit, vegetables, rice, cereals, and livestock products.[46]

---

45. E Acorn, *Learning from Experience: Special and Differential Treatment in the World Trade Organization* (Toronto: University of Toronto, 2006) 16.

46. A Hoda and A Gulati, 'Special and Differential Treatment in Agricultural Negotiations' in G Anania, and others (eds), *Agricultural Policy Reform and the WTO: Where Are We Heading?* (Edward Elgar, 2004) 364.

Developed country tariff rates are often particularly high in the above-quota categories. The above-quota categories are a consequence of the AOA's two-tier tariff system which came about due to the recognition that despite tariff reductions, many tariffs would remain high. Thus, to provide market access for products subject to high tariffs, tariff rate quotas were established whereby a certain volume of imports would be allowed at a much lower rate. In 1999 the European Union maintained a quota tariff rate for 2 million tons of corn imports at a price of 24.45 euros per ton. However, the most-favored-nation (above-quota) rate was 48.45 euros per ton.[47]

Market access continues to be hindered by tariff peaks (the presence of relatively high tariffs amidst generally low tariff levels[48]) and tariff escalation (where tariffs on unprocessed products are disproportionately lower than the tariffs on processed products, creating disincentives against manufacturing and value-added activities). Tariff peaks are frequent in various agricultural sectors, including beef, chocolate, and dairy products.[49] Tariff peaks may, Trachtman suggests, be the result of the principle of nonreciprocity or of simple political economy and a desire to protect the jobs of the relatively poor in rich countries.[50]

Tariff escalation has continued to be a problem for developing countries in the post-Uruguay period, with several studies confirming that tariff escalation remains a major factor in hindering export growth, diversification, and sustainable development in developing countries.[51] Tariff escalation affects both basic food commodities and tropical and horticultural products and may occur both between raw and semifinished products and between semifinished and finished products. In most cases, escalation is greatest between raw and finished products. The United Nations Food and Agriculture Organization (FAO) examined tariffs on 16 commodity chains in the Quad countries (United States, European Union, Japan, and Canada), and found that 12 suffered from tariff escalation. Nearly 60 percent of tariff escalation pairs had tariff wedges (which measure the difference between tariffs in primary and processed stages) of between 1 and 10 percent, while about 10 percent had tariff wedges exceeding 50 percent.[52]

---

47. United Nations Development Programme, *Making Global Trade Work for People* (London and Sterling, Virginia: Earthscan Publications Limited, 2003) 114.

48. Tariff peaks are often referred to as rates that are more than three times the national average and are sometimes also referred to as 'mega-tariffs'. UNCTAD, 'Back to Basics: Market Access Issues in the Doha Agenda' (New York: UNCTAD, 2003) 18.

49. Ibid 20.

50. J Trachtman, 'Legal Aspects of a Poverty Agenda at the WTO: Trade Law and 'Global Apartheid'' (2003) 6(1) JIEL 3, 13.

51. See, for example, N Elamin and H Khaira, 'Tariff Escalation in Agricultural Commodity Markets' (Food and Agriculture Organization (FAO), Rome, 2003). UNCTAD (n 46 above). A Rae and T Josling, 'Processed food trade and developing countries: protection and trade liberalization' (2003) 28 Food Pol 147.

52. N Elamin and H Khaira (note 49 above) 108.

However, it is not only the rich industrialized countries that engage in tariff escalation; an UNCTAD study found that it is present in developing countries as well, thus inhibiting South-South trade.[53]

A number of OECD countries maintain high levels of export subsidies which distort world commodity markets and make it difficult for developing countries to compete.[54] It has been estimated that as a result of export subsidies, farmers in the European Union and the United States are able to export some crops at prices more than a third lower than the cost of production.[55] Market access for developing countries is also impeded by rich countries' domestic support measures that artificially increase production and distort trade. In 2001, the total amount of OECD support in the agricultural sector was $311 billion, an amount approximately equal to the GDP of all countries in Sub-Saharan Africa.[56] A recent study argues that the AOA's disciplines on domestic support are biased toward developed countries who have been able to take advantage of the AOA's 'amber' box. The amber box is a category created by the AOA that applies to domestic policies with a direct effect on production and trade. This type of support is required to be cut back with reduction amounts based on Members' calculation of how much support of this kind they were providing per year for the agricultural sector in the base years of 1986–1988. The United Nations Development Programme (UNDP) argues that 1986–1988 levels were high enough in developed countries that the required reduction has not prevented them from continuing to provide substantial support to domestic sectors. Further, developed countries have been able to increase support for sensitive products of export interest to developing countries (rice, sugar, dairy products) due to the fact that reduction commitments were framed in aggregate rather than product-specific terms.[57]

The Enabling Clause remains in force, which permits developed countries to grant trade preferences to developing countries. However, as in the pre-Uruguay period, while the GSP programs have been found to have had modest benefits, they have not been applied to provide greater market access for many of the products that are most important to developing countries.[58] Further, several factors have diminished the utility of the scheme. These include exclusion of

---

53. UNCTAD (n 46 above) 27.

54. MD Ingco and JD Nash, 'Agriculture and the WTO - Creating a Trading System for Development' (Washington, DC: The World Bank & Oxford University Press, 2004) 10.

55. United Nations Development Programme, *Making Global Trade Work for People* (London and Sterling, Virginia: Earthscan Publications Limited, 2003) 120.

56. Ingco and Nash (n 52 above) 8.

57. United Nations Development Programme, *Making Global Trade Work for People* (London and Sterling, Virginia: Earthscan Publications Limited, 2003) 119.

58. J Trachtman, 'Legal Aspects of a Poverty Agenda at the WTO: Trade Law and 'Global Apartheid'' (2003) 6(1) JIEL 3, 11.

products that are deemed to be 'import-sensitive' (often in response to pressure from domestic industries whose products compete with those of developing countries),[59] increasing conditionality on preferences, ceilings on eligible exports, and graduation of countries out of the schemes.[60] These issues are compounded by the continued erosion of preferences as a result of MFN reductions of tariffs as well as an increase in regional arrangements such as the Cotonou Agreement providing deeper and more secure preferences than the GSP. Also on the *export* side, Article 9 of the Safeguards Agreement provides that developed countries shall not apply safeguard measures against a product originating in a developing country as long as its share of imports of the product concerned in the importing Member does not exceed 3 percent.

On the *import* side, Article 9.1 of the Safeguards Agreement allows developing countries to extend the period of application of a safeguard measure for a period of up to two years beyond the maximum allowed for developed countries. Regarding *flexibility of commitments*, the AOA permits developing countries to offer lower reduction rates with respect to tariffs. Least-developed countries were required to set and bind tariffs but were not required to undertake any reduction commitments.[61] Many developing countries took advantage of the option to offer ceiling bindings so that they would not have to go through the procedure of computing tariff equivalents to quotas and binding those tariffs.[62] Most developing countries chose to implement ceiling bindings at relatively high levels, leaving them flexibility to determine tariff levels at a later date.

With respect to export subsidies, reductions had only to be two-thirds of those offered by developed countries. In addition, Article 6 of the AOA allows developing countries some latitude with respect to domestic support. Article 6.2 provides exemptions from reductions for investment subsidies which are generally available to agriculture in developing country Members, agricultural input subsidies generally available to low-income or resource-poor producers in developing country Members, and domestic support to producers in developing country members to encourage diversification from growing illicit narcotic crops. In addition, Article 6.4(b) sets a higher *de minimus* threshold on domestic support for developing countries, meaning that they are entitled to maintain trade-distorting domestic support up to 10 percent of the total value of production, as

---

59. FJ Garcia, 'Trade and Inequality: Economic Justice and the Developing World" (1999-2000) 21 Mich JIL 975, 1034.

60. J Trachtman, 'Legal Aspects of a Poverty Agenda at the WTO: Trade Law and 'Global Apartheid'" (2003) 6(1) JIEL 3, 11.

61. Article 15.2 of the AOA. LDCs in the WTO are identified according to three criteria adopted by the Economic and Social Council of the United Nations, namely, income levels (Gross National Income per capital under $750), human resource weakness, and economic vulnerability. <http://www.un.org/special-rep/ohrlls/ldc/ldc%20criteria.htm>.

62. Modalities for the Establishment of Specific Binding Commitments, para 14.

compared to 5 percent for developed countries. These provisions have had little practical relevance for most developing countries due to their already low levels of domestic support and export subsidies.[63]

As noted, a new aspect of SDT in the Uruguay Round Agreements covers *transitional time periods* and *technical assistance*. *Transitional time periods* are reflected in Article 15.2 of the AOA which allowed developing countries to implement reduction commitments over a period of up to ten years, compared to six years for developed countries. In practice, this flexibility has proven to be of little real value to most developing countries as they had little to reduce in the way of domestic support and export subsidies in the first place. The new branch of SDT, *technical assistance*, is not covered in the AOA, but is an important aspect of the SPS Agreement. The SPS Agreement is of concern to developing countries due to the potential for developed countries to set strict sanitary or phytosanitary standards which effectively act as nontariff barriers to trade given the difficulties facing developing countries in meeting such standards.

Finally, the 'Decision on Measures Concerning the Possible Negative Effects on LDCs and Net Food Importing Developing Countries' provides for access to concessional financing facilities in the event of difficulties arising in financing food imports, commitments on food aid availability, as well as requiring full consideration to be given to requests for technical and financial assistance to improve agricultural productivity and infrastructure. Unfortunately this instrument has been of very limited value given that it is not legally binding.[64]

Scholars, generally, and governments of developing countries have lamented the limited value of SDT initiatives in the Uruguay Round.[65] Ostry criticizes the Uruguay Round Agreements for providing arbitrary implementation periods, inadequate technical assistance, and 'seem[ing] little more than tokenesque compensation'.[66] Views differ on the reasons for the failure, with explanations including that the provisions were introduced on an ad hoc basis late in the negotiating process and lacked an integrated structure based on a consensus on the trade needs of developing countries or a clearly defined framework

---

63. For export subsidies, the provision of most relevance to developing countries is Article 9.4 which exempts developing countries from having to reduce subsidies given to marketing and internal transport and freight costs on the export of agricultural products. For domestic subsidies, Article 6.2 exempts developing countries from reduction commitments on rural development measures. Seventy percent of developing country notifications to the WTO for 1995 and 1996 indicated recourse to this provision.

64. See United Nations Development Programme, *Making Global Trade Work for People* (London and Sterling, Virginia: Earthscan Publications Limited, 2003) 127.

65. See, for example, J Trachtman, 'Legal Aspects of a Poverty Agenda at the WTO: Trade Law and 'Global Apartheid ''(2003) 6(1) JIEL 3.

66. Sylvia Ostry, 'The Uruguay Round North-South Grand Bargain: Implications for Future Negotiations' (2000) Political Economy of International Trade Law.

for implementation.⁶⁷ Michalopoulos argues that many of the SDT commitments are too broad and general in nature to be of any practical significance.⁶⁸ Many of the SDT provisions, as well, are little more than 'best endeavors' clauses that do not require concrete action from developed country Members but simply encourage them to pay attention to the needs of developing countries.⁶⁹ There is thus no means for developing countries to hold developed countries to the commitments. Finally, there is a strong sense among many commentators and developing countries that historically, governments of industrialized countries have been prepared to extend SDT in favor of developing countries more as a political gesture than out of any conviction that it would make a real difference and that the commitments of developed countries are in practice much less important than they would appear on paper.⁷⁰

In the face of these failures, commentators are divided on the best way forward. Many are skeptical about the continuing relevance or usefulness of SDT, arguing that such policies have done more harm than good to developing countries by prolonging their exclusion from the global economy and denying access to the benefits of openness.⁷¹ In the spirit of Hudec's earlier views, Hart and Dymond argue that SDT is more likely to retard than aid economic development and poverty alleviation and that the full application of traditional SDT measures will be a drag on the participation of developing countries in the trading system. They thus suggest that the appeal of SDT is wholly political and bereft of any economic underpinning.⁷² They are particularly critical of the principle of nonreciprocity. First, it has compounded the difficulty of convincing developed countries to open their markets to products of export interest to developing countries, including agricultural products. Second, the failure to open their own markets to competition meant that most developing countries gained

---

67. M Pangestu, 'Special and Differential Treatment in the Millennium: Special for Whom and How Different?' (2000) 23(9) W Econ 1285, 1292. See also C Michalopoulos, *The Role of Special and Differential Treatment for Developing Countries in GATT and the World Trade Organization* (Washington, DC: The World Bank, 2000) 24.

68. Michalopoulos, ibid 25.

69. P Lichtenbaum, '"Special Treatment" vs. "Equal Participation": Striking a Balance in the Doha Negotiations' (2002) 17 AUIL Rev 1003, 1014.

70. M Hart and B Dymond, 'Special and Differential Treatment and the Doha "Development" Round' (2003) 37 JWT 2, 395, 398. See also C Michalopoulos, *The Role of Special and Differential Treatment for Developing Countries in GATT and the World Trade Organization* (Washington: The World Bank, 2000) 24. Daniel Altman, 'Managing Globalization: Q&A with Charlene Barshefksy', International Herald Tribune Blogs, available online at: <http://blogs.iht.com/tribtalk/business/globalization/?p=342>.

71. JE Stiglitz and A Charlton, *Fair Trade For All: How Trade Can Promote Development* (New York: Oxford University Press, 2005) 88.

72. M Hart and B Dymond, 'Special and Differential Treatment and the Doha "Development" Round' (2003) 37(2) JWT 395, 395.

less than was available to them through active participation in the GATT. Third, they argue that SDT has contributed to corruption through the use of discretionary import and export licensing schemes.[73] Finally, they argue that SDT has contributed indirectly to the status of developing countries as second-rank players with little influence and potential targets of discriminatory policies including gray-area measures such as voluntary export restraints, increasing resort to contingency protection measures, and agricultural protectionism.

The available evidence certainly supports the argument that to the extent SDT measures have endorsed and encouraged inward-looking trade strategies, the results have not been positive. But does this mean that the SDT agenda should, as some scholars would argue, be abandoned entirely?[74] Or does it still have potential benefits for developing countries? A number of commentators argue that it does. Stiglitz and Charlton find continued justification for SDT due to the asymmetry of power in trade negotiations and the severe difficulties faced by many developing countries in making the required adjustments following trade liberalization due to low levels of education, poorly developed financial and insurance markets, weak social safety nets, and poor physical infrastructure.[75] Jensen argues, in the case of Africa, that many developing countries are too small to extract benefits through the regular channels of reciprocal negotiations, and that accordingly there is a continuing role for SDT.[76] Arguments for the continued relevance of SDT that revolve around fairness and equality have particular salience in the agricultural sector which for many communities in developing countries remains the means for food sustenance and subsistence income generation.[77]

Another argument for the continued relevance of SDT is that tariffs ought to be seen not just as distortionary taxes but from the viewpoint of optimal taxation.[78] This, it is argued, would recognize the reality that tariffs are critical

---

73. Ibid 397.

74. See, for example, K Anderson, 'Agriculture, Trade Reform and Poverty Reduction: Implications for Sub-Saharan Africa' (2004) Policy Issues in International Trade and Commodities Study Series No. 22. ZK Wang and LA Winters, 'Africa's Role in Multilateral Trade Negotiations: Past and Future' (1998) 7 (Suppl) J Afr Econ 37. J Bhagwati, 'Reshaping the WTO' (2005) *Far Eastern Economic Review*. A Panagariya, 'EU Preferential Trade Policies and Developing Countries' (2002) 25(10) W Econ 1415.

75. JE Stiglitz and A Charlton, *Fair Trade For All: How Trade Can Promote Development* (New York: Oxford University Press, 2005) 108.

76. MF Jensen, 'African Demands for Special and Differential Treatment in the Doha Round: An Assessment and Analysis' (2007) 25(1) Dev Pol Rev 91, 92. See also Trachtman who argues that the international trade regime has not been special and differential enough. J Trachtman, 'Legal Aspects of a Poverty Agenda at the WTO: Trade Law and 'Global Apartheid"(2003) 6(1) JIEL 3, 11.

77. United Nations Development Programme, *Making Global Trade Work for People* (London and Sterling, Virginia: Earthscan Publications Limited, 2003) 123.

78. See, for example, MS Emran and J Stiglitz, 'Price-neutral Tax Reform with an Informal Economy' (Working Paper, George Washington University, Washington,

for revenue generation for many developing countries who have limited capacity to administer internal direct and indirect taxes (especially where much economic activity is carried on in the informal sector). On average, African countries generate 31 percent of their total current revenues from taxes on international trade, mainly from import tariffs.[79] Given this dependence, Jensen argues for a system of derogations on the basis of individual country assessments of current tax structures and analyses of the trade regime from the viewpoint of optimal taxation rather than trade alone.[80]

Here, we adopt the view that there is, in principle at least, an argument to be made for SDT policies that have the goal of assisting developing countries deal with the adjustment costs of integrating their economies into the world trading regime. Hence for us, the more relevant and difficult question revolves around what kinds of SDT measures can usefully be employed for this purpose, given both the lessons of the past and today's geopolitical environment. It is to the current environment that we turn in the next section.

D. THE DOHA DEVELOPMENT ROUND

i. What is at Stake for Developing Countries?

If we conclude that SDT, in some form, has continuing salience, we must give consideration to what we can realistically expect it to achieve. This first requires consideration of what is at stake in the current negotiations for developing countries in the agricultural sector. Agriculture is of significant economic importance for developing countries. In low-income countries in particular, it accounts for more than 70 percent of employment, compared with 30 percent in middle-income countries and just 4 percent in high-income countries.[81] In terms of world trade, in 2003, developing countries' share of world agricultural exports was 41.5 percent.[82] The share held by Asian countries and Latin America and the Caribbean was approximately 16 and 17 percent respectively, with Africa only holding a 5 percent share.[83] Exports within these regions were largely dominated by a relatively small number of countries: Brazil, Argentina, and Mexico in Latin America;

DC, 2003). MS Emran and J Stiglitz, 'On Selective Indirect Tax Reform with an Informal Economy' (2002) Working Paper, George Washington University.

79. MF Jensen, 'African Demands for Special and Differential Treatment in the Doha Round: An Assessment and Analysis' (2007) 25(1) Dev Pol Rev 91, 96.

80. Ibid 104.

81. United Nations Development Programme, *Making Global Trade Work for People* (London and Sterling, Virginia: Earthscan Publications Limited, 2003) 109.

82. J Bhagwati, 'Reshaping the WTO' (2005) *Far Eastern Economic Review* Table I.2.

83. WTO Secretariat, 'Agricultural Trade Performance by Developing Countries 1990–2003' (Committee on Agriculture, Special Session, WTO Doc No. TN/AG/S/19, 2005) Table I.3.

China, Malaysia, Thailand, India, and Indonesia in Asia; and South Africa in Africa.[84] The WTO Secretariat noted in a 2005 report that overall, since 1990, developing countries have experienced some growth in agricultural exports but that this growth is small relative to the growth in the manufacturing sector where growth has been more than three times that of agriculture.[85] Further, there is a significant concern that some developing countries have moved from a positive net agricultural trade position, with exports exceeding imports by a significant proportion, to a situation in which agricultural imports and exports have been roughly balanced in recent years (with the decline in agricultural exports not offset by a growth in manufacturing exports).[86] Sub-Saharan Africa is of particular concern in this regard. While it remains a net agricultural exporter as a region, it has seen a sharp decline in the share of agriculture in its exports, from about 60 percent in the 1960s to about 20 percent today. Further, it has become marginalized in international agricultural export markets; its share of global agricultural exports has declined from about 10 percent in the 1960s to 3 percent today.[87]

A survey of worldwide agricultural trade patterns reveals that the bulk of trade is conducted between developed countries. About 80 percent of developed country agricultural exports are destined for other developed countries and more than 70 percent of developed country agricultural imports originate in other developed countries.[88] However, developing countries still depend to a large extent on developed countries, both as markets for their agricultural exports and as suppliers of their agricultural imports. Nevertheless, South-South trade has been increasing since the 1990s, with the proportion of developing country agricultural exports going to other developing countries growing from 31 percent in 1990 to 40 percent in 2002, while on the import side, imports originating from other developing countries increased from 36 percent to 45 percent over the same period.[89]

LDCs face particular difficulties in the agricultural sector. Overall, they are much less integrated into the world economy than developing countries as a group, and they face a large and growing trade deficit in agriculture.[90] They also exhibit a low degree of integration of their agricultural sector into world markets compared with developing countries overall.[91]

---

84. Ibid.
85. Ibid.
86. Food and Agriculture Organization (FAO), 'The State of Food and Agriculture: Agricultural Trade and Poverty' (FAO, Rome, 2005) 15.
87. Ibid 16.
88. Ibid 19.
89. Ibid 20.
90. Ibid 12.
91. Ibid 17.

Numerous economic studies have sought to estimate the potential gains to developing countries from agricultural trade liberalization.[92] Prior to the Cancun Ministerial in 2003, the World Bank was very optimistic about the potential benefits of liberalized trade in agriculture, estimating more than $500 billion in developing country benefits from liberalization. One study found that a successful Doha Round conclusion on agriculture would have the potential to benefit developing countries in that sector alone by some $142 billion annually.[93] However, since Cancun, the World Bank has revised its figures downwards with the share of benefits for developing countries dropping significantly. The downward revision is due to several factors, including the use of applied rather than bound tariff rates and recognition of the reality that full global liberalization is not—even under the most optimistic scenario—likely to occur during the Doha Round.[94] In a 2005 study, Anderson, Martin, and van der Mensbrugghe found that developing countries do stand to gain from liberalization of agriculture but that the extent of the gains will heavily depend on the level in cuts of tariffs and subsidies.[95]

A 2007 study by Hertel and others finds that there are potential benefits to developing countries from partial liberalization under the Doha Round. In particular, they find that low-income farm households would benefit.[96] A number of NGOs have sponsored or produced studies that disagree. A 2006 study sponsored by the Carnegie Endowment for International Peace concluded that the benefits of agricultural trade liberalization would flow overwhelmingly to rich countries.[97] It found that while a few developing countries would gain, including Brazil, Argentina, and Thailand, many more would suffer a loss due in large part to the pervasiveness of noncompetitive, small-scale farming in those countries.

---

92. See, for example, WR Cline, *Trade Policy and Global Poverty* (Washington, DC: Center for Global Development, Institute for International Economics, 2004). See also Timothy A. Wise & Kevin P. Gallagher, 'No Fast Track to Global Poverty Reduction' (April 2007) Tufts University, Global Development and Environment Institute, Policy Brief No. 07-02.

93. MD Ingco and JD Nash, *Agriculture and the WTO—Creating a Trading System for Development* (Washington, DC: The World Bank & Oxford University Press, 2004) 16. See also TA Wise and KP Gallagher, 'Doha Round and Developing Countries: Will the Doha deal do more harm than good?' (April 2004) RIS Policy Brief No. 22.

94. Wise and Gallagher, ibid.

95. K Anderson, W Martin, and D van der Mensbrugghe, 'Market and Welfare Implications of Doha Reform Scenarios' in K Anderson and W Martin (eds), *Agricultural Trade Reform and the Doha Development Agenda* (Washington, DC: The World Bank, 2005).

96. TW Hertel and others, 'Distributional effects of WTO agricultural reforms in rich and poor countries' (2007) Econ Pol 289 at 330.

97. S Polaski, *Winners and Losers: Impact of the Doha Round on Developing Countries* (Washington, DC, Carnegie Endowment for International Peace, 2006) 7.

The countries projected to suffer the greatest losses were those in East and Sub-Saharan Africa as well as Bangladesh. Similarly, Jensen and Gibbon argue that the Doha Round Agenda and the objectives of the main negotiating parties in relation to it do not address Africa's trade problems and that the likely benefits for African countries are likely to be minimal, if not negative.[98] Jensen argues that countries who are net food importers are at particular risk of losing out if world food prices rise.[99] Some commentators have suggested that developing countries can expect potential gains from agricultural South-South trade that are three times greater than the gains to be expected from liberalization in industrialized countries.[100] However, as Lichtenbaum notes, increased developing country government assistance to their agricultural sectors could undermine the potential for increased South-South trade by distorting resource allocation.[101]

In the final analysis, it is difficult to estimate exactly what benefits would accrue to which developing countries from further liberalization of agricultural trade. Overall, however, the available studies suggest that there would be some value to developing countries from improved market access through tariff reductions and a reduction in the use of export subsidies and domestic support by developed countries.[102] Conversely, it is equally predictable that some countries will suffer losses as they are unlikely to be able to adjust easily to the liberalization of agricultural markets. If this position is accepted, then it must be asked what developing countries need do in order to achieve such liberalization and in what respects SDT might usefully play a role in helping developing countries reap the full benefits of liberalization and in minimizing the negative impacts of liberalization.

ii. The Doha Development Round Agenda

Despite the failures of SDT to achieve its goals in the past and the conclusions of some economists that it has had perverse effects on developing countries, the

---

98. MF Jensen and P Gibbon, 'Africa and the WTO Doha Round: An Overview' (2007) 25(1) Dev Pol Rev 5, 6.

99. Ibid 9.

100. M Moore, 'The Challenges of the Doha Development Agenda for Latin American and Caribbean Countries' (speech given on February 27, 2002 at the Inter-American Development Bank, available online at the WTO Web site: <http://www.wto.org/english/news_e/spmm_e/spmm78_e.htm> last accessed 22 February 2007).

101. P Lichtenbaum, '"Special Treatment" vs. "Equal Participation": Striking a Balance in the Doha Negotiations' (2002) 17 AUIL Rev 1003, 1030.

102. TW Hertel and R Keeney, 'What's at Stake: The Relative Importance of Import Barriers, Export Subsidies and Domestic Support' in K Anderson and W Martin (eds), *Agricultural Trade Reform and the Doha Development Agenda* (New York: Palgrave Macmillan, 2006) estimate that 90% percent of the gains from liberalizing trade in agriculture would come from the reductions in import barriers and the rest from the reductions in export subsidies and domestic support.

concept has played a key role in the Doha Round Negotiations. The Doha Ministerial Declaration emphasizes SDT in relation to agriculture in paragraph 13 where it states that SDT 'shall be an integral part of all elements of the negotiations and shall be embodied in the Schedules of concessions and commitments and as appropriate in the rules and disciplines to be negotiated, as to be operationally effective and to enable developing countries to effectively take account of their development needs, including food security and rural development'. In addition, the Implementation Decision asks Members to 'exercise restraint' with regard to acting against developing country measures taken for rural development and food security.[103]

Three aspects of SDT have dominated the negotiations.[104] First, questions have been raised as to the extent to which development issues should be addressed through SDT in the context of trade negotiations and the extent to which the development principles on which SDT is based should be incorporated into the WTO's structure. Second, there are various issues relating to SDT under each of the three pillars (market access, export competition, and domestic support) of the Agreement on Agriculture. Third, developing countries have raised a number of implementation and monitoring issues related to ensuring that SDT provisions are effective.

iii. Negotiating Positions

Developing countries are seeking various SDT measures under the AOA. On the *export* side (market access), key proposals have included that developed countries grant duty-free and quota-free access to tropical products[105]; maintenance of preferential margins by preference-giving Members; compensation for the continued erosion of preference margins; increased market-access opportunities for least-developed, net food-importing, landlocked, and small-island developing countries whose economies would potentially benefit from growth

---

103. Doha Ministerial Conference—Decision on Implementation-Related Issues and Concerns (Nov 20, 2001) (WTO Doc. WT/MIN(01)17).

104. Food and Agriculture Organization (FAO), 'FAO Trade Policy Technical Notes on Issues Related to the WTO Negotiations on Agriculture: No. 10. Special and Differential Treatment in Agriculture' (FAO, Rome 2005) 1.

105. Note, however, that there is a lack of consensus among developing countries regarding tropical products. While many Latin American countries want to see tariffs and quotas removed, others—including the African, Caribbean, and Pacific countries—have benefited from preferential access to developed country markets for these products and therefore oppose such liberalization. Bridges Weekly Trade News Digest Vol. 11, No. 9, 15 March 2007. In his introduction to the draft modalities released in December 2008, Chairman of the Committee on Agriculture, Crawford Falconer noted that agreement on tropical products remained wanting, with issues concerning bananas the key stumbling block. Committee on Agriculture in Special Session, 'Revised Draft Modalities for Agriculture', WTO Doc. TN/AG/W/4/Rev.4 (6 December 2008).

of their currently small export sectors; and promotion of access by developing countries to knowledge and technical infrastructures needed to ensure compliance with food safety standards in developed countries.[106] In terms of tariff reduction formulas, developing countries have demanded that any formula and its application should reduce tariff escalation on products of export interest to developing countries, in particular, processed products.

On the *import* side, developing countries have emphasized that they still require flexibility in terms of their own liberalization obligations. Proposals have included the right for developing countries to renegotiate tariff bindings that they consider too low, permission to exclude from market-access commitments products that constitute the predominant staple in their traditional diet, longer time frames for implementation of tariff reductions, and access to a new mechanism to protect their domestic markets against import surges.

Developing countries have also made proposals under the export competition and domestic support pillars of the AOA. In relation to export subsidies, proposals include that until a developing country reaches a certain stage of export competitiveness the support provided to subsistence products and certain other crops not be subject to commitments and that developing countries be allowed to use export restrictions and taxes to address food security concerns. In relation to domestic support, proposals include that existing developing country exemptions be maintained and expanded to include subsidies to encourage diversification from crops considered harmful to health. It has been questioned how important these aspects of SDT are for developing countries, due to the fact that most developing countries do not have the capacity to provide significant trade-distorting support for their agricultural sectors.

In July 2004, the General Council adopted a Framework Agreement to focus the negotiations going forward. On the policy flexibility side, the Framework Agreement would provide SDT with respect to the tariffs, export subsidies, and domestic support rules. Special and Differential Treatment would also allow developing countries to make lower tariff reductions and less tariff-rate quota expansion, give them longer implementation periods, give the flexibility to designate certain products as Special Products; and establish a 'Special Safeguard Mechanism' for developing countries. The special products proposal would allow developing countries to designate certain products that are crucial to their food security and economic and social development as 'special products', for which agreed tariff reductions would not be applied fully. In the Framework Agreement, Members agreed that designation of special products should be based on the criteria of 'food security, livelihood security, and rural development

---

106. Examples of developing country proposals in this and the next paragraph are taken from A Hoda and A Gulati, 'Special and Differential Treatment in Agricultural Negotiations' in G Anania, ME Bohman, CA Carter and AF McCalla (eds), *Agricultural Policy Reform and the WTO: Where Are We Heading?* (Edward Elgar, 2004) 360.

needs'. However, it has been extremely difficult to obtain consensus on how exactly these criteria ought to be defined, the number of special products that countries ought to be allowed, and what SDT treatment such products should receive. Attempts to reach a compromise on these issues have resulted in sharp and continuing disagreement. In particular, the ability of developing countries to gain access to developed country markets depends on them being able to carve out special product exclusions for themselves while at the same time resisting proposals by developed countries to invoke the sensitive product concept to carve out extensive product exclusions for themselves. Under the export subsidies pillar, the Framework Agreement would provide SDT through maintenance of the Article 9.4 exception for developing countries, as well as provision of special consideration for state-trading enterprises in developing countries aiming to preserve domestic consumer price stability and ensuring food security. Under the domestic support pillar, the Framework Agreement would provide SDT through, *inter alia*, longer implementation periods and lower reduction requirements for trade-distorting support, a higher threshold for the definition of *de minimus* support, and exemptions for countries that allocate almost all *de minimus* support to subsistence and resource-poor farmers.

While the concept of special products is designed to provide flexibility with respect to noncompetitive products for developing countries, the proposed Special Safeguard Mechanism is designed to help countries protect products that may be competitive but which can be subject to short-term disruptions resulting from depressed international prices or from surges in imports.[107] A Special Safeguard Mechanism would be for use exclusively by developing countries without proof of injury and would allow governments to intervene temporarily in cases of large increases in food imports and subsequent price falls.

On the *export* side, the Framework Agreement would provide SDT under the market-access pillar by accelerating market access for tropical products and alternatives to narcotic products, addressing the issue of preference erosion, and requiring developed country Members and developing country Members to provide duty-free and quota-free market access for products originating from LDCs.

The 2004 Framework Agreement did not resolve differences between Members on SDT measures, although there is significant agreement among WTO Members that LDCs ought to be both exempted from any further reduction commitments and accorded preferential market access. The fault lines among Members' positions on SDT are best analyzed by examining the ongoing negotiating positions of key players. The Danish Institute for International

---

107. FAO, "The State of Agricultural Commodity Markets" (Rome 2007) at 7.

Studies has conducted such an analysis and has identified various 'clusters' of countries according to their positions on SDT.[108]

The largest cluster they identify is the 'tariff reduction exemptions' cluster, which contains the African Group and a number of other low-income countries in the Caribbean and South Pacific. As well as being the largest, this is also the poorest cluster. The African Group has put forward the most specific proposal regarding SDT.[109] On the *export* side, its proposal focuses on achieving further tariff reductions and quota-free access to products of export interest to developing countries. It sees preferences as critical to ensuring adequate market access and argues that they should be more automatic and durable. The African Group would also extend the ability to grant preferences for developing countries to allow developing countries to grant preferences to other developing countries, opening up a channel for South-South preferential trade. The demand for preferences has not gone uncontested, with discussion in the negotiations on adjustment away from dependence on preferences and suggestions that the problem of preference erosion should ideally be targeted by finding the means of removing supply-side constraints so that preferences are no longer required.[110]

On the *import* side, the African Group wants developing country Members to have the right to use subsidies as 'may be necessary for their economic development', and also wants domestic agricultural support for specific development purposes to be exempt from calculations of total support.[111] It has proposed that developing countries 'shall have the right to modify their commitments if this is found necessary to protect the public interest in ensuring food security and alleviating rural poverty'.[112] The African Group is also a strong supporter of both the proposals for a special products category (where it wants to be able to designate at least 20 percent of all agricultural tariff lines), and a Special Safeguard Mechanism. It considers the latter to be necessary because the current special safeguard provisions under Article 5 of the AOA are only available to 22 developing countries who undertook tariffication during the Uruguay Round. The FAO notes that even for these 22 countries, the provisions are neither simple nor flexible enough for effective use and their use incurs considerable administrative costs. During the period 1995 to 2004, only six developing

---

108. The discussion in this section draws extensively upon the Institute's analysis. The Danish Institute for International Studies & The Food and Resource Economics Institute, 'Special and Differential Treatment and Differentiation between Developing Countries in the WTO' (The Danish Institute for International Studies & The Food and Resource Economics Institute, Copenhagen & Frederiksberg, 2005).

109. WTO, "Special and Differential Provisions", Joint Communication from the African Group in the WTO—Revision (WTO Doc No. TN/CTD/W/E/Rev.2, 2002).

110. Danish Institute for International Studies (n 106 above) 65.

111. WTO, "Special and Differential Provisions", Joint Communication from the African Group in the WTO—Revision (WTO Doc No. TN/CTD/W/E/Rev.2, 2002) at 20.

112. Ibid 13.

countries used the mechanism, representing a mere 1 percent of the potential uses by all 22 countries.[113]

Among developing countries, the Danish Institute identifies two other clusters. First is what it refers to as the 'tariff rate quotas for developing countries' cluster. This cluster contains the Dominican Republic, Honduras, Nicaragua, and Panama and is focused on the export side of SDT through increasing tariff rate quotas for developing country exports to developed countries. Second, the 'domestic support for developing countries' cluster consists of 21 countries, including several Cairns Group members and larger developing countries such as Argentina, Brazil, China, and South Africa. This group seeks to ensure that developing countries have the policy space to support their agricultural sectors through domestic support measures. They also support the elimination of export subsidies on products of export interest to developing countries. The Institute identifies Jordan as constituting its own cluster as it alone has asked for developing countries to be allowed to provide export subsidies and export credits.

Among developed countries, the largest cluster is the 'average SDT position' cluster, which contains 49, mostly developed, countries including the United States and the EU Member States (but excluding Canada and Japan). The countries in this group maintain fairly moderate positions on SDT, neither actively endorsing as strong a form of SDT as the first cluster, nor being too cautious to support such measures. The *United States* has been cautious about proposing any specific SDT measures, while the *European Union* has made a proposal for a 'food security box' which would include establishment of a Special Safeguards Mechanism, an examination of specific domestic support needs, and a revision of the *de minimus* clause so that the *de minimus* percentage provides enough flexibility to support the agricultural sector for development reasons. It also proposes a significant reduction in tariff escalation on products of export interest to developing countries, as well as a phase-out of export subsidies for certain products and has been specific about suggesting elimination of export subsidies for products of export interest to African countries.

A small cluster is made up of Canada and Japan, countries who—as noted—are the least willing to provide SDT. Together they are referred to by the Danish Institute as the 'moderate SDT' cluster. Canada proposes that SDT should come in the form of transitional phase-out and facilitation of access to tariff quotas by developing countries, while Japan has argued for adequate assistance and capacity building for developing countries and the designation of special products. Otherwise, its focus is on lower reductions and longer implementation periods. Neither Canada nor Japan would increase the *de minimus* level for domestic support to benefit developing countries.

---

113. Food and Agriculture Organization (FAO), 'FAO Trade Policy Technical Notes on Issues Related to the WTO Negotiations on Agriculture: No. 9. A Special Safeguard Mechanism for Developing Countries' (FAO, Rome 2005).

Finally, there is the 'special safeguard cluster'. This cluster contains a mix of developed and developing countries who typically support a more liberalized trading regime: namely, Australia, New Zealand, Kenya, India, and Uruguay. These countries support both the proposed Special Safeguards Mechanism and *de minimus* levels of domestic support for developing countries.

Interestingly, the Danish Institute's analysis suggests that the two largest clusters, that containing the African Group, and that containing the US and EU Member States, are not far apart in their proposals. It finds that the most notable difference is the African Group's desire to be able to retain higher tariff rates primarily for revenue purposes.

Despite the Danish Institute's fairly optimistic conclusion, the differences that remain between Members are not proving easy to resolve. This has been highlighted in various communications from the chairman of the Committee on Agriculture, Crawford Falconer, and in the draft negotiating texts released to date. While Falconer has not considered the issues of special products and the Special Safeguard Mechanism to be at the heart of the difficulties faced in the agriculture negotiations, he has acknowledged that the whole negotiations could collapse over these issues.[114] Indeed, the collapse of the summit held in Geneva in July 2008 was the result of a failure of the major negotiating parties to agree on the details of a Special Safeguard Mechanism.[115]

At the time of writing, the latest in a succession of draft negotiating texts (or modalities) had just been released.[116] The December 2008 text states that 12 percent of tariff lines shall be available for designation as special products; up to 5 percent of lines may have no cut, while the overall average shall, in any case, be 11 percent. This text provides more certainty than previous versions when no definitive numbers could be agreed upon. The July 2008 version provided for designation of between 10 and 18 lines, with an overall average of 10 to 14 percent. However, the text also notes that a number of developing country Members have expressed reservations about the numbers specified.[117] Special products would be self-designated, guided by indicators based on the criteria of food security, livelihood security, and rural development.[118]

---

114. Communications from the Chairman of the Committee on Agriculture, First Installment (30 April 2007) and Second Installment (25 May 2007).

115. WTO, 'An unofficial guide to agricultural safeguards: GATT, old agricultural (SSG) and new mechanism (SSM), online at http://www.wto.org/english/tratop_e/agric_e/guide_agric_safeg_e.htm (date accessed: 20 December 2008). On the collapse generally, see 'The Doha Round ... and Round ... and Round' *The Economist* (31 July 2008).

116. Committee on Agriculture in Special Session, 'Revised Draft Modalities for Agriculture' WTO Doc. TN/AG/W/4/Rev.4 (6 December 2008).

117. Committee on Agriculture Special Session, 'Revised Draft Modalities for Agriculture', WTO Doc. TN/AG/W/4/Rev.4 (6 December 2008), paras 120-22.

118. An illustrative list is provide in Annex F, Ibid.

Regarding prospects for a special safeguard mechanism, the December 2008 text provides for a price-based and a volume-based mechanism and proposes options for formulas for these, including possible disciplines to avoid the safeguard being triggered frequently and frivolously. The question which was at the root of the July collapse and which continues to be a source of difficulty is what happens in cases where invoking the mechanism would mean going above the pre-Doha bound rate: when it would be triggered, how high the tariff would go, how long it would last, and when it could be triggered again, and whether it could be triggered when prices are not falling. The Chairman for Agriculture, Crawford Falconer, noted in an additional paper that while progress had been made since July, "the unavoidable reality is that we are still short of a clean text, let alone actual agreement on key matters".[119] Thus the impasse continues, raising the question of what alternative approach might be taken to move negotiations forward.[120]

E. BREAKING THE IMPASSE?

We stated in the Introduction that while there is broad consensus among WTO members as to the desirability of improving the economic welfare of developing countries, commitment on the part of developed countries to actually implementing the policies required to achieve this goal is questionable. Vested interests in the domestic agricultural sectors of developed (as well as developing) countries resist increasing market access to developing countries where they see

---

119. Committee on Agriculture in Special Session, 'Revised Draft Modalities for Agriculture Special Safeguard Mechanism', WTO Doc. TN/AG/W/7, 6 December 2008, para 1. Falconer notes that questions also remain on LDCs, small and vulnerable economies, and provisions for when tariffs do not go above pre-Doha rates. In an analysis of a previous incarnation of the text released in July 2007, Williams argues that developing countries should have sought to protect sensitive and special products by means of the safeguard provisions only, suggesting that they have focused too much on reducing subsidies, thus backing the European Union and G10 into a corner where they can only refuse to concede on sensitive products. D Williams, 'The Falconer Draft WTO Text for the Doha Agriculture Negotiations' (2007) UNSWLJ 30,2.

120. The difficulties of concluding the negotiations may well be exacerbated by recent events, notably the new US administration, and the global food and economic crises. Regarding the food crisis, see A Beattie, 'Poor nations defend import tariff rights', *Financial Times* (20 April 2008) noting that the food crisis might hurt rather than help trade liberalization by encouraging countries to insulate themselves from global markets. In addition, approximately 40 food exporting countries have imposed export restrictions in an attempt to maintain food supplies at home and to keep local prices low. (See 'The world food summit: only a few green shoots' *The Economist* (5 June 2008); J Webber, 'Farmers doomed to pay price for export restrictions', *Financial Times* (17 April 2008) Regarding the economic crisis, see 'Fare well, free trade' *The Economist* (18 December 2008) discussing the political appeal of protectionist policies when times are tough.

this as potentially impacting negatively upon their ability to compete in their home market and possibly export markets. They also demand government financial support for their own domestic production. Faced with pressure at home, governments of developed countries are exceedingly unlikely to strike a trade deal favorable to developing countries unless the deal is also perceived as benefiting their own constituencies (including constituencies in other sectors, especially export interests). This is the *realpolitik* of trade negotiations. Whatever the economic welfare implications of SDT for developing countries, we suggest that it is futile to discuss SDT without recognizing the *realpolitik* within which the negotiations are being conducted. In other words, there should be no sentimental illusions as to the interests and influences driving the negotiating process; compromise will be required of both developed and developing countries alike.[121] Here an analogy may be made with domestic politics, for example, as illustrated by the case of reform of US agricultural policy vis-à-vis cotton. Duranton suggests that unilateral reform of trade in cotton is not politically feasible since it will incur opposition from Louisiana and members of Congress who will support Louisiana in return for future political reciprocity on other issues. He argues that broad trade liberalization measures might also run into trouble for the same reason but compounded by the fact there will be a complete coalition of potential losers. However, he suggests that a deal may be possible by playing winners against losers, explaining by way of example that, 'a trade deal which includes, say, software and cotton will pitch California against Louisiana and some progress might be achieved'.[122] The same principle, we argue, applies in respect of SDT proposals. In other words, if developed countries are going to agree to SDT measures in agriculture, they will need to see a benefit for themselves in some other area of the negotiations.

As noted above, we believe that there is a case for some kind of SDT in the context of agricultural trade. We base this not simply on the notion of fairness—appealing as it is—but also on the basis of economic welfare and the *realpolitik* of trade negotiations. We noted various economic rationales for SDT in Section 2 and noted the concern that rather than helping developing countries, SDT has often hindered their integration into the global economy. Certainly there are strong lessons to be learned from history in this regard. However, we treat these lessons as a caution against an overly broad application of SDT measures rather than a signal that SDT has no virtues. In the agricultural context, we believe there is a case for a reconceptualized form of SDT to mitigate the severe adjustment costs that would afflict some regions and sectors in developing countries

---

121. B Hoekman, 'Operationalizing the Concept of Policy Space in the WTO: Beyond Special and Differential Treatment' (2005) 8(2) JIEL 405, 411.

122. G Duranton (University of Toronto), discussion of TW Hertel, R Keeney, M Ivanic and LA Winters, 'Distributional effects of WTO agricultural reforms in rich and poor countries' (2007) Econ Pol 289, 333.

if further liberalization on the import side was to occur.[123] Finally, there is a political rationale for SDT that stems from the *realpolitik* of trade negotiations to which we have referred above. The rationale is simply that just as rich countries are unlikely to extend offers of SDT without receiving concessions in return, developing countries for their part have made it clear that they will not accept a new trade deal if SDT is not part of it. In other words, developed countries cannot expect to gain the support of the vast majority of WTO Members who are developing countries unless they are prepared to offer some form of meaningful SDT measures. Thus, we believe that the issue is not whether or not SDT should form part of international trade law and policy but how to make it both politically palatable to all parties as well as more effective for developing countries in order to advance their economic and social welfare and development.[124]

We have identified three branches of SDT. We start here with the third branch identified—namely, the financial and technical assistance that is increasingly justified as WTO rules reach behind borders requiring costly changes to domestic regulatory regimes and practices.[125] For example, the SPS Agreement requires changes to a number of domestic regulatory processes including control, inspection, and approval procedures, while the TBT Agreement requires countries to follow prescribed procedures in their preparation, adoption, and application of technical regulations. We also note that many developing countries require assistance not only to deal with these implementation costs but also to overcome supply-side constraints in production, marketing, and trade. The FAO suggests that international assistance is required to help developing countries create an environment where resources can be reallocated to activities where they can be used more productively as well as to improve marketing and trade through better infrastructure and diversification.[126]

Some commentators have argued that this is the most meritorious branch of SDT and should receive the most attention going forward.[127] We agree that this form of SDT is of critical importance in helping developing countries face the adjustment costs of agricultural trade liberalization. The SPS and TBT Agreements already contain provisions requiring technical and financial assistance. Article 9 of the SPS Agreement states that 'Members agree to facilitate the provision of

---

123. See generally JE Stiglitz and A Charlton, *Fair Trade For All: How Trade Can Promote Development* (New York: Oxford University Press, 2005).

124. M Pangestu, 'Special and Differential Treatment in the Millennium: Special for Whom and How Different?' (2000) 23(9) W Econ 1285, 1295.

125. For a discussion of the costs of compliance faced by developing countries, see JM Finger and P Schuler, 'Implementation of Uruguay Round Commitments: The Development Challenge' (2000) 23(4) W Econ 511.

126. FAO, 'The State of Agricultural Commodity Markets' (Rome 2007) 7.

127. See for example C Michalopoulos, *The Role of Special and Differential Treatment for Developing Countries in GATT and the World Trade Organization* (Washington, DC: The World Bank, 2000).

technical assistance to other Members, especially developing country Members', while Article 11 of the TBT Agreement provides that 'Members shall, if requested, advise other Members, especially the developing country Members, and shall grant them technical assistance on mutually agreed terms and conditions'. Unfortunately, these Articles are vaguely worded and are only of a best-endeavors nature, that is unsatisfactory from the perspective of developing countries who have no leverage to insist upon receiving the assistance they require. Such provisions should be strengthened so that they are enforceable by developing countries. Costs of conformity assessments of imports from developing countries into developed countries might be borne by developed countries rather than developing countries or their exporters. Also, a system of independent monitoring is required to ensure that assistance is being provided as necessary and that all developed country Members are fulfilling their obligations. Giving a legal imprint to technical assistance and other aid-for-trade provisions is not without problems. Indeed, Finger argues that "trying to force the extensive international cooperation that is already taking place into a legal straight-jacket would more likely compromise the existing trust and appreciation of shared benefits than bring forward additional money".[128] However, Finger does appear to be receptive to a proposal by former UNCTAD Secretary-General Rubens Ricupero for an implementation audit in the WTO. This would involve identification of the specific investments required by developing countries to meet new obligations so that any agreement could include bound commitments to provide the needed support.[129] While we acknowledge the problems associated with giving binding force to provisions requiring assistance, we would endorse a proposal such as that made by Ricupero.

The other two branches of SDT are, respectively, that relating to *imports* (policy flexibility) and that relating to *exports* (market access). From a *realpolitik* perspective, these two sides of SDT are intimately linked. If developing countries wish to protect certain domestic agricultural sectors, for example, by designating all kinds of special products, they will likely encounter resistance if they also want to receive concessions on the export side, for example, by developed countries designating all kinds of sensitive products. We support the continuation of SDT

---

128. JM Finger, 'Trade and Development: Systemic Lessons from WTO Experience with Implementation, Trade Facilitation and Aid-for-Trade' (24–26 May 2007). Paper presented at 'Developing Countries in the WTO Legal System', University of Minnesota Law School at 29.

129. Ibid 17. Citing R Ricupero, 'Integration of Developing Countries into the Multilateral Trading System' in J Bhagwati and M Hirsch (eds), *The Uruguay Round and Beyond: Essays in Honor of Arthur Dunkel* (University of Michigan Press, Ann Arbor 2000) 9–36; and R Ricupero, 'A Development Round: Converting Rhetoric into Substance' (paper presented at John F Kennedy School of Government Harvard University, Cambridge, MA, 'Symposium on Efficiency, Equity and Legitimacy: The Multilateral Trading System at the Millennium', June 2000).

but subject to the condition that the measures chosen must be far more nuanced and targeted than in the past. By this we mean that SDT measures should be focused on those regions and sectors within developing countries that would face the most severe adjustment costs in the absence of SDT. Special and Differential Treatment should be focused on helping those countries to deal with those adjustment costs. To this end, it is crucial that a way is found to differentiate between countries, regions, and/or sectors.

On the *export* side, developing countries face a number of major market impediments in agricultural trade, including the presence of extremely high tariffs, tariff peaks, and escalation. Rather than relying on SDT to provide preferential market access to exporters from developing countries, it would be highly preferable for developed countries to make a broad across-the-board commitment to improving market access on a MFN basis, in return for a similar across-the-board commitment by developing countries, subject only to longer transition periods and to the general safeguards adjustment regime we outline below. However, at a minimum, developed countries should commit to providing unconstrained market access to the LDCs. A recent study by Oxfam suggests that while industrialized countries have repeatedly pledged to provide free access for all exports from the world's poorest countries, the majority of their initiatives to date have excluded key products of export interest to LDCs.[130] The European Union's 2001 'Everything But Arms' (EBA) initiative was originally designed to provide free market access for all nonmilitary exports from LDCs. However, as a result of pressure from various vested interests, market access for rice, sugar, and bananas has been delayed.[131] Similarly, the US Africa Growth and Opportunity Act (AGOA) purports to provide free-market access for selected products exported by the 39 African LDCs. However, such access does not extend to sensitive products.[132] Providing unconstrained market access to LDCs should be possible from a *realpolitik* perspective because these countries do not export enough to seriously threaten producers in developed countries. That is, little sacrifice is required of those countries or their producers.

For countries above the LDC threshold, we believe it is neither realistic nor helpful for them to expect to receive improved access to developed country markets on a nonreciprocal basis beyond that which is already in place. Thus, SDT on the *export* side should not be applicable to them. While developed countries should reduce tariffs, tariff peaks and escalation in respect of products of export interest to *all* developing countries, they will expect concessions in return. In this regard, we note the importance of the negotiation process itself. It is critical that SDT not be addressed solely within the confines of the agricultural negotiations

---

130. Oxfam, 'Rigged Rules and Double Standards—trade, globalisation, and the fight against poverty' (Oxfam, London 2002) 101.
131. Ibid.
132. Ibid.

but in the context of the wider negotiations. This is important to provide greater bargaining room and possibilities for cross-issue trade-offs, particularly for developing countries who are aggressive exporters in some sectors. For example, if Brazil wishes to gain improved market access for its sugar or cotton into the United States, it must be prepared to provide concessions in other areas which may not be related to agriculture: some industrial sectors, telecommunications, and other services, or restrictions on foreign investment where adjustment costs may be lower. If developing countries are not prepared to consider cross-sectoral concessions, it is difficult to see that developed countries will be prepared to move on market access for agricultural products. This has institutional implications for the negotiating framework where agricultural negotiations are currently cabined within their own 'silo' under the aegis of the Committee on Agriculture.

On the *import* side of SDT, we also consider that LDCs ought to be exempt from further commitments. However, even once we move above the threshold of LDCs, it becomes apparent that developing countries are an extremely heterogeneous group. A number of commentators have suggested methods for differentiating between developing countries for the purposes of SDT. These suggestions stem from the notion that there is no defensible justification for providing the same SDT treatment to a large and/or middle-income developing country such as Brazil or China as to a smaller, more vulnerable (yet non-LDC) country such as Vanuatu or Botswana. Indeed, *realpolitik* would suggest that developed countries are unlikely to support proposals for SDT that provide the same benefits to all developing countries. In particular, they will not agree to providing benefits to middle-income countries or large rapidly growing low-income countries (like China and India) without concessions in return. From an economic perspective, Michalopoulos argues that there is very little reason to suggest that some of the more developed of the developing countries cannot compete in the products in which they have a comparative advantage over developed countries and notes that there is very little political support for extending special treatment to them.[133]

However, there is another side to this argument which means that the larger and higher-income developing countries will not be willing to conclude the negotiations without receiving some commitment on SDT. First, developing countries present a stronger negotiating bloc if they can bargain together, and hence they will be extremely unlikely to support any formal differentiation beyond separation of LDCs. Second, even the higher-income and growing developing countries have regions that remain mired in poverty, and these are often concentrated in areas where households rely on traditional subsistence or small-scale farming. Hertel and others find that in Brazil, agriculture-specialized

---

133. C Michalopoulos, *The Role of Special and Differential Treatment for Developing Countries in GATT and the World Trade Organization* (Washington, DC: The World Bank, 2000) 25.

households have a poverty rate about six times the national poverty rate.[134] While Brazil is a leading exporter in certain areas of agricultural production such as beef and dairy, it is also home to a large number (over four million) of smallholder farms dedicated to subsistence production.[135] A similar situation persists in India where a large number of rural poor live in that country's semi- and tropical regions where shortages of water and regular drought have impeded agricultural development. In Chhindwara, for example, subsistence farming is common, and many farmers depend upon staple goods such as rice, wheat, onions, and poultry, for their livelihood.[136] The existence of this vulnerable sector means that the Indian government is reluctant to cut tariffs on these and other products.

The charity Oxfam has drawn attention to the plight of poor farmers in developing countries who, they argue, have suffered negative impacts as a result of agricultural trade policies over the past decade. They find that the negative effects of agricultural trade policies impact most severely on small, resource-poor, subsistence farmers. In the Philippines, Oxfam reports that trade liberalization in the corn market in 1997 reduced import prices for US corn by one-third. This cheap corn threatened the livelihood of Philippine farmers on the island of Mindanao. An Oxfam study found that many of the poorest households in Mindanao obtained more than three-quarters of their income from domestic corn sales, meaning that any fall in household income would have devastating effects on resources available for food, health care, and education. Thus, the impact of exposing poor corn farmers to competition from heavily subsidized US corn was to leave some of the poorest families even worse off.[137]

A similar scenario has unfolded in Mexico, a country which is often touted as one of the success stories of globalizing economies. It is the world's second-largest exporter of medium-technology manufactured goods, after Korea and ahead of Taiwan, and the sixth-largest exporter of high-technology products.[138] However, in the agricultural sector, farmers have—like those in Mindanao—suffered as a result of an influx of cheap corn imports from the United States. Over 40 percent of corn growing operations in Mexico consist of subsistence farmers who face difficult growing conditions as well as little if any access to technology, credit, storage facilities, and marketing channels. Following implementation of the North American Free Trade Agreement, these farmers were

---

134. TW Hertel and others, 'Distributional effects of WTO agricultural reforms in rich and poor countries' (2007) Econ Pol 289, 302.

135. Rural Poverty Portal <http://www.ruralpovertyportal.org>.

136. 'World trade talks—a pot-holed road', *The Economist* (14 April 2007).

137. Oxfam, 'Rigged Rules and Double Standard—trade, globalisation, and the fight against poverty' (Oxfam, London 2002) 115.

138. Ibid 77.

subject to an influx of US corn being sold at below production costs.[139] The impact on subsistence farmers was severe, given that they did not have the ability to switch production to more profitable crops and has exacerbated unrest in the Chiapas region.[140] Of note, however, is the fact that there was another group of farmers in Mexico who were not impacted in this manner. These were the larger farmers with greater assets and the ability to shift production to capital-intensive fruits and vegetables for export.[141]

Thus, we see a pattern emerging where the sectors most at risk from agricultural trade liberalization cannot necessarily be broken down along country lines. Given the poverty that exists in even the higher-income developing countries and the adverse impacts of trade liberalization on small, resource-poor farmers in their rural sectors, they are not likely to agree to a trade deal that eliminates them from the category of 'developing country'. The adjustment costs in their poorest regions would be too severe. Thus, suggestions that some broad-based formula (such as GDP per capita) be used to categorize developing countries into bands are neither politically realistic nor appropriate. Yet the need for some kind of differentiation remains; surely Brazil should not be able to utilize SDT provisions to protect its beef export industry. On the other hand, it arguably has a case for some SDT measures to assist small farmers in the poor northeast of the country.

We argue, therefore, that on the *import* side, the AOA should make SDT available to sectors where the adjustment costs of liberalization would be particularly severe. As noted above, the infant-industry argument recognized in Article XVIII of the GATT is not readily applicable to the traditional agricultural sector. Further, we strongly believe that any desire on the part of developing countries to apply an infant-industry type argument to underdeveloped agricultural sectors must be resisted. The empirical evidence as to the outcome of infant-industry protection suggests that it is not a recipe for success, and it would be a step backwards to promote such a recipe in the agricultural context. What then is the rationale for SDT on the *import* side? We argue that a rationale can be found in the social and economic desirability of allowing developing countries to protect sectors where exposure to further trade liberalization (and thus increased imports) would likely have significant negative social, economic, and political repercussions. These sectors will be those that are predominantly made up of small, resource-poor farmers who rely on agricultural production for their basic food intakes and subsistence income requirements. In such sectors, displacement caused by imports is not easily softened. Unlike the model used by Ricardo in his famous illustration of comparative advantage where English winemakers could shift to cloth production, many farmers and farm workers in developing

---

139. G Henriques and R Patel, *Policy Brief No. 7: Agricultural Trade Liberalization and Mexico* (Institute for Food and Development Policy, Oakland, CA 2003) 30.
140. Ibid.
141. Ibid.

countries do not have the education, skills, capital, or infrastructure required to move to other sectors, particularly given the high unemployment rates that plague many developing countries.[142] In making this suggestion, we recognize that certain countries such as Korea and Taiwan have liberalized some of their traditional agricultural sectors, although in the recent bilateral trade agreement between the United States and Korea, we note that Korea still insisted on excluding rice from liberalization commitments.

Two fundamental questions arise out the suggested approach. First, how to identify sectors that qualify for protection; and second, exactly what protection countries would be entitled to accord to the protected sectors? The Doha Round Negotiations have, as discussed above, focused on the issues of 'special products' and a Special Safeguards Mechanism, but the negotiations have run into significant difficulties. Our recommendation for SDT on the *import* side would set aside this approach in favor of a simplified mechanism that moves away from the notion of infant-industry protection and focuses instead on what we believe ought to be the key objective, namely, helping developing countries to cope with the adjustment costs that trade liberalization entails by allowing them to protect their poorest and most vulnerable rural regions and sectors. We will refer to this simplified mechanism as the '*Vulnerable Agricultural Sector Protection Scheme*', or *VASPS*.

The VASPS would be analogous in many ways to a safeguards scheme, especially in the sense that its focus would be on containing and dealing with adjustment costs. A key difference would be, however, that rather than the right to protect being triggered by unexpected import surges, VASPS would allow developing countries to designate in advance against specified objective, verifiable and justifiable criteria the sectors it wishes to protect—in effect, an *ex ante* safeguards regime. This would be largely responsive to critiques by Sykes[143] of the conventional safeguards regime in Article XIX of the GATT and the Uruguay Round Safeguards Agreement (and interpretations thereof by WTO Panels and the Appellate Body), which entail extremely stringent requirements in demonstrating unforeseen developments, serious injury or the risk thereof, and causation (such that no safeguard measure has survived challenge before the WTO DSB), by prespecifying these requirements in the agricultural context. Our proposals are based on the reality that in many cases, developing countries already know which sectors will be the most severely impacted by trade liberalization. Rather than having to wait for import surges and having to provide evidence of serious injury, or modifying scheduled commitments *ex post* under Article XXVIII,

---

142. JE Stiglitz and A Charlton, *Fair Trade For All: How Trade Can Promote Development* (New York: Oxford University Press, 2005) 213.

143. A Sykes, 'The Persistent Puzzles of Safeguards: Lessons from the Steel Dispute' (2004) 7 JIEL 523; A Sykes, 'The Safeguards Mess: A Critique of Appellate Body Jurisprudence' (2003) WT Rev 2, 261.

developing countries should instead be able to designate vulnerable sectors in advance in accordance with specified criteria and put protective measures in place accordingly. We emphasize that the rationale underlying this proposal is not to allow infant-industry style protection but to allow developing countries flexibility to control the most severe adjustment costs incurred as a result of trade liberalization.

Key issues are what criteria would trigger eligibility for VASPS and what privileges eligibility would entail. In terms of eligibility, countries would be entitled to designate sectors in accordance with preset criteria. The criteria should be objectively measurable and designed to legitimize countries' identification of seriously depressed and vulnerable sectors that would face high adjustment costs from further liberalization of agricultural markets. There is some precedent for this type of approach in the SCM Agreement. Article 8 of the SCM Agreements (now expired) provides that subsidies will be nonactionable where they provide assistance to disadvantaged regions as defined by objective criteria which must include criteria of economic development as measured over a three-year period relative to the country as a whole (eg, substantial deficits in per capita income or employment rates in the region relative to the country as a whole).

Thus, countries would be required to identify seriously depressed and vulnerable agricultural sectors, based upon objective criteria showing that high adjustment costs are likely to result from liberalization. High adjustment costs will, we argue, result for a particular agricultural sector where producers in that sector have incomes that are significantly below the national average and are unlikely to be able to find alternative income sources should they suffer injury as a result of increased imports.

Production of products in a sector claimed to be vulnerable would be required to account for a minimum percentage (eg, 35 percent) of personal (not corporate) income of the population either across the country as a whole or in one or more clearly defined geographical regions[144] (the 'dependency' criterion). Where such criteria is only met for one or more regions rather than the whole country, the average income of the defined population would have to be below a defined percentage of the average national per capita income (the 'income' criterion). Further, the right to provide protection would be limited to subsidies to those regions, unless those regions together produce more than a certain percentage (eg, 75 percent) of the country's total production of the product in question in which case the full range of measures would be available. We recognize that more specificity is required than our limited sectoral expertise permits in elaborating the quantitative requirements for fulfilling the stated criteria (although

---

144. Which would be required to have a definable economic and administrative identity (as per Article 8.2(b)(i) of the Subsidies and Countervailing Measures Agreement.

here trade negotiations might well benefit from much valuable work already undertaken by the FAO in this context).[145]

The right to provide protection should encompass the use of domestic support and the ability to impose tariffs on imports but should be limited in duration to no more than ten years to provide an incentive to countries to take steps to adjust to trade liberalization in the affected sector. Further, we propose that the right of developing countries to invoke VASPS ought to be subject to offering equivalent compensatory concessions in other sectors such as industrial goods, services, or investment (analogous to compensation required by the traditional safeguards regime under Article XIX of the GATT and to the modification of schedules under Article XXVIII of the GATT). A VASPS measure could only be renewed subject to negotiation of new compensatory trade offsets. If developed countries affected disagree as to the equivalence of the compensation being offered by a developing country invoking VASPS, this disagreement should be resolved by compulsory arbitration under the Dispute Settlement Understanding (as, for example, is currently the case with disputes over the equivalence of retaliation for nullification and impairment under Article 22.6 of the Dispute Settlement Understanding and in cases where countries wish to modify or withdraw their commitments pursuant to Article XXI of the General Agreement on Trade in Services). This contrasts with the current safeguard regime under Article XIX and with the modification of schedules regime under Article XVIII which allow exporting countries to retaliate if negotiations over compensation fail. Trade compensation would be preferable to retaliation which would have the undesirable effect of closing off market access to developing countries, although we recognize that retaliation is unavoidable in the last resort if a developing country fails to implement a negotiated or arbitrated compensatory tradeoff-set package. Requiring compensation and arbitration should act as a constraint on developing countries so that they do not seek to abuse VASPS by seeking to include an inordinate number of sectors within its scope. In order to encourage the use of less trade-distorting measures, in particular domestic support relative to border measures such as tariffs,[146] we would not require developing countries invoking VASPS to provide compensatory tradeoff-sets where the measures they invoke entail only measures of domestic support (which because they are on budget entail their own form of self-discipline).

---

145. See online at: <http://www.fao.org/countryprofiles/default.asp>. The FAO has data on a wide variety of matters. including food deprivation, inequality in access to food and income, diet composition, and health and poverty.

146. See in this regard C Bown and R McCulloch who emphasize the desirability of a safeguards regime that does not reduce market-driven incentives to adjust to new conditions. CP Bown and R McCulloch, 'Trade Adjustment in the WTO System: Are More Safeguards the Answer'? (2007) 23 OREP 415.

F. CONCLUSION

Rather than continuing with WTO-sanctioned, nonreciprocal preferential arrangements, developed countries should make good on their commitment to development in the Doha Round by extending market access in agricultural products of export interest to all developing countries, with particular focus on reducing tariffs, tariff peaks, and tariff escalation. Indeed, such market-access commitments should ideally be extended to *all* countries on a MFN basis. In return, developing countries (other than LDCs) should make across-the-board commitments to agricultural liberalization, subject to longer transition periods and subject in particular to the special *ex ante* safeguards regime that we have proposed. This would focus SDT on protection of exceptionally vulnerable agricultural sectors that would face severe adjustment costs from agricultural liberalization while recognizing the *realpolitik* of trade negotiations by requiring developing countries to provide cross-issue concessions in return for the right to invoke the most trade-distorting border measures to protect their vulnerable sectors.

Finally, we note that VASPS (or some more demanding variant thereof) might also discipline the promiscuous designation of 'sensitive product' sectors by developed countries. Applying a similar *ex ante* safeguards regime to both developing and developed countries would recognize the principle of reciprocity, while at the same time recognize that *de facto* more developing than developed countries will qualify for its invocation because of the asymmetries in adjustment costs that many developing countries face relative to developed countries from agricultural trade liberalization. We hope that Robert Hudec would view these proposals as consistent with the spirit of his critique of traditional SDT in 1987 (which we largely share).

14. TRIPS 3.0
Policy Calibration and Innovation Displacement

DANIEL J GERVAIS[*]

A. Introduction 363
B. Measuring the Impact of TRIPS on Development 369
    I. Overview of Recent Analyses 369
        Selecting proper indicators 370
        The link between IP and FDI 372
    II. Policy Lessons of Recent Analyses 376
        Copyright 376
        Trademarks 377
        Patents 377
C. The Displacement of Innovation 378
    I. The Role of the Demanders 378
    II. The Transfer of R&D to Developing Countries 383
    III. Developing Countries as Global Competitors 386
    IV. Was it TRIPS? 389
    V. Distribution of Innovation Development 390
D. Conclusion 391

A. INTRODUCTION

The TRIPS Agreement[1] is now entering its third phase. The first phase (TRIPS 1.0) began with a well-documented[2] push by the US government, supported by the

---

[*] Professor of Law; Director, Technology and Entertainment Law Program, Vanderbilt University Law School. The author is grateful to the participants in the conference on Developing Countries in the WTO Legal System Papers held at the University of Minnesota, 24–26 May 2007 and in particular to Professor Jagdish Bhagwati and J Michael Finger for their detailed and helpful comments on the initial draft. The author wishes to acknowledge the generous financial assistance of Bell University Labs and the University of Ottawa.

1. *World Trade Organization Agreement on Trade-Related Intellectual Property Rights*, 15 April 1994, *Marrakech Agreement Establishing the World Trade Organization*, Annex 1C, Legal Instruments—Results of the Uruguay Round Vol. 31; 33 ILM. 1197.

2. See D Gervais, *The TRIPS Agreement: Drafting History and Analysis*, (3rd edn Sweet & Maxwell, 2008); SK Sell, *Private Power, Public Law* (Cambridge University Press, 2003) 96–120; C May, *A Global Political Economy of Intellectual Property Rights: The New Enclosures?* (Routledge 2000); P Drahos and J Braithwaite, *Information Feudalism: Who Owns the Knowledge Economy?* (New Press, 2003); and A Koury Menescal, 'Those Behind

European Commission and the Japanese government, to link intellectual property and trade rules in the WTO as part of the Uruguay Round of Multilateral Trade Negotiations, which ended in Marrakesh in April 1994 with the signing of the Agreement Establishing the WTO, Annex 1C of which is the TRIPS Agreement. Arguably, Phase I did not end with the Round. It continued for a few years after the establishment of the WTO, while a number of developing countries (very few of whom had been active participants in the negotiations[3]) began to grasp the detailed scope of their TRIPS commitments.

From the demanders' perspective, Phase I was informed by *addition narratives* according to which adding high(er) levels of intellectual property protection to the laws of developing and least-developed nations (a) would protect the property of intellectual property holders in both rich and poorer countries (and, by generating additional profits, would in turn lead to more research and development); and (b) was necessary to jump-start economic growth in those countries (intellectual property seen as a necessary ingredient of development).

TRIPS 2.0, the second phase in the life of the Agreement, began just before the new millennium. It was characterized initially by highly critical analyses of the TRIPS negotiation process, which was said to have been based on coercion of and/or ignorance by (for many developing countries this was a first complete multilateral trade negotiation, a difficulty compounded by the lack of intellectual property experts[4]), and/or a very bad bargain for the developing world. Indeed, the Uruguay Round was the first example (on such a scale at least) of sectoral reciprocity. To sum it up rather crudely: GATS and TRIPS in exchange for agriculture and textiles. In addition, developing countries accepted as part of the Round package practically the full range of preexisting GATT law, in the form of the Tokyo Round codes (other than the Government Procurement Agreement).[5] From this perspective, the 'great bargain' seemed unbalanced. As Professor Trachtman notes in his chapter, there is little doubt that, initially, at least, the TRIPS Agreement reduced the welfare of developing countries,[6] and that the TRIPS undertakings[7] turned out to be more costly than anticipated for developing countries.[8]

---

the TRIPS Agreement: The Influence of the ICC and the AIPPI on International Property Decisions' (2005) 2 IPQ 155.

3. See Gervais ibid above.

4. Ibid 375.

5. See the chapter in this volume by J Trachtman.

6. See, eg, FM Scherer, 'A Note on Global Welfare in Pharmaceutical Patenting' (2004), 27(7) W Econ 1127–42.

7. JM Finger and P Schuler, 'Implementation of Uruguay Round Commitments: The Development Challenge' (2000) 23:4 The World Economy 511–25. Also available as Policy Research Working Paper No. 2215 <http://www.worldbank.org/research/trade>.

8. Trachtman (n 5 above).

Critics who emphasize a coercion rationale to explain the bargain, point to various threats during the Round to isolate developing countries from the global trading system and/or to impose punitive unilateral sanctions if they did not accede to the demands of the West.[9] Other critics opined that intellectual property was not proper subject matter for the WTO.[10] An extension of this critique sees the Uruguay Round as the last major multilateral trade negotiations round or at least the last in which the West is able to obtain more than it concedes to the developing world, owing specifically to the WTO's foray into the atypical area of intellectual property and the developing world's reaction to it.

However, the majority of critics underscored the absence of empirical data to justify the addition narratives. They also rejected the transfer of (partly) empirically based justificatory theories from industrialized to developing nations. In parallel, many of them tried to demonstrate the inadequacy of Western intellectual property norms to protect certain forms of traditional medicinal knowledge or traditional cultural expressions (sometimes referred to jointly as 'traditional knowledge').[11] This discourse went much further than the casuistry and polite obfuscation so prevalent in international diplomacy; a sense of outrage pervaded many of the discussions. Not surprisingly, it led to a recommendation that TRIPS should be resisted and new norms developed. Phase II was thus informed by *subtraction narratives*: in short, the lesser the impact of TRIPS, the better the situation of developing countries would be.[12] Several books, articles, and reports were published to explain how TRIPS could be 'fought' both within the WTO (for example, by coalescing or insisting on technology transfers) and without (for

---

9. Put differently, TRIPS was perceived by a number of developing nations as a lesser evil than isolation and loss of MFN status. See B Hoekman, 'Services and intellectual property rights', in SM Collins and B Bosworth (eds)., *The New GATT: Implications for the United States* (Brookings Institution, 1994) 113.

10. J Bhagwati, *In Defense of Globalization* (Oxford, 2004) 182–85. Dr Bhagwati's criticism seems to insist mostly on the fact that TRIPS is not proper subject matter for the WTO.

11. JM Finger and P Schuler, *Poor People's Knowledge: Promoting Intellectual Property in Developing Countries.* (World Bank, 2004). On possible solutions within the TRIPS framework, see D Gervais, 'Traditional Knowledge & Intellectual Property: A TRIPS-Compatible Approach' [2005] Mich St LRev 137–66.

12. For a detailed discussion of how Egypt's pharmaceutical industry and access to medicines was done more harm than good by TRIPS, see BI Abdelgafar, *The Illusive Trade-Off: Intellectual Property Rights, Innovations Systems and Egypt's Pharmaceutical Industry* (Toronto: Univ. of Toronto Press, 2006). At 15–23, she discusses the emergence of TRIPS. As J Trachtman notes in that respect:

> The issue of TRIPS and essential medicines is a good example of the frequent result of negotiations between developed countries and developing countries: the developed countries are successful at securing harder legal rights, while the developing countries obtain softer, less realizable, exceptions based on their concerns.

Trachtman (n 5 above).

example, by fostering the emergence of alternative norms in other forums, such as the *Convention on Biological Diversity*).[13] Phase II confronted head-on a fundamental two-prong query, namely (a) what is the causal relationship between intellectual property protection and foreign direct investment (FDI) and (b) does increased FDI necessarily lead to growth in the recipient economy's innovation and its overall development? The query is important because it targets the major underpinning of much of the prointellectual property discourse.

Not surprisingly, multilateral norm making designed to increase protection levels (and reduce some of the flexibilities that remain in the TRIPS Agreement) became increasingly difficult. After the outbreak of the debate between several African and Latin American countries, on the one hand, and pharmaceutical companies, on the other, and the companies' ill-advised attempt to enforce patent rights in the face of thousands of patients unable to afford antiretroviral therapies, increasing multilateral levels of patent protection became practically impossible, at least for the predictable future.[14] Initial suggestions in the Doha Round to strengthen the enforcement section of TRIPS and incorporate two treaties negotiated in 1996 under the auspices of the World Intellectual Property Organization (WIPO)[15] dealing with copyright on the Internet were all but abandoned. Efforts in WIPO to negotiate new treaties (eg, on database protection, harmonization of substantive patent law, rights of broadcasters and webcasters) have met with strong opposition, in particular from developing countries. As an additional sign of the shift brought about by Phase II, while the WTO attempted to address some of the concerns raised by the developing world (eg, by allowing the TRIPS Council to work on the relationship between TRIPS and the CBD and insisting on documenting compliance with the industrialized countries' technology transfer obligations), WIPO started work on a Development Agenda[16] designed to align the organization's work with the interests of the developing world. As of this writing, work on the Agenda was continuing, but its fate and the measurable outcome of the discussions remained uncertain.

---

13. *Convention on Biological Diversity*, 5 June 1992, 1760 UNTS 143.

14. Recent measures announced by the governments of Thailand and Brazil tend to demonstrate that the issue is far from resolved.

15. *WIPO Copyright Treaty*, 20 December 20 1996, CRNR/DC/97, 35 ILM 65; and *WIPO Performances and Phonograms Treaty*, 20 December 1996, 36 ILM 65.

16. WIPO, 'Proposal by Argentina and Brazil for the Establishment of a Development Agenda for WIPO' (27August 2004; WO/GA/31/11); see also 'Report on the Thirty-First (15th Extraordinary) Session" (WIPO, Oct. 5, 2004; WO/GA/31/15) 33-7. This proposal was joined by 12 other member states (Bolivia, Cuba, Dominican Republic, Ecuador, Egypt, Iran, Kenya, Peru, Sierra Leone, South Africa, Tanzania, and Venezuela). See WIPO, Report of the First Session of the Provisional Committee on Proposals Related to a WIPO Development Agenda (20–24 February 2006; PCDA/1/6 Prov.2, including an Annex containing all the proposals).

Yet during the second phase, the TRIPS demanders did not abandon their efforts to continue to increase the international intellectual property baseline. They began using their political ammunition in *bilateral* negotiations to negotiate trade and investment treaties. Recent bilateral agreements signed by the European Union and the United States almost always contain 'TRIPS Plus' norms, including undertakings by developing countries not to use specific TRIPS flexibilities.

Trade Related Intellectual Property Rights has now entered a third phase (TRIPS 3.0)—one that is informed by *calibration narratives*. TRIPS is no longer seen rather simplistically as the enemy of the developing world. The intellectual components of the calibration process that is underway are many: (a) the recognition that developing countries are very different, from Chile to China, from Bolivia to Burkina Faso, or from Egypt to India, and consequently may need different implementations of TRIPS, instead of 'cookie cutter' norm implants; (b) the recognition that below certain developmental thresholds, the introduction of high levels of intellectual property protection will not generate positive impacts (as was evidenced by the extension of transitional periods available for least-developed WTO members); (c) the recognition that intellectual property protection is necessary to develop innovation and foreign direct investment (including technology transfers) but in itself is insufficient to achieve developmental objectives; (d) consequently, the recognition that any complete TRIPS implementation must form part of a broader strategic initiative; and finally (e) the recognition that the sudden introduction of high levels of protection and enforcement may induce significant welfare impacts, which must also be managed.

This multifaceted calibration effort is a reflection of the fact that the negotiation of the TRIPS Agreement incorporated intellectual property in the trade realm as one of many areas of trade negotiations. In the trade world, what matters more is not the protection of private property interests but rather the protection of income and investment.[17] Property protection becomes, as it were, a means to an end. As a result, intellectual property now has to 'square off' against *other trade related rights*. At the same time, all trade related rights, including intellectual property, must fight normative battles with nontrade related rights, such as the right to health and other human rights. These nontrade related rights and their intersection with intellectual property are recognized in Articles 7 and 8 of TRIPS, both of which were also specifically mentioned in the Doha Declaration of 2001. Incorporating the constraints considered until recently exogenous to

---

17. In other words, as the three-step test filter for nationals exceptions to copyright, design, and patent rights—and to a certain extent, trademark rights, as well makes plain, what matters most is not whether an infringement has taken place but whether actual or potential revenue was lost as a result. The protection of rights is therefore indirectly at least tied to a new harm to a market test.

trade arguably will be one of the main challenges of the WTO Dispute settlement system in enforcing TRIPS and other trade related norms and standards.[18]

The TRIPS demanders are not likely to accept a reduction in the level of commitments contained in TRIPS for developing countries (other than much longer transitional periods for least-developed ones) nor indeed to stop asking for higher levels of protection and enforcement. However, there seems to be widespread recognition that the technology transfer and the encouragement of innovation in the developing world are their part of the bargain, enshrined (though perhaps not very forcefully) in Article 66 of TRIPS. Work on Article 66 transparency within the Council for TRIPS was a first step.

Another significant step was taken at the 2007 G8 summit, at which the 'Heiligendamm Process' was agreed. The Process launched 'a new form of co-operation,'[19] with the aim 'to achieve tangible results within two years.'[20] The Summit included a dialogue between the G8 and the so-called 'Outreach 5' (or O5) countries, namely Brazil, China, India, Mexico, and South Africa. According to the program of the Summit:

> 'The planned topics for the Heiligendamm Process are also to be "innovation" and "technology co-operations". The G8 countries are *to share their know-how* with the emerging economies especially when it comes to energy efficiency. At the same time, *agreement is to be reached on more effective international property rights*: protection against replicated machines, copied brand products and counterfeit medications'.[21]

In spite of the process's specific focus on climate change, the intellectual property *quid pro quo* is quite apparent. Given this seemingly unanimous view expressed by all G8 members, this intertwined offer to increase technology transfers while insisting on strong protection will inform Phase III and constitutes the most probable backdrop for both bilateral and multilateral policy discussions for the next few years.

In this chapter, we consider the impact of the TRIPS Agreement on development, including how it can and should be measured (Part B). We will then consider whether the medium and long-term impact of TRIPS might be to cause or accelerate a geographical displacement in innovation (Part C). The Conclusion

---

18. D Gervais, *The TRIPS Agreement: Drafting History and Analysis* (3rd edn Sweet & Maxwell 2008) Part I.

19. 'G8 Summit 2007: The Heiligendamm Process' available at <http://www.g-8.de/nn_92160/Content/EN/Artikel/__g8-summit/2007-06-08-heiligendamm-prozess__en.html>. The OECD will "provide the platform".

20. Ibid.

21. 'G8 Summit 2007: Breakthrough on climate protection. 7June 2007', available at <http://www.g-8.de/nn_92160/Content/EN/Artikel/__g8-summit/2007-06-07-g8-klimaschutz__en.html>.

offers some thoughts on the longer-term role of the developing world on the international intellectual property stage.

B. MEASURING THE IMPACT OF TRIPS ON DEVELOPMENT

The introduction, or updating, of intellectual property norms in all member countries and territories of the WTO, as a result of the adoption of the TRIPS Agreement, sparked a relatively new field of study, namely the impact of the introduction of intellectual property norms on the social, cultural, and economic development of developing and least-developed countries. Two notable institutional efforts include the World Bank's[22] report on the impact of intellectual property on economic development and a report published by the UK Commission on Intellectual Property Rights.[23] There have also been initiatives concerning the origins of the push to have intellectual property included as part of the Uruguay Round package[24] and to provide a deeper understanding of the impact of intellectual property on developing and emerging economies.[25]

i. Overview of Recent Analyses

Major studies[26] discussing the impact of higher intellectual property (IP) protection on developing countries offer a blurred and complex picture. It now seems

---

22. C Fink and KE Maskus (eds), *Intellectual Property and Development* (Washington, DC: World Bank, 2004)

23. Commission on Intell. Prop. Rights, *Integrating Intellectual Property Rights and Development Policy* (2002), available at: http://www.iprcommission.org/papers/pdfs/final_ report/CIPRfullfinal.pdf [hereinafter UK IPR Commission Report].

24. See n 1 above.

25. Many of the contributors to this book have published extensively on this topic. One could also mention S Scotchmer, 'The Political Economy of Intellectual Property Treaties' (2004) 20 JL Econ & Org 415, 435–36.

26. 'The Impact of Trade-Related Intellectual Property Rights on Trade and Foreign Direct Investment in Developing Countries'. OECD Working Party of the Trade Committee, Document TD/TC/WP(2002)42/FINAL, May 28 2003, available at: <http://www.oecd.org/dataoecd/59/46/2960051.pdf>; WG Park and D Lippoldt, 'International Licensing and the Strengthening of Intellectual Property Rights in Developing Countries' (OECD document TD/TC/WP(2004)31/FINAL, 21 December 2004); UK. IPR Commission Report (note 23 above); World Bank study (note 22 above); W Martin and LA Winters (eds), *The Uruguay Round and the Developing Economies* (World Bank, 1995), available at: <http://econ.worldbank.org>; S Scotchmer, 'The Political Economy of Intellectual Property Treaties' (2004) 20 JL Econ & Org 415, 436. OECD Science, Technology and Industry Outlook 2004 (2004); Org. for Econ. Co-operation and Dev., Patents, Innovation and Economic Performance: OECD Conference Proceedings (2004); C Brenner, 'Intellectual Property Rights and Technology Transfer in Developing Country Agriculture: Rhetoric and Reality' (March 1998) OECD Development Centre Working Paper 133, CD/DOC(98)3.

clear that because TRIPS was informed more by the *belief* that introducing 'Western' IP norms would induce development than by actual supporting analyses and data, TRIPS put the policy cart before the empirical horse.[27] We know that a simple equation cannot be drawn between an increase in trade following the introduction of TRIPS-compatible IP protection, on the one hand, and economic development on the other, especially when measured in terms of welfare increases.[28] We also know, however, that innovation (the generation and application of new ideas) is one of five main drivers of economic development and in the longer term perhaps the strongest one.[29]

Selecting proper indicators There are (at least) two principal indicators that are helpful to analyze the impact of increasing protection, namely (a) the increase of trade flows in goods that include a significant IP component (as compared to the physical value of the material and components—for example, a music CD, DVD, or a patented pharmaceutical molecule; such areas may be referred to as 'intellectual property sensitive'); and (b) the increase in FDI concerning goods or services that require a high level of IP protection. A number of studies posit that there is a correlation between FDI concerning goods that require a higher level of intellectual property protection and human development. The underlying assumption, which seems intuitively correct, is that making, selling, or using those goods or services generally requires technology transfer to the recipient country, higher knowledge functions (and the education or training necessary to perform them[30]), or both. This assumption is hard to verify and some authors claim that even if FDI increases. the costs (rent extraction) of moving to higher intellectual property protection outweigh benefits.[31]

---

27. As Park and Lippoldt noted (in ibid 1.):
Reform of the global IPR framework over the last decade has been at least partly motivated by the premise that developing economies will benefit from increased technological inflows as a consequence. However, the theoretical literature does not provide unambiguous predictions about this premise and the empirical evidence is scant, particularly at the firm or enterprise level.

28. C Fink and CA Primo Braga, 'How Stronger Protection of Intellectual Property Rights Affects International Trade Flows' in C Fink and KE Maskus, *Intellectual Property and Development* (n 22 above) 21 ('The implications of IPRs for economic welfare are complex. The simple fact that trade flows rise or fall in response to tighter IPRs is not sufficient for drawing conclusions regarding economic welfare. Both static and dynamic effects need to be considered.). Obviously, an increase in overall economic development may not translate into a reduction of poverty. Other factors, such as wealth distribution and corruption are relevant.

29. The other drivers are trade, finance, migration, and aid. See I Goldin and K Reinert. *Globalization for Development, Revised Edition: Trade, Finance, Aid, Migration, and Policy* (revised edn, World Bank/Palgrave Macmillan, 2007).

30. For the link with innovation, see JL Christensen and BÅ Lundvall, *Product Innovation, Interactive Learning and Economic Performance*. (Elsevier/Jai Press 2004).

31. B I Abdelgafar, n 12 above.

I suggest that (a) to some extent welfare costs can be minimized/managed; and (b) the level of benefits derived from FDI increases will vary greatly from country to country based on, *inter alia*, that country's absorptive capacity. Consequently, while it is true to say that FDI gains in 'higher knowledge' goods and services may not necessarily lead to a globally positive outcome, this type of FDI will assist in leading a country on the path of innovation and the analysis is, therefore, worthwhile.[32]

It is also essential to measure increases in both inward FDI and trade flows (imports) because, to a certain extent, they cancel each other out: a company in country A (export) may have the ability to send goods to country B (import), but it may instead opt for local production (under license) in country B. The main conclusion of the studies under review is that higher levels of IP protection are useful in areas other than fuel (and presumably, raw resources prevalue-added transformation) and, perhaps surprisingly, high technology.[33]

Maskus and Fink suggest[34] five possible explanations as to why there is no measurable positive impact in the case of high technology goods: (1) strong market power may offset the positive market expansion effects of higher protection; (2) higher FDI may lower international trade (as discussed above); (3) it is possible that the impact of intellectual property protection was not accurately measured; (4) factors in the destination country (country of export) may matter more than intellectual property (including first mover advantage); and (5) finally, tariff and nontariff barriers may impede trade flows. It may be also, perhaps mainly in fact, because intellectual property and especially patents are not a dominant consideration in many high technology industries. Waiting three years or more for a patent to be issued may not be a major consideration in deciding

---

32. As the Organisation for Economic Co-operation and Development (OECD) noted in its major report on national innovation:

> New types of policies are needed to address systemic failures, particularly policies directed to networking and improving firm absorptive capacities. Networking schemes put emphasis on improving the interaction of actors and the interplay of institutions within national innovation systems. Such policies stress the role of joint research activities and other technical collaboration among enterprises and with public sector institutions.

OECD, *National Innovation Systems*, (OECD, 1997), available at <http://www.oecd.org/dataoecd/35/56/2101733.pdf>, 41.

33. In fact, those results seem at odds with Professor Mansfield's 1994 study of US. business executives (E Mansfield, 'Intellectual Property Protection, Foreign Direct Investment, and Technology Transfer', Int'l Fin. Corp. Discussion Paper No. 19 (1994)), which found that IP protection influenced mostly executives in high tech. industries. For a discussion, see PJ Heald, 'Misreading a Canonical Work: An Analysis of Mansfield's 1994 Study' (2003) 10 JIPL 309.

34. *Intellectual Property and Development* (n 22 above) 28.

whether to develop new software, for instance.[35] Other factors may include the nature of the innovation process in that industry.[36]

The link between IP and FDI As mentioned earlier, the traditional view on the effect of intellectual property, which is supported by case studies in countries such as postwar Japan, is that higher IP protection, especially of patent rights, will lead to higher inward FDI, which often has a significant technology transfer/intellectual property component.[37] However, in a recent analysis of the

---

35. It has in fact has given rise to the anti-innovation effect known as patent trolls. See RE Thomas, 'Vanquishing Copyright Pirates and Patent Trolls: The Divergent Evolution of Copyright and Patent Laws' (2006) 43 Am Bus LJ 689. Prof Thomas notes (at 730–31):

> The negative impact on small-entity inventors and patent consolidators is why restrictions on a court's ability to grant injunctions are attractive to info-tech companies. Info-tech and other companies that employ low development costs and fast-depreciating patents are strong supporters of this provision because the number of potential patent infringement claims they face is high. In many cases the only requirements for developing info-tech patents are programming knowledge, access to a computer, and time. [. . .]
>
> The reasons that info-tech companies wish to restrict injunctive relief are the same reasons that biotech/pharma oppose such restrictions. Biotech/pharma's interests tend to be closer to those of copyright content holders in that their business model is based on selling products to end users that embody one or a very limited number of patents, whereas info-tech companies are more likely to use their intellectual property as production inputs. (footnotes omitted)

36. 'ICTs and Economic Growth in Developing Countries', OECD Development Assistance Committee, DCD/DAC/POVNET(2004)6/REV1, 10 December 2004, Park and Lippoldt (note 26, above) suggest that in the biotech and electronics groups, stronger patent reform has generally led to greater increases (or fewer decreases) in licensing deals. However, in the computer group, the 'medium' reformers attracted the greatest increase in deals, whereas in the communications group, both the high and low reformers had the most gains in deals. Modest patent reform may be of some benefit to licensing activities in technological fields, such as computers and communications, where the innovation process is cumulative and sequential. Modest patent strength may better enable opportunities for knowledge diffusion and sharing of common pool resources (such as internet tools and data networks). Agreeing with Tim Berners-Lee, Stiglitz notes that in the software field, 'patents stifle innovation', adding that Amazon.com's patent on one-click online purchases is 'not the kind of major intellectual breakthrough that deserve[s] patenting' J Stiglitz, *Making Globalization Work* (Norton 2006), 113–15.

37. Park and Lippoldt explain that licensing transactions are a means by which technology can be transferred from one party to another. Although the details of individual licensing agreements vary, they can include terms referring to technical support, training, and other assistance to be provided by the licensor to the licensee. They can enable the licensee to acquire the right to use new technology (subject to specific conditions) without having to undertake costly research and development (R&D) and to capitalise on the licensor's reputation and expertise. In exchange, the licensor derives fees and royalties, can capitalise on the licensee's local reputation and knowledge, and may obtain reciprocal licenses to

FDI component and its relation to IP, Professor Maskus concluded that many other factors influence FDI and technology transfer decisions, including market liberalization and deregulation, technology development policies and competition regimes, and a low level of corruption.[38] That said, in China's case, the growth of FDI does not seem to be correlated to increases in the level of intellectual property protection or political reforms, suggesting that in some cases at least, there are considerations of geopolitical or 'geocommercial' realities that trump intellectual property concerns.[39]

The conventional wisdom is also that foreign firms invest internationally if there are location advantages and if it is more profitable for them to produce in that country rather than licensing their IP. Firms are more apt to invest in countries that implement strong IP protections (and to bring their IP or allow for licenses in such countries). Transnational firms may also choose to invest in vertical FDI (where different plants produce products that can be used by the plant 'above' it as an input to their product).[40] Yet the IP/FDI correlation is not

---

any technical improvements made by the licensee (eg, grant-backs). Thus, licensing transactions can provide for technology transfer to developing countries, while yielding mutual benefits to both parties. (Executive Summary, p 2)

See also KE Maskus, 'Intellectual Property Rights and Economic Development' (2000) 32 Case West Res JIL 471, 481–85; and KE Maskus and C McDaniel, 'Impacts of the Japanese Patent System on Productivity Growth' (1999) 11 Japan & W Econ 557.

38. KE Maskus, 'Intellectual Property Rights in Encouraging FDI and Technology Transfer' in *Intellectual Property and Development* (note 22 above) 70–71; see also C Fink, 'Patent Protection, Transnational Corporations, and Market Structure: A Simulation Study of the Indian Pharmaceutical Industry' in ibid, 250–51. In his summary of a study by Ginarte and Park (JC Ginarte and WG Park, 'Determinants of Patent Rights: A Cross-National Study' (1997) 26 Res Pol 283, 285–86) Professor Maskus notes that those authors found that the strength of patent rights across countries and over time depended positively on real GDP per capita, the share of R&D in GDP, openness to international trade, and a measure of the freedom of markets from arbitrary and nontransparent government regulation. Human capital, measured by the secondary school enrolment ratio in an earlier period, was a positive and marginally significant contributor to patent rights. (Maskus, 'Intellectual Property Rights and Economic Development' 477).

39. See Y Li, 'Pushing For Greater Protection: The Trend Toward Greater Protection of Intellectual Property in the Chinese Software Industry and the Implications for Rule of Law in China' (2002) 23 UPennJIL 637, 638-"1; KE Maskus, 'The Role of Intellectual Property Rights in Encouraging Foreign Direct Investment and Technology Transfer' (1998) 9 Duke JCIL 109, 115–19 (noting that FDI increased ten-fold in China prior to the introduction of TRIPS-compatible norms); M Schiappacasse, 'Intellectual Property Rights in China: Technology Transfers and Economic Development' (2004) 2 Buffalo IPLJ 164; PK Yu and others, 'China and the WTO: Progress, Perils, and Prospects' (2003) 17 Colum. J. Asian L. 1.

40. See CA Primo Braga and C Fink, 'The Relationship Between Intellectual Property Rights and Foreign Direct Investment' (1998) 9 Duke JCIL 163, 172–73.

universally supported by available data probably because there are several other key factors at play.

The conclusions of Professor Maskus's above-mentioned study are based on data from the International Monetary Fund showing increases in inward and outward FDI between the years 1987 and 1995. Pre-2000 data may not offer ideal parameters to do a full analysis of the current situation. In many cases, IPR protection increased sharply after the TRIPS Agreement entered into force in developing countries, which, except for the least-developed ones, had until January 2000 to comply.[41] Interestingly, in China's case, the date of TRIPS compliance coincided with its becoming a WTO member on 11 December 2001. Another developing-country-specific study that compared African countries to India and China found significantly lower FDI numbers in Africa despite higher levels of IP protection.[42]

The *World Investment Report 2005* prepared by UNCTAD[43] shows that FDI peaked in 1999–2000 (before or coterminous with the TRIPS implementation deadline) and then actually declined significantly in 2001, 2002 and 2003 (by 41 percent, 13 percent, and 12 percent, respectively, before increasing by 2 percent in 2004). However, they also note that 'The difference between inflows to developed countries and developing countries shrank to $147 billion—a significant narrowing of the gap compared with previous years'.[44]

Another study, this one concerning the situation of FDI in so-called 'transition economies',[45] is perhaps more illuminating because those countries were, for the most part, closed to FDI until approximately 1990. The study confirmed intuitive conclusions, in particular that (a) FDI in IP sensitive areas is discouraged when IP protection is weak and that across all sectors; and (b) low IPR protection encourages foreign firms to focus on distribution rather than local production.[46]

---

41. TRIPS, Article 65. For patents on pharmaceuticals in countries where patents were previously unavailable for inventions of that type, the transitional period ended on 1 January 2005 (TRIPS Article 65(4)).

42. S Ragavan, 'The Jekyll and Hyde Story of International Trade: The Supreme Court in PhRMA v. Walsh and the TRIPS Agreement' (2004) 38 URichL Rev 777, 789; and RM Sherwood, 'Global Prospects for the Role of Intellectual Property in Technology Transfer' (2002) 42 IDEA 27, 33–34 (emphasizing the need for proper enforcement mechanisms).

43. Available at <http://www.unctad.org/en/docs/wir2005_en.pdf>.

44. Ibid 3.

45. Essentially, these are countries in Central and Eastern Europe that formed part of the former Soviet bloc. Article 65(3) of the TRIPS Agreement refers to them as '[m]ember[s] which [are] in the process of transformation from a centrally-planned [economy] into a market, free-enterprise economy and which [are] undertaking structural reform of [their] intellectual property system[s]. . . .'

46. B Smarzynska Javorcik, 'The Composition of Foreign Direct Investment and Protection of Intellectual Property Rights: Evidence from Transition Economies' (2004) 48 Eur Econ Rev 39.

In the specific area of pharmaceuticals, available data analyzed in another study on the Indian market illustrates that the introduction of patent protection is likely to lead to increased research and development, price increases, and related welfare effects. However, research also shows that only 10.9 percent of the top 500 pharmaceuticals in that market were patented. Additionally, the government retained certain tools including price controls and, in cases where Article 31 of TRIPS allows, compulsory licenses.[47]

The UK IPR Commission Report[48] presents a picture consistent with the above findings but also stresses that it is important not to consider developing countries as a homogeneous group.[49] In fact, a fairly well developed sequencing phenomenon exists. In an impoverished country, there is little rent that foreign firms can extract and limited innovation potential—with the possible exception of the exploitation of genetic resources or traditional knowledge, a topic to which I shall return below. Furthermore, there is scarce technology to copy or improve on high technology goods, and it is unlikely that the country in question can benefit as an innovator from technology transfer. Foreign Direct Investment is unlikely because of factors unrelated to IP, such as infrastructure, or absence of a viable domestic market. International firms take notice when a country becomes both a piracy threat and a potential market, even if the threat is limited to a fairly small percentage of the population.[50] While countries that implement IP norms may benefit from increased local development and inward FDI, they may also incur job losses in established copycat industries and welfare costs associated with higher local prices. However, consumers benefit from knowing they are purchasing the genuine product, especially in areas where the quality of the goods is essential.

In sum, economic analysis tends to demonstrate that sufficient IP protection is an essential component of increased inward FDI and trade flows in IP-sensitive goods for countries above a certain economic development threshold.[51] The trade

---

47. Fink (n 38 above) 250–51.
48. See n 23 above.
49. Ibid 2–3.
50. For a discussion on the situation in Kenya, see JM Migai Akech, 'The African Growth Opportunity Act: Implications for Kenya's Trade and Development' (2001) 33 NYUJIL & Pol 651.
51. A point made by Professor Cottier: '[TRIPS] rules apply (subject to extended time periods for implementation) across the board and irrespective of real competitive relations. In reality, lack of protection, or inadequate protection, is mainly felt in relation to highly competitive economies and sectors, while it remains without much impact in relation to noncompetitive products. Despite lack of protection, they are not in a position to harm and displace competitive products. Intellectual property does not really matter in such constellations that may frequently be found in DCs, in particular LDCs. On the one hand, the matter could therefore be left to benign neglect of failure to fully comply with obligations. Reality largely follows this model. It is not an accident that WTO disputes on

regime (especially tariffs and nontariff barriers), tax, and competition laws are also potent influences.

ii. Policy Lessons of Recent Analyses

When higher IP rules allow foreign firms to begin exporting IP-sensitive goods and services to a country, local consumers and industries gain lawful access to those products and services. This may result in welfare gains. This may also, however, lead to price increases, especially when goods whose status changes to 'pirate' or 'counterfeit' after the introduction of IPR protection are displaced by genuine goods sold at a higher price. Increased trade flows may lead to new jobs in distributorships and the retail sector, but these are likely to be low-skilled, low-paying positions. There also may be significant gains in terms of product quality and reliability, most notably in the area of pharmaceuticals.

Another lesson learnt is that inward FDI is a more powerful development lever than trade. It transfers technology and usually creates jobs requiring a higher skill level. This may be the case for the manufacturing of technology-intensive goods, which requires engineering and quality-control positions, as well as management and other softer skill sets. In the best-case scenario, some research and development jobs are created, which may have spillover effects in areas such as higher education or local laboratories.

Copyright In the absence of sufficient rights and enforcement options, one may reasonably conclude that in the copyright arena, music, films, and books are unlikely to be distributed, and national cultural industries are unlikely to develop. In these areas, the gains generated by establishing sufficient protection are 'unambiguous'.[52] However, the introduction or beginning of enforcement of copyrights may also lead to the closure of businesses that rely on copying, thus displacing (mostly unskilled) workers. Ideally, some of these workers will be able to find work in the new, creative industry jobs made possible by the adequate protection of copyrights. There is little economic benefit to be derived from selling counterfeit DVDs or luxury goods (whether in terms of jobs or income or sales taxes, which may not be paid). There are however, clear risks in selling counterfeit spare parts for automobiles or pharmaceuticals. Finally, new jobs created by new IP-based industries are likely to pay higher wages and stimulate creativity and reduce the need felt by local creators to live in higher protection countries as exiles.[53]

IPRs mainly exist between developed countries." T Cottier, 'From Progressive Liberalization to Progressive Regulation in WTO Law' (2006) 9 JIEL 779, 802.

52. KE Maskus, 'Strengthening Intellectual Property Rights in Lebanon, in Intellectual Property and Development' (note 22 above) 286–89.

53. If not physically, at least industrially. For example, a book published by an author who is not a national Berne (or WTO) Member country may still be protected if the book

Trademarks Trademark protection is essential to generate higher inward FDI. The purpose of trademarks is twofold. First, trademarks protect the public by indicating the source of goods and services so that purchasers can identify the desired level of quality and receive a similar product or consistent service over time. Second, trademarks protect the trademark owner against commercial misappropriation of the mark and/or the goodwill associated with the mark. The value of a mark stems from the mental link that is created over time in the minds of prospective buyers between particular goods or services and a particular source. Many people will buy a product or service because consciously or unconsciously they associate qualities such as value, excellence, or efficiency with the trademark. A strong trademark is invaluable because the ability of a mark to raise these associations directs a potential buyer toward a company's own product or service rather than those of a competitor. Trademarks are influenced both by sellers' perceptions about buyers' psychology and the public's marketing-influenced perceptions of how goods and services are differentiated. Trademarks also serve an informational purpose: the legal protection of marks gives companies an incentive to invest in making their marks more recognizable and easier to remember so consumers can more easily identify which particular good or service they want.

Introducing trademark protection will, as in the case of copyrights, lead to the closure of businesses producing counterfeit goods. Some of the higher end former counterfeiters may be able to produce noncounterfeit goods (either legal goods of the same class or licensed goods legally bearing the trademark). Counterfeit economic activity may thus be replaced by jobs in distribution, retail, and franchises. These are, however, often low-level, low-skilled jobs. Trademark protection will also benefit consumers who will have access to 'genuine' goods, ie, goods that come with the perceived assurance of quality associated with the mark via domestic or international advertising and reputation. Over time, the experience in product assembly, delivery, servicing, and management acquired through franchise and distributorship arrangements may be transferred to new local businesses.

Patents Patents are also directly relevant. Patents do not ensure that new products will be supplied in the short term. When patent protection is unavailable, products that would otherwise infringe a patent could be made available legally for the domestic market. In terms of FDI, however, the impact is exactly the opposite because global firms relying on patent protection need assurances about the level of protection and enforcement before considering any significant technology transfer. Fully exploiting a patent often requires expertise that is not fully disclosed in the published patent or patent application. Ongoing research

---

is first published in a Member country, thus benefiting the industry of the country of publication.

and variants of the patented inventions may also exist. For this reason, firms also consider the level of protection of trade secrets for information that, for strategic or other reasons, is not disclosed in a patent. In fact, for certain process patents, even in the presence of a presumption that a product not previously available results from a new patented process, many companies prefer not to disclose new processes in patent applications.[54] Direct patent-related inward FDI is often the best way to create high-paying, highly skilled jobs, and it is therefore highly sought after by many governments willing to go to great lengths to attract foreign firms.[55]

Introducing patent protection produces a shock on the economy. Like trademark protection, it will lead to closures of businesses that were copying (legally before patents were issued) products or using processes developed by foreign inventors. In certain cases, they may, like in the area of trademarks, become legal manufacturers. In other cases, it may lead economic players to move from imitation-based models to innovation-based models, thus adding to the Displacement Effect discussed below.

It is also worth noting that introducing patents may not help Research and Development (R&D) efforts based on imitation because exploitation of the results of imitation (at least beyond experimental use) would in many cases require a license. Moving from a lax indigenous imitative base to a 'foreign seed' base model thus arguably favors countries (mostly in the West) that currently own the bulk of global patented knowledge. But shifts remain possible as innovation gray matter builds up faster in some parts of the developing world, where in addition research costs are lower. This is the topic of the next section.

C. THE DISPLACEMENT OF INNOVATION

i. The Role of the Demanders

The multinational companies that successfully lobbied to establish a linkage between IP and trade, first in the domestic US context and then in the WTO,[56] did so because of their desire to increase profit and markets or, to put it differently,

---

54. Article 34(1) of the TRIPS Agreement reads in relevant part: "[I]f the subject matter of a patent is a process for obtaining a product, the judicial authorities shall have the authority to order the defendant to prove that the process to obtain an identical product is different from the patented process". TRIPS, Art. 34(1). See SA Merrill and others (eds), *A Patent System for the 21st Century* (Joseph Henry Press, 2005) 20, 23, available at: <http://www.nap.edu/html/patentsystem/0309089107.pdf>.

55. Javorcik (note 46 above) 60.

56. Their decision to use the multilateral forum may be explained by the lack of alternatives: They could not easily lobby developing countries individually (having, in most cases, little to offer in exchange for higher intellectual property protection).

to maximize rent extraction and increase the number of foreign territories into which they could consider expanding their commercial or industrial activities. They see 'the failure to protect foreign intellectual property rights as an implicit subsidy to domestic production and therefore as a means to promote growth domestically.'[57] Imposing this harsh medicine on developing countries created difficult situations, especially in less industrialized nations.[58] However, as it led to a progressive deindustrialization of the West through outsourcing, it also led to the emergence of new competitors for the same companies that lobbied for TRIPS, as more developing nations at the receiving end of technology transfers and inward FDI develop the ability to innovate and compete. Combined with a healthy dose of economic nationalism,[59] the medium-term impacts of TRIPS and related measures—such as free-trade agreements and bilateral investment treaties, the purpose of which are to bring developing countries into the Western IP system are certainly worth pondering. Consider Japan after World War II and now or China in 2000 and China circa 2025.[60]

There is a consensus assumption that the West will continue to dominate and that the clout that follows from such dominance will allow it to impose its will on the developing world or at least to resist norm-making attempts not supported by Western stakeholders. One might consider WIPO's work on Traditional Knowledge or a Development Agenda (to the extent it tries to influence future norm-making and interpretation beyond capacity building and technology transfer commitments) where work is slow due to lukewarm support by several western countries, as examples of the latter. Bilateral trade and investment treaties would be an example of the former.

If the current rates of economic growth are maintained, this assumption will hold, at least in part.

As the table shows, by 2030 the United States would still largely dominate with a GDP of $25 trillion. China, however, would have moved from fourth to

---

57. Trachtman (n 5 above). He also notes, however that '(a)s the most valuable intellectual property rights are owned by persons or firms based in developed countries, TRIPS denied developing countries the ability to provide these implicit subsidies at foreign expense. It is also important to recognize that TRIPS seems to have resulted in a significant net outflow of cash from developing countries to developed countries. Thus, TRIPS cannot generally be understood as beneficial to developing countries standing alone'.

58. Now subject, however, to the postponement of the deadline to implement TRIPS accorded least-developed nations until July 2013 (TRIPS Council Decision of 29 November 2005, Extension of the Transition Period Under Article 66.1 For Least-Developed Country Members, document IP/C/40.)

59. KJ Vandevelde, 'The Political Economy of a Bilateral Investment Treaty' (1998) 92 AJIL 621, 621–23.

60. J Straus, 'The Impact of the New World Order on Economic Development: The Role of Intellectual Property Rights System', (2006) 6 J Marshall Rev IPL 1, 5–9, where Prof Straus describes 'China's commanding, complex, and almost scary development'.

TABLE 1. GDP

RANK	1	2	3	4	5	6	7	8	
	US	Japan	Germany	China	UK	France	Canada	India	
pop 2006	300	128	82.5	1304.5	60	60.7	32.6	1094.6	millions
GDP 2006	12,455 $	4,506 $	2,782 $	2,229 $	2,193 $	2,110 $	1,115 $	786 $	billion USD
GNI (atlas)	43,740 $	38,980 $	34,580 $	1,740 $	37,600 $	34,810 $	32,600 $	720 $	USD
GDP/cap	41,517 $	35,202 $	33,720 $	1,709 $	36,543 $	34,764 $	34,209 $	718 $	USD
	US	China	Japan	Germany	UK	France	India	Canada	
pop 2030	360	1350	130	85	67.5	68	1400	38	millions
GDP growth/yr	3.00%	6.00%	2.00%	2.50%	2.50%	2.50%	5.50%	3.00%	assumed annual growth (in%)
GDP 2030	25318 $	9,021 $	7,246 $	5,030 $	3,964 $	3,816 $	2,837 $	2,266 $	billions USD
GDP per capita	70,328 $	6,682 $	55,738 $	59,176 $	58,726 $	56,118 $	2,026 $	59,632 $	

Source: World Bank statistics/OECD

second place, ahead of all European countries and Japan, and India would be seventh, ahead of Canada. As was pointed out by the *New York Times*:

> China surpassed Canada in the first two months of this year as the largest exporter to the United States. According to statistics released by the World Trade Organization last Thursday, China also overtook the United States in the second half of 2006 to become the world's second-largest exporter of goods over all, after Germany. China is still nearly 25 times as dependent on exports to the United States as a percentage of its total economic output as the United States is on exports to China. Given that the Chinese economy is less than a quarter the size of the American economy, it is all the more striking that Chinese exports to the United States are worth more than six times American exports to China.[61]

Naturally, one may question growth assumptions, especially after the financial crisis of 2008–09. The growing trade, budgetary, and current account deficits of the United States, the possibility of natural or man-made disasters affecting any country to the point not simply of reducing growth but also of effecting a net GDP reduction, are always possible. However, delving into such contingencies would not be productive for our purposes.

The hypothesis explored here is that we may be on the cusp of a significant displacement of research and innovation to certain developing countries, which should cause a regional spillover effect, which in turn will increase the gravitational pull of such regions for global business and generate new competitors based in such regions. In other words the short-term determinants that drove multinational corporations in the pharmaceutical, software, and entertainment sectors to multilateralize Western intellectual property norms is creating a playing field which allows them to move gradually higher knowledge functions to developing countries with an abundance of brainpower, (Western educated and increasingly some locally trained in excellent institutions), and much lower labor and regulatory compliance costs (from the Sarbanes-Oxley Act of 2002[62] to environmental regulation).

There is increasingly convincing empirical support for this thesis. For example, 'Business Week' reported in May 2007 that 'more than three-quarters of new research and development sites to be set up over the next three years will be in China and India, according to a study by Booz Allen Hamilton and business school INSEAD [. . .] The survey of 186 companies worldwide found a general trend of innovation moving east and 'predicts that China and India are on the verge of overtaking Western Europe as the most important locations for foreign

---

61. K Bradsher, 'China Leans Less on US Trade', *New York Times* (18 April 2007).
62. Public Company Accounting Reform and Investor Protection Act of 2002, Pub. L. No. 107-204, 116 Stat. 745 (codified in 15 USC 7243 (Supp. III 2003)).

R&D for US businesses',[63] adding that by 'the end of 2007 China and India combined will account for almost a third (31 percent) of global R&D staff, up from 19 percent in 2004.

Another sign is the constant string of strategic *governmental* investment in R&D in developing countries. For example, in June 2007, a number of European governments announced a significant investment in research and development in Egypt, ostensibly as a contribution to development but also perhaps to 'stake a claim'. Interestingly, when the investment was announced, officials refused to speak of a 'brain drain', insisting instead of 'brain circulation', recognizing the mobility (in both directions) of scientists.[64]

Then again, under pressure to increase quarterly profits and shareholder value, the multinational companies that sowed the TRIPS seed probably have no choice but to pursue this course of action.[65] A cynic might add that it also explains a possible tendency on the part of some of those companies—and the United States Trade Representative (USTR) in bilateral agreements—not to accompany TRIPS implementation with strong measures destined to optimize local research, development, and innovation in developing countries and thereby support the argument that patents in developing countries are best viewed as market creation and rent extraction tools rather than as innovation incentives (in those countries). In other words, with a high level of intellectual property protection in place, those companies consider these countries first and foremost as new export markets and possibly lower-cost production centers, while maintaining the technological superiority in the West (where R&D is based), and hence, continued economic dominance. According to this view, as Professor Scotchmer noted, 'intellectual property rights are no longer a way to encourage domestic innovation. They also become a strategic instrument to affect profit flows among nations. To affect profit flows favourably, each country wants the strongest possible protections in foreign countries, and the weakest possible protections for foreigners in its own domestic market'.[66]

Yet one may also question the ability of Western companies to prevent technology from being exploited in the recipient countries or indeed their willingness to do so if those countries prove to be innovative, lower-cost environments.

---

63. 'Europe Losing to China and India in R&D', *Business Week* (26 May 2007). Available at <http://www.businessweek.com/globalbiz/content/may2006/gb20060526_804863.htm?chan=search>.

64. D Douara, 'EU backs Egypt's science, technology with LE 135 mln', *The Daily Star (Egypt)* (19 June 2007).

65. Multinational (or perhaps more accurately transnational) corporations "account for a major share of global R&D. Indeed, with $310 billion spent in 2002 (United Kingdom, DTI 2004), the 700 largest R&D spending firms of the world—of which at least 98% percentare TNCs—accounted for close to half (46 percent) of the world's total R&D expenditure and more than two-thirds (69 percent) of the world's business R&D." *World Investment Report 2005* (n 43 above) 119.

66. S Scotchmer, *Innovation and Incentives* (MIT Press, 2004) 329.

ii. The Transfer of R&D to Developing Countries

The TRIPS demanders' plan to increase protection in new export and outsourcing territories was totally understandable from a business standpoint.[67] Yet, it may very well be that the powers of innovation, once unleashed and properly supported, may cut Western dominance short. From this perspective, the end result of TRIPS for many developing countries and global welfare would be very positive overall, especially compared with otherwise bleak economic outlooks. As Michael Ryan noted:

> In the foreword to the 1998/99 World Development Report: Knowledge for Development, [then] World Bank president James Wolfensohn states that "economies are built not merely through the accumulation of physical capital and human skill, but on a foundation of information, learning, and adaptation" and declares that in this new world economy that the "globalization of trade, finance, and information flows is intensifying competition, raising the danger that the poorest countries and communities will fall behind more rapidly than ever before." . . . The WDR recommends that closing knowledge gaps depend upon (1) the acquisition of knowledge through trade, foreign direct investment, and licensing, (2) the absorption of knowledge through education, and (3) the communication of knowledge through advanced information technologies. Developing countries intent upon closing knowledge gaps and reducing information problems will do so with the help [of] intellectual property institutions—trademark to facilitate consumer knowledge, patent to facilitate technology transfer, copyright to facilitate literary, artistic, and informational expression.[68]

---

67. RM Sherwood, 'Some Things Cannot Be Legislated' (2002) 10 Card JICL 37, 39–40. Sherwood explains:
> [A] robust intellectual property regime may indeed not be the objective sought for developing countries by some global elites. The TRIPS level of protection may serve their interests enough to protect their sales into those countries without requiring a level of protection sufficiently robust to encourage local firms and individuals to conduct research and make inventions. In other words, from their perspective, half a loaf for developing countries is just fine. Another way of putting this is to suggest that developing countries are asked by TRIPS to go only half way in protecting intellectual property (primarily the intellectual property of others) without going far enough to fully encourage their own inventors and investors to build national intellectual property prowess.

See also by the same author, 'Global Prospects for the Role of Intellectual Property in Technology Transfer' (2002) 42 IDEA 27, 34 ('[R]obust protection will release a great deal of energy into the economies of many of these countries'.).

68. MP Ryan, 'Knowledge-Economy Elites, the International Law of Intellectual Property and Trade, and Economic Development' (2002) 10 Card JICL 271, 303.

In other words, and as India's 'silicon valley' centered around Bangalore and Beijing's 'Z-Park'[69] have begun to demonstrate, the appropriation process that began by the limited outsourcing of low innovation coding[70] or other functions (eg, 'customer care' call centers) tends to evolve to progressively more complex coding tasks and higher innovation activities, leading to significant innovations in the recipient (outsourced-to) country. The outsourced low innovation becomes a form of technology transfer and serves as a stepping stone to higher innovation functions and eventually to world-class competitiveness.[71] And while a majority of the initial client base of India's programming powerhouse may have been foreign, for most US and European entities, the potential for homegrown innovation-based industries has now increased very significantly. The same could be said of China's manufacturing industries and more recently of the exponential growth of its information technology and telecommunications sectors.[72]

China's R&D efforts are increasingly rapidly, and it plans to match the US innovation levels (relative to GDP) by 2020[73] and should have the largest number

---

69. C Juliette-Beale, 'Z-Park: China's Silicon Valley' *Business Week* (5 June 2007). Available at <http://www.businessweek.com/innovate/content/jun2007/id20070605_039465.htm>. This section focuses on China and India, but similar observations could be made in respect of several other countries—though each one has a different industrial infrastructure—including Brazil, Egypt, South Africa, South Korea, Thailand, and many others.

70. One well-known commentator attributes the acceleration of outsourcing to India to the need of Western companies to deal with the Y2K 'bug', which required extensive but fairly straightforward coding. In that case, the deadline was self-evidently unmovable. See TL. Friedman, *The World Is Flat: The Globalized World in the Twenty-First Century* . (Penguin Books, 2005) 131–37.

71. As UNCTAD's *World Investment Report 2005* noted: 'Research and development (R&D) is one source of innovation (box III.1). In the early stages of technological activity, enterprises need not set up formal R&D departments. As they mature, however, it becomes increasingly desirable to monitor, import, and implement technologies. Research and Development as a distinct activity may appear as early as the second level of complexity, where multifaceted technologies are involved or if local conditions demand significant adaptation. In a developing country, such R&D is feasible once the operation is fairly large scale and the necessary technical skills are available. The role of formal R&D then grows as the firm attempts significant technological improvements to introduce new products or processes'. (n 43 above) 102.

72. Christine Zhen-Wei Qiang, *China's Information Revolution: Managing the Economic and Social Transformation* . (World Bank, 2007). See also above n 69.

73. According to the China Blawg, 'The OECD (see <http://www.oecd.org/document/26/0,2340,en_2649_201185_37770522_1_1_1_1,00.html>) recently announced that this year, China's R&D spending will surpass that of Japan. Estimates have China's 2006 spending of $136 billion edging out Japan's $130 billion investment. . . .The rapid increase in R&D spending in China is one aspect of its current economic development policy that is designed to make China a major innovative force in the near future. The government announced a 15-year plan last February that has R&D spending rising to 2 percent of GDP

of researchers of any country by that date.⁷⁴ Its information technology industry 'has been an engine of economic growth—growing two to three times faster than GDP over the past ten years.'⁷⁵ Multinationals are adapting.⁷⁶

The possibility of very rapid growth of a country to the top of the global innovation scale may be exemplified by the developments in Israel. As Professor Trajtenberg has shown,⁷⁷ Israelis filed less than 100 patent applications per year in the United States Patent and Trademark Office ('USPTO') before 1970. That number now surpasses 1,200. In terms of patents issued per year by the USPTO to foreign nationals, Israel's rate of growth between 1968 and 1997 was 13.3 percent, compared to 5.5 percent for Canada and Ireland, 2.4 percent for Germany, and 3.1 percent for the United Kingdom. Among the few countries and territories that did better than Israel over this period are New Zealand (16.9 percent); South Korea (27.9 percent), and Taiwan (15.7 percent). More important perhaps, Israel has the fourth largest number of patents per capita (after the United States, Japan, and Taiwan).⁷⁸ Another reason for the success of the Israeli innovation strategy is its focus, with 20 percent or more of all

---

by 2010 and 2.5 jpercent of GDP by 2020. This would put China's R&D spending as a percentage of GDP at US levels by 2020". Available at: <http://blawg.lehmanlaw.com/english/archives/2006/12/05/199.html>.

74. According to the same OECD report, 'China, the number of researchers increased by 77 percent between 1995 and 2004. China now ranks second worldwide with 926,000 researchers, just behind the United States (more than 1.3 million)'. The Gartner Group recently ranked India's Infosys as the most innovative software company worldwide.

75. See Christine Zhen-Wei Qiang (n 72 above)

76. According to the *Financial Times*:

Everyone knows that the weight of global power is moving inexorably towards the Asia-Pacific region. China and India are on the rise. Japan is recovering. The US is still a formidable military superpower but its international influence is in steep decline. As The Economist observed in an editorial last week ("Come in number one, your time is up"), the US has been overtaken by China as the world's biggest merchandise goods exporter and is expected to yield the top place in overall economic output in two decades. This shift in the global balance of power is well documented. What has yet to be grasped is the effect on business and the way it is conducted. Multinational companies are the best placed to understand the significance of Asia's rise and several have held board meetings in China or India rather than at home to emphasise their commitment to these fast-growing markets. This is the start of a trend.

Victor Mallet, 'Watch for the new timelords of global business', *Financial Times* (19 April 2007).

77. M Trajtenberg, 'Innovation in Israel 1968–1997' in AB Jaffe and M Trajtenberg, *Patents, Citations and Innovations: A Window on the Knowledge Economy* (MIT Press, 2002) 337–76.

78. Ibid 347–48. Taiwan's per capita number surpassed Israel in 1996. Taiwan would be another interesting case study.

patents issued in only three areas: electronics, computers and communications, and pharmaceuticals.[79]

iii. Developing Countries as Global Competitors

It is therefore not totally unrealistic to see a future where Indian, Chinese, and other companies compete head-to-head with innovation-based Western enterprises (in fact, in certain industries, this process has begun). This innovation displacement effect of TRIPS and TRIPS Plus Agreements may be accelerated when considering that a very significant proportion of researchers in Western laboratories are nationals of developing countries (such as India).[80] Because the West cannot compete on manufacturing costs and less so on productivity than before, if (when) it loses its competitive innovation advantage, the picture of the global economy may be profoundly altered with a shift of the gravity center. To a certain extent, that would prove that those who pushed for the application of TRIPS-compliant norms to the developing world were right (at least for countries counted as success stories). As we have seen, those demanders were largely US and European-based multinationals. It would amount to historical irony if they should end up losing their economic dominance as a result.[81]

Perhaps the plan is that, through investment and acquisition, the same capital, though geographically reconfigured (an issue for Western tax authorities—who may have to move massively to sales-based taxes to replace income-based revenues—but not for the companies involved) will remain dominant in most industries.[82] That would explain why both in bilateral discussions and multilaterally (to the extent that the WTO remains a viable negotiation forum for new

---

79. Ibid 353. Mechanical and chemical patents constitute approximately 10% percent (each) of the total. As of 1994, mechanical patents were still the largest category overall in the USPTO filings, with electronics, computers & communications, and pharmaceuticals standing at 15 percent of less.

80. The *Financial Times* reports that in order to compensate for the shortage of first-rate talent, the 'clamour for brains is driving elite employers in the UK to behave like football talent scouts in India and elsewhere'; A Clegg, 'In Hot Pursuit of the Best Brains', *Financial Times* (14 March 2007).

81. Joseph Stiglitz reports that both the Council of Economic Advisers and the Office of Science and Technology Policy in the White House had deep reservations about TRIPS, and that he believes that "the way the intellectual property regime has evolved is not good for the United States and the EU; but even more, I believe it is not in the interests of the developing countries." (J Stiglitz n 36 above 116–17).

82. One author argues tha, once the proper legal system and protection is in place—and especially what he refers to as the invisible infrastructure of 'asset management'—the conditions required for 'Western' capitalist model to be movable and innovation fully to emerge will be present. See H De Soto, *The Mystery of Capital: Why Capitalism Triumphs in the West and Fails Everywhere Else* (2003).

areas), there is such an emphasis on investment liberalization.[83] However, it may call into question the assumption that governs US bilateral and multinational intellectual property negotiations that US domestic interests are coextensive with those of multinational corporations.[84] Multinational corporations that label themselves as American companies, rightly or not, still need the US government (and occasionally its military arm) to spur growth of new markets and level their outsourcing playing field.

In light of the high mobility of capital and innovation, the relative lack of scientists (especially compared to very high enrollment in science and engineering programs in a number of developing countries including China[85]) and the higher level of business regulation in the United States and associated compliance costs,[86] is it fair to ask whether US prominence in innovation (and its insistence that other countries continually increase their levels of IP protection)

---

83. UNCTAD maintains a database of bilateral investment treaties. The list is impressive. As of 1 June 2006, it listed 48 bilateral treaties involving the United States alone. Available at: <http://www.unctadxi.org/templates/DocSearch___779.aspx>.

84. CJ Forster, *China's Secret Weapon: Science Policy and Global Power* (The Foreign Policy Center, London, 2006) 29–30: 'While policymakers regard S&T [science and technology] as a race between nations in a zero-sum game, businesses see themselves as part of a global information network . . . Government officials are more concerned about stemming the flow of technologies to competitors and possible rivals who might use it for military objectives . . . However, firms and businesses prefer a system that leads to the dissemination of knowledge, including to political rivals'.

85. *World Investment Report 2005* (n 43 above) 159 and foll. One should also consider the number of students from developing countries enrolled in programs in industrialized countries. The World Investment *Report* notes a growth of employment in R&D in developing countries (by local and foreign entities) of 20 percent per year compared to approximately 2 percent on the West. The cumulative effect of this growth over 20 years seems to support the displacement effect theory.

86. One well-known example would be the Sarbanes-Oxley Act of 2002—n 62 above. According to the *Financial Times*, the severe restrictions on immigration after the September 11th attacks, including the major cuts in student and H1-B visas (combined with the extremely unfriendly attitude of immigration officers and excessive, arbitrary deportations—their poll shows that 66 percent of foreign travelers agreed with the statement that a simple mistake or single wrong thing could lead to detention or deportation) are contributing to the shifting of research and development overseas and notes that "presenting an unwelcoming face to the world has political as well as economic implications". G Rachman, 'How to help the huddled masses through immigration', *Financial Times* blog entry (13 March 2007). Available at <http://blogs.ft.com/rachmanblog/2007/03/how_to_help_the.html#more>. Rachman notes: 'A McKinsey report into America's financial services industry, also published in January, warned that New York risks losing its status as the "financial capital of the world" within 10 years. The first two problems it cited were overregulation and fear of litigation. But problem three was US immigration restrictions which are shutting out highly skilled workers'.

will endure.[87] Is it clear that the pharmaceutical companies that drive US foreign intellectual property policy will forever remain 'US companies'? As Chris Patten, former Governor of Hong Kong and European Commissioner for External Relations noted recently: 'If the Western front has fundamentally changed, or been broken by events and cultural disjuncture, what international configuration will emerge during the short interval of years before the rise of China and India reshapes the world's power politics'?[88]

The principal counterargument is the point made by, *inter alia*, well-known business consultants Jack and Suzy Welch. They argue that systemic advantages of the West in general and the United States in particular will continue to outweigh the much faster growth in India and China. They write that the 'US has a *final competitive advantage* that is as powerful as it is unique: its confluence of bright, hungry entrepreneurs and flush, eager investors'.[89] Yet a very significant proportion of new innovators hired in US labs are Chinese and Indian scientists or from other developing countries. And they are mobile. This casts a doubt of the permanent nature of the advantage, especially when the costs of innovation (which, as we are often reminded, is 5 percent gray matter and 95 percent sweat...) are factored in. Jack and Suzy Welch also argue that neither China nor India comes close to the United States in terms of a 'killer app' and that it will

---

87. As of 2003, United States was (still) home for 42.3 percent of the top 700 R&D firms worldwide (*World Investment Report 2005*, note 43 above 121). But the figure is based on dollars spent, which obscures two key factors: how efficiently the research dollars are spent and how far can a research dollar be stretched in one country compared to another—per employee expenditures of US firms are significantly lower in their overseas laboratories (ibid 122), and recent surveys show that cost and lack of manpower in industrialized nations (which slows time to market) have become major drivers of decisions about the location of R&D (ibid 159). The recent announcement by Intel that it was moving design and manufacturing operations to Dalian (China) (though at this stage at least not for the most advanced chips) at a cost of $2.5 billion is yet another example of a trend that is likely to accelerate. See 'Intel given green light for 2.5-billion-US-dollar wafer facility in NE China', *People's Daily* (15 March 2007) available at <http://english.people.com.cn/200703/15/eng20070315_358013.html>). Intel set up Intel China Labs in 2000 and also formed an alliance with Baidu.com, a major Chinese search engine, in April 2006, to develop search applications for laptops, mobile phones, and home PCs. See 'Intel, Baidu to jointly develop search apps", *InfoWorld* (13 April 2006) (available at <http://www.infoworld.com/article/06/04/13/77407_HNintelbaidusearch_1.html>).

88. C Patten, *Not Quite the Diplomat* (Penguin, 2006) 2. Mr Patten also questions the recent by the US government away from multilateral forums: 'There are other and better ways of asserting the primacy of values in which America has always believed than ultimate dependence on exceptionalism: doing whatever America wishes to do because she can get away with it... international agreements and the rule of law offer more effective ways of guiding the international community and protecting America's interest'. (307).

89. J and S Welch, 'Sounds Economics Fuels US Hegemony', *Gulf News* (24 June 2007) 57.

take years of venture capital 'before the Chinese finally let go of their rote approach to work and embrace innovation'.[90] Clearly the venture capital is far more developed and sophisticated in the West.[91] That said, the lower costs (and, consequently, lower financing needs) and governmental support may compensate partly for the lack of risk capital. More important, as innovation grows, so will the market for this type of investment and it would be far from surprising to see the same venture capital firms that operate in the West enter emerging markets very rapidly. Capital is highly mobile, even more so than people. The fragility of the perpetual superiority arguments is readily apparent.

iv. Was it TRIPS?

One may question whether a causal link between increased FDI, outsourcing of increasingly high knowledge functions (and resulting technology transfers), and the development of local innovation that follows actually exists. India's pharmaceutical industry started well before 2005, when it introduced pharmaceutical patent protection.[92] The United States and Europe, among others, began outsourcing to China before that country had achieved a level of intellectual property protection and enforcement they considered sufficient. Indeed, a recent complaint shows that this level has not yet been reached.[93] Clearly, there are geopolitical (or 'geocommercial') factors at play. Government-subsidized research laboratories were also created prior to TRIPS in those countries. Yet, I suggest that TRIPS (a) led to the emergence of what is a relatively new field of study, namely the impact of introducing Western intellectual property protection in the normative, judicial, and administrative fabric of developing countries (at various stages of economic development); (b) by forcing developing countries to adopt intellectual property protection at that level, is prompting them—though in almost all cases after and not as part of TRIPS implementation—to develop or revise their national innovation policy,[94] which is evidenced, *inter alia*, by the

---

90. Ibid.

91. For good *and* bad. It may also be responsible for part of the 'tech bubble'. In addition, traditional venture capital is often criticized for its tunnel vision, ie, it invests in a limited business sector rather than a diversified set of entrepreneurial ventures. See R Gittell and J E Sohl, 'Technology centers during the economic downturn: What have we learned?' (2005) 17(4) Entrepreneurship & Regional Development 293–312.

92. JN Bhagwati and S Chakravarty,*Contributions to Indian Economic Analysis: A Survey*. (Bombay: Lalvani Publishing House, 1972). The same could be said of Switzerland, which introduced high levels of protection of patents after it had developed world-class industries.

93. WTO, 'China—Measures Affecting the Protection and Enforcement of Intellectual Property Rights: Request for Consultations by the United States' (16 April 2007) WTO Document WT/DS362/1.

94. Stan Metcalfe provides a more complete definition: a 'set of distinct institutions which jointly and individually contribute to the development and diffusion of new

recent efforts on WIPO's Development Agenda and global development. In addition, the increase in FDI and outsourcing of intellectual-property sensitive issues is partly dependent on TRIPS compliance, as was shown in the discussion of recent studies. It thus seems fair to link TRIPS to the increased innovation-based activity in several developing nations. Yet the point of this paper is not to prove this causal link, nor *a fortiori* to quantify it. TRIPS is merely used here as a credible flag bearer of the march toward increased protection and awareness among policy makers since its adoption.

v. Distribution of Innovation Development

There is valid assumption that the net effect of TRIPS in several developing nations had been a new outflow of royalty (rent) payments by developing countries to Western interests, whether because of the patent and trademark rights of the pharmaceutical industry or the copyright rights of the software, entertainment, and publishing industries. This was documented in numerous TRIPS 2.0 efforts, and the lessons learned are increasingly applied to calibration efforts undertaken in Phase 3. That said, calibration should mean more than just limiting subtracting, namely the substantial TRIPS welfare and transition costs. It should include developing a national innovation policy to maximize the positives (benefits), in addition to minimizing the negatives. This is, in fact, the very definition of full calibration. The equation is hard to solve because for countries with finite resources, the immediate impact of additional rent payments reduces resources available to develop domestic innovation. However, the emergence of a number of successful examples tends to show that the circle can be squared.

Against that backdrop and for the purposes of this Chapter, I would group WTO Members into four categories:

1. Industrialized nations, beneficiaries of additional rent made possible by TRIPS-compliant protection;
2. Developing countries where innovation benefits outweighs additional rent extraction by Group 1 made possible by TRIPS;
3. Developing countries where additional rent extraction by Group 1 made possible by TRIPS outweighs innovation benefits;

---

technologies and which provides the framework within which governments form and implement policies to influence the innovation process. As such it is a system of interconnected institutions to create, store and transfer the knowledge, skills and artefacts which define new technologies', JS Metcalfe, 'The Economic Foundations of Technology Policy: Equilibrium and Evolutionary Perspectives' in P Stoneman (ed), *Handbook of the Economics of Innovation and Technological Change* (Blackwell 1995). See also Organisation for Economic Co-operation and Development (OECD), *National Innovations Systems*, n 32 above; and D Archibugi and S Iammarino. 'The Globalization of Technology and National Policies' in D Archibugi and BA Lundvall (eds), *The Globalizing Learning Economy* (Oxford, 2002).

4. Least-developed countries, below the threshold at which substantial industrial innovation benefits are likely to develop but now also exempt from most TRIPS obligations[95] (and consequently free from ip-generated additional rent extraction).

We leave out from our analysis Group 1 (because most if not all members were essentially TRIPS compliant before TRIPS and gradually increased their level of protection over several decades) and Group 4, which is not directly concerned by TRIPS at this juncture, though its Members must be borne in mind for the future. I suggest that the aim of a global development agenda should be to move as many countries as possible from Group 3 to Group 2. This can be achieved in part by measures to limit welfare impacts of TRIPS. However, in the longer term, it can be sustained only by developing domestic industrial innovation potential.

It is also essential to note that displacement is not a zero sum game. In other words, not every additional R&D dollar invested in country B means an equal loss in country A. Research can be amplified by the new inputs, vision, and human abilities of researches in country B. Second, globalization is leading to the emergence of mobile researchers, often having the nationality of country B and working in country A for most of their time, but traveling often to their home country and third countries. In a best-case scenario, this should create numerous cross-fertilization opportunities.

D. CONCLUSION

The latest developments in China, India, and others such as Brazil and perhaps Russia[96] beg the question whether imitation is a necessary phase of industrial development (defined here as a movement toward Western-style capitalism with a strong emphasis on innovation). Imitation is still widely practiced in the West, most notably in the form of reverse engineering. Indeed, especially in smaller or less advanced markets, innovation often proceeds along the following sequence: first a country imitates foreign technology (the *imitation* phase) which itself requires some technical skills); then it modifies the foreign technology to suit domestic needs and markets (the *local innovation* phase); and then it produces

---

95. See n 58 above.
96. The four so-called BRIC countries. It seems the term was first prominently used by Goldman Sachs investment bank in 2001 in Global Economics Paper No. 99: Dreaming with BRICs: The Path to 2050, available at: <http://www2.goldmansachs.com/insight/research/reports/99.pdf>. See also 'The BRICs Dream: Web Tour', July 2006, available at: <http://www2.goldmansachs.com/insight/research/reports/report32.html>; and RC Bird, 'Defending Intellectual Property Rights in the BRIC Economies' (2006) 43 Am Bus LJ 317, 347.

innovations (whether new products or processes or improvements of existing ones) which are globally competitive (the *global innovation* phase). A strong intellectual property system will be required to support this last phase. It will also be helpful in the second phase. Conflicts which may arise, however, due to the need to license the foreign technology to which an improvement is made or applied, often can be solved through licensing (market forces) or if that fails, by the issuance of a dependent patent compulsory license (as allowed under TRIPS Article 31(l)).

The imitation phase is essential to internalize the 'global' state of the art in any given field. In other words, before one can begin to innovate, one must ascertain the level of innovation in the field concerned worldwide to determine what can be used without a license and what could be improved upon either by localizing a product or making it better for the global market.[97] Then, perhaps, one can obtain intellectual property protection on such improvements. Naturally, one must have the intellectual, technical, and material tools to access and process this global state-of-the art before improvements or adaptations can be envisaged. This explains the heavy emphasis put on education, training, and technical assistance in recent analyses.

To illustrate the point, the notion of novelty in patent law is generally defined as worldwide novelty, meaning that any element of prior art anticipating the invention claimed anywhere in the world will be sufficient to refuse the application. As a result, and also owing to the global nature of trade flows (especially in ideational goods and services), innovation is necessarily a global business and a huge step up for most developing countries. A possible exception are products and services, including variants of existing ones, developed to cater to the needs of consumers in a specific developing country or region. If that is correct, then those countries that had begun their growth and the imitation phase prior to TRIPS implementation may have benefited from a head start. For now, however, large exporting firms are the clearest winners.[98]

Another related question worth asking is whether the Western economic institutions and capitalism are coterminous or whether they are just an instantiation of a (somewhat 'free') market economy. Perhaps technological innovation

---

97. To benefit from the patent system, innovators must be aware of the global state of the art. To do so, they should familiarize themselves with published patents and applications (most of which are published 18 months after filing). As Jaffe and Trajtenberg's research has shown, patents are a window on the process of technological change and a powerful tool for research on the economics of innovation. Patent records contain a wealth of information, including the inventors' identity, location, and employer, as well as the technological field of the invention. Patents also contain citation references to previous patents, which allow one to trace links across inventions. A Jaffe and M Trajtenberg, *Patents, Citations, and Innovations: A Window on the Knowledge Economy* (n 77 above).

98. E Su, 'The Winners and the Losers: The Agreement on the Trade-Related Aspects of Intellectual Property Rights and Its Effects on Developing Countries' (2000) 23 Hous JIL 169, 214.

can be woven into different social and economic fabrics, thus creating what Charles Taylor refers to as 'multifaceted' capitalism—the South may be redefining capitalism and the broadly held assumption that free market may not exist without certain rights and freedoms (eg, freedom of expression) may very well be proven wrong. Arguably, China, which is much less free than India, has been doing better over the past ten years.

What seems inescapable, however, is the move toward modernity, which I would define for the purposes of this article, and using Taylorian terminology again, as moving to a rational moral order in which 'economic (ie, ordered, peaceful, productive) activity has become the model for human behavior and the key to harmonious existence.'[99] Ideology or religion-based social orders, including those interpreted as excluding women or social classes or fearing innovation and change cannot hope truly to succeed in this scenario,[100] because this child of the Enlightenment we call modernity is not something that innovative societies can easily avoid inviting to their economic dinner table. 'The eighteenth-century transition is in a sense a crucial one in the development of Western modernity. . .[it] generated new, stadial theories of history, which saw human societies developing through a series of stages, defined by the form of their economy (eg, hunter-gatherer, agricultural), culminating in the contemporary commercial society'.[101]

Globalization also has an impact on governance. The globalization of media, in particular the Internet, feeds the various social imaginaries. For one thing, it provides new images of what is, and of what is possible. This is crucial because, as Taylor's insightful analyses have shown, a perception of what is possible widens the array of norms that are realizable. In other words, people don't fight for utopia but can move into action for something they know they can achieve.

The passage of time likely will show that some of the (Western) institutions we associate with an innovation-based capitalist economy are not in fact a necessary ingredient of a society that is able to compete (using the same science of course) with the West. It will be interesting to see whether Western-style democracy is but an idiosyncratic variant of modernity. Put differently, while stadial analysis is indeed inexorable, there may not be a single path forward, and the very direction of technological progress may be altered as a result.

---

99. C Taylor, *Modern Social Imaginaries* (Duke Univ. Press, 2005) 15.
100. To quote Taylor again: "Individualism and mutual benefit are the evident residual ideas that remain after you have sloughed off the older religions and metaphysics". (ibid. 18).
101. Ibid 48.

15. TRADE AND COMPETITION POLICY IN THE DEVELOPING WORLD
Is There a Role for the WTO?

DANIEL J GIFFORD AND ROBERT T KUDRLE[*]

A. Introduction 396
    I. One More Inquiry into the Relation Between Competition Policy and the World Trading System 396
    II. Two Perspectives on Trade Policy: The Advance of Welfare or the Advance of Political Objectives 396
    III. Perspectives on Competition Policy 398
    IV. Competition Law and the WTO 401
        Competition law proposals 401
        Clash of interests between developed and developing nations 402
        Relationships between competition policy and the WTO (and GATT) regimes 404
    V. The Usual Content of Competition Law 405
    VI. Competition Laws and Developing Countries 408
B. Why an International Agreement on Competition Law Policies is Incompatible with the Dominant Producer Interests in Both Developing and Developed Nations 412
    I. National Competition Laws and Market Restraints 412
        Internal market restraints 412
        External cartels 413
        Merger control 414
        Exclusionary restraints 414
    II. What Would an International Competition Law Supply That National Competition Laws are Unable to Supply? 418
        The Case of International Cartels 418
        The case of export cartels 422
        Market power by importers 427
        Intellectual property issues 428
        International differences over merger cases 429
    III. Why an International Competition Law Agreement is Unlikely 431
C. Why International Cooperation on Competition Law will Progress and Why Some Agreement May Ultimately be Reached 434

---

[*] Robins, Kaplan, Miller and Cirisi Professor of Law, University of Minnesota and Orville & Jane Freeman Professor of International Trade and Investment Policy, Hubert Humphrey Institute of Public Affairs and the Law School, University of Minnesota respectively.

A. INTRODUCTION

i. One More Inquiry into the Relation Between Competition Policy and the World Trading System

This paper addresses a topic that has already been repeatedly examined in the trade literature: the possible expansion of the jurisdiction of the WTO to include competition issues. Our treatment of this topic, however, brings several critical concerns together. First, it focuses on the developing nations.[1] We ask whether, and to what extent, such an expansion would further the welfare of the developing nations or would further the combination of domestic interests that are ascendant in their governments and governing institutions. Second, following from the first point, our inquiry distinguishes between welfare and institutionalized national interests, recognizing that it is the latter that effectively determine a nation's objectives. Third, we try to identify differences between the developing nations and their developed counterparts that may be likely to affect their approaches toward an international competition regime. Fourth, we identify differences in established competition policies among the developed nations, and we explore how these differences may affect the position of the developed nations toward the establishment of an international competition regime.

ii. Two Perspectives on Trade Policy: The Advance of Welfare or the Advance of Political Objectives

Myriad commentators have stressed that the foundation of effective trade policy lies in mercantilist notions, summarized by Krugman as '1) Exports are good; 2) Imports are bad; 3) Other things equal, an equal increase in imports and exports is good'.[2] While not ignoring this 'conventional wisdom', ingenious arguments have been developed to link trade policy to the collective national rationality first developed by Harry Johnson,[3] work that Wilfred Ethier calls the 'received theory'.[4]

---

1. Although some scholars have addressed the desirability (vel non) of a multilateral approach to competition policy from the perspective of developing nations, their analyses do not embrace the combination of analytical factors that we employ, eg, A Bhattacharjea, 'The Case for a Multilateral Agreement on Competition Policy: a Developing Country Perspective' (2006) 9 JIEL 293; JS Lee, 'Towards a Development-Oriented Multilateral Framework on Competition Policy' (2006) 7 San Diego ILJ 293; H Nottage, 'Trade and Competition in the WTO: Pondering the Applicability of Special and Differential Treatment' (2003) 6 Int'l Econ L 23.

2. P Krugman, 'The Move towards Free Trade Zones' in *Policy Implications of Trade and Currency Zones* (Federal Reserve Bank of Kansas City, 1991).

3. HG Johnson, 'Optimum Tariffs and Retaliation' (1953–54) 21 Rev Econ Stu 142.

4. WJ Ethier, 'Political Externalities, Nondiscrimination, and a Multilateral World' (2004) 12 Rev Int'l Econ 303, WJ Ethier, 'The Theory of Trade Policy and Trade Agreements: A Critique' (2006, unpublished).

Bagwell and Staiger[5] try to incorporate the collective national interest of states large enough to affect their own terms of trade into a model that also contains elements of familiar trade politics. In this dispute about motivation, many observers have concluded that only the 'conventional wisdom' really fits the facts of actual state behavior.

Most of trade policy and politics appear to be based on bad economics, and much of the reason lies in the subtlety of reasoning behind open trading policies. Paul Samuelson once claimed that the doctrine of comparative advantage is the most important nonobvious proposition in the social sciences.[6] But the neglect of the doctrine of comparative advantage is bad economics only when assessed from the standpoint of each state's aggregate economic well-being and the welfare of the informed median voter. From the standpoint of nonexport producer interests, it is very good economics. And since producer interests are generally the dominant influences upon government, mercantilist motivations often simply reflect those interests.

Robert Hudec articulated a modified version of the conventional mercantilist understanding that bears a striking resemblance to some others developed in political science and economics.[7] Producer interests may dominate, but they are at least partially offset by consumer and general interests. And producer interests themselves fall into two broad classes: those that serve the domestic market and those that export. In *Developing Countries in the GATT Legal System*,[8] Hudec identified an important effect of the GATT legal system as a marginal alteration of the domestic power balances in Member states between those political and business groups favoring free trade and those taking a mercantilist approach. Thus, Hudec looked beyond the relationships of states with each other and with the GATT to the domestic political structures of the Member states as a critical locus of trade policy decisions. In that context, the GATT played a significant role in bolstering the power of officials and domestic interest groups favoring free trade. Although this important aspect of the GATT was widely recognized, it was often underappreciated.

We examine Hudec's emphasis on the importance of the GATT and its WTO successor to the determination of domestic trading policy. We use his insight as

---

5. K Bagwell and RW Staiger, 'An Economic Theory of GATT' (1999) 89 AE Rev 215; K Bagwell & RW Staiger, *The Economics of the World Trading System* (2002).

6. Samuelson was responding to the mathematician Stanislaw Ulam, who had expressed doubt that there were any nonobvious truths in the social sciences. PA Samuelson, 'The Way of an Economist' in *International Economic Relations: Proceedings of the Third Congress of the International Economic Association* (1969) 1–11.

7. RE Hudec, *Developing Countries in the GATT Legal System* (1987). In doing so he anticipated informally some of the political dynamics more formally developed by such writers as Ethier, n 4 above.

8. Ibid.

a starting place for a re-examination of the domestic and international trading policies of both developing and developed nations and of their welfare effects. In this reexamination, we explore the relationships between national economic policies of the WTO Member states, especially those of developing nations, and the overarching structure of the WTO. In particular, we focus on the relationships between interests in the developing nations vis-à-vis competition policy and the WTO. We do not ignore the welfare effects of competition and trade policies, but we look at them separately. Although the world trading system created by the GATT and the WTO is built on the assumption that each nation pursues a mercantilist policy, the multilateral trade negotiations of the GATT and the WTO have advanced global welfare.[9] Is there a parallel in competition policy? Can the WTO nudge interests in the right direction, or can it help in resolving important policy problems that states cannot deal with on their own? We will argue that both of these questions should be answered in the negative.

iii. Perspectives on Competition Policy

By competition policy we mean the practice of enforcing what in American parlance is called 'the antitrust laws' which, according to one prominent source, aim to 'limit the market power exercised by firms and to limit how firms compete with each other'.[10] More specifically, US antitrust laws and the competition laws of most other jurisdictions including the European Union and Japan deal in one way or another with three major concerns: *collusion* among firms that would facilitate 'monopoloid' behavior in making product and pricing decisions; *amalgamation* that would create such power directly; and *exclusion*, which refers to firm behavior designed to disadvantage other participants or to deter entrants. We will argue that the scope of antitrust law and policy is now, and for the foreseeable future will be, sharply circumscribed by trade law and policy. In fact, this provides much of the case for doubting a useful integration of competition policy into the WTO.

---

9. Ethier claims that the 'multilateral trade liberalization of the previous half century may well be the most successful deliberate exercise of economic policy in human history'. Ethier (n 4 above) 1.

10. DW Carlton and JM Perloff, *Modern Industrial Organization* (5th edn 2005) 631. This usage largely conforms to what Hoekman and Kostecki call competition law, but they use competition *policy* as a broader term to encompass 'the set of measures used by governments that determine the conditions of competition that reign in their markets'. BM Hoekman and MM Kostecki, *The Political Economy of The World Trading System: The WTO and Beyond* (2nd edn 2001) 425–26. Thus trade policy is obviously a subset of competition policy. For present purposes, we think clarity of argument is served by using the term competition policy in another way: the actual practice of applying competition law. We will employ trade law and trade policy similarly.

Some have contrasted trade policy with the more enlightened thinking that supposedly informs competition policy.[11] But competition policy has evolved radically over the period since the Reciprocal Trade Agreements Act of 1934[12] or even the General Agreement on Tariffs and Trade of 1947.[13] The United States has undergone what has been described as an 'antitrust revolution' that substitutes the pursuit of economic welfare for the earlier goals of firm rivalry or producer protection.[14] The European states have seen even greater change. There was no European Union in 1947, and antitrust law did not appear until the adoption of the Treaty of Rome, a decade later. Japanese antitrust law was imposed by the US occupation authorities almost simultaneously with the emergence of the GATT but has since undergone significant revision.[15] Few other states had competition policies as late as 1980, and the ones that did often pursued them largely with a focus on producer protection that would not surprise students of trade policy.

Most poor countries first considered competition policy as means of controlling foreign firms as part of the 'New International Economic Order' of the 1970s. As dirigisme gave way to liberalization in the 1980s and 1990s, the UNCTAD assistance that was first sought mainly to bring multinational corporations to heel was redirected to the devising of policies to direct competition more broadly in the domestic market.[16] In addition, virtually all of the political entities that escaped the dominance of the Soviet Union in the 1980s soon developed competition policies.[17] By the early years of the new century, more than 100 competition law regimes were in place.[18]

---

11. Eg, JM Finger and A Zlate, 'Antidumping: Prospects for Discipline from the Doha Negotiations' (2005), Boston College Working Papers in Economics 632.

12. Pub L No 73-316, 48 Stat, 943 (codified at 19 USC § 1351 (2000)).

13. *General Agreement on Tariffs and Trade*, Oct. 30, 1947, TIAS No 1700, 55 UNTS 187.

14. JE Kwoka and LJ White, *The Antitrust Revolution: Economics, Competition, and Policy* (4th edn 2004).

15. See M Matsushita, *International Trade and Competition Law in Japan* (1993) 79–84 (describing the original law and its subsequent amendments).

16. For a persuasive account of the two phases of policy among poor countries and the transition between them, see SK Sell, *Power and Ideas: North South Politics of Intellectual Property and Antitrust* (1996) 141–73, 198–212. For a discussion of the variety of content in the policies development of the developed in the second period, see RT Kudrle and DB Bobrow, 'Competition Policy and Regional Integration: Compatibility and Conflict' (March 1998) J Int'l Pol Econ.

17. W Kovacic, 'Merger Enforcement in Transition: Antitrust Controls on Acquisitions in Emerging Economies' (1998) U Cinn L Rev 66.

18. Much of the great flurry of competition law adoption in the nineties was strongly linked to access-assurance in preferential trade agreements and may involve little activity. See L Cernat, 'Eager to Ink, but Ready to Act? RTA Proliferation and International Cooperation on Competition Policy' in P Brusick, AM Alvarez and L Cernat (eds), *Competition Provisions in Regional Trade Agreements: How to Assure Development Gains* (2005) 1.

The well-established competition policy regimes and the newer, less well-established ones interact with each other in many ways, most notably through the International Competition Network (ICN), a principal purpose of which is to provide assistance from the higher income countries for implementing and strengthening the competition laws in poorer states. The ICN was formed following a 2000 recommendation by the US International Competition Policy Advisory Committee (IPAC), a group set up by the US Justice Department to consider international competition problems.[19] It is open on equal terms to all states with functioning competition agencies; it has neither secretariat nor permanent financing; it aims only to produce 'best practice' proposals and reports; it aims to be effective through demonstration and peer pressure.[20] The ICN's product has so far been almost entirely informational and procedural[21] and in these areas, it has sponsored a large amount of substantive activity. Much exchange and discussion has aimed to clarify, coordinate, and lower the cost of multijurisdictional merger review, a particular concern of the high income countries that are footing the modest cost of the endeavor. But much attention has been directed to 'capacity building' of competition agencies in developing countries, including their role in 'competition advocacy,' ie, making the case for the use of markets among government decision makers in recently liberalized states.

The evolution of competition policy away from producer protection has not been uniform across major states nor has it anywhere unambiguously embraced the total surplus standard that maximizes national income.[22] Nevertheless, from a national or global welfare perspective, it is hard to quarrel with the judgment

---

19. M Janow, 'Transatlantic Cooperation in Competition Policy' in SJ Evenett, A Lehmann, and B Steil (eds), *Antitrust Goes Global* (2000) 29. The ICN was specifically asked to consider multijurisdictional merger review, the trade-competition interface, and the future of international competition agency cooperation. The EU Commission also officially endorsed the founding of the ICN. K von Finckenstein, *Competition Issues in the OECD WP3 And ICN*, presented to the Conference Board's 2002 Antitrust Conference, New York City, March 8, <http://www.internationalcompetitionnetwork.org> (Last visited 30 June 2007).

20. The WTO, UNCTAD, and the OECD along with private practitioners play a role as Non-Governmental Advisors in preparing work products on an equal footing with other participants.

21. A conference is held once a year, hosted by a national competition authority. A somewhat more extensive core organization has been proposed partly to raise sufficient funding for conference participation by a larger number of agency representatives from low-income countries, K von Finckenstein, *Recent Developments in the International Competition Policy Network*, Address to the 2003 Forum on International Competition Law, February 6, <http://www.internationalcompetitionnetwork.org> (Last visited June 30, 2007).

22. See discussion in DJ Gifford and RT Kudrle, 'Rhetoric and Reality in the Merger Standards of the United States, Canada, and the European Union' (2005) 72 Antitrust LJ 423, 446–63.

that competition policy in general now makes much better economic sense than trade policy does. But the history and the political logic of the two policy realms differ dramatically. Much, if not most, successful trade liberalization has been predicated on a quid pro quo from trading partners, making cooperative action essential. Most national competition policy has sprung largely from internal sources with the international economy as a secondary concern. Moreover, as will be seen, international cooperation on competition policy, while desirable, is typically not central, and various means, especially bilateral cooperation, are consistent with meeting the competition policy challenges of growing globalization for the foreseeable future.

We believe that competition policies generally further aggregate welfare and that a carefully crafted international competition regime would enhance global welfare. Yet neither our belief in the welfare-enhancing characteristics of such a regime nor the similar beliefs of other academics will bring such a regime into being. A competition law component will be added to the WTO only if and when states come to believe that such a change will further their protectionist-tilted dominant interests.

iv. Competition Law and the WTO

Competition law proposals The past several decades have seen a range of proposals for establishing an international competition law regime. The United Nations Conference on Trade and Development has been continuously involved in proposals for nonbinding agreements on policy content and cooperation since the late 1970s.[23] At the other extreme, a group of scholars meeting in Munich in the early 1990s proposed a comprehensive international competition law authority.[24]

The OECD proposed in the late 1990s that Member countries ensure that their respective competition laws incorporate effective prohibitions on so-called 'hard core cartels', ie, explicit agreements on price, quantities, or division of markets.[25] This proposal also included recommendations for cooperation in enforcement.[26] Eleanor Fox proposed, as recently as 2003, a similarly modest competition policy approach, but one incorporated into an agreement that would commit its adherents to transparency, nondiscrimination, due process, and an anticartel

---

23. UNCTAD, *The Set of Multilaterally Agreed Equitable Principles and Rules for the Control of Restrictive Business Practices* (1980, 2000).

24. 'Draft International Antitrust Code as a GATT-MTO-Plurilateral Trade Agreement' (BNA Special Supp, Aug 19, 1993) 65 Antitrust & Trade Reg Rep. See criticism of this proposal in DJ Gifford, 'The Draft International Antitrust Code Proposed at Munich: Good Intentions Gone Awry' (1997) 6 Minn JGT 1.

25. OECD, Recommendation of the Council concerning Effective Action against Hard Core Cartels (1998) C(98) 35/Final 2–3 (OECD Recommendation I(A)).

26. Ibid (Recommendation I(B)).

law.[27] This resembled Clarke and Evenett's 2003 summary of the main elements of submissions to the WTO Working Group on the Interaction between Trade and Competition Policy,[28] which closely paralleled the submission of the European Union. The European Union had consistently favored a basic agreement.[29] These positions capture much of the thinking that grew from the ultimately unproductive discussions on a multilateral framework for competition policy following the Doha Ministerial Meeting in 2001.[30] Further consideration of a competition element in WTO trade negotiations, however, was formally abandoned in July 2004.[31]

We believe that it is highly unlikely that any proposal for an international competition law agreement, however minimal, will succeed in the foreseeable future. The task of establishing an international competition law regime is complex and fraught with difficulties. There are numerous components to competition law. Each component affects different nations differently and, within each nation, often affects one or more powerful political interests. Because a range of powerful political interests from around the globe would find themselves threatened by an international competition agreement, no such agreement appears possible without mollifying all or most of those interests. For the reasons that will be set forth, this task appears impossible.

Clash of interests between developed and developing nations In his 1987 book, *Developing Countries in the GATT Legal System*, Robert Hudec reviewed the long-standing conflicting approaches between the developed and developing countries over whether the governing terms of the international trading order should apply across-the-board to all nations or whether they should incorporate special and less onerous provisions applicable to developing countries. When the GATT was organized in 1947, developed countries made up the majority of its membership: only 10 out of the 23 contracting members were developing countries.[32] Developed countries retained their majority through the 1950s.

---

27. EM Fox, 'International Antitrust and the Doha Dome' (2003) 43 Va JIL 911.

28. Additional elements are greater cooperation among WTO members on competition policy issues and unspecified assistance to developing countries on competition issues that would involve other international institutions in addition to the WTO. JL Clarke and SJ Evenett, 'A Multilateral Framework for Competition Policy' in J Clarke and SJ Evenett (eds), *The Singapore Issues and The World Trading System: The Road to Cancun and Beyond, Swiss State Secretariat of Economic Affairs* (2003) 113.

29. EC, 'Dispute Settlement and Peer Review: Options for a WTO Agreement on Competition Policy' (2003) (Communication to the Working Group on the Interaction between Trade and Competition Policy. WT/WGTCP/W/229).

30. WTO, 'WTO Ministerial Conference, Ministerial Declaration' (20 November 2001) WT/MIN(01)/ DEC/1.

31. WTO, 'Doha Work Program—Decision Adopted by the General Council' (1 August 2004) WT/L/579, para 1(g).

32. Hudec (n 7 above) 23.

In its early years, the GATT members saw no need for membership by poor countries because they were not at that time a major factor in trade. Developing countries, however, began entering the GATT on a large scale during the 1960s and by 1970 had outranked the developed country membership by a 2-to-1 ratio.[33] Developing countries had been pressing for special treatment at least as far back as the negotiations over the abortive International Trade Organization. Their efforts began to produce initial results during the late 1950s and early 1960s. The Haberler Report of 1958[34] called for opening rich-state markets to developing countries, and the resulting Action Programme adopted by the GATT trade ministers deprecated the need for reciprocity by developing countries.[35] The Dillon Round negotiations of 1960–1961 generated an acknowledgment that reciprocity from developing countries could not be expected to the same degree as it could from developed countries.[36] By 1968, the United States had voted to support a generalized system of preferences for developing countries in that year's UNCTAD conference.[37] In 1971, the GATT allowed those preferences.[38]

Until the late 1960s, the developed countries were able to extend such 'S&D treatment' to the developing nations at a minimal sacrifice because the developing-country markets still constituted a small part of the global market. As many poor countries advanced economically, however, developed countries increasingly came to resent the S&D terms on which the developing nations adhered to the GATT. Poorer states, with some exceptions (most notably Korea), resisted the abandonment of that special status, which in practical terms had never really been defined and the precise benefits of which, if any, were left to bilateral determination by GATT/WTO members. Developed states began to make judgments about when particular developing nations had 'graduated' from a developing status so that they would lose their special status.[39] When a nation was treated as losing its developing nation status, its protectionist measures would no longer be treated as exempt from generally applicable GATT obligations. A developed country would then be entitled to impose sanctions when it faced now unauthorized trade barriers. For their part, poorer countries tended to see many outcomes of the GATT's Uruguay Round as unequal bargains (most notably its TRIPS Agreement and unfulfilled promises (eg, implementation assistance). These countries were extremely reluctant to make any new WTO commitments.[40]

---

33. Ibid 24.
34. Ibid 41.
35. Ibid 42.
36. Ibid 44.
37. Ibid 63.
38. Ibid 64.
39. Ibid 73, 86.
40. Bhattacharjea (n 1 above) 297.

This smoldering conflict between developed and developing countries over S&D treatment underlies much of the differences of view over competition policy. Although competition policy on its face appears neutral on differences over trade policy, its potential market-opening effects appear to be attractive to developed nations and threatening to developing ones. Yet, as we will show, this possible conflict is muted because the open-textured aspects of all of the competition law proposals make them threatening to developed states as well.

Relationships between competition policy and the WTO (and GATT) regimes In the immediate aftermath of World War II, economists and government officials saw a strong linkage between trade policy and competition policy. In 1946, for example, Edward S. Mason proposed integrating trade and competition policy.[41] Competition policy was viewed as a critical part of the ill-fated plan for an International Trade Organization in 1947, and proposals for its inclusion into the GATT and the WTO have surfaced intermittently ever since. This linkage between international trade and competition policies makes clear sense to economists at a sufficient level of generality. Scherer observes that ideal competition policy and ideal trade policy have the same objective: to 'maximize real income'.[42] But 'ideal' in this context drains virtually all of the usefulness from the observation. As many writers have pointed out over the last 60 years, the two realms are indeed linked by economic logic, but the policies that deal with them are driven by very different political forces. Moreover, the maximization of real income lies far from either the intention or the result of policies pursued in either sphere. And the split is manifest at a practical level as well: Since the Havana Conference and the abortive International Trade Organization, competition law concerns have lurked at the edges of trade law.

Beyond differences in the basic political structure between trade and competition policy and their independent policy realms, there are at least five other important differences that also cast doubt on the appropriateness of a major role for the WTO in competition policy. First, the function of trade policy is overwhelmingly to *control* access to the domestic market while much competition policy attempts to *balance* competing arguments about the structure of markets and the conduct of business firms. Second, trade policy focuses mostly on *government* action while competition policy deals mainly with *firm* action. This difference implies a third: competition policy necessarily involves continuous nonroutine processes while much of trade policy simply aims to remove official interference with market forces. Fourth, open trade is a fairly clear concept;

---

41. ES Mason, *Controlling World Trade: Cartels and Commodity Agreements* (1946). An international agreement dealing with competition policy was also considered at the 1927 Geneva Economic Conference. See DJ Gerber, 'Competition Law and the WTO: Rethinking the Relationship' (2007) 10 JIEL 707.

42. FM Scherer, *Competition Policies for an Integrated World Economy* (1994) 2.

appropriate competition policy in many dimensions remains changing and contested both within countries and among them. Finally, even where competition policy was grafted onto the rest of domestic policy only in recent decades, as in much of Europe, Japan, and all transition and developing countries, both its exact content and its procedures are intertwined with highly idiosyncratic national legal variations.

Although the Doha Ministerial Conference moved competition law concerns onto the formal agenda of trade negotiations, those negotiations appear to have made little or no progress. Today, therefore, competition law remains where it has always been—a subject widely discussed as an adjunct to trade agreements but one that has not yet been absorbed into the world trading system. Moreover, the Doha Round is moribund. Nevertheless, the quest for multilaterally agreed freer trade will never really die because that aspiration is congruent with the advance of global economic welfare. Despite our emphasis on the role of the dominant political interests in the WTO nations in shaping negotiating policy, we believe that policies promoting aggregate welfare, including more formal cooperation on competition policy, will prevail in the long run. But our concern here is the past, present, and the near-term future.

We need to explore the relation of competition law and policy to the ascendant political interests within both the North and the South. This is essential for a broader understanding of the failure of trade negotiators to embrace a competition law component in either the GATT or the WTO. We find that a competition law component has not been added to the world trading system because it is not in the interests of either the developing or developed worlds to do so. In addition, while the national economic welfare interests of the developed and developing nations are not entirely congruent on this issue, the areas in which they diverge are rather small.

v. The Usual Content of Competition Law

As we observed, most anticompetitive behavior involves restraints that involve collusion, amalgamation, or exclusion. Economists also often identify restraints as either horizontal or vertical, depending upon whether they involve action or collusion on the same or different levels of economic activity. Collusive restraints and amalgamations can be either horizontal or vertical. Horizontal restraints arise when competing firms agree with each other either not to compete or to reduce the level of their competition. A horizontal amalgamation occurs when competing firms merge. The paradigmatic horizontal restraint is the formation of a cartel that controls all or most of the supply of a particular kind of good or service. Such a cartel has the power to restrict output and generate a concomitant price increase. The amalgamation or merger of competing firms that control most of the supply of a particular good or service would produce the same effect.

Cartels have been per se illegal under US antitrust laws at least since the early twentieth century.[43] They are also illegal under the competition laws of the European Union and other developed nations. Nevertheless, the United States, the European Union, and other developed nations generally distinguish between the cartels just described that exercise power over supply in order to raise price and to restrict output and other horizontal agreements among competitors that involve cooperative activities designed to reduce costs.[44] Cooperative arrangements among competitors that do not control a significant portion of the industry supply are almost necessarily of the latter type, since only the achievement of cost savings lies within their power.[45] A given horizontal agreement or merger may, of course, both create market power and reduce costs.[46] Such an agreement would involve joint cost reduction by sellers that, in the aggregate, controlled a substantial part of market supply. The competitive consequences of this latter type of horizontal agreement are ambiguous and will be discussed.

Vertical restraints arise from agreements or other arrangements along the chain of production and distribution to final customers. They often involve exclusive commitments by a supplier to its existing dealers or commitments by dealers to handle the products of their supplier exclusively. Both types of restraint are generally designed to generate dealer incentives to promote the supplier's products, effectively reducing distribution costs.[47] To the extent that these agreements succeed, the supplier's output increases. A similar analysis applies to vertical mergers. Nevertheless, as pointed out below, vertical arrangements—if sufficiently comprehensive—can act as barriers to potential entrants wishing to offer alternative sources of supply to final-product producers. United States antitrust law tends to focus upon the efficiencies often generated by vertical restraints and vertical mergers and the likelihood that these vertical arrangements will intensify market competition. As a result, US law tends to be more tolerant of vertical restraints than does EU competition law. Both US and EU law, however, would find vertical restraints more problematic as they covered larger shares of a relevant market.

---

43. *United States v Socony-Vacuum Oil Co* 310 US 150 (1940), *United States v Trenton Potteries Co* 273 US 392 (1927).

44. *Broadcast Music, Inc v Columbia Broadcasting System, Inc* 441 US 1 (1979), *Northwest Wholesale Stationers, Inc v Pacific Stationery & Printing Co* 472 US 284 (1985).

45. See discussion in *Rothery Storage & Van Co v Atlas Van Lines, Inc* 792 F 2d 210, 229 (US Ct of Apps (2nd Cir) 1986).

46. See O Williamson, 'Economies as an Antitrust Defense: The Welfare Tradeoffs' (1968) 58 AE Rev, 18; R Bork, *The Antitrust Paradox: A Policy at War with Itself* (1978) 107–15.

47. *Continental TV, Inc v GTE Sylvania, Inc* 433 US 36 (1977). See L Telser, 'Why Should Manufacturers Want Fair Trade'? (1960) 3 JL & Econ 86 (discussing vertical price-fixing agreements that generate similar incentives).

Exclusionary arrangements are designed to prevent rival firms from entering the market or to raise their costs of doing so, or can produce those effects. Thus, for example, assume that the US widget industry is composed of a small number of domestic producers selling to a large number of widget distributors. The domestic widget producers agree among themselves to obtain the agreement of all or most of the domestic widget distributors not to handle the widgets of foreign suppliers. This arrangement, if successful, could impose a significant barrier to foreign suppliers seeking to enter the domestic market.[48] The agreement would include both horizontal and vertical elements. The horizontal aspect involves agreement among domestic widget producers, and the vertical aspect involves the agreement between the domestic producers and the domestic distributors. Viewed from the point of view of the domestic producers, the ultimate objective of the agreement is horizontal: the exclusion of the foreign suppliers from the market served by the domestic producers. Under both US and EU law, such an agreement would be unlawful. Entry may also be illegally discouraged by incumbent 'predatory pricing' against new or weak competitors, the standards for which vary considerably across jurisdictions.

As developed in Part VI, many of the restraints that would be suspect under the competition laws of the United States or of the European Union would be fostered by some proposed approaches to competition policy for developing economies. Ajit Singh is a well-known advocate of S&D competition laws. He has contended that it would be in the interest of developing nations to follow the techniques employed by Japan during its period of rapid economic growth from 1950 to 1973.[49] These techniques in large part substitute government oversight for competitive-market norms. According to Singh, such arrangements would both encourage needed investment and support the development of export capabilities.

Arrangements that temper competition in the interest of generating profits and/or fostering national champions in export markets would not necessarily run afoul of competition laws based on US or EU models because of an array of technical legal considerations, such as the presence or absence of an agreement and the degree of government involvement.[50] The Japanese practice of 'administrative guidance' appears to foster cartel decision making, although the degree of government involvement might be enough to exonerate the participating firms

---

48. WTO Panel Report, *Japan--Measures Affecting Consumer Photographic Film and Paper* (WT/DS44/R).

49. A Singh, *Competition and Competition Policy in Emerging Markets: International and Development Dimensions* (UNCTAD, G-24 Discussion Paper Series No 18, September 2002) 17.

50. See discussion below and discussion, nn 74–80 below.

under a traditional competition law.[51] Moreover, the Japanese example shows that it is possible to have a competition law while limiting its application so as not to interfere with government supervision or oversight. The types of behavior employed in a Japanese-style development approach are nonetheless antithetical to the policies incorporated in competition laws.

To the extent that developing nations want to embrace approaches to development similar to those described by Singh, they would be likely to resist the imposition of any legal institutions that would impose free market norms on their societies, unless they were sufficiently circumscribed to avoid interfering with government control over key sectors of the economy. First, governments that had assumed directive roles over their economies might well believe that competition laws based upon US or EU models would be unnecessary because government direction rather than competition would perform the resource allocation functions for their economies. Second, even if an array of technical legal factors (or outright exemptions)[52] would prevent a competition law from undermining the government's directive role over an economy, the philosophical underpinning of competition law would be antithetical to government's planning activities, and the competition law (unless its scope were sufficiently circumscribed) might raise a variety of impediments to government direction that could be time-consuming and costly to overcome.

vi. Competition Laws and Developing Countries

The current competition policies of the United States, the European Union, Japan, and many other high-income countries focus on horizontal and vertical restrictions with considerations similar to those outlined above. Do developing countries need something else? Most of the writing on the subject of competition policy in the WTO gives scant attention to this question, but it cannot be avoided. There are two quite different approaches to an affirmative answer. One is that poor countries may need to begin with quite simple competition policies. The World Bank for example, implies that a full-blown competition policy might lie beyond the administrative competence of some states: they should instead simply try to reduce policy impediments to competition, particularly by facilitating trade. In addition, such governments should improve the flow of freely available information so that entry will be encouraged. Going beyond this might create opportunities for corruption and rent seeking. But, if feasible, states should go beyond policy review and disclosure to the adoption and enforcement

---

51. See M Matsushita, *International Trade and Competition Law in Japan*, (1993) 146–47 (describing judicial approaches to administrative guidance in the context of the Japanese Anti-Monopoly Law).

52. The Japanese Anti-Monopoly Law provides exceptions from its coverage for so-called 'depression cartels' and 'rationalization cartels.' Anti-Monopoly Law § 24.3, § 24.4, reprinted in Matsushita (n 51 above) 313–15.

of prohibitions against 'price-fixing and other horizontal restraints' as well as 'restrictive marketing and other restraints'.[53] The urgency of moving to the latter phase has been strongly supported in a recent survey by Frédéric Jenny that documents a vast amount of horizontal conspiracy in poor countries that directly lowers the living standards of the poor.[54]

The other position once ascendant and now much reduced but not negligible, holds that low-income countries should embrace a 'developmental state' in which competition is just one device among many to produce desired social outcomes and may or may not be treated in a sharply defined set of enforceable legal principles. Ajit Singh argues that 'for a developing country the purpose of competition policy cannot simply be the promotion of competition as a good thing per se, but to foster economic development. This would in some instances involve restriction of competition and in others its vigorous promotion.'[55] Perhaps his clearest and most consistent claim is that competition may excessively reduce profits and therefore investment. Instead, he advocates *inter alia* an 'emphasis on dynamic rather than static efficiency', an '"optimal degree of competition" ... to promote long term growth of productivity', an 'optimal combination of competition and cooperation', industrial policy, and selective state support.[56] Moreover, the favoring of local over foreign firms is apparently assumed to be good thing.

Singh's models appear to be the Japanese and Korean economies during their principal (post-World War II) developmental stages. These models involve protection and an array of government actions (including coordination) designed to encourage investment and to foster exports. Singh rejects the emphasis of US competition law upon allocative efficiency in favor of an emphasis upon investment and industrialization. He is especially alarmed by the prospect that an international competition law would interfere with international commodity

---

53. World Bank, *World Development Report* 101 (2003).

54. F Jenny, 'Cartels and Collusion in Developing Countries: Lessons from Empirical Evidence' (2006) 29 W Comp 1.

55. Singh (n 49 above). Singh quotes Jean Laffont: 'It is not always the case that competition should be encouraged in [poor] countries.' JJ Laffont, 'Competition, Information, and Development' (1998) Annual World Bank Conference on Development Economics 237. But the observation is related to the general problems of second best and appears to aim at countries of very low governmental capacity, the apparent polar opposite of Singh's developmental state. Moreover, the citation completely misleads about Laffont's general policy position made only a few pages later (251): 'Although *even more desirable* [emphasis added] in developing countries, the US type competition policy... is not affordable or even implementable. The design of simple and transparent rules for developing countries, in particular for horizontal collusion and abuse of a dominant position, remains I believe a worthy task.' Moreover, Laffont cites with favor the work of Rey who suggests that even some vertical restraints might usefully be subject to *per se* restriction in low income countries. P Rey, *Competition Policy and Development* (1997, unpublished).

56. Singh, ibid 18.

agreements, government supervised, industrial development cartels and other investment and marketing coordination.

Singh suggests that developing economies may wish to encourage investment by fostering high rates of profit that may be possible only when competition is limited. He points out that, in pursuance of such a policy, Japan's Ministry of International Trade and Industry (MITI) fostered high levels of concentration by sponsoring a wide range of cartels and supervising industry entry and exit decisions.[57] In the semiconductor industry, the Japanese government excluded foreign rivals from the Japanese home market, enabling Japanese firms to generate scale economies and to proceed further on the industry learning curve, taking these advantages with them when they entered the world markets.[58] The effective vertical integration that results from long-term relationships between suppliers and final-product producers characterizes important sectors of the Japanese economy such as the automobile and electronics industries. It provides benefits to both input suppliers and producers, but it also operates to exclude foreign suppliers from the input markets.

Singh's claim that the East Asian experience demonstrates the critical role of state policy relates to a vast and complex literature. The active role of the government in Japan and Korea cannot be denied; whether its role was essential or even usually positive can be.[59] Much of this active involvement of the Japanese and Korean governments is related to the traditional infant-industry rationale often employed in its defense and to the insights of the so-called 'new trade theory'.[60] Writing in 1987 when industrial policy debates were at the forefront of public discussion in the United States,[61] Robert Hudec professed skepticism about this approach.[62] He conceded the theoretical possibility that government intervention on behalf of specific industries might produce the intended beneficial effects but doubted that the aggregate effects of such government interventions would be beneficial. Indeed, Hudec believed that governments were institutionally incapable of acquiring and acting upon the information necessary to achieve positive results.[63] Governments are also notoriously slow to act, a major problem in dealing with constantly shifting economic and business conditions, and

---

57. Ibid.

58. See discussion in DJ Gifford, 'Antitrust and Trade Issues: Similarities, Differences, and Relationships' (1995) 44 DePaul L Rev 1049, 1067–70.

59. See, for example, RE Caves and M Uekusa, *Industrial Organization in Japan* (1976); J Mark Ramseyer and M Yoshiro, 'Capitalist Politicians, Socialist Bureaucrats? Legends of Government Planning from Japan' (2003) 48 Antitrust Bull 595.

60. See PR Krugman, *Rethinking International Trade* (1990) 192-98; E Helpman and PR Krugman, *Trade Policy & Market Structure* (1989) 1–9.

61. See, eg, WE Hudson, 'The Feasibility of a Comprehensive US Industrial Policy' (1985) 100 Pol Sci Q 461.

62. Hudec (n 7 above) 146–51.

63. Ibid 148–49.

reluctant to change directions when new conditions warrant.⁶⁴ Moreover, the industries that are the beneficiaries of government intervention do not necessarily respond to government assistance in the ways that the government anticipates: they may devote less, rather than more, resources into efficiency enhancing activities.⁶⁵ Finally, government intervention is subject to massive distortions generated by lobbying and other pressures from potential beneficiaries.⁶⁶

Singh implies that his views are more consonant with a modern view of industrial organization theory than are those of the advocates of Western-style competition policy. He refers to some of William Baumol's work to bolster his case, but the material cited merely champions a longer-term view of the welfare effects of policy or defends certain explicitly sanctioned and limited forms of firm cooperation in industries characterized by rapid innovation—not industries typically found in developing countries.⁶⁷ Other writers on the development of export markets by firms from poor countries have implied or advocated tolerance for firm cooperation.⁶⁸ But all of these specific concerns merely imply exceptions to the overall thrust of competition policy and not grounds for an exceptional competition policy.⁶⁹

We find the 'developmental state' arguments unpersuasive. Indeed, we agree with Hudec's assessment of the general ineptitude of government for bringing about welfare enhancing growth by intervening in particular industries. Arguments to the contrary assume a level of state competence and probity that has proved generally unwarranted, especially in low-income countries. Moreover, their fit with both the history of development and with modern industrial

---

64. Ibid 148.
65. Ibid 149.
66. Ibid 149–50.
67. Baumol's overall approach to industrial organization policy, 'contestability', turns on maximally free entry, not an emphasis congenial to Singh's nationalist protectionism. Moreover, taking the long view must confront issues of risk, uncertainty, and discounting. See DJ Gifford and RT Kudrle, 'Rhetoric and Reality in the Merger Standards of the United States, Canada, and the European Union' (2005) 72 Antitrust LJ 423.
68. A Bhattacharjea, 'Export Cartels: A Developing Country Perspective' (2004) 38 JWT 331; D Rodrik, 'Goodbye Washington Consensus, Hello Washington Confusion? A Review of the World Bank's 'Economic Growth in the 1990s: Learning from a Decade of Reform' (2006) 44 JE Lit 973.
69. Singh also argues that direct evidence that the level of competition in poor countries is worse than in richer countries is somewhat ambiguous. This is true but does not address whether or not poor countries' performance would improve with a competition policy. Bhattacharjea takes a position that rejects the 'developmental state' but that apparently leaves governments with broad discretion about when and where to enforce competition. We have serious doubts about the likelihood that such discretion would be used constructively or predictably; we think exempting some sectors entirely might be a better approach. Bhattacharjea (n 1 above) 317–18.

organization theory[70] and evidence can be seriously questioned.[71] Accordingly, we believe that the adoption of a competition law would advance welfare in most developing countries. The low levels of government competence in some developing countries suggest the need there to begin with a simple competition law limited to outlawing price-fixing cartels. Despite our belief in the welfare enhancing benefits of competition laws, however, we do not believe that the nations of the world are disposed to accept an international obligation to adopt a competition law, for reasons that we set forth in this paper.

B. WHY AN INTERNATIONAL AGREEMENT ON COMPETITION LAW POLICIES IS INCOMPATIBLE WITH THE DOMINANT PRODUCER INTERESTS IN BOTH DEVELOPING AND DEVELOPED NATIONS

i. National Competition Laws and Market Restraints

Internal market restraints National competition laws are generally capable of dealing effectively with restraints that arise within their state's borders. Almost all such agreements among the domestic actors in any nation whether horizontal, vertical, or exclusionary that adversely affect national competition can be legally proscribed by the governing authorities within that state, and those prohibitions are *prima facie* as enforceable as any other domestic law. Whether a state chooses to adopt a competition law, however, depends upon the strength of the different interests that would be affected by such a law. Consumers, of course, benefit from an effective competition law. Large domestic producer interests, however, may oppose the enactment of a competition law, the enforcement of which would weaken their market power. Indeed, to the extent that local producers rely upon government for protection from either domestic or foreign competition, their relationship with government may be complex, engendering support and dependence on both sides. Powerful domestic producers—especially oligopolists—may provide significant support for the government in some

---

70. In questioning a ban on 'hard core cartels,' Singh suggests that 'Economic theory and analysis have a much more sophisticated and nuanced view of cartel price fixing'. A Singh, *Multilateral Competition Policy and Economic Development: A Developing Country Perspective on the European Community Proposals* (2003, unpublished) 10. In fact, most scholars find few respectable exceptions. He also argues that the role of 'temporary monopoly profits' play the same incentive role in markets for private goods and services as in the production of the public good of intellectual property and that 'The argument for some restraint on competition maintaining firms' inducement to investment is an analogous one' (ibid 16). This position seems to conflate a normal (risk adjusted) rate of return on capital with no return at all—unless competition is restrained.

71. For similar recent conclusions, see LJ White, 'The Role of Competition Policy in the Promotion of Economic Growth' (May 2008) Law & Economics Research Paper Series, Working Paper No 08-23, New York University School of Law.

countries, making it difficult for such governments to pursue policies running counter to those domestic producer interests. In such circumstances, the prospects for an effective competition policy would be dim. Although foreign producer interests might well benefit from an increase in competition among their local suppliers, they might nonetheless oppose the enactment of a competition law that their local rivals could use against them. Indeed, under a law based upon an EU model, foreign producers that acquired a significant local market share might be characterized as 'dominant', and the open-endedness of the accompanying 'abuse' concept could subject them to attacks by hostile officials lacking the expertise of their European counterparts.

External cartels The competition law of an importing state could legally prohibit an international cartel from exerting its pricing power on imported products, but it may lack the power to enforce such prohibitions. Large developed economies such as the United States or the European Union can and do prohibit such practices. These jurisdictions also possess the power to enforce those prohibitions. The United States, the European Union, and Japan assert jurisdiction over anticompetitive behavior that produces adverse effects within their boundaries, regardless of where the physical behavior takes place.[72] They also possess the power to enforce their laws against such behavior. Most cartels could not easily abandon selling in these markets, since they are very large and thus likely major sources of cartel revenues. Moreover, these economies are so large that it would be difficult for cartels to avoid exposing substantial amounts of their assets to seizure once the importing government has asserted jurisdiction.

Small or developing nations typically lack the power to enforce their antitrust laws against an international cartel. Even if the cartel members physically carry on operations within the country's borders, such a state may often be effectively powerless to enforce its competition laws against them. Fines are sometimes levied by and paid to such states, but if the penalty exceeds the sum of present discounted value of future cartel profits and the value of the cartel members' immobile assets in the importing country, the cartel may simply withdraw its operations from that state in the face of an adverse judgment. This does not make a small market internationally irrelevant, however. Cartel operations

---

72. United States antitrust enforcement employs an 'effects test' to support jurisdiction against enterprises acting abroad to produce anticompetitive effects in the United States. See Foreign Antitrust Improvements Act, 15 USC § 6a (2000); *Hartford Fire Ins Co v California* 509 US 764 (1993). The European Union follows a similar course. See Case 89/85 *Osakeyhtiö v Commission of the European Communities* 1988 ECR. 5183 (In re Wood Pulp). M Matsushita reports that Japan now also asserts jurisdiction over at least some events that occur abroad and produce an impact in Japan. See M Matsushita, 'United States-Japan Trade Issues and a Possible Bilateral Antitrust Agreement Between the United States and Japan' (1999) 16 Ari JICL 249, 250 (describing 1998 amendment to Chapter 4 of the Antimonopoly Law to extend its application to mergers and acquisitions that occur abroad).

discovered there—perhaps including relevant evidence of activity in larger markets—could trigger investigation and convictions abroad.

Domestic producer interests are not likely to oppose legislation aimed exclusively at foreign cartels, unless those producers are themselves participants in the cartel. As with legislation directed at other restraints, consumer interests would be furthered by such legislation. Local legislation targeting foreign cartels (and only foreign cartels) could expect widespread support.

Merger control The United States, the European Union, and Japan all now evaluate mergers under their respective competition laws for impacts on the domestic market. When firms affecting these markets propose to merge, each jurisdiction conducts a review, and, in effect, the merger must be approved by all authorities.

Differing merger standards pose the most innately intractable problem for international business because the major jurisdiction with the most stringent regulation will prevail, regardless of the strength of the merging firm's case and the possible efficiencies and lower prices that might be experienced all over the world. This presents an area in which only the really large players can veto mergers with a truly global reach. If firms believe their global strategies require a merger, they will likely ignore the views of objecting governments in smaller markets, withdrawing from them completely if that is necessary.

Most economists would probably take the view that aggregate global welfare would be maximized by a single merger standard keyed to the maximization of total surplus. Neither the United States nor the European Union has unambiguously embraced such a standard, however. Moreover, the European Union appears especially reluctant to recognize the efficiency aspects of mergers as positive factors. The conflicting approaches of the United States and the European Union are sufficient to block international agreement on merger standards. It is likely that aggregate producer interests in the United States favor a greater recognition of efficiencies in merger evaluation. It is unclear whether producer interests in the European Union take the same approach or whether they support the current tendency of the European authorities to foster rivalry as such, an approach that (in the merger area) tends to maintain the status quo. Low-income states pursuing an interventionist approach to development, such as that described by Singh, would tend to foster consolidation of domestic industries while limiting and subordinating foreign investment. Accordingly, the governments of those developing nations and their domestic producer interests would probably favor lax merger standards for domestically owned firms and more stringent control over foreigners.

Exclusionary restraints Exclusionary restraints, like the ones described above, that impede foreign entry into a domestic market[73] benefit domestic sellers at

---

73. See text before and after n 48 above.

the expense of domestic consumers and foreign sellers. By definition, in a state where such a restraint exists, the political forces undergirding the government favor the interests of domestic producers supplying the home market. Whether an international prohibition on such exclusionary restraints would be supported by other states depends upon whether the political and social forces in those other states have come to be dominated by some combination of exporter and consumer interests. Therefore, on the usual assumption that producer interests dominate trade politics, support for such a prohibition in any state would *prima facie* turn on the relative power of exporting interests.

Even major exporting states might not support enforceable prohibitions on such exclusionary restraints. Japan, for example, is a major exporter but has been the subject of complaints by the United States and the European Union that domestic exclusionary arrangements impede foreign suppliers from accessing its home market. South Korea, another major exporter, may also harbor private arrangements that impede the entry of foreign sellers. And while developed nations may believe that the existence of private exclusionary restraints undermine the expectations of market access that they had when they subscribed to the GATT and the WTO, there is reason to believe that those expectations are not yet as widely shared in the developing world.

Tight vertical relationships between component suppliers and final-product producers carry many benefits. Final-product producers have an assured source of supply, confidence in the quality of the supplies, and often protection against unexpected price increases. Suppliers likewise benefit from having an assured outlet and protection against sudden price changes. These relationships can facilitate planning by both suppliers and customers, including joint participation in the development of new products and improvements of existing ones. All of these factors have been recognized in US antitrust law as reasons for presuming vertical restraints lawful (they are regarded with more suspicion in the European Union). Yet tight vertical relationships that commit final-product producers to purchase exclusively from particular suppliers also exclude new suppliers from selling their goods to those final-product producers. When exclusive arrangements cover most sales within a market, new suppliers are effectively excluded from that market.

In the 1980s and 1990s, the United States contended that many US-based producers were effectively excluded from the Japanese market. For example, US producers were unable to sell semiconductor chips to Japanese buyers because almost all of the Japanese electronics firms obtained their chips from Japanese sources.[74] Similarly, US producers of automobile parts were unable to sell to Japanese auto manufacturers.[75] These market exclusions, however, were apparently not the result of action by the Japanese government in contravention of its

---

74. L D'Andrea Tyson, *Who's Bashing Whom? Trade Conflict in High-Technology Industries* (1992) 98–101.

75. See Gifford (n 58 above) 1056 and n 53.

GATT obligations. Rather, they appear to be the result of the way that Japanese businesses were organized. Final-product producers developed long-term relationships with suppliers that both parties understood would continue so long as both remained cooperative.[76] Such producers often maintained relationships with several alternative tiers of suppliers, switching among tiers to foster incentives by suppliers to maintain quality, timeliness, and cooperation.

Although the *keiretsu* model of industrial organization had the effect of excluding US and other foreign suppliers from the Japanese market, there was in fact no remedy for this exclusion. The United States could not seek a remedy under the GATT because there was no GATT violation absent Japanese government involvement. The United States wanted to argue that this exclusion resulted from private action that ought to be seen as an antitrust violation under the Japanese Anti-Monopoly law.[77] Yet the American position was weak because these vertical relationships would not have been illegal even under US antitrust law: There was no agreement to maintain exclusivity; there was only an expectation. In addition, US objections to this *de facto* exclusion were further weakened by the fact that these vertical relationships may have been efficient and thus welfare enhancing.

The weakness of the case made by the US government against the market-closing effect of private restraints strongly suggests that the addition of an antitrust component to the WTO trading regime would not produce the market-opening effects that some of its supporters anticipate. Indeed, not only US experience but also that of the European Union indicates that it may be effectively impossible to eliminate private exclusionary arrangements. The United States and the European Union complained repeatedly of such arrangements in Japan,[78] and the United States exerted immense pressure upon the Japanese government to eliminate them. In the *Kodak/Fuji* case[79] the United States even brought a complaint against Japan before the WTO, alleging private, market-closing behavior abetted by the Japanese government. None of these actions produced the desired market-opening results. It may be concluded therefore that private arrangements designed to impede foreign suppliers' access to a state's domestic

---

76. Ibid 1057.

77. eg, Office of the US Trade Representative, 1993 National Trade Estimate Report on Foreign Trade Barriers (1993) 161–63 (contending that the Japanese Anti-Monopoly Law was flawed or it was not being enforced.) See discussion in Gifford, above n 32, 1062.

78. US complaints ultimately led to a series of negotiations in the so-called 'Structural Impediments Initiative.' See Joint Report of the US-Japan Working Group on the Structural Impediments Initiative (1990).

79. WTO Panel Report, 'Japan—Measures Affecting Consumer Photographic Film and Paper' (31 March 1998) WT/DS44/R.

market are irremediable, so long as they receive the tacit support of that state's government.[80]

States pursuing economic development based on strong government intervention might ultimately be able to preserve many directive policies even in the face of a WTO-imposed antitrust regime either through explicit exemptions or for reasons similar to those that prevented the United States and Europe from successfully challenging Japanese exclusionary policies. A WTO-imposed antitrust regime, however, would generate costly and time-consuming conflict over their industrial policy activities. Accordingly, such states can be expected to vigorously oppose global antitrust proposals. In such 'developmental model' regimes, producer interests have already prevailed. They and the governmental policies that they support would likely be averse to adding a competition component to the WTO trading regime for the reasons stated.

In summary, producer interests in developing countries that pursued interventionist policies would be likely to oppose a global antitrust regime that would impose a variety of antitrust restraints incompatible in theory and/or in practice with those policies. Moreover, most poor countries, whatever the level of government intervention and private cooperation, will see likely foreign challenges to domestic practices as an affront to their sovereignty. Producer interests in developed countries would find some theoretical benefits in a set of global antitrust rules that superficially promise market-opening effects. These producers would likely discover, however, that the purported market-opening effects were a mirage because the antitrust policies were effectively impeded by a host of technical legal requirements, which would almost inevitably arise to compensate for what would otherwise be increased foreign advantage—and not just in *dirigiste* poor countries. Finally, many developed nation producer interests, especially those in the United States, would be opposed to a global antitrust regime because of their fear that the open-endedness of typical antitrust provisions, combined with a lack of an antitrust tradition in many developing countries, would contribute to politically based interpretations[81] or to interpretations that would conflict with the values embodied in the Sherman Act.[82] This danger would be exacerbated when the law was enforced by inexperienced or untrained officials.

---

80. It should be stressed that 'market-opening' measures advocated by exporting interests do not always increase world welfare; some of them, eg, American firms demanding a share in the Japanese market, bear some resemblance to local firms that demand what amounts to a right of market participation in the European Union. The difference is that the latter likely damages the home economy while the former may benefit it.

81. See Gifford (n 24 above).

82. An Indian case involving a US Webb-Pomerene Association, the American Natural Soda Ash Corporation, illustrates the problems that would be raised by a global ban on anticompetitive practices in a world in which nations differ in their understandings of what kinds of behavior are, and are not, anticompetitive. In that case, the Monopolies and Restrictive Trade Practices Commission of India alleged that the US Association had

ii. What Would an International Competition Law Supply That National Competition Laws are Unable to Supply?

The case of international cartels In an early exploration of the wisdom and feasibility of including competition policy in the GATT and WTO, Hoekman and Mavroidis cite Sir Leon Brittan as a leading advocate. In 1992, when he was competition commissioner for the European Community, Sir Leon wanted the next international trading round to consider '. . . restrictive business practices and cartels. . . The aim should be to draw up *common* rules, lay down the principle that restrictive arrangements are not enforceable at law and that governments are responsible internationally for the implementation of these rules and procedures'. . .[83]

One expert has estimated that the current chances of a cartel being detected are between 10 and 20 percent if it operates in Europe or the United States and it is negligible elsewhere.[84] Cartel behavior is a violation of nearly all national competition laws in the hundred or so jurisdictions that now have them, yet a compelling case for a connection between WTO institutionalization and a substantially more effective assault on such cartels remains to be made. Sufficient cooperation has already been established among authorities in the United States, the European Union, and Japan, to pursue nearly all suspected global cartels. There is no cartel equivalent of 'tax havens', where lax local regulation stems from an ambition for national gains at the expense of the larger global system.[85] On the other hand, the absence of a definite antisocial incentive does not assure positive government action of any kind, including cooperation. Attention to local aspects of international conspiracies demand resource commitments that go beyond simply having a stricture against cartels in place. So a proposal that

---

encouraged its members to sell in India at prices that covered only variable costs. See PS Mehta, N Nanda and A Pham, *Multilateral Competition Framework: In Need of a Fresh Approach* 20, CUTS Centre for Competition, Investment & Economic Regulation (2005) <http://cuts-international.org /documents/MCF-1feb05.doc>. Although selling at prices covering only variable costs might constitute offenses under antidumping legislation, such behavior is not unlawful under US antitrust laws. See, eg, *Spirit Airlines, Inc v Northwest Airlines, Inc* 431 F 3d 917, 938 (US Ct of Apps (6th Cir), 2005) (pricing above average variable cost is prima facie lawful).

83. BM Hoekman and PC Mavroidis, 'Competition, Competition Policy, and the GATT' (2004) 17 W Econ 121.

84. See JM Connor, 'Global Cartels Redux: The Amino Acid Lysine Litigation' in JE Kwoka and LJ White (eds), *The Antitrust Revolution: Economics, Competition, and Policy* (4th edn 2004).

85. For this reason, we think the term 'haven' in this competition policy context is unfortunate if all the commentator means to imply is lassitude based on lack of sufficient incentive for cooperation. The term brings 'tax haven' to mind, where there are strong positive reasons for a government's failure to cooperate with others. Cf. Bhattacharjea, above nn 1, 304; Clarke and Evenett, above nn 28, 44.

all WTO members adopt a policy against ('hard core') cartels could mean very little.[86]

The United States treats price-fixing agreements as criminal violations, and individuals participating in them are sometimes charged with felonies, though infrequently imprisoned. This severity of penalty puts the United States at the most stringent end of punishment, a difference that complicates international cooperation.[87] Many jurisdictions shun formal ties with the United States because of its criminal provisions and treble damages in civil cases. Nevertheless, informal cooperation on antitrust matters between the United States and a large number of jurisdictions has blossomed in recent years (along with bilateral cooperation between other states), particularly on merger and cartel cases of mutual interest, demonstrating the usefulness of cooperation that does not involve the exchange of confidential information. Such cooperation has not yet involved many non-OECD countries.[88]

Some governments in the South seem to have abandoned the dichotomy between 'good' and 'bad' cartels that underlay their adherence to the 'New International Economic Order' 30 years ago. At that time, southern cartels (or 'commodity schemes') were judged acceptable—India supported OPEC—while any market power visited upon poor countries from the North was condemned. Northern governments have all opposed international cartels in recent decades and are now engaged in unprecedentedly determined—if still highly inadequate—attacks upon them. Yet there are limits to the enforcement capabilities even

---

86. There is additional reason for doubting the significance of a WTO role. Many experts believe that the only really effective path to substantial reduction of the cartel problem lies in the deterrence that could be achieved only by greatly strengthened penalties. For example, careful research has demonstrated that the treble damages provided by the US antitrust laws effectively leave cartelization as a rationally attractive strategy in many industries (Connor, ibid 274). More leverage would certainly be gained by a high likelihood of jail time for perpetrators, but even the US is quite sparing about incarceration (although the maximum penalty for violation of the Sherman Act was increased from thtree years to ten years in 2003), and this option is not available in most other jurisdictions, which typically lack both private action and multiple damages. See discussion of private actions, below, text nn 93–97. American commentators seem uniformly convinced that the deterrent effect of incarceration cannot be easily traded off against increased financial penalties. 'Our defendants routinely offer to pay large fines in lieu of going to jail, a plea that we reject, but they don't offer to go to jail in lieu of paying a large fine.' R Hewitt Pate, *International Anti-Cartel Enforcement* (US Department of Justice, 2004, unpublished).

87. Eg, individuals cannot be sanctioned for competition law violations under EU law; they may be under national statutes. SJ Evenett, A Lehmann, and B Steil, 'Antitrust Policy in an Evolving Global Marketplace' in SJ Evenett, A Lehmann, and B Steil (eds), *Antitrust Goes Global* (2000) 19.

88. An exception was the assistance the US provided Brazil in its pursuit of the lysine and vitamins cartels. See Clarke & Evenett, above n 28, 118.

of the United States and the European Union. Southern governments, therefore, may be especially concerned about cartel behavior that falls outside the scope of the cartel enforcement of the richer countries but which may nonetheless exploit particular vulnerabilities of developing countries.

Clarke and Evenett have recently argued that a cartel will rationally moderate prices where it may be most easily detected.[89] This means not only that existing cartels are likely systematically to exhibit greater moderation in high-income states (nearly all of which have strong laws forbidding such activity) but also that they are likely to exploit their power differentially across poorer states according to whether or not states pursue an 'active' national anticartel policy. But two points are worth noting. It is very likely that the payout from anticartel and antibid-rigging regimes greatly exceeds the cost.[90] On the other hand, simply having a law on the books as opposed to demonstrating enforcement has not been shown to be valuable. The WTO could only assure the former,[91] but self-interest should increasingly draw states to enforcement for their own reasons.

The incorporation of an antitrust component into the WTO could be done on the model of TRIPS,[92] where states would be required to enact antitrust legislation, perhaps limited to the prohibition of 'hard core cartels' but in combination with a provision for private enforcement. The latter frees enforcement policy from government control and removes the need for interest-group pressures directed at government enforcers. As just argued, anticartel legislation combined with effective enforcement is likely to generate substantial social benefits. Insofar as the availability of private enforcement helps to ensure that the legislation is effectively enforced, including a provision for private enforcement in a WTO antitrust provision would be desirable.

---

89. JL Clarke and SJ Evenett, 'The Deterrent Effects of National Anti-Cartel Laws: Evidence from the International Vitamins Cartel' (2003) 48 Antitrust Bull 689.

90. WTO Secretariat, Study on Issues Relating to a Possible Multilateral Framework Agreement on Competition Policy, WT/WGTCP/W228, 2003. Bhattacharjea criticizes the supporting evidence presented by S Evenett (who prepared the study). But Bhattacharjea also acknowledges that many additional benefits of anti-cartel enforcement are left out. Hence he concludes merely that the numerical estimates suggest 'specious precision'. Bhattacharjea, (n 1 above) 306.

91. A state's implied provision of a 'safe haven' for international conspirators (a term we would not choose because of the connotation of purpose rather than lassitude) seems independent of both the existence of a national cartel law or its enforcement for local purposes (although some legal regimes may avoid cooperation where the target is not involved in activity that would be locally illegal). This reflects the obvious fact that the jurisdictional location of the conspiracy may be completely unconnected with any local damage.

92. *Agreement on Trade-Related Aspects of Intellectual Property Rights*, Articles 42–50, 15 April 1994, *Marrakesh Agreement Establishing the World Trade Organization*, Annex 1C, Legal Instruments—Results of the Uruguay Round, vol 31, 33 ILM 81 (1994).

Despite its merits for those seeking remedy, a private enforcement provision would be less acceptable to the membership of the WTO than an obligation to adopt a substantive antitrust law in the first place. Until recently, private enforcement of antitrust laws has generally been unique to the United States. Private suits for damages, however, have begun to be recognized in Europe.[93] The Japanese Anti-Monopoly Law provides for a limited private enforcement but effectively grants the Japanese Fair Trade Commission a veto over the institution of suit.[94] No one has ever won a suit for damages under that law although a few cases have been settled.[95] States that are reluctant to adopt a domestic antitrust law and/or reluctant to support an antitrust addition to their WTO obligations could be expected to resist private enforcement provisions that took control of enforcement out of government hands.[96]

As the previous discussion demonstrated, the effectiveness of every national competition law is subject to challenge by externally imposed restraints that adversely affect that nation's economy. International cartels thus are the prime example of such an external restraint. Large developed economies such as the European Union and the United States are generally capable of meeting that challenge. Most international cartels cannot avoid doing business in either the United States or the European Union and, as a result, are vulnerable to the laws of both jurisdictions.[97] Moreover, it is difficult for cartel members to keep their assets out of the reach of antitrust enforcement authorities in both jurisdictions. Developing nations, however, often cannot effectively enforce their laws against international cartels. In theory, therefore, an international competition law (enforceable by an international body) would fill this gap. Yet the gap may not be as large as these considerations would suggest. To the extent that an international cartel is setting a world price (or a set of prices keyed to regional or country

---

93. W Wurmnest, 'Foreign Private Plaintiffs, Global Conspiracies, and the Extraterritorial Application of US Antitrust Law' (2005) 28 Hastings ICL Rev 205, 214 & n 42 (describing case law recognizing private actions in the United Kingdom, Germany, and Italy).

94. H First, 'Antitrust Enforcement in Japan' (1995) 64 Antitrust LJ 137, 147.

95. Ibid 148.

96. An addition reason for skepticism about the feasibility of mandating the availability of private action is that the standards for intellectual property violation appear more clear-cut than those for even 'hard core' cartels. One difficult issue is evidence. For example, culpability as a conspirator based on the parallel behavior of firms is treated quite differently in various jurisdictions. See Jenny (n 54 above) 136.

97. See the list of international cartels that have been subject to investigation by the United States and European Union antitrust authorities in M Levenstein & V Suslow, 'Private International Cartels and Their Effect on Developing Countries' 63–66, <http://www.worldbank.org/wdr/2001/bkground papers/levenstein.pdf>.

demands but anchored in global collusion) for a product, it is likely victimizing both developing and developed nations.[98]

Enforcement action taken by antitrust authorities in the United States or the European Union is likely to benefit all states in which the cartel does business, including developing nations.[99] United States enforcement action against such cartels is enhanced by the availability of private actions, providing a huge economic stimulus for such actions, and by the recent institution of the US government's leniency policy, designed to encourage informers.

National authorities are cooperating informally and with increasing intensity to battle international cartels. The continuing pervasiveness of the problem seems to stem from a combination of inattentiveness to the pattern of prices across jurisdictions, difficulties of detection, problems of evidence gathering, and insufficient penalties. A critical contribution of the WTO to significant improvement in any of these areas is far from apparent.

The case of export cartels References in the literature condemning export cartels as devices employed by developed nations to exploit importing nations, especially developing ones[100] deserve examination. The US Webb-Pomerene Act,[101] enacted in 1918, exempts agreements among competitors dealing solely with the export market from the antitrust laws. The more recent Export Trading Company Act[102] creates a limited antitrust immunity for joint ventures engaged in export trade. Both acts were intended to enable small exporting companies to exploit scale economies in their export operations.[103] If these acts were to generate the effects for which they were designed, they would lower the cost of exports,

---

98. The regulation of international maritime transport in a way that amounts to *de facto* cartel price fixing hurts both rich and poor countries. A World Bank study has estimated that poor countries likely lose at least $2.3 billion yearly from this cartel activity alone. World Bank, *Global Economic Prospects* (2003) 141–42.

99. The international price variation reported in connection with the vitamins cartel suggests that national authorities may have been insufficiently attentive to the prices they paid, quite independent of their cartel laws. Did purchasing agents attempt arbitrage by buying in lower price areas?

100. Eg, F Becker, 'The Case of Export Cartel Exemptions: Between Competition and Protectionism' (2007) 3 J Comp L & Econ 97, 98–99. See also BE Hawk, 'International Antitrust Policy and the 1982 Acts: The Continuing Need for Reassessment' (1982) 51 Ford L Rev 201, 248 (referring to an 'enforcement lacuna' in developed nations as 'widened by the neutral, and in many instances the positive, position taken toward export cartels that can engage in foreign predation'.) Many scholars, however, have expressed skepticism that export cartels are threats to developing nations, eg, B Sweeney, 'Export Cartels: Is there a Need for Global Rules?' (2007) 10 JIEL 87.

101. Pub L 126, 40 Stat 516 (1918) (codified at 15 USC §§ 61–65 (2000).

102. Pub L 97-290, 96 Stat 1233 (1982) (codified at 15 USC § 4001–21 (2000).

103. See Export Trading Company Act, 15 USC § 4001(a)(4)(7) (2000). On the Webb-Pomerene Act, see *United States v United States Alkali Export Ass'n* 86 F Supp 59, 70 (SDNY 1949).

thus benefiting consumers in the importing nations.[104] Indeed, several developing countries themselves apparently see export cartels as devices to enhance their own benefits from trade, employing rationales similar to those that underlie the Webb-Pomerene and Export Trading Company Acts.[105]

Have the Webb-Pomerene Act and the Export Trading Company Act provided means for US companies to exert monopoly power in the export trade? A priori, it would appear unlikely. First, both acts contemplate associations limited to US producers. Such an association could exercise monopoly power only in a situation in which US producers dominate the entire product market. Otherwise the US firms—even if organized into a single export enterprise encompassing all US producers—would still have to compete with other (foreign) firms in the export market. As a 1993 OECD report observed, 'cartels formed by exporters with only small market share in the importing country are not likely to harm competition there. In fact, an anticompetitive cartel attempted by firms with only a limited [market] share is likely to be harmful to them and self-defeating'.[106]

Second, the Webb-Pomerene and Export Trading Company Acts do not provide antitrust immunity otherwise unavailable to exporters.[107] If an export association organized under either act combined with foreign sellers so that the combined group controlled a substantial part of the world supply, that group would be able to impose monopoly prices on importers. Earlier cases suggest that an export association that combined with foreign sellers to impose monopoly prices on importing nations would lose its antitrust immunity. Analysis under current law, however, indicates that the US antitrust laws are not concerned with activities that do not affect the American market.[108] Accordingly, the exemptions available under the Webb-Pomerene Act and the Export Trading Company Act are effectively redundant as far as immunizing behavior directed solely at foreign markets.

Let's rephrase the inquiry. Apart from a legal analysis of the impact of the Webb-Pomerene and Export Trading Company Acts, we now ask whether in fact export associations organized under either act have been used to impose monopoly prices on importing nations. The answer to this question appears to be 'yes'.

---

104. Compare *Report, Obstacles to Trade and Competition* 19 (Paris: OECD, 1993) ('at least in the United States, export cartels are frequently formed to achieve economies of scale in distribution and in information gathering in order to penetrate a foreign market'.)

105. See Sweeney (nn 88, 92 above); MC Levenstein and VY Suslow, 'The Changing International Status of Export Cartel Exemptions' (2005) 20 AUIL Rev 785, 796 and n 42.

106. OECD Report, above nn 104, 19. See also Spencer Weber Waller, 'The Failure of the Export Trading Company Program' 17 NCJIL & Comm Reg 239, 251 ('The history of the Webb-Pomerene Act suggests that few export associations will have sufficient global market power to exploit foreign markets'.)

107. See nn 114–119 below.

108. See nn 114–119 below.

Both situations described above have occurred. Some Webb-Pomerene associations have been formed in industries in which the United States was the primary source of global supply, in which the US industry structure was oligopolistic, and in which the firms constituting the membership of the association were the largest firms in the industry. This situation occurred in the carbon black and walnut board industries in the 1960s, when US production accounted for 80 percent and 95 percent, respectively, of 'free world' supply.[109] It had occurred previously in the copper industry in the 1920s, when US producers controlling nine-tenths of US output, which in turn constituted two-thirds of world output, joined in a Webb-Pomerene association.[110] We also know that US Webb-Pomerene associations have combined with foreign sellers. Several such cases in which a Webb-Pomerene association affiliated with foreign cartels are known to have occurred prior to World War II.[111] More recently, the *Wood Pulp Cartel* case[112] revealed that US companies belonging to a Webb-Pomerene association[113] joined Finnish and Canadian companies in an effort to raise prices of wood pulp to European buyers.

It should be repeated, however, that neither the Webb-Pomerene Act[114] nor the Export Trading Company Act is necessary to exempt the export trade from the application of US antitrust law. United States antitrust law is concerned only with restraints that affect US commerce. Its primary application is on the domestic market where it protects US consumers, and, secondarily, US exporters. It has no application to restraints in foreign markets that do not adversely impact US consumers or US exporters. This limited application of US law has always been implicit in the so-called 'effects doctrine' articulated by Judge Learned Hand in 1945,[115] and it has been made explicit in the Foreign Antitrust Improvements Act.[116] As the US Supreme Court has recently pointed out,

> The FTAIA seeks to make clear to American exporters (and to firms doing business abroad) that the Sherman Act does not prevent them from entering into business arrangements (say, joint-selling arrangements), however

---

109. DA Larson, 'An Economic Analysis of the Webb-Pomerene Act' (1970) 13 JL & Econ 461, 481, 482, 483.
110. HP Sturm, 'Webb-Pomerene Associations' (1955) 8 West Pol Q 82, 87.
111. Sturm (nn 110, 87 above).
112. *Re Wood Pulp Cartel*, 1988 ECR. 5193, 4 CMLR 901 (1988).
113. Ibid 909–10.
114. 15 USC § 61 (2000).
115. *United States v Aluminum Co of America* 148 F 2d 416, 443–44 (US Ct of Apps (2nd Cir), 1945). See also *Hartford Fire Ins Co v California*, 509 US 764, 796 (1993) (reaffirming the effects doctrine).
116. 15 USC § 6a (2000).

anticompetitive, as long as those arrangements adversely affect only foreign markets.[117]

In 1918 when Congress adopted the Webb-Pomerene Act, the extent to which the US antitrust law covered agreements among American firms engaged in foreign sales was unclear.[118] The standards that would govern the lawfulness of efficiency-enhancing agreements among competitors were also in flux. That Act removed these sources of uncertainty over the export trade. By the time of passage of the Export Trading Company Act in 1982, it was becoming increasingly clear that the antitrust laws were concerned solely with protecting American commerce. It was also becoming increasingly clear that efficiency enhancing cooperative activities among competitors lacking market power would be evaluated under the rule of reason, even when these activities took place in the domestic market.[119] Accordingly, the Export Trading Company Act was probably less essential to the Congressional goals than was its predecessor.

The European Union, like the United States, follows a version of the effects test.[120] The treaty provisions containing the EU's antitrust provisions are directed against restraints that distort trade within the common market and against abuses within the common market.[121] Moreover, unlike the United States, the European Union yielded to arguments against the legality of export cartels with effects beyond its borders: concerns about positive comity, the greater use of such cartels by large rather than small firms, the possibly negative effects on poor countries, and the contribution of exemption to trade friction. Both the EU

---

117. *F Hoffman-LaRoche Ltd v Empagran S.A.* 542 US 155, 161 (2004). Eleanor Fox has advocated making all 'hard core' export cartels illegal calling them the 'hazardous wastes' of antitrust. Failing that, she advocates giving foreigners jurisdiction for discovery including subpoena power 'when the developed country's citizens are the alleged victimizers of the people of developing countries.' E Fox, *Economic Development, Poverty, and Antitrust: The Other Path*, New York University School of Law Public Law & Theory Research Paper Series, Working Paper No 07-12 and Law and Economics Research Paper Series, Working Paper No 07-02, 124. But neither action is likely without a quid pro quo, which would most likely be market access, as argued by Hoekman and Saggi, below, n 124.

118. See *United States v United States Alkali Export Ass'n*, n 103 above, 86 F Supp, 69.

119. In *Broadcast Music, Inc v Columbia Broadcasting System, Inc* 441 US 1 (1979), the Supreme Court made clear in the presence of substantial efficiencies, agreements among competitors would not necessarily be condemned as per-se illegal. Although *Broadcast Music* contained especially appealing facts, the Court's subsequent decision in *Northwest Wholesale Stationers, Inc. v Pacific Stationery & Printing Co* 472 US 284 (1985) indicated that rule-of-reason evaluation would be appropriate for a wide range of agreements among rival firms that, in the aggregate, lacked market power.

120. *Re Wood Pulp Cartel: A. Ahlström Osakeyhtiö v EC Commission*, Cases 89, 104, 114, 116. 117 & 125–29/85, 1988 ECR 5193 [1988] 4 CMLR 901. Common Mkt Rep (CCH) 14, 491.

121. *Treaty Establishing the European Community* (consolidated text) Article 81, 82.

Commission and many Member states have removed exemption for export cartels.[122]

Levenstein and Suslow have recorded a shift in many states away from an explicit exemption of 'export cartels' and toward domestic effects. They note that this may increase the legal ambiguity of such cooperation while, by eliminating the formality of registration, it removes information about activity that could be of use to purchasers in other states.[123] They also recognize that many 'export cartels' are actually efficiency enhancing cooperatives that lack power to impose market restraints.

Overall, 'export cartel' seems a misleading term. An export association in which the member firms lack market power and in which they share the expenses of entering a foreign market would lower export costs and benefit participants and customers alike, as observed above. To the extent that export associations acquire market power, they are simply cartels and subject to antitrust enforcement in any jurisdiction in which they sell.

In addition to a concern about export cartels, developing countries have expressed special concern about cartel prices on products primarily or exclusively sold in their markets and the problem of bid rigging on special orders or projects. Cooperation from the developed countries, in which the perpetrators reside or about whose activities competition agencies have good information, would greatly assist the local efforts of the countries suffering such harms.[124] And, as noted earlier, the higher-income countries may value lower income countries' cooperation in tracking global cartels. This contribution is likely supplementary rather than essential, however. The International Competition Network (ICN) and individual developed country competition agencies now extend some assistance to nascent agencies in lower income countries. It is almost inevitable that cooperation on specific matters of interest to particular poor countries will get a fuller and more sympathetic hearing from officials of agencies that are themselves cooperating on matters of mutual concern—such as global cartels. Moreover, rich states have every incentive to support key investigations abroad with both funding and personnel. So, growing bilateral as well as multilateral cooperation on cartel issues between rich and poor countries appears likely. Moreover, the precise value of any single act of cooperation cannot be accurately assessed a priori by either side, which is probably the most propitious situation for building stronger policy links within an 'epistemic community' of competition policy professionals in a broad range of countries.

---

122. Levenstein and Suslow, above n 105, 794–98.

123. Ibid 806–07.

124. For a discussion of how poor countries might trade greater cooperation for market access, see BN Hoekman & K Saggi, *Trading Market Access for Competition Policy Enforcement* (2003) CEPR Discussion Paper No 4110. The authors conclude that such a bargain is unlikely.

Market power by importers The reverse case of an export cartel, monopsony or oligopsony in buying, including buyer collusion, has generated much concern in the South. A recent paper concerning commodity sales from developing countries into the world economy recalls the monopsony power of the British East India Company and then observes that '... it has become relevant again today with the markets for primary product exports of developing countries increasingly dominated by a small number of multinational buyers.'[125] The authors assign the problem to the atomization of producers that resulted from the widespread abolition of marketing boards in the 1980s coinciding with the increasing concentration of buyers due to economies of scale (which has led to a decoupling of initial foreign purchasing from final-product use). They cite coffee and cocoa as the two prime examples of this development: three firms now control about two-thirds of all global cocoa purchasing, and about ten firms purchase two-thirds of all coffee.[126] Nevertheless, a recent detailed study by Gilbert[127] accounts for all changes in the structure of the 'value chain' between grower and consumer for both commodities in a 20 or 30-year time series (1976–2005 for some countries and 1985–2005 for others) without discovering any increase in market power by commodity buyers.[128] But there is other evidence of buyer power. Orallegara and Özden[129] provide persuasive evidence that concentrated buyers are responsible for the failure of export prices of apparel from newly preferred-access countries to rise more than a fraction of the amount theoretically predicted for a competitive market.

The markets just noted, as well as many others, will undoubtedly come under further scrutiny, but, even if strong buyer power is found, solutions are not obvious. One policy direction builds on familiar theory to employ a national export tax that would move international markets still farther from global efficiency while increasing the welfare of national sellers by moderating the exercise of

---

125. AV Deardorff and I Rajaraman, 'Can Export Taxation Counter Monopsony Power?' (2005) RSIE (Ford School of Public Policy) Discussion Paper No 541 p. 2.

126. It appears that the existence of such monopsony power is widely accepted by policymakers in developing countries. (See, for example, PS Mehta and N Nanda, *Competition Policy, Growth and Poverty Reduction in Developing Countries* (unpublished).

127. CL Gilbert, 'Value Chain Analysis and Market Power in Commodity Processing with Application to the Cocoa and Coffee Sectors' (2006) Universita degli Studi di Trento, Dipartimento di Economia, Discussion Paper No 5.

128. The only hard empirical evidence given by Deardorff and Rajaraman to suggest actual monopsony power is that reported by Fitter and Kaplinsky: a divergence in price variation between coffee purchase prices and those at which coffee is traded (the latter is up; the former is down). R Fitter & R Kaplinsky, 'Who Gains from Product Rents as the Coffee Market Becomes More Differentiated?' (2001) 32 IDS Bulletin 69, 78.

129. M Olarreaga & C Özden, 'AGOA and Apparel: Who Captures the Tariff Rent from Preferential Access?' (2005) 19 W Econ 63.

monopsony power by their customers.[130] A global initiative, echoing earlier efforts that were often very poorly implemented, would be the deployment of collective monopoly power of all producers to countervail buyer power. Success turns on agreement about prices and shares as well as satisfactory monitoring of agreements and ideally penalties for cheating.

Monopsony in the purchase of certain commodities produced predominantly in the South and sold predominantly in the North presents a theoretically clear, but very limited, case of opposed interests; a strong case that this has major practical importance, however, remains to be made.[131]

Intellectual property issues In theory, a global competition law regime might help developing nations deal with anticompetitive abuses of intellectual property rights. Most developing nations have subscribed to the TRIPS Agreement[132] and therefore to an obligation to respect intellectual property rights. Because those rights may be abused, the TRIPS Agreement contains several provisions conferring power on signatory nations to proceed against such abuses. Article 8.2 explicitly confers power on signatory states to prevent abuses of intellectual property rights. Article 40 authorizes legislation against abuses, and Article 31(k) authorizes compulsory licensing as a remedy against anticompetitive abuses.

In a recent article, Aditya Bhattacharjea recognizes that TRIPS provides developing nations authority for dealing with abuses of intellectual property rights, but he fears that they may lack the skills to act to do so.[133] Bhattacharjea elaborates his concern by identifying various forms in which intellectual property rights abuses might occur. These are licensing conditions restricting the licensee's pricing, marketing outside a designated area, sublicensing, tying a license to an obligation to purchase other products, and barring the licensee from dealing in rivals' products or using rivals' technologies.[134] As he observes, the TRIPS Agreement itself provides a list of practices that it recognizes as potentially abusive: exclusive grant-back conditions, conditions preventing challenges to validity, and coercive package licensing.[135] Bhattacharjea recognizes, however, that many of these practices carry both the promise of efficiencies (benefiting both licensor and licensee) or market power, depending upon the surrounding circumstances. His instinct

---

130. Deardorff and Rajaraman (n 125 above) 2.

131. For example, rich country import preferences aim to assist poor states. Any diversion of rent toward importing firms following preferential market access stands as a policy challenge for the rich countries and not an outcome most policy makers could defend. For example, any diversion of rent toward importing firms following preferential market access for poor countries stands as a policy challenge for the rich countries and not an outcome they seek.

132. TRIPS Agreement (n 92 above).

133. A Bhattacharjea, 'The Case for a Multilateral Agreement on Competition Policy: A Developing Country Perspective' (2006) 9 JIEL 293, 301–03.

134. Ibid 301-02.

135. TRIPS Agreement, Article 40(2).

that few of the identified practices can be condemned in advance but must be evaluated in context under a rule-of-reason approach[136] is a correct one. Yet administering a competition law on a case-by-case basis in which the enforcement authority applies a rule of reason may (as Bhattacharjea fears) be beyond the abilities of many developing nations, especially in the areas in which competition law policies and intellectual property law policies appear to conflict.[137]

The issue (abuse of intellectual property rights) identified by Bhattacharjea is another source of conflict, not just between developing nations that want to limit intellectual-property rights abuses, on one hand, and developed nations that want intellectual property rights to be respected, on the other. It also encompasses areas in which the developed nations take different views and therefore reinforces their determinations to reject the prospect for a supranational antitrust agency. Competition law developments in the European Union, for example, imposing compulsory license obligations on intellectual property rights holders[138] do not appear consistent with US law. Again the EU approach to assessing the lawfulness of adding functionalities to an operating system does not appear consistent with US law.[139] It is policy conflicts such as these that have generated a US antipathy toward any global competition regime that would possess authority to resolve these issues in ways contrary to US antitrust policy.

If the developing nations are incapable of carrying out this rule-of-reason inquiry, then developing nations cannot rely upon their own newly adopted competition-law regimes for help but must seek help elsewhere. Since a supranational antitrust authority no longer seems a possibility, they must seek assistance from the antitrust agencies of the developed nations. Whether such assistance will in fact be forthcoming is unclear.

International differences over merger cases As noted earlier, if Australia or even India alone objected to a globally strategic merger and were simply ignored, their only recourse would be an attempt to collect fines from the offending firms, a move that could lead to the withdrawal of firm assets and sales from the penalizing jurisdiction. This action, in turn, would almost certainly leave that jurisdiction worse off than before, destroying the credibility of the threat. But this seeming inequity may not be worth trying to solve. From a global welfare

---

136. Bhattacharjea (n 133 above) 302.

137. The interface between intellectual property law and competition law is a difficult one. United States courts have not always reached consistent results in this area. Compare In re *Independent Service Organizations Antitrust Litigation*, 203 F 3d 1322 (US Ct of Apps (3rd Cir), 2000), cert. denied, 531 US 1143 (2001) with *Image Technical Services, Inc v Eastman Kodak Co*, 125 F 3d 1195 (US Ct of Apps (9th Cir), 1997).

138. *IMS Health GmbH & Co OHG v NDC Health GmbH & Co KG* [2004] 4 CMLR 28; *Radio Telefis Eireann v Commission of the European Communities* [1995] ECR I-743.

139. *Microsoft Corp v Commission of the European Communities* [2007] ECR 00. Compare *United States v Microsoft Corp*, 253 F 3d 54, 80 (US Ct of Apps (3rd Cir), 2001).

point of view, it is hard to construct a plausible merger scenario generating net global losses that would not be scotched by one or more of the United States, the European Union, or Japan. It is much more likely that one of the three will block a merger with widespread benefits. Actions by the European Union disapproving the GE/Honeywell merger and imposing conditions on the Boeing/McDonnell-Douglas merger in the 1990s may well have reduced global welfare.[140]

In the statement cited earlier advocating GATT/WTO action on cartels, Sir Leon Brittan also urged attention to mergers. 'For mergers, common rules should also be established, as well as a common commitment to enforcement'.[141] Some progress has been made over the past 15 years in developing a common approach to mergers across the Triad (United States, European Union, and Japan) and among the developed countries more broadly. The three largest OECD jurisdictions now review mergers using guidelines that derive from those first developed by the US Department of Justice in 1982.[142] Nevertheless, the feasibility of Sir Leon's aspiration still seems nearly as farfetched to anyone familiar with the actual practice of vetting mergers under national competition policies as it must have appeared in 1992.

All merger (and other competition) policies reflect one or more of four broad goals: producer protection, rivalry, and the maximization of either consumer surplus or total surplus.[143] One need only consider US-EU conflicts in the

---

140. Case No COMP/M, General Electric/Honeywell, 2004 O.J. (L 48) 1 (2001); Case No IV/M, Boeing/McDonnell-Douglas, 1997 OJ (L 336) 16, aff'd [2005] ECR II-5527 (Ct 1st Instance). DJ Gifford & RT Kudrle, 'Alternative National Merger Standards and the Prospects for International Cooperation' in DLM Kennedy & JD Southwick (eds), *The Political Economy of International Trade Law: Essays in Honor of Robert E. Hudec* (2002). Disagreements about specific merger cases among various jurisdictions could be clarified by putting them into a common framework. Well-trained analysts can come to different conclusions in at least four major areas: what, when, for whom, and with what degree of certainty. The outcome of allowing or forbidding some market practice or structural change in terms of prices and quantities may be subject to differing best estimates; there may be disagreement about when those changes will take place; gainers and losers may have their outcomes differentially weighted; and the best point estimates of outcomes may be surrounded by varying levels of subjective uncertainty. See Gifford & Kudrle, n 22 above. The epistemic community of competition policy enforcers may well develop such a framework and increasingly common views over time as they share argument and evidence with each other; this is the only plausible route to convergence.

141. Hoekman and Malvoidis, n 83 above.

142. Merger Guidelines, 4 Trade Reg Rep (CCH) 13,102 (June 14, 1982). The guidelines currently governing horizontal mergers were issued in 1992 and modified in 1997. Horizontal Merger Guidelines, 4 Trade Reg Rep (CCH) 13,104 (as amended 8 April 1997). For an overview of the Guidelines, see Kwoka & White, n 9 above, 15–23.

143. Gifford & Kudrle, 'Alternative National Merger Standards', n 140 above.

Boeing-Airbus and GE-Honeywell cases in the 1990s[144] to see the greater emphasis that the United States typically gives to either consumer or even total surplus efficiency by comparison with the European Union's instinct to favor rivalry or even producer protection. And in Japan, very few mergers have yet been blocked despite the supposed shift in the 1990s from a 'harmonization culture' to the Japan Fair Trade Commission's preferred 'competition culture'.[145]

Leaving poor country preferences entirely aside, differences among high-income countries alone would preclude a meaningful WTO agreement on merger policy beyond the expedition and coordination of national approval (or denial) processes, an objective that is already being pursued by the ICN.

iii. Why an International Competition Law Agreement is Unlikely

An international agreement on competition law in any form currently under discussion is unlikely because the developed nations will not find common ground with each other or with the developing countries on the content of any competition law proposal. The principal attractiveness of an international competition law to the developed states lies in its promise as a market-opening device. Yet even on this issue, the rich nations are probably divided. The European Union and the United States would see the market-opening aspects of an international competition law as a positive development. It is unclear whether Japan would take the same view.[146]

The market-opening aspects of an international competition law has been viewed in much of the developing world as an attempt by the developed nations to enrich themselves at the expense of the poor. This is partly an ideological legacy of colonialism, but it also plausibly stems from what many see as the lop-sidedness of the outcomes of the Uruguay Round and its TRIPS Agreement in particular.[147] Moreover, the governing authorities in many developing states are undoubtedly under the influence of domestic producers serving their home markets, who would be threatened by market opening. Finally, the governing authorities in developing nations will also be acutely aware of the social havoc that could be wreaked by the large-scale entry of efficient foreign producers, and they are likely to resist an international competition law that promises market opening precisely because of its likely social effects.

---

144. DJ Gifford and RT Kudrle, 'European Union Competition Law and Policy: How Much Latitude for Convergence ith the United States'? (2003) 48 Antitrust Bull 727.

145. RT Kudrle, 'The Globalization of Competition Policy' in S Vachani (ed), *Transformation in Global Governance: Implications for Multinationals and Other Stakeholders* (2006).

146. See nn 73–80 above.

147. A concise statement of how much of the educated public in the developing world sees TRIPS is provided in J Bhagwati, *In Defense of Globalization* (2004) 82–83, 182–85.

The developed and developing nations would be far more likely to agree on a 'bare bones' attack on 'hard core' cartels, ie, price-fixing or output-restricting agreements, than anything else. Those attempting to mollify poor country concerns in the Working Group discussions stressed that the adoption of a bare-bones competition policy left both foreign direct investment policy and industrial policy (whole sectors of the economy could be made exempt) as *de facto* means of controlling threatening foreign competitors.[148] But even such a bare-bones proposal was apparently feared by some states.

Rich countries have grounds for reservations about even minimum agreement due to definitional and administrative uncertainties.[149] The United States is likely to fear that a prohibition on so-called hard core cartels would be extended by the administering and enforcement authorities to efficiency-enhancing agreements among business firms that lack power over price and supply. And it would be difficult to assuage that fear because US administration of its own antitrust laws is more heavily imbued with economic analysis than any likely international competition law would be. Moreover, the United States would also fear a loss of sovereignty and, more specifically, that an international antitrust enforcement authority might employ its powers for political purposes.

The possibility that an international competition law would produce market-opening effects in the markets of developing nations makes it superficially attractive to export interests in the developed world. But an international competition law might also threaten influential producer interests in both the developed and developing world by undermining the rationale for antidumping laws. Such laws are premised on the assumption that foreign suppliers are selling in domestic markets at below-cost prices or prices that are substantially less than their home-market prices. An international competition law embedded in the WTO trading regime would promote increasingly intense global competition and would tend to threaten the national cartels that facilitate two-level pricing. Probably more important, an international competition law in conjunction with the WTO would make competition a global market norm. Consistency would require that existing antidumping laws be reconfigured to meet this new norm. The only legitimate target for antidumping legislation would be predatory pricing: pricing designed to drive rivals from the market in order to establish a monopoly. Indeed, this was the rationale for the original US antidumping law, The Antidumping Act of 1916,[150] which was directed only at predatory dumping. Indeed, it is a foreign trade counterpart to the original Section 2 of the

---

148. Clarke and Evenett (n 28 above) 114.
149. Gifford (n 24 above) 29.
150. Act of Sept. 8, 1916, ch 463, § 801, 39 Stat 798 (1916).

Clayton Act[151] (enacted two years earlier) that was directed against predatory pricing in domestic markets.[152]

Antidumping may demonstrate more clearly than any other GATT-WTO measure that sensible economic policy typically ends at the water's edge. Antidumping does not just ignore economic logic; it reverses it. Many states gear domestic competition policy partly to minimize damage to those who are offered real or apparent discriminatorily high prices relative to other intrastate buyers[153] (such solicitude is mainly reserved for resellers rather than final purchasers, however). The posture toward foreign trade is superficially the opposite: declared prices are too low. Absent predation, which most competition policy condemns regardless of perpetrator, this is nonsense. The underlying reason in both cases is, of course, predominantly the same: domestic producer protection. Joseph Stiglitz[154] saw a competition policy agreement resulting from the Doha Round as pushing antidumping laws to a predation standard and hence utterly crippling them. As just observed, this would return antidumping in the United States to where it was in the 1916 Antidumping Act. In 1985 the then vice chairman of the US International Trade Commission, Susan Liebeler, argued in a case before that body[155] that the legitimate object of antidumping legislation should be predatory pricing. Such sensible thinking, however, completely ignores the political constituency for antidumping in both the North and the South.[156]

As recently as the initial discussions for the Doha Round, antidumping could be seen, in net terms, as a substantial North-South issue: Although many northern states used antidumping against each other, they also employed it extensively against the South. The reverse was not true. But it is now. India launched

---

151. Clayton Antitrust Act, 38 Stat 730, ch 323, § 2 (1914). The legislative history of Section 2 makes clear that it was directed against predatory pricing. See HR Rep No 627, 63d Cong, 2d Sess, pt 1, at 8 (1914); S Rep No 698, 63d Cong, 2d Sess 2–4 (1914).

152. See discussion in DJ Gifford, 'Rethinking the Relationship Between Antidumping and Antitrust Laws' (1991) 6 AUJIL & Pol 277, 281–82.

153. This is a mistake in our view. See discussion of this point in DJ Gifford and RT Kudrle, *The Law and Economics of Price Discrimination in Modern Economies: Time for Reconciliation?* (2007, unpublished).

154. JE Stiglitz, 'Two Principles for the Next Round or, How to Bring Developing Countries in From the Cold' (2000) 14 W Econ 447.

155. Certain Red Raspberries from Canada, USITC Pub No 1707, Inv No 731-TA-196 (final) (June 1985). The courts subsequently rejected Liebeler's interpretation of US antidumping legislation. *USX Corp v United States*, 682 F Supp 60, 68 (Ct Int'l Trade 1988).

156. Stiglitz writes that 'Competition policy has few supporters within any country other than the economists who realize the central role it plays in making markets work perfectly.' Stiglitz (n 154 above) 61. In fact, public support for competition policy is broad but thin. Antidumping is also popular and is buttressed by very determined interests.

15 percent more antidumping investigations in the first half of 2005 than did the United States (412 versus 358).[157]

The developing countries entered the Doha Round with the ambition, if not the real hope, that antidumping could be largely retained for themselves but softened in its use against them. The European Union declared some willingness to consider antidumping policy changes, while the Americans were determined that the status quo not be substantially altered.[158] Considering the vast reversal of economic logic that underlies antidumping, its enthusiastic embrace by low-income countries over the past decade and their desire to retain their own antidumping policies while reducing them elsewhere brings to mind one of Robert Hudec's main arguments in 1987: The 'GATT's current policy [of allowing greater protectionism for low income states] is harming developing countries more than it is helping them'.[159]

C. WHY INTERNATIONAL COOPERATION ON COMPETITION LAW WILL PROGRESS AND WHY SOME AGREEMENT MAY ULTIMATELY BE REACHED

In the long run, the obstacles to agreement on competition policy that now appear so formidable may be overcome. As low-income countries get richer, the internal advantages of effective and comprehensive competition policies are likely to become increasingly apparent. As domestic consumption grows, consumer political interests will advance accordingly. Moreover, as the economies of developing nations expand, their markets will become increasingly attractive to all producers, including producers in other developing states. These factors will increasingly tip the political balances in much of the developing world in the direction of both trade and competition policies that will foster market opening.

One can predict that the ICN[160] will develop ever-greater commonality among global competition policy officials as the 'epistemic community' approach to global networks predicts.[161] In the short run, this very commonality could either

---

157. WTO Committee on Anti-Dumping Practices, Reports (semi-annual).

158. How supposedly universal antipathy toward cartels can be reconciled with what appears to be increasingly general firmness in support of antidumping must puzzle anyone approaching these subjects for the first time. Absent plausible predation, one policy attacks unnecessarily high prices; the other supports them. And both the domestic and foreign inter-firm coordination that alternatively makes the case for a dumping allegation or responds to it has been shown to generate or bolster cartel behavior.

159. Hudec (n 7 above) 59.

160. See text above, at nn 18–21.

161. For a discussion of the role of epistemic communities in building international cooperation, see PM Haas, 'Introduction: Epistemic Communities and International Policy Coordination' (1992) 46 Int Org 1. For a more recent consideration of many of the same issues, see 'A Slaughter, Global Government Networks, Information Agencies, and

increase the capacity of competition authorities to influence domestic policy or isolate and estrange them from the general thrust of governance. The outcome will likely differ widely across states, but, unless the 'developmental state' makes a strong comeback, setbacks are likely to be only temporary.[162]

Competition policy lacks the characteristics that would make it a promising candidate for inclusion into the WTO.[163] The relevant expertise is unrelated to most of what the WTO does, and even the most rudimentary competition policy rules require enforcement of a kind that would allow for external judgments only about broad forms and not specific cases. Nevertheless, the integrating world economy would benefit from clearer and more consistent competition policies. Some progress is being made despite the stalemate at the WTO. Harmony will increase slowly and uncertainly through cooperation and demonstration. Even a modest central competition authority, however, appears neither feasible nor desirable now.

Disaggregated Democracy' (2003) 24 Mich JIL and A Slaughter, *A New World Order* (2004).

162. Graham has expressed some concern about the ultimate legitimacy of the ICN process based on his study of the OECD's ill-fated Multilateral Agreement on Investment (MAI). EM Graham 'Internationalizing' Competition Policy: An Assessment of the Two Main Alternatives' (2003) 48 Antitrust Bull. But we think the lessons from that episode are twofold. First, the enterprise should be truly global, as the ICN is. Second, convergence should be slow and informal without premature—or perhaps any—attempts at codification. If the ICN is careful and sufficiently open in all of its activities, we think progress can continue. And the fate of the MAI is relevant here too. As Graham makes clear, neither foreign direct investment nor investment policy liberalization has been hobbled by the absence of the MAI.

163. A Bradford (Piilola) has convincingly stressed the advantages of the current 'transgovernmental' approach of cooperation among competition authorities over the 'intergovernmental' approach of incorporating a competition dimension into the WTO. Some of her arguments parallel those made here. Her case for a larger 'transnational' dimension in competition policy involving more participation by civil society is much less convincing, however. Civil society (other than directly affected actors with major stakes) plays very little role in successful domestic competition law and policy. A Piilola, 'Assessing Theories of Global Governance: A Case Study of International Antitrust Regulation' (2003) 39 Stanford JIL 207. Bradford has also constructed a more theoretical case against the efficacy of the WTO in the competition policy area. A Bradford, 'International Antitrust Negotiations and the False Hope of the WTO' (2007) 48 Harv ILJ 383.

16. THE GATS AND DEVELOPING COUNTRIES
Why Such Limited Traction?*

BERNARD HOEKMAN*

A. Introduction 437
B. Reciprocity Constraints 440
    I. Asymmetric Interests 443
    II. Regulatory Constraints 444
C. Could More S&D Treatment Help? 445
D. Alternatives to S&D 447
    I. Political Economy: Redistributing Rents and Dealing with Adjustment Costs 448
    II. Implementing Appropriate Domestic Regulation 449
    III. Improving Domestic Access to Better Services 449
    II. Facilitating Market Access Through Broader Cooperation, Particularly on Mode 4 451
E. Toward Greater Transparency: A Comparative Advantage of the WTO 452
F. Concluding Remarks 454

A. INTRODUCTION

The Uruguay Round was the eighth round of trade negotiations under GATT auspices. To date, it has been the most ambitious round yet, spanning many more issues than its successor, the Doha Round. Among the major achievements of the Uruguay Round were the creation of the WTO, new multilateral disciplines for trade in services and intellectual property, and the reintegration of agriculture into the trade regime. It also led to further liberalization of international trade. In addition to an average 40 percent cut in tariff bindings, there was agreement to abolish quantitative restrictions on textiles and clothing trade over a ten-year period, and for the first time, imposed specific limits on the magnitude of permitted subsidization of agricultural exports and trade distorting production subsidies. Few observers in 1986 had expected such an ambitious outcome to be feasible, and at numerous points during the eight-year marathon, the talks came close to failure.

---

* World Bank and CEPR. An early draft of this paper was presented at the conference 'Developing Countries in the WTO Legal System', University of Minnesota, May 24–26. I am grateful to Richard Steinberg and to participants for comments and suggestions on the conference draft. Parts of the paper draw on joint work with Aaditya Mattoo. The views expressed are personal and should not be attributed to the World Bank.

The move to consider rules for trade in services originated with the United States, which had a large services trade surplus. Many developing countries were opposed to negotiating on services. Once talks had started, they argued that service transactions involving establishment by foreign providers (inward foreign direct investment—FDI) should not be covered by any agreement. These countries also stressed the need for governments to remain unconstrained in their freedom to discriminate against foreign suppliers of services. A consequence was outright rejection of any suggestion that the principle of national treatment apply to services.

Both the European Union and United States took a different stance on how to define trade in services, arguing that all types of transactions required to achieve effective market access should be covered, including FDI. In contrast to the United States, the European Union agreed with many developing countries that a multilateral agreement on trade in services should not involve far-reaching obligations of a generally binding nature. Specifically, it proposed that national treatment be a specific commitment that would be negotiated on a sector-by-sector basis. The eventual compromise that emerged in the design of the GATS involved acceptance that trade in services be defined broadly to include FDI and the movement of natural service providers but that disciplines applying to the various modes of supplying services be mode- and sector-specific. Thus, national treatment applies only if a Member commits to this on a sector-by-sector basis. In contrast to the GATT, it is not a general commitment. In addition, commitments could be made on a limited number of specific policies deemed to restrict access to markets.

The GATS was an important element of what Sylvia Ostry has called a 'grand bargain'. In return for introducing multilateral disciplines on agricultural policies and safeguards, stronger dispute settlement procedures, and the abolition of the Multifibre Arrangement (which restricted exports of developing country textiles and clothing), developing countries accepted new disciplines on services and intellectual property. Whether this was a good deal has been much debated in policy circles and the academic literature, but in the eyes of signatories the Uruguay Round package was better than the threat point or their best alternative to a negotiated agreement.

Developing countries had a significant impact on the structure of the GATS, in particular the positive list approach to coverage of the national treatment and market-access disciplines. A noteworthy feature of the GATS was that S&D treatment of the type incorporated in the GATT did not apply. The GATS contains no provisions similar to Part IV of the GATT on S&D treatment for developing countries or calling for preferential access to markets. Special and differential treatment-type language is limited to Article IV GATS, which states that '[p]articular account shall be taken of the serious difficulty of the least-developed countries in accepting negotiated specific commitments in view of their special economic situation and their development, trade and financial needs',[1] and that negotiations should prioritize sectors that are of export interest to developing nations. In addition, Article XIX GATS specifies, '... liberalization shall take place with due respect for national policy objectives and the level of development of individual Members'.[2]

These are very weak best-endeavor-type provisions, much less specific than what is found in the GATT. A major reason for the weak S&D treatment language is that the structure of the agreement allows members to make differential commitments, permitting calibrated reciprocity. However, the general presumption is that all members will negotiate commitments. This approach accords well with the view expressed by Hudec that S&D treatment and the associated presumption that developing countries should not be expected to reciprocate market-access concessions was not in the interest of these nations.[3]

The newness of the services issue implied that traditional GATT-type reciprocity in market-access terms was not the dominant feature of the negotiations. Instead, the primary focus was to establish a framework for future efforts to liberalize trade in services on a reciprocal basis. Virtually all services commitments made in the Uruguay Round were of a 'lock-in' nature, that is, a promise not to become more restrictive than what was implied by actually prevailing policies for specific sectors. Most developing countries made significantly fewer commitments than high-income nations.[4] No WTO Member came even close to locking in all unilateral reforms that had already been implemented—the (weighted average) coverage of specific commitments as of 1995 did not exceed 50 percent for most countries.[5]

Expanding the coverage of the GATS should be beneficial to WTO Members individually and collectively. First, the potential direct gains from reform of services trade for most WTO Members are likely to be large, given the evidence that barriers to trade and investment in many markets are still high. Second, services reform is needed to enable developing countries to take advantage of goods trade liberalization. Many poor countries lack trade capacity and competitiveness. Improving competitiveness is largely a service agenda: better access to efficient

---

1. General Agreement on Tariffs and Trade: Multilateral Trade Negotiation Final Act Embodying the Results of the Uruguay Round of Trade Negotiations, Annex 1B, General Agreement on Trade in Services, 33 I.L.M. 1125, 1168 (1994).

2. Ibid.

3. R Hudec, *Developing Countries in the GATT Legal System* (Aldershot: Gower, for the Trade Policy Research Centre, 1987).

4. Bhagwati, Hirsh and Croome discuss the negotiating history of the Uruguay Round. J Bhagwati and Mathias Hirsch, (eds), *The Uruguay Round and Beyond: Essays in Honor of Arthur Dunkel* (Ann Arbor: University of Michigan Press, 1998) and J Croome, *Reshaping the World Trading System* (Leiden: Kluwer International, 1999).

5. B Hoekman, 'Assessing the General Agreement on Trade in Services' in W Martin and LA Winters (eds), *The Uruguay Round and the Developing Countries* (Cambridge: Cambridge University Press 1996).

and competitively priced transport, distribution, and many other services. Third, the WTO negotiating process requires countries that seek market-access concessions to offer concessions in turn. Thus, greater ambition in terms of liberalization of agriculture is likely to require greater opening in services, an area of export interest to many of the OECD countries that protect their agriculture sectors.

The stylized fact that looms large here is that with the exception of basic telecommunications, very little progress has been made to date in using the GATS framework to lock in unilateral reforms that have already been implemented, let alone in inducing new liberalization. Developing countries have resisted expanding their specific commitments. Instead of *quid pro quo* bargaining, traditional S&D treatment has become more prominent. Thus, the December 2005 Hong Kong Ministerial Declaration stated that 'We recognize the particular economic situation of LDCs, including the difficulties they face, and acknowledge that they are not expected to undertake new commitments'.[6] Reciprocity does not appear to working very well, contrary to Hudec's presumption.

The question taken up in this paper is why such limited traction? The basic argument is that in the services context, the power of standard reciprocity is constrained (Section B) and that there is a stronger case for S&D treatment of developing countries (Section C). However, the form this S&D treatment should take is not the standard GATT form that was criticized by Hudec. Instead, what is needed is to provide greater assurances that the preconditions for benefiting from services liberalization have been put in place. This is necessary for reciprocity to be able to work. These preconditions are largely regulatory in nature. This suggests, therefore, that what may be needed is to complement the WTO with mechanisms to assist governments design and implement regulation and to monitor the effects of applied policies, both liberalization and regulation (Section D).

B. RECIPROCITY CONSTRAINTS

In a recent paper, Barth, Marchetti, Nolle and Sawangngoenyuang combine data on specific GATS commitments on financial services with measures of actual policy in this sector for 123 countries drawn from Barth, Caprio, and Levine.[7]

---

6. World Trade Orgaization 'Doha Work Programme, Ministerial Meeting' (18 December 2005) WT/MIN(05)/Dec.

7. J Barth and others, 'Foreign Banking: Do Countries' WTO Commitments Match Actual Practices?' (2006) WTO Staff Working Paper No. ERSD-2006-11 <http://papers.ssrn.com/sol3/papers.cfm?abstract_id=950198> accessed 11 August 2008 and J Barth, G Caprio and R Levine, *Rethinking Bank Regulation: Till Angels Govern*, (Cambridge and New York: Cambridge University Press 2006).

They conclude that in practice, applied policy is much more liberal than what was committed to in the GATS. Eschenbach and Hoekman come to the same conclusion for the set of transition economies that were EU accession candidates.[8] Adlung and Roy point out that the provisional (conditional) offers made by WTO members in the six years following the launch of new negotiations on services (mandated by the GATS to commence in 2000 and subsequently folded into the Doha Round) were not ambitious.[9] Essentially, offers were limited to further (still incomplete) lock-in of past liberalization.

These papers suggest there is limited interest in using the GATS as a vehicle to commit to actual liberalization of markets. As noted by Hoekman, Mattoo and Sapir, one reason for this may simply be that numerous countries have taken action to increase competition on services markets by liberalizing FDI, opening access to foreign competition in backbone sectors such as transport and telecommunications, and privatizing state-owned or controlled service providers.[10] If many of the markets that services exporters are interested in contesting were already open, this would certainly help explain the apparent lack of interest on the part of industry to support the WTO negotiations on services.

Because inefficient service industries generate costs for downstream users in many sectors, unilateral reform incentives may be larger than for trade in goods and be less susceptible to rollback, reducing the need to use international commitment mechanisms such as trade agreements. Allowing high-cost, low-quality services to dominate on a market will be detrimental to almost everyone in an economy, with large users having strong incentives to push for measures—such as deregulation, privatization, and liberalization—that generate more competition in the provision of these upstream suppliers of inputs.[11] In practice, the majority of reforms that have been implemented by countries have been autonomous. The extent of unilateral reform that has been observed since the mid-1980s suggests multilateral mechanisms may not be needed as much as in the case of goods trade.

However, there is substantial evidence that numerous barriers to trade and investment continue to prevail in most countries. The consensus view is that the

---

8. F Eschenbach and B Hoekman, 'Services Policies in Transition Economies: On the EU and WTO as Commitment Mechanisms' (2006) 5(3) WT Rev 415–43.

9. R Adlung and M Roy, 'Turning Hills into Mountains? Current Commitments Under the General Agreement on Trade in Services and Prospects for Change' (2005) 39 JWT 1161–94.

10. B Hoekman, A Mattoo and A Sapir, 'The Political Economy of Services Trade Liberalization: A Case for International Regulatory Cooperation?' (2007) 23(3) OREP 367–91.

11. B Hoekman and P Messerlin, 'Liberalizing Trade in Services: Reciprocal Negotiations and Regulatory Reform' in P Sauvé and R Stern (eds), *Services 2000: New Directions in Services Trade Liberalization* (Washington, D.C.: Brookings Institution, 2000) 487–508.

tariff equivalents of these barriers are a multiple of those that affect merchandise trade.[12] Indirect evidence also suggests barriers are still significant in many countries, especially developing nations. Studies that use available information on prevailing policies conclude that further services liberalization would have much greater positive effects on national welfare than the removal of trade barriers.[13] Instead of the 'standard' 1 percent increase in welfare from goods liberalization, introducing greater competition on services markets raises the gains to the 5–10 percent range or more. These large effects of services liberalization reflect both the importance of services in the economy and the extent to which many of them continue to be protected. Thus, there is still great scope to complement the unilateral reforms that have been implemented by WTO Members with multilateral commitments. Unilateral action cannot fully explain the lack of progress on services in the WTO: there are still many barriers to be negotiated away.

As important, there is much that can be done in terms of scheduling status quo policies that are relatively liberal. While what matters for exporters are applied levels of protection, this is not the focus of WTO negotiations. These center on specific commitments ('policy bindings') for services sectors. For many countries, applied services trade policies are much more liberal than what is implied by their commitments in the WTO. Insofar as traders are benefiting from past liberalization and perceive a low probability of governments backsliding (raising protection again), the return to investments of political capital to lock in existing levels of openness may be seen to be low. If this is true, one can certainly question whether corporate interests are excessively optimistic on this front, discounting too much the probability of backsliding. The example of Indonesia is illustrative: in July 2007 the government announced a variety of more restrictive conditions on inward FDI. Given that the prevailing, more liberal situation had not been locked in through the GATS, the government was unconstrained in taking this action.[14]

---

12. No comprehensive, cross-country, comparable datasets exist that allow a summary assessment of the prevailing levels of services trade and investment barriers. B Hoekman, 'Liberalizing Trade in Services: A Survey' (2006) World Bank Policy Research Working Paper 4030.

13. See Konan and Maskus, on one part, on Tunisia and Jensen, Rutherford and Tarr, on the other part, on Russia. DE Konan and KE Maskus, 'Quantifying the Impact of Services Liberalization in a Developing Country' (2006) 81 JDE 142–62 and J Jensen, T Rutherford and D Tarr (forthcoming), 'The Impact of Liberalizing Barriers to Foreign Direct Investment in Services: The Case of Russian Accession to the World Trade Organization', Review of Development Economics.

14. Indonesia announced a 49 percent foreign ownership cap on companies in sectors such as multimedia, ports, airports, and education. Equity ownership caps were reduced for mobile phone companies (from 95 percent to 65 percent). Insurance companies were

Continued high barriers to trade and investment in conjunction with the limited extent to which current policies are bound in the GATS suggests there should be significant scope for quid pro quo bargaining. So why is this not happening? There are at least two possible reasons why the standard mechanisms of reciprocity as developed over 50 years of GATT practice may not readily apply to services: (i) the export interests that are needed do not prevail sufficiently in the services context, and (ii) regulatory concerns impede the ability (willingness) of WTO Members to engage in what Jagdish Bhagwati has termed 'first difference' reciprocity.[15]

i. Asymmetric Interests

In the case of merchandise trade, all WTO Members have clear interests in improving access to export markets. Some countries are more diversified than others, and all have differential specific interests—but all countries are exporters of goods that are subject to trade barriers in partner country markets. Thus, they have exporters that see potential benefits from multilateral negotiations. This is less the case for services. While many developing countries are significant exporters of services, often the associated foreign exchange earnings are derived from activities where the relevant policies are under the control of the government as opposed to trading partners. The most important such 'service' is tourism, where the export revenue generated depends primarily on measures that the tourism destination country puts in place itself.

As far as cross-border trade in services via telecommunications networks is concerned (Mode 1 GATS), developing countries have export interests, but this channel for trade is often not constrained by policy in the importing country (with the exception of services such as gambling where importing countries may reserve the activity to the state or ban it altogether). Most of the business process outsourcing, call centers, etc., that are growth areas for many countries are not constrained by trade policy measures in the destination or importing country. While there is certainly increasing opposition against such trade in high-income countries, outside of government contracts there is little that is currently done to restrict such activities from being 'offshored'.

Turning to FDI (Mode 3 of the GATS or establishment), most developing countries do not have significant 'offensive' interests—they do not have indigenous multinational service providers seeking better access to foreign markets. This is a mode that is primarily of interest to firms based in high-income countries and large emerging economies.

The one mode where developing countries confront particularly high barriers and that is therefore of great relevance to potential exporters is the temporary

---

capped at 80 percent, hospitals at 65 percent, and most construction activities at 55 percent. J Aglionby, 'Indonesia restricts foreign investment' *Financial Times* (4 July 2007).

15. B Hoekman, A Mattoo and A Sapir (n 10 above).

cross-border movement of service providers (natural persons—Mode 4 of GATS). However, Mode 4 is politically extremely sensitive. Insofar as there are no serious prospects for Mode 4 liberalization in the GATS framework, most of the potential export interests in many developing countries are disengaged from the process.

A fundamental problem, as in the case of goods, is that most developing countries—the majority of the WTO membership—are small and therefore not of great interest to the large players in the WTO, constraining their prospects of negotiating significant additional access to major markets.

These considerations imply that a key driver of the reciprocity mechanism—services exporters—is either missing or much weaker in many WTO Members than is true for goods. The exception are large service firms that are based in high-income economies, which have clear interests in selling more services to both OECD and to developing countries. This is mostly a Mode 3 (FDI) agenda. The implication is that if access negotiations are to be restricted within the services arena, deals are likely to be limited to Mode 3 exchanges (largely an intra-OECD/large emerging markets affair) or better access for developing countries through Mode 4 to OECD markets in return for Mode 3 liberalization by developing countries.

However, as argued below, a precondition for making headway may be regulatory cooperation and assistance. Limiting the focus to 'trade policy' concessions may not allow agreement to emerge, ie, reciprocity cannot work by itself.

ii. Regulatory Constraints

In goods, trade barriers apply at the border and are very visible. In the case of services, trade is restricted by a mix of explicit discrimination against foreign providers and domestic regulation that may result in *de facto* discrimination. The prevalence of regulation to address market failures due to asymmetric information, imperfect competition, and network externalities greatly complicates the process of multilateral market-access negotiations. Regulators may be concerned that trade liberalization will impede their ability to enforce domestic regulatory standards. Trade will bring with it regulatory competition if services suppliers are only subject to the norms and standards that apply in their home markets. A critical—and difficult—question is how to differentiate between legitimate concerns relating to quality and performance and regulatory requirements that simply constitute barriers to entry, creating rents for incumbents by raising prices.

In addition to concerns about the ability to enforce national regulatory standards, in developing countries, liberalization may raise an additional regulation-related issue: achieving social equity objectives. The impacts of more competitive market structures following liberalization on access to services by poorer households in developing countries have been mixed. In cases like mobile telecommunications, a positive relationship has been observed in many developing countries because initial conditions were bad—few households had access. However, in other areas like financial services, unless improved regulatory measures are put in place, liberalization may have an adverse effect on access to credit for rural areas and the poor. Putting in place mechanisms to ensure better access to services postliberalization is important from an equity perspective. It is also important from a political economy perspective to bolster support for implementing efficiency-enhancing policy reforms and sustaining them over time. Absent actions to address regulatory weaknesses, countries may not be in a position to fully realize the potential benefits of trade reforms in services (*or* goods).

The prevalence of regulation further complicates and constrains use of the traditional GATT reciprocity mechanism for services because it is very difficult to design multilateral rules and national commitments in a way that clearly separates or distinguishes between measures that are protectionist and measures that have good domestic efficiency or social equity rationales. As the focus of WTO negotiations is not on the welfare of members or on the identification of 'good' policy, regulators may therefore be concerned that market-access negotiating dynamics could adversely affect their ability to design and implement regulatory norms that maximize national welfare.

C. COULD MORE S&D TREATMENT HELP?

The constraints on the use of reciprocity in services are to some extent similar to those that arise in the goods case. Thus, small countries have little to offer in the WTO bargaining process simply because they are small. In economic terms, many developing countries are very small indeed. This was one of the major rationales for the creation of the GSP in the 1960s. Given that small poor countries cannot play the mercantilist trade negotiating game, and have limited export capacity (do not constitute a major threat in terms of 'market disruptive' import competition), offering these countries preferential access to rich markets seems to make good sense: an opportunity to do some good at low (political) cost.

The GSP and similar programs offering nonreciprocal preferential access to markets is one prong of S&D treatment in the GATT. The other is 'less than full reciprocity' and exemptions from provisions that constrain the use of trade policies. The latter was not driven by the fact that small and/or poor countries have little offer—although this was no doubt a major reason why it was not very controversial with the large players in the GATT—but was based on the premise that industrial development required protection of infant industries.

In contrast to goods trade, developing countries do not have nonreciprocal preferential access to OECD service markets. There is no GSP for services trade: preferential access is only on offer in the context of reciprocal trade agreements. Should there be? All the arguments offered by Hudec and the many analysts that have followed in his tracks suggest that preferences will not help address the reciprocity problem. Indeed, these arguments are even stronger for services than for goods.

One reason is that barriers to trade in many services are low: for Modes 1 and 2, trade barriers often do not exist. Instead, what matters are own policies; these will determine competitiveness of services exports. Thus, for preferences to be operationalized, OECD and other large markets will have to subsidize imports—the preferential removal of trade barriers is not available. The likelihood of direct fiscal subsidization being feasible is, however, much lower than preferential removal of trade barriers, notwithstanding economic arguments that in principle, import subsidies would dominate traditional trade preferences in welfare (efficiency) terms.[16] In addition to the lack of political feasibility of subsidies, implementing them for nontangible and nonstorable products offers challenges that are much greater than in the case of trade in goods.

In Mode 3 (FDI), where there may be significant discriminatory policies restricting market access, as discussed above, many (most) developing countries do not have significant capacity or 'export' interest—what matters here is to *attract* FDI. In short, meaningful preferential access can only offered for Mode 4—the (temporary) movement of people (natural persons) who supply services in a host country. But achieving significant preferential liberalization of this mode is politically very difficult, especially for less-skilled workers.

Matters are complicated further by the fact that some OECD countries do have bilateral arrangements with certain developing countries that facilitate and regulate access to labor markets. This is not part of a 'GSP'; these are strictly unilaterally determined and often discriminatory (recall that a feature of the GSP—at least in principle—was that preferences were to be made available to *all* developing countries). Insofar as a country has better access to an OECD member's labor market it may not be very supportive of efforts to move toward the creation of a GSP for services, as existing labor market arrangements (visa or work permit regimes) are not subject to the GATS MFN rule.

Thus, independent of one's views of the economics of preferential access programs, this is not an option that can readily be implemented for trade in services. What about infant-industry protection? Observe that to a significant extent this option is 'built in' the GATS: the positive list approach to coverage of the agreement implies that sectors that a government desires to protect can be protected. Thus, seeking to make this explicit is essentially redundant although it would constitute a clear change from the premise that implicitly underlies the GATS: all countries will benefit from making specific commitments. Turning to the economics of infant protection in services, this has weaker foundations than the standard infant-industry argument for industrial products. Because many

---

16. N Limão and M Olarreaga, 'Trade Preferences to Small Developing Countries and the Welfare Costs of Lost Multilateral Liberalization' (2006) 20(2) WB Econ Rev 217–40.

services—especially so-called 'backbone' services such as the network industries (telecommunications, transport, energy services) are inputs into production of virtually every industry, policies that raise the costs of such services can have much greater negative effects on national welfare. Many services are also still much less tradable than goods and thus involve local production, and thus local demand for labor and other inputs. Liberalization and the associated inflow of foreign providers will generate local employment and over time generate technology transfer as employees and local competitors learn from the new competition.

Although there is little merit in the infant service industry argument for protection, as noted previously, services markets are often characterized by different types of inefficiencies. Both efficiency and equity may require effective regulation of services activities. The capacity to do this may be weak or simply absent in some developing economies. If so, there is a clear case for 'intervention' to build the requisite capacity. And, insofar as liberalization might result in either inefficient or inequitable outcomes that could undermine support for greater competition and contestable markets, there may be a good case for delaying opening up service markets to foreign entry.

This line of argument suggests that instead of old style S&D treatment, which is appropriately not incorporated into the GATS, what is needed are mechanisms that complement the WTO machinery. Other forms of international cooperation—*outside* WTO—may be needed as a 'facilitating device' for reciprocal market-access bargaining to be feasible (mutually beneficial).

D. ALTERNATIVES TO S&D

The focus of the WTO is on market access. Policy advice and assistance for regulatory reform and public investments in services infrastructure are provided by international financial institutions and specialized agencies. There is virtually no link between the two processes. This disconnect persists even though improved regulation, ranging from prudential regulation in financial services to procompetitive regulation in a variety of network-based services, will be critical to realizing the benefits of services liberalization in many sectors. The 2005 WTO Ministerial Declaration requires Members to provide 'targeted and effective technical assistance and capacity building for LDCs . . . . to strengthen their domestic services capacity, build institutional and human capacity, and enable them to undertake appropriate regulatory reforms.'[17] The challenge is to operationalize this commitment and to extend it to a broader set of developing countries.

---

17. WTO Ministerial Declaration (n 6 above).

The agenda goes far beyond technical assistance to help countries make market access commitments, which is the focus of much current assistance (as illustrated. for example. by the language on technical assistance for services negotiations in the Hong Kong Ministerial Declaration). It spans helping countries overcome the political economy factors that impede liberalization, improving domestic regulation, adopting measures that spread the benefits of liberalization to poor and disadvantaged households, support for the pursuit of regional cooperation, and measures that are preconditions for obtaining and exploiting better market access in export markets. What follows briefly discusses possible approaches in each of these areas.[18]

i. Political Economy: Redistributing Rents and Dealing with Adjustment Costs

Poor policies in many countries often reflect standard political economy forces: those who gain (or are not hurt) from current policies are more economically and politically powerful than those who lose. In the case of telecommunications, for example, the incumbent provider may confront an administered price structure (with artificially high international prices and artificially low local prices). Liberalization will require tariff rebalancing to allow the incumbent to compete on the international segment. The resultant increase in local call prices is likely to be resisted by the politically vocal urban consumers, though the prospect of more competitive mobile telephony may dilute such opposition. Putting in place transparent and credible compensatory measures (eg, voluntary retirement schemes, access to cheaper mobile telephony) could help persuade the incumbent's employees and urban consumers to accept reform.

Similar forces play out in other sectors. In Zambia—a country that being landlocked confronts higher transportation costs than many coastal countries—high costs are partly due to restrictions that Zambia imposes on air and road transport. While these are detrimental to exporters, they benefit import competing interests and domestic transport service providers.[19] In accounting, local professionals in Zambia are geared almost entirely toward the lucrative large-firm market and the use of international accounting and auditing standards. Although these are recognized to be excessively burdensome (costly) for small firms, the accounting profession has an interest generating the revenue associated with audits.[20]

---

18. What follows draws on B Hoekman and A Mattoo, 'Regulatory Cooperation, Aid for Trade and the GATS' (2007) 12(4) Pac Econ Rev 399–418.

19. Eg, foreign entry in cabotage activities is prohibited and international transporters may move products between two foreign countries only if they pass through their own country.

20. A Mattoo and L Payton (eds), *Services Trade and Development: The Experience of Zambia* (Washington DC: Palgrave/McMillan and World Bank, 2007).

Identifying the magnitude and incidence of the costs and benefits of prevailing policies that inhibit competition from foreign providers and developing mechanisms to assist losers is one area where aid for trade resources can make a difference in helping governments deal with vested interests that resist changes to the status quo.

ii. Implementing Appropriate Domestic Regulation

As noted previously, regulation is often needed in services sectors to achieve efficiency and equity objectives. Designing appropriate regulatory standards and institutions takes time as they often must be tailored to national circumstances to be effective and attain the desired objective. An increasing body of evidence has shown that a 'one size fits all' approach—including international 'best practice' norms—may not be appropriate. Reverting to the example of Zambia, in addition to the accounting example just mentioned, burdensome regulatory requirements for banks relating to documentation, collateral, and money laundering restrict access to credit for small enterprises and the rural poor, while not much affecting large firms or the urban rich. A fear of being blacklisted generates a chilling effect on the incentives for banks to explore or propose less burdensome alternatives to regulatory requirements.

The Zambia case illustrates the types of complementary measures that will have the most effect in increasing the gains from liberalization and showing that they will not be uniform across countries. Barth, Caprio, and Levine, in the first comprehensive cross-country assessment of the impact of the Basel Committee's influential approach to bank regulation, conclude that there is no evidence that any single set of 'best practices' is appropriate for promoting well-functioning banks.[21] There is need, therefore, for a high degree of country specificity in both diagnosis and remedial action. This is more time- and labor-intensive—ie, expensive—than is the adoption of (international) norms 'off the shelf'.

iii. Improving Domestic Access to Better Services

For the poorest countries in particular, the desired investment response to liberalization (entry by foreign providers) may be muted and take long to materialize. Structural factors such as economic size or location may imply that some countries or parts of countries will not be attractive enough to induce entry by private firms, whether foreign or domestic. Or, the market may be too small to allow vigorous competition. Such situations will result in limited access, if any, for many poor households or rural communities. Improving the distribution of access to services could be achieved by targeting aid for trade on service providers to encourage them to provide services in remote and disadvantaged regions in poor countries and/or to lower the prices of such services below what would

---

21. J Barth, G Caprio and R Levine (n 7 above).

be needed to cover costs. This could be an important dimension of an effective 'aid for trade' strategy to complement and support multilateral trade reforms. Such aid need not imply fiscal investment or entry incentives of the type offered by virtually all developing countries to foreign investors. These are costly and of dubious value. Instead, the idea is to use development aid funds to induce services firms, foreign or nationally owned, to provide specific services to households that otherwise would not be served.

The experience of a number of countries in the last decade has improved our understanding of how universal access policies can be used to complement market-based reforms to improve access for the poor to infrastructure services. In network industries such as telecommunications or electricity, private providers could compete for performance-based subsidies related to providing services to the poor. This would ensure that for the poor to reap some of the benefits of competition, and while minimizing outlays for the government, the 'reverse auction' process allows it to discover the true cost of service provision. Countries such as Chile, Peru, and Uganda have put in place such mechanisms, which have helped to expand services to areas that otherwise would not have access. Based on the Chilean experience,[22] Kenny and Keremane estimate that an upper bound on the amount needed for achieving universal access to basic telecommunications using competitively awarded subsidies to private providers in developing countries is some $5.7 billion. Of this amount, $1.8 billion could not be supplied by a reasonable tax on existing providers and would need to be generated from outside the sector. Most of this—some $1.5 billion—would be needed in Africa.

An international arrangement that replicates the key elements of successful national schemes may be one way to use additional aid for trade resources to increase support for procompetitive reforms. This could involve countries (or regions) that are willing to eliminate barriers to investment being given assistance to put in place both the necessary regulatory reforms *and* granted access to a 'universal service provision fund' in instances where the investment response from domestic and foreign firms had been inadequate. Funds would be made available to provide a subsidy to firms to create infrastructure and/or provide services in the relevant region or country at prespecified terms. Along the lines of the policies put in place in Chile, the Dominican Republic, Peru, and Uganda, these terms could be established as the result of an reverse auction or bidding process under which firms would indicate the minimum level of subsidy they

---

22. The subsidy needed to provide universal access in Chile varied across subregions, with poor, sparsely populated areas requiring a larger per capita subsidy. Income density explains over 60 percent in the variation of subsidy cost. C Kenny and R Keremane, 'Toward universal telephone access: Market progress and progress beyond the market' (2007) 31(3) Telecommunications Policy 155–63 therefore use income density data for other countries to estimate what would be needed to achieve universal access.

would require to fulfill the mandate set out by the government. Note that this form of assistance does not target specific industries or firms, as would industrial policies or trade preferences. Rather, the objective would be to improve the availability and quality of services for all firms, farms, and households in areas that would otherwise be underserved.

iv. Facilitating Market Access Through Broader Cooperation, Particularly on Mode 4

Facilitating regulatory cooperation could help deal with apprehensions about liberalization on all modes. In financial services, for example, confidence in cooperation by the home country regulator of suppliers could facilitate greater openness to both commercial presence and cross-border trade by host countries. Similarly, in international transport services, confidence in the enforcement of home-country competition law may increase the willingness to liberalize in importing countries.

The area that is probably of greatest interest to many developing countries—whether large emerging markets or the LDCs—in direct trade terms is to achieve progress on Mode 4. To date, Mode 4 has been (another) millstone for the services negotiations. To support a positive outcome on Mode 4, Members need to recognize that simply asserting that Mode 4 is about trade in services and *not* about migration cannot dispel the deep-rooted fears raised by the entry of foreign providers in many countries. Whatever one's views of the legitimacy of those fears, to make progress they have to be acknowledged and addressed.

Immigration authorities in host economies must be assured that source countries will cooperate to screen services providers, to accept and facilitate their return, and to combat illegal migration. The approach pursued to date in the WTO by developing countries has been to request that potential host countries make binding commitments on an MFN basis, regardless of the conditions that prevail in source countries or measures that governments in such countries should implement in order to manage Mode 4 trade. One way to take a more cooperative and less antagonistic approach to Mode 4 is to draw upon the experience of a few relatively successful bilateral and regional trade agreements. Greater progress might be feasible if more is done to also impose obligations on source countries. This is a key element of regional agreements (eg, APEC) that have facilitated mobility of skilled workers and bilateral labor agreements (eg, between Spain and Ecuador, Canada and the Caribbean, Germany and Eastern Europe) that have to a limited extent improved access for the unskilled. Source country obligations in these agreements include premovement screening and selection, accepting and facilitating return of workers, and commitments to combat illegal migration. Cooperation by the source can help address security concerns, ensure temporariness, and prevent illegal labor flows in a way that the host country is incapable of accomplishing alone. In effect, such cooperation constitutes a service for which the host may be willing to 'pay' by allowing increased access.

How might such elements be incorporated in a multilateral agreement? One possibility is that host countries commit under the GATS to allow access to any source country that fulfills certain prespecified conditions, along the lines of mutual recognition agreements in other areas. Even if these conditions were unilaterally specified and compliance determined unilaterally, it would still be a huge improvement over the arbitrariness and lack of transparency in existing visa schemes. Although negotiating these conditions multilaterally and establishing a mechanism to certify their fulfillment would be an improvement over the unequal, nontransparent, and potentially labor-diverting bilateral context, this is simply not feasible in the short run. Given the large differences in the ability of source countries to satisfy whatever conditions are put in place, there is a clear case for high-income countries also providing assistance to poorer countries to attain them. This is an area where regulatory cooperation between host and home countries, supported by development assistance from rich countries, could do much to assuage fears on the part of voters and governments in the North that Mode 4 is simply another form of long-term migration.

E. TOWARD GREATER TRANSPARENCY: A COMPARATIVE ADVANTAGE OF THE WTO

Much of the attention directed at the WTO tends to center on the process of negotiations and the dispute settlement mechanism. However, the functions of the WTO extend beyond rule making and enforcement. One of its tasks is to increase the transparency of member trade policies through the TPRM (Article III WTO). The objective of the TPRM is '... achieving greater transparency in, and understanding of, the trade policies and practices of Members ... [through] the regular collective appreciation and evaluation of the full range of individual Members' trade policies and practices and their impact on the functioning of the multilateral trading system. It is not, however, intended to serve as a basis for the enforcement of specific obligations under the Agreements or for dispute settlement procedures, or to impose new policy commitments on Members'. Annex 3 WTO, Section B, states further that 'Members recognize the inherent value of domestic transparency of government decision-making on trade policy matters ... and agree to encourage and promote greater transparency within their own systems, acknowledging that the implementation of domestic transparency must be on a voluntary basis and take account of each Member's legal and political systems.'

Services are included in the ambit of the TPRM. Indeed, the WTO is currently the only multilateral body that has the mandate to review all the services, trade related policies of countries. Greater investment of resources in enhancing the transparency of applied services policies and analysis of their effects (economic impact, distributional consequences) is a way that the WTO can complement aid for trade in services provided by development agencies and the private sector. A goal could be to monitor not just national trade- and investment-related policies but also the 'performance' of both the country concerned and the provision and effectiveness of the aid provided by donor countries. Over time, this could reduce uncertainty regarding the value of making specific commitments to countries, as these would be based on the experience obtained in implementing domestic policies for the sector concerned.

An implication is that in addition to being primarily a lock-in device for negotiated policy reforms, the WTO could also become a focal point for considering the international dimensions of national services policies on a regular basis, a mechanism for increasing the transparency of policy and outcomes, and a vehicle for monitoring the provision of development assistance. No other organization has as strong an incentive to monitor services trade and investment policies. Moving down this path does not imply ceasing to negotiate binding disciplines. Instead, it would put greater stress on the identification and pursuit of a national services policy agenda and link this to development assistance.

The small size of many WTO Members has implications not just for their ability to obtain market-access concessions. It also has implications for the enforcement of negotiated commitments. Small countries may not be able to credibly threaten retaliation if needed. Moreover, of probably greater importance is that very small countries are much less likely to be the subject of disputes than larger ones. This can reduce the value of GATS commitments (and, indeed, WTO membership) for such countries. As the threat of disputes is the main enforcement mechanism in the WTO, smallness may imply that governments are able to violate WTO disciplines and commitments with impunity.[23]

Little empirical analysis exists documenting the scale of this potential problem.[24] However, the poorest countries in the WTO system are almost completely disengaged from enforcement of market-access rights and commitments through formal dispute settlement litigation. Although more advanced and larger

---

23. C Bown and B Hoekman, 'Developing Countries and Enforcement of Trade Agreements: Why Dispute Settlement is Not Enough' (2008) 42(1) JWT 177–203.

24. Eschenbach and Hoekman provide some suggestive findings. They compare GATS commitments of 16 transition economies with actual policy in these countries. They find an *inverse* relationship between the depth of GATS commitments and the 'quality' index of actual services policies. The most far-reaching commitments were observed for Central Asian countries. These also had the worst applied policies in the sample. Moreover, over time these countries saw the least improvement in services policies. For these countries the GATS appears to have been either a failure—in not helping to promote improvements in services policies in the period following accession—or irrelevant in the sense that commitments were made that governments either did not intend to implement or could implement without resulting in a significant change in actual policies. F Eschenbach and B Hoekman, 'Services Policies in Transition Economies: On the EU and WTO as Commitment Mechanisms' (2006) 5(3) WT Rev 415–43.

developing countries have started to use the DSU—eg, Central American countries have initiated cases against each other, India has challenged the European Union, Brazil has taken on the United States—the LDCs are mostly absent, whether as complainants, respondents, or third parties.

Given that many (if not most) of the gains to trade liberalization of a particular import market accrue to domestic consumers (and consuming industries) through access to lower priced services and greater variety, the failure of the WTO system to enforce commitments in many developing countries has sizable costs *within* those countries. While governments may complain about having their policies challenged under WTO dispute settlement, the process is needed for commitments to be supported by domestic industries and firms.

Greater transparency of policy—not just identification of the existence of policies but assessments of their effects—may help offset the weakness in the enforcement incentives that are inherent in the status quo. More frequent and in-depth analysis of services trade policies in WTO Members, as well as the extent to which high-income countries have provided assistance to address priorities that were identified by developing countries (mentioned earlier), could support more constructive engagement of business and NGOs with the WTO and the GATS. If WTO Members were to expand the transparency mandate of the organization to make the WTO a focal point for multilateral discussions and assessments of the state of members' service sectors, the institution could do much to help address the needs of its poorer members by raising the policy profile of the services agenda in these countries and identifying where investments/ assistance are needed.

By combining its commitment and monitoring 'technologies' to mobilize liberalization commitments that are conditional on assistance and monitoring the delivery and effectiveness of such assistance, the WTO could play a useful role in both helping Members and expanding the coverage of its agreements. Greater efforts to ensure transparency do not necessarily have to involve the WTO itself. Research and public interest bodies can do much to help shed light and build consensus by identifying good (better) policies; their economic impact, including distributional effects within and across countries; and whether alternative instruments exist that could attain governmental or societal objectives (more) efficiently.

F. CONCLUDING REMARKS

There are significant limits to the power of reciprocity to induce greater developing country participation in GATS. This reflects a mix of 'fundamentals' about which little can be done and legitimate concerns regarding the likely magnitude and distribution of the costs and benefits of services liberalization. A fundamental constraint for many countries is that the export interests that must drive the

WTO negotiation process are simply missing or too weak. While this does not apply to larger developing countries—the emerging markets—it is a factor affecting many WTO members. Reversion to traditional GATT types of S&D treatment is not the answer; preferences and nonreciprocity (opting out) will not help developing countries. In part, this is for the same reasons that were laid out in Hudec, but matters are worse in the services context in that S&D simply cannot have the desired effects even in theory.[25] The characteristics of services are such that traditional S&D treatment cannot work.

To address the legitimate worries regarding regulation and regulatory preconditions for liberalization—a distinct feature of the services agenda that differentiates services trade from trade in goods—another type of S&D treatment is arguably needed. Complementing traditional reciprocal bargaining on market access with mechanisms combine analysis and dialogue based on full transparency, and development assistance to strengthen regulatory capacity could do much to enhance the value of WTO membership for many developing countries. While not addressed at any length in this paper, the regulatory concerns and constraints affecting liberalization of services trade are not limited to the group of smaller and poor countries. They also pertain to the set of countries that have the capacity to utilize the reciprocity mechanism. Thus, the 'alternative S&D treatment' options sketched out may also be of benefit to these countries.

---

25. R Hudec (n 3 above).

17. DEVELOPMENT BY MOVING PEOPLE
Unearthing the Development Potential of a GATS Visa

SUNGJOON CHO*

A. Introduction 457
B. A Balance Sheet of Temporary Migration of Workers 459
    I. Benefits 459
    II. Costs 461
C. What the GATS Mode 4 Regime Offers (and Fails to Offer) 463
    I. Definition: Temporary Movement of Specific Service Providers 463
    II. Main Problems: Poor Levels of Commitments 464
D. Rethinking GATS Mode 4: A GATS Visa 466
    I. Overview 466
    II. Three Challenges 466
    III. How to Meet the Challenges 467
        Temporariness 467
        Legal binding 469
        Substantial levels of commitments 470
    IV. How to Negotiate on a GATS Visa: A Proposal for a Three-Step Approach 471
        The first step: Building confidence 471
        The second step: Extending the scope of Mode 4 liberalization 471
        The final step: Hardening (legal binding) 472
E. Conclusion 473

A. INTRODUCTION

The recent surge in the international migration of workers, in particular the migratory flow from the South to the North, symbolizes both a problem of and a solution to development. First, it eloquently demonstrates a widening income gap between poor and rich economies, marking a 20 or 30 times difference.[1] At the same time,

---

* Associate Professor of Law, Chicago-Kent College of Law, Illinois Institute of Technology. I would like to extend my deepest gratitude to Professor Jagdish Bhagwati for his extraordinary guidance and support on this paper. I also thank Professors Michael Trebilcock, Joel Trachtman, Richard Steinberg, Chantal Thomas, and other participants of the Conference on Developing Countries in the WTO Legal System held at the University of Minnesota Law School on 24–26, May 2007, for their valuable comments on an earlier draft. Sean Donohue and Deborah Ginsberg provided excellent research assistance. Finally, I dedicate this paper to the late Robert Hudec whose pioneering and field-defining work on trade and development still remains powerful and inspiring. All errors are mine.

1. Global Commission on International Migration, *Migration in an Interconnected World: New Directions for Action* (2005) 12.

however, the international migration of workers holds tremendous potential for poor economies' development. Remittances from these workers currently mark the second biggest source for hard currencies in poor countries, second only to foreign direct investment.[2] Rich economies also benefit from this factor (labor) mobility, dramatically reducing their production costs. It is estimated that replacing only 3 percent of rich countries' workforce by foreign migrant workers will create a global income gain of $150 billion annually, which is much larger than the $100 billion per year earned through a complete liberalization of trade in goods.[3]

Despite this gigantic developmental potential, this issue has seldom been discussed in the current Doha Round under the auspices of WTO[4] mainly on account of its immigration-related political implications and other 'unfortunate concomitants of national sovereignty'.[5] Heated debates on immigration policies in major developed countries, including the United States, may disqualify this subject as an agenda for international trade negotiations. Yet what is happening should be happening: these ever-increasing migrant workers can be an essential contributor to development, benefiting both home and host countries.

Against this backdrop, this paper explores practical strategies for promoting the international migration of workers under the WTO parameter, ie, free movement of natural persons (Mode 4) of the GATS.[6] Many scholars and researchers emphasize that GATS Mode 4 liberalization will greatly profit developing countries when it concerns the temporary movement of low-skilled service providers.[7]

This paper first identifies both benefits and costs of temporary migration while it highlights that those costs may be manageable. It then analyzes to what extent GATS Mode 4 could manifest development potential embedded in GATS. It observes that the 'GATS visa' proposal could deliver this development potential in GATS and suggests that WTO Members should tackle three main challenges (temporariness, legal binding, and levels of commitments) to succeed in the GATS visa program. The paper also contends that WTO Members should first gain confidence in the GATS visa system through voluntary experimentation on a limited scale before they negotiate on the expansion of the covered list or on any legally binding mechanism.

---

2. World Bank, *Global Economic Prospects: Realizing the Development Promise of the Doha Round* (2004) 148.

3. See discussion below in Part B(i).

4. *Final Act Embodying the Results of the Uruguay Round of Multilateral Trade Negotiations* (the 'WTO Agreement') (Marrakesh, 15 April 1994; 33 ILM 1140, 1144–53).

5. JN Bhagwati, 'Splintering and Disembodiment of Services and Developing Nations" (1984) 7 World Economics 133, 141.

6. The WTO Agreement, article XXIV, annex 1B (Marrakesh, 15 April 1994; 33 ILM 1140, 1144–53). My main concern in this paper is unskilled (or semiskilled), nonprofessional service providers who have largely been excluded in the current GATS commitments of most developed countries.

7. See A Winters and others, *Liberalising Labour Mobility Under the GATS: Economic Paper* (2003) ch 3.

B. A BALANCE SHEET OF TEMPORARY MIGRATION OF WORKERS

i. Benefits

The temporary migration of workers[8] brings to both home and host countries significant benefits through multiple channels, such as the efficient allocation of human resources, remittances, and brain circulation.

First, the increasing temporary migration from South to North is a natural phenomenon driven by two salient factors. There exists a very substantial gap in average wages between developed and developing countries. For example, the average hourly wage in the manufacturing sector in Germany is $30, while in some parts of China and India it is only 30 cents.[9] Like the law of gravity, workers from developing countries tend to seek better-paying jobs in developed countries. Second, the continuing demographic change—aging population and low birth rate in developed countries and the opposite phenomenon in developing countries[10]—is also responsible for the surge in temporary migration these days. Out of 83 million annually added to the world population, 82 million are from developing countries.[11]

This phenomenon, ie, the ever-increasing temporary movement of workers from developing to developed countries, may be interpreted as economically sound in that it tends to achieve the efficient allocation of human resources. It certainly helps reduce unemployment in the home (labor-dispatching) countries.[12] On the other hand, producers in labor-receiving (developed) countries can redress the labor shortage as well as save production costs by paying low wages to foreign workers.[13] This is a

---

8. The taxonomical distinction on this temporary labor migration (currently GATS Mode 4), vis-à-vis permanent immigration, had already been discussed even before the Uruguay Round Negotiation began. For example, Jagdish Bhagwati referred to it as 'temporary-factor-relocation-requiring' service. JN Bhagwati, 'Economic Perspectives on Trade in Professional Services' (1986) UChig Leg For 45, 47 Bhagwati observed that temporary migration, which is subject to the 'utilitarian calculus', is free from the communitarian argument in favour of the 'right to exclude' permanent immigrants. Ibid 52. Regarding the general discussion on the taxonomical distinction of temporary migration of service providers, see GP Sampson and RH Snape, 'Identifying the Issues in Trade in Services' (1985) 8 W Econ 171; G Feketekuty, 'Trade in Professional Services, An Overview' (1986) UChig Leg For 1.

9. World Bank, *Global Economic Prospects: Realizing the Development Promise of the Doha Round* (2004) 145–46.

10. Ibid.

11. Ibid.

12. Organization for Economic Cooperation and Development, *Service Providers on the Move: Labor Mobility and the WTO General Agreement on Trade in Services*, (2003) 3; T Conway, 'Trade Liberalization and Poverty Reduction' (February 2004) Overseas Development Institute 17 (observing that the very poor workers in the home countries can fill in the vacuum generated by the migration).

13. Organization for Economic Cooperation and Development, *Service Providers on the Move: Labor Mobility and the WTO General Agreement on Trade in Services*, (2003) 3.

TABLE 1. EUROPE AND AFRICA DEMOGRAPHY (1800–2050) (SHARE OF WORLD POPULATION: %)

	1800	2000	2050
Africa	8	13	20
Europe	20	12	7
World Pop. (Bils.)	1	6	9

Source: Martin (2003)

classical example of a win-win situation, which Jagdish Bhagwati had aptly illustrated in a simple, two-country economic model.[14]

In this context, economists concluded in unison that even a small degree of liberalization in this field would mean a substantial welfare gain to the world economy.[15] TL Walmsley and A Winters observed that both developed and developing countries would realize an overall gain of $150 billion each year in case developed countries were to raise their quotas on temporary foreign workers to only 3 percent of their labor force.[16] Dani Rodrik also came up with a similar projection. He contended that if the temporary movement of foreign skilled and unskilled workers were to be capped at 3 percent of the developed countries' labor force, direct income gains of $200 billion dollars can occur.[17] Yet from a development standpoint, the largest gains would result from the movement of low-skilled workers because those workers are "spread more evenly over the economy, benefiting more sectors" than a high-skilled labor force.[18]

---

14. Bhagwati demonstrated that under a normal condition of diminishing returns any service labor shortage in one country will be addressed by migration from another labor abundant country until marginal returns of a specific service in question in both labor-receiving and labor-dispatching countries become equalized at a certain equilibrium point, provided that there exist no government regulations preventing such migration. At this equilibrium, both countries achieve their respective welfare gains. JN Bhagwati, 'Economic Perspectives on Trade in Professional Services' (1986) UChig Leg For 50–51.

15. See B Hamilton and J Whalley, 'Efficiency and Distributional Implications of Global Restrictions on Labor Mobility' (1984) 14 JDE 61, 62.

16. TL Walmsley and AL Winters, 'Relaxing the Restrictions on the Temporary Movements of Natural Persons: A Simulation Analysis' (2003) Centre for Economic Policy Research Discussion Paper No. 3719.

17. D Rodrik, 'Feasible Globalizations' (August 2002) National Bureau of Economic Research Working Paper W9129.

18. See Organization for Economic Cooperation and Development, *International Mobility of the Highly Skilled* (2002) 2–4.

More direct benefits of temporary migration to developing countries originate from remittances. Remittances increasingly play an essential role in securing necessary foreign currencies in developing countries. India's remittances in 1996 ($7.6 billion) were nearly three times as high as net direct investment inflows in the same year and equal the contributions by the textile and clothing industries to its GDP.[19]

The development effect of remittances is more salient in low-income developing countries. They are the second-largest source of foreign currencies next to foreign direct investment (FDI). In 2001, workers' remittances to low-income developing countries were considerably higher than major funding sources, such as FDI inflows, total private capital inflows, and official development assistance.[20] Considering that this statistic covers only what has been reported, the actual volume of worker remittances, including those from undocumented workers, may be larger than what has been reported.[21]

ii. Costs

Temporary migration might accompany negative effects similar to those which permanent migration tends to inflict on the host countries, including national security concerns.[22] In particular, domestic workers could be replaced by foreign workers if the latter's wages are considerably lower than the former's wages without severely sacrificing the quality of the job. While it is true that temporary migration could generate these 'adjustment stresses' to domestic workers,[23] the OECD observes that complementarity between foreign and native workers prevails over substitution between the two.[24] According to one study, even a 10 percent increase of immigrants had few effects on the wages of US workers.[25]

---

19. Council for Trade in Services, Presence of Natural Persons (Mode 4): Background Note by the Secretariat (8 December 1995) S/C/W/75 <http://docsonline.wto.org>.

20. World Bank, *Global Economic Prospects: Realizing the Development Promise of the Doha Round* (2004) 148.

21. Ibid.

22. R Walters, 'Managing Global Mobility: Free Trade in Services in the Age of Terror' (2006) 6 UC Davis Bus LJ 15 (describing various restrictions on global labor mobility due to the September 11 terrorist attacks).

23. LA Winters, 'The Economic Implications of Liberalizing Mode 4 Trade' (2002) (Paper prepared for Joint WTO-World Bank Symposium on Movement of Natural Persons (Mode 4) Under the GATS, 11–12 April 2002).

24. Organization for Economic Cooperation and Development, *Service Providers on the Move: Labor Mobility and the WTO General Agreement on Trade in Services* (2003) 3.

25. JB Grossman, 'The Substitutability of Natives and Migrants in Production' (1992) Review of Economics and Statistics No. 64. See also 'Myths and Migration' (8 April 2006) *The Economist* 76; I Arieff, 'Migrants Help More Than Harm Their New Lands-UN' (29 November 2004) *Reuters*.

At the same time, the temporariness of migration tends to save the hosting country government tremendous costs for providing social safety nets to foreign workers, such as health care, education, and welfare payments. Moreover, since foreign workers need not fully integrate themselves into the hosting society, the possibility of sociocultural tensions would be relatively lower than under the permanent migration.[26]

Another possible concern for hosting countries is 'overstaying' or a switch from migration to immigration. Conservative commentators often criticize a temporary (guest) worker program through a paradoxical argument that 'nothing is more permanent than temporary'.[27] However, 'overstaying' is also a concern for other types of temporary movement, such as tourist visas.[28] If home and host countries closely cooperate in managing the temporary flow of workers to and from these countries, it not only prevents overstaying problems but also reduces the number of illegal immigrants by making more room for documented workers.[29]

Finally, some critics point out that scarce skilled labor in developing countries would be 'drained' to developed countries via temporary migration of these workers. Yet many commentators seem to be skeptical of this brain drain phenomenon.[30] In fact, the opposite phenomenon has happened. Through technology transfer and human capital reinforcement, temporary migration has served as a ladder to higher-skilled jobs[31] in many developing countries. As the OECD defined as 'brain circulation', a number of Indian information technology (IT) workers who have worked in Silicon Valley with a temporary visa, such as H1B, returned to India and started up huge IT enterprises, boosting Indian IT exports from $150 million in 1990 to $4 billion in 2000.[32] More important, this brain

---

26. LA Winters, 'The Temporary Movement of Workers to Provide Services' (GATS Mode 4) 3.

27. P Martin, 'There Is Nothing More Permanent than Temporary Foreign Workers' (April 2001) Center for Immigration Studies, available at: <http://www.cis.org/articles/2001/back501.html>.

28. Organization for Economic Cooperation and Development, *Service Providers on the Move: Labor Mobility and the WTO General Agreement on Trade in Services* (2003) 3.

29. Ibid. See also F Emmert, 'Labor, Environmental Standards and World Trade' (2003) 10 UC Davis JIL & Pol 75, 155.

30. Organization for Economic Cooperation and Development, *Service Providers on the Move: Labor Mobility and the WTO General Agreement on Trade in Services* (2003) 3; World Bank, *Global Economic Prospects: Realizing the Development Promise of the Doha Round* (2004) 158–59.

31. World Bank, *Global Economic Prospects: Realizing the Development Promise of the Doha Round* (2004) 161.

32. Organization for Economic Cooperation and Development, *Service Providers on the Move: Labor Mobility and the WTO General Agreement on Trade in Services* (2003) 5. See also S Rudrappa, 'Working Borders: Linking Debates about Insourcing and Outsourcing of Capital and Labor' (2005) 40 Texas ILJ 691, 761–62 (aptly observing that insourcing and outsourcing is 'part and parcel of the same phenomenon'); M Jansen and R Piermartini,

drain problem rarely exists in low-skilled labor, which is abundant in many low-income developing countries.[33]

In sum, even if temporary migration may involve certain costs/risks, they are inevitable ones which any temporary movement of people, such as tourists, may generate. Also, those risks in the case of temporary migration tend to be more manageable than under permanent migration. Last but not least, brain drain is not a major problem to the movement of low-skilled labor in which low-income developing countries have great stakes.

C. WHAT THE GATS MODE 4 REGIME OFFERS (AND FAILS TO OFFER)

i. Definition: Temporary Movement of Specific Service Providers

Temporary migration within the meaning of GATS is defined as Mode 4, ie, 'the supply of a service by a service supplier of one Member, through presence of natural persons of a Member in the territory of any other Member'.[34] Although this provision is subject to multiple interpretations due to its ambiguity, the nature of GATS tends to characterize temporary migration under GATS in two critical ways: temporariness of duration and functional specificity.

First, Paragraph 2 of the Annex on Movement of Natural Persons Supplying Services under the Agreement (Annex) provides that 'the Agreement shall not apply to measures affecting natural persons seeking access to the *employment market* of a Member, nor shall it apply to measures regarding *citizenship, residence* or *employment* on a permanent basis'.[35] The Annex basically carves out immigration issues, such as permanent residence, and employment from the scope of GATS. Then what about temporary employment? Does Mode 4 allow service providers to seek jobs in the host country's labor market *after* they enter into the host country? Since GATS Mode 4 does not actually guarantee access to the host country's labor market, service providers are likely to be preemployed by the host country's industries and screened by the host country's government *before* they come to the host country. In sum, Paragraph 2 tends to convert the already very limited US commitments on Mode 4 into a null ('Unbound').

Second, Paragraph 1 of the Annex stipulates that 'this Annex applies to measures affecting natural persons who are service suppliers of a Member, and natural persons of a Member who are employed by a service supplier of a Member, in

---

'The Impact of Mode 4 Liberalization on Bilateral Trade Flows' (November 2005) Staff Working Paper ERSD-2005-06, 2.

33. I thank Joel Trachtman for raising this important point.

34. The WTO Agreement, article XXIV, annex 1B (Marrakesh, 15 April 1994; 33 ILM 1140, 1144–53) article I para 2(d).

35. Annex on Movement of Natural Persons Supplying Services under the Agreement (Annex), para. 2 (emphasis added).

respect of the supply of *a* service'.[36] Critically, what GATS Mode 4 covers in terms of temporary migration is the movement of providers of specific services, which are not interchangeable among sectors.[37] It does *not* concern manufacturing or agricultural workers,[38] which constitute an important subject of temporary migration under domestic immigration policies (eg, an H-2A visa category for seasonal farm workers in the United States).

ii. Main Problems: Poor Levels of Commitments

Article I:2 (d) of GATS, as it stands, seems to suggest that any service provider from a developing country may freely get access to developed countries' service markets. However, an ostensibly liberal definition by itself should not be translated into actual market access on Mode 4, which depends on a national schedule of commitments of each Member (host country). Unsurprisingly, most developed countries register minimum commitments on Mode 4 in nearly all service sectors. Therefore, despite the legal possibility under Article I:2 (d), development potential embedded in Mode 4 fails to materialize.

The ratio of full liberalization in Mode 4 market access ranges from 0 to 4 percent compared with 18–59 percent in Mode 1 (cross-border, such as e-commerce), 24–69 percent in Mode 2 (consumption abroad, such as foreign outpatients), and 0–31 percent in Mode 3 (commercial presence, such as foreign subsidiaries).[39] In particular, most developed countries, including the United States, adopt 'horizontal' restrictions which apply across all service sectors. Under these horizontal restrictions, developed countries generally refuse to commit, ie, are 'unbound' by, Mode 4 liberalization—except for the aforementioned movement of 'intra-corporate transferees' between parent companies and their foreign subsidiaries, and 'corporate executives and managers'—which mostly concerns developed countries' own economic interests. This narrow exception accounts for nearly 90 percent of their current commitments in GATS Mode 4.[40] As a

---

36. Ibid para 1 (emphasis added).

37. Council for Trade in Services, Presence of Natural Persons (Mode 4): Background Note by the Secretariat (8 December 1995) S/C/W/75 <http://docsonline.wto.org> 4.

38. Organization for Economic Cooperation and Development, *Service Providers on the Move: Labor Mobility and the WTO General Agreement on Trade in Services* (2003) 2; Organization for Economic Cooperation and Development, 'Service Providers on the Move: A Closer Look at Labor Mobility and the GATS' TD/TC/WP(2001)26/FINAL (20 February 2002) 6.

39. Organization for Economic Cooperation and Development, 'Service Providers on the Move: A Closer Look at Labor Mobility and the GATS' TD/TC/WP(2001)26/FINAL (20 February 2002) 30; World Bank, 'Global Economic Prospects: Realizing the Development Promise of the Doha Round'(2004) 144.

40. World Bank, *Global Economic Prospects: Realizing the Development Promise of the Doha Round* (2004) 144; J Nielsen, 'Service Providers on the Move' (2002) Evian Group Compendium, Lausanne: Evian Group 144.

result, providers of low-skilled services from developing countries never get access to potentially lucrative markets in developed countries under the current GATS regime.

Moreover, the liberalization of underlying services is also modest in general.[41] Even for the very limited Mode 4 commitments to be truly effective, Mode 3 commitments should also be incorporated in the national schedule so that service providers can establish certain types of commercial presence in order to actually perform their services in the host countries once they enter into the market.[42] For example, the United States' commitments on Mode 4 mostly regard 'intracorporate transferees', which may be qualified for an L visa status. These transferees can come to the United States only when their branches or subsidiaries (commercial presence) have already been established in the United States under its Mode 3 commitments. Yet in many sensitive service sectors, Mode 3 liberalization is still limited, with some exceptions of telecommunication and financial services.[43]

Finally, as discussed above, an open-ended regulatory reservation, especially under Paragraph 2 of the Annex, tends to potentially restrict the actual level of movement of service providers. The host (labor-receiving) country can find effective ways to regulate temporary migration flows (Mode 4) through measures 'affecting' employment or other normal immigration policies which are exempt from GATS and thus stand alone.

In conclusion, one might reasonably attribute such limited scope of liberalization in Mode 4 to a wide array of political resistance, ranging from labor unions' opposition and national security concerns. Due to this resistance, enormous welfare benefits, such as consumer welfare for developed countries and development gains for developing countries, remain largely immaterialized under GATS.[44]

---

41. R Self and BK Zutshi, 'Temporary Entry of Natural Persons as Service Providers: Issues and Challenges in Further liberalization under the Current GATS Negotiations' Joint WTO-World Bank Symposium on Movement of Natural Persons (Mode 4) Under the GATS (11–12 April 2002) 18–19.

42. Ibid 11.

43. Ibid 18–19. See also R Chanda, 'Movement of Natural Persons and the GATS: Major Trade Policy Impediments' in B Hoekman and others (eds) *Development, Trade, and the WTO: A Handbook* (2002) 304, 305 (observing that restrictions on foreign direct investment (FDI) may impede Mode 4).

44. Council for Trade in Services, Presence of Natural Persons (Mode 4): Background Note by the Secretariat (8 December 1995) S/C/W/75 <http://docsonline.wto.org> 7.

D. RETHINKING GATS MODE 4: A GATS VISA

i. Overview

Out of a variety of reform proposals on GATS Mode 4, a GATS visa has recently gained salience. The nitty-gritty of the GATS visa proposal is to create an independent visa category solely for the purpose of GATS Mode 4, ie, the temporary movement of service providers, for which applicants bear minimum administrative burdens. India provided a basic framework of the GATS visa program.[45]

According to the Indian proposal, which is similar to those proposals submitted by the US and European businesses,[46] a temporary visa for service providers under GATS may be issued within strict timeframes (2–4 weeks maximum) in a transparent and streamlined manner. A GATS visa is designed to avoid any unnecessary delays and administrative burdens which are the norm in the normal (permanent) immigration process.[47] Under the GATS visa system, applicants will be informed of causes of rejection and requirements to be met in the case of reapplication. A GATS visa, once issued, will be easily renewed under certain circumstances. Certain safeguard mechanisms will be included in this system to prevent its abuse, ie, shifting to permanent residence or employment after its expiration.

The GATS visa proposal is similar to the guest worker program that the Bush Administration has proposed in that it is a temporary visa system that is renewable, yet has end dates; may offer economic incentives to return home; and that it can coexist with conventional immigration policies.[48] Nevertheless, the main target of the US guest worker program is farm or manufacturing workers, falling within the rubric of the traditional Bracero or H2 program, not service providers under GATS.

ii. Three Challenges

While the proposal of a GATS visa may sound plausible, its actual implementation is prone to certain formidable challenges. First, the risk of overstaying always exists. Second, once bound, a host country *must* issue GATS visas in terms of legal obligation under GATS. Third, a GATS visa alone will be of little

---

45. WTO, Council for Trade in Services, Special Session, Communication from India: Proposed Liberalisation of Movement of Professionals under General Agreement on Trade in Services (GATS) (24 November 2000) S/CSS/W/12.

46. R Self and BK Zutshi, 'Temporary Entry of Natural Persons as Service Providers: Issues and Challenges in Further liberalization under the Current GATS Negotiations' Joint WTO-World Bank Symposium on Movement of Natural Persons (Mode 4) Under the GATS (11–12 April 2002) 25.

47. C Ng and J Whalley, *Visas and Work Permits: Can GATS/WTO Help Or Is a New Global Entity Needed?* (September 2004) 7.

48. The White House 'Fact Sheet: Fair and Secure Immigration Reform' (7 January 2004).

use to developing countries unless developed (host) countries significantly expand their current level of commitments in Mode 4.

First, overstaying is a serious concern to immigration authorities, although it is a problem beyond a GATS visa. In fact, nearly a half of illegal immigration originates from legal entries such as tourist visas.[49] Once admitted, they do not return after their legal duration expires. Likewise, service providers from developing countries may turn into illegal immigrants after their GATS visas expire after one or two years. Overstaying is a setback even to home countries of those service providers-turned-illegal immigrants since it may result in some kind of 'brain drain'. Instead of building human capital in their home countries, they may become a part of the labor force in host countries.

Second, any migration policy, including the GATS visa system, tends to claim maximum discretion and flexibility due to the volatile nature of domestic labor markets. Yet if Mode 4 liberalization through a GATS visa is bound as a legal obligation, domestic migration policies may lose such discretion and flexibility. This is one of the main reasons why the developed countries' current level of commitment in Mode 4 does not even match their current practices.[50] They may want to scale down the current level of migration without any legal restraints if future circumstances force them to do so.

Third, the GATS visa proposal is basically a *procedural* agenda. It purports to facilitate temporary movement of service providers by creating a separate visa category with a fast-track approach. Yet this procedural proposal would be of little practical help to developing countries unless it is accompanied by a substantive increase of market access to developed countries' service markets via Mode 4. Although a GATS visa does not guarantee employment in the host countries,[51] a GATS visa without a work permit would be of no use at all.

iii. How to Meet the Challenges

Temporariness To maintain the temporariness of a GATS visa will ultimately determine its success. Developed countries will gain confidence in this program if their demands for foreign labor are met without the serious side effect of overstaying. Commentators such as Alan Winters propose various policy instruments to

---

49. See JG Gimpel and JR Edwards, Jr., *The Congressional Politics of Immigration Reform* (1999) 81.

50. R Self and BK Zutshi, 'Temporary Entry of Natural Persons as Service Providers: Issues and Challenges in Further liberalization under the Current GATS Negotiations' Joint WTO-World Bank Symposium on Movement of Natural Persons (Mode 4). Under the GATS (11–12 April 2002)10; WTO, Council for Trade in Services, Presence of Natural Persons (Mode 4): Background Note by the Secretariat, S/C/W/75 (8 December 1995) 10.

51. Annex on Movement of Natural Persons Supplying Services under the Agreement (Annex), para 2.

secure the return of GATS visa holders to their home countries. Host countries may withhold partial income or social security tax of foreign service providers during their stay and return this amount after they go back to their home countries.[52] The fee (wage) parity between home and host countries should be maintained to discourage host countries' service buyers (employers) from illegally extending service providers' stay.[53]

In the same context, Dani Rodnik observed:

> One potentially Pareto-efficient solution is to institute a system of temporary contract employment in the host countries, with various penalties on the migrant and/or his employer to ensure that there is repatriation after a set number of years. In principle, the return migrants would then be in an even better position to contribute to the development of their home economies.[54]

It should be noted that cooperation between home and host countries is essential to implement any of these policy instruments. Both countries should realize that maintaining the temporariness of a GATS visa serves their mutual interests. Labor-receiving (host) countries want to avoid the risk of overstaying, while labor-dispatching (home) countries fear the risk of brain drain. Therefore, both countries retain strong incentives to have foreign service providers to return to their home countries after the expiration of their GATS visas.

Based on these incentives, both home and host countries should share the visa database and comonitor an inflow and outflow of service providers.[55] Naturally, this regulatory cooperation necessitates technical assistance from developed (host) countries to developing (home) countries, ranging from the precertification of service providers in home countries to the repatriation of their remaining income or social security contribution from host countries on their return. Host countries may want to assist home countries in establishing a 'national roster' of precertified service providers which satisfy the relevant regulatory requirements of the former countries and thus can be eligible for their GATS visas. Home countries may also contract private 'labor brokers' who secure the temporariness of the GATS visa by holding up new visa holders' entry until old visa holders return home.[56]

---

52. LA Winters, 'The Temporary Movement of Workers to Provide Services' (GATS Mode 4) 48–50; PL Martin, 'Managing Labor Migration: Temporary Worker Programs for the 21st Century' (September 2003) International Institute for Labor Studies 28.

53. LA Winters, 'The Temporary Movement of Workers to Provide Services' (GATS Mode 4) 48–50.

54. D Rodrik, 'Comments at the Conference on "Immigration Policy and the Welfare State"' (2001) <http://ksghome.harvard.edu/~.drodrik.academic.ksg/papers.html> 2.

55. Global Commission on International Migration, *Migration in an Interconnected World: New Directions for Action* (2005) 17.

56. D Ellerman, 'Policy Research on Migration and Development' (August 2003) World Bank Policy Research Working Paper No. 3117; PL Martin, 'Managing Labor

Another issue in temporariness regards the nature of service provided. While developed countries need both high- and low-skilled services from foreign providers, most low-income developing countries are incapable of providing these high-skilled services. Hence, most available service providers from poor countries are in low-skilled, labor-intensive services in which they hold comparative advantages. However, the risk of overstaying is generally higher in low-skilled service providers than in their high-skilled counterparts, which makes potential host (rich) countries allergic to this type of temporary migration.

One possible solution to this dilemma is to shorten the duration of stay in GATS visas for low-skilled services, such as building and cleaning, packaging, construction, refuse disposal, and transportation. A GATS visa for these kinds of services may only be valid for less than a year and cannot be renewed. Such nonrenewable,[57] short-term visas may minimize any overlapping with preexisting temporary working visas, prevent overstaying problems, and maximize the number of beneficiaries in the labor-dispatching countries. If GATS visa holders want to seek further stays in host countries, they should follow conventional immigration procedures such as H1B visas.

Legal binding The frustratingly low level of commitments in Mode 4, which is much lower than the actual practice, largely stems from the fear of legal binding, ie, the loss of future policy discretion to control an inflow of foreign service providers due to legal obligation. However, such a fear seems to be exaggerated considering an overriding mechanism embedded in the Annex. For example, Paragraph 4 of the Annex specifies that:

> The Agreement shall not prevent a Member from applying measures to regulate the entry of natural persons into, or their temporary stay in, its territory, including those measures necessary to protect the integrity of, and to ensure the orderly movement of natural persons across, its borders (. . .).

If this built-in policy discretion is insufficient to relieve host countries, they may introduce certain measures to potentially expand further discretion and thus mitigate risks from legal binding. Host countries may monitor and control the volume of GATS visa issuance through various screening mechanisms, such as a preemployment requirement and other licensing requirements, an economic need test (ENT), or a safeguard mechanism.[58]

Migration: Temporary Worker Programs for the 21st Century' (September 2003) International Institute for Labor Studies 28 (n 39).

57. PL Martin, 'Managing Labor Migration: Temporary Worker Programs for the 21st Century' (September 2003) International Institute for Labor Studies 3 (discussing the 'rotation principle').

58. Organization for Economic Cooperation and Development, 'Service Providers on the Move: A Closer Look at Labor Mobility and the GATS' TD/TC/WP(2001)26/FINAL (20 February 2002) 55–56. GATS provides that WTO members undertake a multilateral

Admittedly, mitigating the legal rigor in the GATS visa regime may risk generating a culture of indiscipline in this area. Nonetheless, considering the current status quo in Mode 4 liberalization, this compromise in legal disciplines seems to be necessary to move otherwise reluctant developed countries, which are potential GATS visa issuers, in favor of a GATS visa. The point here is to gain confidence in this targeted—and thus manageable program on temporary migration under GATS before it is ready to be hardened as a matter of legal obligation.

Substantial levels of commitments As discussed above, without a substantial improvement in most developed (host) countries' concessions on Mode 4, a GATS visa is of little use in generating development benefits to developing (home) countries. A GATS visa must be tied with the creation of certain quotas in low-skilled service jobs in host countries. For instance, if the United States issues 100,000 GATS visas for refuse disposal services, it must commit itself under GATS Mode 4 to this effect. This sector-specific commitment under the GATS visa will override any horizontal restrictions on Mode 4 to the extent of conflicts between the two in accordance with the principle of *lex specialis*.[59]

While setting an appropriate volume of GATS visas is a daunting task for domestic regulators, domestic industries that need foreign service providers may work with their governments to signal the level of their demand as well as to facilitate the implementation process. The United States Coalition of Services Industries and the European Services Forum have already echoed their support for Mode 4 liberalization and thus are in a good position to work with their governments to set the proper threshold of GATS visas.[60]

Domestic waste management companies may submit their annual demand for foreign refuse disposal service providers to the government and may be prequalified as 'sponsors' of GATS visa in this sector if these companies can demonstrate that they are of good standing and these foreign service providers

---

negotiation on safeguard measures for trade in services. *See* GATS, n 6 above, Article X. *See also* JN Bhagwati, 'Economic Perspectives on Trade in Professional Services' (1986) UChig Leg For 45, 56 (proposing a GATT Article XIX-type safeguard mechanism to hedge against any unexpected large influx of migratory workers).

59. Organization for Economic Cooperation and Development, 'Service Providers on the Move: A Closer Look at Labor Mobility and the GATS' TD/TC/WP(2001)26/FINAL (20 February 2002) 7.

60. R Self and BK Zutshi, 'Temporary Entry of Natural Persons as Service Providers: Issues and Challenges in Further liberalization under the Current GATS Negotiations' Joint WTO-World Bank Symposium on Movement of Natural Persons (Mode 4) Under the GATS (11–12 April 2002)17. The former USTR Robert Zoellick has urged US service industries to lobby Congress in favor of Mode 4 trade in services. CS Rugaber, 'Zoellick Urges Service Sector to Push Congress on Temporary Entry' (30 September 2004) 21 *International Trade Reports* 1587.

benefit the host countries' economy.⁶¹ Through this prequalified sponsor system, the government can have a clear picture of the demand for foreign service providers in each sector, which helps the government set an appropriate quota for GATS visas. In addition, the government may put on these sponsors certain administrative responsibilities in managing these foreign service providers and reporting their statuses.

In particular, from a development standpoint host countries must pay special attention to the LDCs. Host countries may create a labor version of the GSP when issuing GATS visas. Low-skilled service providers from eligible countries may be granted preferential quotas for GATS visas vis-à-vis other WTO members. Some might argue that this scheme might violate the MFN principle under GATS. Yet this 'labor GSP' scheme is still consistent with GATS to the extent that the Annex on Mode 4 endorses ample discretion on host countries in regulating this field.

iv. How to Negotiate on a GATS Visa: A Proposal for a Three-Step Approach

The first step: Building confidence The GATS visa system must be implemented on a voluntary, experimental basis for at least a couple of years. During this period, WTO members adopting this new system should be granted full policy discretion without any grave binding obligations. They are expected to test any accompanying administrative burdens and learn lessons via trial and error.⁶² At the same time, government officials in this field are strongly encouraged to network with each other and conduct dialogues, seminars, and brainstorming sessions under the auspices of relevant international organizations such as WTO and OECD.

The second step: Extending the scope of Mode 4 liberalization Once major WTO members witness the tangible benefits of the GATS visa system and thus gain confidence, they may want to extend the scope of its operation through a grand bargain between developed and developing countries. Since GATS Mode 4 excludes manual labor such as manufacturing or farm workers, a minimum level of skills or professional requirements would be necessary to apply for a GATS visa. This will in turn boost up demands for various educational or vocational services in the labor-dispatching countries. Developed countries' companies may want to set up training camps in the source countries and train applicants to equip themselves with skills required for the GATS visa before they

---

61. Australia has introduced this system ('prequalified business sponsors') in the temporary migration of professional service providers. OECD, 'Current Regimes for Temporary Movement of Service Providers, Case Study: Australia' TD/TC/WP(2002)22/FINAL (6 February 2003) at 15–16.

62. Organization for Economic Cooperation and Development, 'Service Providers on the Move: A Closer Look at Labor Mobility and the GATS' TD/TC/WP(2001)26/FINAL (20 February 2002) 49.

TABLE 2. COMPARISON OF W/120 AND ISCO-88

W/120 Service Sector Classification		International Standard Classification of Occupations (ISCO-88)
B. Computer and related Services	213	Computing professionals
		Computer systems designers and analysts
		Computer programmers
		Computing professionals not elsewhere classified
	312	Computer associate professionals
		Computer assistants
		Computer equipment operators

Source: WTO

apply. This would be yet another GATS Mode 4 from developed to developing countries, in addition to further liberalization on the Mode 3 front. Hence, a win-win situation would exist for both developed and developing countries.

The final step: Hardening (legal binding) Even after the GATS visa program earns a status of practicability, legally binding it in the national schedule of commitments under GATS would be difficult mainly due to its potential implications for immigration policies. Instead, members may want to keep this program on an ad-hoc basis within their domestic legal system. They may create quotas for GATS visas through sporadic legislation when seasonal demands emerge. They may even use special exemptions to conventional immigration statutes to create room for the GATS visa.

Although concrete scales of GATS visas are hard to bind in the national schedule of commitments, improving the current method of writing schedules may serve as the *de facto* institutionalization of extensive use of the GATS visa. As the OECD and the Indian government have argued,[63] replacing the current W/120 Service sector classification by the International Labor Organization's (ILO) International Standard Classification of Occupation (ISCO-88), especially in Group 3 (Technicians and Assistant Professionals), would effectively expand the potential scope of GATS visa holders since the latter criteria is more accommodating to low-skilled services than the former. For example, using the ISCO-88

---

63. Organization for Economic Cooperation and Development, 'Service Providers on the Move: A Closer Look at Labor Mobility and the GATS' TD/TC/WP(2001)26/FINAL (20 February 2002) 7, 38–42; WTO, Council for Trade in Services, Special Session, Communication from India: Proposed Liberalisation of Movement of Professionals under General Agreement on Trade in Services (GATS) (24 November 2000) S/CSS/W/12.

in the area of computing and related services tends to expand the realm of this category to less-skilled service providers, such as technical support personnel.[64] This new approach parallels what Jagdish Bhagwati coined as a 'dualistic' structure in which both sophisticated and unsophisticated services exist within the same service sector spectrum.[65]

E. CONCLUSION

GATS Mode 4 certainly retains sizable development potential, which a certain institutional imagination such as the GATS visa system, can materialize. While the system can make the rich richer, it can also expose the poor to the nascent global labor market,[66] prevent further marginalization, and thus deliver a true sense of development to them. However, its effectiveness will hinge on experimental institutionalization maintaining maximum policy flexibility before major developed (host) countries gain full confidence in this novel proposal.[67]

The former United Nations Secretary-General Kofi Annan once observed that 'historically, migration has improved the well-being, not only of individual migrants, but of humanity as a whole'.[68] His historical observation rings true even more clearly for the future, considering that over the next decade, developing countries will generate 700 million young members of the labor force[69] and that these young people, if unemployed, are vulnerable to recruitment to violent and illegal activities such as terrorism and organized crimes.[70] Development means not only prosperity but also peace and security, on a *global* scale. In this regard, GATS Mode 4 and a GATS visa can certainly contribute to global peace and prosperity through their development aptitude.

---

64. Organization for Economic Cooperation and Development, 'Service Providers on the Move: A Closer Look at Labor Mobility and the GATS' TD/TC/WP(2001)26/FINAL (20 February 2002) 7.

65. JN Bhagwati, 'Economic Perspectives on Trade in Professional Services' (1986) UChig Leg For 45, 54.

66. 'The Coming Global Labor Market' (February 2007) *The McKinsey Quarterly Chart Focus Newsletter*.

67. R Self and BK Zutshi, 'Temporary Entry of Natural Persons as Service Providers: Issues and Challenges in Further liberalization under the Current GATS Negotiations' Joint WTO-World Bank Symposium on Movement of Natural Persons (Mode 4) under the GATS (11–12 April 2002) 25.

68. KA Annan, 'In Praise of Migration' (5 June 2006) *Wall Street Journal* 10.

69. Organization for Economic Cooperation and Development, *Service Providers on the Move: Labor Mobility and the WTO General Agreement on Trade in Services* (2003) 2.

70. ILO/04/36 (11 August 2004) available at <http://www.ilo.org/public/english/bureau/inf/pr/2004/36.htm>.

18. JUSTICE, THE BRETTON WOODS INSTITUTIONS, AND THE PROBLEM OF INEQUALITY

FRANK J GARCIA[*]

'He who lends, commands'.[1]

A. Introduction 476
B. International Justice and International Economic Institutions 480
    I. International Justice as Fairness 480
        Liberal theory and multilateral institutions 480
        Rawls and domestic justice as fairness 481
        Adapting the theory for international application 482
    II. Mapping the Theory to International Economic Law 483
    III. Bretton Woods Institutions and International Justice as Fairness 485
        Operationalizing justice as fairness: trade law 485
        The Bank, the Fund, and global inequality 486
C. International Justice and the Work of the Bank 487
    I. The Bank's Role in International Justice 488
        Toward a theory of just international development lending 489
    II. Operational Implications of a Theory of Just International Development Lending 492
        The Bank's mission and priorities 493
        The Bank's role in the domestic social policy of borrowers 496
D. International Justice and the Work of the Fund 500
    I. The Fund's Role in International Justice 500
        Toward a Theory of Just International Monetary Policy 501
    II. Operational Implications of a Theory of Just Monetary Policy 504
        The Fund's mission and priorities 504
        Conditionality 505
E. Conclusion 509

---

[*] Professor, Boston College Law School. I want to thank the participants in a 2003 World Bank legal staff workshop for their generous and insightful comments on an early draft of this paper. The author would also like to thank the editors, Joel P Trachtman and Chantal Thomas, as well as Jeffrey Dunoff, John Linarelli, and participants in the University of Minnesota Conference on WTO Law and Developing Countries, for their comments. Thanks also to Daniel Blanchard, Matthew Hoisington, and Michael Garcia for exceptional research assistance.

1. E Galeano, *Open Veins of Latin America* (1973) 299.

The Bretton Woods Institutions are, together with the WTO, the preeminent international institutions devoted to managing international economic relations. This mandate puts them squarely in the center of the debate concerning development, inequality, and global justice. While the normative analysis of the WTO is gaining momentum, the systematic normative evaluation of the World Bank and the International Monetary Fund is comparatively less developed. This essay aims to contribute to that nascent inquiry. How might global justice criteria apply to the ideology and operations of the Bank and Fund? Political theory offers an abundance of perspectives from which to conduct such an analysis; this essay will focus on Rawls's theory of justice as fairness adapted to international institutions by the author in connection with the WTO and extend it to the remaining 'legs' of the Bretton Woods 'stool'. This essay will ask what difference it would make for the Bank and Fund if an explicit global justice framework informed their international lending activities.

A. INTRODUCTION

It need hardly be pointed out that we live in a world marked by profound inequalities. Both within countries and between them, the distribution of natural and social resources is dramatically skewed.[2] Taking income alone, the World Bank's Web site declares that

> [w]e live in a world so rich that global income is more than $31 trillion a year. In this world, the average person in some countries earns more than $40,000 a year. But in this same world, 2.8 billion people—more than half the people in developing countries—live on less than $700 a year. Of these, 1.2 billion earn less than $1 a day.[3]

Many studies suggest as well that the degree of inequality is, in fact, worsening.[4]

These facts and trends led me in 1997 to begin considering the role of the WTO and trade law generally in relation to the problem of inequality.[5] Elsewhere I have

---

2. United Nations Development Programme Web site <http://www.undp.org> (last visited 29 May 2008).

3. The World Bank, 'About Us—What is the World Bank'? <http://web.worldbank.org/WBSITE/EXTERNAL/EXTABOUTUS/0,,contentMDK:20040558~menuPK:34559~pagePK:34542~piPK:36600,00.html> (last visited 29 May 2008).

4. See, eg, 'In the Shadow of Prosperity' *The Economist* (1 January 2007) <http://www.economist.com/displaystory.cfm?story_id=8548661> ('A host of big economic shifts, such as rising income inequality, are blamed on global integration'.).

5. See FJ Garcia, 'Trade and Justice: Linking the Trade Linkage Debates' (1998) 19 UPenn JIEL 391; FJ Garcia, 'Trade and Inequality: Economic Justice and the Developing World' (2000) 21 Mich JIL 925; reprinted in A D'Amato and J Abbassi (eds), *International Law Today* (2006); reprinted in LA Cunningham (ed), *Heights of Justice* (2006).

written about how liberal theories of justice might apply to international trade law.[6] This sort of normative inquiry is also urgently needed in other areas of international economic relations. Global social policy[7] is currently managed through a variety of institutions in addition to the WTO, including in particular what are popularly called the Bretton Woods Institutions (BWIs): the International Monetary Fund (IMF or the Fund), and the World Bank Group (WBG).[8]

In this chapter, I propose to use the normative analysis I developed for trade law as a model for beginning a different inquiry, into the relationship between justice and the work of the BWIs. Specifically, I want to consider the role of the WBG and the Fund as institutions which form part of the 'basic structure', those institutions which discharge a fundamental allocative role in society and are therefore subject to the constraints and obligations of justice.[9]

The WBG consists of several interrelated institutions and affiliates. The WBG began when the International Bank for Reconstruction and Development (IBRD), one of the WBG's two lending institutions, was created in 1945 to help finance the reconstruction of Europe. Its mission quickly broadened into supporting

---

6. FJ Garcia, *Trade, Inequality and Justice: Toward a Liberal Theory of Just Trade* (2003); reviewed in C Wittayawarakul, 'Book Review: Trade, Inequality and Justice' (2007) 4 Manchester JIEL 159; J Pauwelyn, 'Book Review: Just Trade' (2005) 37 Geo. Wash. ILR 101.

7. By global social policy, I mean (broadly speaking) policies designed and/or implemented at the transnational level which affect the creation and allocation of social primary goods (such as wealth, income rights, opportunities, privileges, status, legal standing, etc.), and the elaboration of secondary social goods (such as education, employment, health care, sustenance, security, etc.). In this essay I am focusing on social primary goods and the institutions which influence their allocation through their policy decisions. Such policies are obviously formulated and affected by domestic institutions, but also increasingly by global institutions as well. For a comprehensive and insightful overview of the institutions which manage global social policy, see B Deacon, 'Social Policy in a Global Context', in A Hurrell and N Woods (eds), *Inequality, Globalization and World Politics* (1999) 211–47.

8. Both the World Bank and the International Monetary Fund were conceived at the Bretton Woods Conference in 1944 to serve complementary roles in the postwar economy, together with the International Trade Organization, which did not come into existence except in limited form as the GATT. Considering the WTO as in some sense its successor, these three institutions together are the pre-eminent institutions for international economic relations today. See generally GRD Underhill, 'Global Issues in Historical Perspective', in R Stubbs and GRD Underhill (eds) *Political Economy and the Changing Global Order* (2000).

9. The global 'basic structure' consists of those 'major social institutions' which at the global level 'distribute fundamental rights and duties and determine the division of advantages from social cooperation'. J Rawls, *A Theory of Justice* (1979) 7. For an overview of the concept of a global basic structure and its role in the global justice debate, see S Caney, 'The Global Basic Structure: Its Nature and Moral Relevance' (2 September 2004) <http://www.allacademic.com/meta/p58933_index.html> (paper presented at the annual meeting of the American Political Science Association).

development investment on a global scale, and the IBRD continues to carry out what is often considered the Bank's core activity: development lending at preferential (but near-commercial) rates. The second lending institution, the International Development Association (IDA), was created in 1960 to focus on assisting the WBG's poorest clients through concessional (zero-interest) lending and outright grants and shares the same office, staff, and project evaluation standards as the IBRD.[10] However, the two institutions differ in important ways when it comes to their source of funds. The IBRD finances its lending activities primarily through sales of bonds on the international capital market whereas the IDA is funded primarily through donations from member states.[11]

The work of these two institutions is complemented by three affiliates which focus on private sector investment: the International Finance Corporation (IFC), which invests in emerging markets; the Multilateral Investment Guarantee Agency (MIGA), which offers investment guarantees for private transactions; and the International Centre for the Settlement of Investment Disputes (ICSID), which offers investment-related dispute resolution.[12] In this essay, I will focus on IBRD and IDA and refer to both collectively as the Bank, except where I focus specifically on one or the other institution.

The IMF was created to bring stability to the exchange rate system and in general to facilitate cooperation on international monetary matters in the wake of the Great Depression. The exchange rate aspects of its operation changed significantly in the 1970s when first the United States and then other states abandoned the so-called Bretton Woods system of gold-pegged exchange rates. Today, the most active and publicly known facet of its operations involves monitoring and intervening in the global distribution of hard or 'trade' currencies. The IMF engages in short- and medium-term lending in response to balance-of-payments difficulties (with accompanying IMF 'conditions' involving domestic policy reforms), although the IMF continues to monitor and investigate member states' exchange rate policies and work to encourage members to remove any exchange controls.[13] The IMF carries out this lending through a variety of distinct lending programs or 'facilities', each with different terms and conditions suited to different categories of borrowers in different types of needs.[14] The IMF's activities are funded from both member states' quota subscriptions and from the IMF's own line of credit with banks and governments.

---

10. B Ghazi, *The IMF, the World Bank Group and the Question of Human Rights* (2005) 24.
11. Ibid 26. This distinction will be significant as will be discussed below.
12. For a discussion of the WBG, see generally I Shihata, *The World Bank in a Changing World: Selected Essays* (2000).
13. S Hagan, IMF General Counsel, Proceedings of the 93rd Annual Meeting, ASIL (24–27 March 1999)
14. Ghazi (n 10 above).

The primary task of this essay is to develop a normative framework through which to analyze the work of the BWIs with respect to global distributive justice.[15] In normative terms, I will argue that, as part of the basic structure, the mission of the BWIs is to deliver justice. Now, what do I mean by justice? Justice is a structural matter, involving an inquiry as to what principles social institutions should follow in their decision making in order to reach normatively defensible outcomes. In the case of the BWIs as institutions which allocate social resources, the relevant field is distributive justice. The question becomes: what normative principles should guide the BWIs in their allocation of international development capital and international hard currency resources?

I am going to suggest a framework for evaluating the Bank and Fund based on principles of distributive justice drawn from the Western tradition of political and moral theory, specifically liberalism. By liberalism I mean that tradition of political and moral theory which maintains that the individual is the ultimate unit of value. However, as I will discuss below, by grounding my approach in liberalism, I do not mean to suggest that all BWI member states necessarily adhere to liberalism nor that these principles are limited to the liberal tradition or relevant only if one adheres to this tradition.

What are liberal principles of justice? How do they apply internationally? And to the point, how would liberal principles of justice relate to the work of the BWIs? These questions form the substance of the present inquiry, but let me briefly summarize them at the outset. Insofar as the Bank and Fund are social institutions, charged with making decisions involving the allocation social resources, their activities are the direct subject of justice theory. The fact that the Bank and Fund are international organizations does not alter this fundamental point. International liberal justice would dictate that in their policies and operations, the Bank and Fund respect and promote the welfare of all affected individuals. It then becomes a political question for the community of states as to whether the Bank and the Fund will explicitly embrace their tasks from this normative perspective and adopt the framework of justice as their explicit ideology, policy goal, and operational guide.

---

15. I have couched this inquiry in terms of global justice, although I believe a true theory of global justice requires either cosmopolitan or communitarian grounding, or both, and I offer neither here, relying instead on a more traditional international law/'society of states' model of justice. See FJ Garcia, 'Globalization and the Theory of International Law', 11 Int'l Leg Theo 9 (2005) (surveying arguments regarding normative basis of global justice in globalizing social relations). Thus what I am actually engaging in here is more properly an international justice argument, or justice between states and with their citizens, although I will continue to speak in global justice terms, both because that is the generally accepted term for this entire line of inquiry and because in this case I believe the substantive conclusions would largely be the same.

B. INTERNATIONAL JUSTICE AND INTERNATIONAL ECONOMIC INSTITUTIONS

In this chapter I will present in summary form my approach to the generation of an international normative application of domestic political theory, based on my work applying Rawls's theory of justice as fairness to international trade law.[16] This will form the basis for the specific application of the theory to the Bank and the Fund in the sections which follow.

i. International Justice as Fairness

The initial task is to choose a particular body of normative political theory through which to develop the analysis of the obligations of justice as they apply to the BWIs. For a variety of substantive and strategic reasons, I think liberalism is the best normative language for modern secular international law. Within liberalism, I have chosen Rawls's 'justice as fairness', despite its complex relationship to international justice, because of its approach to the problem of inequality.

Liberal theory and multilateral institutions For reasons I have expanded upon elsewhere, liberalism, in particular liberal egalitarianism, is a powerful vehicle through which to examine inequality problems.[17] To begin with, liberalism is the normative tradition of many of the most wealthy and powerful states, which are primarily Western or Western-style liberal democracies.[18] Moreover, the BWIs themselves have roots in the same tradition of liberalism, in particular liberal internationalism. First, they are creatures of international law, which grew out of the same tradition that gave us political liberalism, namely that of western European states.[19] Moreover, the genesis of the BWIs reflects the postwar tradition of liberal internationalism.[20] Finally, in political terms, the BWIs are controlled by states which consider themselves part of the liberal political tradition. This further reinforces the compliance pull, if you will, of liberal theories of justice in this arena.[21] This is important on topics of international justice

---

16. FJ Garcia, 'Developing a Normative Critique of International Trade Law: Special & Differential Treatment' Working Paper Series, University of Bremen Transformations of the State Research Centre, <http://www.sfb597.uni-bremen.de/pages/pubAp.php?SPRACHE=en> (forthcoming); Garcia (n 6 above).

17. Garcia (n 6 above).

18. J Rawls, *Political Liberalism* (1995) XXIV.

19. On the intertwined roots of political liberalism, liberal internationalism, international law, and the modern state system, see AM Slaughter, 'International Law in a World of Liberal States' (1995) 6 EJIL 1, 5–0.

20. See, eg, Deacon (n 7 above) 223 (acknowledging liberal internationalist roots of IMF).

21. The fact that we are talking about international justice does raise the problem of cultural relativism since both participating states and client states of the BWIs come from other traditions. Some could object that we are forcing a particular system, or by choosing

because if you develop arguments for justice in this language, it is harder for such states to ignore them.

Rawls and domestic justice as fairness Rawls is the leading liberal political theorist and a natural place to begin considering liberal international justice. I am going to assume familiarity with the outlines of Rawls's basic theory and only note a few issues of significance for international economic law. Rawls is particularly concerned with inequalities that arise in the distribution of social primary goods, such as rights, privileges, wealth, income, status, opportunities, etc. Inequalities in the natural distribution of natural primary goods (such as for individuals—intelligence, health, and imagination); while they deeply affect people's life chances, they are not themselves the subject of justice. Rather, it is how a society responds to such inequalities that forms the basic subject of justice.

The fundamental problematic of distributive justice is that inequalities in natural primary goods often lead, through the operation of social institutions, to inequalities in the social distribution of social primary goods.[22] Such inequalities in social primary goods are not deserved because they are deeply influenced by an underlying natural inequality untouchable by categories of moral responsibility and entitlement.[23]

---

one system, confining our conclusions to a narrow set of states. On the contrary, I am concerned with the obligations which liberal states, and liberal institutions, have toward others, *not* in trying to force others to be liberal. I also think one can find support for the principles of liberal justice in all the major religious traditions of the world (Islam, Buddhism, Christianity, and Hinduism share doctrines of mercy, compassion, and almsgiving). See R Bhala, 'Theological Categories for Special and Differential Treatment' 50 Kansas L Rev 635–93 (2002). The fact that there are different value systems in the world does suggest, however, a potential role for human rights as a sort of consensus normative basis for international justice.

22. Inequalities in the distribution of social goods can also result from the degree of effort and ambition we apply to our level of natural resources. This is the problem of ambition, and Rawls's failure to take adequate account of the role of ambition in distributive justice is one of the main criticisms raised by Dworkin and others. Dworkin maintains that it would be unjust to redistribute wealth in accordance with inequalities resulting from differences in ambition—in other words, that a theory of justice must be 'ambition-sensitive.' See Garcia (n 6 above) 61.

23. To the extent that inequalities in social primary goods also result from differences in ambition, and not from differences in natural endowments, such inequalities might be said to be 'deserved'. However, I believe it is fair to read Rawls as referring here more narrowly to the social advantages which attach to the particular circumstances of our birth and not those which we develop in life. In any event, my approach here accepts the validity of Rawls's assumption that arbitrary inequalities in natural primary goods render the unequal distribution of social primary goods undeserved. It is this assumption, of course, which is the chief point of contention for libertarian critics.

Rawls argues that as a result, the basic structure of society must be arranged 'so that these contingencies work for the good of the least fortunate'.[24] The distribution of natural talents is to be considered a common asset and society structured so that this asset works for the good of the least well-off. He develops this view into the theory of justice as fairness, which includes the 'Difference Principle', which states that inequalities in the distribution of social primary goods are justifiable only to the extent they benefit the least advantaged.[25] Satisfying this criterion could entail a variety of social measures, ranging from altering the structure of incentives to reward actions which benefit the least advantaged, such as the charitable gifts deduction of the tax code, to the outright redistribution of private wealth through progressive tax and welfare legislation. Rawls contends that a society so organized would meet the basic Kantian obligation of mutual respect-to treat each other as ends and not as means.[26]

Adapting the theory for international application Having identified an appropriate body of normative political theory to work with, the next step involves adapting the theory for use in an international context involving economic law. This involves as a further preliminary matter that one address any theoretical issues raised by the application of the theory across national boundaries. Applying justice as fairness internationally poses one such issue, namely Rawls's own refusal to extend the argument of *A Theory of Justice* to international distributive problems.[27] For reasons I expand upon elsewhere,[28] I am going to proceed, as many other commentators have,[29] to nevertheless apply Rawls's theory internationally.

---

24. Rawls (n 9 above).
25. Ibid 303.
26. Ibid 179. On the Kantian aims of Rawls's project, see Garcia (n 6 above) 77–84.
27. In *A Theory of Justice* Rawls limits his theoretical enterprise to principles of justice for what he assumes to be a closed domestic society. Even by 1979 the validity of this assumption was being seriously questioned. See C Beitz, *Political Theory and International Relations* (1979) 143–49.
28. See Garcia (n 6 above) 133–44.
29. Globalization and other developments in international relations generally, and in international economic relations in particular, have in the view of many commentators rendered such assumptions untenable today. For example, in his study of the concept of fairness in international law, Franck concludes that the requisite level of community has emerged at the international level to sustain a fairness analysis. See T Franck, *Fairness in International Law and Institutions* (1998) 12–13. For similar reasons, Pogge argues that Rawls's bifurcation of the choice problems into separate domestic and international ones is untenable because the international environment in which states actually operate will significantly affect the nature of domestic societies, something representatives should know in the original position if they are to ratify their choices post-veil of ignorance. TW Pogge, *Realizing Rawls* (1989) 255–56. C Beitz, *Justice and International Relations*, in *International Ethics* (1985) 282–311.

ii. Mapping the Theory to International Economic Law

A Rawlsian theory of international distributive justice will require three elements: establishment of the facts of inequality, an examination of the choice problem faced by those in the original position, and identification of the principles of justice which result.

As mentioned above, there are many forms of inequality at work in the world today. The key normative assumption underlying a Rawlsian account of inequality is that differences in natural endowments and consequent differences in the allocation of social goods are unmerited. In Rawls's terms, they are morally arbitrary.[30] Setting aside the issues of migration and conquest, states and their citizens must in general accept the extent of resources to be found within their territories.[31] At the individual level, people are simply born into existing states, the resource levels of which they could neither choose in advance nor influence. These national boundaries and the resource endowments they encompass have a profound distributional impact on individuals' life prospects.[32]

This is precisely the pattern of natural and social advantage which, at the individual level, requires justification according to principles of justice. The fact that a particular state should be favorably situated with respect to natural resources and that this fact results in advantages in the acquisition of social goods through the operation of domestic and international social institutions does not by itself justify that state's claim to the benefits arising from that happy fact of geography. To accept the status quo without further justification would be to endorse a system of natural liberty as one's principle of justice, which Rawls rejects as unjust precisely because it allows arbitrary advantages too much sway in determining life prospects.

Together, these natural inequalities, the arbitrariness of their distribution, and their social consequences form the subject of international justice. The task of international justice is to furnish principles that will serve both as a standard for evaluating the social response to natural inequalities and as a guide to social institutions for making distributive allocations that will justify social inequalities.

In a Rawlsian approach to international justice, those principles are to be chosen through a heuristic device he calls the original position, in which representative individuals must choose principles that will govern their future social relations under conditions of limited knowledge of the general human condition

---

30. Ibid 72.

31. Migration and conquest could be envisioned as individual and collective responses to the arbitrariness of international borders and the particular resource 'bundles' they circumscribe, but this notion is destabilizing and could easily be manipulated.

32. TW Pogge, 'An Egalitarian Law of Peoples' (1994) 23 Phil & Pub Affairs 195, 198 [hereinafter *An Egalitarian Law of Peoples*] (borders have tremendous distributive impact which requires justification).

and ignorance as to their particular future socioeconomic situation. When the choice problem is one involving the choice of principles governing states, then the representatives are present on behalf of states whose future intercourse will be governed by the principles chosen by that assembly.[33] Representatives of states know only that natural and social goods are necessary for the realization of domestic cooperative schemes, that inequalities exist between states, and that such inequalities are highly correlated with resulting differences in wealth and other social advantages enjoyed among states.

Under those conditions, Rawls's argument in *A Theory of Justice* dictates that the representatives of states should choose principles of justice which maximize the minimum bundle of social goods they are likely to receive in the face of life's inequalities.[34] In the domestic original position, the representatives chose two principles, a principle of equal liberty and a principle of distributive justice—the Difference Principle. In Rawls's account of the international choice problem, representatives of states do not in fact choose a principle of distributive justice.[35] However, as has been argued by Beitz, Barry and others, 'there is no reason to think that the content of the principles would change as a result of enlarging the scope of the original position'.[36] Parties to this international original position would view the distribution of resources in the same manner that parties in the domestic original position viewed the distribution of natural talents: as morally arbitrary.[37]

---

33. Rawls has been criticized for bifurcating the original position into a second, separate choice problem for interstate principles of cooperation and for failing to take into account the evolution of contemporary international law to recognize nonstate actors, including individuals. See L Brilmayer, 'What Use is Rawls' Theory of Justice to Public International Law?' (2000) 6 Int'l Leg Theo 36; F Tesón, *A Philosophy of International Law* (1998) ch 4. This second original position could be modified to include, for example, representatives of significant NGO's and international institutions; or, as Beitz and Pogge suggest, collapsed into the first, thus forming a single cosmopolitan original position. Pogge (n 29 above) 246–47; Beitz (n 29 above) 150–51. I will proceed along Rawlsian lines and argue in terms of a second 'statist' original position in order to illustrate that, even closely following Rawls's original approach, one is led to an international difference principle. *An Egalitarian Law of Peoples* (n 32 above) 197 (international egalitarian concerns can 'easily' be accommodated within Rawls's own two-step format).

34. Ibid 152–57.

35. See FJ Garcia, 'Review: *The Law of Peoples*,' (2001) 23 Hous JIL. 659, 671–76 (reviewing Rawls's arguments and conclusions regarding international principles of justice).

36. *An Egalitarian Law of Peoples* (n 32 above); Beitz (n 29 above) 151; B Barry, *The Liberal Theory of Justice* (1973) 131 ('I can see no reason why within Rawls' theory the representatives of different countries should not, meeting under the conditions specified, agree on some sort of international maximin'.); D Richards, 'International Distributive Justice', in JR Pennock and JW Chapman (eds), *Nomos XXIV* 288–92.

37. Beitz (n 29 above) 137; Pogge (n 32 above) 247.

I therefore follow these theorists and suggest an international difference principle drawn directly from Rawls's own domestic elaboration: **International social and economic inequalities are just only if they result in compensating benefits for the least advantaged states.**

iii. Bretton Woods Institutions and International Justice as Fairness

Operationalizing justice as fairness: trade law Having sketched out how in Rawlsian terms it can be argued that international economic relations are subject to the Difference Principle, it remains to develop a normative critique of specific aspects of international economic relations law in terms of the theory. Once the basic principles of justice have been identified, the next step according to Rawls is 'to choose a constitution and a legislature to enact laws, and so on, all in accordance with the principles of justice initially agreed upon'.[38] In the case of international trade, we already have the equivalent of a constitution and a legislature, albeit imperfect ones, in the GATT/WTO system and its attendant rounds of international economic negotiation and diplomacy.[39]

Turning to such a system's regulatory output, I have argued that as with any other allocative social institution, trade law is subject to justice theory.[40] Using Rawls, I have further argued that in order for trade law to be just, it needs justification according to the Difference Principle: it should make inequalities work to benefit least advantaged. Liberalizing trade is essential to the justification of such inequalities. By allowing the principle of comparative advantage to operate, free trade moves the trading system in the direction of operating to the benefit of the least advantaged, by affording them the opportunity for welfare increases through specialization.

However, the Difference Principle also suggests that just trade cannot consist only of free trade. Normatively, free trade alone is essentially a libertarian system of equality of opportunity (reciprocal free trade rules) and subject to the same shortcomings as libertarian theory.[41] Empirically, we see many places in which a

---

38. Rawls (n 9 above) 13.

39. On the constitutional and law making function of trade institutions and their shortcomings in this regard, see EU Petersmann, 'Constitutionalism and International Organizations' (1997) 17 Nw JIL & Bus 398; but see JL Dunoff, 'Constitutional Conceits: The WTO's 'Constitution' and the Discipline of International Law', (2005) 17 EJIL 647 (arguing that Petersmann's account is descriptively inaccurate and normatively undesirable).

40. I think it is most consistent with Rawls's view of institutions as cooperative schemes for mutual benefit to examine the justice of each institution's operations.

41. The reality of gross inequalities in international endowments undercuts the possibility of effective equality of rights among states (sovereignty). See Garcia (n 6 above).

system of liberalized trade does not seem to be working—despite free trade theory—to the benefit of the least advantaged states.[42]

The key lies in understanding the way many of the natural and social inequalities among states translate into the relative strengths of different states' markets.[43] With respect to trade, states that are rich in natural resources and have developed significant social resources such as wealth, industrial capacity, and technology will generally have as a result a strong consumer market as manifested in per capita income, and a strong production base as manifested in per capita GDP. States that are poor in resources will generally have a weak consumer market, manifested in low per capita income and a weak production base manifested in low per capita GDP.

This means that market access becomes a key variable in any attempt to address inequalities through trade law. The International Difference Principle applied to trade requires that market access be organized in such a way that it benefits the least advantaged. This is where the trade doctrine of special and differential treatment comes in. At its core, special and differential treatment is the practice of asymmetric trade liberalization to secure the benefit of developed country wealth and resources for the least advantaged states through nonreciprocal market access. By opening their markets to developing country exports on a preferential basis, developed countries in effect place the consumption power of their larger, richer consumer market at the service of the developing country, which can increase its exports and thereby strengthen its economic base. Such policies can, if properly designed, help justify inequalities with respect to trade by making sure they benefit the least-advantaged states.[44]

The Bank, the Fund, and global inequality In order to apply justice as fairness to the work of the BWI's, a similar process must be undertaken. After mapping domestic theory onto the international subject and generating an international form of the Difference Principle, one must examine the specific nexus between the policy context and the normative system (ie, what is the institution allocating?). As allocative social institutions, the Bank and Fund make distributive decisions about social primary goods, in this case about the way international

---

42. See Robert Hudec, *Developing Countries in the GATT Legal System* (Aldershot: Gower, 1987) 40-1 (GATT seen as failing to promote export growth for developing countries).

43. Garcia (n 6 above) 149.

44. S&D as constituted is very imperfect, and there is much debate as to whether it makes any contribution to smaller economy well-being. See Garcia (n 6 above) 156–92; Hudec (n 42 above) 208–24; Dunoff chapter in this volume. However, the very fact that S&D as implemented is so flawed means that the empirical literature questioning its effectiveness may well be documenting the effects of a flawed instrument and not resolving the larger question as to the promise of S&D. Elsewhere I suggest reforms which are suggested by the normative analysis, which might also lead to different empirical results. Garcia (n 6 above).

development capital and hard currencies will be distributed.[45] Their core operational commitment, and therefore the appropriate policy nexus, is lending—development lending in the case of the Bank and balance-of-payments lending in the case of the Fund. Therefore, generating a normative theory of international development and balance-of-payments lending will involve analyzing the lending activities, terms, and policies of the Bank and the Fund with reference to distributive justice criteria.[46] I will develop this analysis for the Bank in Part C and for the Fund in Part D.

C. INTERNATIONAL JUSTICE AND THE WORK OF THE BANK

The first step in critically analyzing an international institution from the perspective of political theory is to develop an international normative theory, by mapping domestic normative theory onto the international subject. That step was accomplished in Part B. To restate, we arrived at an international difference principle: **International social and economic inequalities are just only if they result in compensating benefits for all states, and in particular for the least-advantaged ones**.

The second step is to articulate how this basic principle of international justice applies to the work of the institution, by examining the specific policy nexus between normative theory and the work of the institution. In the case of the Bank, this is development capital lending, in the same way that trade liberalization was for the WTO. This is the task of the following section.

---

45. As mentioned at note 7 above, there are other important social primary goods subject to institutional allocation; and there are many public and private entities and institutions at both the national and international levels which make decisions influencing the allocation of these two specific examples of social primary goods, development capital, and hard currencies. The Bank and the Fund stand at the confluence of these two factors, as the principal international institutions allocating these two kinds of social primary goods—hence my focus on them here.

46. I want to emphasize that in this analysis, I am taking as a given that these two institutions exist and arguing that given their allocative roles, their operations are subject to the International Difference Principle. I am not arguing that the International Difference Principle *requires* the existence of these two institutions nor am I arguing that these institutions are the only, or even best, mechanism through which to address the inequality in distribution of development capital and hard currencies. Rather, given that states have created (for rational reasons, as I suggest below) global markets for development capital and currency exchange, and these institutions in particular, the appropriate next question is how justice might influence their operations.

i. The Bank's Role in International Justice

The starting point is to recall that the Bank is a social institution whose core activity is to allocate a primary social good: wealth, specifically development capital; and the terms of access to such capital, which terms are themselves a social good.

Development capital is a socially produced resource. A country's supply of development capital reflects a complex blend of natural and social factors. It reflects the country's natural resource endowment and the complex blend of its history, policies, institutions, and trade relations, all of which affect the capacity of the system to generate surplus capital for development and the amounts of such capital.

Given these factors, it is no surprise that the distribution of development capital is unequal since states' original resource allocations are unequal, and their socioeconomic histories varied. In this sense, the distribution of development capital reflects a complex interaction among natural and social inequalities. Moreover, under natural conditions, states will be in a state of dynamic instability with respect to the supply of development capital: at a given point in time they will either have too much, too little, or just enough. It is unlikely that any state can safely assume that it can be entirely self-sufficient in the matter of development capital.

All of the forgoing leads to a rational policy choice for states: it is useful to create an international market for development capital. Through such a market, development capital can be made available in the form of investment capital and lending capital from private banks at rates set by the market. Such a market serves the self-interests of borrowers and lenders alike. Lending states put their surplus capital to work, generating interest and future economic opportunities for themselves, as well as contributing to stability in foreign relations through support for other states' development aspirations. Borrowing states have access to levels of development capital they could not develop domestically.

However, the facts of inequality mean that, just as in trade reciprocal market access could not in all cases benefit the least advantaged, in the case of development capital a private market would not be equally beneficial to all states. Due to the same kinds of natural and social inequalities which affect a state's capacity to generate development capital, not all states can afford to borrow sufficient development capital on commercial terms in the private market. For this sort of reason, states created the Bank, which draws its capital from the same sources (in the case of the IBRD through bond sales to the private market) but is institutionally oriented to meet the specific development lending needs of less wealthy states and can lend on other than commercial terms.[47]

---

47. For example, the conditions set out in Article 3 Section 4 of the IBRD Articles of Agreement reflect the particular needs and available credit resources of states.

Since the Bank's core function with respect to these resources is to allocate them among states through its lending decisions and policies, this intimately involves the Bank in distributive justice concerns: by what principles and rules are these social goods allocated, and to whose benefit? To normatively evaluate this, we need a theory of Just International Development Lending. That is a book in itself, but I can suggest here what I think the core of such a theory would be, based on my work in trade law.

Toward a theory of just international development lending The second step in the overall process of applying normative theory to international economic institutions is to derive from the International Difference Principle a set of 'constitutional' principles regarding how the basic structure of a given area of institutional policy or practice should be oriented as a matter of ideal theory; from this we would proceed to develop policy-specific guidelines with a normative valence. Together, these two steps allow us to identify the core implications of the International Difference Principle for Bank activity.

As when with trade law we looked at the function of market access, here we look to the Bank's role as a lender, specifically a development lender, which suggests we focus on access to development capital.[48] As an initial matter, access to development capital is a function of the private capital market. The Bank itself (here I am referring specifically to the IBRD) acquires its funds from this private market through the sale of bonds to private investors, and in turn makes the funds available to states which for one reason or another cannot meet their needs through the private sector of the capital market.

However, as a social institution governed by states, the Bank is subject to normative constraints and criteria in allocating these resources that would not necessarily apply to private sector financial institutions. Put another way, the Bank as an international institution has a unique role to play in seeing to it that the market for development capital effects a just allocation of the relevant social resources.[49]

The key normative implication of justice as fairness for development lending is that states do not categorically deserve their relative supply of development capital, insofar as it is a product, in part, of natural inequalities which are morally arbitrary, compounded by social inequalities.[50] This means that states cannot be

---

48. Hockett suggests a further theoretical link between justice and lending, or as he puts it between justice theory and finance theory, on an insurance model, namely, that both involve risk allocation under conditions of uncertainty. R Hockett, 'From 'Mission Creep' to Gestalt Switch: Justice, Finance, the IFIs, and Globalization's Intended Beneficiaries' (2005) 37 Geo Wash L Rev. 167, 179–81.

49. Ibid 194 (discussing the necessity of both markets, and justice, to the possibility for international financial institutions to deliver on their social promise).

50. In this respect, we do face the problem of how to account for the fact that good social policies contribute to an abundance of development capital, or the problem of

presumed to be entitled to their particular supply of development capital and that resulting inequalities in the distribution of development capital must be justified.

Applying this principle to the Bank's role as development capital lender, we can posit the following, as an application of our basic principle of global distributive justice to the work of the Bank: **In order to justify inequalities in the distribution of development capital, states must ensure that access to development capital is structured so as to benefit the least advantaged.**

How does this square with the work of the Bank? The very essence of the Bank's mission is to make wealthy states' abundance of development capital available to states with less development capital. As a first matter, this in itself is consistent with the International Difference Principle. By putting surplus capital to work on near-commercial terms in the economies of states without adequate indigenous supplies of capital, the Bank is conferring a benefit on less-advantaged states. It is true that the Bank is not the sole source of development capital for undercapitalized states—today it is increasingly easier for states to borrow development capital on attractive terms from commercial banks and the international capital markets.[51] However, whenever there is a general economic crisis or a country-specific crisis, it is much harder for certain states to borrow needed development capital. Moreover, the demand for development capital exceeds capital-poor states' ability to pay commercial rates, so if the only access to development capital was through private banks at commercial rates, their capital needs could go underserved.[52]

This brings us to the issue of the *terms* on which the Bank makes development capital available. The terms of access to this development capital are themselves a social resource. In other words, the terms on which the IBRD makes its development capital available (preferential rates) and the terms on which the IDA makes its credits and grants available (concessionary rates) are themselves a further socially produced, and socially allocated resource.

In this sense, the Bank's IBRD lending is similar to the principle of free trade in WTO—helping to equalize opportunity to development capital in a manner consistent with the basic requirements of justice as fairness. However, in the same manner that with respect to trade, a system of purely free trade was not enough due to the facts of inequality; so in development lending a system of pure private market commercial lending, or even a blended system of private bank commercial lending and Bank preferential lending, would not be enough. Recall that according to the International Difference Principle, the international

---

ambition-sensitivity. See Garcia (n 6 above) 61. Hockett, for example, suggests in this regard that global distributive justice by BWIs should focus on what he calls 'ethically exogenous' benefits and burdens only. Hockett (n 48 above) 193.

51. Ghazi (n 10 above) 36.
52. Ibid 24. This was one reason for the formation of the IDA.

economic system is only just if the inequality in distribution of wealth operates to the benefit of the least advantaged. Because the least-advantaged states have limited domestic capital formation capabilities and limited resources to borrow capital on the market, they cannot get enough through these avenues, meaning that the overall inequality in capital will not work to their advantage. Continuing the analogy to free trade from the previous section, IBRD-style lending is therefore necessary, but not sufficient, for international justice. It is not enough that capital is made available, even at below-commercial terms—the International Difference Principle asks much more. It asks that capital be made available under such terms and in such a manner, that it benefits the *least* advantaged.

In this respect, it is significant that the Bank has bifurcated its roles between the IBRD and the IDA. The IDA's specific mission is to make development capital available to the least-advantaged states on deeply preferential terms, involving concessional lending and outright grants. Internation Development Association credits are typically repaid on a very long term (35–40 years), with a ten-year grace period on any principal repayment.[53] Complementing IDA lending is the initiative for Heavily Indebted Poor Countries, or HIPC, about which more will be said later,[54] which consists of outright loan forgiveness for the most heavily indebted countries as their IDA credits become due.

International Development Association grants and credits constitute a further social resource allocated by the Bank, of particular interest to the least wealthy states: the concessionary access to capital. Moreover, HIPC loan forgiveness is itself a social resource as well. In distributive terms, the Bank's mission is to allocate these particular social resources, which by virtue of the nature of the international economy are those of greatest value to the least advantaged. Therefore, the IDA's programs have the most potential for justifying inequalities in development capita, by making them work for the benefit of the least advantaged.

In terms of the International Difference Principle, this suggests the following corollary: **In order that access to development capital benefit the least advantaged, states must offer concessional access to development capital.**

In this sense, in the lending context the IDA's policies and programs are the structural analog to the WTO's special and differential treatment policies reviewed in the trade justice analysis set forth above—concessional access to capital as a tool for justifying inequality. It is that specific aspect of the Bank which directly addresses the inequality in development capital from the perspective of the least advantaged.

The normative importance of concessional lending raises a further question: why can't the Bank just give all the money away? Even assuming *arguendo* that

---

53. Ibid 26.
54. See note 64 below and accompanying text.

this would in fact be in the best interests of the least advantaged (and it is not clear that it would be), this would ignore the fact that development capital is an exhaustible social resource. It is generated and regenerated by social activity, but it is not limitless.[55] This means that it must be treated as an exhaustible resource and must be renewed and conserved if it is to be available in the future.

It also means, fundamentally, that it is normatively defensible for the Bank to be a bank and not a pure aid institution, ie, to maintain a balance between development capital redistribution and sustainability and preservation of capital. In other words, it is legitimate for the Bank to expect its loaned funds to be repaid and to exercise that degree of oversight with respect to its concessional lending and grants consistent with a duty of prudence and the preservation of capital.

In summary, then, the Bank's basic mission is consistent with the normative implications of the International Difference Principle: development lending on near-commercial terms is itself a benefit to those less-advantaged in terms of capital resources. However, in order to fully reflect the International Difference Principle, the Bank must go a step farther and offer concessional lending programs that will benefit the *least* advantaged, which it currently does through the IDA. How this can best be carried out at the operational level, in a manner that *will* benefit the least advantaged, is the question for the next section.

ii. Operational Implications of a Theory of Just International Development Lending

Recall that the fourth step in developing a normative theory for the Bank is to apply the 'constitutional'-level principle derived above to develop more specific guidelines that can be used to both structure and critique actual institutional practice. In other words, we need a set of nonideal criteria for how such practice should be structured in the real world, both refining the theory and developing a policy-specific normative critique. As discussed earlier, there are many aspects of the Bank's operations which would seem to meet the injunction of the International Difference Principle, at least at a general level: there is the Bank's very existence and basic mission and the fact that the Bank operates exclusively on either preferential or concessionary terms.

However, a thorough evaluation of the justice of the Bank's operations and the full development of a theory of just international development lending

---

55. This is particularly true with respect to funds used for HIPC loan forgiveness because by definition, these amounts represent funds which will not go back into IDA coffers for future loans, grants, or HIPC loan forgiveness. This is even more significant as the Bank broadens out its debt relief efforts with sister institutions toward 100 percent debt forgiveness for eligible states through the Multilateral Debt Relief Initiative (MDRI), which will intensify the need for increased member contributions to the IDA. World Bank, 'The Multilateral Debt Relief Initiative', <http://web.worldbank.org/WBSITE/EXTERNAL/TOPICS/EXTDEBTDEPT/0,,contentMDK:20634753~menuPK:64166739~pagePK:64166689~piPK:64166646~theSitePK:469043,00.html> (last visited 29 May 2008).

would require taking this general principle and deepening the analysis through a program-by-program evaluation of the Bank's operation: Are they actually structured to benefit the least advantaged, and do they in fact operate this way? And what does the way the Bank actually works suggest in turn about how principles of just-development lending operate in the real world?

This is of course a large undertaking; a definitive analysis of such a topic would require a book-length study.[56] As a preliminary matter I will introduce two areas of inquiry: (1) the Bank's mission and priorities and (2) how the Bank determines the nature and extent of its involvement in the domestic policies of borrowing state.[57] For each of these, I will suggest at least the initial formulation of a specific policy criterion based on the application of the basic principle derived above, to the particular aspect of the Bank's operations in question. In many cases, it will be seen that the Bank is in fact doing much that is consistent with the mandate of the International Difference Principle but that it could and should do more. More particularly, the International Difference Principle can offer normative guidance as to precisely what more the Bank should do.

The Bank's mission and priorities Simply stated, the Bank's mission is development. Now, as is well-known, there is in reality nothing simple about the term 'development'. The Bank's articles do not define 'development'. In fact, 'development' is an evolutionary term, and its definition has evolved in international law and in Bank practice.

The current international consensus on the meaning of development, albeit somewhat tautological, can be expressed as follows: development means sustainable and equitable development. As the Copenhagen Declaration states it, development must incorporate democracy, social justice, economic development, environmental protection, transparent and accountable governance, and universal respect for human rights.[58]

Bank officials have stated that the Bank agrees with this comprehensive statement of the international community's position.[59] This can be seen, for example, in the Bank's adoption of the Millennium Development Goals. The Millennium Development Goals explain what sustainable and equitable development means for Bank policy. They identify—and quantify—specific gains that can be made

---

56. This essay is intended as the beginning of such a project.

57. Other promising areas of inquiry for future work includes criteria employed by the Bank in selecting projects, participation by the least advantaged in Bank decision making and project design, and how the Bank evaluates success in terms of the least advantaged sectors of borrowers' societies. See generally JW Head, *The Future of the Global Economic Organizations* (2005) 111–66 (reviewing and evaluating critiques of Bank practices).

58. 'Copenhagen Declaration on Social Development', in *Report of the U. World Summit for Social Development*, UN Doc A/CONF.166/9 (1995).

59. D Bradlow, 'The World Bank, the IMF and Human Rights' (1996) 6 Transnat'l L & Cont Prob 47, 53–54 (citing remarks by Shihata and Wolfensohn).

by 2015 to improve the lives of the world's poor. Their overall aim is to reduce poverty while improving health, education, and the environment.[60]

As a function of its institutional commitment to the Millennium Goals, the Bank is already committed to addressing the problem of inequality through development and poverty eradication—what does a justice perspective add? A justice perspective can be a powerful tool for complementing any evaluation of the Bank's success on its own terms. Moreover, using the normative framework of global justice may itself be a subtle but significant change in emphasis—one commentator has called it a 'Gestalt shift'[61]—that may have valuable substantive and political benefits.

When viewed from the perspective of justice as fairness, many aspects of the Bank's operations seem like moves in the right direction: for example, the existence of the IDA, the 'LICUS' project for particularly fragile states,[62] and in particular the HIPC Initiative.[63] However, the International Difference Principle requires us to go a step further and ask if these programs are in fact structured so as to operate to the benefit of the least advantaged.

Let me begin with just one example: debt forgiveness and least-advantaged states.

Since 1996, the Bank has begun to tackle debt relief through the HIPC Initiative. Through HIPC, 26 poor countries have received debt relief which the Bank estimates will save them $41 billion over time.

The creation of HIPC represents a considerable achievement, but the inquiry cannot end there. justice as fairness requires that we ask ourselves whether the mere existence and current extent of this type of program is enough. Should it be expanded? Should it become a higher priority among the Bank's activities?

In terms of resource commitments, the Bank's current priorities can be summarized as follows: 1) IBRD lending on preferential terms, 2) IDA lending on concessional terms, and 3) HIPC debt forgiveness.[64]

---

60. 'Millennium Development Goals' <http://ddp-ext.worldbank.org/ext/GMIS/home.do?siteId=2>. The MDGs were endorsed by 189 countries at the September 2000 UN Millennium General Assembly in New York. They provide a focus for the efforts of the World Bank Group, governments, and other partners in the development community.

61. Hockett (n 48 above) 169.

62. Licus LDC, <http://web.worldbank.org/WBSITE/EXTERNAL/PROJECTS/STRATEGIES/EXTLICUS/0,,menuPK:511784~pagePK:64171540~piPK:64171528~theSitePK:511778,00.html>(task force providing low income countries under stress with advice).

63. HIPC, <http://web.worldbank.org/WBSITE/EXTERNAL/TOPICS/EXTDEBTDEPT/0,,contentMDK:20260411~menuPK:64166739~pagePK:64166689~piPK:64166646~theSitePK:469043,00.html> (Bank initiative providing debt relief to the world's poorest nations).

64. According to the 2006 World Bank Annual Report, as of the end of fiscal year 2006, outstanding IBRD lending commitments totaled $420.2 billion, IDA commitments

Justice as fairness requires us to evaluate this scheme with reference to our normative touchstone, namely, is this prioritization benefiting the least advantaged? In other words, what is the normative significance of, despite the evident inequality in the global distribution of development capital and in the borrowing power of states, the fact that most of the Bank's activities involve loans, not grants, and most of these loans are preferential and not concessional?

In this respect, let me suggest that the International Difference Principle could require a complete inversion of the Bank's priorities. Certainly, both the existence of such programs as the IDA and HIPC and the level of resources committed demonstrate that the Bank is at some meaningful level committed to poverty reduction for the least well-off.[65] However, at the macrolevel, we must still look at the overall balance of Bank activities and ask if more of the Bank's lending should be IDA lending instead of IBRD lending, if more IDA lending should be grants instead of credits, and if HIPC debt should offer forgiveness instead of credit repayment.[66]

Application of the International Difference Principle to the Bank's mission and priorities might therefore suggest the following: **The Bank should emphasize debt forgiveness and concessional lending as its primary mission, followed by IBRD lending.**

This would suggest a reorientation of the Bank's programmatic priorities as follows: 1) Debt forgiveness—HIPC—as the Bank's primary mission, 2) Concessional lending—IDA—as its second priority, and 3) IBRD lending—as the third priority.

Such a reorientation must be compatible, of course, with sustainability and prudential considerations, in view of the Bank's stewardship role with respect to development capital.

Such a reprioritization would be consistent with the Bank's own efforts to reorient its activities in view of the increasingly liberal access to development

---

totaled $170 billion, and HIPC commitments totaled $62 billion. <http://web.worldbank.org/WBSITE/EXTERNAL/EXTABOUTUS/EXTANNREP/EXTANNREP2K6/ 0,,menuPK:2838586~pagePK:64168427~piPK:64168435~theSitePK:2838572,00.html>.

65. The creation of HIPC is part of an overall trend in Bank lending toward poverty reduction. Since the 1960s the Bank has shifted its resources more toward poverty reduction and the poorest countries (Ghazi estimates from 37 percent of total average commitments before 1968 to 61.3 percent in 1989–1990). However, as Ghazi points out, during that time and since, inequality has increased as a function of globalization, so the policies are certainly not enough and may not be working. (n 10 above) 76.

66. At the microlevel, we should ask certain questions of the Bank's culture: what type of involvement does the Bank's internal culture reward? Are programs involving concessional lending, loan forgiveness, and outright grants seen as the cutting edge of the Bank's work and highly rewarded institutionally? Or is the action elsewhere for ambitious Bank employees?

capital from the private sector enjoyed by more and more states.⁶⁷ Embracing this would mean significantly increasing the amount of Bank resources devoted to nonrenewing types of loans, meaning that donor countries would have to significantly increase their level of contributions to the IDA.⁶⁸ This would require a further political commitment on the part of the Bank's donors.

The Bank's role in the domestic social policy of borrowers This aspect of the inquiry concerns the Bank's involvement in the domestic social policy of borrowing states. Consistent with its prudential obligations, the Bank has a role in evaluating the degree to which the domestic social policies of borrowing states are themselves part of the problem of inadequate capital and the degree to which such policies help or hinder the project goals and risk squandering development capital, which is after all an exhaustible social resource.⁶⁹

This has been one of the most controversial aspects of the Bank's operations, particularly with respect to its participation in Structural Adjustment Programs or SAPs, through which the Bank seeks in concert with the IMF to 'improve resource allocation, increase economic efficiency, expand growth potential and increase resilience to shocks'.⁷⁰ This criticism is largely due to two factors: the leverage the Bank has by virtue of its role to insist on domestic policy reforms and the controversy surrounding the soundness and ideological basis of the Bank's approach to domestic policy.⁷¹ The former will not change; it is in fact essential to the Bank's proper stewardship. However, the latter is, and should be, a constant source of inquiry and criticism both within and without the Bank, as its experts search for the appropriate blend of policies for each borrowing state.⁷²

Taking HIPC as an example, in order to qualify for HIPC, countries have to be eligible for concessional assistance from the Bank and Fund, face an unsustainable debt burden beyond available debt relief mechanisms, and have established a record of reform and policies which the Bank and Fund judge

---

67. Ghazi (n 10 above) 36.

68. As discussed above, the Bank's expansion of debt relief efforts through the MDRI will increase this demand for additional funds. World Bank, 'The Multilateral Debt Relief Initiative', <http://web.worldbank.org/WBSITE/EXTERNAL/TOPICS/EXTDEBTDEPT/0,,contentMDK:20634753~menuPK:64166739~pagePK:64166689~piPK:64166646~theSitePK:469043,00.html> (last visited 29 May 2008).

69. Hockett refers to this as the 'stick' aspect of Bank operations, or the ways in which the Bank and other BWI's implement their policies. Hockett (n 48 above) 195.

70. 1990 Bank paper cited in Ghazi (n 10 above) 47.

71. I am referring here most recently to the Bank's neoliberal approach, which has been the subject of much criticism. Ghazi (n 10 above) 47; see generally Head (n 57 above).

72. Naturally, the more demonstrably sound and ideologically minimal the Bank's policies are seen to be, the less its leverage will be resented.

as 'sound'.⁷³ A justice perspective means we need to look carefully at these conditions for participation.

For example, justice as fairness requires us to inquire into what goes into a determination that a HIPC candidate's economic policies are 'sound'. What conditions are imposed on participants? Do these conditions bear a demonstrable relationship to the overall policy and normative goal of debt relief and benefit to the least advantaged? Or are there disguised preferences built in favoring other Bank constituencies?

In this respect, it is significant that civil society critics have argued that the structure and disbursement of HIPC lending in fact disproportionately benefits the wealthy elites within HICP borrowing countries and multinational enterprises, thus furthering 'the globalization agenda of the donor governments of the industrialized North'.⁷⁴ This raises the possibility that with respect to its actual operation, HIPC may not be fulfilling the requirements of either the Bank's mission or of international distributive justice—the program is not in fact operating in a manner that meets our core normative criteria: benefiting the least advantaged. Instead, it may be further benefiting the already advantaged.

As a general matter, in order to be consistent with both the International Difference Principle, which focuses on least advantaged states, and the domestic Difference principle, which focuses on the least advantaged *within* states, the Bank's domestic involvement should focus on the degree to which such policies affect the welfare of the poorest segments of a borrower's society.⁷⁵ Moreover, the Bank should exert its policy influence to redirect such policies toward ensuring that the poorest segments benefit from the Bank's lending.⁷⁶ But does such a focus on the poorest segment within a society impermissibly intertwine the Bank in domestic politics? Must not the Bank stay out of basic political issues like a country's wealth distribution policies? Both the Millennium Development Goals and the principles of justice as fairness have something to say about this.

The Millennium Goals are quite broad in their scope. This could mean that, in principle, all aspects of a borrowing country's social policy come within the Bank's purview. This cannot be the case. In fact, the issue of the proper scope of the Bank's operations has a long and fraught history. The Bank has in fact taken

---

73. Ghazi (n 10 above) 78.

74. Ibid 79 (citing report by CorpWatch).

75. This form of a two-step obligation, both international ('statist') and domestic, is consistent with Rawls's own formulation. See note 33 above. Cosmopolitans would collapse the two and argue that the International Difference Principle focuses entirely on least advantaged individuals, whatever states they are found in. I will maintain the two-step formulation for the time being, and defer to another day a fuller treatment of the cosmopolitan model. I believe for out purposes they arrive at the same place.

76. Current Bank practices have been criticized for failing to take into account the redistributive effects of Bank policies. Ghazi (n 10 above) 49.

the opposite position, namely that as a specialized economic agency of the United Nations, it has a limited mandate, restricting its permissible activities to the economic aspects of the development process.

Support for this view can be found in the Articles, specifically the so-called 'political prohibition':

> The Bank and its officers shall not interfere in the political affairs of any member, nor shall they be influenced in their decisions by the political character of the member or members concerned. Only economic considerations shall be relevant in their decisions, and these considerations shall be weighed impartially in order to achieve the purposes stated in Article I.[77]

Taken together, this prohibition, coupled with the Millennium Goals, establish a complex framework within which the Bank must pursue its mandate of promoting sustainable and equitable development. How does the Bank pursue this mandate when development involves so many issues that one could say are political in nature? How should the Bank determine which considerations are appropriately within its mandate?

At this juncture, it is useful to recall that the Bank has discretion to interpret the political prohibition selectively.[78] The issue becomes the Bank's determination of its own jurisdiction. What principles or criteria will guide its decisions? According to this analysis, it should be the International Difference Principle, restated for this specific issue as follows: **The Bank must ensure that its involvement in the domestic policy of borrowers operates to the benefit of the least-advantaged states and the least advantaged within states.**

According to commentators, the Bank's position is that it will focus exclusively on economic considerations, and economic considerations are any factors having a 'direct and obvious' economic effect relevant to the Bank's work.[79] The literature suggests the Bank follows a three-part test for 'direct and obvious': clear and unequivocal, preponderant, and of such impact and relevance as to make it a Bank concern.[80]

Most commentators consider this test inadequate by itself—it is underdetermined. In other words, it allows too much room for too many judgments: What counts as an economic effect? What makes it sufficiently strong and relevant to the Bank? For these reasons, commentators suggest application of the test is difficult and has been arbitrary.[81]

This approach could be usefully supplemented by employing a normative principle such as the International Difference Principle to guide this discretion. The criteria for determining what makes up economic factors and considerations

---

77. IBRD Articles, Article IV, Section 10; IDA Articles, Article V, Section 6.
78. Bradlow (n 59 above) 54–55.
79. Shihata (n 12 above) 53–97.
80. Bradlow (n 59 above) 61.
81. Ibid.

must be tied to the basic criteria for just international development lending: does it put development capital to work for the benefit of the least advantaged? I would offer the following definition of 'economic considerations': **'Economic considerations' include all social factors which influence the degree to which Bank projects will in fact operate to the benefit of the least advantaged.**

This means the Bank must be prepared to address questions of domestic social responsibility as related to its projects, on issues such as privatization, the use of competition law, and the social responsibility of corporate and investor conduct.[82]

I believe this approach is consistent with the Bank's own responsibilities and Articles. The purpose of the prohibition is to ensure the Bank acts impartially: to prevent discrimination based on politics and the application of leverage through the Bank by one Member against another.[83] So interpreted, the political prohibition means recognizing that inequalities of distribution of wealth within states are not internal political matters—they are the essential basis for the Bank's existence.[84] To look at the way in which a country's social resources are distributed internally among its Members is not to act with partiality. Internal inequalities in wealth are matters of economic justice, which are squarely within the Bank's mandate. Inequalities in wealth distribution affect stability, levels of education, life expectancy, levels of health care, job training, etc.: in short, the factors which are already the subject of Bank activities.

These are the sorts of factors which have led the Bank to invest in governance projects, for example, on the argument that they impact the borrower's investment prospects.[85] These are also the reasons why the Bank has moved away from its traditional approach to SAPs, by collaborating with the Fund to create Poverty Reduction and Growth Facilities based on each borrowing country's Poverty Reduction Strategy Paper. Moreover, in 2001 the Bank and the Fund together began a program of 'social impact analysis' (SIA) through which to 'assess the consequences of policy interventions . . . on the well-being of different social groups, with a special focus on the vulnerable and the poor.'[86] However, the Bank's efforts continue to be criticized as inadequate in this area,[87] and the International Difference Principle suggests avenues for possible reform.

---

82. If intervention by the BWIs through programs like Structural Adjustment is allowed to protect the international financial system, there is no principled reason not to allow intervention to protect the world's least advantaged.

83. Bradlow (n 59 above) 54 (citing legislative history of the political prohibition).

84. See Hockett (n 48 above) 202 (constitutive documents should be interpreted in the context of the broad global human rights constitution within which the BWIs operate).

85. Bradlow (n 58 above) 61.

86. Fact Sheet, Ghazi (n 10 above) 72.

87. Ibid 49. Hockett argues that BWIs need to take a stronger public position on the normative justification of such social insurance programs. Hockett (n 48 above) 198.

D. INTERNATIONAL JUSTICE AND THE WORK OF THE FUND

Having suggested what a normative analysis of Bank activities according to the International Difference Principle might look like, it remains to offer such an analysis of its sister institution, the Fund.

i. The Fund's Role in International Justice

As with the Bank, the Fund is a social institution whose core activity is to allocate a primary social good, also a form of wealth: hard currency reserves and the terms of access to such reserves. Hard or 'trade' currencies are an exhaustible social resource.[88] As with market size in the case of trade and capital supply in the case of development, the socioeconomic factors which influence the market's determination of which currencies are hard and which are soft, reflect a complex blend of natural and social inequalities, including the arbitrary distribution of natural resources and good or bad luck; and contingent social factors such as sound or unsound policy choices, historic patterns of economic development, exploitation, or oppression, etc.

The fact that certain currencies are considered hard and others are not necessarily creates inequalities in the distribution of hard currencies. This inequality is in part a function of the fact that currencies are national in nature, and those countries whose economic policies and performance support the hardness of their currency have a built-in advantage in the supply of that currency.[89] This inequality also reflects broader contingent historic factors such as the colonial legacy of the global economic system, which contribute to the hard currency attributes of some economies and undercuts such attributes of others. Those states whose currencies are hard have an abundance and a capacity to self generate, whereas those states whose currencies are soft are always at risk of scarcity and cannot create this resource indigenously.[90]

---

88. Accord RM Lastra, 'The International Monetary Fund in Historical Perspective', (2000) 3 JIEL 507, 516 (Fund resources are finite hence their use is subject to oversight). While it is true that countries whose currencies are hard could in theory print more money, it is in the very nature of hard currency countries that they not pursue such policies or risk the tradability of their currency. Therefore, hard currency is in essence exhaustible even for hard currency countries.

89. The fact that in today's floating exchange rate environment, most currencies are freely convertible does not itself alter the preference on the part of international firms and central banks for those currencies considered 'hard' when seeking settlement of trade debts or reserve currencies. Thus the demand for such currencies, the genesis of balance-of-payments problems, and the advantage which those jurisdictions have in supplying their own demand for it.

90. I am setting aside for the moment the issue of whether by making better policy choices they could harden their currency. This would not in any case deal with natural inequalities or historical contingencies.

This leads states to the rational decision that it is useful to create an international market for hard currencies to supplement national economic mechanisms which influence a state's supply of hard currencies. Through such a market, hard currencies can be made available at rates set by the market. Such a market serves the self-interest of borrowers and lenders alike. Lending states put their hard currencies to work in the satisfaction of trade debt owed to their own producers, generating export volumes and future economic opportunities for themselves, as well as contributing to stability in foreign relations through support for other states' commercial activities. Borrowing states have access to needed goods and services through hard currency supplies they could not generate domestically.

However, the facts of inequality mean that just as in trade it is the case that reciprocal market access could not in all cases benefit the least advantaged, so in the case of hard currencies a private market would not be equally beneficial to all states. Due to the same kinds of natural and social inequalities which affect a state's capacity to generate a supply of hard currency, not all states can afford to borrow needed hard currencies on commercial terms in the private market. For this sort of reason, it is rational for states to create an institution such as the Fund, which draws from the same sources (ultimately from hard currency states themselves),[91] but is institutionally oriented to meet the specific currency lending needs of less wealthy states and can lend on other than commercial terms.

Since the Fund's core function with respect to these hard currency resources is to allocate them, this intimately involves the Fund in distributive justice concerns: by what principles and rules are these social goods allocated, and to whose benefit? To determine this, we need a theory of Just International Monetary Policy.

Toward a Theory of Just International Monetary Policy As with trade law, we looked at the function of market access, here we look to the Fund's role as a lender, specifically a balance-of-payments lender, which suggests we focus on access to hard currencies.[92] As an initial matter, access to hard currencies is a function of the private currency market. The Fund exists to make these currencies available to states which for one reason or another cannot meet their needs

---

91. The IMF's activities are funded from both member states' quota subscriptions and from the IMF's own line of credit with banks and governments. See Head (n 57 above) 25–26 (discussing quota subscriptions); Ghazi (n 10 above) 8 (Fund is also authorized to obtain currency from private market sources but it has never done so).

92. Hockett suggests a further theoretical link between justice and lending, or as he puts it between justice theory and finance theory, or an insurance model, namely, that both involve risk allocation under conditions of uncertainty. See Hockett (n 48 above) 179–81.

through the export operations of their private sector, their own central bank reserves, or through the private currency market.[93]

The key normative implication of justice as fairness for hard currency lending is that states do not in a categorical sense deserve their relative supply of hard currency, insofar as it is a product, in part, of natural inequalities which are morally arbitrary, compounded by social inequalities.[94] This means that states cannot be presumed to be entitled to their particular supply of hard currency and that resulting inequalities in the distribution of hard currency must be justified.

Applying this principle to the Fund's role as manager of international currency reserves, we can derive the following as an application of our basic principle of global distributive justice to the work of the Fund: **In order to justify inequalities in the distribution of hard currencies, states must ensure that access to hard currencies is structured so as to benefit the least advantaged.**

How does the Fund look from this perspective? As was the case with the Bank, the very existence and mission of the Fund suggest that the Fund plays a normatively justifiable role, making wealthy states' abundance of hard currencies available to states with less access to trade currency. By putting hard currency to work on near-commercial terms in the economies of states without adequate indigenous supplies of such currencies, the Fund is conferring a benefit on less advantaged states.[95]

However, whenever there is a general economic crisis or a country-specific crisis, it is much harder for certain states to generate or borrow needed hard currencies. Moreover, the demand for hard currency exceeds currency-poor states' ability to pay commercial rates so that if the only access to hard currency was through private banks at commercial rates, economic opportunities would go unrealized.[96]

This brings us to the issue of the *terms* on which the Fund makes hard currency available. The Fund offers two basic types of facilities: 'regular' or nonconcessional facilities, which are not in fact loans but purchase and repurchase agreements;[97] and concessional facilities, which are truly trade currency

---

93. Ibid 194 (existing necessity of both markets and justice to the possibility for international financial institutions to deliver on their social promise).

94. As with development capital supplies, this raises the problem of ambition sensitivity, namely how to account for the fact that good social policies contribute to both to the hardness of one's currency and to an adequate supply of others' hard currencies. See note 50 above.

95. Head (n 57 above) 95–96 (documenting the considerable wealth transfers which IMF facilities have effected for the benefit of the least-developed members).

96. Exporting states would lose sales, importing states much-needed goods and services, and less advantaged states would be tempted to employ currency controls, devaluations, etc., destabilizing the international monetary system to the detriment of all.

97. See Head (n 57 above) 24 (describing operation of SBA and EFF purchase/repurchase obligations).

loans to developing countries.[98] The Fund's regular facilities consist of four main lending programs: Stand-By Arrangements, the Extended Fund Facility, the Supplemental Reserve Facility, and the Compensatory Financing Facility.[99] All have varying eligibility criteria and repayment terms and charge interest that is slightly below, but keyed to market rates.[100] The Fund's concessional facilities consist of the Poverty Reduction and Growth Facilities (PRGFs), which replaced the earlier SAPs and Enhanced SAPs, and charge only 0.5% interest per year.[101]

The terms of access to such currencies through each facility are themselves a social resource. In other words, the terms on which the Fund makes its currencies available through regular facilities (preferential rates) and the terms on which the Fund makes its currencies available through concessional facilities (concessional rates) are themselves a further socially produced, and socially allocated resource.

In this sense, the Fund's regular facilities lending is similar to the principle of free trade in WTO and to the Bank's preferential lending through the IBRD—helping to equalize opportunities to access hard currencies in a manner consistent with the basic requirements of justice as fairness. However, in the same manner that with respect to trade, a system of purely free trade was not enough due to the facts of inequality; so in hard currency lending, a system of pure private market currency transactions, or even a blended system of private bank commercial currency transactions and Fund preferential lending, would not be enough. Because developing countries have limited domestically generated supplies of hard currency and limited resources to borrow such currencies, they cannot get enough through these avenues, meaning that the overall inequality in currency supplies will not work to their advantage.

Continuing the analogy to free trade from the previous section, private market and regular Fund facility lending is necessary but not sufficient for international justice. It is not enough that hard currencies be made available, even at below-commercial terms. The International Difference Principle asks that hard currencies be made available under such terms and in such a manner, that it benefits the *least* advantaged.

---

98. See Lastra (n 88 above) 517–18.
99. See generally Head (n 57 above) 24–25 (reviewing types of facilities).
100. See Ghazi (n 10 above) 13.
101. Ibid. (One commentator suggests that the category of concessional facilities also includes special facilities such as the oil facility, accelerated procedures such as the emergency financing mechanism, and exceptional facilities such as the supplemental reserve facility and contingent credit line for sudden and disruptive events). See Lastra (n 88 above) 519–20. I will follow the narrower approach and restrict my attention to the PRGFs since the rest charge higher, near-market rates.

In terms of the International Difference Principle, this suggests the following corollary: **In order that access to hard currencies benefit the least advantaged, states must offer concessional access to development capital.**

The PRGFs are, in the balance-of-payments lending context, the structural analog to the WTO's S&D Treatment policies in trade and the Bank's IDA lending: concessional access to hard currencies as a tool for justifying inequality. They represent that specific aspect of the Fund which directly addresses the inequality in the distribution of hard currencies from the perspective of the least advantaged. It is the Fund's responsibility to see that this most valuable social good—concessional access to hard currencies—is in fact structured so as to benefit the least advantaged. How can this be carried out at the operational level?

ii. Operational Implications of a Theory of Just Monetary Policy

There are many aspects of the Fund's operations which would seem to meet the basic thrust of the International Difference Principle, at least at a general level. To begin with, there is the Fund's very existence and basic mission. Moreover, there is the fact that the Fund operates through all of its facilities almost exclusively with countries that are in some stage of development.[102] Finally, there is the fact that the Fund does indeed offer concessional hard currency lending through its PRGFs.

However, a thorough evaluation of the justice of the Fund's operations and the full development of a theory of just international monetary policy would require taking this general principle and deepening the analysis through a program-by-program evaluation of the Fund's operation: Are they in fact structured to benefit the least advantaged, and do they in fact operate this way? And what does the way the Fund actually works suggest about principles of just monetary policy in the real world?

As with the Bank, I am going to focus in this essay on two areas: the Fund's mission and priorities and its involvement in domestic policies.[103]

The Fund's mission and priorities As discussed above, the Fund's resources are made available under two types of arrangements: regular facilities and concessional facilities. The PRGF's specific purpose is to make hard currencies available to the least-advantaged states on deeply preferential terms. Poverty Reduction Growth Facility's loans are typically repaid on what is for the Fund

---

102. It can also be said that the majority of the Fund's personnel budget is dedicated to pay for staff devoted to addressing developing country needs. Conversations with Fund executives, 25 October 2007.

103. Other promising areas include the Fund's system for allocating SDRs, its decision making structure, and its system for choosing and evaluating projects. See generally Head (n 57 above) (summarizing critiques of IMF policies and practices in these areas).

a very long term (up to 10 years), with interest at 0.5 percent per year.[104] Moreover, PRGF funds come from a different source: a Trust Fund consisting of funds generated by prior sales of IMF gold assets, and loans and grants from wealthy members.[105]

In terms of resource commitments, the Fund currently emphasizes its regular facility lending, with PRGF lending a miniscule portion of its portfolio.[106] justice as fairness requires us to evaluate this scheme with reference to our normative touchstone, namely, is this prioritization benefiting the least advantaged? The PRGF program has the most potential for justifying inequalities in hard currencies by making them work for the benefit of the least advantaged. However, despite the evident inequality in the global distribution of hard currencies and in the borrowing power of states, most of the Fund's activities nevertheless continue to involve preferential and not concessional lending.[107]

In this respect, application of the International Difference Principle could in fact require a complete inversion of the Fund's priorities, along the following lines: **The Fund should prioritize those activities which most benefit the least advantaged. This means, in particular, that the Fund should emphasize its PRGF concessional lending as its primary mission, followed by its regular facility lending programs.**

Such a reorientation would put the PRGF, that aspect of the Fund's activities which most benefits the least advantaged, at the center of the Fund's priorities. This would need, of course, to be consistent with sustainability and prudential considerations in view of the Fund's stewardship role with respect to currency resources.

Conditionality This second aspect of our inquiry concerns the Fund's involvement in the domestic social policy of borrowing states. Consistent with its prudential obligations, the Fund has a role in evaluating the degree to which the domestic social policies of borrowing states are themselves part of the balance-of-payments problem and the degree to which such policies risk squandering Fund currency reserves, which are an exhaustible social resource.[108] The Fund

---

104. See Ghazi (n 10 above) 10–13.

105. See Head (n 57 above) 24 (discussing Trust Fund and PRGF funding sources in general).

106. In 2006 PRGF lending represented 1.5 percent of total IMF lending. IMF, 'IMF Annual Report 2006' (2006) <http://www.imf.org/external/pubs/ft/ar/2006/eng/index.htm>.

107. See C Abugre, 'Still SAPping the Poor: A Critique of IMF Poverty Reduction Strategies' (2000) <http://www.wdm.org.uk/resources/reports/debt/stillsappingthepoor01062000.pdf>(citing declining economic conditions and increasingly inequitable distribution of wealth in numerous countries despite IMF activity).

108. This is the 'coercive' aspect of Fund operations. See Ghazi (n 10 above) 5; Hockett (n 48 above) 195.

exercises this role through what it calls 'conditionality', which it defines as the link between 'the approval or continuation of the Fund's financing and the implementation of specified elements of economic policy by the country receiving this financing.'[109]

Conditionality functions in IMF lending as a substitute for collateral through the imposition of policy restrictions on borrowing states as a condition of releasing credit tranches.[110] When a Fund member needs to draw on the Fund for hard currencies in excess of its own reserve account, such draws are subject to conditions negotiated between the Fund and the drawing country. Such conditions can include such sensitive domestic issues as wage rates, levels of public expenditures, budget deficits, and export levels.[111] Similar conditions are also imposed as a function of a borrower's participation in the Bank's HIPC program, through the link between HIPC and participation in the Fund's PRGF.[112]

Conditionality has been one of the most controversial aspects of the Fund's operations. The conditions the Fund imposes as a cost of its intervention have a tremendous impact on the domestic policies and development strategies of recipient countries.[113] Criticism has been particularly strong with respect to the Fund's Structural Adjustment Programs or SAPs and the successor Enhanced Structural Adjustment Facility.[114] Such criticism is largely due to two factors: the leverage the Fund has by virtue of its role to insist on domestic policy reforms[115] and the controversy surrounding the soundness and ideological basis of the Fund's approach to domestic policy.[116]

Although the Fund has begun to acknowledge shortcomings in its conditionality and Structural Adjustment Programs,[117] justice as fairness requires more than a recognition of problems in the implementation of the Fund's policies—it requires a radical reexamination of the Fund's conditionality program.

---

109. IMF, 'Conditionality in Fund-Supported Programs—Overview' (June 8, 2007) <http://www.imf.org/external/np/pdr/cond/2001/eng/overview/index.htm>.

110. Lastra (n 88 above) 517.

111. See generally Ghazi (n 10 above) 16–7.

112. C Abugre, 'SAPping the Poor: Structural Adjustment—the Forgotten Issue' (1999) <www.wdm.org.uk/resources/reports/debt/sappingthepoor01061999.pdf> (citing link between HIPC participation and PRGF).

113. See generally Hurrell and Woods (n 7 above) 30–33 (surveying impact of IMF).

114. See Ghazi (n 10 above) 47 (1990 Bank paper).

115. But see Head (n 57 above) 75 (downplaying the leverage aspects of conditionality in view of borrowing countries' formal right to say no).

116. I am referring here to the Fund's ideological approach, which has been called 'unrepentant neoliberalism'. Deacon (n 7 above) 220; see generally J Stiglitz, *Globalization and Its Discontents* (2003). But see Head (n 57 above) 61–63, 69–75 (summarizing and rejecting the ideology, or what he calls the 'bad medicine', critique).

117. See Head (n 57 above) 72–73 (discussing 2002 reforms to Fund conditionality policies).

What principles or criteria should guide this reevaluation? According to this analysis, it should be the International Difference Principle. As was the case with the Bank, in order to be consistent with both the International Difference Principle, which focuses on least advantaged states, and the domestic Difference principle, which focuses on the least advantaged *within* states, the Fund's domestic involvement should focus on the degree to which such policies affect the welfare of the poorest segments of a borrower's society.[118]

Current Fund practices have been criticized for failing to adequately take into account the redistributive effects of Fund policies.[119] While the Fund has begun to publicly note the distributive impact of its policies[120] and develop new approaches to conditionality,[121] such policies continue to be criticized,[122] and require a sustained normative reevaluation according to the International Difference Principle, so that the inequality in international currency resources can be effectively put in the service of the least advantaged.[123]

This suggests that that the Fund consider reconfiguring its approach to conditionality along the following lines: **The Fund should ensure that its involvement in the domestic policy of borrowers operates to the benefit of the least advantaged. In particular, Fund conditionality must be tailored toward enhancing those domestic policies most likely to benefit the least advantaged states and the least advantaged within borrowing states.**

---

118. See supra note 76.

119. See, eg, Head (n 57 above) 81–84 (summarizing and largely endorsing the distributive critique of Fund policies). Hockett, for example, argues that BWIs need to take a stronger public position on the normative justification of social insurance programs. Hockett (n 48 above) 198.

120. Hockett (n 48 above) 223.

121. The Fund now guides its PRGF lending through Poverty Strategy Reduction Papers, designed in consultation with borrowing states, and supplemented since 2001 by the 'social impact analysis' (SIA) program, through which the Fund attempts to assess the consequences of its conditionality policies on the well-being of different social groups, with a special focus on the vulnerable and the poor. IMF, 'IMF Annual Report 2003' <http.//www.imf.org/external/pubs/ft/ar/2003/eng/index.htm>. However, these reforms do not specifically address the most critical issue highlighted by the International Difference Principle, namely that conditionality policies be specifically tailored to benefit the least advantaged. Even the SIA is intended more to mitigate adverse effects rather than to make the benefit of the least advantaged a policy priority.

122. See, eg, Ghazi (n 10 above) 72; Abugre (n 107 above); but see Head (n 57 above) 82 (equity criticisms understate Fund efforts in this area).

123. See, eg, N Wahi, 'Human Rights Accountability of the IMF and the World Bank: A Critique of Existing Mechanisms and Articulation of a Theory of Horizontal Accountability' (2006) 12 UC Davis JIL & Pol 331 (critical of conditionality from a human rights perspective); O Eldar, 'Reform of IMF Conditionality: A Proposal for Self-imposed Conditionality' (2005) 8 JIEL 509 (proposing that conditionality be entirely borrower-driven, with Fund approval).

The Fund has attempted to address this issue by shifting away from its traditional approach to SAPs through creation in 1999 of the Poverty Reduction and Growth Facility, based on each borrowing country's Poverty Reduction Strategy Paper (PRSP).[124] A country's PRSP is supposedly developed primarily by the borrowing country and involves input from all country stakeholders, presumably contributing to fuller consideration of distributive effects.[125] The PSRP process was supplemented in 2001 by the 'social impact analysis' (SIA) program, through which the Fund attempts to 'assess the consequences of policy interventions . . . on the well-being of different social groups, with a special focus on the vulnerable and the poor'.

Most recently, in 2002 the Fund announced a new approach to conditionality, through which conditionality policies are to follow four principles: national ownership, parsimony, tailoring to member circumstances, and clarity or transparency.[126] Through the PRSPs and the SIA program, the Fund hopes to 'assess the implications of key policy measures on the well-being of different social groups, especially the vulnerable and the poor'.[127]

While these laudable reforms seemingly address several of the most prominent critiques of IMF conditionality, criticisms of Fund efforts in this area continue.[128] In the words of one commentator largely sympathetic to the Fund, 'the IMF still does not give enough attention to issues of distributional and social justice'.[129] In particular, with respect to the subject of this essay, these reforms do not specifically address the most critical issue highlighted by the International Difference Principle, namely that conditionality policies be specifically tailored to benefit the least advantaged. The Fund's 'social impact analysis' program does seem designed to at least assess impact on the least advantaged, but it is intended more to mitigate adverse effects rather than to make the benefit of the least advantaged a policy priority.[130] Instead, following the International Difference

---

124. PRSPs are intended to guide all Bank and Fund activity in the borrowing country, including both implementation of the PRGF and any other conditionality imposed as a function of Fund lending.

125. But see Head (n 57 above) 78 (questioning the value of increased public input into what are highly technical IMF decisions).

126. See IMF Guidelines on Conditionality <http://www.imf.org/external/np/pdr/cond/2002/eng/guid/092302.pdf >; Head (n 57 above) 73).

127. *IMF Annual Report 2003* (n 121 above) 44.

128. See, eg, Ghazi (n 10 above) 72; Abugre (n 107 above); but see Head (n 57 above) 82 (equity criticisms understate Fund efforts in this area).

129. See Head (n 57 above) 83.

130. Moreover, the Fund response to finding threats to the least advantaged include policies which have not worked particularly well even in wealthy societies, such as cash subsidies, price controls on essential commodities, and job retraining.

Principle, the Fund should use its 'enforcement' powers[131] to pursue conditionality policies more specifically tied to the benefits of the least advantaged.[132]

E. CONCLUSION

To review, this normative analysis of Bank and Fund lending activities began with the following statement of an international principle of justice drawn from Rawls's justice as fairness: **International social and economic inequalities are just only if they result in compensating benefits for the least advantaged.**

From this, we derived normative principles more closely tied to the institution's responsibilities in international economic relations, as established by the states which founded and control them. With respect to the Bank's role in development capital lending, this means: **In order to justify inequalities in the distribution of development capital, states must ensure that access to development capital is structured so as to benefit the least advantaged.**

With respect to the Fund's role in balance of payments lending, this means: **In order to justify inequalities in the distribution of hard currencies, states must ensure that access to hard currencies is structured so as to benefit the least advantaged.**

The next step was to begin to consider how, given the facts of inequality, access to development capital and hard currencies might indeed benefit the least advantaged, which yielded the following suggested directions for policy reform. In terms of mission: **The Bank should prioritize those activities which most benefit the least advantaged. This means in particular, that the Bank should consider emphasizing IDA debt forgiveness and concessional lending as its primary mission, followed by IBRD lending.**

The Fund should prioritize those activities which most benefit the least advantaged. This means, in particular, that the Fund should emphasize its PRGF concessional lending as its primary mission, followed by its regular facility lending programs.

In terms of conditionality: **The Bank should ensure that its involvement in the domestic policy of borrowers operates to the benefit of the least advantaged. This means, in particular, that 'economic considerations' include all social factors which influence the degree to which Bank projects will in fact operate to the**

---

131. Bradlow (n 59 above) 728. Bradlow suggests that the Fund use its 'implementation powers' through surveillance and technical assistance to collect information and offer expertise supporting such policies.

132. Outgoing IMF Managing Director Michel Camdessus offered a broad vision for 'social conditionality' shortly after leaving office in 2001. M Camdessus, 'The IMF at the Beginning of the Twenty First Century: Can We Establish a Humanized Globalization'? (2001) 7 Global Governance 363, 374–77.

benefit of the least advantaged states, and the least advantaged within borrowing states.

The Fund should ensure that its involvement in the domestic policy of borrowers operates to the benefit of the least advantaged. In particular, Fund conditionality must be tailored toward enhancing those domestic policies most likely to benefit the least advantaged states and the least advantaged within borrowing states.

Some may be quite uncomfortable with the breadth of the agenda outlined above, by casting the Bank and Fund in roles that looks suspiciously like governance, whereas the Bank and Fund are not intended to be governments. There is a core of truth to this discomfort, but governance without government is the central characteristic of the challenge facing states and their institutions in the global era. Globalization can be understood as the triumph of market society at the global level, and markets need governance. Given the weaknesses of individual states in a globalizing environment and the comparatively underdeveloped level of international institutions, this means there is a regulatory gap between global market and regulatory institutions. International organizations like the Bank and the Fund must step in.

Failure by the Bank and Fund to comprehensively organize their efforts according to the benefit to the least advantaged could result in projects which fail to achieve their original goal, or in fact put the least advantaged in a worse position. A justice framework allows us to understand that this is not just a technical failure but an injustice which renders the entire international economic system that much less just. The Bank and Fund cannot simply lend on the assumption that eventually it will benefit the least advantaged if it benefits everyone else. By virtue of their activities, the Bank and Fund have a responsibility to ensure that their projects do in fact benefit the least advantaged.

INDEX

ACP-EC Partnership Agreement Arbitration, 210n39
Adjustment costs, dealing with, 448–49
Advisory Centre on WTO Law (ACWL), 195, 204–6, 229, 237, 300n46
Africa, Caribbean, and Pacific (ACP), former colonies in, 8
Africa, Caribbean, and Pacific (ACP) countries, 267
Africa, trade data for, 244–45
African Group, 97, 348
African Growth and Opportunity Act (AGOA), 53–54, 330, 355
Agarwal, P., 38n81
Aggregation, fallacy of, 26
Agreement on Agriculture (AOA), 334–41, 346
  SDT and, 334, 338–41, 345, 358
Agreement on Development Facilitation (ADF), 294
  adjustment to tariff bindings, 306–8
  case for, 301–3
  extension of special treatment for LDCs, 316
  regulatory elements, 302–3
  S&D provisions, 304–6
  setting procedures to monitor and enforce commitments under Part IV of GATT, 303–4
  subsidy treatment, 308–9
  suspension of antidumping measures, TRIMS and TRIPS Agreements, and, 310–16
Agreement on Textiles and Clothing (ATC), 31
Agreement on Trade Related Aspects of Intellectual Property. *See* TRIPS Agreement
Agricultural Biotechnology.
  See EC-Agricultural Biotechnology
Agricultural subsidies, 124
Agricultural trade, SDT in, 323–26, 362.
  See also Agreement on Agriculture

breaking the impasse, 351–61
Doha Development Round, 341–51
from Geneva to Uruguay, 326–33
negotiating positions, 345–51
what is at stake for developing countries, 341–44
"Aid for trade," 91
  basis of concern for, 94–95
  rise and fall of, 94–95
Aid for Trade Task Force, 95, 102
Airbus-Boeing (US-EU), 207
Aircraft. See Canada-Aircraft
Alcoholic and Malt Beverages.
  See US-Alcoholic and Malt Beverages
Alcoholic Beverages. See Chile—Alcoholic Beverages; Japan-Alcoholic Beverages
Amalgamation, 398
Amsden, Alice, 15, 17
Annan, Kofi, 473
Anti-Dumping Agreement (ADA), 158, 160t, 225
Antidumping Act of 1916, 432–33
Antidumping Measure on Shrimp from Ecuador. See US-Antidumping Measure on Shrimp from Ecuador
Antidumping measures, 433–34
  suspension, 310–12
Antidumping or countervailing measures (AD/CVM), 281, 284, 285, 286t, 287
Antitrust laws, 398, 399
Appellate Body (AB)
  balance of payments and, 119–20
  Dispute Settlement Understanding and, 238–39
  GSP programs and, 115–16
  James McCall Smith on, 252
  nondiscriminatory treatment and, 8
  reciprocity and, 7–8, 115–16
  right to give testimony before, 248
  Shrimp Turtle II and, 31
  zeroing, antidumping regulations, and, 225

Argentina-Footwear Safeguards, 279t
Asia, trade data for, 243, 244

Balance of Payments (BOP)
  Committee, 120
  exceptions, 11
  lending, 487
  measures, 12–13, 119–20, 295
Balassa, Bela, 84
Banana Regime. See EC-Banana Regime
Banana Tariff Arbitrations. See EC-Banana Tariff Arbitrations
Bananas III. See EC-Bananas III
Barshefsky, Charlene, 325
Baumol, William, 411
Belgian Family Allowances case, 137
"Best practice" norms, 449
Bhagwati, J. N., 22, 25–27, 31, 460
Bhagwati-Hudec thesis, 22
Bhattacharjea, Aditya, 428–29
Bilateral (complainant/respondent) trade disputes, 279–81. *See also* Dispute Settlement (DS) system
  defined, 154
  distribution, 156, 156t, 157t
  importance of discriminatory nature of initial allegation, 281
  outcomes of claims made in, 179–85
Bilateral investment treaties (BITs), 313
Bilateral opportunism, problem of, 288
Bindings, 84–85
  tariff, 306–8
Boeing. See Airbus-Boeing
Bown, Chad P., 208, 249–50
Bradford, A., 435n63
Bretton Woods Institutions (BWIs), 476–79
  and international justice as fairness, 485–87

Canada-Aircraft, 253
Canada-Patent Protection of Pharmaceuticals, 253, 279t
Capacity-building, 300
Capitalism, 393
Caribbean. *See also* Africa, Caribbean, and Pacific
  trade data, 245–46

Caribbean Basin Initiative (CBI), 52
Cartels, 406, 412n70
  export, 422–26
  external, 413–14
  international, 418–22
Ceiling bindings, 84–85
Central Asia, trade data for, 243
Certain Paper. See Korea—Certain Paper
Chang, H., 25n17, 33–34
Chile—Alcoholic Beverages, 253
China, 25, 26
  research and development efforts, 384–85
Claims Settlement Declaration (CSD), 219
"Class action," 196
Coffee. See EC-Coffee
Cold War rivalry for developing countries' loyalty, 79
Collective national rationality, 396
Collusion and monopoloid behavior, 398
Colonial era, 26
Committee on Trade and Development (CTD), 299–302. *See also* United Nations Committee on Trade and Development
Comparative advantage, doctrine of, 397
Competition advocacy, 400
Competition law proposals, 401–2
Competition law(s)
  developing countries and, 408–12
  international *vs.* national, 418–31
  market restraints and national, 412–17
  usual content, 405–8
  why an international competition law agreement is unlikely, 431–34
  why international cooperation on competition law will progress, 434–35
  WTO and, 401–5
Competition policy
  appropriateness of a major role for WTO in, 404–5
  GATT/WTO regimes and, 404–5
  perspectives on, 398–401
  world trading system and, 396
Concessional lending, 495
Consultations, 250, 251
Contingent derogation mechanisms, 121–22

Copyright, 376. *See also US-Copyright*;
    *US-Section 110(5) of the US
    Copyright Act*
Core Group proposal. *See* W142
Costa Rica, 262
Cottier, T., 41, 42n99, 375n51
Cotton, 124–25
Cotton and Man-Made Underwear. *See
    US-Cotton and Man-Made Underwear*
Cottrell, P. M., 40
Council for the Trade of Goods, 213
Council for Trade and Development
    (Development Council), 294
  case for, 301–3
  development-assistance policy
    implementation, 317
  instituting and supervising
    committees, 318
  regulatory monitoring, 303–4, 317–18
  role of, 303–4, 316–18
Countervailing duties (CVDs), 308

Davey, William, 254n28
Debt forgiveness, 495
"Deep integration," 9
Developing (DEV) countries, 155, 167–68.
    See also specific topics
  clash of interests between developed
    countries and, 402–4
  definition and scope of the term, 101
  as global competitors, 386–89
  support for liberalization of, 103
*Developing Countries in the GATT Legal
    System* (Hudec), 117. *See also* Hudec;
    Preference/preferential programs;
    Preferences
  audience, 72
  contributions to trade literature, 46
  GATT and, 77, 78, 81
  hidden costs of the rhetorical strategy
    of, 68–72
  historical narrative in first part of, 47–50
  in light of recent literature, 71–72
  methodological commitments, 59–68
  overview, 21–22, 45–46, 72–73, 111–12,
    129–30
  recommendations, 82–83
  results of 1987, 81–82
  second part of, 50–59

  theoretical orientation, 59
  Trachtman on, 23
  world changes since the writing of, 111
Development, economic. *See* Economic
    development
Development Agenda, 366
Development assistance, from rhetoric to
    action, 318–19
Development-assistance provisions,
    294–99, 317
Development Council. *See* Council for
    Trade and Development
Development-Facilitation Subsidy (DFS),
    294, 309
Development-Facilitation Tariff (DFT),
    294, 307
Development lending, theory of just
    international
  operational implications of a, 492–99
  toward a, 489–92
"Development safeguard" mechanism,
    118–19
Difference principle, 484–86. *See also*
    International difference principle
"Differential and More Favourable
    Treatment, Reciprocity and Fuller
    Participation of Developing Countries,
    The." *See* Enabling Clause
"Diplomat's economics," 88
"Dirty tariffication," 87n35
Dispute Settlement (DS) system, 152–55,
    165–66, 187–90, 266. *See also* Small-
    claims procedure; Third countries
  description of number of claims per
    provision, 169–71, 173, 175, 177
  distribution of bilateral disputes across
    groups, 156, 156t, 157t
  distribution of claims across groups,
    156–58
  distribution of claims across provisions/
    agreements, 158–59, 159t, 160t
  distribution of outcomes, 160–62t,
    160–63, 164t
  nation size, biases, and, 151–52, 193–94,
    209
  outcomes of claims made in bilateral
    disputes, 179–85
  and variation in exports across WTO's
    membership, 193

Dispute Settlement Understanding (DSU), 11, 106–7
  alternative WTO dispute settlement mechanisms, 209–14
  economic impact on third countries, 277–78
  empirical research literature on, 266n1
  and the right to give testimony, 248
  threshold for profitable use of, 202
Doha Declaration of 2001, 123, 324
  2004 Work Program on S&D treatment, 92–93, 93f
  review called for in, 93
  S&D treatment and, 5, 50, 114
Doha Development Agenda (DDA), 2–3, 16, 90, 106, 113, 292, 300
Doha Development Round, 325. *See also under* Agricultural trade
  agenda, 344–45
Doha Mandate, 114–15
Doha Ministerial Conference, 405
Doha Ministerial Decision on Implementation-Related Issues, 91, 92, 114
Doha Ministerial Declaration, 95, 345
Doha Round, 108, 294
Doha Round Negotiations, 94, 115, 120, 123, 213
Domestic access to better services, improving, 449–51
Domestic reform and poverty reduction, 5–6
Domestic regulation, implementing appropriate, 449
Domestic resource cost, 83
Dominican Republic, 254
Dumping. *See also* Antidumping measures
  defined, 310n88

Early settlement, 248, 249
East Asia, trade data for, 243
EC (European Communities), 7–8, 115. *See also ACP-EC Partnership Agreement Arbitration*
  European Small Claims Procedures, 217–18
EC-ACP preferential agreement, 210–11
EC-Agricultural Biotechnology, 235

EC-Banana Regime, 272–73, 278, 279t, 280t
EC-Banana Tariff Arbitrations, 232n95
EC-Bananas III, 154, 247, 249, 250n12, 251, 261, 284n26
EC-Coffee, 279t
EC-Grains, 280t
EC-Measures Affecting the Exportation of Processed Cheese, 275–76
EC-Oilseeds, 280t
EC-Sugar Regime, 267, 268
EC-Tariff Preferences, 7–8, 10, 115
EC-Unbleached Cotton Fabrics, 280t
EC-Wood of Conifers, 280t
Economic development, 119
  trade and, 292–94
Economic regulation, 117–18
Ecuador, 247, 261. *See also EC-Bananas III*
Effective protection, 83
Effects doctrine, 424–25
Enabling Clause, 42, 49, 298, 329
  requirement for nondiscriminatory treatment, 8
Equal treatment rule. *See* Most favored nation (MFN) rule
Europe, trade data for, 243
European Communities. *See* EC
European Court of Justice (ECJ), 252
European Grouping of Societies of Authors and Composers (GESAC), 234n101
European Small Claims Procedures, 217–18
European Union (EU), 53, 195, 198
  hybrid governance and, 148–49
Everything But Arms (EBA) initiative, 316, 330, 355
Exclusion, 398
Exclusionary restraints, 414–17
Export cartels. *See* Cartels, export
Export Measures Affecting Hides and Skins. *See Pakistan-Export Measures Affecting Hides and Skins*
Export restrictions, disputes alleging respondent engaged in excessive, 276–77
Export subsidies, 13
Export Trading Company Act of 1982, 422–25

Exports. *See also specific topics*
  GDP and total, 198, 199f
  how many developing third countries increase, 282, 283t, 284–85
  relative importance of $1 million of, 194t
  share of export below $1 million, 202f
  share of export below $10 million, 202f
  size of exporting nation and, 201t
  total export *vs.* diversity of, 199–200, 200f

Falconer, Crawford, 350, 351
Federal Rules of Appellate Procedure, 224
Feminist trade theory, 29
Finger, J. Michael, 5
Finger, M. J., 354
Fink, K. E., 371
Footwear Safeguards. See Argentina-Footwear Safeguards
Foreign Antitrust Improvements Act, 424
Foreign direct investment (FDI), 438. *See also* GATS, Mode 3
  intellectual property protection and, 312, 366, 370–79, 389–90
  remittances and, 461
  in transition economies, 374
"Foreign seed" base model, 378
Forster, C. J., 387n84
Framework Agreement, 346–47
Free trade skepticism, 23, 24, 32, 43
  ethical and political objections, 28–30
  historical and economic objections, 24–28
  nature and character of GATT/WTO and, 30–32
Fuji. See Kodak/Fuji

GABB (General Agreement on Better Bargaining), 137–38
Gathii, J. T., 27, 32
GATS (General Agreement on Trade in Services), 17, 438. *See also* Services sector
  Article IV, 438–39
  Article XIX, 38, 439
  Mode 1, 443
  Mode 3, 443, 444, 446, 472
  Mode 4, 443–44, 446, 451–52, 463–67, 471–73
  reciprocity constraints and, 440–43, 454–55
  services sector and, 36–39
  unilateral *vs.* GATS liberalization, 36
GATS visa system, 462
  challenges in implementing, 466–71
  legal binding, 469–70, 472–73
  overview, 466
  substantial levels of commitment, 470–71
GATS visas
  how to negotiate on, 471–73
  temporariness, 467–69
GATT (General Agreement on Tariffs and Trade), 1, 8, 9, 11, 14. *See also Developing Countries in the GATT Legal System*
  Article XVIII, 16, 112, 118–21, 295–96, 328
  Article XXII, 247, 251–52
  Article XXIII, 247, 251–52
  Articles XXXVI-XXXVIII, 296–98
  Balance-of-Payments Provisions (BOP Understanding), 12
  beyond, 33–43
  and domestic policy making, 57
  Hudec's analysis of first 40 years of, 76–82
  individual sacrifice for the common good, 77
  market-opening obligations, 116–17
  retrospective/historical perspective on, 70, 103
GATT Decision of 5 April 1966, 211–12
"GATT Legal System, The" (Hudec), 135–42
"GATT or GABB?" (Hudec), 137–38
"Gender-blind" trade theory, 29
General Agreement on Better Bargaining (GABB), 137–38
General Agreement on Tariffs and Trade. *See* GATT
General Agreement on Trade in Services. *See* GATS

Generalized System of Preferences (GSP), 7, 53, 446
  application, 7
  arrangements for "better than GSP" treatment, 115
  and beneficiary state exports, 54–55
  benefits for developing countries, 331–32
  dangers of relying on GSP programs, 7
  developed countries extracting policy concessions in exchange for, 8, 116
  economic effects, 54–55
  Hudec on, 9
  limitations, 7, 9
  nonreciprocity principle and, 7
  nontariff barriers, rules of origin, and, 332
  S&D treatment and, 5
Geneva, 106, 107, 300
GESAC. *See* European Grouping of Societies of Authors and Composers
Global growth, 2
Global innovation, 392
Global legal space and the future of governance, 142–49
Global space
  functions and features of law in, 132–35
  Hudec and, 140, 142, 144–46, 148
  law of, 131–33
  legalization of, 130–31
Globalization, 393
  and governance, 393
Goods and services liberalization, 116
Government Assistance to Economic Development. *See* GATT, Article XVIII
Graham, E. M., 435n162
Grains. *See* EC-Grains

Haberler Report of 1958, 81
Harmonised Commodity Description and Coding System (HS), 198–99, 201*t*
Heavily Indebted Poor Countries (HIPC), 491, 492n55, 494–96
Heiligendamm Process, 368
Hikino, T., 17
Hoekman, Bernard, 41, 114
Honduras, 254
Hong Kong Declaration, 93, 94

Hong Kong Ministerial meeting, 38–39, 114, 123, 125
Horizontal restraints, 405, 406
Howse, R., 31n46
Hudec, Robert, 5, 83, 150, 410–11. *See also Developing Countries in the GATT Legal System*
  analysis of first 40 years of GATT, 76–82
  on Article XVIII, 118–19
  and clash of interests between developed and developing nations, 402
  on Cold War rivalry for developing countries' loyalty, 79
  Cottier on, 42n99
  Dani Rodrik and, 144–46
  dispute settlement and, 152, 153
  on GATT and domestic trading policy, 397
  "The GATT Legal System," 135–42
  "GATT or GABB?", 137–38
  global space and, 140, 142, 144–46, 148
  on governance issues, 135–42
  Harold Koh and, 142
  on infant-industry protection, 144–46
  model, 118
  on nonreciprocal treatment, 75–76, 79, 82, 111–12, 328
  overview, 45
  on preferential/S&P treatment, 40, 75–76, 79, 93–94, 102, 111, 113–14, 323–24
  on trade liberalization, 57, 58, 111
  trade rules and, 144, 148
Hybrid governance and European Union, 148–49

Imitation phase (industrial development), 391–92
Immigration, switching from migration to, 462
Impartiality constraint, 204
Import liberalization. *See also* Liberalization
  and developing third-country exporters, 277–88
Import promotion, disputes alleging respondent engaged in excessive, 275–76

Import protection, disputes alleging respondent engaged in excessive, 272–75
Import subsidies, 13
Import substitution, 121
India, 37nn75–76
India—Measures Affecting Export of Certain Commodities, 276
India—Quantitative Restrictions, 12, 119
Indian information technology (IT) workers, 462
Indonesia, 442
Industrial development, 391–92
Industrialized (IND) countries, 155, 167. *See also* Dispute Settlement (DS) system
Industry, 121
Infant-industry protection, 144–45, 296, 446–47
Innovation process, 393. *See also under* TRIPS Agreement
 phases, 391–92
Institution building, 143
Integrated Framework, 108, 125
Intellectual property (IP). *See also* TRIPS Agreement
 foreign direct investment and, 370–76
Intellectual property rights (IPRs), 116–17, 314–16
International Bank for Reconstruction and Development (IBRD), 476–77, 488, 489, 491, 503
International Centre for the Settlement of Investment Disputes (ICSID), 478
International Competition Network (ICN), 400, 426, 434–35
International Development Association (IDA), 478, 491, 495
International difference principle, 486–87, 489–93, 497, 498, 503–5, 507–9. *See also* Difference principle
International Finance Corporation (IFC), 478
International justice. *See* Justice, international
International Monetary Fund (IMF), 477, 478, 509–10
 conditionality, 505–9
 global inequality and, 486–87

 mission and priorities, 504–5
 role in international justice, 500–509
International monetary policy, theory of just
 operational implications of a, 504–9
 toward a, 501–4
International Trade Organization (ITO), 76
Investment measures, 117
Iran-US Claims Tribunal, 218–20
Ismail, Faizel, 115
Israel, innovation in, 385–86

Japan, 251, 407–10, 415–17
Japan-Alcoholic Beverages, 234
Japan-Leather, 280t
Japan-Photographic Film, 205
Japan-Taxes on Alcoholic Beverages, 232n96, 234
Japanese Anti-Monopoly Law, 421
Jensen, M. F., 340, 341
Justice, international
 as fairness, 480–87, 489, 497, 502, 503
 international economic institutions and, 480–87
 International Monetary Fund and, 500–509
 World Bank and, 487–99
"Justice as Fairness" (Rawls), 480–85

Kant, Immanuel, 28
Kennedy Round Negotiations of 1964, 79
Knowledge, 107–8
Kodak/Fuji, 416
Koh, Harold, 142
Korea—Certain Paper, 161

Latin America, 97
 trade data, 245–46
Law. *See also* Global space
 functions, 132
Least developing countries (LDCs), 125, 155, 167, 298, 299. *See also* Dispute Settlement (DS) system
 extension of special treatment for, 316
 technical assistance and capacity building for, 447
Leather. *See Japan-Leather*
Legal aid, 195

Legal claims, defined, 154
Legalization. *See under* Global space
Liberalism and liberal principles of
    justice, 479
  multilateral institutions and, 479–81
Liberalization. *See also* Trade liberalization
  of developing countries, support
    for, 103
  goods and services, 116
  import, and developing third-country
    exporters, 277–88
  MFN, 16, 114
  standards, 116
  unilateral *vs.* GATS, 36
Lippoldt, D., 372nn36–37
Litigation. *See* Dispute Settlement (DS)
  system; Small-claims procedure
Local innovation, 391–92

Managerial approach, 140–42
Market access
  in developing countries, 6–8
  facilitating, through broader
    cooperation, 451–52
Market restraints
  internal, 412–13
  national competition laws and, 412–17
Maskus, C., 371, 373
*Measures Affecting Export of Certain
  Commodities. See India—Measures
  Affecting Export of Certain Commodities*
*Measures Affecting the Exportation of
  Processed Cheese. See EC-Measures
  Affecting the Exportation of Processed
  Cheese*
Merger control, 414
Metcalfe, J. Stan, 389n94
Multi-Fiber Arrangement (MFA), 87
Multi-Fiber Arrangement (MFA) quotas,
  gain/loss from elimination of,
  87–88, 88f
Michaelopoulos, C., 356
Middle East, trade data for, 244
Migration. *See* Temporary migration of
  workers
Millennium Development Goals (World
  Bank), 493–94, 497
Monopoloid behavior, 398
Monopsony, 428

Most favored nation (MFN)
  principle, 273, 281
  rule, 269, 273, 278, 281
  status, 4, 10, 22
  GATT/WTO membership and, 287
  liberalization, 16, 114
  tariffs, 64, 65
Multilateral Agreement on Investment
  (MAI), 435n162
Multilateral Investment Guarantee Agency
  (MIGA), 478

Needs assessment, 100
Negotiation, decentered deliberation
  and, 134
New International Economic Order
  (NIEO), 9, 111, 114, 399, 419
Newly industrializing countries (NICs),
  7, 293
Non-Agricultural Market Access (NAMA)
  Negotiations of the Doha of
  Round Trade Negotiations, 23,
  28, 33–35
Nondiscrimination, 83
Nondiscriminatory policy of import
  protection, 288
Nonreciprocal treatment. *See also*
  Preferential treatment
  Hudec on, 75–76, 79, 82,
    111–12, 328
Nonreciprocity
  as path of least resistance/easy way out,
    78–79
  policy of, 22, 78
  principle of, 7, 8, 115, 328–29,
    339–40
Nonreciprocity doctrine, 142
North Africa, trade data for, 244
North America, trade data for, 243

Oilseeds. See EC-Oilseeds
Olarreaga, M., 427
"One-size-fits-all issue," 90, 91
Organization of Petroleum Exporting
  Countries (OPEC), 8
Ostry, Sylvia, 89n40, 90
Overstaying (immigration), 462
Özden, C., 65–66, 427
Özden/Reinhardt study, 65–66

Pacific. *See also* Africa, Caribbean, and Pacific
  trade data, 243
Pakistan-Export Measures Affecting Hides and Skins, 276
Park, W. G., 372nn36–37
Participatory alliance, 248
Patent law, novelty in, 392
Patent protection, 122, 377–78
Patent Protection of Pharmaceuticals. See Canada-Patent Protection of Pharmaceuticals
Pharmaceuticals, 253, 279t, 375
Photographic Film. See Japan-Photographic Film
Piilola, A. *See* Bradford, A.
Political economy, 61–68
  as alternative to S&D treatment, 448–49
Political prohibition (World Bank), 498
Poverty, 1–3
  trade liberalization and, 3–10
Poverty reduction
  domestic reform and, 5–6
  role of S&D treatment in, 3–5
Poverty Reduction and Growth Facilities (PRGFs), 503–5, 508
Poverty Reduction Strategy Paper, 508
Preference/preferential programs
  features that limit their reach, 52–54
  reauthorization, 52
  reform *vs.* elimination of, 56
  as reinforcing protectionism in developing states, 65–67
Preferences, 46
  dysfunctional debate over, as a diversion, 67–68
  economic approach to assessing the efficacy of, 51–56
  Enabling Clause and, 49
  history of the idea of, 47–50
  political economy approach to how they work, 56–59
  as politics *vs.* economics, 50–59
Preferential trade agreements (PTAs)
  limits to the use of, 329
  preference schemes as leading to, 62–65

Preferential treatment, 46n2. *See also* Special and differential (S&D) treatment
  forms of, 46n2
  Hudec on, 82
Price-fixing agreements, 419
Prosecutor, WTO public, 195
Protection, 13
Protectionism, 118
  developed country, 31
"Public choice" approach, 2

Quantitative Restrictions. See India—Quantitative Restrictions

Rachman, G., 387n86
Rawls, John
  and domestic justice as fairness, 480–85
"Rebalancing," 90
"Received theory," 396
Reciprocal control mechanisms, 15
Reciprocity, 48, 83, 86, 114–15, 295. *See also* Nonreciprocity
Reciprocity constraints in services sector, 440–45
Regional trade agreements, 63n66
Regulation
  right to regulate, 117
  types of, 117–18
Regulatory constraints in services sector, 444–45
Regulatory cooperation, facilitating market access through broader, 451–52
Reinhardt, Eric, 65–66
Rents, redistributing, 448–49
Research and development (R&D), 378, 382
  transfer to developing countries, 383–86
Ricupero, Rubens, 91, 92, 103n73, 354
Rodrik, Dani, 10–11, 143–46, 460, 468
Ruggiero, Renate, 319n121
Ruhnka, J., 216–17
Ryan, Michael, 383

Safeguards (SG) Agreement, 158, 160t, 337
Sanitary and Phytosanitary Measures, Agreement on. *See* SPS Agreement

Sanitary and phytosanitary (SPS) measures, 159
Schuler, Philip, 103*n*73
Scotchmer, S., 382
Self-assessment, 98, 100
Serious prejudice, 14
Services Council of WTO, 146
Services sector. *See also* GATS
  asymmetric interests in, 443–44
  defining trade in, 438
  reciprocity constraints in, 440–45
  regulatory constraints in, 444–45
Sherwood, R. M., 383*n*67
Shrimp. See US-Shrimp
Shrimp Turtle II, 31
Singh, A., 409–12
Small claims
  definition in WTO context, 223–27
  in international dispute settlement, 218–20
Small Claims Legal Advisor Program (California), 216
Small-claims procedure, the case for a, 196–98
  alternative WTO dispute settlement mechanisms, 209–14
  litigation costs and internal expertise, 203–9
  trade stakes, 198–203
Small-claims procedures, 214, 218–20, 239–41. *See also* Dispute Settlement (DS) system
  adaptation to WTO context, 221–39
  aims and practices at national and supranational level, 191–97
  concerns regarding, 216–17
  costs and finances, 195–96
  creation for a trial period, 239
  "estimated" litigation cost, 205, 206*t*
  EU regional context, 217–18
  filing distribution, 208, 209
  institutional issues: panels, appeals, and procedures, 236–39
  introducing simplified, less costly litigation procedures, 196
  limiting access to certain WTO Members, 228
  national context, 214–17

no precedential effect and cap on remedies, 230–36
  open to certain WTO Members, 227
  premises underlying the case for, 197–98
  who could use, 227–30
Smith, Adam, 32
Social impact analysis (SIA) program, 507*n*121, 508
South Asia, trade data for, 244
Special and differential (S&D) provisions, 294, 298–99
  why they are not sufficient to meet developing countries' development needs, 299
Special and differential (S&D) treatment (SDT), 22*n*8, 91–93, 102, 113–16, 455, 486*n*44. *See also* Agreement on Agriculture (AOA); Agricultural trade; Preferential treatment
  Agreement on Development Facilitation and, 304–6
  alternatives to, 447–52
  beneficial aspects, 4–5
  branches, 353–55
  historical development of SDT policies, 326–33
  Hudec on, 323–24
  impact of more, 445–47
  principle of, 39–43
  rationales for, 352–53
  role in poverty reduction, 3–5
  small-claims procedure and, 228, 241
  in Uruguay Round, 8–10
Special Products, 346
Special Safeguard Mechanism, 346–48, 350, 351
SPS
  Agreement, 106, 121–22, 147, 159, 338
  committee, 147–48
  measures, 159
Standards liberalization, 116
Steel Safeguards. See US-Steel Safeguards
Stiglitz, J., 372*n*36, 386*n*81, 433*n*156
Structural adjustment programs (SAPs), 496, 506, 508
Sub-Saharan Africa, 342
  trade data, 244
Subsidies, 13–14

Subsidies and countervailing measures
    (SCM), 158
  Agreement, 10, 13, 14, 124, 308,
    309, 360
Substantial interest *vs.* substantial trade
    interest, 251
Sugar Regime. See EC-Sugar Regime
Systemic interest to be joined in
    consultations, 251

Tariff bindings, 306–8. *See also*
    Bindings
Tariff peaks, 6, 335
Tariff Preferences. See EC-Tariff Preferences
Tariff reduction exemptions, 348
Tariffs, 340–41. *See also specific topics*
Taxes on Alcoholic Beverages.
    See Japan-Taxes on Alcoholic Beverages
Taylor, Charles, 393
TBT Agreement. *See* Technical Barriers to
    Trade (TBT) Agreement
Technical assistance, 338
Technical Barriers to Trade (TBT)
    Agreement, 106, 353–54
Telecommunications, 448
Temporary migration of workers. *See also*
    GATS, Mode 4
  benefits, 459–61
  costs, 461–63
  defined, 463–64
Textiles. See Turkey-Textiles; US-Textiles
Third countries (in trade disputes)
  developing country performance as
    implicitly interested, 286*t*,
    286–87
  disputes with many implicitly interested
    developing, 278–79, 280*t*
  how many also increase exports, 282,
    284–85
Third-country export, size of increases in
    developing, 286–87
Third-country exporters
  economic performance of developing,
    282, 283*t*, 284–87
  import liberalization and developing,
    277–88
Third-country exporters (in trade
    disputes), 272–73, 273*f*, 275–77
  identifying the developing, 281–82

Third-country importers (in trade
    disputes)
  of disputed product, 273*f*, 274–77
Third-country interests in trade disputes
  involving alleged excessive export
    promotion, 275, 276*f*
  involving alleged excessive export
    restrictions, 276–77, 277*f*
  involving alleged excessive import
    protection, 272–74, 273*f*
Third parties at WTO
  developing countries and, 258–63
  DSU allowances regarding, 250–52
  how they shape rulings, 252–58
  reasons Members join disputes as third
    parties, 249–50
  ways they increase main litigant's
    bargaining costs, 253–54
  trade disputes with many developing
    countries intervening as third
    parties, 278–79, 279*t*
Third-party interest in GATT/WTO
    dispute, economic reasons for,
    270–77
Third-party interventions *vs.* implicitly
    interested third parties, 278–79
Thomas, R. E., 372
Tobacco. See US-Tobacco
Trachtman, Joel P., 23, 36, 42, 308*n*73,
    331, 364, 365*n*12, 379*n*57
Trade Act of 1974. *See US-Section 301-310*
    of 1974 Trade Act
Trade Act of 2002, 27
Trade and Development, Council for. *See*
    Council for Trade and Development
Trade and Development, WTO Committee
    on, 114
Trade data, 243–46
Trade disputes. *See also* Bilateral
    (complainant/respondent) trade
    disputes; Dispute Settlement (DS)
    system; Third countries
  categories of, 270–71
  economically successful outcomes, 271
Trade facilitation, 95–96, 102–3
  assistance mechanics of proposals,
    98–99
  identifying concrete implementation
    needs/support, 96–98

522 INDEX

Trade Facilitation Register, 98
Trade liberalization, 77, 114, 289, 343–44, 358–60. *See also* Liberalization; Most favored nation (MFN) status, MFN liberalization
  and economic success in bilateral disputes, 281
  Hudec on, 57, 58, 111
  poverty and, 3–10
Trade of Goods, Council for the, 213
Trade policy. *See also specific topics*
  advance of welfare *vs.* political objectives, 396–98
Trade Policy Review Mechanism (TPRM), 452
Trade regime, paradox involved in constructing an international, 61
Trade Related Aspects of Intellectual Property, Agreement of. *See* TRIPS Agreement
Trade-Related Development Assistance Report (TDAR), 304, 317, 318
Trade Related Intellectual Property Rights. *See* TRIPS Agreement
Trade Related Investment Measures (TRIMS) Agreement, 10, 14, 310, 312–14
Trade rules, need for flexibility in application of, 143
Trademark, 377
Transitional time periods, 338
Transparency, toward greater, 452–54
Trebilcock, Michael J., 31n46
TRIMS (Trade Related Investment Measures) Agreement, 10, 14, 310, 312–14
TRIPS Agreement, 9–10, 14–15, 31, 88, 122–23, 310, 313–15
  abuse of intellectual property rights and, 428
  and distribution of innovation development, 390–91
  and geographical displacement in innovation, 378–90
  measuring its impacts on development, 369–78
  phases, 363–68
Trubek, David M., 40
Tuna. *See US-Tuna*

Turkey-Textiles, 279t
Turtle. *See US-Shrimp-Turtle*

Unbleached Cotton Fabrics. *See EC-Unbleached Cotton Fabrics*
United Nations Committee on Trade and Development (UNCTD), 317. *See also* Committee on Trade and Development
United Nations Compensation Commission (UNCC), 218–20
United Nations Conference on Trade and Development (UNCTAD), 79, 80, 401
United States. *See* US
Upland Cotton. *See US-Upland Cotton*
Uruguay Round, 11, 31, 113, 437
  active non-mercantilist-developing country participation in, 83–86
  asymmetry, 106–8
  as "Grand Bargain," 105
  "grand bargain" struck at, 86–87
  implementation, 91–94, 102
  implementation problem, 89–90, 102
  mercantilism and the outcome of, 86–90
  motivation for developing countries, 83–84
  post-Uruguay Round tariff rates, 85–86, 86t
  reductions in MFN tariffs for PTA products during, 64
  results, 84–87
  S&D treatment and, 50
  S&D treatment in, 8–10
  story of, 76–81
  tariff concessions given and received, 84–85, 85t
  unbalanced outcome of, 87–89
  under-developed economics and, 80–81
  Understanding on Balance of Payments, 119–20
  well-developed politics and, 79–80
  WTO response to, 90–91
Uruguay Round Agreements, 298–99
Uruguay Round of Trade Negotiations, 11, 31
US-Alcoholic and Malt Beverages, 280t
US-Antidumping Measure on Shrimp from Ecuador, 280t
US-Copyright, 232n95, 234

US-Cotton and Man-Made Underwear, 280t
US-Section 301-310 of 1974 Trade Act, 279t
US-Section 110(5) of the US Copyright Act, 210n39
US-Shrimp, 278, 280t, 280n24
US-Shrimp-Turtle, 235, 279t
US-Steel Safeguards, 274
US-Textiles and Apparel Products, 279t, 280t
US-Tobacco, 280t
US-Tuna, 279t
US-Tuna II, 279t
US-Upland Cotton, 275
US-Women's and Girls' Wool Coats, 280t
US-Woven Wool Shirts and Blouses, 280t
"User fees" for smaller trading nations, 194–97

Van Duzer, J. A., 36n72
Vertical mergers, 406
Vertical restraints, 406
Visas. *See* GATS visas
Vulnerable Agricultural Protection Scheme (VASPS), 359–62

W137 (proposal), 98
W142 (Core Group proposal), 98–100
Washington Consensus, 9, 11, 16, 112–13, 121
Water Framework Directive (WFD), 148–49
Webb-Pomerene Act, 422–25
Williams, B., 351n119
Wolfensohn, James, 383
Women's and Girls' Wool Coats. *See US Women's and Girls' Wool Coats*
Wood of Conifers. *See EC-Wood of Conifers*
Wood Pulp Cartel, 424
World Bank, 78, 343, 509–10. *See also under* Justice
  global inequality and, 476, 486–87
  and international justice, 487–99
  mission and priorities, 493–96
  role in domestic social policy of borrowers, 496–99
World Bank Group (WBG), 476
World Development Report (WDR), 383
World Intellectual Property Organization (WIPO), 363
World Trade Organization (WTO), 1, 3. *See also specific topics*
  communications and facilitation through councils and committees, 146–48
  comparative advantage, 452–54
  equity in, 108
  General Council, 146
  Ministerial Declaration of 2005, 447
  Ministerial Meeting in Cancun 2003, 95
  obligations, 90
  organizational apparatus in, 299–300
  proposals to reform, 143–46
  protection and, 13
  and the right to regulate for development, 10–15
  Services Council, 146
  Task Force on Aid for Trade, 95
  Working Group on the Interaction between Trade and Competition Policy, 402
World Trade Organization (WTO) law
  challenges to, 222
  as complex and open to interpretation, 222
  government-to-government character of, 221
World Trade Organization (WTO) Members, classification of, 155, 167–68, 390–91
Woven Wool Shirts and Blouses. *See US-Woven Wool Shirts and Blouses*

Zambia, 448, 449